1812

THE GREAT RETREAT

'The habit of victory cost us even dearer in retreat. The glorious habit of always marching forwards made us veritable schoolboys when it came to retreating. Never was a retreat worse organised.'

Caulaincourt.

'Extreme misery knows not the law of humanity. One sacrifices everything to the law of self-preservation.'

Louise Fusil, at the Berezina.

'I have never, to this day of writing in 1828, seen an account of the retreat that could be described as exaggerated. Indeed I'm sure it would be impossible to exaggerate the misery endured by those who took part in it.'

Lieutenant Vossler.

'For the honour of humanity, perhaps, I ought not to describe all these scenes of horror, but I have determined to write down all I saw. And if in this campaign acts of infamy were committed, there were noble actions, too.'

Sergeant Bourgogne.

1812

THE GREAT RETREAT

told by the survivors

Paul Britten Austin

Greenhill Books, London

Stackpole Books, Pennsylvania

Greenhill Books

1812: The Great Retreat
first published 1996 by
Greenhill Books, Lionel Leventhal Limited, Park House,
1 Russell Gardens, London NW11 9NN
and
Stackpole Books, 5067 Ritter Road,
Mechanicsburg, PA 17055, USA.

© Paul Britten Austin, 1996
The moral right of the author has been asserted.

British Library Cataloguing in Publication Data
Britten Austin, Paul
1812: The Great Retreat
1. Napoleonic Wars, 1800–1815—Campaigns—Russia
I. Title
940.2'7
ISBN 1-85367-246-7

Library of Congress Cataloging-in-Publication Data
Austin, Paul Britten
1812 : The Great Retreat / Paul Britten Austin
464 p. 24 cm.
Includes bibliographical references and index.
ISBN 1-85367-246-7 (hbk)
1. Napoleonic Wars, 1800–1815—Campaigns—Russia
—Personal narratives, French 2. Russia—History, Military—
1801–1917—Sources 3. Napoleon I, Emperor of the French,
1769–1821—Military leadership 4. France. Armée—History—
Napoleonic Wars, 1800–1815—Sources. I. Title.
DC235.A86 1996
940.2'7—dc20   96–29074

Designed and edited by DAG Publications Ltd.
Designed by David Gibbons; edited by Michael Boxall.
Printed and bound in Great Britain by
Clays Ltd, St Ives plc

CONTENTS

To the English-speaking world's
two greatest Napoleonic scholars of our century,
Professor David Chandler, D. Litt. (Oxon)
and
Colonel John R. Elting (USA. Rtd)
this volume is dedicated in admiration and gratitude
for all their kindness and generosity.

PREFACE

I have really nothing to add to the prefaces of the first two volumes of this work: *1812 – the March on Moscow* and *1812 – Napoleon in Moscow* – except to say that this volume completes the drama of the Russian disaster, as experienced by the invaders and described by them in their own words. For my translation and other methods of presenting my 'word film' the patient reader should turn to the prefaces of those volumes.

The story has of course been told innumerable times. But apart from Sergeant Bourgogne's immortal classic, whether the sheer magnitude of the event has wearied authors or their publishers, it has always been, for understandable reasons, in résumé. As the reader will see, there are many first-hand accounts; indeed the body of material I've drawn on, some 160 participants, has been almost too great, and the fewer the survivors the more detailed their narratives become. First and last my project has been to reconstitute, in maximum close-up, a fragment of past time. Even this, of course, is an illusion. The most objective and circumstantial account adds up to only a millionth part of the reality. Hundreds, perhaps thousands, of other participants must have kept diaries that perished with them in the snows. The mind boggles at the task that would have presented itself if they hadn't! The relevant surviving details have been what has fascinated me. If some are too gruesome for the tender-minded reader I can only suggest he – or she – skip them; but not their implications. To have omitted them would have been intellectually dishonest. *Bellum dulce inexpertis,* says Erasmus: 'How charming is not war to those who've never been in it!'

Despite the ever-growing mass of first-hand material (I've used no others, and new memoirs are always being unearthed), I've tried to let the whole compose itself into what is, I hope, a kind of outsize symphony, whose first brilliant bars were struck by all the trumpets and drums of the Imperial Guard at the Niemen on that Midsummer's Day of 1812 – only to end in the few survivors' frozen 'cello tones of horror and despair.

Lastly, on a personal note. My book has taken almost 25 years to compose. If I've persisted – I might almost say had the fortitude – long enough to complete it, it's not been because of any abiding obsession with military history as such; but because of the striking and manifold glimpses into human nature it affords, until at times the 1812 story has even seemed to be a tragic paradigm of human existence: – the outset's overweening optimism, not to say arrogance – the flawed calculations – the horrific results – the raw egoism of survival – the staunchness of some, the cowardice and fatuity of others, the heroism and true greatness of a few – the friends left by the wayside ... *Homo lupus hominem* – the leopard, alas, hasn't changed its DNA, as our own 'unforgivable century' has all too amply shown. No philosopher of the pessimist school could want a better instance of what Dr Johnson called 'the vanity of human wishes', here geometrically demonstrated by what might be called the aesthetic of its own historical logic. I've had to make nothing up.

My gratitude goes to my publisher Lionel Leventhal for his devotion to a project which in the upshot has run to as many words as there were men in the Grand Army. It was in his office, long ago, our project was conceived. And with it – and with me – he has had almost half a working lifetime's patience. We are both of us grateful to three experts who have given the text their critical attention: namely, Philip J. Haythornthwaite, Digby Smith and John R. Elting, all themselves distinguished authors in the Napoleonic field. Their keen eyes and immense knowledge have eliminated many an error, larger or smaller. I should also particularly like to thank Assistant Professor Algirdas Jakubcionis of Vilnius University for his ready help in suggesting and providing illustrations; and, once again, Peter Harrington of Brown University, Providence, Rhode Island, USA, for helping with the illustrations.

Dawlish, S. Devon, 1996

SOME IMPORTANT EYEWITNESSES

Pierre Auvray, captain, 23rd Dragoons.

Louis Begos, captain adjutant-major, 2nd Swiss Infantry Regiment.

Vincent Bertrand, carabinier sergeant, 7th Light Infantry, Gérard's division, I Corps.

Honoré Beulay, sous-lieutenant, 36th Line, Partonneaux's division, IX Corps.

Hubert Biot, captain, ADC to General Pajol.

Guillaume Bonnet, captain, 18th Line, Razout's division, III Corps.

Jean-François Boulart, major, Guard artillery.

A.-J.-B.-F. Bourgogne, sergeant, Fusiliers-Grenadiers, Young (Middle) Guard.

Paul de Bourgoing, lieutenant, 5th Tirailleurs of the Guard, interpreter to General Delaborde, Young Guard.

Heinrich von Brandt, captain, 2nd Regiment, Vistula Legion.

Jean-Marc Bussy, voltigeur, 3rd Swiss, Merle's division, II Corps.

Jean Calosso, regimental sergeant-major, 24th Chasseurs à Cheval, Castex's brigade, II Corps.

V. E. B. Castellane, captain, orderly officer at IHQ.

Armand de Caulaincourt, general, Master of the Horse, responsible for IHQ transports and the courier service.

Désiré Chlapowski, colonel, 1st Polish Guard Lancers, Colbert's lancer brigade.

Jean-Nicholas Curély, regimental sergeant-major, 20th Chasseurs à Cheval, Corbineau's brigade, II Corps.

Dedem van der Gelder, general of brigade, ex-diplomat, attached to IHQ.

François Dumonceau, captain commanding a company of the 2nd ('Red/Dutch') Guard Lancers, Colbert's lancer brigade.

Victor Dupuy, colonel, 7th Hussars, Bruyère's division, 1st Cavalry Corps.

B. T. Duverger, captain, paymaster to Davout's I Corps.

Henri-Pierre Everts, major, 33rd Line, Dufour's division, I Corps.

Baron A.-J.-F. Fain, Napoleon's Second Secretary.

G. de Faber du Faur, major, commanding reserve artillery, Ney's III Corps.

Raymond Faure, surgeon, Grouchy's 3rd Cavalry Corps (prisoner).

Fezensac, duke, colonel, 4th Line, Razout's division, III Corps.

Charles François, 'the Dromedary of Egypt', captain commanding the 30th Line's grenadier company, Morand's division, I Corps.

Jean-David Freytag, general of brigade, III Corps.

Louise Fusil, actress, travelling with IHQ.

Gaspard Gourgaud, baron, colonel, 1st *officier d'ordonnance*, IHQ.

Lubin Griois, colonel of horse artillery, 3rd Cavalry Corps.

J. L. Henckens, NCO, acting adjutant-major to the 6th Chasseurs à Cheval, Chastel's division, 3rd Cavalry Corps.

Dirk van Hogendorp, baron, general, ADC to Napoleon, governor of Vilna province.

Porphyre Jacquemot, lieutenant, 5th Company, 5th Artillery Regiment, at Vilna.

Henri de Jomini, baron, general, military theorist, governor of Smolensk city.

von Kalckreuth, lieutenant, 2nd Prussian hussars, Niewievski's brigade.

Bellot de Kergorre, war commissary in charge of a Treasury wagon, marching with IHQ.

Captain Eugène Labaume on staff of Prince Eugène's IV Corps, author of the first published account of the campaign (1814).

D.-J. Larrey, baron, Surgeon-General, IHQ.

Cesare de Laugier, adjutant-major of the Guardia d'Onore of the Kingdom of Italy, IV Corps.

Thomas Legler, lieutenant, 1st Swiss Regiment, Merle's division, II Corps.

L.-F. Lejeune, baron, general, until Borodino one of Berthier's ADCs; thereafter chief-of-staff to Davout.

C. F. M. Le Roy, lieutenant-colonel, 85th Line, Dessaix's division, I Corps.

M.-H. de Lignières, count, captain, 1st Guard Foot Chasseurs.

G. L. de Lorencez, general, chief-of-staff to Marshal Oudinot, II Corps.

J.-E.-J.-A. Macdonald, marshal, Duke of Taranto, commanding X Corps.

A.-A.-A. Mailly-Nesle, count, sous-lieutenant, 2nd Carabiniers, riding with IHQ.

Marcelline Marbot, colonel of the 23th Chasseurs, Castex brigade, II Corps.

Albrecht von Muraldt, lieutenant, 4th Bavarian Chevaulegers, Ornano's light cavalry brigade, attached to IV Corps.

Amédée de Pastoret, marquis, war commissary at Witebsk.

Pierre Pelleport, viscount, colonel, 18th Line, Razout's division, III Corps.

François Pils, 'grenadier', artist, batman to Marshal Oudinot, II Corps.

A.-A. Pion des Loches, major, Guard foot artillery.

Planat de la Faye, lieutenant, secretary to General Lariboisière, artillery staff.

F.-R. Pouget, baron, general, governor of Witebsk.

D.-G.-F. Dufour de Pradt, bishop, ambassador at Warsaw.

Jean Rapp, general, ADC to Napoleon.

Roch-Godart, baron, general, governor of Vilna city.

L.-V.-L. Rochechouart, émigré count, serving under General Langeron in Tchitchakov's army.

Franz Roeder, captain, Hessian Footguards.

François Roguet, baron, general, commanding 2nd Division, Imperial Guard.

Heinrich von Roos, surgeon, 3rd Württemberg Chasseurs.

Abraham Rosselet, captain, 3rd Swiss Regiment, Merle's division, II Corps.

M.-J.-T. Rossetti, colonel, ADC to Murat.

N. T. Sauvage, lieutenant of the Train, VIII Corps.

Philippe de Ségur, count, general, assistant prefect of the Palace, in charge of IHQ's mules.

T.-J.-J. Séruzier, baron, colonel of horse artillery, 2nd Cavalry Corps.

Roman Soltyk, count, captain, attached to IHQ's Topographical Department.

Karl von Suckow, captain, Württemberg cavalry, III Corps.

Maurice Tascher, lieutenant of chasseurs à cheval.

F.-A. Teste, baron, general, governor at Viazma.

Auguste Thirion, regimental sergeant-major, 2nd Cuirassiers, Saint-Germain's division, 1st Cavalry Corps.

L.-J. Vionnet, major, Fusiliers-Grenadiers, Young (Middle) Guard.

H. A. Vossler, lieutenant, Prince Louis of Prussia's Hussars.

Jakob Walter, private in a Württemberg infantry regiment, III Corps.

R. Warchot, captain, 8th Polish Lancers.

C.-A.-W. Wedel, count, general, VI Corps.

Sir Robert Wilson, general, the British government's liaison officer at Kutusov's headquarters.

J.-H. Zalusky, captain, 1st Polish Guard Lancers.

For bibliographical details of these and other sources I refer the reader to the comprehensive bibliographies in *1812 – The March on Moscow* and *1812 – Napoleon in Moscow*. Any additional sources are given in the Notes.

Note:
First references to the eyewitnesses whose accounts make up this 'documentary' of Napoleon's retreat from Russia appear in *italic*.

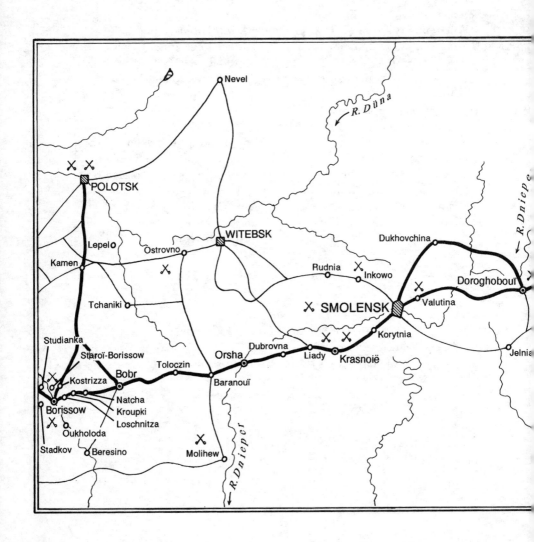

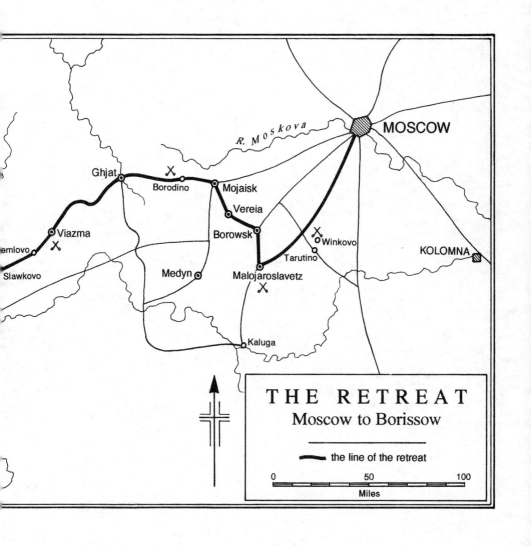

R. M O S K O V A

MOSCOW

Ghjat

Borodino

Mojaisk

Viazma

Vereia

emlovo

Borowsk

Winkovo

KOLOMNA

Slawkovo

Tarutino

Medyn

Malojaroslavetz

Kaluga

THE RETREAT
Moscow to Borissow

the line of the retreat

0   50   100

Miles

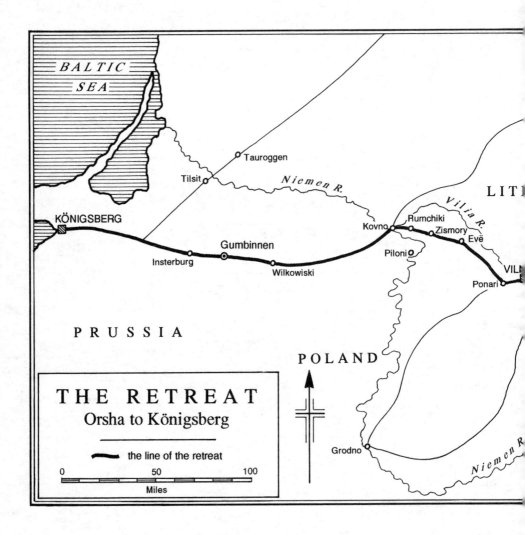

BALTIC
SEA

Tauroggen

Tilsit

Niemen R.

LITI

KÖNIGSBERG

Vilia R.

Kovno

Rumchiki

Zismory

Evë

Insterburg

Gumbinnen

Piloni

VIL

Wilkowiski

Ponari

PRUSSIA

POLAND

THE RETREAT
Orsha to Königsberg

the line of the retreat

0   50   100

Miles

Grodno

Niemen R.

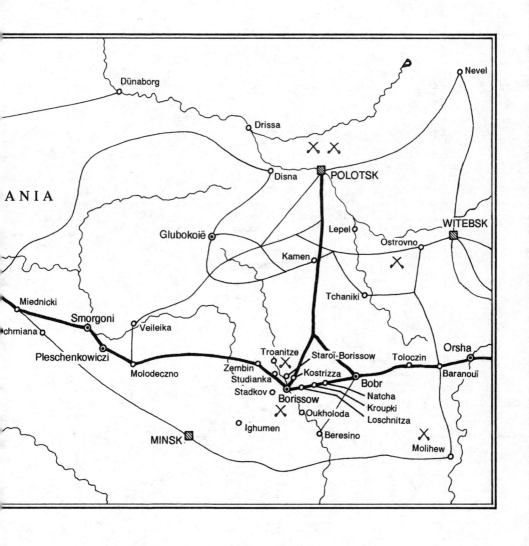

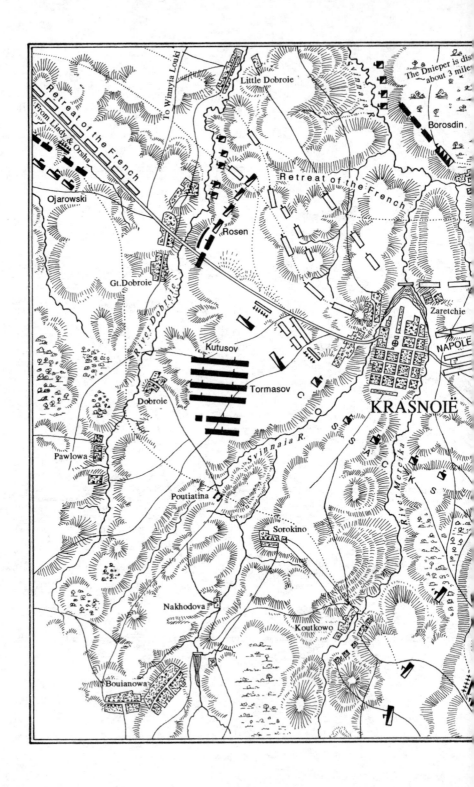

Little Dobroie

To Winnyia Louki

Svinnaia

The Dnieper is dist
— about 3 mile

Borosdin

Retreat of the French

From Liady & Orsha

Ojarowski

Rosen

Retreat of the French

Zaretchie

Gt. Dobroie

River Dobroie

NAPOLE

Kutusov

Tormasov

KRASNOIË

Dobroie

C
O
S
S
A
C
K
S

Pawlowa

Svinnaia R.

Poutiatina

River Mereïka

Sorokino

Nakhodova

Koutkowo

Bouianowa

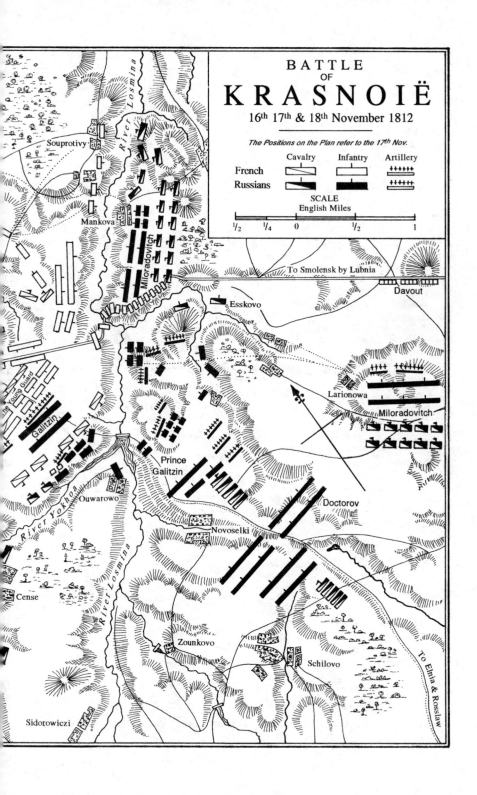

BATTLE
OF
KRASNOIË
16th 17th & 18th November 1812

The Positions on the Plan refer to the 17th Nov.

	Cavalry	Infantry	Artillery
French			++++++
Russians			++++++

SCALE
English Miles

½   ¼   0   ½   1

Souprotivy

River Losmina

Mankova

Miloradovitch

Esskovo

To Smolensk by Lubnia

Davout

Larionowa

Miloradovitch

The Young Guard

Galitzin

Prince Galitzin

River Yokhoa

Ouwarowo

Doctorov

Novoselki

Cense

River Losmina

Zounkovo

Schilovo

To Elnia & Rosslaw

Sidotowiczi

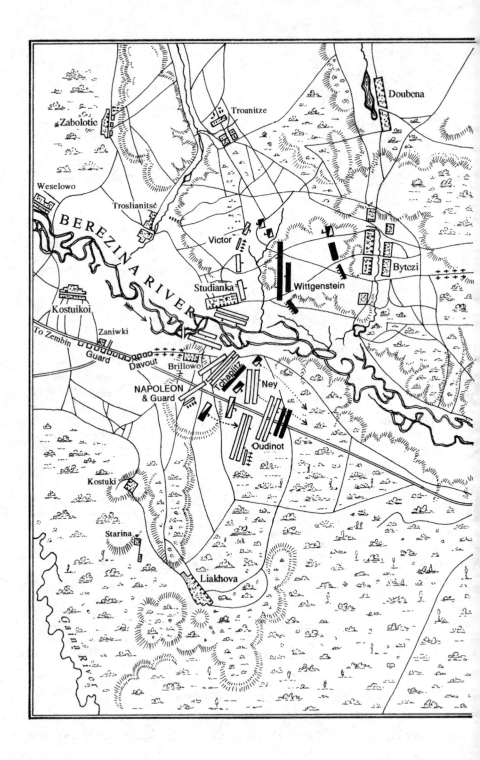

Vougly

To Orsha

Zasténok

Staroi Borissow

Platov

BORISSOW

Wittgenstein

BEREZINA RIVER

Nowoï Stakhov

To Bobr

Bridgehead
Dymki

...roi Stakhov

Tchichakov

...choï Stakhov

Brodnia R.

...chichakov

THE CROSSING
OF THE
BEREZINA
26th 27th & 28th Novr 1812.

	Cavalry	Infantry	Artillery
French			+++++
Russians			+++++

SCALE

1   ½   0   1   2

English Miles

THE EVENTS SO FAR

In the midsummer of 1812 Napoleon had crossed the Niemen with nine army corps: a third of a million men, the largest and most redoubtable, not to say multi-national, army in European history. To effect liaison between their two corps the Russians, refusing him the battle he sought, had hastily withdrawn into the interior until, on 14 August, they'd stood and fought at Smolensk, which had gone up in flames. A pyrrhic victory for the French. The main 'Moscow' army had already lost so many men and horses en route that what should have been the crucial battle (Borodino, 7 September) had been indecisive. Moscow, evacuated by Kutusov and occupied by the French (14 September), had been set in flames by its governor Rostopchin.

For five illusory weeks Napoleon waited in the Kremlin, hoping that the Tsar would make peace, while his advance guard at the Winkovo camp had literally starved. On 18 October the Russians attacked it, and only Murat's prompt action had saved it from annihilation. Next day Napoleon had marched out southwards for Kaluga and the unravaged Ukraine with some 110,000 men and a vast baggage train glutted with the spoils of Moscow. On 24 October 22,000 Italians, Frenchmen and Croats of Eugène's IV Corps ('The Army of Italy') had run into and defeated 70,000 Russians at Malojaroslavetz. Once again Kutusov withdrew, and in the dawn mists next day Napoleon himself was within an ace of capture by Cossacks. Reluctantly deciding the Grand Army had 'done enough for glory' he'd ordered a retreat via the devastated Mojaisk–Viazma road to Smolensk, where he hoped to go into winter quarters before fighting a second campaign in the spring of 1813. 'Towards midnight the two armies turned their backs on each other, marching in opposite directions.'

PHASE ONE
TO SMOLENSK

CHAPTER 1

'A WORD UNKNOWN IN THE FRENCH ARMY'

'Suddenly everyone seemed indifferent' – 'the retreat of the wounded lion' – the Cossacks – the loot of Moscow – contents of a wagon – plight of the wounded and prisoners – Mailly-Nesle keeps singing – Ney's corps at Borowsk – Dumonceau sacrifices his cart – a cock goes into Le Roy's cookpot – Davout's protest – Napoleon as seen by Dedem – growing food shortage – an imperial outburst – plight of the Mojaisk wounded

After a second night in the weaver's cabin Napoleon rides out again toward Malojaroslavetz. Looks out over its smoking ruins and, through the smoke-haze, to the plain beyond. Has Kutusov really retired? The reports are confirmed. And this, his Second Secretary A.-J.-F. Fain notices, removes his final objections to a retreat via the main Mojaisk–Smolensk highway. At least Kutusov's withdrawal will give the army a chance to get clear away. And at 9 a.m. 26 October, 'beside a fire lit at the roadside, he sends the order to everything left at Gorodnia to retire on Borowsk,' a dozen or so miles to the rear; and at 11 a.m. himself turns his back on this foe who has so long and so successfully eluded him.

Only once before has he ever retreated. It is an operation of which he has little or no experience. Everyone knows instinctively what it means. And is depressed by the insight. Hadn't he sworn he'd never retire by the route he'd come by – through 'the desert we ourselves created'?

Between Moscow and Smolensk, as the self-appointed war artist *Albrecht Adam*, who's had his bellyful of campaigning and gone off home, already knows,

'everything was devastated for more than 300 miles. The villages were ruins. The towns were starving hospitals. The few barns or houses were filled with corpses of men and domestic animals, some half-rotted. You only had to follow the cadaverous stench to be sure you were on your right road.'

The few men the ex-cakemaker and his travelling companions had encountered, 'stragglers following the army and lacking all nourishment, were straying hither and thither in utmost distress' in a countryside 'infested with Cossacks and peasants'. Several times they'd 'only escaped them by a miracle'.[1]

Morale is low. Everyone knows how the Emperor, in that hut at Gorodnia, had 'sat for a whole hour pondering his fateful decision'; and how, at dawn yesterday, he'd blundered into a swarm of Cossacks,[2] and could easily have been captured. Though IHQ has done its best to hush up the shocking episode 'by evening next day the whole army knew about it, and was retrospectively trembling with fright'. Also at a rumour that Platov, the Cossacks' supreme hetman, has been 'seized with such violent hatred of the French after his son had been killed in an affray between Cossacks and Polish Uhlans at Vereia that he'd ordered all short fat Frenchmen to be brought before him for special viewing, and even promised his daughter's hand in marriage to anyone – be he only a simple Cossack – who brings Napoleon before him, dead or alive.'

This rumour the Dutch ex-diplomat and general of brigade *Dedem van der Gelder,* who'd incurred Berthier's dislike for the way he'd stood up for foreigners and been told curtly at the Kremlin 'if you aren't satisfied you can go home', is sure 'disquieted Bonaparte'. Though how he knows it he doesn't say. At all events the word 'retreat', which this scathing critic of military behaviour had been told at Witebsk in July 'didn't exist in the French army', has become the grim reality.

Hardly have the units about-faced and marched off one after another down the Borowsk road than it seems to Major *A. A. Pion des Loches,* of the Guard Artillery, that 'everyone seemed seized with indifference'. The newly promoted major, too, is a chronic dissident and a considerable know-all. And to him the 'indifference' already seems to be 'turning our retreat into a rout'. In charge of the Guard Foot Artillery's 1st Company, the 2nd of the Young Guard's and a part of the Train, he's deeply shocked when the Guard Artillery's chief-of-staff General Lallemand comes riding up and orders him

'to abandon the ammunition wagons by preference and destroy the ammunition as I lost horses. In vain I put it to him that it was useless to keep the guns without their supplies: "The Emperor", he said imperiously, "doesn't want a single gun abandoned." What wisdom! Did that man think the guns falling into the enemy's hands would be the only witnesses of his retreat? But his order was carried out.'[3]

As it is, they're already 'abandoning the ammunition wagons, and this without any formal instructions. Each of us was following his own whims.' It doesn't occur to Pion des Loches that while Napoleon will be able to replenish his ammunition at Smolensk, with its immense stocks of everything, cannon are another matter. Lallemand's order will be almost the last he'll receive in Russia.

Naturally not everyone loses heart. Colonel *Lubin Griois* is filled with admiration for the 'rare cool-headedness and courage' of his corps commander General Grouchy, whose 3rd Cavalry Corps is covering the army's rearguard, formed by Davout's I Corps. Griois' horse artillery was the last to cross the bridge over the Luja Gorge:

'Present everywhere, with a serene calm air, he inspired so much confidence, so much assurance in such mounted troops as still remained that the enemy, despite reiterated attempts, could neither overcome nor discourage him. It was the retreat of the wounded lion.'

Yet he has hardly recovered from the wound he received at Borodino. And of his cavalry, after starving for a month at the Winkovo camp,[4] all too little's left. It's a brilliant sunny day. Griois' horse-gunners are having incessant brushes with ever-growing numbers of Cossacks:

'They came and caracoled around us, at times even to within pistol range. Whenever they put too much liveliness into their attack, we halted; and several discharges or a charge by a few platoons sufficed to drive them off. But this meant slowing down, and did them too great an honour. So we limited ourselves to making them respect us by sending them some grape and musket shots as we went on marching.'

Easy enough to identify, even from afar, 'from the disorderliness of their masses, the obscure colour of their horsemen's clothing and the motley of their piebald horses', the Cossacks too have artillery:

'They were crowning all rises in the ground, debouching from all roads, and advancing in all directions. So we faced to all sides. Our guns replied to theirs. And at all points a minor war commenced between our light cavalry and theirs.'

No one's the least bit intimidated by these 'barbarians', whom the troops scornfully refer to as '*les hourrassiers*' (cf. cuirassiers) on account of their 'hurrahs'[5] as they brandished their lances.

'Now and again some of our platoons charged through these clouds of horsemen, who dispersed in front of them, to return at a gallop at some other point to recommence their howlings and provocations.'

There are even single-handed combats,[6]

'a veritable jousting. Each combatant tried to show off his brilliant courage and skill in the eyes of his comrades. Above all our Poles distinguished themselves. Their way of fighting and their shouts, very much the same as their adversaries', added something more lively and picturesque to the noise of the cannon or exploding shells. Alternately pursuing and pursued, depending on whether some comrades came to join them or they had to do with new assailants, they caracoled in little troops between the two armies,'

a truly superb spectacle, Griois thinks, which recalls what he's read about ancient wars. But some of his men are wounded. And these, the first to fall, he puts on to his ammunition wagons:

'But the more gravely wounded, who couldn't keep up with us with their comrades' aid, them we had to leave behind to the Cossacks. Their entreaties, their cries, pierced my heart. But there was nothing else we could do, short of carrying them on our shoulders.'

Cossacks are indeed everywhere. Dedem van der Gelder, relieved of his command since Moscow and attached to Imperial Headquarters, is remembering how, as he'd galloped along this same road 'carrying the Emperor's orders to the Viceroy' during the Malojaroslavetz action, they'd 'put paid to two of my hussar orderlies and I'd only owed it to my horse's swiftness that I hadn't suffered the same fate'. Now he hears they've even surprised Dufour's (ex-Friant's) division and 'taken some cannon'.

Autumn days in Russia aren't meant to last. By and by the sky clouds over, and the weather turns to a depressing drizzle. Through a rain-sodden, heavily wooded countryside of oaks, ashes and silver birches almost stripped of their last leaves and a sombre background of conifers deep green against all these tones of brown and grey, the army rides, trundles or trudges back along the Borowsk road it has just advanced by. Soon the leading units run head on into its grossly swollen baggage train,

'a disorderly caravan of every kind of vehicle, military carriages, little cars, *calèches, kibitkas, droshkis,* most of them attached to little Russian horses ... most opulent and elegant carriages, sutler carts, wagons, barouches, diligences, coaches of every variety, including state coaches,'

that until yesterday had brought up the rear, but now are forced to turn their horses' heads and become its van. Already, en route for the unattainable Ukraine, some 20,000 of its vehicles have either broken down, tangled their spokes with one another's wheelhubs, lost their horses or, getting in the way of the guns, have had to be burned. Whereupon their

'precious objects, pictures, candelabras, whole libraries, gold and silver crucifixes, ciboria or chalices, beautiful carpets, tapestries and wallhangings and cloths embroidered with gold and silver, pieces of silk of every colour, embroidered and brilliant clothes, both men and women's, such as are only seen in the courts of princes ... precious stones, cases filled with diamonds or rolls of ducats'

in a word, all the fantastic loot of Moscow – have been tipped into ditches.[7] Yet there are still masses of vehicles jamming up the road.

If there's one man who's utterly furious with Kutusov for missing out on the 'glorious golden opportunity' he'd been offered at Malojaroslavetz and, in general, for the one-eyed Field Marshal's sloth and *fainéantise,* it's the British government's special envoy and liaison officer at his headquarters, General *Sir Robert Wilson.* The Russian army, he's noting in his *Journal,* so far from being weakened, has actually 'been reinforced by numerous militia and all had fought with determination'. And now here's its senile, or perhaps even treacherous commander letting Bonaparte, that enemy of mankind, give him the slip!

It's enough to drive any right-thinking man mad.

To the retreating army, however, more important by far than its booty are the foodstuffs also stored in its baggage train. And many a foreseeing officer has his well-stocked wagon jolting along with the regimental ones. En route for Moscow, as a mere captain, Pion des Loches had had to share one 'half-filled with my company's effects and reserve shoes' with his lieutenant. Now, promoted major, he's entitled to one of his own, 'smaller, it's true, but sufficient for my victuals for a retreat of 3 to 4 months'. Among other things it also contains a singularly fine Chinese porcelain dinner set which had taken his fancy, and,

'against the eventuality (which I regarded as inevitable) of a winter cantonment on the left bank of the Niemen, a case containing a rather fine edition of Voltaire and Rousseau; Clerc and Levesque's *History of Russia;* Molière's plays, the works of Piron; Montesquieu's *L'Esprit des Lois* and several other works such as Raynal's *Philosophical History*, bound in white calf and gilded on the spine.'

His no less ample larder consists of

'100 cakes of biscuit a foot in diameter, a sack holding a quintal of flour, more than 300 bottles of wine, 20–30 bottles of rum and brandy, more than 10 pounds of tea and as much again of coffee, 50–60 pounds of sugar, 3–4 pounds of chocolate, some pounds of candles.'

For 80 francs he's also bought himself 'one of the most beautiful furs that have been brought back from Moscow'. This chilly day his foresight is seeing itself rewarded: 'I was keeping open house. We were rarely fewer than seven or eight at dinner.' One of his subalterns even has a tent,[8] to which he has access in exchange for sharing his provisions:

'Before leaving we had copious boiling hot soup. I'd put some bread and sugar in my pocket. On me I had a bottle of rum. At the midday halt some glasses of wine; in the course of the day some bits of chocolate, of biscuit, to keep our strength up.'

Surgeon *Louis-Vincent Lagneau* of the Fusiliers-Grenadiers of the Young Guard, too, has a tent, 'very likely', he thinks (erroneously) 'the only one in the army'. He'd had it made at Moscow of striped canvas and got his men to make its pegs and poles:

'My ambulance wagon was big and very heavy. We'd loaded it with wine, rice, biscuits, sugar, coffee and many other supplies, either in small casks of the kind carried by our *cantinières* or else in large sacks. This was to be our viaticum for the retreat.'

Neither has I Corps' paymaster, Captain *P. T. Duverger*, forgotten to look after Number One:

'I had a fortune in furs and paintings. I had any number of cases of figs, of coffee, of liqueurs, of macaroni, of salted fish and meats. But white bread, fresh meat and *vin ordinaire* I had none.'

He too can give a dinner for sixteen of his comrades, among them a general: 'We solemnly toasted the success of the coming campaign and our entry into St Petersburg.'

All this is in crude contrast to the plight of the ordinary ranker. Unless he's a free-enterpriser who's 'hired a retinue of others to care for themselves and their horses and the handling of as many as four carriages in their train', all he has is what he can carry on his back.[9] And Smolensk, with its huge magazines, filled with supplies brought up from the distant rear, is at least ten days, perhaps a fortnight away. Yet even the ranker is to be envied, compared with the sick and wounded. After his narrow escape during yesterday's Cossack flurry – where Napoleon could so easily have been captured – General Pajol's normally healthy ADC Captain *Hubert-François Biot* had been overcome with faintness and collapsed in a ditch. Luckily Pajol had found him there and had him put into 'a wagon driven by the wife of one of his orderlies, a trumpeter of the 11th Chasseurs'. And now Biot's jolting along on top of some sacks of flour.

Even this is to be preferred to the fate of the 2,000 or so Italians, Spaniards, Croats and Frenchmen who'd been wounded at Malo-jaroslavetz. For, General *Armand de Caulaincourt*, Master of the Horse, sees there's no longer any medical service, except perhaps residually in the Guard. Dr *Réné Bourgeois*, also of 3rd Cavalry Corps, had seen the wounded being

'hastily laden on to ambulance wagons and their belongings passed to the *vivandières*. Deprived of all help or food they painfully followed the army.'

Still worse is the plight of the Russian prisoners, of whom several hundreds, too, are being herded along. Yet not quite so brutally, perhaps, as are the tens of thousands of French and allied prisoners who are being herded eastwards: those of them, that is, who've been lucky enough not to have been sold off 'at 2 frs a head' to be tortured and killed by enraged peasants. Of the 1,400 sick and wounded Marshal Mortier's had to leave behind in the three Moscow hospitals as 'too weak to have been transported with their comrades', some have been

'thrown on to wagons to be taken to Twer. All perished from cold and misery, or were assassinated by the peasants charged with driving them who cut their throats to take their coats. The rest were left in the hospitals with the French surgeons who'd stayed to look after them, but were given neither food nor medicines.'[10]

At least one Frenchman, however, is glad he's fallen into British hands. For a mixture of family and political reasons, Wilson has offered to get the nephew of Napoleon's war minister Clarke exchanged. But the young man, realising what would be in store for him, has declined

'until the French were out of their present embarrassments, as he'd "had enough of horse-flesh and Cossack iron". I then despatched him, with a very strong letter of recommendation to all Russians, a good cloak and two hundred roubles.'

Few prisoners have either. Fezensac's dictum about how 'for a prisoner the difference in the way officers and the rank and file are treated can be the difference between life and death' is applying in all its rigour. A few miles away to the south-east Surgeon *M. R. Faure* of the 1st Cavalry Corps, captured in the desperate mêlée at Winkovo,[11] is noticing – with winter coming on any day now – how sure his guards are that the Grand Army's hated *sabacky franzusky* are doomed. At first the officers, at least, aren't being too badly treated:

'A prisoner chief-of-staff came and brought each officer of his corps [the 2nd Cavalry Corps] six ducats from Prince Kutusov, who was acting towards the prisoners with all the generosity and all the greatness of soul to be expected of a man of superior merit. Among all the Russian officers we saw a kind of fraternity reigned that witnessed to a good spirit in an army, and which should be conducive to beautiful actions on campaign.'

Faure's party had left the Winkovo battlefield 'satisfied with the Russians' conduct, under the orders of an officer we had no reason to complain of.'

En route southward for Kaluga they'd found the roads congested with transport vehicles making for the Russian army:

'All day on the third or fourth day we'd heard a cannonade which lasted until ten or twelve that night. It was the Malojaroslavetz affair, three or four leagues [9–12 miles] distance from us.'[12]

They also see masses of peasants who've been forced to evacuate their villages. Reaching Kaluga, 35 miles beyond Malojaroslavetz, Faure sees all its well-to-do inhabitants have fled, just as they'd done at Moscow:

'Those merchants who hadn't yet left were ready to do the same. The governor had made all preparations, in the event of our army threatening it, to set it on fire. He came to feast his eyes on the prey being brought to him. He complained loudly that we wore an air of being in good health. He'd been told the French army lacked victuals, and to have satisfied him we'd have had to be as thin as he was.'

The governor 'abuses' a Pole who'd had a leg carried off at the thigh at Winkovo, and this causes the common folk to follow suit. But Faure forgives them, blames only the governor. Most shocking of all at Kaluga is the brutality being shown to some wounded soldiers who've 'fallen into very bad hands' and are herded together into a filthy building:

'Battered and bruised and no longer having the strength even to cry out, they're wrenched off the carts. A wretch, an inferior officer, charged with conducting them, had had two or three shot en route because they'd seemed to want to escape.'

Only when a superior officer turns a blind eye and lets Faure's comrades go shopping do they momentarily forget their indignation. But even then two or three of them are insulted by 'a Russian wearing a sword'. All this, however, is only the beginning of the prisoners' sufferings.

As always, privileged connections make all the difference. Almost optimally comfortable (apart from his wounded shoulder) is a certain aristocratic sous-lieutenant of the prestigious 2nd Carabiniers, the young Count *A.-A.-A. Mailly-Nesle*. If he and Prince Charles de Beauveau, son of one of Napoleon's chamberlains, are swaying along (none too strongly escorted against Cossacks, he thinks) ahead of the imperial baggage train in one of the Emperor's own carriages, it's because he's a relative of the once famous Marshal Mailly.[13] Like so many other 'whites', Mailly-Nesle has rallied, at least temporarily,[14] to the new regime. But he 'hates the despotism and tyranny weighing on France' and 'sees himself condemned to lead this soldier's life':

'So here I am in an excellent carriage with one of my friends, a footman at my orders, and what's more with three doctors to care for us and bandage our wounds. We had six horses to pull us, with two postilions. I thought I'd got myself out of trouble.'

Since being wounded at Winkovo, the insouciant Mailly-Nesle has bought himself 'a fox pelt, which was very useful to me'. He also has

'a certain plank which was serving us as desk or dining-table by day and for a chandelier in the evening, and which, by placing it across the two seats, served me for a bed'.

From a 'M. Lameau, attached as a geographer to the Emperor's cabinet' he has borrowed Voltaire's *History of Charles XII* of Sweden – the very same 'pretty little volume, morocco gilded on the spine' Napoleon had been reading in the July heats at Witebsk and kept on his bedside table in the Kremlin. In it Mailly-Nesle can read all about how that royal hero's entire army had been wiped out at Poltava, not very far from here, in 1709. Between chapters he sings lustily, to keep his own and his friend Beauveau's courage up. But who's this now, coming toward them – in the wrong direction – if not

'L——, radiant and smart as if he'd just come out of the Tuileries. I asked him why he hadn't stayed on his estates, shooting hares. He replied he'd had to do *his duty*.'

Italics for irony! Snug Mailly-Nesle may be in his comfortable if overcrowded carriage – the only flies in his and his fellow-passengers' ointment are some bugs that are causing them to itch and scratch. Yet 'many of us were badly dressed, still wearing summer trousers. There was a lack of gloves and other items of clothing.'

After spending three days at Czsirkovo, at the junction of the Podolsk and Fominskoië roads, Ney's III Corps have left that village at midnight, 25/26 October, to bring up what they're still assuming is the army's rear. Struggling on through bottomless lanes is newly-promoted Major *Guillaume Bonnet.* He'd gone down with a fever on the eve of leaving Moscow and on the morrow of III Corps' departure had 'left the city, alone, in a *droschka* through streets where no Frenchman was to be seen' but fortunately caught up with his regiment some fifteen miles along the Kaluga road. Now he's noting in his diary how the Cossacks, who're prodding at them to see how they'll react, keep their distance 'with 2 bad cannon, firing 20 roundshot, which as yet haven't hit anyone' – perhaps thanks to 'Guardin's and Beurmann's light cavalry, who've been ordered to set fire to all the villages'. When Ney's men reach Borowsk in the evening they find it too in flames.

A link between III Corps and the main army, these last few days, has been Colbert's Guard Lancer Brigade, consisting of the 1st (Polish) and 2nd (Dutch) Regiments. Himself also ordered to fall back six miles to Borowsk, Colbert has sent his young Belgian Captain *François Dumonceau,* commanding 6th Troop of 2nd Lancers' 2nd Squadron, on ahead to tell Ney about his regiment's near-disastrous affray with a huge horde of Cossacks at Ouvarovskoië.[15] Outside Borowsk he finds

'the head of the Marshal's column peacefully bivouacked. The general in charge there was little moved by my account, and, despite my remonstrances, only slowly got his men under arms to receive us.'

At 8 a.m. on 26 October the always efficient Colbert has sent out a reconnaissance southwards toward Malojaroslavetz. No Cossacks has it seen. But instead, to its dismay, run into a 'long convoy of wounded coming toward us'. Its conductors' statements make it seem likely that the entire army is following in their wake:

'We were all painfully affected. After the success of the day before yesterday we couldn't conceive that it could be a question of a retrograde movement.'

Only now, in the evening, do Ney's men learn that the army's retreating. The news comes as a considerable shock to Bonnet and the Württemberg Major *G. Faber du Faur*, in charge of the 12-pounders of Ney's reserve artillery. And orders come for III Corps to leave for Vereia, the next town along the Mojaisk road. Just as the units are getting ready to leave the Cossacks attack. And Ney's men have to face about and 'in very open country and the plain, stripped [of everything]' draw up in line of battle. Not that Cossacks are anything for an entire army corps to worry about: 'A brief discharge of artillery and a charge by the cavalry of the [Württemberg] Royal Guard sufficed to drive them off.' How many vivid close-ups do we not owe to Faber du Faur's engravings! 'At Borowsk', it seems to him, 'our luck seemed to turn; and in the afternoon of the 26th we began our retreat.'[16]

Bonnet's diary is always succinct. That evening he makes one of his cursory jottings: Though only 1,100 men of its original strength are still with the colours, the 18th Line is still two battalions strong. Only at 7 p.m., as Ney's regiments are leaving their campfires, does the situation dawn on him:

'We must give up [the idea of] marching south. Doubtless we've been repulsed, or the Emperor is manoeuvring – I don't know how.'

At this moment Colbert's men arrive, ride up on to a plateau near the burning town, and bivouack in the midst of 'several infantry units and various parks' squatted around the thousands of campfires. Out there in the darkness Cossacks are still hovering about at the foot of the hill. Yet no one bothers – only his Dutchmen are jittery, so it seems to Dumonceau: somewhat naturally so after their private battle of the 25th: 'We were all more or less demoralised by our setback.' Only when IHQ and the other Guard regiments come marching into Borowsk does a staff officer come and tell Colbert to prepare for an immediate departure for Smolensk. 'News that fulfilled all our wishes. It soon effaced the impression of a retreat.' Perhaps quite a few of Dumonceau's Dutchmen, too, have had their bellyful of campaigning? At least in Russia?

After the Ouvarovskoïe affray they've a lot of wounded to take with them. Keen observer and recorder of events though he is, the 26-year-old Dumonceau is neither emotional nor very tender-hearted. Nevertheless he distributes his food between his favourite mare Liesje,[17] his second horse and his servant Jean's rough-haired '*konya*' (Russian pony), and sacrifices his cart and other contents. And when, next morning, when the Lancer Brigade rides off to its usual position at the head of the Guard column, the cart, with three wounded lancers on it, moves off escorted by a corporal.

Only for safety's sake is the 85th Line's newly promoted Lieutenant-Colonel *C. F. M. Le Roy*[18] travelling with it and I Corps. Promoted by Davout for his efficiency, he's going back to France to the regimental depot. With him, meanwhile, he has his best friend, Lieutenant Jacquet, the only confidant he's ever had, and his ugly-faced but devoted servant Guillaume. Their treasured iron cookpot, which has followed them all the way from Glogau in Prussia, turns this trio into a quartet. The portly Le Roy's abiding concern, namely, is to secure his dinner each day.

What's sauce for the goose is sauce for the gander. Ever since Smolensk the Russians have burnt down their villages, and in the end even their sacred capital. To delay Kutusov's pursuit Napoleon has ordered every village, every house, every cottage, every barn along the route to be fired. Nothing's to be left standing for his men to take shelter in, should they too follow this already devastated route. Strictly speaking it's I Corps, bringing up the rear, that's to carry out this order. But it's being anticipated by the Imperial Guard, heading the column. That night the bald-headed, bespectacled Iron Marshal and his staff sleep

'in a big timber château, furnished and adorned with mirrors and which seemed to offer its proprietor everything desirable and agreeable.'

And in the evening Le Roy joins his men in a hunt for wildfowl. He needn't have troubled himself. Finds his dinner under the straw he's sleeping on in the shape of 'a big cock'. But though it 'begins to raise the devil's own shindy' its protests avail it nothing. It goes straight into the iron cookpot. As for the château, when they wake up next morning 'all that had vanished. Like the village, it was put to the flames. It was the matter of an instant.'

Davout, some people are thinking, is being altogether too methodical with his routines. Should be moving faster. After resting there all day, not until evening are the 85th:

'ordered to advance near a wood where we lit big fires to deceive the Russians. Just before midnight we retired and recrossed the river at the same point as had served us the previous day. Our march would have been concealed had it not been for the imprudence of our scouts who, in withdrawing, set fire to two large villages and so displayed all our movements to the enemy. So closely were we pursued by Cossacks, we were able to fire a few shots at them.'

Shelter's important. Waking up that morning at Borowsk, Dumonceau had found it was snowing. As yet only lightly. Even so, he's been sleeping under

'a thick layer of snow. It was the beginning of winter, which had come to stay. Our march, resumed this time at the head of the whole Imperial Guard, went on under a sombre and misty sky across snowy morasses of mud.'

Now Borowsk, where 'the several bridges over the Protwa had been finished too late', a big traffic jam has been left behind for Davout to cope with. Four miles further on Dedem's called for. He finds Napoleon 'warm-ing his hands behind his back at a bivouac fire made up for him beside a little village on the Vereia road'. With him is Marshal Berthier, his chief-of-staff and the army's major-general. Napoleon orders Dedem to go back and direct both IV and I Corps to take a parallel road to the left of the main column:

> 'He personally expounded his intentions. While the Prince of Neuchâ-tel was explaining His Majesty's intentions to me I had a chance to study the face of this extraordinary man. Then, suddenly turning to the Prince of Neuchâtel, he said: "But he'll be captured." And this in a tone of indifference which struck me, for it wasn't a question of myself but of a general movement of the whole army. Napoleon had the air of one of those chess-players who, seeing the game is lost, finish it honestly and say to themselves: "Now let's have another".'

Dedem doesn't like Napoleon,

> 'because he'd ruined my country. At Borodino I'd witnessed his indif-ference and terrifying stoicism. I'd seen him furious and taken aback when entering Moscow. Now he was calm, not angry, but also not depressed. I thought he'd be great in adversity, and this idea reconciled me to him. But here I found in him the man who sees disaster and realises the whole difficulty of his position, but whose soul isn't a whit put down, and who tells himself: "It's a setback, we must clear out. But they'll meet me again."'

Dedem evidently carries out his mission; for after riding onwards for two or three hours Dumonceau's surprised to see the head of another column appear to his left 'beyond a little stream'. And Colbert sends an adjutant to find out who they are. Yes it's IV Corps. following a cross-country road, doubtless the one Napoleon has indicated. Coming back, the adjutant tells Dumonceau how the Army of Italy had been saddened to see dead lancers from the 2nd Regiment lying on the ground at Ouvarovskoïë 'but been cheered to see so many Cossacks among them'. By then Ouvarovskoïë itself, like all the other villages, was in flames. And in its ashes Captain *Eugène Labaume* on the Viceroy's staff, had been shocked to see

> 'the corpses of several soldiers or peasants, children whose throats had been cut, and several girls massacred on the spot where they'd been raped'.

As for Ouvarovskoïë's magnificent château 'although of timber, of a size and magnificence equal to the most beautiful ones of Italy and full of exquisite furniture and chandeliers', Eugène's gunners had placed some powder wagons on its ground floor and blown it sky-high. Then, marching for Borowsk, IV Corps had left behind it the whole of I Corps and Chastel's cavalry division, which Griois' artillery belongs to, to cover the army's retreat at the distance of a day's march. Some of IV Corps' artillery having got stuck in a ford at Borowsk, it had been necessary to march with the rest of it – and its powder wagons – through the burning town. But, says Adju-tant-Major *Cesare de Laugier* of the Italian Guardia d'Onore, 'we got through without incident. Everywhere we'd seen ammunition wagons abandoned for lack of horses to draw them. Such losses at the very outset of our retreat gave us a premonition of the future in the most sombre colours. And those who were carrying with them the loot of Moscow trembled for their booty.'

After being seriously held up by the immense baggage train, Razout's division of III Corps reaches Vereia, 6 hours' march from Mojaisk, at about midday on 27 October. Following closely in the wake of IHQ are 25 Treasury wagons, stuffed with the imperial spoils from the Kremlin, but also with millions of gold '*napoléons*' (20-franc pieces). The one in the care of the 28-year-old Breton war commissary *A. Bellot de Kergorre* is heavily laden. In a ravine just before Vereia he has to put the brakes on all its four wheels. But this doesn't prevent it, no more than all the other vehicles, from rushing down the steep slope, blocked by the artillery. 'Other carriages, even ammunition wagons, followed our example.' Vereia itself turns out to be

'a pretty little palisaded town which, apart from a fight between Poles and Russians' [its Polish garrison had been taken by surprise and massacred], had only faintly suffered the horrors of war. It was the more unfortunate in that it lay a little off the main road and had momentarily flattered itself it would escape them.'

Its fields haven't been ravaged at all. 'Its well-cultivated gardens were covered with all sorts of vegetables, which in an instant were carried away by our soldiers.' Bonnet's men instantly baptise it Cabbage Town.[19] But Kergorre is upset to see

'men stealing the timbers from barns where generals were sleeping, so that the latter awoke to find themselves under the bare sky'.

Although the weather's decidedly chilly, Napoleon declares: 'The winter won't be on us for eight more days.' But how to gain the shelter of winter quarters at Smolensk before then?

Warming his hands at a campfire that evening is one of Napoleon's aristocratic staff officers: Squadron-Leader Count *V.-E. B. de Castellane*, ADC to Count *Louis de Narbonne*, who in turn is ADC to the Emperor. The day after the army had marched out from Moscow Castellane had been sent off on mission to the 1st and 2nd Battalions of the Spanish Joseph-Napoleon Regiment, stationed at Malo-Viazma,[20] on the main Moscow–Mojaisk highway. And it had been Castellane's business to liaise with them at Prince Galitzin's superb country house, where their task had been to protect the convoys of wounded retiring westwards from Cossack incursions. After doing '40 miles by cross-country roads' he'd found

'adjutant-commandant Bourmont, a very amiable man, the one who'd served with the Chouans. But for the last two years he'd been serving with the Emperor's army and as yet hadn't been given the cross, though it had been requested for him. Under his orders he had two battalions of the Spanish Joseph-Napoleon Regiment and two of Bavarian chevaulegers.'

On 22 October they'd left Malo-Viazma and marched to the village of Koubinskoë:

'Soon after we'd got there the Cossacks appeared and carried out a hurrah against a convoy of wounded. The isolated men escorting it had behaved badly. Colonel de Bourmont called his men to arms, I carried the order to the Bavarian colonel to charge with his brigade. He answered that his horses were too exhausted to gallop. During that expedition the only use he was to us was to exhaust 50 infantrymen a day to protect his forage and, to the Spaniards' great annoyance, to eat sheep from the flock they'd collected. I asked the Joseph-Napoleon regiment to provide me with 50 men of goodwill to go on ahead a couple of miles and save more of the [wounded] men. Those 50 grenadiers marched at the double toward the enemy. We rescued 100 well-armed men who'd hidden in the woods, without firing a shot.'

Now five days have gone by. After hearing about IV Corps' exploits at Malojaroslavetz, Castellane and the Spaniards' Major Doreille are talking over their own experiences. With some difficulty. Doreille, namely, is a native of Tarascon, and 'can't speak French', only Provençal. The 39-year-old Doreille tells the handsome young aristocrat from Napoleon's staff how

'he'd had six brothers killed since the beginning of the revolutionary wars. He was the sole support of his old and poverty-stricken mother.'

On this snowy morning of 27 October even the *Intendance-Générale*, escorting the Treasure, has to depart in a hurry. 'The Cossack guns were at half-range.' But his servants having found a chicken and some onions, Belot de Kergorre, loth to abandon his stew, delays departure until the last possible moment. And indeed, though it's only a week since the army left Moscow, food's beginning to be in short supply. As yet Colonel *Montesquiou de Fezensac* of the 4th Line (III Corps) is noticing there are large discrepancies between various units:

'One regiment had kept some oxen and had no bread; another had flour but lacked meat. In the same regiment some companies were dying of hunger while others were living in abundance. And though the superior officers ordered them to share and share alike, egoism employed every means to outwit their supervision and escape their authority.'

I Corps' horses, Paymaster Duverger is distressed to see,

'always on the march, had nothing to eat and were collapsing from fatigue and abstinence. The collapse of a horse was our good fortune. The poor beast was hacked to pieces. Horseflesh isn't bad for the health. But it's hard and fibrous. Some preferred the liver. The nights were beginning to be long and cold. We were sleeping on a damp and frozen soil. The ideal bivouac was one in which we could stretch out softly on a little straw in front of a fire of dry wood, sheltered by a pine forest. If there was horse stew, some wheatbread, and a flask of aquavit to pass around, it was a feast.'

'From the second day of the retreat,' Davout's reluctant chief-of-staff, the future artist Baron *Louis-François Lejeune*, says:

'a cold fine drizzle came to add itself to our mental torments, the difficulties of the route and the inconveniences of the bad weather. The cold damp nights spent in bivouac, the inadequate nourishment from unleavened munition bread or badly cooked broth began to give the troops dysentery.[21] The sick no longer had the strength to keep up with their units and were falling behind.'

Even the 7th Hussars' new colonel *Victor Dupuy* is having to subsist all day on a cup of sugared coffee for breakfast. All the long way from the Niemen to Moscow his regiment had been in the extreme van. Then they'd starved in the Winkovo camp. Had no share in Moscow's culinary riches. Now Roussel d'Hurbal's brigade of Bruyères' light cavalry division of Nansouty's 1st Cavalry Corps is forming IV Corps' rearguard. Arriving at the regiment's bivouac Dupuy walks to and fro beside the road,

'waiting until some Polish marauders should pass. I bought some rare and furtive provisions for their weight in gold. A bit of pork grilled on charcoal, or some fistfuls of flour dipped in melted snow helped me and my companions to believe we weren't hungry.'

Unfortunately this windfall only upsets their stomachs. But then Dupuy has a real stroke of luck:

'I saw my former farrier of the élite company of the 11th Chasseurs, Bouton by name, and now sergeant-major of the Chasseurs of the Imperial Guard. He was escorting a wagon. He offered me some sugar and coffee. I emptied all my dirty linen out of my portmanteau and furnished it with these provisions, very useful to me thereafter. Having taken a good dose of coffee in the morning, I didn't feel hungry all day.'

Everyone's feeling more and more miserable. Particularly so sous-Lieutenant *Pierre Auvray* of the 23rd Dragoons, escorting the baggage hour after hour,

'without any rest from 2 a.m. to 11 p.m. and at each moment being attacked by peasants dressed as Cossacks who charged the column to get hold of the superb carriages many officers had supplied themselves with in Moscow. These carriages, laden with gold, silver and victuals, drew the attention of peasants whom the fires had deprived of their asylums. Every day they took some, along with their drivers, whom they stripped and sent back again.'

Mailly-Nesle hears a new word in the French language, '*se démoraliser*'. Defines it as 'a kind of nostalgia'. Another officer who dates its first outbreak from this second day of the retreat is Lieutenant *N. L. Planat de la Faye*, general factotum and 'man of letters' to General Lariboisière, supreme commander of the army's artillery. IHQ and the artillery staff has just got to Vereia when

'after dinner an officer came in who'd had nothing to eat since morning. Though by nature compassionate and disposed toward everything called sacrifice and devotion, I myself hadn't been exempt from the barbarism and brutal egoism,' now beginning to prevail. 'We had nothing left to give him except a little bread or biscuit and a glass of bad brandy.' Irritated, the officer lodges a formal complaint. Since it's Planat's comrade and friend Honoré de Lariboisière, the general's surviving son, who's responsible for distributing rations, he goes to his father to explain. But ever since his other son Frédéric's death after Borodino[22] old Lariboisière has been deeply depressed. And all Honoré gets is a furious upbraiding. That day, too, Planat loses – for all futurity – another friend, on account of a 'little piece of meat not quite equally divided'.

IV Corps headquarters has spent the night in a hut in the miserable hamlet of Alféréva. Only Prince Eugène and his divisional generals have been able to get some shelter. His staff-captain Labaume, too, dates the disintegration of morale from that day. Any army – as Napoleon had memorably pointed out but seems temporarily to have forgotten – marches on its stomach. And Lieutenant *Albrecht von Muraldt* of IV Corps' 4th Bavarian Chevaulegers is shocked to notice how quickly the spreading food shortage is affecting obedience and military discipline:

'Men were beginning to leave the ranks without permission, and anyone who wasn't present when the others bivouacked was hardly asked after when leaving next morning. Yet this was only the beginning!'

Two days later Lieutenant *Louis-Joseph Vionnet*, also of the hitherto so well-disciplined Fusiliers-Grenadiers of the Young Guard, will be noting how

'the habit of stealing was establishing itself in the army. From now on nothing was safe except what one wore on one's own person. Men were taking portmanteaux from horses and pots off fires,'

placing Le Roy's and Jacquet's great iron cookpot in perpetual danger. Already men are withdrawing into the forest to eat such little bread as they still have left. Here and there a unit seems to be miraculously intact. From his carriage Mailly-Nesle admires a regiment of Portuguese light cavalry as it comes trotting across the fields. 'Their excellent condition, the rested air of these men in chestnut brown uniforms, their handsome faces, serious and brown, provoked our admiration.'[23] Only the exiguous Pion des Loches, it seems, is snug:

'In the evenings we raised our tent. I undressed, I lay down on bearskins and there, in my sleeping-bag, covered by my fur, slept as soundly as at any bivouac. My servant Louvrier, a strong robust man, looked after my horses. Thanks to the precautions I'd taken at Moscow I had less to suffer from than anyone.'

Just outside Vereia the retreating army runs into Marshal Mortier's two Young Guard divisions. They'd left Moscow, four-fifths of it in ashes, at 7 a.m. on 22 October, with orders to march for Borowsk via Vereia, after blowing up the Kremlin. Not until 11 p.m. that evening had the last unit left the city. While Mortier had been making his preparations something extraordinary had happened. Curious to see what was going on, General

Winzingerode, the commander of the Russian forces north of the city, had taken it into his head to walk into it dressed in a civilian overcoat. Upon his trying to chat up a post of the 5th Tirailleurs,[24] its lieutenant, who'd had his wits about him, had arrested him despite his 'vain attempt to save himself by pretending he'd come to parley and waving a white handkerchief,' and sent him to Mortier. Winzingerode's ADC, a Captain Narishkin, wondering what had become of his chief, had insisted on also being taken prisoner.

Mortier's force consists of General Delaborde's Young Guard division with its artillery, some sappers, a brigade of 500 cavalry who still have their mounts, and Carrière's scratch brigade of 4,000 troopers who haven't. As they join the column, Dr *Heinrich von Roos* of the 3rd Württemberg Chasseurs notes these provisional units are

'armed like infantrymen with muskets from the Moscow arsenal. This armament was so little to their liking that when they saw the great disorder prevailing among us they threw away both muskets and ammunition and each went aside on his own, his portmanteau on his back and holding the ramrod in his hand like a stick, without any officer being able to prevent them.'

Just as Napoleon's getting off his horse Winzingerode and Narishkin are brought before him. And instantly he's anything but the calm self-possessed person Dedem had seen. The Emperor of the French has a long memory.

'"Who are you?" he shouts at Winzingerode, unleashing on him all his frustration at the turn the campaign has taken:

'"A man without a country! You've always been my personal enemy. You've fought with the Austrians against me, then asked to serve with the Russians. You've been one of the greatest perpetrators of this war.[25] Yet you were born in the kingdom of Württemberg, in the states of the Confederation of the Rhine! You're my subject! You aren't an ordinary enemy, you're a rebel, and I've the right to bring you before a court. Do you see this desolate countryside, Monsieur, these villages in flames? Who ought to be reproached with these disasters, who are they due to? To fifty adventurers like yourself, suborned by England, which has thrown them on the Continent. You've been taken with weapons in your hand. I've the right to have you shot!"'

Winzingerode tries to explain that since the French had anyway been on the verge of evacuating Moscow there'd been no point in further hostilities. His attempted parley had aimed at avoiding useless bloodshed and above all at preventing any further damage to the city. He denies he's one of Napoleon's subjects, not having been in his native country since he was a child. If he's serving Tsar Alexander it's out of personal devotion.

'The more M. de Winzingerode tried to justify himself, the angrier the Emperor became, raising his voice so loud that even the picket could hear him.'

Present at the stormy interview are Caulaincourt, for four years ambassador at St Petersburg and explicitly against the war from the outset. The middle-aged Berthier, who's beginning to have had enough of wars of any kind. And, at a more respectful distance, other staff officers.[26]

> 'At first the officers of his entourage had withdrawn a little. Everyone was on tenterhooks. Glancing at each other, we could see in every eye the distress caused by this painful scene.'

Berthier, standing closest to his master, is most distressed of all, as the others can

> 'see in his expression, and his remarks confirmed it when, on some pretext, he was able to join us. The Emperor called for the gendarmes to take M. de Winzingerode away. When no one passed on this order, he repeated it so loudly that the two men attached to the picket stepped forward. The Emperor then repeated to the prisoner some of the charges, adding that he deserved to be shot as a traitor.'

Stung by this word Winzingerode,

> 'who'd been listening with eyes lowered to the ground, drew himself up, raised his head, and looking straight at the Emperor and those standing nearest to him, said loudly:
>
> '"As whatever you please, Sire – but not as a traitor!"
>
> 'And walked away of his own accord, ahead of the guards, who kept their distance.'

Now Murat arrives on the scene and tries to calm his raging brother-in-law who's

> 'walking to and fro with nervous hurried steps, summoning now one of us, now another, to vent his anger. He met only with silence.'

Caulaincourt, who has witnessed many an imperial rage, has 'never seen him so angry.' Clearly Winzingerode's life's in danger. General *Jean Rapp*, Napoleon's favourite ADC, 'is sure he'd have been in despair if this order, obviously dictated in a furious rage, had been carried out'; and joins with others in begging him to postpone it. This only sets Napoleon off inveighing against the Russian nobility 'which had dragged Alexander into making war:

> '"The weight of this war is going to fall on those who've provoked it. In the spring I'll go to St Petersburg and throw that town into the Neva."'

Berthier, 'beside himself', sends an ADC to the headquarters élite gendarmes, ordering them to treat their prisoner with consideration. 'Everyone,' says de Ségur,[27] 'hastened to wait upon the captive general to reassure and condole with him.' But neither Berthier nor Caulaincourt have

> 'ever seen the Emperor so completely lose control of himself. A little way off we could see a fine large house. The Emperor sent two squadrons to sack and fire it, adding: "Since these barbarians like to burn their towns we must help them."'

An action which strikes Caulaincourt as peculiarly shocking:

> 'It was the only time I'd ever heard him give such an order. As a rule he tried to prevent such destruction as only harmed private interests or ruined private citizens. He returned to Vereia before nightfall. Not one inhabitant remained.'

To Bessières' ADC Major Baudus, too, the scene has come as 'one more proof that the Emperor perfectly realised the depths of the abyss to whose edge he'd let himself be drawn'. The wounded Rapp and all the staff are sorry for the 'traitor' and do what they can for him and for his loyal and self-sacrificing ADC. Narishkin, says Dedem, 'was shown more consideration'.

Napoleon usually doesn't give a fig for Berthier's views – his job is simply to implement the commander-in-chief's orders. But now even Berthier makes so bold as to point out that Winzingerode *isn't* in fact one of the Emperor's subjects. Together with Caulaincourt he urges Murat to have another word with him. By now Caulaincourt's anyway becoming easier in his mind about the outcome 'in proportion to the Emperor's annoyance. Princes, like other men, have a conscience which bids them right the wrongs they've done.' And by and by he's sent for.

'"Has the courier arrived?"' Napoleon asks.

The question's a good omen. Napoleon knows very well it's still too early in the day,[28] and is already 'much quieter'. But still needs to vent his spleen. Winzingerode's behaviour, Caulaincourt hastily agrees, has been 'most irregular'; but surely His Majesty has 'used his prisoner so sternly in words that no further punishment is needed?' Won't further severity only look like an act of personal act of malice against the Tsar, whose ADC Winzingerode is? Rulers, Caulaincourt makes so bold as to observe,

'"have no need, after so many cannonballs have been exchanged, to come personally to grips with each other".

'The Emperor began to laugh, and affectionately pinched my ear, as was his habit when he tried to coax people.

'"You're right. But Winzingerode's a bad character, a schemer, a secret agent of the London government and Alexander's been at fault in making him his ADC."'

But he, Napoleon, won't be equally at fault in treating him badly:

'"I'd rather they'd captured a Russian. These foreigners in the service of the highest bidder are a poor   catch. So it's for Alexander's sake you're taking an   interest in him? Well, well, we won't do him any harm."

'The Emperor gave me a little tap on the cheek, his signal mark of affection. From the outset I'd seen he only wanted an excuse to go back on his words.'

And in fact Napoleon tells Caulaincourt to 'try to persuade Narishkin to dine with us'. As for Winzingerode,

'"I'll send him to France, under a good escort, to prevent him from intriguing throughout Europe with three or four other firebrands of his sort."'

At dinner Napoleon turns to Narishkin:

'"What's your name?"

'"Narishkin," the young officer replied.

'"Narishkin! With a name like that one is too good to be adjutant to a defector."'

'This piece of rudeness upset us extremely,' Rapp says, 'and we did all we could to make the general overlook it.' Still speaking to Narishkin, Napoleon tells him what an excellent moment it is for making an honourable peace, "the French army's movement being in some sort a retreat". Evidently he's intending to send Narishkin to Alexander.

Was the calm feigned, and the rage a real explosion of fury and frustration? Or vice versa? 'The trouble with Napoleon', writes Caulaincourt, 'was that he never for a moment stopped playing the great emperor.' In what concerns Narishkin, he changes his mind. For next day both men are sent to the head of the column to set out for France with an officer and an élite gendarme. Caulaincourt, who's already given Narishkin some money, sends his valet after him with one of his own overcoats, against the increasing cold.

In sharp contrast to the indiscipline prevailing among the 4,000 dismounted cavalry, Delaborde's division is in good shape. But his well-educated interpreter Lieutenant *Paul de Bourgoing* is oddly hatted; having unaccountably lost his own hat on eve of quitting Moscow, he's had to replace it with a doctor's head-dress. With him he still has his faithful and enterprising servant Victor, the plucky 13-year-old Parisian street-urchin who'd so dearly have liked to enlist as a drummer-boy, but been found too puny of stature, and whom Bourgoing out of pure kindness had taken on as his 'philistine'. Delaborde's nature, too, is generous and hospitable. His little household has grown to include four French civilians from Moscow and two actresses from the French Theatre in Moscow. Also a painter named Lavanpierre, and a tutor ('a learned grammarian') named Lardillon. Mme. Anthony, one of the actresses, is sure she'll never see France again, and is often in tears.[29] 'The day we left Vereia,' Planat de la Faye goes on,

> 'began our embarrassments caused by the quantity of useless vehicles encumbering the army. In the defiles the military police and artillery officers overturned and smashed several of these carriages to right and left of the road. Above all they were pitiless toward such sutlers' wagons as didn't belong to any regiment. One of them being overturned, a magnificent harp and books bound in morocco and gilded on the spines fell out, to a great burst of laughter from all present.'

More and more guns and ammunition wagons are having to be left abandoned. All their horses have to eat is mouldy thatch off the one-storey timber cottages. Pion des Loches is shocked to see how

> 'superior officers first had the abandoned ammunition wagons parked, then burnt. The men were throwing away their weapons and packs to march more easily.'

Soon, he thinks, the army won't even be able to defend itself.

Terrible things happen in the evening of 28 October as Davout's corps reaches Vereia, greatly upsetting the cultured and humane Griois:

'At the entrance to the town some infantry battalions had halted to the left of the road. In front of them I saw their divisional general Friederichs, telling his men to take three Russian peasants they'd just seized to a certain distance and kill them. I trembled when I heard this order given at the top of his voice. The peasants thought they were being taken to some post to be guarded – I can still see them with their great overcoats and their cloth caps on which was sewn a Greek cross, impassively walking to their deaths as they didn't know what their fate was to be.'

Does such a cross worn on the headgear of the *opolchni* conscripts make them liable to pain of death if captured? Evidently Friederichs thinks so. They only have to go 40 paces from

'the general, who was following them with his eyes. I heard their cries. All three had had a bayonet thrust into the small of their backs just as they were entering a little straw hut. There they all fell down together, and the fire being put to it stifled their groans. I only knew this General Friederichs by sight. He was certainly one of the handsomest men in the army. But this abominable trait ever afterwards made me regard him with horror.'[30]

Although marching on ahead, even the Guard is obeying the order to burn everything, leaving it to III, IV and V Corps to 'set fire to the few houses that had been left'. This of course is leaving no shelter at all for I Corps. That evening Davout writes to Berthier from Vereia and asks His Serene Highness

'to give such orders as may be needed so that the troops marching ahead of the advance guard shall not burn the villages, thus destroying the resources the rearguard has such great need of.'

He even makes so bold as to point out that 'it alone should be charged with burning the villages it abandons'. And adds: 'The Emperor's army will have great benefit of this.' The order, Griois says, was rescinded. But the practice went on.

Not entirely, it seems. A big village has been left for the 85th to set fire to: 'Though it had offered us good shelter, it was none the less delivered over to the flames. As it lay in a dell we remained on the other slope while it burnt. On the far side was the enemy, indifferently watching this act of destruction.'

The same day 'some ammunition wagons were set fire to and blew up. In the distance the hollow projectiles, bursting one after another, emulated the sound of a battle.'

As for Vereia itself, that little palisaded town of muddy streets whose culinary delights Le Roy had earlier sampled when he'd visited it under more idyllic circumstances with a large detachment just before reaching Moscow,[31] 'though its gardens still offered us some vegetables the town itself no longer existed'.

I Corps is on its way from Vereia's blackened ruins towards Mojaisk where everyone knows they'll be rejoining the main Moscow–Smolensk highway, when suddenly the 85th are 'almost surrounded by enemy cavalry who seemed disposed to disturb us. It was then we, for the first time, made use of our regimental 4-pounders, which kept the enemy at a respectful distance.'

After Vereia comes Mojaisk. 'We'd passed through it 51 days ago as victors.' Since then it's been occupied by the sorry remnant of the Westphalian VIII Corps. Its commander General Junot, having lost the campaign for Napoleon at Valutina,[32] had been forbidden to show his face at the Kremlin. At Mojaisk, despite Commissary Kergorre's heroic disobedience to orders in his efforts to feed them and the plentiful harvest, the insouciant and selfish attitudes of Junot's staff had let any number of the Borodino wounded starve to death.[33] But now room must be found on the army's transports for the 2,000 or so who've survived and fill Mojaisk's remaining houses. What about the 200 wagons that have been brought from Moscow expressly for the purpose?

'Having left Moscow already full of refugees, women and children, the vehicles had had to take up the men wounded at Winkovo and Malo-jaroslavetz. And now these at Mojaisk!'

Hastily carried out and put on carts and carriages

'drawn by men from the hospitals, they were placed on the top-seats, on the fore-carriages, behind on the trunks, on the seats, in the fodder-carts. They were even put on the hoods of wagons if there wasn't any room underneath. One can imagine the spectacle our convoys presented. At the smallest jolt the least securely placed fell off. The drivers took no care. And the driver who followed after, if not distracted or in a stupor or away from his horses, or even for fear of stopping and losing his place in the queue, would drive on pitilessly over the body of the wretch who'd fallen.'

The weather's fine but chilly. 'Fortunately the keen frost preserved us from the infection the great numbers of dead men and horses would otherwise inevitably have caused.' Even so, IHQ skirts the town at a distance, for safety's sake, and presumably neither Planat nor Honoré Lariboisière visit the 'spot in the ruinous town wall' where they'd placed the mortal remains of young Ferdinand.[34] Do they cast a glance in that direction? Never, says Planat, will he forget its exact location.

When on the morrow Davout's regiments also 'skirt Mojaisk to avoid the last houses which had just been set fire to', they see how in the end only the church tower 'white amid black swirling smoke' is left standing, 'its clock still striking the hours after the town no longer existed'.

CHAPTER 2
BORODINO REVISITED

At Napoleon's bedside – the grim field of Borodino – 'cursing warfare, he predicted the Emperor himself would be abandoned'– ruthless vivandières *ditch the wounded – who shot the Russian prisoners? – Lejeune saves his sister – Davout's rearguard at Kolotskoïë abbey – a windfall at Ghjat – a heroic carabinier – Griois defends his cart – a devastated countryside – Colonel Chopin's robber band – a helpful Russian*

Spending the night of Wednesday, 28 October (the one Davout spends at Vereia) in the ruined château of Ouspenskoïë, just beyond Mojaisk, Napoleon, at 2 a.m., sends for Caulaincourt. 'He was in bed.' Telling the Master of the Horse to make sure the door's properly closed, he says he's to sit down at his bedside. 'This wasn't habitual with him.'

A long conversation follows. He asks Caulaincourt to speak his mind frankly about the situation. Wise from his four winters as ambassador at St Petersburg, Caulaincourt predicts the effects of extreme cold, and reminds him of 'the reply Alexander was said to have given when he'd got the peace proposals from Moscow: "My campaign's just beginning."'[1] The allusion irritates Napoleon, as does any reminder of Caulaincourt's personal knowledge of, and friendship with, the Tsar:

'"Your prophet Alexander's been wrong more than once," he retorted. But there was no lightness in his reply. His troops' superior intelligence would somehow enable them to protect themselves against the cold – they'd be able to take the same precautions as the Russians did, or even improve on them.'

And then there are the 'Polish Cossacks' that Ambassador Pradt's[2] certainly been drumming up in Warsaw. Any day now he's expecting to run into 1,500 or 2,000 of them. They'll change the situation entirely. Flanking the army, they'll enable it to rest and find food. Caulaincourt notes Napoleon's – as it seems – incurable optimism. After talking for an hour about one thing and another, he comes suddenly to the point. As soon as he has 'established the army in some definite position' it's 'possible, even likely' that he'll leave it and go back to Paris. What does Caulaincourt think about the idea? What effect will it have on morale? Caulaincourt, who's least of all a yes-man, agrees that it's an excellent idea, the best way of re-organising it and keeping a firm hand on Europe. He should date his orders of the day, like his decrees, from the Tuileries; but be careful about choosing the right moment to leave.'It was 5.30 when the Emperor dismissed me.'

If only they'd left Moscow a fortnight earlier, instead of hanging about waiting for peace overtures from the Tsar! That's what many people are thinking as they slowly pull out on to the main Smolensk road. Then they'd already be ensconced behind those medieval walls on which even the Grand Army's 12-pounders had made no impression, living off the well-stocked magazines and protected by Marshal Victor's IX Corps! True, the frozen Dnieper will no longer provide a line of defence. But, welcomed by its light infantrymen lining the surrounding hills, no one doubts the army's ability to hold out until the spring, far off though it be, five or six months away! And by then Marshal Augereau's XI (Reserve) Corps and Schwarzenberg's Austrians, together with many thousands of 'Polish Cossacks', will have come up and re-established the situation. And if the Tsar still doesn't make peace – why, then they'll march on Petersburg. It too is inflammable!

But from Mojaisk to Smolensk is 80 leagues,[3] well over 200 miles.

Meanwhile where's Kutusov? Fastest melting away of all is the cavalry – Lieutenant *von Kalckreuth*'s regiment, the 2nd Prussian Hussars, for instance, which had performed so brilliantly at Ostrovno in July,[4] now counts only twenty troopers and officers. And without cavalry reconnaissance an army's blind and deaf. So it's impossible to know. In fact Kutusov's main body is some 30 to 40 miles away to the south, following the road to Medyn (where Wilson's diary will rejoice on 30 October, 'The Cossacks have defeated the advanced guard of Prince Poniatowski.'). By now 'the English general', as Wilson always styles himself, is beside himself with fury at Kutusov's sloth, his indifference to his opportunities to annihilate the infamous Buonaparte, once and for all; and by making 'a false movement, occasioned by his personal terror rather than by an error of judgement', having made 'a circuit of near 80 versts [50 miles]' and losing sight of the French:

'I can scarcely behave with common decency in his presence. His feebleness outrages me to such a degree that I have declared, if he remains Commander-in-Chief, that I must retire from this army.'

Probably nothing would please Kutusov more. Pestered by all and sundry, he's beswarmed with intrigues. And his army too is extremely short of rations as it struggles along the Medyn road.

At least the Smolensk road is better. 'Leaving the ploughed fields which had cost us more than 10,000 vehicles', the army begins moving off down it. First, the pitiful remains of Junot's (Westphalian) VIII Corps. Then the Imperial Guard. Then III Corps. Then Eugène's IV Corps. Last – a day's march behind – Davout's once so formidable I Corps. Each in turn crosses the broken ground beyond Mojaisk – those ravines where, on 8 September, Murat's impulsiveness had thrown away the lives of so many of his troopers – and plunges into the forest beyond. Beyond that, everyone knows, lies the terrible battlefield.

There have been others where Napoleon has held commemorative parades – Austerlitz, for instance. No one thinks of holding one here.

Emerging from the forest they first see to their right 'the remains of the cabins where Kutusov had camped' and where he'd made his fateful decision to retreat and, if necessary, even abandon Moscow. But most of the mournful scene is spread out to their left: 'It was a cold day,' Lieutenant von Muraldt of IV Corps' 4th Bavarian Chasseurs will always remember, 'and a furiously whirling snow, whipped up by an icy wind, did nothing to dispel our gloomy thoughts.'

Dumonceau, riding on as usual ahead of the rest of the Guard and 'crossing the Borodino bridge where so many had fallen',[5] can just make out

'the former redoubts, covered in snow. Standing out white against a murky horizon, they were no longer visible except as shapeless hillocks. This plain, once so noisy and animated, was now only a vast solitude.'

The sole sign of life he can see is 'a horseman, doubtless looking for some souvenir or memento'. Also, 'the immense flocks of carrion crows which for several days now had constituted our habitual cortège, as if following a prey they could be sure of' and whose sinister activities are marked all along the roadside 'by messy reddened snow from which protruded the hideous remains of half-eaten corpses'.[6] Mailly-Nesle and his favoured companions, looking out of their carriage, notice that many of the dead are

'as yet hardly decomposed, and had kept what one might call a physiognomy. Almost all had their eyes fixedly open. Their beards had grown out of all measure for this epoch. And a bricklike and Prussian-blue colour, marbling their cheeks, gave them an abominably filthy and messy aspect.'

Following immediately behind with IHQ, another aristocratic officer, Quartermaster *Anatole de Montesquiou*, is horrified to see

'a Frenchman wounded at this battle who'd been left without help. He'd sat down with his back to a tree beside the road and was waiting for the Emperor to pass. As soon as he recognised him he advanced on all fours and reproached him for all he'd suffered by being so cruelly abandoned. He went on cursing war and predicting that the Emperor himself would be abandoned and forgotten. The Emperor showed only pity. Turning to his officers who were following him he said: "Have this poor fellow put in a carriage and lavish every care on him."'

Captain *K. F. E. von Suckow*, who'd had to leave his dead Württembergers unburied, finds

'the famous battlefield in exactly the same state as we'd left it in on 8 or 9 September. More than 20,000 corpses of men and horses in a more or less advanced state of decomposition were lying where they'd fallen'.

The only difference, Surgeon-Major von Roos of the 3rd Württemberg Chasseurs notes, is that 'the grass had grown since that sanguinary day'. Not far from the Great Redoubt, the bloodiest spot of all, von Suckow sees an object sticking up. Curious, he rides over to take a closer look. It's

'a simple pine trunk stuck in the earth, and bearing a noticeboard, on which was written in ink already half-effaced by the rain, these words, which I've faithfully preserved: *"Here lies General Montbrun. Passer-by, of whatever nation you may be, respect these ashes! They belong to the bravest soldier in the world. This feeble monument has been raised to him at the orders of his faithful friend the Marshal Ney."*'[7]

Farther on the Italians see 'rising up like a pyramid in the midst of a desert' the famous Great Redoubt.[8] Leaving Eugène's staff, Labaume too rides over and climbs what can only be a heaped up mass of corpses. From the summit of the so fiercely contested redoubt he sees a solitary soldier whose 'motionless figure produced in the distance the effect of a statue'. But he also hears unfortunates crying out for help:

> 'One of these was a French soldier who'd lost both legs and for two months been living off the stream and herbs, roots, and a few bits of bread he'd found on corpses, and at nights had been sleeping in the bellies of eviscerated horses. A general took pity on him and placed him in his carriage.'

Reaching the Kolotchka stream, IV Corps crosses it at least as precipitately as it had done when moving in the opposite direction to storm the Great 'Raevsky' Redoubt, at first ineffectually, then with success:

> 'The slope down to the little river was so steep and the soil so slippery that men and horses instantly fell on top of each other. On all sides were only horses' carcasses and half-buried corpses, blood-stained coats, bones gnawed by dogs and birds of prey, and the debris of arms, drums, helmets and cuirasses. There we also found the shreds of standards. From the emblems on them one could judge how much the Muscovite eagle had suffered on that sanguinary day. Crossing the theatre of their exploits our men proudly showed the places where their regiments had fought.'

'Yet', reflects von Muraldt, grimly contemplating the scene,

> 'the masses of blood that had flowed on this soil and the advantage gained by such convulsive efforts hadn't led to anything except a retreat, with unexampled difficulties and sufferings!'

The dead at least are at rest. A couple of miles farther on beyond these scenes of horror comes another, in its way even more ghastly. The enormous walled and turreted edifice of the Kolotskoïë monastery which the Italian Guardia d'Onore's Adjutant-major *Cesare de Laugier*, when he'd first glimpsed it in the distance on 5 September, had taken for a whole town and which during and after the battle had been the army's hospital where Surgeon-General Baron *Dominique-Jean Larrey* had made so many amputations, strikes Colonel Fezensac as 'nothing but a vast cemetery'. All its monks had fled. Only some 2,000 of the 20,000 wounded collected there have survived. Though Larrey finds the dressing-stations he'd set up there,

> 'no one had bothered to use the fine weather to evacuate the wounded. They were squatting in a stinking infectious barn, surrounded on all sides by corpses, almost never receiving any rations and obliged to eat cabbage stalks boiled with horseflesh to escape the horrors of famine. Because of a severe shortage of linen, their wounds had seldom been dressed. The surgeons were themselves having to launder the bandages and compresses.'

The Belgian surgeon *D. de Kerkhove* is so horrified that his 'pen refuses to describe the sufferings the sick and wounded had been reduced to'. What's become of the supplies of medicines and food, etc., sent back from Moscow? He's sure those who'd already died are happiest. As III Corps arrives in the wake of the Imperial Guard, Napoleon immediately orders a brigade of 200 Württemberg chasseurs and light infantry to lift all the wounded on to sutlers' carts. Surgeon Roos sees his Württembergers carrying them out and their officers indicating where they're to be placed. Although the men complain of this imposed fatigue,

> 'the order was carried out in the most punctilious fashion, and all was finished in an hour and a half. Every carriage, whether it belonged to a marshal or a colonel, every wagon, every *cantinière*'s cart or *droschka* had to take one or two.'

Even the fastidious Mailly-Nesle and his fair companions have to move over: 'One of the Emperor's footmen, Mouet by name, had been detailed off to take care of them, which he did meticulously.' Dumonceau, waiting a long time outside the main gate, sees Larrey himself standing there, 'presiding over their departure and reassuring them with encouraging remarks'. Although most have to 'to drag themselves along on foot, some on crutches', all strike the Belgian captain as 'joyful and resolute to resume their journey'. Perhaps they realise instinctively that they're luckier, at least for the time being, than those placed on carts?

For these the journey's going to be short. 'However good the Emperor's intentions,' the mild and pious Surgeon Roos exclaims, horrified,

> 'it turned out badly for the poor wounded. They fell into the hands of crude-minded coachmen, insolent valets, brutal sutlers, enriched and arrogant women, brothers-in-arms without pity, and all the riff-raff of the Train. All these people only had one idea: how to get rid of their wounded.'

From the inept cavalry general Lahoussaye – travelling along in his carriage and apparently doing nothing to help Grouchy, his superior, at the rearguard – Murat's Neapolitan ADC, Colonel *M.-J.-T. Rossetti*, hears that 'the *vivandières*, whose carts were laden with the loot of Moscow and who hadn't accepted them without murmuring at this extra weight' are deliberately falling behind and letting the column overtake them. 'Then, waiting for a moment when they were alone, they threw all these unfortunates who'd been confided to their care into the ditches. Only one survived sufficiently to be picked up by the first carriages to pass.' Never has the Master of the Horse seen, nor will ever see,

> 'a sight so horrible as our army's march 48 hours after Mojaisk. Every heart was closed to pity by fear of starvation, of losing the overladen vehicles, of seeing the starving exhausted horses die. I still shudder when I tell you I've seen men deliberately drive their horses at speed over rough ground, so as to get rid of the unfortunates overburdening them. Though they knew the horses would mutilate them or the wheels crush them, they'd smile triumphantly, even so, when a jolt freed them from of one of these poor wretches. Every man thought of himself and himself alone.'

It's Mojaisk all over again. When Larrey hears about wounded men being dumped in ditches he complains to Napoleon. Who has some of the worst offenders shot.

All that 'long and painful day' Rossetti and others at IHQ are 'hearing detonations at every instant. It was ammunition wagons that were being blown up for lack of horses to pull them.'

Somewhere towards the head of the column 3,000 Russian prisoners are being herded along, though no one has any food for them:

'Parked like cattle, they weren't being allowed to go a yard from the spot. Laid out on the ice [*sic*], all those who didn't want to perish were eating the flesh of their comrades who'd just expired from their miseries.'

And now, 'three miles before reaching Ghjat', here's another terrible sight, heavy of sinister import:

'Lying to the left of the road were about 200 Russians, who'd just been killed. We noticed that each of them had his head shattered in the same way and his bleeding brain was spread out beside him.'

They've just been shot by their Spanish and Portuguese escort. 'Each of us, depending on his character, approved or remained indifferent. The Emperor kept a sombre silence.' Not so Captain *Josef Zalusky*, who's already seen them as he's riding along at the head of the Polish Guard Lancers beside their CO, General Krasinski:

'We were horrified. Indignant, Krasinski galloped forward to the officer in charge at the head of the column, a Portuguese colonel. Krasinski reproached him for his barbarous cruelty that nothing justified. The Portuguese took these observations very much amiss and replied in an improper manner. It was neither the moment nor the place for a discussion. Krasinski hastened to the Emperor's staff and told them how the prisoners had been treated. The Emperor immediately sent his *officier d'ordonnance* Gourgaud to obtain clarification of this incident.'

The Polish count and artillery officer *Roman Soltyk*, marching with IHQ's Topographical Department, has actually heard the shots:

'To my horror I'd been told straggling prisoners were being shot by their Spanish escorts. In vain the Spanish soldiers had pushed them on with blows of their musket butts; in the end they fell down exhausted. Whereupon these barbarians fired bullets into their ears to finish them off.'

Roos counts 'eight of these corpses' and on reaching Ghjat is told the cold-blooded massacre had been the work of 'some Baden grenadiers' [9] who'd been cruelly ordered to kill 'all prisoners who might become exhausted and unable to go on'. Fezensac, too, hears they'd been shot by troops of the Confederation of the Rhine:

'I owe the men of my regiment the justice of saying that they were indignant. They realised too what cruel reprisals the sight of such barbarism would expose any of them to who might fall into the enemy's hands.'

Soltyk, a fervent admirer of Napoleon, is clearly unable to believe his hero can condone such murders: 'As soon as he was told of these horrible executions he showed his extreme displeasure and put an instant stop to them.' And both Rossetti and Roos notice that 'these executions ceased from the next day, when the Cossacks began to harass us between Ghjat and Viazma.'

Everyone feels that the retreat, crawling along at a snail's pace, is going far too slowly. And it's the unpopular Davout who gets the blame – though others, Labaume says, defended his method:
> 'Too hasty a retreat would have redoubled the enemy's audacity. If the rearguard had refused to stand and fight, their light cavalry would have been able to cut it to pieces.'

Actually I Corps has left Mojaisk this morning, followed by ever-increasing swarms of Cossacks, who're trying delay if not actually cut it off. Just after leaving what's left of Mojaisk, its chief-of-staff Lejeune sees them
> 'trying to force a passage across our path, but without success. They had to restrict themselves to pursuing and briskly cannonading one of our big convoys which, considerably delayed, had to pass across their front as it emerged from the town. Their roundshot was doing horrible work among the convoy, several hundred ill-harnessed vehicles, carrying many wounded as well as the wives and children of French businessmen resident in Moscow who'd been pillaged and were obliged to flee from the Russians. There was even the personnel of the Moscow French theatre.'

In that convoy, he knows, is his own half-blind sister. The carriage in which he'd sent her on ahead from Moscow was one of his own; and he'd
> 'taken care to furnish it with food and furs and harnessed it to three good horses with good grooms and under the protection of some of our wounded generals and, even more, under the aegis of Providence'.

Now he's so lucky as to be able to snatch it – and her – out of the panicking convoy:
> 'Her coachman assured me the three horses were still excellent and full of vigour. So I asked my sister: "Are you up to braving the guns?" Trembling she replied: "I'll do whatever you wish." At once I told the coachman: "Cross this plain at the gallop, the cannonballs will pass over your head. In this way you'll reach the head of the convoy, after which you can get on unopposed and without stopping." My advice was good and he succeeded.'

Hearing Cossack cannon for the first time during the retreat, Le Roy, marching with the 85th Line, knows how to interpret the sound:
> 'We were going to be relentlessly pursued by the enemy's army and by the entire population of this savage countryside. We'd only be able to count on our own courage and tenacity to escape out of the hands of these barbarians.'

Coming to the Kolotchka stream with the extreme rearguard, Griois finds the
> 'fragile bridge we'd built over it[10] broken. We ourselves forded it easily. But it wasn't the same for the guns. They had a lot of trouble getting

clear of its muddy bed and climbing up its steep banks. Several vehicles remained there. Only when we were out of this fix did we realise we were on the battlefield we'd left seven weeks ago. No more illusions now!'

Running his glance over the 'ravines still covered with weapons, roundshot and debris', he too has some

'sad reflections. The future had darkened. I recognised the various positions I'd occupied during the battle. Silence, solitude reigned, replacing the noise of the thousand guns and innumerable masses which had smashed into each other there two months ago.'

While waiting for his artillery to ford the stream – 'but fatigue and the draft horses' bad nourishment didn't allow us to do so very promptly' – he hears less ghostly guns firing to the rear. It's the rearguard (evidently he's been relieved) 'standing firm to halt the enemy who was pressing us too hard, and to give the artillery and baggage encumbering the ford to get clear of it'. A little way away he sees Davout himself, on foot, urging on 'the isolated units preceding his rearguard'. Davout tells him to get a move on. It's easier said than done. But by and by he and his friend the witty if not exactly amiable Colonel Jumilhac bivouac in a ravine near the monastery walls, which protect them from the biting wind. 'Not far from there General Grouchy had established himself under a tent. It was the last time I saw him during the retreat. The ground was completely frozen over.' Griois too sees the abandoned wounded – 'some who'd been evacuated from Moscow; also those who'd been brought there after the battle'.

Le Roy, Jacquet and Guillaume bivouac on the actual battlefield. 'The famous redoubts were on our left. Of Borodino itself only the church was still standing.' So does the Dromedary of Egypt. The 30th's passage across the Kolotchka is particularly dreadful. 'After a slow painful march of eighteen miles across the snow that everywhere covered the ground' Captain François and his men haven't

'a blade of straw to lie down on. Nor could we make up a fire, the wind being so violent it put it out as soon as we tried to light one. My horses were still carrying a few victuals for me, but there was no longer anything to feed them on except the few rotten leaves they nosed about for under the snow. The French cursed their sad destiny and impatiently waited for sunrise to get on the march again, without having taken the least nourishment to restore their strength.'

Next morning Davout's last unit, the 7th Light Infantry, crosses the battlefield and Carabinier-Sergeant *Vincent Bertrand* finds:

'thousands of bits and pieces of weapons and *matériel* belonging to both armies under our feet. Here and there the remains of our comrades fallen on the field of honour. The redoubts, though breached, were still standing, and we recalled the alternative options in that battle of giants. This one we'd taken at bayonet point, that one over there had repulsed us. Glorious but dolorous memories!'

And when, an hour later, he too reaches the abbey, the 7th Light take up position there. 'The enemy attacks us in force.' In fact there's a sharp

engagement. The whole of Platov's force, with cannon, falls on the 30th
Line. Captain François' men

'can't go a thousand paces without having to halt and face about, albeit
without firing – the mere movement's enough to send these fanatics flying. They come up till they're a hundred paces from us and deafen us
with their hurrahs. Sometimes we fire a few salvoes of cannon fire at
them. As we approach the village of Kolotskoïë,[11] they unite themselves
into a vast body and attack our army corps. We fight them off, after
they've killed a few men and taken five ammunition wagons.'

The fight costs the 7th Light

'a few killed and wounded. The latter no longer re-appeared with the
flag. The few wounded in the abbey, [although] almost cured, were
abandoned too.'

(Did it perhaps cost more than that? Or is the 'the agreeable news' that
reaches Kutusov's headquarters of Platov's men having captured '20 cannon and two standards and the destruction of two battalions at the convent
of Kollodiy [sic] near Borodino' exaggerated, as so many Cossack claims
turn out to be?)

Anyway it's the end of the 2nd Prussian Hussars. Under the monastery
walls its officers are told that their regiment's dissolved. Erased from the
list of combatants, they're free to proceed as they like, each take his own
orderly or, if he prefers, attach himself to some general of his choice.
Before quitting the position Lejeune wishes,

'to find out how many of the enemy were turning up in the plain. So I
went forward and stood on a terrace of the monastery, and found myself
in the presence of 100 or so Cossacks who were approaching to reconnoitre. Seeing me, they took to their heels; but realising I was on my
own, soon came back, and I, in my turn, hardly had time to rejoin our
own men who'd left and were already far off.'

'From Borowsk to the main Smolensk highway there'd been no real road.
We'd made our way across forests, fields and swamps.' But the Moscow
highway's both broad and well-paved. Yet now they've reached it, Cuirassier
Captain *Bréaut des Marlots* is distressed to see everyone beginning 'to march
more or less on his own account'. First Corps' Paymaster Duverger sees 'all
the villages within our reach are burning. We moved toward Smolensk
between hedges of flame – a measure necessary, it was said, to slow the
enemy's pursuit.' Nor can the abandonment of so many wounded be helping morale. Each unit', Ségur confirms, 'seemed to be marching on its
own. There was no staff, no order; no common knot to bind all the units
together.' 'There's not a man isn't terrified at the thought of what awaits
him,' Captain *Charles François* is thinking as he limps along in the rear with
the 30th Line:

'Here we are, only 120 miles from Moscow, in the middle of a devastated
countryside where we fight only by the light of burning buildings.
Today, the ranker, if he has anything to eat and who used to share his

morsel of bread with his comrade, is carefully hiding the little he has.'
Murat's ADC Rossetti is certainly not the only one to be feeling a nip in the
air. Winter's on the way:

'A mere gust of wind lasting a few minutes is enough to bring it on,
rough and biting. In an instant everything changes – roads, faces, men's
courage. The army's becoming sombre, its march painful, and consternation's beginning to spread.'

Lejeune orders those horses which, on a highway littered with vehicles,
have dropped from sheer inanition and can be put on their feet again to
be

'immediately harnessed up to carts laden with the wounded. But
scarcely had they dragged themselves a few paces than they died. So our
wounded remained there, abandoned. And as we went off and left them,
averting our glances, we had to harden our hearts to their cries. This day
[30 October] was very long and dreary. We had to march all night long,
in a cold that was beginning to feel very keen, because we had to get to
Ghjat before the enemy, who was forcing his marches by cross-country
roads to get there first.'

Until two months ago, 'one of the most flourishing commercial towns in
Russia, where leathers, canvas, tar and ropes needed by the navy were
manufactured', Ghjat has already been reached by IHQ yesterday evening
– only to find that all its timber houses, carelessly reduced to ashes on the
eve of the battle, have 'vanished almost without trace. One would have
thought one was on the site of a forest fire.' Only its main street of stone
houses still stands. The weather may be cold, but it's brilliantly sunny.
Caulaincourt, who ever since Vereia has been marching on foot 'and finding it to my advantage, as I didn't suffer from the cold', notices how the
temperature has fallen:

'At Borowsk we'd begun to feel the cold. Only the surface of the ground
had been frozen. The weather had been fine, and the nights quite
endurable in the open if one had a fire. Here at Ghjat the winter was
already more noticeable.'

But here at least is an unexpected windfall, if only for IHQ. Part of a convoy partly pillaged by Cossacks 'in charge of two footmen, are the remains
of a consignment sent from France for the Emperor's household'. Since
the horses are beginning to fail and they've no means of taking its surplus
with them, they distribute it among themselves, 'and there was abundance
at headquarters. Clos-Vouillet and Chambertin were the commonest wines'
– luckily for Napoleon, who drinks nothing else:

'We stored up our strength and a sense of well-being against the days of
real privation ahead. Everyone still had a few provisions. A small biscuit
ration was issued. In spite of the cold nights and several patches of
ground where a brief thaw had made the going difficult, the men were
standing up well to the long marches.'

But it's different with the horses. Caulaincourt's prime duty is to keep
them operational:

'They were worn out by having to go six miles from the road to forage and because of the wretched quality of what, at cost of so much danger and exhaustion, was being brought back. All but the strongest were dying. The reserve horses were being harnessed up: but since they no longer sufficed, we were already beginning to abandon some of the vehicles.'

One of Ghjat's still standing stone buildings has been used as a hospital; and when III Corps gets there its colonels are ordered to go and identify any wounded from their regiments. 'The sick', Fezensac is shocked to see, 'had been left without medicines, without food, without any help. Amidst all the refuse of every sort encumbering the stairs, the corridors, and the centre of the halls,' he can hardly get inside, but is 'delighted to be able to save a few men' of the 4th Line. But what's the good? Shortly afterwards Dr Réné Bourgeois, too, is horrified to see no one's really bothering about these sick men. Already it's as much as a healthy one can do to stay alive, and the *vivandières* and officers' servants driving the carts and wagons

'soon got rid of them either by offloading them by the roadside or intentionally forgetting them at the bivouacs. Not one of them would reach Smolensk.'

Wounded generals, of course, are another matter. Never has Rapp never seen so many:

'General Friant, whose wounds still hadn't healed, General Durosnel, who was almost all the time suffering from nervous fever and delirium; General Belliard [Murat's chief-of-staff], who'd been hit by a musket ball at Borodino ...'

or, more exactly, at the Mojaisk ravines. To his list Rapp could have added Dedem, whose chest bruise, dating from Smolensk in August, still hasn't healed properly and is causing him ever worse pain.

And here's something shocking, that bodes ill for the future. Invited by some grenadiers of the Old Guard to share their campfire beside a half-demolished wall, von Suckow witnesses something that not only astounds but also deeply worries him:

'Hardly had I installed myself than one of those staff officers in such an elegant uniform – blue with red waistcoat and silver hussar-style aiguil-lettes – came up to my grenadiers and invited them to leave their nice warm spot and cede it to General NN and the officers of his staff. How stupefied was I – a German officer used to the severest discipline – to hear one of the grenadiers, getting up, say in a loud voice:

'"*Mon officier*, there are now no longer any generals. There are only unfortunates. We're staying where we are."

'The other retired without a word.'[12]

That evening Surgeon Roos is surprised to bump into an officer who – quite voluntarily – has collected a party of his chasseurs and, wanting to see Moscow, brought them all the way from the Niemen:

'But he'd arrived too late. We were still gathered around our fire when we heard that our king had arrived from Stuttgart, bringing money for the rank and file, decorations and sabres of honour, gold medals and money for officers and men who'd distinguished themselves.'

All of which may be gratifying but in the present circumstances isn't the least use. By contrast Roos sees that many men are belatedly trying to rough-shoe their horses against the winter. But within a 6 or 7-mile band of devastated countryside on either side of the route there's 'not a straw of hay' to feed them with. Though Major Bonnet, getting to Ghjat, is sent out with 300 men of the 18th Line to maraud, he finds not a grain or any forage in the villages: 'The inhabitants and quadrupeds had decamped. We brought back absolutely nothing.' Ghjat is 'surrounded by small streams flowing through lakes.' The 85th Line, getting there next day with I Corps, finds

'the bridge badly rebuilt and we'd a lot of trouble getting across, because of the congestion of teams and vehicles. The jam and the lack of order at the rivers soon caused the two wretched hastily reconstructed bridges to cave in. The swampy ground around them couldn't support the vehicles' weight. A great number got stuck there.'

Among them Le Roy sees to his dismay 'a wagon belonging to my former battalion, with my trunk inside it'. But the resourceful Guillaume rescues much of its contents.

By now III Corps' Württemberg infantry division is reduced to only two platoons. Next morning it leaves what had once been the 'pretty little town of Ghjat' and until late in the evening manages to hold off the Cossacks until the panicking mob of stragglers have passed on. One of von Suckow's feet is becoming frost-bitten. Wearing 'a red velvet dressing-gown with rabbit skin linings' he hitches a ride in a yellow carriage led by a barefooted Russian girl and driven by a French businessman with a blunderbuss across his knees. Inside are two young French ladies.

Then the ruins of Ghjat, too, are left behind.

Riding ahead with Prince Eugène's staff, Labaume sees a

'countryside trampled by thousands of horses, which seemed never to have been cultivated. The farther we advanced the more the earth seemed to be in mourning.'

The marching regiments are all jumbled up with convoys of various kinds. The Prussian lieutenant *Heinrich August Vossler*'s convoy of 100 Württemberg wounded from Borodino ('including some 50 fit for duty') had almost reached Moscow when they'd had to turn back and been caught up in the retreat's chaos:

'Day by day the column was growing, for anyone travelling along that road was seeking safety in attaching himself to our contingent, whose defensive strength increased proportionately. In a matter of days we found ourselves in the company of generals and officers of every rank, and every arm of the service was represented. Few were fully equipped. Some carried an odd assortment of weapons. Most were unarmed. But

all, without exception, were burdened with a rich collection of loot, ranging from worthless rags to finest shawls, from tattered sheepskins to costly furs, from rickety carts to gilded coaches. For the rest, certain distinctions still prevailed. The infantryman was still marching on foot, the trooper either rode a *konya* or shared some kind of vehicle with several others, or at least as long as it could keep its feet drove in front of him his galled nag, loaded with his weapons. Apart from Frenchmen there were Spaniards, Portuguese, Germans, Poles, Dalmatians, Illyrians, etc.'
Now Sergeant Bertrand is realising that not all wounded who fall behind are reappearing, 'something which from this moment onwards was becoming the invariable rule'. 'Right now', Captain François goes on,

'the army's position is horrible! As for me, since leaving Moscow, despite my two bullet-holes in my left leg and several other wounds which still haven't formed scabs, I've been marching all the time with my right foot in a down-at-heel shoe. But like all my brothers-in-arms I foresee such ills, and don't dream of bothering about my wounds. I no longer dress them, and my good leg goes on as if it were a machine.'

And always there are

'cannon at our heels, as well as irregular Cossacks, barbarians, who were joining up with the peasantry to do us as much harm as possible. The latter, riding lamentable nags, were armed with a long stick at the end of which they'd fixed an iron lance point or a long nail. From this moment we had to fight one against ten. A carabinier of my regiment, grievously wounded in the head during our defence of the Kolotskoïë abbey, was marching on his own to the left of the column formed by our [Gérard's] division. Assailed by three Cossacks, he's stricken by several lance thrusts and falls. These savages were trying to carry him away. But he, having held on to his sabre, gets up and puts himself on guard, intending to resist to the death. An unequal combat starts. Happily the Cossacks' yells reach his comrades who're flanking the column. A corporal goes back to help the wounded man. Tries to shoot. His musket misfires. So he attacks with the bayonet, and, seconded by the carabinier, soon puts one of these Cossacks *hors de combat* and takes the other two prisoner.'[13]

At one moment Griois, too, has to defend himself almost single- handed. All his remaining possessions, notably 'the little food we still had, and our kitchen outfit, a stew pot, a mess-tin and a camp-kettle' are 'in a little Russian go-cart I'd found en route'. But he's wearing a bearskin coat, the second he has bought en route, his first having been stolen – it's still possible to buy one for 30 or 40 francs. Having gone on ahead of his artillery, he's riding along together with his 'adjutant-major, two gunner orderlies, my Bavarian servant and a soldier of the Train' who's leading the cart some 500 or 600 paces ahead of them; when across the plain they catch sight of some horsemen, whose 'irregular way of riding and lances' show they're Cossacks:

'As soon as the soldier of the Train caught sight of the enemy he tried to turn back. But either this cart didn't turn easily or he was too precipitate, the pole-bolt holding the front carriage broke, and our baggage rolled out in the middle of the road. However little the booty tempted them, the Cossacks advanced. But it was our last resources which were in question! My adjutant and I draw our sabres and grasp our pistols. We place ourselves in front of our overturned cart, thoroughly determined to defend it, and I order my servant and the soldier of the Train to at least save what was most precious, i.e., the food; which they did with ardour and not letting themselves be intimidated by the presence and shouts of the enemy. It wasn't the same with the gunner orderlies, on whom I was counting even more. One went off on the pretext of finding help; the other fled.'

But though there are now only two of them, and they poorly armed, Griois and his adjutant-major show themselves so self-assured that, together no doubt with the sight of 'some infantry platoons that appeared in the distance', the Cossacks are sufficiently impressed, after 'prancing about in front of us and threatening us with their shouts and lances', and clear off. By and by, after taking the best of the cart's contents on to their horses for a while, Griois and his adjutant-major find an abandoned empty ammunition wagon to replace it:

'That evening my two gunners rejoined me, very much ashamed of themselves, and I treated them according to their deserts. However, I kept them by me, because one did the cooking and the other served me as secretary.'[14]

Others are in no position to defend themselves. Lieutenant Auvray of the 23rd Dragoons, for instance, is suffering

'from dysentery caused by the bad things we were being forced to eat so as not to die of hunger. We couldn't have passed along a stream, a pond or a ditch without drinking from it. To cap it all, I had a boil as big as an egg on my right thigh, which gave me great pain for eight days. Neither able to walk nor sit my horse, I had to lie across its saddle.'

Dedem, 'still living off the provisions we'd brought with us from Moscow', notes how troublesome any little stream can be:

'Since it hadn't been intended to take the Smolensk road again, no one had given a thought to rebuilding the little bridges the Russians had destroyed while retiring on Moscow and which we, during our advance, had passed by quite easily thanks to the drought and the summer heats.'

But now these bridges are a repeated source of ill-affordable delays:

'Now that the rains had begun again they'd become indispensable for the artillery and carriages; and all the time our march was held up by the need to rebuild them. It was frightening to see the immense quantity of carriages parked *en masse* and which could only get over one by one and very slowly. Woe to those vehicles which got stuck in the mud! They were promptly turned over and the owner, who had all his resources in them, thereafter saw himself exposed to lacking his basic needs!'

There are resourceful and not always scrupulous officers who're determined not to so expose themselves. Colonel Chopin, for instance, commander of 1st Cavalry Corps' artillery, whom Griois knows slightly and at whose bivouacs he, together with his friend Jumilhac and his adjutant-major, can be sure of enjoying some good soup,

'a bit of meat, and to round it off some coffee, a rarity, and, something even rarer, a bottle of hydromel a drink [made from honey] which, without being the equal of wine, is drinkable. A true devil-may-care of a fellow, persuaded that the vital thing is to stay alive and that one must above all think of oneself, since the retreat had started Colonel Chopin had gathered round him a dozen of his most alert gunners, most fertile in resourcefulness. A well-harnessed wagon followed him, and every evening it was the place of assembly to which each of his gunners brought whatever he'd managed to get hold of, either in the villages or, or at the expense of isolated men whom they, by force or persuasion, had stripped of part of their provisions. Thus the colonel's robber band (the only name one can give to it) lacked for nothing. The wagon was well-filled, and to see or listen to its purveyors, it'd never be empty. Chopin himself gave me these details. I hadn't the courage to blame the way in which he'd acquired the dinner we were eating, but could never make up my mind to resort to the same methods on my own account.'

But the best-stocked wagon can break down – indeed, the more heavily laden the more it is likely to do so. As Surgeon Lagneau's now does. Before leaving it behind, his party load their provisions on to the ambulance horses, 'in sacks suspended on either side'. Even his famous tent is

'loaded, together with its pegs, etc., on a little Cossack horse which was gallantly living on pine or willow bark and went up and down the ravines just like a little dog. His unshod hoofs had grown down so they had a very good grip on the ice.'

Reaching each night's halt, the party pitch their tent. To get out of the icy north wind 'which took our breath away', everyone – the general, the adjutant, the quartermaster, the paymaster and Lagneau himself – lends a hand. 'This done, we unloaded the provisions and stored them in the tent.' Some sappers under their command are good amateur cooks and have their share of the soup. While it's getting ready 'we sheltered in our tent and were as snug as in some billet in Germany'.

Almost no one else is. A captain of the 18th Line, Viscount *Pierre de Pelleport*, seeing wagons and carriages of every kind being abandoned because their hungry teams can't take another step on a road covered in ice, has the 18th Line's battalion wagons opened:

'The officers could do what they liked with their effects. I had the military chest counted. It contained 120,000 gold francs. I divided it up into several parts. Each of the officers, NCOs and men received a small sum, promising not to abandon this deposit confided to his honour, and to hand it over to a comrade if about to succumb.'[15]

When Delaborde's Young Guard division had left Moscow the weather had at first been so pleasant that young Paul de Bourgoing's little servant Victor had laid his overcoat on his horse and tied it to Delaborde's carriage. Suddenly both are stolen. 'All Victor now had against the winter was a waistcoat of grey broadcloth.' But Madame Anthony, following on in a calèche, takes pity on her little compatriot. In her theatrical baggage she finds Victor a triple-collared greatcoat, one of the garments perhaps Prefect of the Palace de Bausset had provided for the troupe's performances in Moscow. Paul de Bourgoing too is shivering by their bivouac fire. How cold the nights are getting! What a fool he'd been, instead of one of 'the excellent black bear pelts, or wild or white wolf skins' which, after the Moscow fire, had been so plentifully available to anyone who could pay for them, to buy himself a pretty – but pitifully ineffectual – fur-lined hooded cape,

> 'a very pretty *polonaise* in dark blue cloth, richly adorned with silken fringes and lined with black astrakhan, most elegant in shape and colour'.

Also of the party is a Russian who'd stayed behind in Moscow and been Delaborde's guest but is fleeing from what he imagines will be his compatriots' vengeance. Bourgoing's just cursing himself for a vain young fool when the Russian comes up and offers to swap the *polonaise* for his own thick red fox fur:

> 'Believe me,' he said, 'You won't be able to stand our 25 degrees of frost.'

Gratefully but reluctantly, Bourgoing accepts. 'What a difference in warmth!' Next morning the Russian has vanished. Had he been a spy? Anyway they'd been good friends, and he'll owe him his life. As for the two women, they're rarely getting out of their carriage except to join the circle at Delaborde's fireside in the evenings:

> 'We heard their voices, often trembling with disquietude, calling out to us from afar. Anyway they were accompanied by one of our group, whom they'd had fallen in with on the march.'

Already the column looks more like a masquerade than a retreating army. And Paymaster Duverger too wraps himself up 'in a woman's fur, lined with yellow taffeta. The sleeves were too long for my arm. The surplus served me as a handkerchief.' Now anything in the way of a fur is in acute demand and will command almost any price. Among the Württembergers everyone's envying von Suckow his rabbit-lined dressing-gown:

> 'An eminent Westphalian general, obliged for the time being to hoof it like a mere lieutenant, several times returned to the charge and offered me fantastic sums for it. But by this time money no longer had any value, seeing we found nothing to buy.'

Even at IHQ, with its dozens of horses, mules and carriages, all traces of imperial splendour are vanishing. At nightfall, 5 p.m., on 30 October Napoleon reaches 'the pretty château of Weliczewo:

> 'Not a window frame remained. With difficulty, enough of its debris was assembled to make one passable room for the Emperor and another for Berthier. The woodwork of the billiard table was the only intact piece of furniture.'

CHAPTER 3
GETTING THROUGH AT VIAZMA

Apprehensions – Teste at Viazma – shooting of Russian prisoners – Captain Roeder mounts guard outside Napoleon's office – the Guard loots the magazines – 'I'm no ordinary general' – Miloradovitch attacks – the Battle of Viazma – Ney takes over the rearguard

By now, as the van approaches Viazma, that 'newly built city of 15,000 inhabitants, remarkable for the elegance of most of its buildings' where the army in late August had feasted so plentifully on geese and fish, everyone who remembers its topography is getting apprehensive. Viazma, namely, lies at the junction of the Mojaisk and Medyn roads. And since Napoleon's rejection of the latter for his retreat, the Russians are certainly following it, aiming to cut him off. Leaving Rouibki in the afternoon, Fain hears en route that

'our advance guard still hasn't reached it. It seems that Konownitzin, who's just replaced Platov, has been trying to gain a few hours on us. We're hoping Viazma will offer us some resources. But the enemy is being so slow in yielding it to us we fear he's preparing another fire.'

At 5 p.m. IHQ halts 'at the nearest château [Weliczewo], on the heights three leagues in front of the town.' To the south, with 30 miles more to go, Wilson's hopping mad at Kutusov's sloth:

'We have 50 versts to reach Viazma and I fear much that we shall not arrive there in time. Had we moved on Jouknow after we had quitted Malojaroslavetz, as we all besought the Marshal to do, we should have been now in an impregnable position facing Viazma, and the golden glorious opportunity lost at Malojaroslavetz might have been retrieved.'

General Baron *F. A. Teste*[1] had been wounded at Borodino. Relieved of his brigade, he'd presented himself at the Kremlin with his arm in a sling and been amiably received:

'I'm going to assign you a post well worth a brigade,' the Emperor said. 'Make yourself ready to leave for Viazma, where you'll replace Baraguay d'Hilliers as governor. There you'll find 8,000 men of all arms.'

Arriving with a convoy of wounded at this town 'surrounded by ravines and situated on a fine plateau which equally dominates the plain and the mouth of the defile traversed by the Smolensk–Moscow road' on 12 October, Teste had found

'not a single inhabitant. Before we'd appeared there in August,[2] it had counted 20,000 souls. Out of 20 houses which had escaped the fire, only five or six are at a pinch inhabitable.'

Keeping one as a hospital, he'd turned all the others into stores and sent out large marauding parties, protected by cavalry. All had returned without mishap. And even after most of this cavalry had suddenly been taken from him, on 16 October, he'd gone on industriously filling up his magazines with 'a great amount of foodstuffs, destined for the numerous detachments we were told should be coming from Smolensk to join the army'. One of his marauding parties had been commanded by Major *H.- P. Everts.* Getting there as recently as 22 October, Everts' battalion of the (mostly Dutch) 33rd Line[3] had escorted a convoy of the Imperial Treasure to Doroghoboui – the next town along the Smolensk highway – and then come back.

All this time Teste had heard nothing from Moscow. And not a word about the army's retreat; only from a convoy that had passed through on the 18th 'that communications were becoming more and more problematic'.

Also at Viazma are the Hessian Footguards. A month earlier, at 6 a.m. on 21 September, they'd marched out from Witebsk,[4] bound for Smolensk, to form part of its garrison. Captain *Franz Roeder* had taken with him his cart and pony, 'two servants, a dog and two goats, one black, one white with crooked horns' to provide milk for his coffee. Gradually, much to the temperamental Roeder's fury, starvation, exposure to bad weather and – not least – incompetent officers who thought the lash the answer to everything and who constantly incensed the humane but fiery-tempered Roeder by their indifference to their men's welfare, had begun to dissolve the crack regiment's discipline. Reaching Smolensk they'd still numbered 'about 600 combatants, including bandsmen, the 1st Battalion of the Prince's Own about 500, the 2nd Battalion a third less'. But from there they'd been ordered forward to Viazma; and on 7 October to their surprise had met

'a munitions convoy escorted by the Flanker Regiment returning to Smolensk. The commander told us that all the convoys had received or would receive orders to turn back, and this would be the case with ourselves.'

The Flankers[5] belong to the Young Guard, to which the Hessians are also attached. Roeder, a man for whom campaigning is a veritable passion, hungering as he always is for new experiences, had found it 'vexatious' not to have a chance to see Moscow, that legendary city. On the other hand he'd long ago become pessimistic about the campaign's outcome, and therefore seen the convoy's return as

'good news, for it must either signify a cessation of hostilities with the possible hope of peace, or that the Emperor is returning to winter quarters in Poland and doesn't intend to expose us all to the winter at a point so far forward in Russia.'

But then something more sinister had begun to happen. Roeder's diary, 9 October:

'Today we found on the road a Russian soldier who'd not long been shot – a prisoner who, from weakness, illness, or perhaps only a wounded foot, had been unable to go further and so, in obedience to orders, was shot by the escort!'

The previous day the Hessians had met the unit that had carried out these executions:

'400 Italians of the 2nd Regiment. The commandant at Doroghoboui allowed 30 prisoners to be shot while we there because, being ill, they could go no further.'

Roeder, like any other officer in his senses, had immediately realised the implications. 'That the Russians would be justified in taking reprisals upon the prisoners they take from us appears to have struck nobody.' Yet another such massacre of prisoners had taken place at Viazma on the 10th. And on the 16th

'news went round that a few hundred armed peasants and Cossacks who had their base of operations five leagues from here had seized the baggage of a Westphalian regiment and murdered the escort. Captain von Storck was sent out to reconnoitre with two officers, eight NCOs, eight Schützen and 120 men.'

Next day – with understandable haste – this commando had returned without having seen either Cossack or armed peasant. Finally, on 24 October, Teste had received an urgent order to

'inspect the highways northwards as well as southwards and to seek out roads running parallel as far as Doroghoboui, along which an army or great host might pass, see what accommodation there was for troops suitable to the cold season and such sustenance as the country may provide.'

It had been left to him to figure out why he should do all this. But his report was to be sent in to Berthier by 30 October at the latest. Whereupon a detachment of four companies of the Hessians, with no fewer than 300 armed men and 50 troopers (20 French dragoons plus 30 Portuguese chasseurs) had been detailed off. After escorting the elderly Baraguay d'Hilliers – sick, mean and talkative – to Doroghoboui, the Hessians had carried out their reconnaissance. The main road has been stripped of everything edible; but some distance away from it they'd found plenty of everything that farms could provide or forests conceal. Safely back at Viazma, Roeder's half-witted and irascible Colonel Follenius had wanted him to write out his report in quadruplicate. But Roeder, who's not feeling very well, had refused. More important, it seems to him, is to lodge a violent protest against some Portuguese chasseurs who, though themselves utterly scared of Cossacks, had maltreated some villagers. This done, Roeder's just about to turn in for the night, when suddenly – at 4 p.m. on 31 October – the whole situation changes.[6]

Who's going to get to Viazma first, the French or the Russians? An ADC of Caulaincourt's dead brother Auguste, official hero of Borodino, has been sent ahead to order Junot and his Westphalians 'to carry the town at daybreak, taking all possible precautions to preserve it'.[7] Eugène, too, a few miles to IHQ's rear, is worried. And has sent one of his ADCs, Squadron-Leader Labédoyère, on ahead. Also, to make assurance doubly sure, Staff Captain Labaume. Overtaking IHQ, Labaume's surprised to see Napoleon, in lieu of his famous Swiss-style civilian hat, wearing a fur-trimmed bonnet.

Evidently Eugène's as anxious as anyone else to get to Viazma before the Russians do. And in fact Labédoyère only gets back to his headquarters after running into all sorts of dangers. That morning at Weliczewo will stand out in Planat's memory as

'one of the pleasantest of the retreat. There was only a single hut [*sic*] occupied by the Emperor. We were bivouacked a little way off, sleeping as best we could, around a fire of green wood. That morning, before daybreak, I heard the *diane* being beaten. It indicated the existence of a regular service in the midst of the army's commencing disorganisation. The drum I'd heard was that of a battalion of the Old Guard, bivouacked in square around IHQ. Daylight was just beginning to appear, and I saw that battalion under arms, splendidly turned out and with a good countenance.'

And at crack of dawn Napoleon himself goes on ahead. At 2 p.m. Teste's 'on horseback inspecting my outposts on the Ghjat road' when 'an ordnance officer presents himself and announces to me the Emperor's arrival'. Teste gives all necessary orders to the Viazma commandant (orders apparently not passed on swiftly enough to reach Roeder two hours later) and, as protocol requires, rides out eastwards to meet the Emperor,

'whom I wasn't slow to recognise, though contrary to his habit he was wearing a tunic of green velvet with gold brandenburgs.[8] He was advancing at the head of a group, where Murat and Berthier were in the front line. "There's Teste!" exclaimed the King of Naples. – "Well, Teste," said the Emperor, "what's new here?" – "Sire, nothing, absolutely nothing" – "Have you got some food for us?" – "Our magazines are provided with everything we've been able to collect from 8 to 10 leagues around."'

Pleased, Napoleon tells him the Guard's following on immediately behind him:

'"It's been given food for five days. See to it that it doesn't get any distribution at Viazma. Keep everything for the wounded, who should be reaching you the day after tomorrow."'

And with these words he rides on into the town, and 'at 4 p.m. dismounts at my predecessor's former lodging'.

Of all the Hessian officers Roeder alone can speak fluent French. Sick or not, he's ordered to take 100 of his best men, augmented by those of the Lifeguards' 2nd battalion, and mount guard over 'the Palace', Napoleon's lodgings:

'I posted two grenadiers in the antechamber, in accordance with the adjutant's orders, and stationed the smaller posts as I thought fit. I'd stationed six sentries in pairs in the antechamber and at the head and foot of the stairs, but didn't let them load, like outdoor sentries, partly because such a sentry can't make immediate use of such a shot anyway, and partly because one might go off by mistake. The adjutant observed this and remarked that with such strong fellows the bayonet was the best and only weapon of defence. I also saw to the barricading at all points with such reinforcements as might be necessary, especially at the rear of the house, sending out patrols to watch and listen, doubling the sentries, etc. In short, everything was done to render impossible any surprise attack by an intrepid enemy who might have been informed by the locals.'

All of which is rewarded by the duty adjutant with a curt 'good' and a 'very good', and even by a few words from Berthier himself, 'whom I hadn't seen since Tilsit' [in 1807]. As he posts his sentries in front of the audience chamber, Roeder hears Napoleon's 'loud voice'[9] ordering all sick and wounded to be instantly evacuated to Smolensk – and having himself so recently come from Smolensk along a road no one's done the least thing to keep up, he reflects privately that none of them will get so far. Soon, from that upstairs room, he hears His Majesty dictating other orders. One, to be carried by one of the officers who come stumbling downstairs between Roeder's pairs of sentries, is to General Charpentier, governor of Smolensk, to tell him that 'on 3 November the army will be at Doroghoboui':

'Full details of all stores at Smolensk are to be forwarded thither. Other orderlies and ADCs are being sent off to Witebsk and Molihew, with orders to bake every loaf of bread those towns are capable of.'

A courier, too, has arrived. Bearing letters, Fain sees, posted from Paris (on 14 October), Vilna (26 October), and two more from Saint-Cyr (19 and 20 October) in charge of II Corps and his own Bavarian VI Corps at Polotsk, as well as from Victor, 'the most recent being dated 24 October'.

In a flash everyone from Berthier down to the sentries knows that Victor, so far from being at Smolensk, as everyone's been assuming, and ready to come to their aid, is marching northwards to support the long-suffering but still intact II Corps which, if Napoleon's orders have been obeyed, is withdrawing inwards from the Polotsk region on to the Moscow army's line of retreat.[10]

During the early part of the bright cold night, with -3° to -4° Réaumur (-2° C) and some ice on the Viazma river where it flows through the town, and fields covered with thick frost, Roeder and his sentries hear and see some Guard artillery and cavalry come marching straight through the town without halting. Since they're commanded by Murat this makes them wonder just what's going on. But Napoleon just works on:

'Reports kept on going in to him. He was still busy at midnight. It wasn't quiet in his room until 1 a.m. and I saw him up again at 3.30.'

Then, at 9 a.m., the Old Guard arrives. The Emperor stands on the balcony, watching it march past. Obliged to cede their barracks to it, the Hessians have to go out to the western suburbs and bivouac out in the icy cold.

All that day [1 November] Napoleon spends at Viazma dictating orders as he waits for what he, with increasing annoyance, regards as Davout's dilatory rearguard and for the rest of the army to catch up. As usual if he has a spare moment he reads the newspapers, brought presumably by the courier. But what's this? His kid brother Jérôme, King of Westphalia[11] has gone and turned Cassel's principal Protestant church into a Catholic one!

– Write! And at top speed Fain, sitting in a corner of the room at his little portable desk, takes down in his scribbled shorthand a letter to Vilna, for Maret to forward to Cassel. He's to tell Jérôme

'it's very dangerous indeed to touch matters of religion and that it only embitters the population. That Cassel's a Protestant town and he must leave its Protestants in peace.'

At about midday on 2 November it's up and off. Grooms and escorts dash for their horses. Caulaincourt appears with the imperial riding whip; Napoleon stumbles down those narrow steep stairs; the sentry at the door shouts '*l'Empereur!*'. The brown imperial berline draws up outside. And IHQ leaves 'for Semlovo, where he was to set up his headquarters'. Teste continues,

'I joined the escort for as far as a league from the capital of my government, where I got my last orders from the Emperor's mouth.

'"You'll tell Marshal Ney that as soon as I Corps has passed through Viazma he's to be responsible for the rearguard. Davout's to support him."'

But when Teste gets back to Viazma he's met by a sight so shocking that for him it will be

'the cruellest memory of my career. During my two-and-a-half hour absence, the [rest of the] Imperial Guard, which had only been expected that evening, had entered Viazma, forced the sentries, and pillaged all our magazines. In a few instants the provisions we'd had so much trouble to gather in were dissipated, dispersed, annihilated by men who, though already supplied with food for five days, were acting like starving lunatics.'

All Teste can do that evening is to send on an indignant report to Berthier, protesting at the Guard's abominable – but customary – behaviour. And when,

'in the morning of 3 November, the big convoy of wounded reached us, it went straight on towards Smolensk, since we'd no more distributions to give it. That evening[12] the Guard followed this convoy in the same direction, and I appealed to the gentlemen, its officers, to act so that their troops should hand over some small part of their provisions to come to the aid of these brave men.'

When the Young Guard turns up the Hessian Footguards are rejoined by the other battalion of the Prince's Own, returning from Moscow with clothing, coffee, sugar, tea and food – some 80 head of cattle! After which they too are swept up in the retreat.

The crush outside the town gate is immense. As the Old Guard leaves the town Commissary Kergorre, who's had to bivouac beside the gate, has the headquarters police place a wounded Dutchman on his Treasury wagon,

'to serve us in certain circumstances as a safeguard. The road being blocked by the Guard and its teams, we had to pass through Viazma by impracticable paths, cross deep ditches, wells and courtyards and gardens, and even clamber over demolished houses.'

Fortunately Kergorre's horses are still in good nick, and he even regains the Smolensk road to find

'the Old Guard passing by. But this road being very broad the greater the jam inside Viazma became the better we marched. Marshal Lefèbvre was in command of it. Seeing me on foot beside my wagons, he called me over and chatted a long while with me. I walked on beside his horse. We spoke at length of the present circumstances, of the Administration at such moments. He was full of consideration and politeness.'

But the language of the miller's son who'd risen from the ranks in the old Royal Guard to be Duke of Danzig is by no means that of the drawing-room.

'That morning he'd expected to be attacked by Platov, and had made this harangue to his troops, drawn up in the square:

'"Grenadiers, Chasseurs! The Cossacks are over there, and there, there and there [pointing to the four points of the compass]. If you don't fol-low me the whole lot of you are done for. I'm no ordinary general, and it wasn't for nothing that the Army of the Moselle called me the Eternal Father. Grenadiers, Chasseurs, I tell you again: If you don't follow me you're all f....d. For the rest, I don't give a damn, go and get f....d!"'

The ex-hussar Marshal Ney also has a blunt way of speaking – sometimes, Teste thinks, a good deal too blunt. During the morning of 4 November, the ex-Governor's preparing to depart when he sees

'III Corps arrive, with its chief, to whom I transmitted Napoleon's orders. When I told him it was Davout who was to support his rearguard, Ney said to me: "Oh? As for that, we know what kind of support *he* pro-vides." He deplored, in terms I shan't reproduce, the Guard's conduct.'

IHQ reaches Semlovo at 7 p.m., followed by the Guard. 'An hour's march from the spot where we were to spend the night', one of Pion des Loches' gunners comes to tell him his wagon's axle is broken.

'My officers' desolation was even greater than mine. It was carrying all our provisions and the axle's specification wasn't the same as those of our other vehicles. What was to become of us? How begin repairs, at night, in the extreme cold. Where find some workmen even? Fortu-nately Levrain, the best sergeant of our company of workmen was marching with me at the head of the Train. He ran back to the tail and we'd hardly reached our bivouac before he brought me my wagon, fit-ted with an ordinary axle.'

Pion des Loches rewards him with six bottles of Bordeaux. 'It would give him life for several days.'

But though IHQ bivouacks at Semlovo, and next morning (3 November) marches on towards Slawkovo, which it reaches at 3 p.m., Poniatowski, Eugène and Davout's corps are all still on the wrong side of Viazma. And Kutusov's van is still nearing that 'highly defensible position'. This time it's Planat de la Faye who's sent back to tell Davout to stir his stumps. In Moscow, Planat, that man of a delicate constitution, had been so taken up with his duties that 'unlike so many other officers I hadn't been able to get myself either a fur or double shoes'[13]. Now, shivering in his inadequate clothing, he sets out. Finds Viazma, so far from being congested, utterly deserted. Mission accomplished, he halts there 'to find something to eat, for I was dropping for hunger' – evidently Davout, as usual, hadn't shown any normal hospitality:

'Having strayed about awhile among the ruins without finding a living soul, I spotted, in the corner of a tumbledown cottage, a man squatting in front of a small fire.'

Planat's astonished to find that it's a Captain Burgstaller,

'whom I'd been much attached to in Berlin, a true philosopher, without a care in the world, taking things as they came and men as he found them. Burgstaller had lost nothing of his good humour. In his pot he was cooking a bit of horsemeat, seasoned with some gunpowder, and for half an hour he entertained me with his striking buffooneries and gay reminiscences from the past.'

Then he rejoins de Lariboisière's headquarters at Slawkovo.

Since before dawn, the Army of Italy, preceded by the Polish V Corps, and followed by I Corps 'albeit at a distance', has been pursuing its march in a dense fog. Near the demolished village of Tsarewo-Simiche it has to cross

'an earthen causeway over which the main road used to pass, but which the guns' passage has deteriorated to a point where it was no longer practicable. And to continue on our way we had to go down into a swampy plain, bisected by a broad stream. Although the first only crossed it thanks to the ice, they broke it in doing so, and then one either had to expose oneself to wading the river or else wait for wretched hastily constructed bridges to be finished. From the moment the head of the column had got there more vehicles were constantly arriving. Thus the artillery, carriages and *vivandières'* carts were all spread out on the road, while their drivers, as their habit was, took advantage of this moment to light fires and warm their numbed limbs.'

Everyone's in this seemingly secure state when suddenly,

'out of a thick wood to our left, Cossacks yelling frightfully, came out and fell on this unfortunate mass. At this sight, each man, driven by fear, acts on impulse. Some take refuge in the woods, others run to their vehicle and whip up their horses, and without knowing where they're going disperse over the plain; and there, stuck in the swampy ground, fall an easy prey to the Cossacks.'

The more fortunate entrench themselves behind the mass of vehicles and await deliverance, 'which duly arrived with the infantry'. Meanwhile the employees of IV Corps' baggage train are beginning to pillage it. 'Now one was no more in safety even among one's own people,' Labaume will remember bitterly, 'than one would have been among enemies.' Theft, indeed, is becoming endemic. Last night even Sergeant Bertrand 'driven by hunger' has indulged in it. On reaching the 17th Light's bivouac and seeing some men of the Train sleeping under shelters around a rousing fire, he had 'profited by their cook's absence to jump over these sleepers and make off with one of their well-filled pots, which comforted us, my comrades and me'. Now, at about 8 or 9 a.m., through the 'cold, very dense fog, which prevented us from seeing ten paces ahead, but in greatest safety' Griois and his witty friend Colonel Jumilhac are still riding on some distance ahead of his artillery, somewhere ahead of I Corps and IV Corps' rear,

'when some roundshot whistled past our ears. After a few moments an extremely lively fire of guns and musketry started up on our left.'

That first shot makes Prince Eugène (he'll tell Wilson one day) 'start with more alarm than he'd ever felt in his life, as he instantly foresaw the fatal consequences'. The neighbouring infantry units come to a bewildered halt:

'The generals didn't know what to do or which way to face. We were being blasted by an enemy we couldn't see. Finally a few battalions deployed. Others formed squares against cavalry, which soon fell on us, and our fire answered the enemy's. Little by little the fog broke up under the guns' detonations, and at last we were able to see who it was we had to do with. It was the entire advance guard of the Russian army, led by Miloradovitch, whose masses, protected by the thickets of wood and the fog, were bordering the road we were following. They'd waited to attack us until the greater part of IV Corps had already passed through Viazma, or anyway reached it, and until I Corps offered them its flank.'

Both IV and V Corps have left the troublesome Tsarewo–Zalomitsch defile behind them when

'a strong detachment of Cossacks suddenly throws itself on to the highway, momentarily cutting us off from Poniatowski's corps. The Royal Guard, in the van today, loses no time in putting them to flight. But at the same time the cavalry of the enemy's advance guard attacks the left flank of our last columns and tries to bar the road to them. The Guard forms column, makes a bayonet charge and frees our companions.'

Preyssing's handsome Bavarian cavalry brigade, attached to IV Corps ever since June, and whose elegant manoeuvrings the Italians had so admired in July[14] but is now 'reduced to about 200 horses', is approaching the town when

'ahead of us cannon suddenly began banging away, and on some high ground in the town's vicinity we spotted some troop masses firing several guns at an enemy still invisible to us. They belonged to Poniatowski's corps, and the Russians were trying to cut communications between it and our own. But since they were rather low down we couldn't see them.'

As soon as they do, von Muraldt goes on, IV Corps – 'not without noise and confusion' – draws itself up in line of battle to the left of the route. The victors of Malojaroslavetz, Frenchmen and Italians, are in an increasingly desperate state. More and more of their men have been straggling, and Cesare de Laugier, throwing anxious glances over his shoulder, has been seeing how

'a great number of sick or wounded or men too feeble to keep up with their units are just throwing away first their packs, then their muskets, hoping to march better and rejoin their regiments. Pell-mell, In disorder, they're still struggling on, making superhuman efforts not to lose sight of the rearguard. Finally they fall. God knows what will happen to them!'

Twelve or even fifteen emaciated horses, he sees, are now being needed to pull even one cannon. I Corps, which consists of only 11,000 or 12,000 of its original 79,000 combatants, is in no better state. It's just about to pass through the Tsarewo defile when Miloradovitch 'taking advantage of the gap between I and IV Corps' attacks with swarms of light cavalry:

'It came and fell on the column of unarmed men and passed through it several times, without however doing much harm to this dense mass which had huddled together like a flock of sheep at the approach of a wolf. Only a few isolated men were stabbed by their lances.'

For a while Davout's rearguard clings to the village of Federowskoï, but Paskewitch's cavalry finally drive it out and are pursuing it along the Viazma road. And for a while the whole of I Corps is in danger of being overwhelmed by Miloradovitch's 19,000 men.

While all this is going on, another Russian corps, approaching by the Medyn road, is trying to seize Viazma itself. But since the town's defended on that side by two rivers in a semi-circle, and Ney's leading divisions are already in occupation, this isn't easy. Fezensac sees how

'Ledru's division took up position on the plain dominating these streams, and prevented the enemy from forcing a passage, while Razout's division fell back to help I and IV Corps force their way through.'

Things aren't going well for Davout,

'who's being attacked by considerable forces. The Viceroy, informed of the danger he's in, orders our columns to fall back, assembles them and forms them up to fly to the Marshal's assistance. Poniatowski too retraces his steps and takes up position in front of Viazma, to the left of the road.'

Placing Ornano's Bavarian chevaulegers – 'the few cavalry still available' – to the Poles' right, Eugène has to withdraw his divisions quite a long way before they can take up a position on some high ground and threaten Miloradovitch's left flank in rear:

'We position our artillery, and our sharpshooters, under the protection of hedges, attack the enemy lines. At the same time Davout's main body goes into action to open a passage.'

After the Italian light infantrymen have forced the Russian gunners to clear off at a gallop 'the Viceroy sends a column of infantry through the brushwood to the Russian left'. This forces them to face about and, attacked on all sides, to relinquish their position astride the road. But just as the two corps, in contact again, are about to resume their march toward Viazma, Lejeune sees some 50 Russian guns 'again open up a very keen cannonade'. The Italians resist with courage; 'but Davout's corps,' Laugier's alarmed to notice, 'demoralised by the fatigues and all kinds of privations endured since Malojaroslavetz, no longer has the fine bearing it's had since the campaign's outset'. Labaume and Eugène's staff notice it too:

'The men were observing but little discipline and most were wounded or sick with fatigue and swelled the mob of stragglers.'

Griois, meanwhile, has been cut off from his guns and obliged to take refuge in a square formed by a regiment of General Nagel's brigade of the Italian 3rd Division, the 92nd Line. At every instant he sees how difficult the ever-growing mob of civilians and stragglers is making it even for orders to be heard, let alone carried out:

'This mass of isolated men, recognising neither chiefs nor discipline and only heeding its thirst for pillage, was sorely tried. At the first cannon shots it had halted, not knowing where to go in the fog that surrounded it. Swollen by the greater part of the employees whose administrations no longer existed, by *vivandières* and a multitude of little carts laden with children and foodstuffs, it was throwing itself now to one side, now to the other, according to where the last projectile to strike in its midst had come from. This flux and reflux of roundshot, ploughing furrows in every direction and from which arose screams of despair, presented a horrible spectacle. For very good reasons the units that were fighting repulsed these fugitives who were trying to take refuge in their midst, so that the poor wretches found themselves exposed to the enemy's fire and sometimes to our squares' too. They floated in disorder over terrain littered with dead, wounded and shattered vehicles.'

Seeing all this, Laugier goes on,

'the enemy become bolder, redouble their gunfire. On our side the wretched state of our horses delays the artillery's manoeuvres. Sure of his superiority, Miloradovitch tries another vigorous attack to outflank us. But the Italian chasseurs, the Bavarians, and the Polish [line] lancers (though very badly mounted) face the Russians boldly and put them to flight. At long last, thanks above all to our cavalrymen, the infantry reaches the high ground covering Viazma town.'

By now it's about midday and the fog has cleared. For two days Victor Dupuy has 'only taken coffee and some grains of gruel, which some hussars of the 8th had invited me to eat with them'. General Jacquinot sends him to halt and reunite all scattered officers or troopers of what had been his light cavalry division who may already be passing through Viazma. 'I fell in with a light artillery captain, Crosnier by name. He told me to follow him.' Crosnier introduces him to

'one of the French families who'd fled from Moscow, whom the Emperor had told him to take back to France. It consisted of a mother and her two daughters, aged twelve and fourteen.'

But Dupuy's too hungry to be sensitive to their charms, 'A leg of mutton hung up over a rousing fire drew my attention more particularly. What a long time it had been since I'd been at such a feast!' Crosnier even fills Dupuy's pockets with bread and rum, which he duly shares with Jacquinot and Tavernier, his chief-of-staff. In the midst of all the hurly-burly von Suckow, too, has two strokes of luck. Not only does he fall in with some of his armed companions, but he buys a pot of jam from a Jew which, he suspects, has come from some marshal's wagon – 'but we didn't demand a certificate of origin' – and a cake of the kind for which Viazma is noted.

East of the town, meanwhile, the fighting's still heavy. IV Corps' 13,000 men are drawn up at right angles to the road, more to its right, now, than its left, 'with its left flank forming a hook to face the Cossacks all round us'. I Corps is on its right. At last Griois' artillery – he's been worried for its safety – turns up, but at I Corps' extreme rear. Ney, too, has sent back a brigade to flank Davout on his other side, the whole positioned 'at a very acute angle to the post road'. A second line is formed by Poniatowski's 3,500 Poles and the remainder of 1st Cavalry Corps. Although the French side outnumbers Miloradovitch's 19,000 men, the weather's getting colder every minute, and in the ranks of the Guardia d'Onore – any number of its wounded officers have 'bandaged heads or arms in slings' – many men who haven't eaten for days are fainting and collapsing; 'others, hardly able to carry their weapons, are keen to fight to warm themselves or are hoping for death to deliver them from this long agony'. Griois sees the redheaded Marshal Ney

'coming back at a gallop. I can see him still, at the spot where the fighting was hottest, speaking to the men, indicating to the generals what dispositions they should take up, animating all hearts with the confidence that flashed from his glances. He made an effect on me I don't know how to describe. The King of Naples in the thick of the fire had never seemed to me more handsome.'

And indeed it's Ney who, by coming back to the other corps' assistance, has stabilised the whole situation:

'Throughout the action he was present in person and for a long while marched with the Viceroy and the Prince of Eckmühl to confer with them on what dispositions they should adopt.'

But then, just as Cesare de Laugier is staring at 'all three of them together on some high ground near the Royal Guard to the right of the post road, trying to concert their operations', the Russian columns again renew their attack. 'All along the line the firing resumes with extraordinary vigour,' so that among other things the 85th's 2nd Battalion, in square near a forest where there's a fresh clearing, is driven in by combined Russian cavalry and artillery. 'One minute,' Le Roy sees to his horror,

'sufficed for it to vanish. Its commander, whose name was Centenier, had called on the 1st Battalion to support it. It was 200 yards closer to our cavalry and under its protection. Otherwise it would certainly have suffered the same fate. It received into its square the wreckage of the 2nd Battalion which, though most of its men were wounded, had escaped from the enemy's hands. The 1st Battalion's commander had his throat cut by a piece of grapeshot which laid him out dead, while each man, after firing his musket, was trying to flee and escape this massacre. Only our obstinacy got us as far as the town, so as to give the vehicles and the column of disarmed men time to pass through it and gain the protection of III Corps, drawn up in line of battle at the town's exit.'

Preyssing's light cavalry brigade is ordered to charge the 'numerous Russian guns, if possible seize them, or at least reduce them to silence.' An impossible task. But

'regardless of our weakness and the exhausted state of most of our horses, we carried out our order with such determination that the Russians were put to flight, yet without our being able to take any of their cannon. On our exhausted steeds we were only able to attack them at a trot.'

At about 3 p.m. the light begins to fail, and the rest of the 85th, after being blasted by heavy-calibre roundshot, withdraw slowly, Le Roy says, towards the town. So, just before 4 p.m., does IV Corps. Marching through its flames, Le Roy sees III Corps drawn up in line of battle on the plateau beyond.

The 85th may have withdrawn slowly. Not so many of Davout's other units. Watching the battle from the Russian positions Wilson sees how I Corps, though covered by Ney's corps,

'broke and rushed to the points of passage in great confusion. A regiment of Russian grenadiers charged his rearguard into the town, bayoneting all who resisted.'

And all the time, Lejeune says, 'the Russians hadn't ceased to aim 50 guns on our unfortunate convoys, which kept moving on during the battle.' To Major Bonnet, whose 18th Line, part of Razout's division, has been protecting I Corps' retreat, it's the Italians' retirement that's looked more like a rout, and I Corps to have retreated in somewhat better order. If so, it's partly thanks to the staunchness of the 7th Light, which for part of the day has been engaged with regular Russian cavalry. Sergeant Bertrand's had two muskets shattered in his hands, 'one while I was charging it, the second when priming'. Now, at nightfall, the regiment's been ordered to cover the bridge over the steep-banked, swift-flowing river:

'Menaced by cavalry, the four battalions form a massed close column by divisions, our effectives by now being much weakened. Towards 9 p.m., at the moment when, seated on our packs, we were taking a well-earned rest, we were warned of the enemy's attack by the firing of our outposts, one of which was carried off. It was cavalry. Colonel Romme closed us up on the head of the column, the last division [i.e., two companies] faced about, the files of the wings to right and left, and thus we had a full and compact square, in complete defiance of all regulations, but well suited to the circumstances. The firing began immediately from all its four faces, and more than one Russian trooper met his death under our musket balls or on our bayonets. Only a few men were wounded by pistol shots.'

Colonel Romme is complimented by Gérard, his divisional general. But still their job isn't finished. An hour later they march for the bridge, and the first battalions cross. But Bertrand's own carabinier company is ordered to guard the river bank on the far side until the whole column has got over:

'My captain Moncey (son of the Marshal)[15] sends me upstream to reconnoitre with a few men of my choice. After 20 minutes I'm fired on. I establish myself on the fringe of a wood to reply and send a corporal to warn the captain. The whole company, and even all who hadn't crossed the bridge, come running to my aid. But the enemy have disappeared. And we cross to the other bank. It was already well into the night.'

The Italian Royal Guard has bivouacked 'about two and a half miles from the town' near a convoy of sick and wounded in the vast forest beyond which is 'serving them as a hospital and a tomb. The difficulty of making the horses move had forced their drivers to abandon everything'. Facing the enemy, on the left of the highway and finding any amount of firewood, the Italians 'light enormous fires', which burn through the night. 'The Viceroy had his tent in the middle of the regiment of Vélites, who in front of the prince tried to put on a pretence of gaiety very far', their adjutant-major notes, 'from everyone's hearts'. Now and again he hears Ney's guns banging away at the Russians across the river and, looking back, sees what's left of Viazma's houses going up in flames. In the flaming horror of Viazma as 'the Russian general Tschlogokoff marches into it, drums beating and flags flying'[16] several hundred French sick and wounded are being burnt to death in a church after some abandoned shells have exploded in it – the very same church, perhaps, where in August Napoleon had ordered a posse of the Imperial Guard to complete the funeral obsequies of its venerable bishop?[17] But Wilson's gratified to see 'a Swiss family, consisting of a mother with her two daughters, most beautiful girls, saved, and honourably conducted in safety to a sheltering post'.

In 'the English General's' embittered opinion Miloradovitch's failure to cut Davout off has been entirely due to Kutusov's having stacked arms at Biskowo, where he'd 'remained inflexible, saying "the time has not yet come",[18] and to his consequent failure – or even lothness – to hasten on beyond Viazma and cut off all three corps, as Miloradovitch had suggested. 'Had the Marshal marched at 8 a.m. or even 10 or 12, Viazma might have been seized, the bridges destroyed, and the corps of the Viceroy, Poniatowski, Davout and Ney would have had no alternative but dispersion, ensuring destruction or surrender.' But he hadn't. And Ney had been free to stabilise the situation.

In Colonel *T.-J.-J. Séruzier*'s view the struggle to get through Viazma has 'cost the French 4,000 men, and the enemy twice that number'. Wilson, who thinks the French have lost 6,000 men, says the Russians took 2,000 prisoners, – the Russians themselves will afterwards estimate them at 3,000 – one standard and three guns.[19] Thousands of stragglers and vehicles have had to be abandoned for lack of horses. And any number of officers have fallen. Cesare de Laugier admiringly records their names. 'It was in this engagement', writes Lejeune, 'that Colonel Banco, the Viceroy's ADC, commander of the 2nd Italian Horse Chasseurs, had his head carried away by a cannonball.' Among the Russians' prisoners is the 35-year-old General Pelletier, commander of Poniatowski's artillery. He's of the same opinion as Pion des Loches, de Lariboisière and other gunners, and tells his captors so:

'Napoleon's made a great mistake in keeping more than 100 pieces of artillery. He'd have done better to discard 500 cannon to get to Smolensk with the whole of his army. Instead of which he's been obliged to remain in support during the daily brushes he's no longer able to escape, his cavalry being as exhausted as his teams.'

Von Muraldt's 4th Bavarian Chevaulegers' last charge has cost them nine-tenths of their men and horses:

'Our brigade, bivouacked by a wood by the wayside, had been so badly mauled, we counted only 30-40 horses left. Over and above the dead and wounded we also lacked some officers who'd gone off during the battle to find a place of safety or fodder for their mounts. Now, next morning, these reappeared; and our general, Preyssing, now surrounded mainly by an insignificant group of officers, saw himself obliged to report to General Ornano that from now on his brigade must be regarded as dissolved.'

But Ornano, a divisional general who so far has inspired but little confidence, either in young von Muraldt or in anyone else,[20] just shrugs:

'"What d'you expect me to do about it? Everyone's got to get out of this affair as best he can." This consoling observation freed us from further duties. The common bond which had assembled officers and men under the same flag and placed on them their mutual duties, was dissolved. But there was some consolation in the thought that the regiment had asserted itself in its last fight.'

Von Muraldt's is by no means the only cavalry regiment that no longer exists. In Laugier's eyes, too, 'the saddest result' of the battle for Viazma 'was that almost all the cavalry's horses succumbed, not being up to such fatigues'. The numbers of Italian infantrymen who've thrown away their muskets, too, are greater than ever. The battle has also cost Le Roy his last few possessions, including his portmanteau, which he'd entrusted to his batman, who now doesn't even dare appear before him. But as usual Le Roy is philosophical. Tells his faithful Guillaume:

'Oh well, you see, my friend, I've not long been encumbered by my most precious possessions, which would have caused me a lot of worry and which I'd anyway have had to get rid of later on. That fellow's done me a great service. If you see him again, give him a 5-franc piece to drink my health.'

From now on, he decides, he'll dispense with all personal aids and accessories. And begins by making 'two big pockets which I crudely fitted inside my greatcoat', and also in the tails of his uniform coat,

> 'putting into them a razor, a well-stocked travelling case, some thread, some buttons, a box of tea and my knife. Sometimes I stuffed it all inside my shako. The greatcoat's pockets did duty as a larder. It took me several days to fix things up in my own way; and when all was ready I waited to see what would happen next.'

CHAPTER 4

HANDMILLS AT DOROGHOBOUI

Fezensac's strictness with stragglers – retreating chesswise – 'naked wretches flying from the peasantry' – a ridiculous masquerade – end of the cavalry – the loot of Moscow – handmills but no corn – how the Polish Lancers coped – playing the Cossack – Napoleon waives protocol – Le Roy's walking wardrobe – boeuf à la mode – destroying guns

Although Ney has taken up a good overnight position at the edge of the great Viazma forest with the river in front of him, and is fending off the Russians coming from Medyn, Fezensac's deeply shocked at the demoralised state of I and IV Corps: 'The Italian Royal Guard was almost alone in marching in good order.' As for the stragglers, of whom there are thousands, it's more than he can do to persuade them to go on ahead:

'It was important to them to gain a few hours' march; and anyway we couldn't allow them to mingle with our ranks and hinder our movements. I did my very best to persuade them to leave without waiting for the rearguard.'

All in vain:

'Weakness or laziness made them deaf to our advice. Hardly had daylight appeared than III Corps took up its arms and got going. At this moment all the isolated men quit their bivouacs and came to join us. Those who were sick or wounded stayed by their fires, begging us not to abandon them to the enemy. We had no means of transporting them and had to pretend not to hear these plaints we could do nothing about. As for that flock of wretches who'd abandoned their flags though still in a state to fight, I ordered them to be repulsed with blows of musket butts. If the enemy attacked us, I warned them, I'd fire on them at the least embarrassment they caused.'

'Massed at 200 to 300 pace intervals' Ney's battalions 'march off down the road'. Taking turn and turn about with the 4th and 7th Light, it's Major Bonnet who's commanding this 'rearguard of the rearguard' retreating by stages '*à reculons*' or 'chessboard fashion'[1] – 'a new experience' for his men as they

'fall back by battalions 100 or 150 paces. So as to alternate defence with offence the even battalions of the second line, instead of falling back at the same time as the even battalions of the first line, may form columns by divisions, at either close, half, or whole distance behind the first division, the right in front, and then advance outside the right of the first line's even battalions as they retreat and form up into line a few fathoms to the rear of the left of the first line's uneven battalions.'

Is the 18th Line actually manoeuvring, over and over again, in this intricate fashion? Bonnet doesn't say. Neither does Bertrand, nor Fezensac, who of course take all such matters for granted. But it can hardly be the most habitual of drill movements?

Stragglers! By now there are so many thousands the Cossacks aren't even bothering to take prisoners, a task they're leaving 'to the peasants and the militia', who're carrying it out with extreme cruelty. Wilson, who at Viazma has just seen how 'fifty French, by a savage order, were burnt alive' and heard how 'fifty more from another village' suffered the same fate, even sees a brave French drummer boy leap first among his comrades into a common grave where furious peasants are burying them, too, alive. 'The English general', ordinarily so smug and self-satisfied, witnesses horrible scenes as he follows on with the Russian advance guard, and 'as a man and an Englishman' does what he can to help

> 'a French woman, naked to her chemise, with black, long, dishevelled hair, sitting on the snow, where she'd remained the whole day and in that situation had been delivered of a child, which had afterwards been stolen from her. This was the extreme of mental anguish and bodily suffering.'

He even sees scenes of cannibalism where stragglers, before dying, have tried to eat a dead comrade; and among the starving

> 'a veteran French grenadier. I was just putting a bit of biscuit into my own mouth when I turned my eye upon his gaze. It was too expressive to be resisted; I gave him what I designed for myself. The tears burst from his eyes, he seemed to bless the morsel, and then, amidst sobs of gratitude, expressed his hope that an Englishman might never want a benefactor in his need. He lived but a few moments afterwards.'

Sentiments unknown either to the peasants or to their other enemies, the Cossacks. In 'the air enveloped in flame and smoke' he sees how all prisoners are being

> 'immediately and invariably stripped stark naked and marched in columns in that state, or turned adrift to be the sport and the victims of the peasantry.'

He also hears

> 'the prayers of hundreds of naked wretches, flying from the peasantry whose shouts of vengeance echoed incessantly through the woods; the wrecks of cannon, powder-wagons, military stores of all descriptions, and every ordinary as well as extraordinary ill of war combined with the asperity of the climate, are forming such a scene as probably was never witnessed to such an extent in the history of the world'.

Meanwhile the stragglers' column 'marked by flocks of black crows, forever circling overhead, pursued by hordes of dogs which had been following them all the way from Moscow and were living off the dead and dying' is plundering the wagons that are continually being abandoned:

> 'They took the horses and ate them and dressed themselves in whatever warm garments they'd found in the wagons. Here began the ridiculous, terrible masquerade into which the entire French army was soon transformed. Yet this was only the beginning. Such was the army's condition as we approached Doroghoboui.'[2]

Once out of the forest, with Razout's 2nd Division still forming the rearguard and 'each division's left at its head', III Corps marches all day west-

wards. 'The officers and generals, all at their posts, directed its movements.' Only of the cavalry hardly any are left:

'Already half destroyed by our stay at the outposts at Winkovo,[3] a fortnight of marching and fighting had finished off its disorganisation.
Almost all the horses were dead of starvation or fatigue. Such feeble
troops as were still left and whose number was daily dwindling were
marching in isolation, no longer forming either divisions, or brigades,
or regiments, and hurrying on, as far as their mounts' weakness permitted, to cover the distance between one bivouac from the next.'

Even the admirable Grouchy[4] 'who alone would have been able to keep a
certain order in 3rd Cavalry Corps' but still hasn't recovered from his
Borodino wound, is unable to prevent it dwindling away. As for his inept
subordinate Lahoussaye, who has replaced him, 'ill, almost speechless',
he's incapable of restoring order or inspiring confidence. So its dismounted troopers, unable to follow their units, 'went to swell the flock of
unfortunates who were marching in disorder, without discipline or commanders'. And Griois, 'getting no orders from anyone, having to take
everything on to myself, march and choose direction as I thought most
advantageous,' is on his own. As for the isolated groups of troopers,

'we didn't usually ride along the road, but a bit to one side of it, where
we still found farms whose inhabitants had fled, leaving some grains of
corn for our horses. Besides, the highway, from being so marched on,
had become so slippery it looked like a skating rink. Even the most
insignificant slopes called for trouble and effort. Often both men and
horses slipped backwards, and that several times over. This was particularly the case with the French horses which, as is known, have no frost-
nails to their shoes, and which were therefore incredibly wearied. There
you have the explanation why the French cavalry melted away so quickly.'

Lieutenant von Kalckreuth of the Prussian hussars again falls in with

'a Horse Grenadier of the Guard. At Viazma his handsome regiment
had seemed rather strong to me. But a few days later he assured me it
was already wholly dismounted. The Cossacks' repeated attacks, too,
were doing much to ruin the French cavalry. One only had to say the
word *Cossack* rather loud for everyone to look behind him and trot on
ahead, even though no Cossack was to be seen.'

Caulaincourt too is dismayed to see how the army's horses are falling like
flies for lack of winter shoeing. Only the Polish Guard Lancers, familiar
with winter campaigning conditions in the north, are 'always managing
well' as they ride on ahead of IHQ. At least their wealthy colonel Count
Désiré Chlapowski,[5] scathing though he is about his colleagues of the Dutch
Lancers' ability to defend themselves, is satisfied with them:

'Our lancers always rode the little peasant horses we kept with us, so as
not to fatigue our own. The officers always slept amidst the lancers.
Those ordered to find forage in neighbouring villages rarely returned
empty-handed. Since we were always near IHQ and kept running into
convoys of cattle coming to join the army, provisions sufficed. When we

got to the place where we were to pass the night our lancers occupied
some building or other and kept a lookout to see the French didn't set
fire to it to warm themselves.'

Von Muraldt's little group is far from being the only one to go marauding.
Leaving a road incessantly blocked by fallen horses, broken wagons, carriages and guns, they're

'free to settle for the night wherever they like. For the most part men left
the road (particularly if they were mounted), and found their way to
some village or farm as yet unoccupied that might offer them a roof over
their heads and fodder for their horses. Even so it often happened that
after riding far afield we had to camp under the bare sky. If, on the other
hand, did get under a roof, one was in danger of being attacked and
taken prisoner by the Cossacks. Very often, too, one had to defend one's
night quarters, fruit of such a search, sabre in hand against similar little
units. Those who were more numerous or stronger showed no pity to
the weaker, but thrust them out into the cold, and on top of it even
seized such victuals as they might have with them.'

Some groups even

'play the Cossack. Spotting at a distance some village others have already
occupied, they began shouting 'Hurrah!' and in this way frightened
them away, and then took their places. It was the boldest who were generally managing best.'

It's every man's hand against his fellow. The Polish Lancers' foraging expeditions, however, are being organised in collaboration with those of the Vistula Legion,

'most often of its 2nd Regiment, under the orders of Malczewski, and a
detachment of our cavalry. Spreading out over the neighbourhood they
brought back some food for the men and forage for the horses.'

Above all the regiment is guarding Chlapowski's cook

'like the apple of its eye. Helped by a dozen troopers, Garolinski got
busy preparing our food as best he could. Our men undertook to find
some meat and flour. He had the meat cooked, and with the flour made
various kinds of biscuits which he grilled slightly. Unfortunately there
was a grave shortage of salt. Almost every morning before leaving each
horseman got one of his Garolinski's hot *galettes* and a bit of meat, which
had to suffice for the day.'

But Zalusky has had to sacrifice, one after the other, the two cows he's been
bringing along to provide cream for his coffee. Certain precautions are still
being taken. The Young Guard, Sergeant *A.-J.-B.-F. Bourgogne* of the
Fusiliers-Grenadiers is noticing, is 'almost always being made to march
behind the cavalry and artillery' so that there shall be some horseflesh for
them, as for other Guard units, to eat at the day's end:

'Always there were always plenty of dead and dismembered horses. A still
greater number, though still alive and on their feet, but stupefied, had
been left behind and were letting themselves be killed without flinching.'

Although platoons of Russian cavalry and infantry are marching parallel across the immense plain, nothing happens until the evening of 3 November, when the Russian units try to prevent the rearguard getting through a defile. But Fezensac's regiment, supported by two guns, defends it and gives the others time to get through, leaving behind two voltigeur companies, who only retire after nightfall. But hardly have Bonnet and his men

'begun to get some rest than the Russians threw some shells at our bivouacs. One hit a tree at whose foot I was sleeping. No one was hurt, and there were a few moments of confusion in some of the 18th's companies. I've always noticed that shots fired at night do little harm; but they strike the imagination and give the men the idea that the enemy are being prodigiously active.'

Next day – not a very cold one, Pion des Loches is glad to find – Ney resumes his methodical retreat:

'The Emperor wanted to march slowly to preserve the baggage. In vain Marshal Ney wrote to him that there was no time to be lost, that the enemy were pressing the rearguard hard, that on our flanks the Russian army was making long days' marches, and we should be afraid he'd get to Smolensk or Orsha before us. For the rest, the weather was fine and fairly mild for the season, and we were hoping to arrive safely at Smolensk, which should be the term of our wearisome efforts.'

Bridges are still among the most serious obstacles. Coming to one which, like so many others, has collapsed under the vehicles' weight, notably of course of the ammunition wagons, the nimblest men of the 85th

'jumped it easily, the stream being no more than 4 or 5 feet wide. But the pedestrians spread themselves upstream and downstream, so as to cross more easily without having to take their shoes off. Yet this crossing held us up almost all day! Fortunately several wagons got bogged down and broken. They served us as a support to cross this gutter.'

And all the time, on either flank, Lejeune too, also marching on ahead with Davout's headquarters, sees

'many columns of Russian cavalry and artillery trying to overtake us and wait for us at the defile beyond Doroghobouï.'

Sometimes they see a break in the column or some convoy, and pounce. Even IHQ's baggage, though it's going on well ahead, isn't immune. Among vehicles which aren't going to make it to Doroghobouï are all Murat's remaining carriages and wagons – among them no doubt the one containing his many perfumes. Already on 18 October, seeing that his carriages were holding up the chaotic retirement from the Winkovo battlefield, Murat had ordered the men to burn them and 'laughed at the urgency they, having emptied them of their contents, put into carrying out his order'. This loss of his remaining carriages is more problematic. Yet his spectacular wardrobe seems to have survived it, for Surgeon Roos sees him wearing

'over his French general's uniform a Spanish cape, sometimes red, sometimes green, with silver tassels. His hat was ornamented with several white plumes, and he was wearing Hungarian boots, red, green, or yellow.'

Duroc, Grand Marshal of the Palace, has been exigent, so Castellane's thinking, in his choice of employees for the imperial household. 'Thanks to the constant efforts of the *maîtres d'hôtel* and the cooks' everyone at IHQ is 'almost always getting something to eat, better or worse. Not on a par with our hunger, it's true, but no less astonishingly for that.' Normally, only Berthier dines at Napoleon's table. But now Murat, no longer having a table of his own to dine at, also takes his place at it. But 'his ADCs and all the officers of his suite' including Rossetti, are 'obliged to take pot luck elsewhere.' Not too disastrously that first day. However ill-seen by the impe-rial devotees Dedem van der Gelder may be, his culinary status is still excel-lent:

> 'The King went to dine with the Emperor. In the evening, since I was still affluent and well provided for, I offered his staff officers a splendid sup-per, with Madeira and Bordeaux wines, and an abundance of mocha cof-fee and liqueurs from the isles of the Indies! My cook, who'd stayed at Drontheim, prepared horsemeat marvellously and all my guests thought I was serving them beef!'

Alas, it's the swan-song of Dedem the diplomat's career as a host:

> 'Next day my *calèche* was crushed by the artillery; and a nice little well-harnessed *droshka* well supplied with provisions and belonging to the Count de Castel-Bajac, one of my ADCs, was carried off by the Cossacks, who thereupon tasted our wine, carried off the carriage and drove away the coachman, telling him to tell his master they'd found our wine excellent.'

But he still has his wagon left 'and my mobile kitchen. My ADCs escorted it.' Otherwise

> 'only the Emperor was well served; that's to say, he always had white bread, linen, his Chambertin, good oil, beef or mutton, rice and beans or lentils, his favourite vegetables.'

Caulaincourt notices how few are the Emperor's personal demands.[6] A lieutenant of the 1st Company of the Chasseurs à Cheval, *J. M. Merme*, who'd served in Egypt and has 'the privilege of lighting a fire for him at each of his halts', notices it too:

> 'One day as I was preparing to make up the Emperor's fire, I put my hand-kerchief over my busby to keep the cold out a bit. Seeing him approach, I made to take it off. But he said to me: "We aren't at the Carrousel here. It's colder than usual today, so keep the handkerchief on your head!"'

Merme himself is making a point of never warming himself at a fire and 'consequently never had a limb frost-bitten'.

As the years have gone by it has progressively been the practice for regi-ments, particularly cavalry regiments, to leave their regimental Eagles at home. The danger of these sacred objects being captured by France's ene-mies is too great. The flags are less sacred. Leaving Viazma with a party of his wounded Württembergers, surgeon von Roos has had his taken off their poles and wrapped around the bodies of the strongest marchers (a 'precaution thanks to which I'd afterwards discover the Württemberger troops hadn't lost a single one of their flags in Russia'). Also in the endless column a dwindling group of dismounted 2nd Cuirassiers are escorting Sergeant-Major Thirion, who's carrying their eagle on its blue pole. 'Having had nothing to eat for two nights except bark off the trees it had been tethered to,' his poor horse, which he's been dragging behind him, has dropped from hunger and fatigue:

> 'I'd cut short this good companion's agony with a shot through its head. Not wishing to leave my cuirass and sabre to the enemy, I'd thrown them under a bridge; shouldered the standard and a double-barrelled shotgun I'd bought in Moscow; and continued the retreat on foot.'

At every step the 'bronze eagle with spread wings, at the end of a rather long staff' is getting heavier:

> 'Under the eagle, nailed to the staff, was a square flag of white satin surrounded on three sides by a gold fringe of heavy gold, the length and thickness of one's finger. It was embroidered with the words: The Emperor to his 2nd regiment of Cuirassiers. The reverse bore the names of all the battles the regiment had been in, and on every square inch of satin left blank by these inscriptions was a swarm of bees half the size of one's thumb. A white satin cravat was tied to the eagle's feet. It hung down for a foot and a half, and at each end had a tassle made from twisted fringes larger than a finger, all in gold. The whole was furled in a morocco sheath.'

All this has long been cutting into Thirion's shoulder. So he points out to Colonel Dubois that even if he sacrifices his life defending it, there's a danger of it being captured by Cossacks. And is given leave to hide it. 'I unscrewed the eagle, which was placed in Adjutant Millot's portmanteau. Flag and cravat were folded and put in the colonel's. And the staff was burnt.' Thus relieved, 'both morally and physically', Thirion, that man of steel, trudges on.

At last Doroghoboüï, in its 'vast amphitheatre overlooking the Dnieper' comes into sight at the end of the long straight highway – the one the army had advanced along in open order through the terrible August heats.[7] A mile or two before reaching it its van runs into a Dutch unit, marching for Viazma. After escorting a treasury convoy from Smolensk to Doroghoboüï, Major *Henri-Pierre Everts'* battalion of the 33rd Line is marching eastwards – how keenly he's looking forward to seeing Moscow! Instead what he sees – 'I'd never seen so striking an example' – is a 'confused mass of all units, prey to an extreme panic and disorder'. Someone assures him the 33rd's other two battalions under his Colonel de Marguerye will be arriving that very day with the Emperor and the entire Moscow army! 'It was superfluous for me to go any further. I made an about turn and waited for the Emperor at Doroghoboüï.' When IHQ turns up he goes to Jomini,

> 'who was responsible for directing troop movements. From his adroit and judicious questions I realised immediately that this was an officer

absolutely equal to the situation. He seemed to me to be a most reflective person and very calm. It's absolutely impossible to give any idea of the way in which at each moment everyone, prey to the most intense over-excitement, was coming to ask him questions.'

Advised by Jomini to wait for de Marguerye, he also meets

'our brigade's former general Barbanègre who, despite his character of officer of a crack regiment, was also marvellous at playing the role of courtier, a bit to please the Emperor, a bit to encourage the troops'.

Over and over again Barbanègre assures Everts 'that this flight (taking place amidst the most utter disorder) was a beautiful, remarkable retreat'. At about 10 o'clock next morning, amidst utter disorder, all jumbled up with

'generals, wounded officers and men, commissary wagons and other employees, the wreckage of the corps' ammunition trains, the carriages of COs and everything else of the sort one can imagine ...'

the 33rd's two other battalions arrive, escorting a big artillery park. The first thing de Marguerye asks Everts is, has he any food? Everts shows him his carts full of barrels of rice, bread and salt, and a small supply of *votki* [*sic*], which Marguerye delightedly distributes to the whole regiment 'as promptly as ever possible. It went without saying', and the colonel tells Everts all about the fight at Malo-Viazma in September,[8] when a squadron of the Guards Dragoons had been wiped out but most of his Dutchmen had survived.

Waiting there with a convoy of wounded, Lieutenant Vossler, too, is astounded to see 'the first trickle of retreating soldiers', i.e., the army's monstrous vanguard of loot and looters from Moscow:

'We were amazed at their appearance. Many carried no weapons. Others were armed after a fashion, but either their muskets were unserviceable or they'd run out of ammunition. These men were no longer soldiers, but marauders and camp followers, mostly burdened with bales of wool, linen, silk of every colour and description, with men's and women's furs ranging from sable to sheepskin, hats and caps of every shape and size, fashionable boots and shoes, kitchenware of copper, brass and iron, silver and tin cutlery, pewter plates and dishes, glasses, goblets, scissors, needles, thread, waxed twine, and so on and so forth. In short, with every kind of object which the well-equipped peacetime traveller, on horseback or on foot, whether gentleman, journeyman, merchant, artist or whatever, could possibly require. Most were mounted, usually on wretched little Russian ponies, others on carts, barouches, diligences and coaches of every variety.'

Even the captured state carriages are still rolling along, having evidently got through at Viazma.

Orders have been given that Doroghoboui, too, shall be burnt to the ground; and no sooner has the Guard entered it than it tears down its houses to make up its bivouac fires. By the time the other corps begin to arrive,

'nothing was left except a house or two. Its stores had been pillaged, the brandy there'd been so much of was flowing in the streets, while the rest of the army was dying for lack of *spirituosa*.'

III and IV Corps have been attacked by Miloradovitch while still two miles outside the town. When Eugène's men get there Labaume's shocked to see men

'straying about like cattle, sleeping under vehicles, or setting fire to the few remaining houses where generals are trying to warm themselves'.

The weather's horrible. 'As yet we hadn't had such bad weather since leaving Moscow,' thinks Griois, arriving soaked to the skin by a 'cold and humid wind and clouds of sleet which, piercing our clothes, numbed all our limbs'. Bourgogne's comrades are in like state – he particularly so, being bitten all over by lice, which he gets rid of by shaking out his garments over a fire. But what's this, arriving from the opposite direction? If not the long-awaited convoy bringing the handmills on which Napoleon had lavished so much detailed attention in the Kremlin?[9]

'Early next morning [5 November] before setting out, a distribution of handmills was made in every regiment of the Guard, in case we found any corn to grind.'

All the other corps, too, are exhorted to take their share. 'This offer of mills, when there wasn't a single grain at our disposition' seems 'a bitter mockery' to Griois: 'So all these useless pieces of furniture remained stored, at the disposition of the Cossacks.' Bourgogne's men find 'the mills very heavy; we got rid of them before twenty-four hours were over.'

Before leaving again, Le Roy, methodical as ever, passes his wardrobe in review. It consists of

1 pair of string shoes

1 pair of linen underpants, same length as my trousers

1 pair of trousers of blue broadcloth

1 pair of stable boots over the trousers

1 flannel waistcoat against my skin

1 shirt and a knitted woollen waistcoat over it, given me by Colonel Schultz at Vilna

1 waistcoat of blue cloth, with gold braid on front and pockets

1 blue frock coat and my epaulettes hanging down on my chest

1 strong broad cape collar hanging down over its shoulders

2 capacious pockets sewn into the interior 'serving me for a larder'. Two cords prevent the collar from being whipped up by the wind: it's also attached by two brandenburgers.

2 black silk handkerchiefs, the sturdier one protecting my ears and nose. To this end I had lined it with furs; the other served as a necktie.

1 shako, covered over with oilskin cover, containing needles, thread, scissors, soap and razor

1 sabre in its sheath, the handle resting under my left armpit

1 strong knife, with an ivory handle, with a pocket knife and corkscrew

1 notebook and pencil

1 black silk bonnet under the shako

1 bottle sheathed in wicker

Finally, as pocket handkerchiefs, my two hands.[10]

But Griois' amusing comrade and fellow artillery colonel, the aristocratic Jumilhac, 'violent and choleric towards his inferiors, but amiable, witty and excellent towards his comrades', wanders away into the night and doesn't come back.

When I Corps gets under way early next morning, Lejeune has to leave behind the cows that have so far been traipsing along with Davout's head-quarters:
>'Leaving Doroghouï, we made a long march, and at nightfall halted in a big forest where General Jouffroy had been forced to halt with the many ill-harnessed guns he was in charge of. This night was employed to fill the ammunition wagons which could still be put in motion, blowing up those we were abandoning, and burning the wheels and carriages of guns we couldn't drag any further.'

To Davout's unwilling chief-of-staff and future painter of elegant battle-scenes, who has found in the excitements of warfare a unique sensation of pleasure beyond all others, there's something tragic about these
>'ever-multiplying explosions, the signals of our catastrophe. They tore at our heart just like a mother's is torn by the knell of a church bell sound-ing for her child's funeral.'

To console him General Jouffroy has a tent put up and invites Lejeune to supper – 'A supper! Oh God, what luxury in our misery!' Which among other things acquaints him with curry – something he's never tasted before:
>'So far I hadn't been reduced to eating horsemeat. But the only dish the general could offer me was spiced horseflesh, a stew known as *boeuf à la mode*. This flavouring made this black, insipid, scraggly meat, full of sinews that resist even the sharpest incisors, very edible. An insipid yel-low fat, saffron-coloured, gives this dish a repulsive appearance. Yet we were very happy to eat this excellent meal, washed down with a bottle of good wine taken from some great Muscovite lord.'

In vain, in a temperature which is falling sharply – Larrey, wearing a thermometer attached to his buttonhole, sees its mercury's at -16° Réau-mur (-10° C) – Captain François, the 'Dromedary of Egypt', exhorts his men to 'remember' the Egyptian campaigns where I'd suffered even more acutely', and tells his comrades:
>'"One can be even worse off! Here we've horseflesh to eat. In the deserts of Syria we often hadn't anything at all! You're complaining how cold it is, but I suffered more from the heat in the middle of Arabia's burning sands. Patience and courage!"'

But, he adds sadly,
>'they scarcely listened to me, and we marched a whole day in deepest silence. Many of our guns and almost all our baggage were being aban-doned along the road. The cavalry, so beautiful six months ago, being almost wholly without mounts, the men disperse and have no more dis-

cipline. Subordination is despised, the military hierarchy comes to an end. The general officer's no longer able to occupy himself with the soldiers who've made his glory for him, and the misery of these brave fellows causes them to despise their commanders' voices. They just wander away from them or ask them to kill them. This request was made to me several times! What could I say to revive their courage?'

But though he himself and some others are keeping up an unbroken morale, this doesn't prevent them from being tortured by hunger:

'A horse falls, they throw themselves on it, quarrel over strips of its flesh. To find firewood to cook this meat we have to go deep into the countryside, at risk of being massacred. Thus our rest halts are consumed by finding something to cook this disgusting food with.'

The oft-wounded François, marching with

'a boot and slipper on my feet, a crutch in my hand, covered in a pink fur lined with ermine and the hood over my head, with my faithful batman and my two horses who went on as they liked, without losing sight of us,'

pays a grenadier of the Guard a gold napoleon.[11] Otherwise he's eating only

'half-cooked horseflesh, in such fashion that the fat and blood spattered me from my chin to my knees. My face was blackened with smoke, my beard long, and I looked like a Mayence ham, and despite my situation I often laughed both at my costume and at that of my brothers-in-arms. We walked on with long icicles hanging from each hair of our beards, the skins that covered us half-burnt at such rare campfires as we were able to light. Those who had neither knife, sabre nor axe and whose hands were frost-bitten couldn't eat. I saw soldiers on their knees and others seated near shacks biting at horseflesh like famished wolves. Thanks to my batman I never lacked this resource, and each day I ate two or three pounds of this meat without salt or bread.'

But the result is 'dysentery'. Melted snow, which is all most men have to drink, is as bad for them as it is for the horses. Larrey, agreeing with Caulaincourt that it's hunger, not cold, that's killing the army, explains why:

'The little heat left in the viscera was absorbed. In particular it killed those who'd grown thin from abstinence and lack of nourishing food. In such people death was preceded by constrictive pains in the epigastric region, by sudden fainting fits, by a painful constriction of the throat, and by obvious anxiety – all symptoms of hunger.'

Even the Surgeon-General himself will have to march for the next three days on only 'two or three cups of pure coffee without sugar'. Then a friend gives him 'a glass of Bordeaux which I drank with indescribable pleasure'. And is immediately quit of his hunger pangs.

More and more, Smolensk is the magic word. There, everyone's saying to encourage himself as much as his neighbour, 'there's any amount of stores. Victor's IX Corps, fresh from Germany, is waiting for us', and will form the army's rearguard, enabling it to go into winter quarters in Poland. 'At least,' writes that amateur soldier, the sapient Dedem van der Gelder, 'that's how the multitude reasoned. Those who saw farther took care to keep their wisdom to themselves.'

That morning Wilson's Cossack escort, coming on the site of a French bivouac, see

'a gun and several tumbrils at the bottom of a ravine, with the horses lying on the ground. Lifting up the feet of several they call out, run and kiss the English general's knees and his horse, dance about and make fantastic gestures, like crazy men. When the delirium had somewhat subsided, they pointed to the horses' shoes and said: "God has made Napoleon forget that there is winter in our country." It was soon ascertained that all horses of the enemy's army were in the same improperly shod state, except those of the Polish corps, and the Emperor's own, which the Duke of Vicenza [Caulaincourt] with due foresight had kept always rough-shod.'

CHAPTER 5

SNOW

'We were assailed by whirlwinds of snow' – 'their limbs gradually stiffen' – doing a bear – Ney at Doroghoboui – Malet's conspiracy – Mother Dubois gives birth – plight of the amputees – Bourgogne hides nine potatoes – 'very well, I'll wait' – eating live horses – importance of cookpots – why southerners survived better – a grotesque masquerade – 'the way the Russians defreeze fish' – Louise Fusil kisses a gendarme

For several days the landscape's been 'swathed in cold vapours'. Le Roy, approaching Doroghoboui and bivouacking in a barn (sole relic of a hamlet) is sure 'everything boded snow for the morrow'. And sure enough, on 5 November

'the mists get thicker. An immense cloud, pressing down, falls in huge snowflakes. In the great black forests the wind begins to whistle and howl. It's as if the sky were coming down. Suddenly everything becomes confused, unrecognisable. Objects change their aspect ...'

The Russian winter Napoleon had so trivialised in spite of Caulaincourt's warnings yet whose onset he'd almost exactly predicted at Viazma, blasts the army with its icy breath. Scarcely have Dumonceau's men installed themselves in a hamlet on the forest edge than 'the temperature becomes glacial and a furious wind pounces' on them, driving before it thick whirlwinds of snow:

'No shelter protects us. Our fires could no longer warm us. The harsh north wind pursued me even in under my bearskin coverlet. Frozen on one side, grilled on the other, stifled by the smoke, agitated by the tempest's roarings as they violently shook the dense woods,'

he has to get up and run about all night, gets no rest. Already two nights before, on 2 November 'this suffering of a kind we'd so far not experienced' has already stricken I Corps' rearguard. Its chief-of-staff, spending it with Gérard's division in a big forest where the thermometer was showing -8° to -9° Réaumur (-5°C), had seen

'what a disastrous effect the snow was already having. When the moment came to leave, many men, stunned by the cold, couldn't get to their feet. We had to leave them where they were.'

In the most frightful cold Lieutenant Vossler sees

'men only lightly clad, without fur or overcoat, toiling along the road. It's visibly overpowering them. Their limbs gradually stiffen. They fall. Pick themselves up painfully, stagger on a few paces and fall once more, never to rise again. Some were showing their naked toes through their torn shoes or boots, first purple, then frozen dark blue or brown, and finally black.'

Dumonceau sees men sit down to rest by the roadside with their backs to trees or a heap of stones:

'At first they seem merely drowsy. But soon they become agitated, make futile efforts to get up; struggle convulsively, eyes haggard and glazed, the mouth fringed with froth, intelligence visibly extinct.'

Even veterans who've taken 2,000-mile marches from Spain and Italy in their stride and marched through many another blizzard – but then they hadn't been starving – are 'doing a bear'. Going suddenly headlong they fall on their faces. Or else death announces itself

'by strange symptoms. Here you're approached by someone with laughter in his eyes, his face beaming. He shakes you effusively by the hand – he's a lost man. Here another looks at you gloomily, his mouth uttering words of indignation and despair – he's a lost man.'

For Ney's rearguard to traverse Doroghobouï's blackened ruins is far from easy. Although he has 'managed to reach the town and blow up the bridge', and is all the while heavily engaged, he knows that half-way to Smolensk the army must cross a bridge over the Dnieper; and it's his intention to hold up the Russians all day on 8 November, to enable it to do so in some kind of order. But the night is

'the coldest we'd had so far. Snow was falling in abundance, and the wind's violence prevented us from lighting fires. Besides which the heaths we were encamped on offered few resources for our bivouacs.'

Next morning, in a thick mist, the 4th and 18th Line (Joubert's brigade) withdraw into the remains of Doroghobouï, closely followed by Cossacks. Fezensac details Joubert's dispositions for holding up the Russians:

'Doroghobouï is situated on a height, has its back to the Dnieper. The 2nd Division, ordered to defend it, was disposed like this: two cannon in battery at the end of the lower road, supported by a post of the 4th Regiment. To the left, a company of the 18th on the Dnieper bridge; to the right, on high ground, in front of a church, 100 men of the 4th, commanded by a major; the rest of the division in the courtyard of the castle, on the same height; the 1st Division in reserve, behind the town.'

But all these sage dispositions come to nought:

'The Dnieper bridge was captured, the church post thrown back. General Razout, shut up in the castle courtyard with the rest of the division and delivered over to his habitual indecision, was going to be surrounded when he, at long last, gives us the order to march. There wasn't a moment to lose. I carried off my regiment at the *pas de charge*, and we threw ourselves at the enemies occupying the town's heights.'

Up to their knees in snow which breaks up their formation, the 4th attack in open order with the bayonet, fighting the Russians man to man:

'The Russians' progress had been held up, but soon the enemy penetrated into the lower part of the town, and General Razout,[1] afraid of being cut off, ordered the retreat. I fell back slowly, reforming my platoons and always facing the enemy. The 18th, which had seconded our efforts, followed this movement. Leaving the enemy masters of the town, the two regiments came and reformed behind the 1st Division. Marshal Ney, dissatisfied with the ill success of his plan, took it out on Razout, on Joubert, on everybody. He maintained that the enemy forces hadn't been big enough to have driven us out of Doroghobouï, and asked me how many I'd seen. I permitted myself to reply that we'd been too close to count them.'

Nor does Ney succeed in recapturing two ammunition wagons which have accidentally been left in the town. No sooner has the 99th Line, under Colonel Henin, set off to do so, than it's forced back by Russian cannon fire. And Ney angrily 'resumes his retreat in good order'. Rapp:

'The army recrossed the Dnieper, the Emperor took up his headquarters in a ravaged château 120 kilometres from Smolensk and fifteen beyond the river. At this point its banks are rather steep and it was covered in ice-floes.'

Does he have any idea how many of his guns, 'not a single one of which was to be abandoned', are all the time having to be blown up or left behind? There are moments when Captain François, limping about on his one good leg, is even having to 'harness up fifteen horses to pull one field-gun'. And when the Württembergers have to spike eight of Faber du Faur's 16-pounders, von Roos sadly, for the last time, contemplates their gun-carriages:

'Everyone present was deeply moved. It seemed we were abandoning a parent or a friend in distress. These were the first guns the Württemberger troops had lost since the beginning of the war.'

Worried how the artillery will get across the Dnieper, Napoleon sends Rapp to Ney, telling him to hold off their pursuers until it's all across:

'All night we were busy getting the guns over. The last was still being pulled up the slope on the other side when the enemy came into view.'

In the ensuing fight several hundred men are wounded and have to be left behind:

'They bemoaned their lot, uttered pitiful cries, begging us to kill them. But what could we do? It was a heart-rending sight. Each of us was staggering under the burden of his own life. One could hardly stand upright. None of us had the strength to help anyone else.'

And all the time it's getting colder.

A few hours after IHQ has left Doroghoboüi at 8 a.m. on 6 November and is nearing the village of Mikhailowska, it's met by a courier 'at a gallop, asking for the Emperor'. He has frightening news from Paris. Count Daru, the army's *Intendant-Général*, brings the locked leather portfolio to Rapp, who's on duty:

'A long time had gone by since any dispatches had come – and I opened these for the Emperor. He ripped open the packet, glanced at its contents, and lit on a number of the *Moniteur* which he glanced through. The first article he read contained an account of Malet's *attentat*; but since he still hadn't read the dispatches, he couldn't make head or tail of it.

'"What's this? What plots, which conspiracies?"

'He opened the letters. They contained all the details of the attempted coup. He was astounded. This police which is aware of everything, guesses everything, had let itself be fooled. It was more than he could explain:

'"Savary in the La Force prison! The Minister of Police seized, arrested!"' 'I went out to distribute some orders. The matter was already known. Amazement, dismay, was written on every face.'

And in fact the news seems to be instantly known even to the Fusiliers-Grenadiers, who've seen the courier arrive. And to everyone else. Halting at a house in Mikhailowska which has been serving as a posthouse, Napoleon exclaims again and again to Caulaincourt and others that Savary should rather have let himself be killed than seized. Most alarming of all is that during the brief episode – it had only lasted from 4 a.m. to 11 a.m. on 23 October – no one had evidently given a thought either to the Empress or his son the infant King of Rome. So frail, at the political level, is his regime![2] Truly, as Talleyrand had whispered to the Tsar at Erfurt in 1910, the colossus has feet of clay – a realisation which certainly strengthens his intention to quit the army as soon as possible.

But there's also more urgent news. Marshal Victor's IX Corps, for instance, instead of attacking Wittgenstein, has been withdrawing in front of him. Two letters are swiftly dictated and sent off, urging Victor to resume the offensive and save the Moscow army's communications.

All day long on 6 November the snow falls heavily, freezing damp clothes to marching bodies:

'An envelope of ice seizes their bodies and stiffens all their limbs. A sharp violent wind grabs their breath even as they exhale it. Cutting it short, it forms icicles which hang by their beard around their mouths. Everything's becoming an obstacle.'

Many tumble into the unparapeted wells typical of Russian villages, and now invisible in the snow. Muskets are becoming

'insupportably heavy to their numbed limbs, slip from their hands, break, or get lost in the snow. Others' fingers freeze fast to them. The poor fellows drag themselves along, shivering, until the snow, clinging to their feet like a stone, or some bit of debris, a branch, or the body of one of their companions, causes them to trip and fall. There they groan in vain. Soon the snow covers them. Slight mounds show where they lie. There's their tomb! The whole road is strewn with these undulations, like a churchyard.'

Few, in this blizzard, have the strength to heed a fallen comrade. 'Even the most intrepid or the most indifferent', Philippe de Ségur sees as he plods on with IHQ's mules, covered with their purple horsecloths,

'are affected. They hurry by, averting their glances. In front of them, around them, all is snow. Their gaze loses itself in this immense dreary uniformity where the only objects that stand out are the great pines, funerary trees, with their funereal verdure, and the gigantic immobility of their black trunks and huge sadness. The whole army's being swathed in an immense winding sheet.'

It's so cold no one's riding a horse. Mailly-Nesle's companions, male and female, get out of their fine carriage and to keep warm 'walk onwards bent almost double, with our hands thrust in under our armpits, the part of the body we notice stays warmest'.

As in June's summer heats[3] there are many suicides. Lejeune keeps hearing 'musket shots on either hand, men were shortening their sufferings'. Some even do a friend the same service. Hearing a shot ring out behind them, Dumonceau's company turn their heads. It's a Württemberger who's blown his friend's brains out. And then 'without even a backward glance' trudges on.

If the day's terrible, the night's worse. After making only seven miles or so the men of the 85th discover how hard it is to set fire to living pine. 'This wood only burns as long as there's resin in its branches, after which it turns black and gives off a thick suffocating smoke.' Von Muraldt's party too are finding it

> 'slow and wearisome work. First you had to fell a tree with your sabre (axes were rare or non-existent), or at least lop its branches, for no dry wood was to be found. And even then, for hours on end, you had more smoke than fire. Only when it had at last begun to burn and we'd cleared away the surrounding snow could you begin making your wretched meal. Horsemeat was grilled at sabre-point and then eaten half-raw and bloody and without salt.'

Anyone still possessing a modicum of flour tries to make 'galettes, a kind of thin cake we kneaded together with icewater and tried to bake over the fire' to go with their horsemeat. 'But usually we were so tormented by hunger we couldn't wait until they were thoroughly done, but ate them up much too soon.' With stomach ache and diarrhoea as a result. Duverger takes up the miserable tale:

> 'After we'd restored our stomachs a little we chatted for a few moments. Each talked of his ambitions and while doing so sleep came to numb our limbs.'

Captain Count *M.-H. Lignières* of the 1st Foot Chasseurs of the Guard describes his night:

> 'There was scarcely any fire. The snow built up on one's back. When you quit your place to heed a call of nature or warm yourself by walking about a bit, you saw in front of you a mountain of snow, from whose midst emerged a scarcely perceptible cloud of smoke. When you went back to take your place again it was thick with snow you had to get rid of.'

Sleeping beside such a campfire, the staff of the Imperial Household find 'the snow, melting on our bodies, seeped into our furs and then, freezing again, turned them into heavy mantles of ice, comparable to those horrible leaden capes described by Dante.'

The Fusiliers-Grenadiers have bivouacked near a wood. All that 'sad day' its sick have been making 'supernatural efforts' in hopes of reaching Smolensk, only to die in the evening.

'A moment after, our *cantinière*, Mother Dubois, the wife of our company's barber, was taken poorly. Our Colonel Bodel did all he could, lending Mother Dubois his own mantle to cover the shelter where she was courageously putting up with her trouble. The regiment's surgeon spares no efforts. And in the end all turns out happily. In a jiffy, while the snow's falling, she gives birth to a big boy – unhappy predicament for a woman.'

'That night', Bourgogne adds, 'our men killed a white bear, which was instantly eaten.' The bivouac is also fatal to the horses:

'One usually had to go some distance and break the ice to water them. Then one needed a bucket to draw the water. Arriving at night, where find a river or a well? A surface of water was indistinguishable from the surface of the ground. Ice, broken only with difficulty in the evening, would be frozen hard again in the morning. Furthermore, even to break it we needed an axe or iron rod, and all implements were scarce. A driver, arriving half dead with cold in the evening and scared of getting lost, would try to find some way of lighting a fire, finding some shelter and getting something to eat. More often than not he just left the horses where they were.'

Tethered to snow-laden pine or silver birch trees, the wretched animals try desperately to break the ice with their hoofs; can't, and die of thirst and cold. And when morning comes their drivers 'set out without even having unharnessed' the survivors. Those without horsecloths, Larrey sees, are the first victims. 'It was above all at night they perished, mostly for lack of water, trying to make holes in the ice with their hoofs.' Thanks to Caulaincourt's foresight, however, the hundred or so drawing IHQ's carriages are 'still numerous and in tolerably good condition' – proof to the Master of the Horse that it's not cold that's killing army's horses, 'but lack of proper care, food; and above all drink.'

After that freezing horrible night the Fusiliers-Grenadiers are on their feet long before dawn. 'As yet the *diane* ['dawn' = reveille] hasn't been beaten'; but Bourgogne, who's come by a whole bear skin, is

'already awake. Seated on my pack I foresee a terrible day from the wind that's already beginning to whine and whistle. I make a hole in my bear skin and put my head through it, so that the bear's head dangles on my chest. The rest covers my pack and back, but it's so long its tail drags along the ground.'

Frozen to the bone and aching all over, Paymaster Duverger and his comrades don't want to get up. 'The heat of one's body had melted the ice on the spot where one had slept, and you could count our places.' When they do get up,

'many just went on sitting there. Thinking they were asleep, we gave them a shove. They were dead. At first we only thought they were drowsy, stunned by the cold. But then, shaking them to wake them up, we found they were dead or dying.'

Every unit's bivouac is

'marked by rings of soldiers lying stiff and dead. The surroundings were encumbered by the bodies of several thousand horses.'

After spending the night in a barn, General Kerner of the Württembergers wakes up to find *all 300* of his men frozen stiff around their campfires. 'No help could save them,' Dumonceau goes on:

'We had to leave them lying there, beside the fires. There could be no question of burying them. Time and means were lacking, and the frozen ground too hard. In this way I lost my chief sergeant-major. We'd found him dead with his feet burnt up to the ankles and the upper part of his body frozen.'

But at last the *diane* is beaten, then the *grenadière* ['stand to arms'!]; and though it's not daylight Bourgogne's comrades set out. 'We got up,' Duverger goes on,

'and like the old nags who'd been condemned to drag numbered carts and the cuckoos[4] from Paris, hesitantly put one foot in front of the other. With oblique and uncertain step we move on.'

Dumonceau's lancers, too, resume their march on foot, 'dragging our horses by the bridle, to warm ourselves by the exercise'. Likewise the Fusiliers-Grenadiers: 'Then the blood begins circulating again. We get warmer as we march, and begin living again.' This morning Mother Dubois, 'covered with the greatcoats of two of the company's men who'd died in the night', is riding on Colonel Bodel's horse, holding her baby wrapped in a sheepskin. After marching for about an hour in the dark and catching up with the unit ahead of it the regiment makes a brief halt:[5]

'Mother Dubois wanted to use this moment of repose to give her new-born the breast. Suddenly she gives a cry of pain. Her babe is dead, hard as wood.'

The men try to console her by saying it's a blessing both for the baby and for herself, and

'despite her groans and though she's pressing it to her breast, take it from her; place it in the hands of a sapper who, together with the child's father, goes a few paces aside from the road and with his axe digs a hole in the snow, the father meanwhile on his knees, holding his child in his arms. When the hole's ready he kisses it, lays it in its tomb. Then they cover it, and all is over.'

Many much longer lives are being granted no such obsequies.

Now the Young Guard's column, its 'lips glued together' as it follows on behind the Guard Artillery, is marching through a thick fog:

'Our nostrils or rather our brains froze. We seemed to be walking on through an atmosphere of ice. All day the snow, blown by an extraordinary wind, was falling in flakes so big no one had ever seen the like of them. Not merely could we no longer see the sky, we couldn't even see the men ahead of us.'

Already in this struggle to survive

'there were no more friends. We looked suspiciously at each other, even became ungrateful toward one's best comrades.'

Near the 'wretched village' of Mikhailowska there's a dispute over a loaf of newly baked bread Bourgogne's obliged a surgeon-major to sell him for 5 francs, only to have it grabbed by his comrades 'leaving me only the bit I was holding between my thumb and two first fingers of my right hand'. Now everyone's only thinking of himself. Seeing a man surreptitiously boiling some potatoes for his general, Bourgogne forces him to sell him nine of them. And slips them – no less surreptitiously – into his cartridge pouch.

'To let oneself be affected by pity at the deplorable scenes one witnessed was to doom oneself. Those who were so fortunate as to find enough strength in themselves to resist the many evils were the ones who developed the coldest sensibility.'

Duverger sees what's happening to those who don't:

'They fell on the road and didn't get up again. We saw their legs begin to tremble, and their body leaning forward augured death. Their companions followed them with their eye and speculated on how soon they'd fall. Still alive, they were stripped naked. We quarrelled over their clothing, snatching from them what feeble resources they still had left.'

A ranker begins pulling the clothes off his general who's collapsed and is dying by the roadside. The general begs him weakly at least to wait till he's dead: 'Very well, *mon général*,' replies the grenadier stolidly. 'I'll wait.'

Hard-heartedness is going to incredible lengths. Réné Bourgeois sees[6] a captain of engineers who's fallen by the wayside appealing to the passers-by for help:

'"I'm an engineer captain, help me!" A grenadier turns round, stops in front of him, and in a voice half-serious half-mocking, says, "What, you're an engineer captain? Well, then, draw up your plan."'

The cruel iron law of survival is the order of the day. And Napoleon's order from Doroghobouï for the army to march

'as we did in Egypt, with the baggage in the middle, a half-battalion in front and at the rear, and battalions in file on either flank ... units at short intervals, with artillery between',

is falling on snow-filled ears. Likewise the order: 'No man may leave his unit or lack a musket.' All around, Cossacks and armed peasants, dodging about in the steadily falling snow, are

'pushing their audacity to the point of penetrating our ranks, carrying off pack horses and wagons they suppose to be loaded with the greatest treasures. Our men haven't the strength even to resist these abductions'

and are too busy trying to steal from one another. Only the horses of the wounded, Victor Dupuy's glad to see, are still being respected by 'soldiers of all ranks'. Not that their owners can use them. It's too cold. 'They'd have frozen within a few hours.' He leaves to our imagination

'the plight of the sick and wounded, more especially of amputees. Piled up pell-mell in wagons whose horses were succumbing to fatigue and inanition, the unfortunates were abandoned in the bivouacs and on the roads, and died raving. Those who had the strength to do so killed themselves. Their companions, the friends of these sad victims, couldn't help them. They averted their eyes.'

Fezensac sees an exception is still being made for women and children:

'Everyone was doing his best to succour them. For a long while our drum-major carried a child in his arms. Officers who still had a horse shared it with these poor people.'

Perched on a gun-carriage Le Roy recognises a commissary's wife who'd been most theatrically attired in Moscow but has lost her husband:

'The silk shawl she was wearing was all scorched, her eyes dulled and red, her face fallen, witnessing to this poor woman's physical and moral sufferings.'

Even veterans for whom comradeship is the one great ethic of a military life are failing to honour it. During that second icy night in the snow, Sergeant Bourgogne, so far from telling his starving comrades about his treasure trove of potatoes, has slept clutching them tightly. And at the next halt 'like an egoist' goes aside into the thickest part of the wood, takes some out – only to find they're

'just ice! I try to bite into them. My teeth slip on them without being able to detach the least bit. It's then I regret not having shared them yesterday with my friends.'

He goes and rejoins them, shamefacedly,

'still holding in my hand what I'd tried to eat, all red with my lips' blood. They ask me what I've got. Without replying, I show them the potato and the ones in my cartridge case.'

Where's he found them? He gestures toward the wood. They run into it, hoping for more. In vain. And Bourgogne's potatoes, when boiled, just melt away like ice. His comrades however, who've cooked a whole pot of horse's blood,

'invited me to have my share. Which I did without being asked twice. I've always reproached myself for acting like that,' he confesses. 'They've always thought I'd found my potatoes in the wood, and I've never disabused them.[7] But all this is only a sample of what we'd see later.'

Cold and hunger have made everyone so insensitive to others' suffering that not even the horses are being allowed to expire before being torn to pieces. Those left behind or killed during the night

'were frozen so hard it was impossible to cut anything from them. As soon as a horse dropped, no one tried to help it to its feet again, but instantly we saw the soldiers throw themselves at it, open up its flanks to tear out the liver, the least repulsive part; and without having bothered to kill it before sacrificing it like this, we saw them, I say, get irritated over the animal's last efforts to escape its executioners.'

Lejeune sees some men hitting a dying horse and shouting as they try to dismember it: '*Coquin!* [Rascal!] Why can't you lie still?' Kergorre too sees how horses 'still alive, from which a large part of the rump had been removed, were weeping as they watched themselves being dissected, and no one thought of finishing them off!' Captain François, who's marching with IV Corps, sees a young woman rush in among some soldiers who've just disembowelled one. Though she's wearing a marten fur lined with white satin she plunges her hands into the animal's belly to tear its liver out. But having no knife has to put her head inside and use her teeth instead. Sergeant-Major Thirion's little party of dismounted cuirassiers cut slices from the horses' rumps as they trudge on through the snow:

'It was too cold to kill them and cut them up. Our hands would have refused to perform this service, they'd have frozen. The wretched animals gave not the least sign of pain, proof positive how numb and insensitive they were from the extreme cold. Under any other conditions these slices of flesh would have brought on a haemorrhage and death. But with 28 [*sic*] degrees of frost this didn't happen. The blood froze instantly and arrested the flow. We saw some of these poor horses walking for several days with large pieces of flesh cut away from both thighs.'

The sergeant-major himself has a little pannikin

'which I wouldn't have exchanged for a fortune. Inserting a knife blade as gently as possible between the ribs, I held up my little casserole to catch the blood, and then cooked it – a black pudding I'd nowadays consider insipid, but which I thought delicious.'

Born survivors like Thirion have their own techniques:

'When I halted with my dismounted cuirassiers at the place where we were to spend the night, I unclasped my cape and threw it on the snow, laid my carbine and helmet on it and, very tired though I was and suffering from a wound in my foot, I started dancing what in choreography is called "pigeon's wings". My comrades thought I'd gone mad, but I reassured them by saying it was to keep my spirits up; or rather, to prevent them from weakening.'

Others, like Commissary Kergorre, are applying no less sophisticated survival techniques:

'As long as I'd any boots I never failed to take them off in the evening and don a pair of linen slippers, which in the daytime I put in my pocket. When morning came I was a great deal less exhausted, my feet not being swollen, and thus I preserved my footwear which otherwise I might have burnt while asleep at the bivouac.'

As for Pion des Loches, he's positively smug about his elaborate arrangements. And who cannot but admire the sangfroid and sagacity of a certain general G***,

'who'd no one left of his brigade, had lost all his horses too, whose servants all had frost-bitten limbs, and who'd lost all his remaining baggage. Out of all his possessions he took a simple cooking pot. Armed as he was with this modest and precious utensil, everyone who had nothing to cook their food with wanted him to join them.'

Installing 'the owner of this treasure in the best spot close to the fire,' they give him a good part of its contents 'and return it him, well cleaned. The gallant general loaded it on his shoulder again and continued on his way, not worrying about his night or his supper, thus always assured to him.'

As for Le Roy and Jacquet's treasured iron cookpot that had so nearly gone missing at the Niemen in June, their ugly-faced young servant Guillaume is guarding it jealously . 'Anyone', says von Muraldt, 'who still owned a little flour, rice, coffee or sugar, and thereto any vessel to cook with, was a millionaire. Everyone fawned on him.' His own 'most precious treasure' too, is 'an iron pot, which never left me. Not many had anything of the kind with them, or else had lost it.' At I Corps' headquarters Duverger and his comrades are

'taking turns at the cooking. It wasn't my kind of task. My stew always smelt of the pot. It wasn't always we had some horsemeat or aquavit. Often no pure water. It was then we prepared our thin Spartan broth. Here's the recipe: Melt some snow – and you'll need plenty to get only a little water. Put in some flour. Then, for lack of salt, some gunpowder. Serve up hot and only eat when you're really hungry.'

Observant individuals like Thirion are noticing how some types and nationalities – Frenchmen, Spaniards, Italians and Portuguese – are, most unexpectedly, surviving better than others:

'Brown subjects of a bilious-sanguine temperament, almost all from southern countries of Europe, put up a better resistance than blond subjects, almost all from the northern countries – which is the opposite of what is usually supposed.'

Dupuy too thinks the southerners are surviving better, and ascribes it to their livelier temperament. An idea also shared by Larrey.[8] 'The former's circulation', he explains,

'is doubtless more active. Their vital forces have more energy. It's also probable their blood, even under the influence of extreme cold, retains much better the principle of the heat identified with its colorative part. From the same cause the moral strength is so much the better sustained. Courage doesn't abandon them, and by understanding how to care for their own preservation they know better than the usually apathetic inhabitants of cold and humid climates how to avoid pitfalls.'

His theory is that southerners have a more vigorous circulation and are therefore of a darker complexion and by the same token have greater moral resources. 'Thus we'd see Dutchmen of the 3rd Grenadiers of the Guard, 1,787 men strong, both officers and rankers, perish almost to a man. Only 41 got back to France.'[9] Surgeon Roos, for his part, is convinced from experience that those who seem to be surviving best tend to be those who're

'best at muddling through, and those most used to privations, no matter what nation they belonged to. Young men, on the other hand, inexperienced, feeble or lazy, or simply spoiled children used to being waited on, who from the outset had been unable to stand the summer heats and most of whom had remained in the rear, were the first to succumb.'

Sometimes there are unburnt houses along the way. Woe betide anyone who sits too long in an overheated room! Soon he finds his limbs swelling, due – Larrey supposes – to

'an expansion of the capillary blood vessels of the interior members, to which the latent heat and life seemed to retreat. The meninges becoming similarly inflated results in heavy headaches, lesion of the mental faculties and an alteration in those of the sense organs. The individual was stricken with general weakness and an extremely painful anxiety. He started a cough, which grew quickly worse. More or less violent, it was accompanied by mucous, sometimes bloody expectorations. Often a diarrhoeic flux occurred at the same time: a desire to vomit, with colic pains. The pulse became feverish, the skin dry. The sick man felt a painful swelling in his members, cramps, fits and starts, and a prickly heat in the soles of his feet. Sleep was laboured and accompanied by sinister dreams. The vessels of the conjunctive injected themselves. Fever developed, with aggravations in the evening. The beatings of the carotids and of the temples became noticeable to the naked eye. Delirium or lethargic drowsiness set in, and danger was imminent. Such were the main symptoms that accompanied his affliction, which could be called *catarrhal ataxia from congealment*. Its course was more or less swift, according to the subject's constitution, his age and his degree of vigour.'

Nor is it only the landscape that's changed its aspect. The army itself has become a grotesque masquerade. Everyone, from generals down to privates, has donned whatever costly silks and furs he's brought from Moscow. 'Each soldier was wearing whatever he'd found in the pillage,' Louise Fusil, *soubrette* of the former French theatre in Moscow, notes with expert eye, as her carriage (property of Caulaincourt's nephew) rolls slowly onwards through the blizzard under its owner's protection:

'Some are covered with a moujik's caftan or some plump kitchen wench's short fur-lined dress. Others a rich merchant's coat and – almost all – in the fur-lined pink, blue, lilac or white satin mantles of the kind all the common people here make into articles of luxury (respectable Russian women wear black ones).'

Nothing would have been funnier, the intrepid actress goes on,

'if the circumstances hadn't been so sad, than to see an old grenadier, with his moustaches and bearskin, covered in a pink satin fur. The poor fellows protected themselves as best they could against the cold; but even they laughed at this bizarre spectacle.'

The staff of 5th Division, I Corps, have christened General Compans, its commander, 'the Tartar' because of his 'cap of crimson velvet edged with sable' given to him at Hamburg by his new wife. Now he's wearing it over

'a dress coat without embroidery or epaulettes, blue breeches, top boots, and an ample greatcoat lined with very good fox fur and trimmed with sable tails. Its collar covers my ears and, reaching down to my ankles, lets nothing be seen except my cap and my booted feet. Over this

I'm wearing my sword, hanging from a gold-embroidered crimson velvet belt. Only the triple stars on the sword-knot indicate my rank. Such is the full-length portrait, my dearest, of Compans the Tartar,'

he'll shortly be writing to his bride.[10] As for the rank and file, some are making themselves boots out of old hats:

'Very few had any furs, mantles or greatcoats, so as soon as they took the least rest they were overcome with stupor. The young men, being the most inclined to sleep, succumbed in great numbers. Most of our men would be mutilated by gangrene due to coming too close to the fires.'

The only cure for frost-bite – a remedy Larrey repeatedly applies to himself – is to rub the white numb skin areas with snow,

'or, if these means didn't suffice – the way Russians defreeze fish – to plunge the affected part into cold water, soaking it until air bubbles are seen rising from the frozen part.'

'It was a Friday [6 November] and we were almost at Smolensk,' Louise Fusil goes on:

'The officer in the coach by which I'd left [Moscow] had ordered his coachman to get there by evening. This latter was a Pole, the slowest and clumsiest I've ever come across. He spent all night – as he maintained – searching for forage. In the meantime he'd let his horses freeze at their leisure, with the result that they could no longer move their legs when he wanted to get them moving again; and we lost two. Those two once dead it was impossible for us to make headway with the two others. We got stuck at the entrance of a heavily encumbered bridge until Saturday the 7th. I was wondering what to do, and made up my mind to abandon the *calèche* as soon as day dawned and cross the bridge on foot to go and ask the general in command at its far end for help or a seat in some other carriage. But just then the Pole returned with two horses he said he'd "found". Of course I realised he'd stolen them; but nothing was commoner.'

Theft, particularly of horses, has become universal:

'Everyone was robbing everyone of everything with perfect impunity. The only risk was to get caught red-handed, because then one risked a thrashing. All day long one heard "*Ah, mon Dieu*, someone's stolen my portmanteau! Someone's taken my pack! Someone's stolen my bread, my horse!" – and this from the general officer down to the ranker. One day Napoleon, seeing one of his officers wearing a very fine fur, said to him, laughing: "Where've you stolen that?" – "Sire, I've bought it." – "You've bought it from someone while he was asleep!" The witticism was repeated throughout the army.'

A joke to Napoleon perhaps, not to the lone straggler, for whom it can mean death. Only because Lariboisière, seeing her in tears, tells a gendarme to include her *dormeuse* among Davout's carriages does Louise get across a congested bridge:

'This gendarme – I don't know why – took me for the wife of General Lauriston and lost himself in beautiful words. As we finally crossed the bridge it was lined on either side by generals, colonels and an officer who'd long been waiting there to hasten the march. The Cossacks, as I've heard later, weren't far off.'

Alas, a quarter of the way across the horses go on strike:

'Any carriage blocking the route in a difficult passage – the order was positive – was to be burnt. I saw myself worse off than I'd been the day before. On all sides the shout went up: "this carriage is preventing us from passing, it must be burnt!" The soldiers wanted nothing better – because they'd loot it. They too shouted: "Burn it! burn it!" But then some officers took pity on me and shouted: "Come on, men, put your shoulders to the wheels!" And so they did, and they themselves were so good as to hustle them into doing so.'

Once in the clear, a laughing Louise rewards the gendarme with a kiss – 'and he was most content'.

Today the Red Lancers, still riding ahead of IHQ, are taking a pause when desperate shouts arouse them from torpor. A 'hurrah' of Cossacks has attacked the mob of stragglers – presumably from VIII Corps. The Dutchmen mount hastily, gallop forward, form up in line – but don't bother to try and recover the few wagons the Cossacks are making off with. 'Hands and feet numb with cold and hardly bellicose,' they just sit there shivering on their horses. But the Cossacks are circumspection itself, 'and this helped to guarantee us against their undertakings'. While 'skirmishing' in this lackadaisical manner, the Red Lancers are overtaken by IHQ,

'and for a few moments its numerous escort was a powerful support to us. Instead of his usual grey overcoat the Emperor, riding his usual beautiful white horse and imperturbably preserving his calm serenity, was wearing a green velvet pelisse with a rich fur lining and enhanced with gold brandenburgs. Near him we spotted the brilliant King of Naples, wearing his Polish sky-blue tunic, also fur-lined and decorated with gold tresses, both otherwise having his neck and the lower part of his face wrapped up to the nose in a broad Indian shawl, and on his head, as always, his Polish toque surmounted by a bouquet of floating feathers. After him came the Duke of Istria [Duroc], always white-powdered and his long stock wig immaculately set, as if to appear in a drawing-room. He was simply dressed in a deep blue mantle, maintaining his strictly regulation appearance.'

After them come Berthier and various generals and orderly officers, uniformly dressed in mantles, 'the only non-regulation feature being turned up collars and scarves around their noses'.

Surprisingly, no one, or almost no one, as far as Kergorre can see, is overtly accusing Napoleon of the disaster that's obviously overtaking the army:

'It's been said that the soldiers insulted Napoleon during the retreat. I, who saw His Majesty in the most painful circumstances, think I can assure you it's not true.'

Dumonceau, unemotional as ever, agrees:

'A few higher-ranking pessimists in fits of bad temper might reason differently; but instances of this among the rank and file and the subalterns were rare, and our devotion remained absolute. Our confidence in him was still intact. No one among us dreamed of reproaching him for our setbacks, and in our eyes he still retained the prestige of a supreme arbiter.'

'The rank and file, it's true,' Kergorre adds, 'were no longer shouting "*Vive l'Empereur!*" But they said nothing.' 'Such was the respect the Emperor was held in and the devotion to his person that no one in his suite,' Caulaincourt affirms, 'not even his servants were ever insulted.' His testimony, he claims, is 'worth something' because ever since Vereia he's always been marching on foot,

'sometimes with the Emperor, sometimes ahead of him, sometimes behind; but always among groups of uniformed men, without my riding-coat and wearing my uniform hat. Unquestionably any discontent among the soldiers would have shown itself in the presence of a general in uniform. The behaviour of the unfortunate men freezing to death by the roadside, I admit, often amazed me. But I wasn't alone in admiring it.'

Even Dedem – critical though he is and though he's beginning to hear the rank and file swear at their officers – never hears

'any soldier swear at the man they owed all their ills to. All I heard was men of the Old Guard saying; "Ah, Moreau[11] would have led us better!"'

Is this really true? Of the soldiers perhaps. Perhaps not of the Administration, etc. Cavalry surgeon René Bourgeois sees one such employee

'who'd had both legs crushed by the wheels of a carriage that had knocked him down. There he lay on the road, prey to terrible pains, at the moment when Napoleon passed by at the head of his Guard. Seeing him, he raised himself up, and gathering all his strength to make his voice as loud as possible, overwhelmed him in abuse:

'"There he is," he said, "that miserable puppet who for ten years has been leading us about like automata. Comrades, he's mad! Don't trust him! He's turned into a cannibal. The monster will devour you all!"'[12]

If there are angry feelings, they're among the top brass. Caulaincourt's shocked to see,

'they were so weary of warfare, had such a craving for repose, for the sight of a less hostile country, for an end to these far-flung expeditions, that most of them let themselves be blinded as to the present fruits and future consequences of our disasters by the thought that they'd prove a useful lesson to the Emperor, and cool his ambition. This was the common view.'[13]

The diary of Secretary Fain, that student of human nature, confirms it:

'Around the Emperor the courtesan's smile has fallen from those lips most accustomed to wearing it. All faces have fallen. The strong minds, which have no mask to lose, are the only ones whose expression hasn't changed.'

Caulaincourt's for instance. Or Duroc's. Dumonceau's men having found a ford,

'the Grand Marshal of the Imperial Court joined us to profit from it. He was riding a very fine horse, was dressed as if for a parade, in white breeches, well-waxed stable boots and all the rest of that kind of costume, only wearing over it neither mantle nor greatcoat, but only a spencer [short-tailed jacket], tight to the body, indifferent to the cold. Otherwise he seemed cheerful. Most amiable to all who approached him, he was on his way to go and prepare the Emperor's lodging, accompanied by some officers and élite gendarmes. All had been provided with horses in good condition.'

Thanks to Caulaincourt's foresight at Moscow, as Wilson will afterwards hear, all the 73 headquarters horses are rough-shod – an obvious precaution that's otherwise only been taken by the Poles. As soon as Duroc's party have crossed the ford he leaves with it 'at a gallop'.

The Guard Horse Chasseurs, too, still have 600 men mounted. And when 300 fresh horses are 'sent forward by a Polish nobleman "to help the Emperor during his retreat"' they're sent to the senior cavalry regiment as remounts. IHQ's spirits also rise during its last day's march before Smolensk when a convoy of provisions intended for Ney's rearguard is seen coming toward it.

'Recalling other times and other ideas, it raised the morale even of the most despondent. Everyone believed in abundance and thus in reaching his goal. The Emperor flattered himself on it more than anyone, and said so several times.'

But when the Red Lancers rejoin the column shortly thereafter they have to come to the rescue of the

'infantry escort who're being attacked and their convoy pillaged by the mob of disbanded men. There was a lot of vociferation on our account but most of the convoy was saved and able to go on its way.'

Did any of its contents ever reach Sergeant Bertrand and his men, executing their chequerboard retreat for four days on end?[14] These two blizzard-stricken days (6–7 November) have destroyed one-third of the Moscow army. 'From this day onwards,' Labaume will write in his history of the campaign,[15]

'it lost its strength and military bearing. The ranker no longer obeyed his officers, the officer abandoned his general. Disbanded regiments walked along any old how. Struggling to keep alive, they spread out in the plains, burning and sacking everything they came across.'

Yet all the time Lejeune sees men like Captain François who 'though riddled with wounds remained full of energy' never lose their morale. And if there's one thing Thirion's noticing it's that

'any man who thought it impossible for us to make the remaining 100 or 150 leagues [3–500 miles] to get out of Russia was a man lost. Two or three days later he'd disappeared.'

CHAPTER 6

DISASTER AT THE WOP

Griois buries two guns – 'winter had fallen on us in all its severity' – IV Corps marches for Witebsk – a new command – Del Fante plunges in – the guns are lost – a day's rest

On 7 November, while still at Doroghobouï, IV Corps has been ordered to leave the main column and march for Witebsk. Witebsk, 'an infinitely important strategic point on the Vilna–Petersburg road at a distance of 24 leagues [75 miles] from Polotsk and 30 from Smolensk' where Napoleon had left a weak garrison in August, but where large stores have been accumulated, is known to be under threat. Crossing the Dnieper by the pontoon bridge at 6 a.m., Eugène's men[1] have peeled off to the right along the Witebsk road. Along this less devastated route, they hope, there'll at least be more to eat.

Grouchy's 3rd Cavalry Corps no longer exists – the 'inept, almost dazed' Lahoussaye[2] is just riding along in his carriage, indifferent to everything' and Grouchy himself seems to have 'disappeared', and for several days now Griois' horse artillery has been marching on its own. Having friends among Eugène's artillery staff[3] he decides to follow on after IV Corps. That night, after crossing the Dnieper, he bivouacs

'under a mere roof on four posts, a sort of barn, open to every wind, but a fine lodging, even so, compared with the ones I'd so long been occupying'.

After his gunners have made up a big fire in the middle of it he lies down to sleep, surrounded by his horses. Waking up at daybreak he finds he's

'covered in thick snow, likewise the whole landscape. It wasn't falling any longer; but the cold sky was icy. Everything was frozen. The mud had frozen hard during the night. Winter had fallen on us in all its severity.'

It's almost impossible to get his guns and ammunition wagons moving:

'In vain our poor exhausted horses tried to drag them out. Only after doubling the teams, using levers to prise the wheels loose, and by joining their efforts to those of the horses, did our gunners and the men of the Train succeed in getting part of the artillery on the move.'

Griois has to triple his teams. And to do this – each caisson now only having four horses to drag it – two guns and two wagons have to be abandoned. All the woodwork is stacked up in a hangar and burnt, and the

'guns entombed in the ashes. It was the first time I'd left behind loaded wagons and guns. So it was with sadness in my soul I got going again on 8 November, to catch up with IV Corps.'

But even then the snow, icy and hardened, frustrates the horses' hooves:

'We had plenty of ice-nails in reserve, but as yet hadn't used them to shoe the horses. Yet even this wouldn't have been enough. After a few hours march their diamond-shaped heads would have been worn down, and they'd have become utterly useless – as we soon found out.[4] Calkins are a lot better, but we'd have needed more time and resources than we possessed.'

The bad road surface still further slows his march. And all the time Cossacks, flanking his column with light guns mounted on sledges, flit from one bit of high ground to the next; fire at his men; kill a few; and then, when his guns laboriously begin to reply, move on to the next eminence. Ahead of him, but steadily nearer as the whole procession slows down, is IV Corps' reserve artillery:

'Our sixteen 12-pounders had long been trying to climb a long and steep hill, surfaced with thick ice. In vain we doubled and tripled the teams. Some of the vehicles had managed to take a few steps, but then come to a halt. The drivers' whiplashes and oaths, the efforts of the gunners putting their shoulders to the wheels, were of no greater avail. Only with greatest difficulty had part of the divisional artillery, lighter and better harnessed up, been able to surmount this obstacle.'

Griois has just caught up with it when its commander, General C.-N. *Anthouard*, is hit by a roundshot which 'after killing the orderly officer at his side' (von Muraldt hears) has 'fractured his thigh'. 'If it hadn't been for his chief-of-staff Colonel Berthier,'[5] Griois reflects, 'who carried him to his carriage on his shoulders, he might have stayed there on the snow, like most men wounded that day.'

Only after 'infinite toil and reinforcing the teams with the horses of four wagons' which Griois again resigns himself to abandoning, does his artillery get up the hill 'and reach the château of Zazelé' whose 'charming position, vast and opulent outbuildings' he'd admired when coming this way before, en route for Moscow:

'Now, covered in snow, shrouded in a dense fog which hardly enabled us to make out its walls, it was encumbered with troops and carriages and looked very different. Happy the first-comers! No shelter remained for anyone else.'

Himself being one of them, he's looking for some nook or cranny where he can get out of the cold and make up a fire, when he hears the seriously wounded Anthouard is asking for him. He finds him lying on some straw in a peasant's hut. A certain Colonel Fiéreck (Anthouard tells him) should normally succeed him. But the elderly Fiéreck just now evidently having no taste for command and also, in Eugène's opinion, 'not being active enough', he has proposed to the Viceroy that Griois should take over IV Corps' artillery. In this new capacity he joins Anthouard's adjutant-commandant[6] in a little low room in the château.

The Italian, Spanish, Croat and French regiments' hopes of finding better conditions along the Witebsk road have been cruelly dashed. But their baggage train is still considerable and 'as yet we didn't feel our losses in this respect'. But ruin and Cossacks are everywhere. 'Everywhere during that night at the château of Zazeló [*sic*] von Muraldt's party of disbanded Bavarian officers, clinging to the Italian Royal Guard, see 'people dying of hunger and cold, and horses, tormented by thirst, trying to break the ice with their feet to find water'. And just ahead, he knows, barring tomorrow's march, 'a little river,' von Muraldt remembers, 'so inconsiderable that we hadn't even noticed it when we'd crossed it during our advance.'[7]

The Wop.

Like many others, Cesare de Laugier's certainly reflecting, as he approaches it, how swiftly it flows between its steep and marshy banks 'and is difficult to ford'.

Already Eugène has sent on a party of engineer-geographers under General Sanson, accompanied by some cannon, to find out what state it's in and seize the bridgehead. Sanson sends back a report that they've already found Cossacks 'infesting all its banks' – and himself is immediately captured. So that evening Eugène sends on General Poitevin with 'the company of sappers that's marching with his headquarters' to throw a bridge. 'We left at first dawn [9 November),' Griois goes on:

'The weather was cold and a thick mist prevented us from hardly seeing anything ten paces ahead of us. We didn't even see the Wop until we'd reached the deep ravine which it flows at the bottom of. A considerable crowd, pressing together at the same point, indicated that the bridge was on that side. I dismounted and went on in that direction. Soon I was sorry I had. But it was too late. I had to follow the crowd I was entangled in. Finally I got to the entrance of the bridge, a frail planking.'

After a few paces everything comes to a halt. Shouts are heard ahead, but no one understands why;

'until the terrifying news is passed from rank to rank that the far end of the bridge is broken, or rather has never quite been completed. The unfortunate first-comers, fooled by the fog, had tumbled into the torrent.'

And in fact the Viceroy's sappers,

'either for lack of time or *matériel* and workmen, exhausted or hungry and cold, had had to leave the bridge as they'd found it. There was no time to think of re-establishing it. We had to make up our minds to ford the river.'

The pursuing Cossacks, with their sledge-guns, promptly open fire on this confused mass. And Eugène, after sending out some fresh troops to support the light infantry that's trying to stave them off, realises 'someone from his household will have to set an example of courage by being the first to cross'. And orders his *officier d'ordonnance* (senior staff officer) Colonel Del Fante[8] to do so at the head of the Royal Guard. Flowing swiftly between its steep banks of frozen mud, the Wop's covered by 'a thin layer of ice'. Up to his waist and almost swept off his feet by ice-floes, Del Fante struggles across to the far bank, followed by Guilleminot, Eugène's staff and the Guard.

'General Pino, wounded and on horseback, Adjutant-commander Del Fante, General Théodore Lecchi, turn to the grenadiers of the Vélites who, formed up by platoons at the head of the columns, were anxiously awaiting their orders on the steep river bank. "Let's save the army," they shout. "Follow us!"'

These 'young men from the best Italian families, each being supported by his family with a Line lieutenant's pay,' their Adjutant-Major goes on,

'needed no further exhortations. The drums beat the charge, and the Royal Guard, followed by other regiments, throws itself into the river. The men have water up to their shoulders and break the ice-floes as they cross over. But many get stuck in its mud and disappear. The blood of others, gripped by the cold, freezes.'

Some perish under the weight of their weapons. As for those who do get over,

'their feet slip on the icy bank. The men roll down over each other. Some fall back into the river. Lastly, those who reach their goal, streaming with water, pierced with cold, their only thought is to hold out their hands and their musket to their comrades coming on behind them. It's impossible',

writes Cesare de Laugier, his pen refusing 'to depict the troops' situation after this crossing, either the physical torments they endured, or the pains caused by this bath of ice.' The river not being all that deep, the first vehicles don't manage too badly. But their wheels churn up its muddy bottom, and their successors are soon in trouble:

'Only by taking time and at the price of great efforts, by doubling and tripling the teams, could a gun or caisson be got over.'

The carriages are another matter. The ford has been

'reserved for the artillery. Repulsed from it, they were trying to cross at other points. But there the river was even more steeply embanked. They got stuck deep in the mud, where their horses remained motionless, half-frozen.'

Griois, on horseback, crosses and recrosses 'at least ten times, keeping the gunners and soldiers of the Train at their pieces, calling, shouting, swearing encouraging some, inciting others'. His trousers are soaked through,

'but I was so agitated I didn't even notice it. I still see those brave soldiers of the Train – they had to begin by breaking the ice-floes all round them – having to remain for hours together with their teams in the middle of the water, and then, having dragged out a gun or an ammunition wagon, having to begin the same efforts all over again, endure the same fatigues. Their horses' traces, stiff with ice, were scarcely pliable.'

Finally, by dint of endless effort, four guns are got across. But then everything gets stuck. And in no time, on the left, eastern bank,

'a mass of cannon, powder wagons, vehicles of every kind, had piled up, covering the river bank farther than the eye could see. Sutlers, everyone who owned any kind of vehicle, were running hither and thither with anxious shouts, trying – if possible – to find some way across. Gunners, seeing no hope to get the heavy pieces across the swampy, ice-covered river, begin blowing up their caissons and spiking their guns. Everyone who hasn't a horse has to plunge into the water. The broken ice-floes can scarcely be thrust aside, and men have the icy water up to their bellies –'

Griois says to their armpits. His four cannon, once across, have been
'immediately ranged in position on the far bank to keep the Cossacks
under control and secure the crossing for the troops, the numerous
marauders and non-combatants still on the other bank. But the muddy
bottom is all churned up and makes it impossible to proceed. One vehicle gets stuck. Others add themselves to it. And everything comes to a
halt. Instantly this, the only practicable ford, is encumbered with ammunition wagons and all kinds of vehicles carrying the little that's left of
our provisions from Moscow.'
The Viceroy, seeing there's not a ghost of a chance of getting the bulk of
his artillery across – some 70 guns and their trains – orders it all to be abandoned. Officers, too, realise the last moment's come for their carriages and
wagons. Extracting their most precious contents – i.e. any foodstuffs – they
hastily load them on to their horses – that is, if their men give them time
to do so:
'The ground was littered with portmanteaux, war chests and papers. A
quantity of objects hidden away in Moscow and which a justifiable sense
of shame had kept hid, again began to see the light of day.'
In the gloaming Staff-Captain Labaume's shocked to see how the Italians
have begun pillaging their officers' carriages and wagons – but only 'sur-
reptitiously' Griois says, 'under cover of dark' – 'hardly giving its owner
time to select what he wants from it'. Labaume, like Griois, like everyone
who hears it, is appalled by
'the shouts of those crossing the Wop and the consternation of those
about to do so, whom we at each moment see plunging with their
mounts down the steep and slippery bank. A *vivandière* had five small
children and all the fruits of her industry. Reaching the Wop, she looks
with stupor at this river which is forcing her to leave her whole fortune
on its banks and her family's sole means of subsistence. A long while she
runs to and fro looking for a new way across. Finding none, she comes
back, much depressed, and says to her husband: "*Mon ami*, we'll have to
leave it all behind. Don't try to save anything but our children."'
Which they do:
'The women's desolation, their crying children and even the soldiers'
despair turned this passage into a heart- rending scene, the very memory of which strikes terror into all who witnessed it.'[9]
The Viceroy himself sits his horse until nightfall, superintending the crossing. Only then does he cross over. That freezing night Griois is horrified to
see
'nothing but people, desperate at having lost everything, frozen to the
bone by the ice which covered their soaked clothing, having neither
shelter to repose their head, nor the tiniest spark to warm themselves
with. Shivering with cold, the soldiers, who'd all forded the river with
water up to their shoulders, went off in all directions to find some food
they could carry off or a house to pull down [for firewood].'
Himself, all things considered, he's not too badly off. His artillery staff,

'after walking a long while across the fields, were so fortunate as to find an isolated cottage, where we settled in. Part of it we demolished for a fire which dried our clothes.'

Two or three bottles of wine that have survived from an abandoned carriage, together with a few fistfuls of flour and 'some sauerkraut we were so lucky as to find in the cottage' make up their dinner and 'in the end we fell asleep. Yesterday, certainly, we'd been badly off for victuals. But now it was a lot worse.'

At dawn on 10 November Eugène sends Labaume back to Broussier's 14th Division, left to cover the crossing, to see what's going on the far bank and save whatever can be saved:

'For more than three miles all one saw was ammunition wagons and guns. The most elegant calèches from Moscow were piled up on the road and along the river bank. Objects taken from their carriages but too heavy to carry off had been scattered far and wide over the countryside, where they stood out only the more boldly for being scattered on the snow. There one saw costly candelabras, antique bronze statues, original paintings, the richest and the most highly esteemed porcelain. A porringer caught my eye. It was of the most exquisite workmanship, painted with the sublime composition of a Marcus Sextus. I took it, and out of this cup drank the muddy icy waters of the Wop. Having used it, I indifferently threw it away near the spot where I'd picked it up.'

Captain François, whose 30th Line forms the rearguard, sees 'the Cossacks laughing like madmen at all this confusion'. For Broussier it's no laughing matter. He's 'obliged to spike 60 guns, which were left behind, together with a mass of artillery vehicles'. 'Except for the four guns which had got across,' von Muraldt sees,

'not merely was the whole of IV Corps artillery lost, but all the vehicles of every kind we'd been dragging with us, as well as a lot of prisoners. All became the Cossacks' prey.'

Some of Broussier's gunners, says Ségur,[10] echoing Griois' account,

'laid a train of powder up to beneath the ammunition wagons that had come to a halt at a distance behind our baggage. Waiting until the greediest Cossacks came running up, as soon as they saw them in numbers, all maddened with pillaging, they flung a flame from a campfire on to this gunpowder. The fire ran, and in an instant reached its goal. The wagons are blown up, the shells explode, and those Cossacks who aren't annihilated scatter in terror!'

How many guns does Broussier really save? Some sources say twelve, others fourteen; but none say how he got them across the Wop. 'Together with those the prince still possessed, these sufficed to keep the Cossacks at bay.' Like everyone else Labaume is full of contempt for the 'cowardice' of the Cossacks, who

'never attacked able-bodied troops. Though surrounded with loot, they still stripped their prisoners, leaving them naked on patches of snow.'

And Broussier can no longer prevent them from flinging themselves on the many sick, feeble and wounded who've got to be left behind.

IV Corps' condition as it resumes its march is now utterly deplorable,

'the men without shoes, almost without clothes, exhausted and famished, sitting on their packs, sleeping on their knees and only rousing themselves out of this stupor to grill slices of horsemeat or melt bits of ice.'

But Eugène himself, 'the most perfect model of military behaviour', never loses his head. The 14th Division brings up the rear and the Royal Guard is vanguard. With them are only 'some armed platoons, the feeble remains of 13th Division and of the Bavarian chevaulegers and a mob of employees and *vivandières*, to whom yesterday had added a terrifying mass of soldiery marching in hurrying waves, without weapons or order.'

That day (10 November) the village or 'small town' of Dukhovchino comes into sight, the way to it barred by a broken bridge and more Cossacks besides those who're at IV Corps' heels,

'walking their sledge guns from position to position. So we were attacked from ahead and behind. Any hesitation would have been fatal. But the Prince Viceroy made haste to form up the Italian Guard in square and press forward,'

together with what Cesare calls 'the Bavarian dragoons and lancers'. 'The mounted officers,' Griois goes on,

'some orderlies on horseback, even the servants, formed a squadron, commanded by General Guyon, and supported the Guard's movement. This squadron's composition was as ridiculous as could be. One saw horses of every height, men in all sorts of uniforms, mostly without weapons. I'd joined it, as had several of my comrades. To close my file I had my Bavarian servant armed with a riding whip, and myself I only had a sabre with a broken blade. But seen from afar this troop gave the effect of the light cavalry we lacked; and after a few unsuccessful hurrahs and discharges of their guns the Cossacks vanished.'

To set an example to his by now thoroughly demoralised troops, Eugène even puts his own hand to the work of rebuilding the bridge. 'Towards 2 or 3 p.m. we entered Dukhovchino in peace.' Up to now the small town of wooden houses has

'only known the passage of Grouchy's cavalry corps and Pino's division during the advance; and hadn't suffered greatly. It was in much the same state as when I'd left it six months ago. As then, the inhabitants had fled at our approach. But their houses were at our disposition, and to us these furtive little timber cabins seemed to be palaces raised by good genies in the midst of these frozen deserts. Each of us got hold of whichever lodging seemed best to him. To cap our happiness we also found some potatoes which had escaped the Cossacks' greed. To us Dukhovchino seemed a land of Cockayne.'

Better still, though the corps is expecting to continue its march on Witebsk tomorrow morning, Eugène orders a day's rest. And Griois and his companions make up a raging fire in their stove:

'These stoves, seven or eight feet square, are built of timber faced with argil clay, and shouldn't be fuelled without care. But we who'd got there pierced through with cold, we had no thought to anything but stuffing it with everything that could burn – doors, shutters, three-legged stools, ladders ...'

The artillery staff sit or lie down around their cookpot, waiting for it to boil. 'The conversation wasn't in the least degree coloured by our sad situation – so quickly do a few moments of well-being make one forget past miseries! A military man's adventurous life makes him so trust to luck and bother so little about the future!'

But there's another reason for Eugène's halt. What's the state of affairs at Witebsk? He has sent off a Polish spy to find out.

CHAPTER 7

HOW WITEBSK WAS LOST

Pouget hops about on one leg – an impatient Jomini – pretty but exalted Polish châtelaines – 'what a garrison!' – Witebsk's indefensibility – countermanded orders – flagrant disobedience in the face of the enemy – Pouget fights a single-handed battle – Eugène's night march for Smolensk – 'Each night she belonged to anyone who'd feed her'

A former colonel of light infantry, the 45-year-old Baron *François-René Pouget*, newly promoted general of brigade, has only one complete foot. In 1809 he'd lost most of the other at the Isle of Lobau but – like his colleague Teste and 'though M. Larrey's opinion in surgical matters should be regarded as final' – had refused to have it amputated. In August, at the First Battle of Polotsk, he'd been wounded again, this time in the leg. After which he'd followed the – also wounded – Oudinot's example; handed over his command and gone back to Vilna. Although he adores only two objects in this world – the Emperor Napoleon and the 26th Light, whose colonel he'd been since 1805 – he'd written to Berthier at Moscow for permission to go to take the waters in France

'this having been prescribed for me, on pain of always having one leg
bent behind me without being able to straighten it'.

At the same time he'd confided to Oudinot he was afraid of missing out on any further rewards or promotion:

'I knew any officer, no matter what his rank, who left the army's cadres,
even on account of his wounds, was totally forgotten.'[1]

The good-natured Oudinot had comforted him, saying he'd already written him down for a 20,000-franc grant. While waiting for Berthier's reply Pouget had presented himself to the province's governor, the Dutch General *Dirk van Hogendorp*, and also made the acquaintance of his sparring partner, the Swiss General *Henri de Jomini*, governor of Vilna town.[2] Jomini, 'young, full of talents and ardour' and one day to become the age's most eminent military theorist, had 'seemed greatly preoccupied' at being left so far to the rear while great events were going forward. But then Napoleon's peremptory order had come that he should second Charpentier[3] as governor of Smolensk city, pending Marshal Victor's arrival in the theatre of war.

Temporarily out of cash but impatient to be off, Jomini hadn't known where to get hold of a wagon for his and his ADC's effects. Pouget, hopping about Vilna on one leg, prides himself on his habit of trusting fellow-officers; and against a mere verbal promise of future payment 'without even a receipt' sells Jomini his own. So Jomini, certainly to Hogendorp's intense relief, had departed.

Berthier's reply to Pouget's application, on the other hand, had come as a shock. One foot or two, wound or no wound, he was instantly to take over from Charpentier the governorship of Witebsk. After some thought he'd 'decided to obey'. And though his ADCs are still having to half-lift him into and out of his carriage, he and they had woven their way from one Lithuanian château to the next, where the party had found all the Polish *châtelaines* – each prettier and more 'exalted' than the last – passionately devoted to the 'national' cause.

> 'September 27, dined and slept at Bogdanow, in the home of Madame the widow Omoliska, who had two big beautiful daughters. I think it was the most exalted family in all Poland. I can still see the mother getting up at table to drink to the Emperor's health and the re-establishment of the Kingdom of Poland, adding that she was prepared to shed her blood for her country. One of her girls told me: "Yes, *M. le Général*, if we have to make war to reach this goal my sister and I will take up arms in man's clothing."'

Why, they all ask, hasn't Napoleon restored the Kingdom of Poland? A question Pouget naturally can't answer.[4] Only at the deserted château near the Ostrovno battlefield[5] do he and his aides, instead of wrestling with political matters and fervent protestations, have to wrap themselves up in their mantles and sleep on straw. Reaching Witebsk on 30 September they'd found Charpentier[6] so eager to be off as to begrudge his successor even one more day to initiate him into his functions. Next day Pouget, almost fainting with pain from his wounded leg tendon, had mounted his horse to inspect the town and found it 'divided into two unequal parts by the Dvina, the less considerable of these, situated on the right bank, almost exclusively inhabited by Jews'. But here's a shock:

> 'Open on all sides like a village, this town, the most important in White Russia, hasn't even the resource of some gardens surrounded by walls or hedges which, at a pinch, could favour its defence.'

To guard it he'd need 6–7,000 cavalry and infantry. As for its garrison ... what a garrison!' All he has are

> 'some 900 isolated men, made up of all the marauders, stragglers and men who'd come out of hospitals, the refuse of all the armies, the most furtive, dirtiest and worst soldiers in the world. Clad in rags and shreds of clothing, without either officers or NCOs, most of them had straggled ever since crossing the Niemen and never seen the enemy.'

Absent as they are from their units, they're getting neither clothing nor pay, 'not a kopek for a shave, for their laundry, to set themselves to rights, nor even for a glass of brandy. Their hosts had to feed and wash for them.' Pouget doesn't know which is worse, the pain in his leg or this monumental pain in the neck:

> 'No one ever saw anything provide a worse service than these isolated men. Each time they mounted guard one had to create a commandant for it, a sergeant, a corporal, and take even *them* at face value. No tasks done properly. No reconnaissances carried out. Rounds at a standstill. The sentinels just sat around their fire with the *chef de poste*. Their weapons were in a bad state, and as for what might happen in the vicinity they couldn't care less. Such were the troops charged with the

defence of an administrative capital, one of the most important points in our line.'

All of which confirms Major Everts' experience from the Minsk area: 'A great fault of this campaign was to leave too few troops in the rear and on the flanks, the more so as we knew the Russians there were still in force.'[7] Fortunately Pouget also had 300 men 'from various detachments, made up of Hessians[8] and other men of the Young Guard, sixteen military police-men commanded by an officer, two 4-pounders, a section of gunners and one of pontoneers'. But indifference to the Russian army's propinquity is massive:

> 'We were only five leagues [fifteen miles] from the Russian advanced posts at the little town of Gorodok, who often pushed parties to within sight of Witebsk, where we were on the *qui vive* day and night.'

And there's nothing Pouget can do about all this – except to profit from an order received by Charpentier, and evacuate 400 men towards Moscow, keeping only the élite. 'My God! what an élite! I'd have needed one.'

Ten days had passed. He does his best to ingratiate himself with the locals. 'I raised no contributions in my own personal interest.' All he asks the magistrates for is some furniture for the timber residence on the main square that Napoleon in August had found utterly bare of any:

> 'In the name of the town they offered me a basket of French wines con-taining 20 bottles and ten of liqueurs, which I'd thought I shouldn't refuse.'

None of these amiable measures, however, bring him much help. The administrative commission 'richly composed of princes and counts' set up by Napoleon during his 8-day stay has evaporated. The man whose job it is to get in provisions from the province is Pouget's 29-year-old Intendant *Amédée de Pastoret*.[9] 'Of all the intendants I know,' Pastoret will write on 28 October to his friends at Vilna,

> 'I am the unhappiest. The Emperor of the French has given me twelve districts to govern, but the Emperor of Russia has thought fit to admin-ister eight of them himself or through his generals, and, what's worse, isn't leaving me in peace in the others. M. de Wittgenstein, whom you certainly know of, has outposts six leagues away from me. Quite near me, it's true, I've two Marshals of France and three army corps. But judge for yourself how much they must consume of all sorts of things. My brave subjects haven't the least desire to fight, nor are they much inclined to give away their money. So I can expect little help. From another aspect, the administrative commission the Emperor made me president of has vanished away like a vain cloud that passeth and cometh not back. Imag-ine a poor young man',

the letter goes on (only to be intercepted by Cossacks),

> 'all alone in a country virtually unknown to him. Put enemies ahead of him and nothing behind his back. Suppose him to have neither money nor military forces; suppose him to be finding neither zeal nor goodwill around him – and you'll have a faint idea of our situation. *Ma foi!* I'm

not exaggerating, but I'm having a lot of trouble putting up with it.'
Even before Pouget's arrival most of the local officials, knowing what's in
the wind, have already quit. Prompt suppression of unruly peasants earns
him the gratitude of local Polish landlords and he fancies he can rely on
their sentiments. With the Witebsk Jews, on the other hand, 'always', as he
puts it sarcastically, 'on the side of the stronger' (somewhat naturally, they
having no political power to protect themselves in any other way) he has a
lot of trouble. Notified by Berthier in October of the Moscow army's
retreat, he's ordered to construct '36 ovens and provision the town with
corn, barley, oats, hay and straw' – something he does

> 'with all speed. Soon the requisitions filled the magazines, and the ovens
> were built.'

And all the time he's keeping Saint-Cyr (at Polotsk) and Victor (at
Smolensk) informed of Russian movements around Gorodka, whence
two squadrons of Russian dragoons and Cossacks keep reconnoitring in
his direction. One day, with his sixteen gendarmes, he even has to fight
a little battle with them in the town's outskirts. 'The other day,' Pastoret
writes, 'some Cossacks came and dined for the third time in Witebsk's
suburbs.'

Then, on 19 October, had come a dispatch from Saint-Cyr, under heavy
pressure from a reinforced Wittgenstein. He's obliged, the newly fledged
Marshal writes, to evacuate Polotsk. And a messenger instantly goes off
from Witebsk to Smolensk to notify Victor of Saint-Cyr's urgent need for
support from IX Corps:

> 'So as not to attract attention my Polish messenger travelled on foot. He
> was so energetic he covered the 30 leagues [90 miles] separating me
> from Smolensk in 30 hours. But got there too late, even so. II Corps had
> already carried out its withdrawal, during which – as General *Lorencez*[10]
> put it when he informed me of this beautiful retreat – the French hadn't
> lost "a single nail from any of its vehicles". Nevertheless it exposed my
> left flank.'

However, here comes a reinforcement in the shape of Daendels' division
of Victor's IX corps. For a while Daendels takes over responsibility for
defending Witebsk and advises Pouget to send 400 of his ill-organised men
to Surash and Veleiz to gather in more supplies. By and by Daendels leaves
again, for Sienno. All he has to bequeath Pouget as garrison is his weakest
battalion,

> 'conscripts who'd never fired a shot or seen an enemy, soldiers from
> Berg who, even so, lacked their grenadier battalion, which was guarding
> Victor's carriages!'

On 4 November an order comes from Victor. Obviously there's been a
scare. Pouget's to evacuate Witebsk and march his garrison to Smolensk:

> 'I began by evacuating the hospitals and sending off the administrations,
> giving them a 200-man escort, with orders to wait for me at Falkowitz, 20
> versts [12½ miles] from Smolensk, and if I myself didn't get there next
> day, to keep going.'

But they've only been gone four hours when a new order countermands. Now, Victor writes, he's *not* to evacuate the town, 'or, if I'd already done so, to get back into it, even by force, because it seemed the enemy had no designs on Witebsk.' Congratulating himself on already having shed his lame ducks, Pouget orders

'the pontoneers to prepare combustible materials to burn the bridge. I took out of the gymnasium 24,000 pikes deposited there by the Russians, had them burnt and their iron points thrown into the Dvina's deepest depths. And waited to see what would happen.'

First and foremost he's anxious about the Ostrovno road, leading to Beschenkowiczi.[11] And here comes the Beschenkowiczi commandant, an officer named Descharmes, bringing a second letter from Lorencez, telling him to evacuate his administration to Smolensk and cover their retreat. From its date Pouget can see it's been delayed several days. Since only one is needed to get to Witebsk from Beschenkowiczi, Pouget wants to know the reason why. Oh, replies a nonchalant Descharmes, surely the matter isn't all that important? An irate Pouget sends him back with a flea in his ear, four chasseurs and a corporal, to Ostrovno, twelve miles down the Beschenkowiczi road, to keep an eye on the enemy's movements. To his amazement Descharmes refuses. Not until 'I threatened to send him to the Marshal, bound hand and foot, to have him brought before a court-martial and punished for disobedience in the face of the enemy' does a disgruntled Descharmes get going.

Next day, to Pouget's amazement and even greater fury, here's Descharmes back again, having simply ignored his mission:

'How can this man have merited the confidence of the army's Major-General and been put to command at Beschenkowiczi? He was a traitor who was losing everything for me and for everything military and patriotic at Witebsk.'

Pouget instantly orders him back to Ostrovno. Next day two squadrons of light cavalry – Pouget, still painfully moving about on his unhealed leg, has every need of them – turn up from Smolensk. But by now Victor's 'putting eighteen more leagues [50 miles] between himself and me. I saw I had nothing more to hope for.' And here in the evening comes a letter from General Castex, commanding the light cavalry of Victor's rearguard[12] – with news which Pouget communicates to, among others, Intendant Pastoret. His outposts, Castex writes, are currently between Ostrovno and Sienno. If he, Pouget, doesn't hear anything more from him by morning it'll mean he has retreated.

The night, though it lasts until 7 a.m., passes quietly – 'except for a timber house catching fire, whether by malevolence or to serve as a signal to the Russians, or in hopes that I'd send some troops to put it out', Pouget can't judge. But then, at dawn, just as he's telling Rollin, his reliable gendarme officer, he has nothing to fear from the Ostrovno road,

'the barrier at the bridgehead opened to let through the fifteen men who were guarding it, and whose captain was sending them to occupy the Riga Gate during the day. Hardly had they been replaced by two sentries than the latter found themselves surrounded by Russian infantry. They retreated quickly to inform me. One of their horses fell and its rider was taken prisoner. The other escaped and warned the big post at the bridgehead, who had the barrier closed. The enemy, who'd known all about our movements, were waiting for the fifteen men who'd been sent to the Riga Gate, turned them and, without a cartridge fired by either side, made them lay down their arms. At the bridgehead were 50 men. Their captain had orders to have all the bridge's timbers that formed its floor on the right bank thrown into the river, and to stand firm, retiring to their left. I had them replaced by the Berg voltigeurs.'

Now a lot of firing breaks out among the houses, and Pouget withdraws to the town castle. It's there, in its courtyard, he has his two 4-pounders:

'They fired a few shots at the columns arriving by the Gorodok road. But now the enemy skirmishers were so close that they kept hitting the gunners at their pieces. The left bank, where my guns were in position, was a steep gradient 20 feet above the right bank.'

So his two cannon are anyway useless. 'Their projectiles couldn't make any hits there except by passing over the roofs of the houses on the left bank and firing at maximum range. So I had to order a retreat.' Pouget sends to inform Rollin, in command of his sixteen gendarmes, and Colonel Chavardès on the Surash road, that he's fixing a point on the Smolensk road outside the town where everyone's to rally:

'I was still greatly astonished and most worried not to hear anything from M. Descharmes at Ostrovno. Because that was where the real danger was coming from. So far I'd only been attacked from the front. I got out of the town in good order, didn't leave a man behind.'

Not thinking that there was anything definitive about the situation and that 'the *Grande Armée*, as it fell back on Witebsk, might still profit from them, I'd forbidden any of them to set fire to any of the magazines' which Amédée de Pastoret's emissaries had so diligently wrested from the peasantry, doubtless condemning them to starve during the winter. Now they'll be consumed by Wittgenstein's troops.

A mile and a half outside the town Pouget orders a halt, assembles all his men, and waits for his rearguard. But as he does so sees Russian units, appearing along the Surash and Ostrovno roads, who're engaging his men. His two cannon are playing on the Russian cavalry when their commander comes and begs him to cease fire – for lack of matches. 'It wasn't the moment to reproach him for having deceived me.' And besides

'the men of the Train were such bad horsemen they couldn't even handle their guns without dismounting. I'd never seen the like of it. They needed ten times more time than anyone else to execute the least movement.'

Chavardès and a dozen men are captured, but the rest of his rearguard rejoins:

'I got going by platoons in double column, my artillery in the middle. For my rearguard I'd a few brave fellows of the Imperial Guard, who'd arrived three days ago. I'd done my four last campaigns as a colonel of light infantry, and was so used to seeing, being charged by and repulsing enemy cavalry, that I thought I could succeed again. More than once I've seen and found by experience that it's good troops which make their generals famous,'

observes Pouget, thus contradicting – very naturally in the circumstances – his adored Emperor's famous dictum that 'there's no such thing as bad troops, only bad officers'. But though he detaches skirmishers to keep off the Russian cavalry that's now appearing on all hands,

'these wretched soldiers from Berg knew no better what they were doing than their officers did. Instead of dispersing and spreading out, they were marching *en masse*, at one moment too close to my column, at the next too far from it. I had to send one of my ADCs to direct and command them.'

Knowing full well that there must also be Russian infantry and artillery in the offing, he tries to hasten his pace. But can't, because

'half the men in my column were convalescents who could only walk with difficulty, but whom I didn't want to abandon. At each instant I was seeing them being sabred or captured by the enemy. Nevertheless I made 20 versts [12½ miles] or four leagues, always firing and always closely pressed and harassed. The Russians saw what kind of troops it was they had to do with, and became steadily bolder. I was everywhere, at the head, at the tail, encouraging and calming these conscripts, telling them I'd get them to Smolensk providing they obeyed me and kept calm.'

But that's just what they can't do. Finally, charged on all sides at once, he has to form square. But its badly aimed volleys don't add up to 50 shots and despite his orders won't even present its bayonets to the enemy,

'so it was easily overwhelmed. Most of it threw itself into a forest clearing. If it had gone on firing from there it could still have done the cavalry a lot of harm and dispersed it. But it took good care not to. Furious at such conduct, I resolved to defend myself personally. I passed my sword between my thigh and my saddle so as to draw my pistols and break out through the cavalry. First I killed a dragoon. A second presenting himself with raised sword, I fired off my second shot. I saw him put his hand on his chest, like a man who's been severely wounded. I flung my excellent horse into the mêlée to break through sword in hand, but in the same instant saw I was surrounded by more than 30 dragoons, and felt a sabre blow on my left shoulder. I saw all their swords pointed at me. One of these men grabbed me by my left wrist and wrenched my arm up so sharply it put my shoulder out of joint. Others dragged at me by one of my cloak's multiple collars and tore it.'

Realising that it's all up with him – the Russian troopers are infuriated by their two comrades' deaths – he does what many a senior officer would do in such a crisis:

'I let them know who I was by opening my cloak and showing them my gold lace. I was wearing a fatigue cap garnished with martin, not quite so tall as those worn by our chasseur officers. It could be the enemy had taken me for a mere subaltern. The sight of my uniform impressed them. I asked in German to see the troop's commander.'

He sees several, among them a German-speaking Livonian RSM, who takes him under his protection: 'The dragoon who'd put my shoulder out of joint ripped off a gold star of the Legion of Honour of the smaller format' and the sergeant-major makes him give his captor his

'purse, two watches in gold watchcases and their chain, my pocket handkerchief and my portfolio; but not finding anything valuable in it, gave it back.'

Although his 'protector' keeps searching him anew for more possessions and relieves him of his two gold rings, 'one my wedding ring, the other given me by a Witebsk lady whose château and village I'd saved' they don't treat him too badly as they set off back to Witebsk, holding his horse's bridle. But as they pass through the town

'my escort shouted hurrahs that were only repeated by some Jews. The old Poles, Russian subjects since the First Partition [of Poland in 1772] didn't respond.'

All this has happened on 7 November, some twelve miles from Falkowitz. Reaching Witebsk, Pouget is much better treated than his miserable garrison:

'The Russian general Tscharba, who'd been in Witebsk while we French had been there, came and embraced me and with permission of the general in command offered to take me to his house.'

Which he does. And gets back his two watches and his Cross for him. Whereon Pouget, seeing the miserable look on the Livonian's face, presents him with one of the watches, keeping 'the one my wife had given me before going off on the first Austrian campaign'. Altogether Pouget ascribes his good reception at Witebsk – by everyone except its Jews – and 'the sympathy of its inhabitants to the memory of the gentleness with which I'd treated them during my governorship'.

Five days go by. Then, just as he's to leave by sledge to be taken to Wittgenstein's headquarters, a local lady bestirs herself to buy back his Cross 'for 50 roubles, which was more than it was worth'; and the Russian commandant grants his request that his departure shall be 'at night, so as not to be a spectacle a second time for the Witebsk populace, which is the same in Russia as it is in all countries'.[13]

Obviously there's no sense in IV Corps' struggling on to Witebsk and trying to save its stores, which have fallen to Wittgenstein. When Eugène's Polish spy gets back to Dukhovchino and tells him all this, he at once sends off an officer to Smolensk 'to inform Napoleon of the disasters at the Wop' and notify him that IV Corps, less its artillery and baggage train, is rejoining the main army. That evening his artillery staff are 'sitting or lying around our mess tin, watching our pot boil, and cooking some bits of meat we (most exceptionally) had been able to get hold of, and whose unaccustomed odour flattered our sense of smell,'

when Griois hears shouts and shots:

'It's those devils of Cossacks who, repulsed at midday, are reappearing at 3 p.m., hoping for better luck as it gets dark! They're attacking our posts at the end of the town, close to our house.'

They all rush out. As ever, a few musket and cannon shots suffice to drive off 'the barbarians'. But when, three-quarters of an hour later, Griois and his comrades get back to their snug fireside it's to find the house 'thick with smoke from the stove which, too vigorously heated, had caught fire'. Officers and servants try to 'master the flames, which finally split the stove apart. In no time the wooden walls, the thatch and wattle roof, had all caught fire.' Only in the nick of time are they able to free their horses from the outhouses. 'But what was irremediable was the loss of our good soup.' Similar fires are breaking out elsewhere; and when, that evening, the march is resumed – toward Smolensk – even those of Dukhovchino's houses that aren't on fire are 'set in flames before departing'. Captain François and his comrades of the 30th Line, though accustomed to such sights, can't help being astonished at

'the horrible but superb spectacle a snow-covered forest produces in the shadows when lit up by torrents of flames. All the trees, wrapped in a bark of ice, astounded our eyes and produced, as if in a prism, the most vivid colours and subtlest nuances. The silver birch branches, which are like weeping willows, bent down to the ground in the shape of garlands, and all round us the icicles, stricken by the light, offered a rain of diamonds, rays and sparklings.'

Now all that is left behind, and the night, by contrast, is pitch black, 'only illumined, as by the Aurora Borealis, by the light of other burning villages'. Only a few such villages, 'black spots against a white surface', lie too far from the road to be safely approached, and aren't molested.

That black night many a frozen and starving veteran feels he can go no further. A grenadier of the Royal Guard, collapsing by the roadside, hands in his Cross of the Iron Crown of Italy to his officer. 'Disdaining, like many others, to ask for any other help and stoically seeing death approach, he says to one of his comrades who wants to try and pick him up: "It's no use. All I desire of you is that you'll do me the pleasure of handing my Italian decoration to my captain. I won it fighting against them at Austerlitz and don't want it to fall into their hands."'

Already Cesare de Laugier, concerned as he'll always be for the honour of the Army of Italy and more especially for its Guardia d'Onore, has

'five of these decorations, belonging to as many vélites, in the leather bag I'm wearing round my neck, and General Théodore Lecchi has several more in his keeping that have come to him in the same way'.

But not everyone's being so heroic. Trudging on in the midst of his little column with one of his gunners holding his horse's bridle, Griois is horrified to see for the first time 'an act of barbarism which later would so often be repeated and in so many guises that I paid no more attention to it, but whose atrocity struck me during that night march. A Bavarian chevauleger, overcome by fatigue or weak from his wounds, fell almost senseless in the middle of the road. Not merely did his comrades, his friends, not try to help him up. One of them who'd been throwing a covetous glance at the poor fellow's boots, and despite his complaints and his *"Mein Gott!"*, uttered in a supplicating voice, halted to wrench them off him. I saw it and I shuddered. But all sensibility was already so emulsified [*sic*] among us that I didn't say a word, and 20 other officers, many Bavarians among them, contented themselves, like I did, with hurrying on so as not to hear the unfortunate man's groans.'

'Nothing's so sad or sinister,' Griois is thinking,

'as a night march during a retreat. Taciturn, discouraged, the men march painfully on. All one hears is their oaths and the monotonous sound of their footsteps in the snow.'

Staff-captain Labaume, who is feeling particularly sorry for

'the Frenchwomen who'd come with us from Moscow, mostly on foot in cloth slippers, dressed in wretched silk or cotton cambric dresses and who'd covered themselves in furs or soldiers' greatcoats taken from corpses',

is shocked to hear an unnamed general cruelly abuse a wretched Russian girl, Pavlowna by name, whom he'd callously seduced under promise of marriage. Although she's pregnant and loyal to him, he tells her to

'go back to Moscow, because he's married already anyway, and there perhaps find the husband her parents had destined for her. The girl fainted, and the general marched off into the night toward Smolensk.'

Labaume is especially touched by the plight of the

'young and touching Fanni. Pretty, sweet, amiable, witty, speaking several languages – in a word, possessing all qualities seductive to the most insensitive man – she was reduced to begging for the slightest service, and usually the bit of bread she obtained obliged her to requite it in the most servile way. She implored our help and we abused her. Each night she belonged to anyone who undertook to nourish her.'

As they approach Smolensk he sees her again,

'but no longer, alas, able to walk. The unfortunate girl was having herself dragged along behind a vehicle, and when her strength gave out she fell down into the snow, which no doubt became her winding sheet, without her having aroused anyone's compassion nor anyone throwing her so much as a pitying glance, so brutalised were our souls and so extinct our sensibility. Misery no longer had any witnesses. We were all its victims.'

CHAPTER 8

SMOLENSK AGAIN

A fire-blackened ruin – Napoleon: 'Stop shoving!' – 'Their eyes, sunk in their orbits, were melancholy and motionless' – 'If I dared to I'd have them all shot!' – the Old Guard's jumble sale – IV Corps arrives – Murat 'a friend nursing a friend' – 'now I've nothing, not even hope' – the Hessians wait in the cold

On the day of the Wop crossing, a day so cold no one had been able to sit a horse or ride in a carriage, IHQ had 'painfully circumvented the slopes at Valutina and in the distance caught sight of the high walls of Smolensk. Napoleon, Fain had noted in his diary, 'was walking, and so were all his lot'. Ahead of them the fire-blackened skeleton of Russia's third largest city lay covered in snow:

'The heights it stood on showed the domes of the venerable cathedral majestically over their summit. But this building stood almost single amidst heaps of ruins.'[1]

Outside the Dnieper Gate there's soon a huge, ever-growing crush. Paymaster Duverger, sent on ahead by I Corps' chief-of-staff to get hold of some horses and victuals and bring them back to Davout's headquarters, finds the Treasury and trophies convoy – 25 wagons, according to Vionnet – 'stretching right up to the gates'. Its officials are under orders 'to prevent any kind of vehicle getting in among our wagons. A magnificent berline, harnessed with four horses, advances swiftly.' Kergorre signs to the coachman to halt.

'He refuses and goes on. My comrades and I seize his horses' bridles and the carriage is already at the edge of the ditch when a woman appears at its window. She's young and beautiful. Her clean costly garments, the luxury surrounding her, indicate her as being the object of some mysterious protection, exempting her from the common misery. In the name of the Emperor, of the Major-General, she signs to us to let her pass. We refuse. She insists. Has to step down even so, and is reduced to walking. What was the lady's name, her status? I don't know.'

Certainly it isn't Louise Fusil, though a Guards colonel holds up her carriage, too:

'It was holding up his regiment. My servant did his best to convince him the carriage belonged to M. de Tintignier, nephew of the Master of the Horse. "D'you think that worries me?" he replied. "You'll go no further." The noise of this discussion woke me up and doubtless it was at this moment that the colonel caught sight of me; for he said: "Oh, I'm sorry, I didn't realise there was a lady inside." I looked at him and, seeing him covered in a blue satin fur, began to smile.'

This reminds the colonel of his odd appearance, for he bursts out laughing:

'"A colonel of grenadiers dressed in blue satin," he said, "is certainly comically got up. But *ma foi!* I was dying of cold and bought it off one of the men." We chatted for some while and he ended by inviting me sur-reptitiously to share some provisions still left to him. A fire was lit, spruces cut, and what he called the cabin of *Annette and Lubin*[2] was erected. Alas, its dreary verdure didn't do much to help the "shepherds" occupying it to get out of the cold, and the song of the nightingale was replaced by a crow's lugubrious croaking.'

But in the end Louise too has to abandon her carriage and, never expect-ing to see it again, at 3 p.m. she finally gets through the Dnieper Gate. Even Napoleon himself it seems has some difficulty in getting in. Dedem's strug-gling in the crush when 'a man in a grey overcoat' just in front tells him sharply to stop shoving – turns round – and he sees who it is!

'As soon as the Emperor had entered, the gates were shut and the army was forced to camp under the town walls.'

Passing through the 'entirely demolished' New Town, Dumonceau sees many new bivouacs and carriages and 'preceded by a mob of disbanded men, clamouring to be let in' reaches the hard- frozen river and its bridge, only to find the gate closed in his face. No one's to be allowed in, the mil-itary police are insisting, except the Old Guard. Its infantry are to preside over the distributions. No one's to get any who doesn't first rejoin his unit. Colbert's lancers cross the Dnieper over the ice and in a freezing mist that seems to promise a thaw, follow on downstream in the gloaming behind some dismounted Guard Dragoons:

'Scattered and covered in their big white mantles, they seemed like so many phantoms. Although hardly able to drag themselves along and vis-ibly overwhelmed with weariness they none the less marched on with exemplary perseverance.'

After following the left bank for six miles, Dumonceau cantons in a fully intact village.

The Hessians too have been among the first units to arrive. Franz Roeder, who's been 'remembering the armies at the Berezina and on the Dvina – 80,000 combatants with newly arrived reserves – and still believing in good winter quarters in Poland', is instantly disillusioned:

'In the bitterest cold we stood about until 10 p.m. on a bit of ground in front of the bastion, as though no one knew what the Young Guard's first division was supposed to do next. At last word came that every man was to fend for himself. Everybody rushed off and I crowded my entire company into one small house.'

Pion des Loches, who'd 'left Moscow with 101 vehicles, and only had 24 left, but faithful to my orders' has kept 'all his guns'. But even the Young Guard artillery isn't let in and he has to bivouack outside the city walls.

All these units have of course had to cross the Valutina battlefield of 19 August. To Dumonceau's eyes it was only marked by snow-covered mounds. But the Fusiliers-Grenadiers have to bivouack there on the ground,

'still covered with dead and debris of all kinds, and out of which legs, arms and heads stuck up. Almost all were Russians, for we'd done what we could to give burial to our own.[3] But as it had been done in haste the subsequent rains had uncovered part of all this. We made up our fires with the debris of weapons, caissons, gun-carriages.'

The stream's water still being putrid with corpses, Bourgogne has to go back almost a mile to 'the very spot where on the morrow of the battle King Murat had aligned his tents' to get some that's drinkable; then, with a friend, 'as far as the ravine to visit the battlefield. As at Borodino, a legless French grenadier is rumoured to have survived inside a dead horse.'

Napoleon meanwhile is in a furious bad temper. The news of Malet's conspiracy is still festering. But something more immediately worse has happened. While obeying his order to march out along the Medyn road to meet the retreating army, one whole brigade of Baraguay d'Hilliers' scratch infantry division, 3,000 men newly arrived from France and commanded by General Augereau, brother of the Marshal, has just surrendered. Assailed by 5,000 Russian cavalry and the villagers of Yazvino, Liakhovo and Dolghomostoë, Baraguay himself – he who'd entertained Roeder with his reminiscences en route for Viazma – had been nine miles to the rear with his guns and convoys. And Augereau, unable to hold out until Baraguay could come to his assistance, had simply capitulated. Whereupon Baraguay, old and sick, had promptly retreated head over heels to Smolensk. Everyone agrees that his behaviour had been utterly incompetent. And a furious Napoleon places him under arrest and sends him back to France under escort.[4] He also, most unjustly, makes him scapegoat for an insufficiency of supplies.

Even worse news is the fall of Witebsk. Informed of it by Pastoret who, unlike the captured Pouget, has managed to reach Smolensk, Berthier exclaims 'three or four times: "not possible!"' And sends him to Napoleon, whom he finds alone with Murat. Pastoret assures Napoleon that there'd been supplies enough at Witebsk to feed the entire army for ten days or maintain a whole army corps for the rest of the winter. Abandoned by his Polish aides, he'd had no little difficulty in gathering them in.

'"What! You were all alone?"

"All alone. And I beg Your Majesty to excuse me if I for this reason haven't carried out your intentions."'

At the time of Witebsk's hasty evacuation, he tells Napoleon, Saint-Cyr had at most 30,000 men. Napoleon retorts that he's got at least 50,000 and Wittgenstein only 20,000. But Pastoret replies 'firmly' that 'from spies and frequent reports' he knows that Wittgenstein has 50,000. He also feels obliged to tell His Majesty of what seems to him to have been Victor's sloth and failure either to support Oudinot or save Witebsk. Whereupon Napoleon bursts out:

'"No, that Victor fellow isn't in a state to command even a division, a regiment!" Approaching the map on the table, he bursts out in a tirade against his marshals:

'"See how they sacrifice the safety of my armies to themselves! All of them, you see? Davout's half-mad and no further use. This Victor comes to Smolensk to destroy to no purpose the stores prepared here. Augereau [in

Germany] hasn't wanted to move, and thinks he's doing me a favour by obeying me. Yet obey me they shall, even so! They know who I am and I know what they are. No, no, there isn't one of them one can entrust with anything. Always, always I have to do everything! Very well, I *shall* do everything. But let them execute it, let them obey! They'd better take care, I'll know very well how to dispense with them!'"

To the Polish General Krasinski he says:

'"If I dared to, I'd have them all shot." He was particularly furious with Davout.'

'Fortune had so long showered her favours on him,' Caulaincourt reflects, 'he couldn't believe she'd deserted him.'

But where are all the 'immense supplies' that should be here at Smolensk? The officer responsible tells him – what *Honoré de Beulay* had seen in September how

'the bands of stragglers left behind by the advancing army had enveloped Smolensk in terror and destruction and intercepted many of the convoys en route. Finally, the heads of long food convoys, assembled in Germany, had appeared – all those that had managed to cross the sands of Lithuania – but as yet had only brought 200 quintals of flour and rice.'

And how on arrival several hundred German and Italian cattle, dying of hunger and fatigue and 'loth either to march or to eat' had had to be slaughtered:

'Their eyes, sunk in their orbits, were melancholy and motionless. They'd let themselves be killed without trying to avoid the blow. At Krasnoië a park of 800 cattle had been carried off by the Russians.'[5]

Then Victor had had to supply IX Corps before leaving for Polotsk to support Oudinot.

None of these excuses are accepted. And in fact Fain notices 'a big discrepancy between what had been ordered and what had been done'. Larrey, too, is furious with the dishonest war commissaries who've intercepted reports from his officers on the peculation of medical supplies. And when *Henri Jomini*, the city's newly arrived governor under Charpentier, governor of Smolensk province, excuses Commissary Siaufat on grounds that armed peasants have made foraging impossible, Napoleon orders Siaufat to be shot. Which, according to Jomini, he is (though no records confirm it).

But worst of all is the strategic situation. Victor's failure to hold Witebsk, Napoleon declares, has wrecked his plan of putting the army into winter quarters.The simple fact is the Moscow army is in no condition to maintain itself at Smolensk or anywhere else. The retreat must go on ...

"Wittgenstein has everything to gain by remaining where he is," Napoleon tells Fain afterwards in his office, "and the Duke of Bellune everything to lose." Just as he's dictating the second of two notes to Victor, one of his ADCs, a Colonel Château, is announced. What His Majesty has just ordered, he explains diffidently, is precisely what his chief's trying to do. Without even being given time to rest up Château is sent back to tell Victor the army will shortly be marching for Orsha, i.e., be keeping to the Dnieper's south bank. Two hours later, in a third dispatch, Napoleon assures Victor it's mostly only militiamen he has to deal with behind the Dwina: 'You haven't a moment to lose!'

Fain, certainly familiar with Napoleon's anxieties, notes in his journal: 'We're even fearing for our main road to Vilna!' And Generals Eblé and Chasseloup of the Engineers are sent on ahead with a strong detachment to check up on road conditions and the state of the bridges between Smolensk and Orsha and report back to Berthier on what supplies are available at depots en route. Likewise on alternative roads. Jomini can keep them company.

That first night, Daru tells Dedem, 'the Emperor had no other lights but some wretched candles stuck in a bottle'. And another officer, *E. Lemoine-Montigny*, only has to

'push the door ajar to contemplate this man who'd made so many kings tremble, asleep, almost alone, hardly even guarded. The room he was resting in was at many points exposed to the open air. Lauriston, on duty that day, was stretched out on a *chaise longue*. It's not there you meet with a double row of courtiers.'

After pillaging the Viazma stores, the Old Guard isn't sparing the far larger ones at Smolensk. It's looting them. Several of the magazines around the main square, Major *von Lossberg* sees to his own satisfaction, 'contain enough flour and fodder for a fortnight'. Planat de la Faye, who's been starving on a handful of rice for breakfast and a biscuit for the rest of the day, sees

'immense resources in provisions of every kind; and if anyone could have put any order into the distributions the men would easily have been able to provision themselves for 15 or 20 days'.

But now, after turning up at 9 a.m. on 10 November and again ousting the Hessians from their lodgings, the Old Guard is turning everything upside down:

'Already the disorganisation, despite the Emperor's presence, was so great that the magazines were pillaged. The corps coming on behind us wouldn't be able to find anything.'

'With the help of our servants and four gunners' one of Planat's fellow-officers manages 'to get hold of a little most intelligently selected supply, made up mainly of rice, biscuits, salt and fat, plus a little barrel of brandy'. The artillery staff place them, together with their cookpot and kitchen utensils, on a very light little Muscovite *teleg* (two-wheeled cart) ready to resume the long icy march.

Down at the Dnieper Gate, meanwhile, only one fatigue party from each line or Young Guard regiment is being allowed in at a time to get its share.

Colonel de Marguerye details off Major Everts and 'a sous-adjutant of the 33rd Line, all the quartermaster-corporals and such rankers as were needed' to go and get what they can. They're

'to calm the monstrous famine, which had gone beyond the uttermost limits. The distribution was being made during the night and since we could foresee the many difficulties and ill-will it would be carried out with, a senior officer from each regiment was charged with presiding over it. When I got to the town gate there were already men from some other units there, and every instant their number was growing. Not merely was each party doing its best to get in first; all this led to a general mêlée which we all, senior officers and adjutants, sabre in hand, had to contain.'

Finally the 33rd's emissaries come across a church where a commissary and his employees are distributing sacks of flour

'in the midst of such an effervescence that not being able to stand his ground he had another replace him. They had a numerous guard to protect them, yet it was only with great difficulty the commissaries were to some extent able to keep the upper hand.'

Everts' group of Dutchmen get eight sacks of flour and two small barrels of vodka:

'As we came out of the church, other starving men tried to snatch them from us. The adjutant and the sergeants-major stood up to them with drawn sabres, all of us hitting out to right and left as I cleared a way for us. You'll easily conceive,'

Everts ends, all out of breath and 'harassed and exhausted by this troublesome stint', how when they get back to the 33rd's bivouac outside the walls, 'that this feeble distribution could only bring slight relief'. No one, for lack of the famous handmills, even has means of turning the flour into an edible paste; and the Cossacks, who've left the column in peace for several days, are already in presence again and firing at them from several sides

'with our own artillery, which they'd picked up on the roads, and were promptly using to dispute our stay in Smolensk and the positions around it'.[6]

The 33rd are sent to a hilltop on the city's western side where, despite a plethora of firewood, some 60 of them succumb during the night. 'At daybreak they looked to our eyes like stone statues.' So Everts is sent to General Friederichs to deplore their exposed position. He finds that general, so merciless to Russian peasants, with his headquarters staff in a pig-sty which 'had escaped the fire and was fortunately still standing'. Friederichs takes pity on his Dutchmen, lets them move down to the foot of the hill, leaving only pickets at its summit.

Not even all Guard units are being allowed in. Like Colbert's lancers yesterday, Major *J. F. Boulart's* artillery, attached to the Chasseur brigade, has to pass under the great walls along the river bank between the Old Town and the New. After which, 'turning left, with much effort we climbed the heights and passed underneath the citadel – where Gudin's corpse was resting in one of the ramparts'.[7]

There Boulart's guns and wagons go and place themselves

'on a kind of esplanade near the Krasnoië gate, whose trees were almost as useful in providing shelter from the snow as they'd been in summer against the sun. We received a ration of bread, biscuit and meat.'

Out in their populated village[8] Colbert's men, well away from the crowd, are freely entertained to 'several delights we'd lost the habit of', and in the cellar of a barn Dumonceau and two of his lieutenants light a nice fire of the kind which 'according to the custom of the country with their smoke help dry or finish ripening the harvest hung up under the roof'. Thereto abundant 'bread, flour, grain, salt and brandy' reach them from the Smolensk stores. Dismounted troopers find remounts and his regiment is even joined by 100 fresh lancers, who'd just arrived from France with Baraguay d'Hilliers' division. But back in the ruined city even the 1st Foot Chasseurs get 'almost nothing'. And on the field of Valutina Lejeune spends the night

'on the banks of the Dnieper beside the bridge where General Gudin had died. Soon our campfires were surrounded by the stragglers, turning up without their weapons, covered in fur-lined silks and women's clothes, ampler than men's and of every colour. Many were wearing what they'd stripped from their comrades en route. Stunned by hunger and cold, they came to ask for a little place at the fires of those who'd still enough strength to light one.'

But the latter begrudge them even 'the tiniest bit of these rays of reviving warmth' and the newcomers, standing perforce behind them, soon

'sag under the weight of fatigue, fall to their knees. Then we see them sit down, and then, involuntarily, lie down. This last movement is the harbinger of death. Their colourless eyes open to the sky. Their lips contract in a happy laugh – one might have thought some divine consolation was softening their agony, indicated by an epileptoid spittle. None of these stragglers hesitated to sit down on the chest of some man lying on the ice until the latter breathed his last.'

None will ever enter Smolensk:

'In the same instant as he stretched out his limbs with an appearance of being in heavenly bliss, the man who was still standing made himself a seat out of the dead man's panting chest and remained like that, reposing his whole weight on him in front of the fire, up to the moment when he himself, unable to get up again, soon ceased to live. The snow only partially covered the terrors of this spectacle!'

Kergorre's convoy has been two whole days in the rear but has halted

'by a big artillery park, where we found Colonel Neigre, our director-general, who was having his horses rough-shod for ice and had the goodness to tell his farrier to do the same for ours.'

Reaching the city gate on 11 November,

'the Dnieper bridge kept being repeatedly blocked by the jam and the gates closed, we had to turn to the right with the rest of the army. Bivouacking at the foot of the wall we were given biscuits, rice, flour and even a sack of oats for our horses.'

When at last the Young and Middle Guard are allowed in, Sergeant Bourgogne wanders about all night in search of food. Loses his footing as he follows a Badener who's clutching a brandy flask, flies down an icy slope and tumbles into a cellar occupied by

'one of those gangs which, multiplying as they went, had been prowling about ever since the great cold had begun'.[9]

In an urgent whisper a poor woman the gang's been forcing to keep them company ever since Viazma tells him how they particularly hate men of the Imperial Guard. So he leaves in a hurry, wanders about among the walls of ruined houses and is within an inch of falling 50 feet from the ramparts into eternity. Everywhere he stumbles over 'corpses which, even two and a half months after the disaster, we saw still lying all over the place in the streets and a great number of others heaped up to a height of one metre at the foot of the town walls' – though Berthier, on 16 August, had asked Napoleon to let him use Russian prisoners to get them all buried he hadn't succeeded in his task. Around a church they're lying particularly thickly. And what's that – if not organ music? Wherever Bourgogne turns it haunts him so that he assumes he must be hallucinating. But upon entering this church he's actually been circling around all the time he finds it's filled with

'the men of my company. Some of them were singing, and others, several of the regiment's musicians, were playing on the organ. They were all dreadfully drunk!'

Next morning Bourgogne remembers his promise to go back to the cellar to rescue his benefactress. 'But the birds had flown.'

In the main square the Old Guard, whose pillage has been less inspired by necessity 'than of greed and arrogance', is holding – as at Moscow – a gigantic jumble sale, 'a veritable bazaar of everything one desires in the way of luxury and demanded by necessity, an incredible quantity of things.' Major Lossberg, buying 'half a pound of butter for a five-franc piece' from one of the Smolensk Jews who're 'pushing in most impudently and buying as well as selling', wonders whether they'll be able to keep their profits:

'Hundreds of soldiers, most of them from the French Guard, were dealing in plunder they'd got hold of during the campaign, particularly in Moscow. It consisted mostly of clothing, women's shawls and scarves of all kinds, as well as articles stolen from churches. An NCO in a green uniform – probably Italian to judge by his looks and way of speaking French – asked 2,000 francs of me for a church ornament which – if he was telling the truth (he talked knowledgeably about diamonds, explaining the various stones' value) – was worth at least ten times as much. The throng of soldiers of all nationalities was so great that one had difficulty

in pushing through them. For 20 francs I bought a yellowish brown beaver cloak with a double collar, and put it on at once.'
Slipping into a house that's still standing, Captain Lignières of the 1st Foot Chasseurs gets 'for a gold napoleon and 20 francs some 20 loaves of bread, which I distributed to my company'. And indeed food is really the only thing anyone's interested in. That jovial giant of a man, Marshal Mortier, makes General Pajol a present of a sack of wheat and half an ox.[10]

'Here a *vivandière* was offering watches, rings, necklaces, silver vases and sometimes precious stones. There a grenadier was selling brandy or furs. Farther on, a soldier of the Train was trying to sell Voltaire's *Complete Works* or Emilie de Desmoustier's *Letters*. A voltigeur was exposing some horses and carriages for sale, and a cuirassier kept a shoe and clothing shop.'

The imperial vintner, 'having speculatively imported a great quantity of wines and liqueurs into Smolensk' is selling off his entire stock for its weight in gold. 'Even the rank and file spent all they had to get hold of a bottle of brandy.' All of which, thinks a shocked Amédée Pastoret, horrified to see 'officers treating the men they did business with as equals', must surely be inimical to discipline? 'Having discussed or shared profit and loss with them, it caused them to lose all respect.' But though the men are beginning to take liberties with their officers – yes, and even swear at them – Dedem never hears them 'swear at the man to whom they owed all their ills'. Dedem himself, spitting blood and still suffering from the chest bruise from a spent musket ball that had hit him as he'd marched up to the Malakhofskaia Gate at the head of his brigade on August 18, is being personally cared for 'as a child' by Daru, who's 'working ceaselessly and showing much energy and courage'.[11] In Moscow, Dedem had taken on an intelligent and resourceful stable-hand who,

'full of zeal, had been driving my carriage, gone off foraging with rare boldness and with no fear of the Cossacks, and sometimes cooked my supper'.

In a word, another Victor. 'Everybody admired my little gunner's intelligence and energy.' But now here's a quandary, a real surprise:

'In a moment of impatience I struck him, and he revealed his identity. It was girl of fourteen or fifteen, of good family and education, but with a marked taste for horses. She'd left her parents' home to go off with a French artillery officer she'd fallen in love with.'

Dedem buys her a horse of her own on which to continue the retreat.

Greatly to Louise Fusil's surprise, her carriage does turn up after all; but not unlooted by its owner's servants:

'Everything I possessed and my trunks, which I'd placed on wagons belonging to officers, had been taken by the Cossacks. All that was left me was a chest containing shawls, some jewellery and silver.'

Captain *Bréaut des Marlots* of the cuirassiers still has all his steeds with him, 'the finest in the army, and certainly the best. I'd made great sacrifices to save them'. Now, ousting some Polish hussars from a house in the outskirts, he has

'plenty to eat and drink for two days, and so did my horses. It was a great blessing for me, as at that moment my feet were rather frost-bitten. The colonel's cook waited on me. She was a very beautiful woman. However, she made not the least impression on me, my heart was of ice.'

Vossler, the wounded Prussian hussar lieutenant, has no such female attendant. His servant has thought him dead en route. However, he joins some other Württemberg officers who're burning furniture from neighbouring empty houses to warm themselves. 'By now the city was little more than a heap of rubble, for not a night passed without several houses going up in flames. Not a single inhabitant was left.'[12]

Mostly demoralisation reigns. True, one of Mailly-Nesle's fellow-officers of the 2nd Carabiniers has turned up 'exhausted by fatigue' but with the regiment's standard in his pocket. But his aristocratic friend Louis L****, he who'd preferred campaigning to partridge shooting, and who'd been so bright and lively on his unexpected arrival from France, is suffering from

'the dreary silence all round us, the apathy of some and the agony of others, and lastly this snow enveloping all the earth and seeming likely to engulf us. All this concurred to induce lugubrious thoughts and carry fear and terror into the most resolute souls. I'm happy to be able to say, however, that Beauveau and I didn't lose an opportunity to laugh and from time to time sang full-throatedly. To bear the misfortunes of war with courage and gaiety there's nothing like being a Frenchman, being young and, perhaps, also being a gentleman?'

Particularly, perhaps, the last. The ugly little dragoon captain *Henri Beyle*, one day to become known as the great novelist Stendhal, is at this time only a commissary of foodstuffs and certainly no gentleman – at least not in Mailly-Nesle's sense of the word. But he's no less certainly a Frenchman, despite his criticisms of his compatriots. On 2 November, after 'three or four times a day swinging from extreme boredom to extreme pleasure' he'd reached 'attractive Smolensk, a trifle spoiled by snow' with the rest of his convoy of 1,500 wounded, or as many as had survived. His normally rather comical appearance hadn't been improved by the journey; for when he'd knocked at his hosts' door and on entering had held out his hand to a colleague of the Administration, he'd been

'taken for an insolent lackey. We're far removed from Parisian elegance. I'm reckoned to be the most fortunate because I've saved my carriage by means of money and by flying into a rage with any wagons that came close. That is, if one can call having only four shirts and one greatcoat 'saved'. Those who aren't stout-hearted are full of bitterness. But the ranker lives well. He has cups full of diamonds and pearls. They're the happy ones in the army, and as they're in a majority, that's as it should be.'

All this persiflage he'd sent off in a letter to a Parisian lady friend. His diary will be lost in the snows.

If Heinrich von Roos is feeling more cheerful it's partly because the weather's momentarily not quite so cold, partly because a decoration awarded him by the King of Württemberg has unexpectedly reached him. Anyway, pious and resourceful, he's finding his three-day stay at Smolensk 'very supportable'. The third night, after dining on kidneys given him by a Pole who firmly believes the French will be victorious again, he 'for the first time since the war started' even sleeps – luxury of luxuries – in a bed.

Although ill-housed Napoleon certainly isn't idle.[13] 'The Emperor rode out each day, visiting the town and its surroundings as though he'd have liked to keep them too.' Caulaincourt thinks that 'the state in which he saw the army during its march through the town convinced him that our plight was worse than he'd been willing to admit to himself.' Optimistic as usual, though, he doesn't doubt he'll be able to go into winter quarters as soon as he's joined up with Schwarzenberg, Oudinot and Victor:

'He was expecting the arrival of the Polish 'Cossack' levies he'd announced we'd find near Smolensk. Was he misled in this respect, or did he announce this reinforcement to create an illusory hope in everyone else's mind? I don't know.'

Attempts, mostly fruitless ones, are being made to reorganise the army. And certainly there are reinforcements. Fezensac finds his 4th Line 'reinforced by the 129th Line and a regiment of Croats'. Pion des Loches runs into Colonel Pelgrin, commanding his artillery park, who'd come no further than Smolensk and whose *matériel* is under the walls:

'I received 27 loaded ammunition wagons, and sufficient horses in a very good state to draw them were fetched for me from distant villages. They bivouacked beside my park, but the cold was so fierce they were visibly perishing.'

By 12 November everyone's getting ready to leave. Hoping for the remount price of 15 gold louis/napoleons, Franz Roeder sends his horse to the artillery – 'a pony will serve me as well'. But his horse can't get through the press and comes back to him. Those of the 'cuirassiers and the heavy cavalry generally' fill Dedem with horror:

'The French cavalry horses were in a frightful state, whilst those of the Prussians, Saxon and Württemberg regiments were still in quite good shape. Their horses' wounds were being regularly attended to, and their superior officers never left their units.'

Caulaincourt himself is 'employed day and night in reorganising the Emperor's carriages. I'd sent orders ahead to forge shoes with three calkins for all the horses'; and he bribes the arsenal workmen, who're working for the artillery by day, to work for him by night. Although Napoleon can hardly be brought to consent to it, he consigns a lot of superfluous vehicles to the flames but stocks the rest 'with all the provisions I could obtain for cash'. The only carriages he conserves are 'those of Messieurs de Beauveau, de Mailly, and de Bausset', the fat major-domo, who's suffering from gout.

131

Of the 11,000 men of III Corps who'd left Moscow hardly 3,000 are left. 'What Frenchmen there used to be in our army corps are reduced to one quarter,' Major Bonnet writes in his newly resumed diary. 'The foreigners have vanished. Not one left.' Fighting their everlasting rearguard action on the Dnieper's bank, Ney's men, who're 'devilishly cold', are feeling they've been forgotten by those they've been protecting. 'No question of relieving us as rearguard. While we were staving off the enemy, the other corps had finished off the magazines and pillaged them.' All that reaches them is 'a few biscuits'. Inside the town Mailly-Nesle can hear 'the cannon firing all the time' as Davout throughout 12 and 13 November has to help Ney fight off the Russians, 'a sound repeated by the echoes from these huge old walls'.

By the time the already depleted 111th Line, having helped Ney hold the bridgehead, withdraws into the city it has lost 20 officers and 449 men and both the 15th Light and the 33rd Line have been reduced from 4 battalions to one, i.e. from 4,500 to 450 men. In the morning of 13 November I Corps,

'with Marshal Davout at its head, passes through Smolensk in considerable numbers and takes up position beyond it in the western suburbs, bivouacking in gardens where the assault had taken place'.

But though Sergeant Bertrand's young Captain Moncey sends him back 'into town to find some victuals' he too finds that 'the Emperor's foresight in accumulating food, clothing, linen and shoes' has been made nonsense of by

'the employees who've abandoned their posts. It was a mob of wounded from all arms, frozen men, stragglers going on ahead of the column, who, in inexpressible disorder, were pillaging all these resources. And the cold was at -23° !'

(Larrey's thermometer, more accurate no doubt, is registering between -19° and -20° Réaumur [12.5° C) Nevertheless Bertrand gets hold of '5 to 6 kilos of flour and some broken biscuit' and putting himself at the head of his two carabiniers and sword in hand 'defending these meagre provisions against those who, with the most horrible threats in their mouths, wanted to wrench them from us,' takes them back to 60 surviving grenadiers.

But what's this – if not the head of Eugène's bedraggled column appearing over the hills along the Petersburg road? After a 50-mile march some 4,000 men, all that's left of IV Corps, are arriving by the icy road from Dukhovchino. Sliding down the last steep slope, Griois and his party joke at their 'long skids and frequent falls. The idea that the term of our ills was close to hand had given us back a kind of gaiety.' Luckily the gate just then happens to be open. Climbing the steep icy main street to the main square they everywhere see groups of men and packed houses – and realise they haven't a ghost of a chance of finding any shelter. So going straight through the town and out by the opposite gate they find the

Guard Artillery bivouacked on its 'esplanade' and their 'little caravan' is promptly established in 'a kind of half-roofed hangar' its horses have been occupying. 'For us it was a veritable palace.' Whereupon Griois goes to see

'Colonel [*sic*] Boulart, commanding a battalion [*sic*] in the Guard, who'd invited me to supper. He was under a tent, and I enjoyed a meal I'll never forget as long as I live: wine, bread, meat, coffee, all things I'd long lost the habit of. So I did them every honour, despite the extreme cold [-28°]. It was so great we had to break our wine by hitting it with a hatchet and putting it over the fire.'

This gives the hospitable Boulart – who's under orders to leave tomorrow morning – 'the satisfaction of entertaining some of my comrades to some passable cooking'. Griois goes back to his hangar, where his comrades 'at risk of being suffocated by the mob' have procured some food from one of the magazines. 'Without having supped as well as I had, they'd shared with some friends in the Guard.'

He has, however, an uneasy conscience. Not merely has IV Corps lost all but four of its last remaining guns – should he, who really belongs to Grouchy's 3rd Cavalry Corps, ever have joined it with his own horse artillery at Doroghoboui? Feeling he must justify himself to Grouchy's superior, the inspector-general of cavalry, he asks the whereabouts of General *A.-D. Belliard*'s headquarters. Climbing the little staircase of 'a rather vast building destroyed by the fire before it had even been completed', Griois, 'without meeting either servants or orderlies' pushes open a half-shattered door, and in front of him sees the King of Naples and Belliard, his former chief-of-staff,

'chatting joyously. Belliard, still suffering from the wound he'd got at Mojaisk [on 8 September], was lying on a wretched pallet, part of which was occupied by Murat. The picture wasn't uninteresting. A king – for that, after all, is what he was and was recognised as such – in the company of one of his wounded generals, in guise of a friend who nurses a friend.'

That, he thinks, 'is a rarity, and I confess I felt touched by it'. But since his bad news is

'agreeable neither to tell nor hear, and anyway no longer had any importance at all, I retired without them noticing me. Murat merely asked who was there. I didn't reply.'

After a lot of searching about among the benighted crowds he finally locates Eugène's headquarters, only to hear he's with the Emperor. Eugène's report on the state of IV Corps, Caulaincourt notes, comes as a considerable shock. So Griois has to wait:

'The session in Napoleon's room was a lengthy one, and to me seemed all the longer as the hall where I was open to all the winds, and the cold glacial despite the fire the officers were carefully keeping up. At last the door opened, Eugène appeared and with him Murat. Murat seemed extremely gay, and no one would have divined our sad situation from his noisy guffaws [*ses bruyants éclats*]. Parting from him, Eugène came over to me.

'"My dear Griois," he said, "before daylight you must be out on the road we've just come by. I'm going there too. Broussier's division, which I've left in position, is surrounded by the enemy. We must clear a way for him. See you tomorrow!"'

Dismayed by this unexpected order Griois goes back to his hangar, rouses his chief-of-staff. 'It was about midnight. And at 5 a.m. we had to be on our feet. Wrapping myself in my mantle I threw myself down on the straw and fell asleep.'

That cold blustery night the whole of the 85th Line lodges in two or three of the suburb's remaining houses. A howling gale's battering the window panes (amazingly, some are still intact) of Le Roy's tiny room. The regiment's ever-cheerful, ever resourceful *adjutant-sous-officier* is an NCO who's always been equal to all thinkable situations. Long ripe for promotion, Sergeant-Major Ballane has already bought a gold epaulette, gold lace and all the other accoutrements proper to a *sous-lieutenant* from a lacemaker who's followed the army. These precious symbols of his future commissioned self he keeps wrapped up in a little bag

'which he never allowed out of his sight, hung it round his neck with a good rope and several double knots, containing as it did all his fortune, all his happiness'.

Alas, how easily snatched from us are our symbols of promotion! Bellane's just been doing the cooking in a room occupied by the officers of the 85th Line, Le Roy has just shaved Jacquet, and their precious cookpot – that more than symbolic means of survival they've been keeping their eyes on ever since the Niemen – is bubbling on the stove, when Ballane, laying his bag on the window sill, goes off to fetch them some stores and some rum. Alas the windowpane is one of the many thousands the glaziers of Davout's corps[14] have lacked time or inclination to repair; and window there is none. Suddenly Ballane notices his bag's gone. And rushing outside sees some remnants of IV Corps marching by. But, alas, no sign of his bag! Stricken, he comes back into the room. *Sic transit gloria mundi.* Though everyone tries to console him, this exemplary soldier cracks. Bursts into tears: "Now I've nothing left me," he sobs, "not even hope."

'He began weeping, and lay down. Despite all our entreaties and arguments he ate nothing all day. From this time onwards we'd notice how he lost his activity, became indifferent and in the end succumbed to his chagrin.'

Back at his bivouac in the western suburb, Sergeant Bertrand sees all the neighbourhood's houses packed with officers and men who've lit fires in them to warm themselves. Among them is one of his comrades. 'Foreseeing what's going to happen, I implore him to come out.' But though the officers and some of the men 'already stupefied by the heat and incapable of a decision' do as he says, his comrade won't:

'Soon a mob throws itself on these houses. The ones inside try to defend their repose. A horrible fight starts up, and the weak are pitilessly crushed. I run to the bivouac to register these atrocious scenes. I've hardly got there before the flames devour these houses and everyone inside.'

But the carabinier company bivouacks apart

'with the colonel and other officers. We set fire to ambulance wagons abandoned for lack of teams, and passed a good night of sleep and happiness, which however wasn't complete, since we had to defend ourselves, musket in hand, against those accursed Cossacks, even around our nice bright fire.'

When morning comes nothing's left of the houses. 'We see only ruins and corpses.' But the trio from the 85th have passed the night with Le Roy's friend Captain Gouttenoire of the 1st Foot Chasseurs:

'The Guard was lodged beside us, in houses near the rampart. The wind was very strong, the cold excessive and the snow went on falling in big flakes.'

Le Roy also pays a visit to another friend, Colonel Schmidt of the Illyrian regiment [III Corps], whom he finds has been charged with the task of blowing up the Smolensk fortifications before Ney's rearguard leaves:

'When we parted he took me aside and confided to me several thousand-franc notes and 150 francs in silver to give to his wife. He foresaw a catastrophe which, he said, couldn't fail to happen to him while blowing up the fortifications at the enemy's approach.'

Schmidt also gives him food for several days, including 'a little sugar loaf which I hid in one of the pockets of my greatcoat, as well as part of the rest of our breakfast,' *inter alia* a chicken.

At 5 a.m. Griois and Colonel Berthier, both frozen to the bone and unable to ride their horses over the ice, have gone back through the city and 'not without several tumbles' descended the slope to the Dnieper Gate. Mounting 'with even greater difficulty, in 25-28 degrees of frost', the even steeper gradient they'd so cheerfully slithered down yesterday, they've found it 'lined with dead men from IV Corps 'covered in wounds and frozen solid, who'd yesterday been attacked by Cossacks' and reached the hilltop at dawn. There they find the Royal Guard facing to the rear – it too has been closely followed by 'numerous regiments' of Cossacks, who've thrown themselves on the stragglers, the remains of IV Corps' baggage and on Broussier's rearguard.

Eugène's men have absolutely no idea of the state of affairs in Smolensk, and from moment to moment Laugier's comrades are

'expecting Victor's troops to come out and replace us. Completely ignorant of what's been happening in the rear, we're amazed they're taking so long to do so.'

Already the indomitable Eugène is standing there to the right of the road with some of his staff officers. Griois goes up to him:

'The weather was superb; but the sun's pale rays only seemed to make the cold more piercing. The prince had detached some troops to protect the retreat of Broussier's division and was awaiting the outcome'. For to the rear a minor battle has developed around a chapel on the hilltop. Broussier, together with 'the few Bavarian horse still with us', is fighting a heroic rearguard action. Pino's division too, marching after the rest of IV Corps, has had to 'fight its way through Grekoff's division, near Kamenka'. Although the Cossacks have massacred the stragglers, 14th Division has established itself in a village, with a nearby palisaded château as a kind of entrenchment. There Broussier, 'resigned and generous,' says Cesare de Laugier, has awaited his fate:

'Late into the night we'd had to stay put in the position indicated to us. Imagine these soldiers standing completely immobile on very high freezing ground where the wind buffets them furiously, in -29 degrees, without food, without hope, and their only prospect to freeze to death rather than abandon the flag – and all the while seeing Smolensk far off in the distance!'

Isn't that a scene, he asks, that Plutarch would have preserved for posterity? 'Honour to so many illustrious warriors who there sleep their eternal sleep!'

Already Eugène has sent '50 soldiers, skeletons of two companies, to attack a hillock crowned by Cossacks'. Scorning the grapeshot and lance-jabs, this handful of brave men 'reaches the height like a troop of lions'. And in the end Broussier retires 'in good order but with extreme difficulty' from the village, now in flames from Platov's shellfire, and manages to cover the withdrawal of what little remains of IV Corps' baggage and its stragglers.

But the cold's so intense that 32 of the Guard grenadiers have dropped dead in the ranks while awaiting the order to leave. Perhaps at the terrible, the shattering, news Eugène has told them: *There's to be no halting at Smolensk.* At 8.30 that same morning 'the Emperor has left, accompanied by the Old Guard and preceded by three hours by the Young Guard'. It's a stunning blow. At least the sweet Fanni has been spared the horror of this final, most cruel disappointment. 'If lightning had struck at our feet we couldn't have been more stupefied.' For the first time the Adjutant-Major sees men who simply 'refuse to believe' it leave the ranks and go down to the town to find out the truth of the matter for themselves. But then, by the Dnieper, 'a horse lying in the ditch, strips of whose flesh were being fought over by some soldiers, destroyed or at least reduced to very little the hopes we'd been flattering ourselves with' and they return and confirm the ultimacy of the disaster.

'At that moment a new scene of horror presents itself to our eyes. Any number of soldiers belonging to the rearguard division, lots of employees, servants, disbanded men who've fallen behind, try to rejoin us and go down into Smolensk. Wounded, streaming blood, pursued by Cossacks, they run toward us howling and imploring us to help them. The road's thick with these unfortunates.'

So steep is the slope and so dangerous the ice that

'all these unfortunates, hardly able to stand up, let themselves roll down it, most of them only to perish in a veritable lake of blood and render up their last sigh under these walls which have been the unhappy object of their longings'.

Although poorly mounted, some cavalry officers and some remaining dragoons of Eugène's escort, unable to contain themselves at the sight, throw themselves at the Cossacks – luckily its commander General Lecchi has had the Guard infantry fall back for the best part of a mile – put the Cossacks to flight and rescue some men of their prey. Only then, leaving Broussier's and Pino's divisions on the heights of the Petersburg road,[15] do the Royal Guard and the dismounted cavalry at last march down towards Smolensk.

They meet Ney's men at the junction of the Doroghobouï and Valutina roads, and envy them for

'not having crossed the Wop and having kept a large part of their artillery and vehicles. The numerous baggage, flowing in from all directions, mingled with the cavalrymen and infantry and caused so much confusion that people were cutting each other's throats to get in.'

The Italians have to wait for three hours. And when they at last reach the charred remains of Smolensk's suburbs it's only to be told that 'all the stores had been consumed'.

To get up the main street, where officers like Dumonceau had gone sightseeing in the August heats, Staff-Captain Labaume has to 'get down on all fours and hang on to the points of rocks jutting up out of the snow'.

And it's a fact. Napoleon and the Guard have left that morning (14 November). After Roeder's men – nominal members of the Young Guard – have been belatedly issued with some flour and rice – certainly not enough for the six days it's supposed to last – that irritable officer's been kept awake until midnight by noisy distributions of 'shoes, leggings, shirts and wicker brandy flasks, but, alas, no bread!' Up at 2 a.m. after only two hours' sleep, the Hessians, though told they'll march out at 4 a.m., have to draw up in the main square and wait and wait. Berthier, whose pampered Neuchâtel 'canaries'[16] are also to leave with the Young Guard, takes pity on them:

'Seeing no orders for departure come from the Emperor he assembled some men from the bands under the Emperor's window and told them to play the air *Where Can One Better Be than in the Bosom of One's Family?*[17] They'd scarcely begun, when the Emperor appeared on the balcony and ordered them to play *Let's Watch over the Safety of the Empire*. The men had to play it, in spite of the cold, and immediately the order to leave was given.'

Just as Napoleon's about to leave, Lejeune goes in to him and again begs to be relieved of the onerous job he'd never wanted in the first place:

'The Emperor agreed and nominated General Charpentier, no longer governor of Smolensk, to relieve me. But although I no longer either had the title or the salary I still went on with the work, as this general, by no means anxious to come and take up a post of whose difficulties he was only too well aware, managed to evade reporting for duty.'

Finally the Hessians, consisting now of eight sergeants, one drummer, seven *Schützen* and 42 guardsmen (ten of them sick), get the order to march. 'Of course,' Franz Roeder caustically concludes in his diary,

'we didn't march out until 9 a.m. in -18° [-11.25° C], the men with empty stomachs and no sleep. This is wreaking terrible havoc. We might have been able to get our strength back here if only we'd been given enough to eat and hadn't had to observe that murderous vigil.'

In a freezing wind the Italians wander about the streets, looking for something to eat. Evidently the magazines still have something to offer, for the pillage follows as before:

'Men flung themselves on the food stores. These were smashed in, looted. There men were killing each other, suffocating each other. As for ammunition, there were no horses to carry it. At least weapons could have been given to this mob of soldiers who'd thrown their own away or lost them. They took good care not to come and find some more. A small number were being distributed to some men of good will and to gunners whose cannon had been left behind in the ice. I had some carbines given to all from IV Corps who formed a kind of battalion.'

That evening of 14 November 'having had a dinner at Lariboisière's which was far from coming up to Boulart's', Griois, returning to his hangar, is told that IV Corps is to leave tomorrow morning.

The 'hospitals', now to be abandoned, are full to overflowing. Because of the failure of this promised land that was to have been Smolensk, writes Labaume,

'despair seized our hearts. Each man, thinking only of his own existence, became oblivious of honour and duty or, more properly, no longer let it consist in submitting to the orders of an improvident leader who hadn't even thought of giving bread to those who were sacrificing their lives for him.'

Although Cesare de Laugier certainly wouldn't agree with such treasonable sentiments, even he, with ice-cold fingers, writes in his diary:

'Assailed by terrible doubts, but determined at all costs to survive, many of us are losing what's left of our military bearing.'

Invited by Sébastiani's ADCs to share a piece of roofing, Victor Dupuy ties up his horse with theirs. Passing 'in front of the house the Emperor had occupied' and seeing 'the remains of his stocks of wine being sold off' he buys 'two bottles of wine, and for 12 francs a soldier sold me a munition ['issue'] loaf pillaged from the magazines.'

Phase Two
TOWARDS THE BEREZINA

CHAPTER 9

THE ICY ROAD TO KRASNOIE

An icy day – courageous women – 'she came back, caressed me, went away again and disappeared' – Roeder loses his inkpot ... and Napoleon his maps – Cossacks outside Krasnoïë – Boulart forces his way through – Louise leaves her carriage – Prince Eugène's bivouac

Junot's 1,800 Westphalians had marched out early in the morning of 14 November at the heels of the dismounted cavalry, followed by the Poles of V Corps and the 900 men of the Vistula Legion escorting the Treasure, IHQ's baggage and the trophies. Now, on the 15th, the Guard, amounting to upwards of 9,000, leaves behind it the city's fire-blackened skeleton and marches for Krasnoïë, 35 miles away. In hopes of avoiding confusion and retarding Kutusov, IV, I and III Corps have been ordered to follow on, in that order and at one-day intervals – a plan, as we'll see, fraught with dire consequences. To bring news, likewise at one-day intervals, of how the city's holding out, IHQ has left behind four of its staff officers.[1]

Hearing that 350 guns have so far been abandoned, Cesare de Laugier, in an off-the-cuff estimate of the state of the army, thinks that more men than not are still under arms. But Secretary Fain, better informed, notes that 50,000 men under arms are now protecting 60,000 without any.

Leaving under a sombre sky – to Planat it looks 'completely black against the snow' – Larrey consults his little Réaumur thermometer dangling from his coat lapel and sees it's fallen to -19° (-14° C). And Planat's comrades' hearts, hearing 'the rearguard's guns rumbling in the distance', ache 'at the thought of so many brave fellows getting themselves killed for our sakes, perhaps never to rejoin us'.

Outside the town gate this freezing morning Mme Domergue, wife of the producer of the French theatre at Moscow (whose husband is currently enjoying himself in captivity with sundry Russian ladies,[2]) is sitting dejectedly on a gun-carriage with her little son 'feeling sad and trying to calm my son's crying' when she sees Napoleon

'now on foot, now on horseback, giving orders to his ADCs. He came up to me and said:

"You're suffering a great deal, aren't you, Madame? But take courage, you'll see your husband again, and I'll recompense you for your misfortunes."

"Sire," I replied, "at this moment your goodness makes me forget them."

'He was always as much master of himself as when things were going well. His attitude was calm and his face serious.'

On the other hand she's upset to see the Emperor is unusually clad:

'Over his grey overcoat he was wearing a kind of Polish pelisse, trimmed with marten. His little hat had been replaced by a green velvet bonnet also trimmed with fur, from which a gold tassel escaped. This head-dress was fixed by two black ribbons under his chin.'

This she, 'being a woman and superstitious', feels is a sinister portent:

'I was struck by the sight of these ribbons of lugubrious hue and at not seeing his hat on his head, that talisman which seemed to protect his brow and his genius.'

Roustam, always in close attendance, sees two more of the troupe's actresses, 'one old and one young and pretty', warming themselves by a fire, made up by some Sailors of the Guard who're 'using the most virulent expressions' as they 'impute all their ills to the Emperor for bringing them to this infernal country'. The older woman exhorts them to

"Show more courage, have more energy. Brace yourselves against adversity. Remember you're soldiers and Frenchmen."

Duverger sees yet another actress, Madame Adnet, 'weeping for her family, killed by the cold'. And remembers how in Moscow she and Louise Fusil had taken the lead roles in *Marton et Frontin,* a performance he'd found 'a sad parody of our Parisian theatres'.[3]

Only Mailly-Nesle, riding on ahead as usual in his carriage, seems to take any interest in the grisly relics of the battle of 16/17 August,[4] lying 'in fragments in a terrible pell-mell so that one couldn't walk without sending bones rolling or crushing rotting flesh'. After 'spending a few nights under a roof, something that hadn't happened since time out of mind and a trifle' compared with the snug winter quarters they'd been looking forward to, Colbert's lancers have emerged in the early hours from their village and been delighted to see the road 'clear of the mob which had previously been encumbering it'. Yet it's already littered with fresh corpses, presumably Westphalian or Polish. Flanking the Guard again, the Lancers

'ride alongside over the fields. The Emperor was marching on foot at the head of the column of his old grenadiers, followed immediately by his travelling *coupé,* harnessed to four bays.'

Three or four times he and Berthier get into it, 'but without going on ahead, and after getting some rest' get out again. But the road's a sheet of ice, and Napoleon has to 'lean now on Caulaincourt's arm, now on Berthier's, now on someone else's.'

Everything that depends on horsepower is in a very bad way: 'Neither the artillery nor the cavalry had a single rough-shod horse – most of our losses,' Dedem sees,

'must be attributed to want of shoeing: i.e., to our lack of foresight. The gunners had been warned in vain. The forges had been abandoned on the road. Our farriers had no nails, and could lay their hands neither on iron nor coals.'

No sooner has Pion des Loches helped to their feet the fine new horses he's just been given in Smolensk, than their hoofs slither beneath them and they slip and fall again:

'I harnessed up as many as 20 to save one of my field-forges, and still didn't succeed. That day I lost 27 of my ammunition wagons.'

Only Private *Jakob Walter*'s *konya* can 'always help itself up again', even has 'the good custom, when we went downhill, of sitting on its rump, bracing its forefeet forward, and sliding into the valley without my dismounting. The other German horses' shoes were ground entirely smooth. Nor could those irons be torn off, since no one had a tool for that.'

'If my officers had been as zealous as myself,' Pion des Loches goes on, he'd have saved a good part of the ammunition wagons. 'But what could one expect of depressed men who'd no longer any authority over their subordinates?' Dreadfully upset and shamefaced, he goes and tells Sorbier. But all the commander of the Guard reserve artillery, 'seeing how embarrassed I was, most obligingly' says is:

"That's desolating for you. I couldn't give a damn. It makes little odds whether you lose your ammunition wagons today or tomorrow. The sooner you lose them, the more the gunners are worth who're killing themselves trying to save them. You won't get a single vehicle to go as far as the Niemen, no matter what trouble you go to. Not", Sorbier adds, "that I'd say that to everybody."'

If whole teams of horses are dropping dead between their traces and the steep gradients are 'littered with abandoned horses that hadn't been able to scramble to their feet', Dedem sees it's 'not for lack of food, since we still had oats to give them. It was due to their own unavailing efforts' to drag guns and caissons uphill. But above all, Caulaincourt's thinking – agreeing with Pion des Loches – it's due to Napoleon's obsession with keeping every gun, whether or not there are any horses to draw it:

'The sensible thing would have been to distribute a certain amount of artillery to each corps before leaving Smolensk; make sure it was properly mounted, even supply it with reserve horses; and sacrifice all the rest. As it was, the tiniest frozen slope in the undulating road was fatal.'

Lariboisière, supreme commander of the Grand Army's artillery, his surviving son Honoré and the latter's close friend Planat de la Faye have every reason to 'follow the route in silence'. The Guard Artillery 'which is mounted best' is crawling along at hardly more than one mile per hour. And despite Lariboisière and Chasseloup's strict orders that all abandoned guns are to be burnt, nothing's being done about it. Everywhere Mailly-Nesle sees:

'guns piled up on top of each other. The frost had glued, or rather cemented, the wheels to their axle-trees. On the detestable surface ice the wheels slid without being able to turn. From this came a continual groaning noise, produced by the rubbing of the iron of the felloes,'

so that the Guard Artillery takes thirteen hours to cover the fifteen miles between Smolensk and its next bivouac, at the 'miserable hamlet' of Korytnia.

More tragic than guns, many of the women are being abandoned – for instance a commissary's wife Dedem had seen clinging to a gun-carriage shortly before reaching Smolensk:

'Their sufferings only added to those of the men. Whilst that sex, much more humane than ourselves, gave evidence of compassion and interest in the midst of indescribable sufferings, I saw distinguished officers heartlessly and barbarously abandon amiable and interesting women. In this way a *vivandière* of the 9th Hussars fed me for several days, and the wife of one of the Emperor's coachmen, whose husband had served me at Mecklemburg, often brought me supper and even wine.'

Otherwise masculine egoism, already rife, has become worse. Having come from Witebsk, Intendant Pastoret has not yet seen anything of the retreat and is deeply shocked at the way privileged persons' carriages and other vehicles are always pushing ahead of the guns, which 'should have had right of way; but no one was respecting it'. On the other hand Franz Roeder is appalled to see

'how little protection is being given to the carriages, the baggage trains, the artillery, even the Imperial Treasure – how bridges are never being repaired, even when this could be done in a couple of hours – how no detachment is ever being stationed to cover the defiles and crossings – how men are being stricken down and murdered on the least pretext – how everyone's riding or driving through the troops, whilst these, never for a moment safe from stumbling, must toil and struggle on in the press.'

After having been ridden through thick snow inside one of the Young Guard's squares, Roeder's own horse finally collapses on the highway, 'a victim to my batman's monstrous negligence, to thirst, hunger and fatigue'. To make matters even worse, he hears to his dismay that 'the wagon with the officers' effects has sunk in a swamp at almost exactly the same moment!' But here at least is a bit of luck. His Sergeant Bruck, whom he'd saved from a flogging back in July, has snatched his valise from the sinking wagon – one of only two survivors. Roeder rewards Bruck with a *louis d'or*, but, just as he's giving it to him, here comes another Cossack 'hurrah'. So, hastily saving 'the writing case with Sophie's letters, my sash and orders, uniform, spyglass, epaulettes, money and a few eatables such as coffee and sago' – he flings his valise back to his sergeant, and trudges on.

No one knows where Kutusov is, or what the Russians are doing. 'Not a single cavalry brigade' apart from the Guard Lancers and fragments of its other

'much reduced regiments remained in a state fit to cover our movements. Unless we took horses from the Guard we weren't strong enough even to make a reconnaissance at a distance or bold enough to get definite news of the enemy's whereabouts. Indeed we weren't even trying to.'

With Napoleon leaning on his arm, Caulaincourt sees all his direst prophesies about the Russian winter being fulfilled.

Le Roy, Jacquet and their Guillaume have gone on ahead, 'being no use to the regiment, where there were already as many officers as rankers'.

Besides, the 85th's newly fledged lieutenant-colonel has orders to return to its depot in France. Tramping onwards through the frozen wreckage of men and horses, caissons and field-forges with his Guillaume beside him 'holding my horse tied to his arm ... the poor beast gnawing such pine branches as came within his reach' Le Roy has reason and enough to reflect on his favourite philosophical theme – the vanity of life. Even his bitch quits him. 'I whistled. She came back, caressed me, went away again and disappeared.' This, in their present circumstances, is enough to make the usually so unemotional Le Roy, a man for whom a good night's sleep and a hearty breakfast had sufficed to get him over the shock of his son's death,[5] begin to wonder whether he too soon won't be 'a little hump, barely perceptible under the snow'. Won't 'some observer soon be saying "there's another fellow who'll never see his family again."?' So forcibly does the thought strike this highly professional soldier who'd begun his military career 'by chance but continued it by taste' that, despite stoic efforts to restrain his tender feelings, he begins 'sobbing silently, but so strongly that my poor Guillaume, thinking something must be amiss with me', tugs at his waistcoat, asks what's up:

'"Nothing," I said. "I'm done for [*rompu*]. Let's get going."'

Overtaking IHQ, he notices its personnel are expecting an enemy attack; and decides to make tracks for Krasnoië – and Vilna – as fast as ever he can.

Cossacks are at everyone's heels. Even of the Guard Artillery. One of Pion des Loches' subalterns, who'd lingered in company with another to 'drink a few glasses of hot wine' while he lightened his wagon 'his horses no longer being able to pull it', only rejoins his unit thanks to the fleetness of his steed and to report that his comrade has been 'Cossacked'; likewise that

'Captain Lavillette, marching at the convoy's tail to get two inadequately harnessed guns to follow on, had succumbed to the same fate. Thus in one day I lost two good officers, one for his having given in to a gourmand's temptation, the other for having been zealous in his duty.'

So hilly is the road and so far have the imperial carriages fallen behind Claparède's advance guard that IHQ overtakes them as they're struggling on at Korytnia. Three miles and an hour farther on they hear that the expected attack has materialised – against a small artillery park and the convoy that's been bringing back the Moscow trophies, together with

'the Emperor's carriages, which had just joined this park. The Cossacks had taken advantage of the moment when the column had halted to double up its teams so as to get up one of the steep icy slopes, thus opening a gap between the head and the rear, with the result that the small detachments guarding it hadn't been able to defend it as a whole.'

Kergorre's Treasury wagon is mixed up in the affray but escapes:

'A defile, approached by a narrow road across a little frozen lake, was blocked by the baggage train. Some vehicles had tried to get through it. The first had got across, but the others had fallen into the water. One of them was the wagon with trophies, among them the famous cross of the church of St John which Rostopchin had said Napoleon must never set eyes on, and which the latter had therefore had taken down from its bell tower.'[6]

Not merely do the Cossacks make off with upwards of a dozen horses, they even loot some of the imperial transport vehicles, whose terrified drivers upset them into the ravine and 'dropping everything that hampered their flight' have simply taken to their heels. 'The Cossacks scattered everything but took little,' Caulaincourt hears. 'It could almost all have been recovered if there hadn't been a second flurry at the column's head.' Among the wagons lost is 'the one containing the maps'. Likewise a not inconsiderable amount of the Imperial Treasure. Kergorre, who's already given up his own carriage to save a friend who'd straggled, estimates 10 millions – Denniée, doubtless more accurately, 1,294,000 gold francs. The artillery park has 'lost half its teams, and most of the IHQ officers their personal effects – myself', Caulaincourt adds succinctly, 'among them' – all this a mere six normal hours' march out of Smolensk.

Napoleon, the Master of the Horse notices, shows no annoyance with his servants for losing his maps. And the incident at least has one good effect. Everyone at once becomes

'more cautious. For 48 hours or so it brought back many who'd left the road. But such was our situation, one can't help asking oneself whether it was really a good thing to rally in wretches we couldn't feed' and who still further slow up the march. 'And we had to hurry.'

That morning Franz Roeder loses something – to him – far more precious. His inkpot. Relic of his beloved and deeply mourned Sophie, it has frozen and broken. 'So writing, too, will soon be at an end.'

If Napoleon and the Guard have left Korytnia precipitously and before daybreak (leaving a surprised Colbert to follow on with his lancers), it's been because of some alarming news. Fifteen hundred Russians under Ojarovski have just occupied Krasnoïe and 'carried off the remains of an Italian battalion and some dismounted troopers of Sébastiani's corps'. But then better news comes back. The Vistula Legion has flushed them out and secured the little timber-built market town of narrow streets perched on a hilltop.

Nowhere between Smolensk and Krasnoïe does Larrey see 'a single habitation. Everything had been burnt down.' But thanks to the Poles' prompt action Krasnoïe itself is intact. So, no less important, is the 'narrow trembling bridge' over the Krasnoïe ravine. Approached by a 'steep, boxed-in road with sharply sloping sides even more difficult because of the ice' – a serious bottle-neck – the ravine is only 30 paces wide.[7] As General Count *François Roguet,* commander of the Young Guard's 2nd Division, sees at a glance, 'no more favourable point could be imagined for holding up a retreating army'. Why hadn't Ojarovski blown it up?

Marching towards it the Guard encounters no opposition. But the IHQ carriages, going on ahead all too lightly escorted, do. As Mailly-Nesle's – the only one apart from Napoleon's own and those of a few other high-ups to have got so far – has still about a mile and a half to go to reach the ravine, its occupants see Russian light cavalry, 'with guns mounted on sledges, which helped them to aim at us':

'The Cossacks' hurrahs, the disorder being caused by roundshot and shells, the postillions' and drivers' shouts and the *cantinières'* shrill screams were causing everyone to lose his head. Everyone wanted to get away. The wheels get hooked into each other. Horses struggle. Carriages turn over.'

To Dedem's admiration his little female groom attacks a Cossack single-handed and grabs back his loot. But soon afterwards disappears for ever. Planat, following on with Lariboisière's remaining son Honoré in charge of his carriage and wagon, runs on

'ahead of the stragglers, who'd taken to their heels but some of whom had kept their muskets. I exhorted them not to scatter and to march slowly. As long as the Cossacks saw a gun or a bayonet, I said, they wouldn't attack. My efforts were fruitless. Each man sought his own safety in flight. This was the signal for the Cossacks' hurrah.'

Mailly-Nesle sees 'the enemy cavalry cross the road at a gallop, killing everything it meets with'.

'Honoré had already ordered our carriages to turn off by themselves to the right. Being well-harnessed, they quickly – by driving across country – reached a little village on the Krasnoië ravine. The little stream was completely frozen. The carriages crossed it easily. But the wagon, being much heavier, broke the ice and fell into the water to above its axles. Two of its four horses were drowned, and the lead horses were only saved by cutting the traces. All the artillery's papers were in this wagon and were lost.'

So are all Planat's personal belongings, all his diaries and years of correspondence. Mailly-Nesle is more fortunate; his carriage isn't attacked:

'A few infantry had come to our aid, restoring order among us and forcing the enemy to retire. M. Montaigu, an *officier d'ordonnance*, had climbed into our carriage. The Emperor and his Guard came up, and together we arrived in Krasnoië, where we parked in the square opposite the church. The air inside the carriage was so cold that our breath was falling in icy flakes.'

By the time the Lancer Brigade approaches Krasnoië in a 'calm and luminous evening' Dumonceau sees in the distance away to his left something more serious than Cossacks: namely, heads of Russian infantry columns debouching on to the high plateau that slopes toward the Losima stream. 'Already Ojarovski's corps was threatening the left of the Maleiwo road.' Napoleon, of course, has seen them too. Halting on the highway as the Guard's leading infantry units cross the shaky bridge and march up the icy incline toward Krasnoië, he orders Roguet

'to put his grenadiers into the houses of the town's eastern suburb. Leaving the road, the Emperor assembled the Old Guard's officers and NCOs and told them he wasn't going to see his grenadiers' bearskins in the midst of such disorder: "I'm counting on you to do great things, just as you can count on me.'"

When Rapp arrives. his head bruised by one musket ball and his horse having been killed by another, he tells him: "'Now you can stop worrying. You aren't going to be killed during this campaign."

"I hope Your Majesty's prophecy comes true. But you assured poor Lannes the same thing, yet he had to go to it."

"No, no, you won't be killed.'"

All Krasnoië's inhabitants have fled, and the Guard infantry packs itself into their houses. But the cavalry's sent off to find night quarters in the environs, and Dumonceau finds himself in the very same hamlet, six miles outside Krasnoië, that his men had occupied on 14 August.

At the bottle-neck at the ravine, meanwhile, a 'prodigious blockage of all kinds of vehicles' is piling up. Escorted by Kirgener's engineers, Boulart's Guard batteries reach it at nightfall and have to park and 'wait for three hours while men and horses ate what they could'. Time passes. Nothing budges. Only the Cossacks are still pressing in from the left. Finally Boulart, exasperated, quite simply decides to

'force my way through this disorderly mass of vehicles. Ordering all mine to follow, tightly closed up and leaving no gaps so as not to be cut off, I place myself at the head of our column. By dint of my men's main force I either straighten out those vehicles which are in my way or else overturn them. Moving slowly, either smashing or crushing everything in our way, and without for one moment allowing cries, shouts, tears or groans to arrest our march, after a thousand evils, the head finally reaches the bridge and gets through to the head of the jam.'

But even this isn't the end of his troubles:

'The road, it's true, is free; but thereafter it climbs sharply and the surface is icy. I have the ice spiked, some earth taken from the embankments of the road, which is here hollowed out of the hillside; throw the soil down in the middle of the road; manhandle the wheels, myself setting the example; and by hook or by crook get the vehicles one by one to the hilltop. Twenty times, going either up or down this hill, I fall heavily. An hour before dawn all my artillery's up there.'

For Pion des Loches, too, it's a terrible night:

'The guns could only pass one after another down the very steep slopes. We were on our feet all night; and it was morning before the turn came to my batteries.'

But Colonel Séruzier's already inside the town and has posted his horse artillery at the exit to every main or side street. By the time Boulart reports to a delighted Sorbier he's been given up for lost.

For Louise Fusil getting into Krasnoië is a traumatic experience. Caught outside with some of the other headquarters vehicles – among them, just ahead of her own, Narbonne's famous yellow carriage[8] – an officer advises her:

'"I fancy, Madame, the Cossacks are very close to us. Just now an officer came and spoke in a low voice to a wounded colonel who's been in my calèche. After stammering out his excuses he's got on horseback, even though he can hardly stay in the saddle."'

So Louise and her fellow-actresses have to get out of their carriage:

'Cannon balls were crossing the road, so we made up our minds, got on the horses and for lack of beaten paths made our way across country in the snow. The poor horses, who hadn't had anything to eat all day, were in it up to their bellies, and had no strength left. So here I am on horse-back, at midnight, no longer owning anything but what I have on me, not knowing which road to follow, and dying of cold. At 2 a.m. we reached the column [Boulart's?] that was dragging along some cannon. I asked the officer in command whether we had far to go to rejoin impe-rial headquarters. "Oh, easy on!" he said, annoyed. "We shan't be rejoin-ing it, because if we aren't taken prisoner tonight we shall be tomorrow morning. We can't escape."

'No longer knowing which way to go to get on, he halted his unit. The men wanted to light some fires to warm themselves; but he wouldn't let them, saying their campfires would give them away to the enemy. I got off my horse and sat down on some straw they'd laid out in the snow. There I experienced a moment of discouragement. But the coachman having recovered our carriage, we went on very slowly all night by the light of burning villages and the sound of gunfire. I saw unfortunate wounded men leaving the ranks. Some, exhausted by hunger, asked us for something to eat. Others, dying of cold, begged us to take them into the carriage, implored any help we could give them. But there were such a lot of them! Camp- followers implored us to take the children they no longer had the strength to carry – it was a desolating scene. One suf-fered both from one's own miseries and others'. When we were in sight of Krasnoië the coachman told me our horses could go no further. I got out, hoping to find IHQ in the town. It was just beginning to grow light. I followed the road the soldiers were taking and came to a very steep slope. It was like a mountain of ice, and the soldiers went sliding down it on their knees. Loth to do the same, I made a detour and got there safely.'

The decision to have IV, I and III Corps leave Smolensk at one-day inter-vals, Caulaincourt's thinking, 'shows how far the Emperor was deluding himself as to the army's situation and the dangers menacing it'. Above all the scheme is causing dangerous gaps to arise between the various corps. Already a first gap has opened up between the Guard and the Army of Italy. Leaving Smolensk in the early hours of 15 November, Eugène had delayed IV Corps' departure 'a good hour' by gathering all his non-walking wounded into one place and providing them with victuals. 'A wise mea-sure', in Cesare de Laugier's eyes; but one that gives rise to an agonising scene. The non-leavers had 'clenched their fists in despair, flung their arms round our legs, sobbed, screamed, clung to us, begged us to find them some means of transport:

'"For pity sake don't leave us to the Cossacks, to be burnt alive, be butchered as soon as they come in. Comrades, comrades, friends, for pity sake take us with you!"

'We go off with heavy hearts. Whereupon these unfortunates roll on the ground, lashing about as if possessed.'

Staggering to his feet before dawn after a sleepless night even colder than yesterday's, Griois had been horrified to discover he was half-blind from the smoke of his campfire. And when his last handful of guns had left the shattered city he'd been 'obliged to take the arm of a gunner' – he knows them all by name – 'who guided me'. After a while his sight had cleared, but he's still feeling very weak: 'the reverberation of the [light on the] snow and the prickings of an infinity of little needles of ice filling the air' make his eyes smart.

IV Corps too has abandoned most of its women 'whose sufferings only augmented our own'. And the groans and screams of deserted comrades, resounding in Cesare de Laugier and his comrades' ears 'a good part of the route', will only be forgotten 'at the thought of the new perils already surrounding us on all sides'. Pursuing its way in silence along the icy Kras-noië road, all he hears is

'the sound of blows to the horses or their drivers' curt oaths, frequent when they find they're on an icy slope they can't cope with. Again, despite the drivers' admirable zeal, were having to abandon vehicles, ammunition wagons and guns. Expiring horses covered the road, and entire teams, succumbing to exhaustion, fell all at once on top of each other. All the defiles the vehicles hadn't been able to get through were filled with arms, helmets, shakos and cuirasses; stove-in trunks, half-open valises, and clothes of all sorts were scattered in the valley.'

Laugier's shaken to see how the whole Krasnoië road is

'littered with ammunition wagons, carriages, abandoned guns no one has thought of blowing up, destroying, spiking or burning. Here and there, dying horses, weapons, all kinds of effects, pillaged trunks, evis-cerated packs are showing us the road followed by those ahead of us. We also see trees at whose foot men have tried to light a fire; and around their trunks, transformed into funerary monuments, the victims have expired after futile efforts to get warm.[9] The waggoners are using the corpses, numerous at every step, to pave the road by filling in ditches and ruts. At first we shudder at the sight; then we get used to it. Anyone who hasn't good horses and faithful servants with him will almost certainly never see his own country again. Far from exciting our sensibility, such horrors just hardened our hearts.'

The Guardia d'Onore's Colonel Battaglia having died on the eve of leaving Smolensk, Major Bastida has detailed Cesare de Laugier to the 'dangerous and most painful task of bringing up the regiment's rear and making sure no one straggles' – a task which 'furthermore made me a spectator of all our column's misfortunes'. Leaving Smolensk at the very last moment to chivvy on his vélites,

'and mounted on my exhausted horse, I'd hastened to rejoin. But not being rough-shod against the ice he kept falling. I saw Cossacks appearing to the left and on the heights around Smolensk and was afraid I'd become their prey.'

One of these falls dislodges the entire saddle and saddlecloth, but with 'hands numb with cold and freezing feet' he manages to fix them as best he can and starts 'running, holding my horse to get warm'. At every step the poor beast slithers on the ice which drags him this way and that and opens sores on his swollen feet. Catching up at long last with the column, Laugier entrusts his horse to a sapper named Maffei, with orders not to let him out of his sight. And that's the last Laugier sees of his horse or his few possessions.

Bivouacking for the night at 'the miserable village of Lubnia' where Napoleon, during the advance, had celebrated his 43rd birthday,[10] Eugène's staff occupy one of its two remaining half-demolished shacks, the Viceroy the other:

'Under a wretched shed, hardly covered, a score of officers, jumbled up with as many servants, crouched around a little fire. Behind us all the horses were ranged in a semi-circle to serve us as a shelter against the furiously blowing wind. The smoke was so thick we could hardly even see the faces close to the fire, busy puffing at the cinders where their food was cooking. The rest, wrapped up in furs and mantles and flat out on their bellies on the ground, were lying on top of each other so as not to feel the cold so much, and they only stirred in order to abuse anyone who trod on them; to curse the horses, which were moaning; or snuff out a fire some sparks had lit in their furs.'

Griois sees Eugène's hardly better lodged than his officers, and respects him for it:

'I found him lying on a wooden bench in a little partly destroyed cabin, the best preserved even so in the village. We passed a terrible night. An icy wind and whirlwinds of snow nothing protected us from kept us awake all the time; anyway the terrible cough Colonel Fiéreck was being tormented by would have been enough to prevent us from getting a wink of sleep.'

In the early part of the night they hear a man groaning outside the shack, 'but not one of us gave a thought to alleviating him by bringing him closer to our fire. To make a place for him would have been to disturb ourselves. And why take pity just on him, rather than on so many others no less wretched?'

MOVEMENTS OF THE VARIOUS CORPS, 13–20 NOVEMBER

Date	Guard	IV Corps	I Corps	III Corps	VIII Corps, V Corps and Vistula Legion
13	In Smolensk	Reaches Smolensk	Enters Smolensk		Leave Smolensk
14	Leaves Smolensk	Rearguard action on heights north of Smolensk	At Smolensk	Fights rearguard action east of Smolensk	At Korytnia
15	At Korytnia	Leaves Smolensk	At Smolensk		Vistula Legion ejects Russians from Krasnoïe
16	Evening; reaches Krasnoïe; Young Guard fights night action	At Korytnia Breaks through to Krasnoïe at night by *ruse de guerre*	Leaves Smolensk		At Krasnoïe
17	Young Guard's battle to defend Krasnoïe	In support of Young Guard	Breaks through to Krasnoïe and forms new rearguard	At Korytnia	Leave Krasnoïe with Treasure followed by Guard
18	Marching for Orsha	Marching for Orsha	Marching for Orsha	Ney, held up by Russians, marches for Dnieper and crosses by night	Reach Orsha
19	Marching for Orsha	Marching for Orsha	Marching for Orsha	Rearguard actions against Cossacks	At Orsha
20	At Orsha	At Orsha	Reaches Orsha	Early morning; Ney reaches Orsha	Leave Orsha for Toloczin and Bobr

CHAPTER 10

THE GUARD STRIKES BACK

A crucial decision – the Young Guard's night action – 'he was the worst man I've known, and the cruellest' – Eugène refuses to surrender – Colonel Klicki has his wits about him – the Iron Marshal loses his bâton – 'a snail, carrying my all on my back' – 'how about some apricots in brandy?' – the Young Guard's heroic battle – Davout breaks through – François saves the Eagle – 390 heroic Dutchmen – a courteous captor – massacre of the wounded – Kutusov talks to Intendant Puybusque – 'the baggage taken was enormous'

Having failed to exploit Napoleon's five-day halt at Smolensk, Kutusov is belatedly lining up some 90,000 men 'including 500 guns, well-mounted like their cavalry in strength'[1] along the low hills south of the Krasnoïe road. A totally out-matching force, that is, to cut off IV, I and III Corps.

Napoleon is faced with a crucial choice. What shall the Guard do? Abandon the rest of the army, hurry on to Orsha and seize the Dnieper bridges? Or make a stand that'll give Eugène, Davout, perhaps even Ney, a chance to catch up? Not once during the campaign has the Guard 'given' (*donné*), as the expression goes. Some people like von Kalckreuth are even wondering whether by dint of almost never fighting its pampered regiments haven't become 'mere parade ground troops'. Their 'only achievement in this campaign', Hencken thinks, has been 'to impress the enemy' – for instance at Borodino. Even there it hadn't been unleashed.[2] This is why the Young and Old Guards together still have upwards of 20,000 men,[3] and it's against just such a moment as this they've been conserved. They're going to teach the Russians a lesson.

Evidently Napoleon's plan is to stake all on a lightning blow with the entire Guard:

'Drouot's strong batteries had been placed in position, and everything was prepared for battle and he didn't doubt he'd succeed, believing, as in happier times, that his luck would hold. He was full of confidence in his veterans, whom he'd doubtless been keeping in reserve for just such a desperate venture.'

But prudence prevails. Caulaincourt sees him return to what, apparently, has been his original plan. A two-phase operation, more efficacious and less risky, especially in view of the hazards of a night operation. 'There's nothing more terrible than a battle at night,' Bourgogne knows, 'when fatal mistakes can often occur.'

That evening Napoleon sends for Rapp. Tells him:

'"We've Russian infantry quite close. So far they've not been so audacious. At midnight you must attack them at bayonet-point. Surprise them, and take away their taste for coming so close to my headquarters."'

Rapp has all the Young Guard[4] placed at his disposal. He returns to his headquarters 'a miserable house in the town, thatched with straw' and is just about to plan the movement when Narbonne appears; 'His Majesty doesn't want you to get yourself killed in this affair,' he tells him.

Mortier, the Young Guard's commander, is evidently more expendable. And it's he who's to take over in chief, while Roguet executes the actual movement. On guard outside Roguet's headquarters with fifteen Fusiliers-Grenadiers, Sergeant Bourgogne is congratulating himself on his 'luck to be under cover and near a fire we'd just lit' and has just put his men 'into a stable' when everything 'turns out quite otherwise'. The regiment is to take part in the night operation, together with Roguet's Grenadiers, the Fusiliers-Chasseurs, Voltigeurs and Tirailleurs. Although the Young Guard includes many veterans like Bourgogne and Paul Bourgoing of the 5th Tirailleurs, very few of its 18-year-old conscripts have ever been under fire before; and en route for Moscow thousands, for instance from the Flankers, have died of sheer physical exhaustion.[5] But at 9 p.m. comes the order to

'surprise and seize the villages of Chirkowa, Maliewo and Bouianowo, about three miles along the Smolensk–Krasnoië road and occupied over a distance of 400 *toises* [about 800 yards][6] by sizeable forces of infantry, artillery and Cossacks.'

'At 11 p.m.,' Bourgogne goes on, 'a few detachments were sent ahead to find out exactly where the Russians were. We could see their campfires in the two villages they were holding.' At about 1 a.m. Roguet comes to him and says 'in his Gascon accent:

'"Sergeant, leave a corporal and four men here in charge of my quarters and the few things I still have left. Yourself, go back to the bivouac and rejoin the regiment with your guard." To tell the truth I was very much disgusted at this order. I don't mean I was afraid of fighting, but I terribly begrudged the time lost for sleep.'

It's a pitch-black night. But Roguet's able to adjudge the enemy's position 'by the direction of his fires. The villages,' he'll recall, 'crowned a fine plateau behind a deep ravine. I formed up three columns of attack.' Some time between 1 and 2 a.m.[7] they get the order *'En avant! Marche!'*

'We began to move forward in three columns – the Fusiliers-Grenadiers and the Fusiliers-Chasseurs in the centre, the Tirailleur and Voltigeur companies to right and left. The cold was as intense as ever. With the snow up to our knees we had the greatest difficulty in marching across the fields.'

Trudging through it at the end of his rank Bourgogne hears several of his men muttering that they hope this'll be the end of their sufferings – they can't struggle on any longer. Roguet goes on: 'Noiselessly, the units to right and left got as close as they could to the enemy masses. Then, at a signal given by me in the centre, we, without firing, flung ourselves on the Russians at bayonet-point.'

Evidently the surprise isn't complete, for Bourgogne sees some Russian units have had time to form up:

'On our right a long line of infantry opened a murderous fire on us. On our left their heavy cavalry was made up of cuirassiers in white uniforms with black cuirasses. After half an hour of this, we found ourselves in the midst of the Russians.'

Roguet:

'Immediately the two wings engaged toward Bouianowo and Chirkowa. In the middle of the night it was so intensely cold that the Russians were exposed even in their shelters.'

The Fusiliers-Grenadiers, it seems, have no experience of Russian 'resurrection men'.[8] As the Young and Middle Guard move forward they pass over several hundred 'dead or seriously wounded' Russians lying on the snow:

'These men now jumped up and fired at us from behind, so we had to about-face to defend ourselves. Unluckily for them, a battalion in the rear came up from behind, so that they were taken between two fires. In five minutes not one of them was left alive.'

But neither are the Fusiliers-Grenadiers by any means unscathed:

'Poor Béloque was the first man we lost. At Smolensk he'd foretold his own death. A ball struck his head, and killed him on the spot. He was a great favourite with us all, and in spite of the indifference we were now feeling about everything, we were really sorry to lose him.'

'The fleeing Russians,' Roguet is noticing, 'though surprised and not knowing where to defend themselves' are 'moving from their right to their left.' As for the cuirassiers to Bourgogne's left,

'though they howled like wolves to excite one another, they didn't dare attack. The artillery was in the centre, pouring grapeshot at us. All this didn't in the least hold up our impetus. In spite of the firing and the number of our men who were falling, we charged on into their camp, where we made rightful havoc with our bayonets.'

By now, Bourgogne goes on,

'the Russians who were stationed farther off had had time to arm themselves and come to their comrades' help. This they did by setting fire to their camp and the two nearby villages. We fought by the light of the fires. The right- and left-hand columns had passed us, and entered the enemy's camp at its two ends, whereas our column had taken it in the middle.'

Divided and in disorder, the Russians have only had time to throw down their arms and fling their guns into the lake at the head of the Krasnoïe stream. And Roguet, judging it unwise to pursue the mass of fugitives too far in the dark, orders a cease-fire. But to order it in the darkness and confusion is one thing, to obtain it another. By now the Fusiliers-Grenadiers, in one of the burning villages the Russians are trying to get out of but can't, and 'blinded by the glare of the fires' have lost all idea of their whereabouts. And when some Russians who're on the verge of being roasted alive in a burning farmhouse offer to surrender, the Fusiliers-Grenadiers' adjutant-major, too, orders the cease-fire. But French blood is up, and a wounded sapper, 'sitting in the snow all stained with his blood', refuses:

'He even asked for more cartridges when he'd fired his own. The adjutant-major, seeing his orders disregarded, himself came over with a message from the colonel. But our men, now frantic, took no notice, and still went on firing.'

The trapped Russians, no less desperate, attempt a sortie,

'but our men forced them back. Unable to endure their situation, they made a second attempt. But scarcely had a few of their number reached the yard than the building collapsed on the rest, and more than 40 perished in the flames, those in the yard being crushed as well. When this was over we collected together our wounded and with loaded weapons gathered round the colonel, waiting for daybreak. All this time the rattle of musketry was going on continuously all round us, mingled with the groans of the wounded and dying.'

In the grey dawn Bourgogne helps a dying Russian to a more comfortable position. The man had tried to kill him, but in the nick of time he'd shot and badly wounded him, after which he'd been run through by adjutant-major Roustan's sword:

'All the houses in the village and the entire Russian camp were covered with half-burnt corpses. The Tirailleurs and Voltigeurs had lost more men than we had. After this bloody contest the Russians abandoned their positions, and we remained on the battlefield, but all the time staying on the *qui-vive*, unable either to get a moment's rest or even warm ourselves.'

Then, in the Fusiliers-Grenadiers' freezing bivouac, something very odd happens:

'After daybreak, while we were all talking together, Adjutant-Major Delaître came up. He was the worst man I've ever known and the cruellest, doing wrong for the mere pleasure of doing it. I don't think there was a man in the regiment who wouldn't have rejoiced to see him carried off by a bullet. We called him Peter the Cruel.'

But now Delaître begins to talk, and

'greatly to our surprise, seemed much troubled by Béloque's tragic death. "Poor Béloque!" he said. "I'm very sorry I ever behaved badly to him." Just then a voice said in my ear (*whose* voice I never knew): "He'll die very soon." Others heard it too. He seemed sincerely sorry for all his nasty behaviour to those under him, especially to us NCOs.'

It's this shock that is enabling Napoleon to wait for Eugène, for Davout, and – hopefully – even for Ney. It has also served notice on Kutusov that the name he's so afraid of is still really to be feared. The Imperial Guard, at least, can still bite back.

At crack of dawn IV Corps – 'scarcely 4,000 men under arms' – but 'in hope of being better off tomorrow night'[9] – makes haste to leave its icy bivouac at Lubnia. All Griois now possesses is his sole surviving change of shirt and, as a last possible recourse, a precious loaf of white bread given him at

Smolensk by General Desvaux, commander of the Guard Horse Artillery. Cesare de Laugier's doing his best to keep up with the slowly trudging column, when

'a man, passing close at a canter, knocks me over, and in my fall my cold sores open up. There I lie, stunned by the shock, mad with rage and realising how powerless I am, unable to stir. Two Italian soldiers who've fallen behind pick me up and lay me on the bank to the right of the road. I feel all my blood freezing, see death approaching, and gradually lose consciousness.'

But his luck holds. A Frenchman named Dalstein, also a captain-adjutant-major and serving with the Italians, sees him lying there; brings him to; encourages him; forces him to get up and come along with him.

All that morning IV Corps marches slowly on without meeting any particular obstacles. 'The weather was fine,' Griois goes on,

'the cold less keen, and the sun, despite the pallor of its rays, was cheering up the snow-covered countryside a little. It was about midday. I'd dismounted at a place where the debris of carriages, weapons and effects showed there'd been a recent hurrah, and while walking onwards I was running my eye over some papers I'd picked up, when two or three roundshot whistled past my ears. They came from a little wood, not far to our left. We saw the puffs of smoke but as yet no unit had appeared. At this unexpected attack everyone rallied to the nearest platoons – but just at the moment no one was expecting to run into the enemy. There was little order in our column, which was widely spread out over the terrain.'

Griois immediately jumps on to his horse and joins Eugène, 'who was quite a way ahead of his troops and waiting for them', accompanied, Labaume says,

'by his staff, some companies of sappers and some Sailors of the Royal Guard who were going on a couple of miles ahead of the divisions.'

Soon Cossacks appear from the woods and cover the high ground to right and left. The gunfire multiplies. Then – Labaume gives the time as 3 p.m. –

'the Viceroy catches sight of the disbanded and isolated men who've been marching ahead of him and occupying the road for a great distance running back. They're being attacked by Cossacks.'

Among those who come galloping back is General Count Ornano, now without any of his Bavarian cavalry, but who's 'been wounded or thrown off his horse'.[10] They'd found the road barred by a body of troops. Eugène turns his horse, gallops back to his main body, halts its column and, haranguing it, explains what a critical position it's in. Immediately, says Cesare de Laugier,

'all who've a weapon, though devoured by fever or annihilated by the cold, come and take their place in the ranks. And the Viceroy deploys his battalions.'

He also does what he did at the Wop, but this time with greater difficulty:

namely, scrapes together some ranks of mounted officers to look like cavalry, von Muraldt among them:

'But a few roundshot falling among us broke us up. After which, in open order. we rode over the snowy icy field, trying to find a hollow to protect us from the enemy's fire.'

Meanwhile chief-of-staff Guilleminot has assembled into companies all the advance party of isolated men who still have weapons, so that together with his sappers and sailors they add up to 1,200 men. 'The disbanded men, administrators and even the women' – evidently some haven't been left behind at Smolensk – 'come pressing in on them from all around. Superior officers who have no men are seen proudly joining the ranks.' The sailors insist on being commanded by one of their own officers, 'but every other platoon is commanded by a general'. One against ten, they're being bombarded by Russian guns and musketry from the surrounding high ground.

What to do? To press on is impossible. After a council of war, Guilleminot, seeing no sign of the main body yet coming to his aid, decides to fall back on to it. Forms up his little force in square – and marches straight through the intervening Russians!

'At first the Russians, stupefied, open up a path for them. Then call out to them to halt. Their only reply is resolutely to continue their march in a disdainful silence, only presenting the points of their weapons. Whereupon all the enemy fire opens up on them at once; and after a few paces half this heroic column litters the ground. The remainder pursue their way in good order – a truly incredible outcome for a force composed of such heterogeneous elements.'

They're welcomed with the Italians' joyful shouts. Seeing that the road passes through a wood, Eugène, to fend off the Cossacks, orders Guilleminot to collect the disbanded men in it, together with his sapper companies and the marines. At that moment, according to Laugier and Ségur,

'a Russian officer, Colonel Prince Kudacheff, Miloradovitch's ADC, preceded by a trumpeter sounding for a parley, comes forward towards the Viceroy's group. The Emperor and the Imperial Guard, he tells them, have been defeated the previous evening:

'"You're surrounded by 20,000 Russians, supported by Kutusov's entire army," he says. "Nothing remains for you but to surrender on the honourable conditions Miloradovitch proposes."

'Already several officers, to prevent the Viceroy being recognised, are going forward to answer. But he thrusts them aside:

'"Hurry back to where you've come from," he tells the spokesman, "and tell whoever's sent you that if he has 20,000 men, we've got 80,000!" And the Russian, at the sight of this handful of such proud men, astounded at such a reply, retired.'[11]

'At the sound of the guns,' Griois goes on,

'the troops hastened their steps, and as they turned up the prince

157

formed them up in line of battle. Detached, my gunless gunners act as tirailleurs and draw up the guns which still remained to IV Corps – i.e., the two or three belonging to the Broussier division, served by my regiment, and six or eight of the Italian Guard's.'

Meanwhile Eugène has placed the Royal Guard in the centre of IV Corps, the 2nd [14th] Division (comprising what's left of the 2nd and 4th Battalions of the Spanish Joseph-Napoleon Regiment)[12] to the left of the road, and the 1st [13th] Division to the right, with Pino's [15th] Division in reserve, all in squares. Attacked first by cavalry, then bombarded by a much stronger artillery than he can muster – by now Eugène only has two guns left – he 'sends the Royal Guard to attack the Russians' right flank'. Repulsed by 'terrible' grapeshot, decimated and forced to retire, it again forms square to drive off an attack by dragoons against its left flank. The Russian masses are far too great to be fought off without artillery. Even the two Italian guns only manage to fire a few rounds 'for lack of ammunition'. Whereupon Eugène 'orders [his ADC] Adjutant-Commandant Del Fante, followed by 200 volunteers, to advance along the highway to rejoin and cover the retreating 1st Division.' Del Fante succeeds, but falls, seriously wounded:

> 'M. de Villebranche, an auditor of the Council of State, seeing him get up all covered in blood, offers him his arm and helps him drag himself to a wood where there are some disbanded men. At that moment a roundshot hits the brave Del Fante, shatters his shoulders and decapitates M. de Villebranche.'[13]

All his men are massacred. 'As for the gunners, they let themselves be killed at their guns rather than surrender.' Having run into such a wall of fire, Labaume says, Eugène is forced

> 'to pretend to wish to prolong the fighting on our left by re-animating and uniting the 14th [Broussier's] Division. And upon the Russians concentrating the greater part of their forces to roll it up, the Prince ordered all who remained to profit by the failing daylight to slip away to the right with the Royal Guard.'

Despite the Russians' huge numerical superiority and considerable losses, IV Corps flushes them out of the woods.

> 'We gained ground against them. But new enemies appeared, outflanking us on all sides. Their crossfire and the charges of their cavalry, which we had none of our own to oppose, caused us to suffer a lot.'

But November days are short, and by 4 p.m. the light is failing:

> 'We kept up the fight until nightfall without being driven in. It was high time. One more hour of daylight and we'd probably have been wiped out.'

All this happens so near to Krasnoïe that Napoleon, 'uneasy at IV Corps' delayed arrival' but hearing the gunfire, has ordered his ADC General Durosnel to take 600 men – two squadrons of the Polish Guard Lancers and a battalion of Old Guard light infantry, with two guns, and facilitate

Eugène's breakthrough. Just outside Krasnoïe Durosnel runs into Cossacks and sees masses of Russian cavalry 'marching to the left of the road to manoeuvre more easily'. Forms square. Fires a few shots. Sends off three of his Polish lancers to circumvent the Krasnoïe ravine and tell Eugène to do the same. And marches on. But then he too runs into such massive opposition that, realising he's done all he can, he beats a retreat back to Krasnoïe:

'The Emperor was perturbed at the thought of part of his Guard being in action and cut off from the main body of the army.'

Durosnel gets back just as Latour-Maubourg and all that's left of the cavalry is about to set off to his relief. Delighted at this detachment's safe return, Napoleon invites Durosnel to supper.

By now some of Pino's Italians and Dalmatians, waiting behind as rearguard, are feeling so discouraged that they refuse to leave their campfires. So do the fragments of the improvised 'cavalry':

'In vain we were told the crucial thing was to try to deceive the Russians as to our camp's position – our most urgent need was for fire to protect us against the biting cold. Our situation was desperate anyway. We were expecting to be taken prisoner on the morrow and our only hope lay in a reasonable capitulation. Our despondency was also the worse for a rumour that the Emperor had left Krasnoïe with his Guard, abandoned us to our fate.'

The order goes round: 'No campfires!' Even so, IV Corps is soon in trouble again with Cossacks who can easily pick out its black mass against the snow. And fires, though forbidden, glimmer faintly, so that in the grim freezing night one or another roundshot keeps falling among them. 'The enemy', Griois resumes,

'was only 600 yards off. He was occupying the road we must follow and was only waiting for morning to bring about our final defeat. Overwhelmed by cold and hunger, regarding retreat as impossible and our loss as certain, we were anxiously waiting to see what course the Viceroy would adopt, when, towards 10 p.m., the order was passed down *sotto voce* to form the ranks and get going, and Prince Eugène, at the head of the Royal Guard, followed by some debris of [the other] battalions, marched off into the night. There was no need to recommend silence; each of us realised it unbidden.'

Eventually the secret night march gets under way:

'In this march across the fields, over thick snow, in profound darkness, one hardly heard some raucous but stifled coughs the men couldn't suppress, and the clickings of their weapons against each other during their frequent falls.'

For the second time in two days the Italians have to leave their wounded behind, this time lying on the blood-stained snow:

'A former vélite named Vignali, whose comrade I'd been when I'd entered that unit, had had his side shattered by a roundshot. I'd have given my life to save him, but there was no vehicle nor anyone willing to help me carry him. Each movement I made to help him caused him a frightful spasm of pain. "It's impossible," he said. "I'll never move again. Do me the kindness of finishing me off with a shot, or pass your sabre through my body so I die instantly."'

But this is more than Cesare can bring himself to do. Exhausted by his efforts, he's obliged to leave him: 'My eyes close as I remember it, I still fancy I can hear his sad complaints, his voice which broke my heart.'[14] By now almost nothing is left of those 'scions of the best families in Italy', the once ardent Vélites of the Guardia d'Onore. Griois too has to 'abandon the little baggage and artillery we still possessed'. The column hasn't gone very far when

'an enemy sentinel, placed at some distance to our left, gave us the *Qui vive?* in Russian. We'd been detected, and each of us made ready to give a hot reception to the hurrah which would doubtless soon fall on us.'

Labaume – he can only have been a few feet away – takes up the thread of Griois' account:

'Colonel Klicki,[15] who knew Russian, was marching at the head of our column when he was halted by an enemy scout who, in Russian, called out to him *"Qui vive?"* This didn't trouble this intrepid officer in the least. Going straight up to the sentry, he said to him in his own language: "Shut up, you fool. Can't you see we're Ouvarov's corps and that we're off on a secret expedition?" At these words the soldier fell silent and let us pass under cover of night.'

But now the moon's up, brightly illumining the wide snowy expanses. Griois and everyone else is sure the Russians must see them:

'In its bright light, which in any other circumstances would have been so useful to us but was increasing our perils, didn't the enemy easily see our column standing out against the snow's whiteness?'

In fact, Cossacks do approach, but 'probably believing we were troops of their own nation' don't interfere. And in the dim dawn light the Italian infantry again sets off, 'without knowing whither'. Hurriedly its few remaining mounted officers attach themselves to it,

'following the dark line winding away across the snow. For a while this march went on in perfect silence. After an hour or two we, after a left turn, rejoined the main Krasnoïe road, leaving the enemy behind us. A discharge of musketry received us at the town's approaches. It was an outpost placed out ahead of the Young Guard's bivouac that, taking us for an enemy, had fired at us. We declared ourselves and reached the foot of the rather steep hill where Krasnoïe's situated.'

The weather, it seems, is thawing slightly – the ice on the Losima, flowing through the ravine, keeps breaking. Although Griois' horse gets across all right, his adjutant-major Lenoble's doesn't:

'The ice broke beneath him and the poor animal, stuck in the mud up to his breast, struggled for over half an hour, and after we'd tried in vain to save him we had to abandon him, to the great regret of his master, who lost in a puddle of water a handsome and good horse which the

Above: A Cossack *pulk* prepares to swoop from high ground. Their blood-curdling 'hurrahs!' (the Cossack word for 'death') caused the French to call them sarcastically '*les hourrassiers*'. Though the least show of resistance sufficed to drive them off, they starved the Grand Army to death by forcing it to keep to the road. Lithograph by Engelmann after a drawing by Lebach.

Below: Nothing had changed on the field of Borodino except the aspect of the dead. The Belgian captain François Dumonceau saw that the former redoubts, 'covered in snow and standing out white against a murky horizon, were no longer visible except as shapeless hillocks. This plain, once so noisy and animated, was now only a vast solitude.' Engraving by Faber du Faur.

Above: The Battle of Viazma, 3 November. Carabinier Sergeant Vincent Bertrand of the 7th Light Infantry was in Davout's rearguard, seen in the background. The church [right] must have been the one where Napoleon, during the advance, had insisted on Guard grenadiers attending the bishop of Viazma's funeral obsequies. Oil painting by V. Adam.

Opposite page, top: Witebsk. Hopping about on one leg, its governor, F. R. Pouget, found it impossible to defend, certainly not with the 900 'marauders, stragglers and men out of hospitals' at his disposal: 'the refuse of all the armies, the most furtive, dirtiest and worst soldiers in the world. Clad in rags and shreds of clothing, without either officers or NCOs, most of them had never seen the enemy.'

Right: 'En route near Pnewa, 8 November. Do you recognize the man in the grey coat,' the artist Major Faber du Faur asks us in doggerel verse, 'that gleaming meteor who so often had led us to war and victory and who alone was wearing a fur-brimmed cap? It's the Emperor!' – 'Yesterday I'd been the conqueror of the world', Napoleon would tell his Council when he got back to Paris, 'and commanding the finest army of modern times. Next day nothing was left of all that.'

Opposite page, top: Smolensk: 'The heights it stood on', J. T. James would see in 1813, 'shewed the domes of the venerable cathedral majestically over their summit. But this building stood almost single amidst heaps of ruins. The main street, the great square, all had suffered the same destruction.' *Views of Russia, Sweden and Poland,* 1824.

Above: Württemberg gunners destroying most of the cannon that by dint of great efforts they had dragged as far as Smolensk (12 November). One of Smolensk's 32 towers can be glimpsed in the background. Next year J. T. James would see French and allied artillery of all calibres 'beginning with the heaviest' on display outside the Kremlin. Engraving by Faber du Faur.

Left: 'Between Korytnia and Krasnoïe, 15 November.' After spiking their last four 6-pounders, the remains of the 25th (Württemberg) division and a horde of unarmed men and women forced their way past Miloradovitch's 'dark lines' to join the Imperial Guard at Krasnoïe. Engraving by Faber du Faur.

Right: The second battle of Krasnoië, 17/18 November. The anonymous artist has focused on the wreckage of the baggage train, pillaged by Cossacks. It was here Davout lost his bâton – only for someone to filch it mysteriously during the victory celebrations at St Petersburg! Nineteenth-century steel engraving.

Below: Grenadier Pils' on-the-spot watercolour of Marshals Oudinot and Victor on a gloomy overcast November afternoon as they try – but signally fail – to coordinate II and IX Corps' movements.

Right: Portrait, painted on a mug, of Captain Franz Roeder of the Hessian Footguards. A temperamental stickler for justice and humanity, he wrote the most vividly personal of all surviving diaries. By kind permission of Miss Helen Roeder.

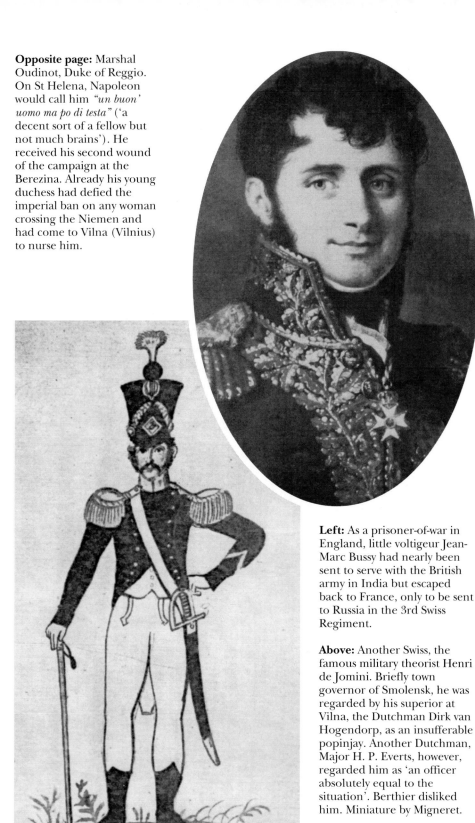

Opposite page: Marshal Oudinot, Duke of Reggio. On St Helena, Napoleon would call him *"un buon' uomo ma po di testa"* ('a decent sort of a fellow but not much brains'). He received his second wound of the campaign at the Berezina. Already his young duchess had defied the imperial ban on any woman crossing the Niemen and had come to Vilna (Vilnius) to nurse him.

Left: As a prisoner-of-war in England, little voltigeur Jean-Marc Bussy had nearly been sent to serve with the British army in India but escaped back to France, only to be sent to Russia in the 3rd Swiss Regiment.

Above: Another Swiss, the famous military theorist Henri de Jomini. Briefly town governor of Smolensk, he was regarded by his superior at Vilna, the Dutchman Dirk van Hogendorp, as an insufferable popinjay. Another Dutchman, Major H. P. Everts, however, regarded him as 'an officer absolutely equal to the situation'. Berthier disliked him. Miniature by Migneret.

The émigré Count L. V. L. Rochechouart served with Tchitchakov's army. He played a part in wresting the Borissow bridge from Dombrowski's 17th (Polish) division, only to be almost trapped in Borissow town by Oudinot's advance guard and swept away by Doumerc's Cuirassiers on 18 November.

Marshal Michel Ney, Duke of Elchingen, Prince of the Moscova, hero of the retreat. By rejoining at Orsha with the remains of his rearguard 'he had executed', wrote Captain François – the 'Dromedary of Egypt' – 'one of the finest and most courageous movements ever attempted by so feeble a corps. It would be to show oneself lacking in the esteem every military man ought to have for Marshal Ney not to recognize his rare talents.' But Colonel Montesquiou de Fezensac was shocked at his lack of feeling for others' sufferings.

Below: Marshal Macdonald, commander of X Corps, two-thirds of which were Prussians. He was of Jacobite ancestry. In late December his Prussian subordinate General Yorcke signed a convention of neutrality with the enemy that triggered off a Prussian rising against the French.

Above: General Count de Lorencez, Oudinot's chief-of-staff. They had married two sisters on the eve of the campaign. Lorencez strongly defends Oudinot's strategies and handling of the preliminaries to the Berezina crossing.

enemy's fire had so often respected. Half way up the hill we met the Guard artillery, Colonel Drouot at its head, on its way to take up position on the Smolensk road we were arriving by.'

General Triaire, commanding Eugène's rearguard, keeps halting and facing about. As usual, the Cossacks don't dare attack. Half an hour after the wreckage of IV Corps has joined up with the Young Guard a mile and a half outside Krasnoïe, Triaire's men finally catch up,

'and you can imagine our joyful surprise, when without realising how it had happened, we suddenly caught sight of a town lit up by bivouac fires and immediately afterwards of the Imperial Guard's familiar bearskins.'

In fact the whole market town's a blaze of light:

'There were twenty times as many people in it than it could contain. Also, the brightness of the lights shining out through each house's doorways and windows, the noise the soldiers were making, the considerable number of those less happy ones who had had to camp out of doors,'

all this at once removes any thoughts Griois and three of his fellow-officers may have had of finding shelter. Worn out, shivering to death, they slip in among the crowd on the market place

'near a bivouac of élite gendarmes [headquarters police], where several assembled beams of wood made up a sparkling fire. The expression on the faces of the gendarmes as they saw four obviously suffering and needy officers approach was hardly encouraging. But it wasn't the moment to be sensitive, and despite their patent ill will we occupied the ends of the beams. We could hardly even see the fire, but in revenge the wind blew all its smoke at us.'

How inhospitable can one be? The gendarmes spread out and consume whole cooking pots full of soup, round off their meal with ample coffee, tea and wine. 'Such was the degree of insensibility we'd reached,' adds Griois forgivingly, 'we, in their place, would probably done the same.' Only when his servant turns up with a *konya* can they mix themselves some rye flour and scarcely boiled water before wrapping themselves up in their ragged furs and getting a little sleep.

Davout too must be rescued. Perhaps also Ney. But just how far in the rear is I Corps and how big is the gap between them? No one knows.

Davout too had delayed leaving Smolensk at dawn on 16 November. Adjudging it 'vitally important to provision his troops in order to prevent them deserting, he hadn't regarded it as his duty to hurry'. And when I Corps had marched out it, too, had dragged with it masses of stragglers. Outside 'the same ramparts as earlier had witnessed our triumph' Lejeune had seen 'an immense quantity of guns, all parked and having to be abandoned to the enemy' – those taken from Sauvage's regiment perhaps among them. Along the road to Lubnia 'entirely covered with guns and ammunition no one had had time to spike or blow up', through the cluttered defiles, marching, riding, slithering or trundling over the corpses of predecessors which would 'have entirely obstructed the road if they hadn't so often been used to fill up ditches and ruts' its chief-of-staff Lejeune sees 'trees receding into the distance, at which soldiers had tried to light a fire' but died while doing so. 'We saw them in their dozens around some green branches they'd vainly tried to ignite.'

Once I Corps had been 'a rival to the Guard'. But since the Viazma débâcle its morale is prey to 'an egoism not yet seen in the French armies'. And when a swarm of Don Cossacks swoops on its baggage train its drivers do as IHQ's had done – 'unharness their horses and make off with the most precious contents'. Among vehicles lost in this way is Davout's personal wagon, containing his Marshal's bâton, clad in purple velvet and beswarmed with imperial gold bees. Also a now wholly redundant map of India.[16]

One of the fugitives who tries to rejoin 'across fields, woods and precipices', with his two remaining wagons ('naturally enough, seeing they each contained part of my resources') – one his unit's accounts wagon, the other the property of his colonel – is Lieutenant *N. J. Sauvage*, of the Train.[17] After an hour and a half he meets up with his 'most zealous protector and most faithful companion' Captain Houdart:

'Like many others he'd been relieved of the vehicles he'd been trying to save. All his booty was his two horses and a little portmanteau. More fortunate than myself, he'd extracted from one wagon a little barrel containing almost a gallon of brandy I'd been keeping in reserve since Moscow. At our first encounter we looked each other in the eye without knowing what to say. Each looked to the other like a fox who'd eaten his hen.'

Ever since Doroghoboui Sauvage has foreseen that he'll lose his effects . So he too is troubled. What upsets him most is 'the loss of victuals all the gold in the world couldn't replace'. After a couple of swigs the two Train officers have just joined the ever-swelling column of isolated men when, noticing that the plain to their left is covered with Russian cavalry, they, 'like everyone else who'd just abandoned more than 80 vehicles of all kinds containing a large part of the staff's treasures' hurriedly join 'two companies of engineer sappers, 140–150 men in all' already drawn up to the right of the road.

'Already formed up in square, they were being charged by four strong columns of Cuirassiers of the Russian Guard.'

Houdart manages to get inside the square with his two horses, but Sauvage has to abandon his *konya* Coco, counts himself lucky to get in at all, even though he's half crushed to death. Attacked on all its four faces, the gallant sappers fend off the four cuirassier squadrons,

'at the front rank's bayonet tips, which remained immovable, whilst the second and third ranks, though their muskets often misfired, kept up a well-nourished fire, flinging their murderous lead at the Muscovite troopers. These, unable to penetrate the square, and after briefly slashing at the defenceless mass, have to retire, leaving more than 50 of their corpses along the square's faces.'

Sauvage is just getting out of the square again when, 25 yards away, he sees his Coco calmly nibbling at a few blades of straw sticking up through the snow half way between it and the rallying Russian squadrons. He's just making a dash to grab her when he hears the order given for a new charge – thinks better of it – and nips back into the square, which had already got under way again. 'So in less than two hours I'd lost horse, portmanteau and trunks, and found myself reduced to the lot of the snails, unembarrassed and carrying my all on my back.'

Not all Davout's men are as resolute. Some individuals in a detached body that's making its way back in hopes of joining up with Ney even let themselves be enticed with the spoils of the Korytnia affray, 'brandy, peaches and liqueurs, biscuits from Reims, apricots in brandy, and spiced bread, all destined for the Emperor's table'. Among the happy captors of 'a wagon containing 60,000 gold napoleons' are four Russian officers – 'one had got drunk and lost all his share during the night!' But though some of Davout's men are enticed to lay down their arms, the head of the column, 'consisting of 300 or 400 officers' goes on its way 'to shouts of *Vive Napoléon!*' The Russians couldn't help admiring their devotion, for their loss was certain.'

But it takes all sorts to make a world. Ever since Mojaisk, von Roos has had his eye on a certain German light infantry officer who, though dragging with him a whole wagon-load of tea – 'as one transports grain' – has only been letting his batman brew it out of used tea leaves! But now, Roos is glad to see, poetic justice is done: the Cossacks take both the German and his tea.

At Krasnoië, meanwhile, the Guard has fallen in, ready to fall back at first glimpse of I Corps coming down the Smolensk road. This makes accommodation suddenly available for Griois and his three friends, who're able 'to enter one of the houses they were abandoning and get warm'. But the Red Lancers, ordered to be at Krasnoië before daybreak, have left their hamlet, reach their rendezvous on the town's eastern outskirts, and find

'the Imperial Guard already drawn up under arms. Its fires had been doused. All we could make out in the profound darkness was confused crowds, motionless. A lot of men seemed to have caught colds, because all round us we heard dull coughing. Riding past them we were led ahead to the left of the town; then drew up in line of battle, facing the enemy, whose fires could be seen afar off on the other bank of the Losima stream.'

It's the whole Russian army, Dumonceau hears, that's in presence, outflanking the French position, whose front is the frozen brook. He also hears how yesterday, thanks to the Middle Guard's night action at Kontkovo, Eugène had broken through. It's still pitch dark.

The Hessian Footguards have been standing to arms since 3 a.m. Franz Roeder sees his own company (originally 442 men and 26 officers) is now down to only seven sergeants and 27 men, and the Prince's Own to 450 men and 23 officers. 'What a brigade of Guards, of only four battalions!' Yet, he consoles himself, 'we're much stronger than the French units!' And now the great moment – the climax, from his point of view, of the whole voluntarily undertaken campaign – has come. With the rest of the Young Guard the Hessians are to fall back along the Smolensk road and form Napoleon's battle front. Taking his personal dispositions Roeder writes a brief farewell letter to Sophie, his second wife, who's providing a mother for his and his deeply loved Mina's children. Generously he presents Prince Wittgenstein with a Göttingen sausage he's come by, 'so that he might have something for [the 20-year-old] Prince Emil[18] in the impending battle.' Then Roeder too, with many of his men dropping from fatigue, trudges back out into the snow along the Smolensk road, and 'after two hours', drawing up by battalions in line of battle to the left of the highway and suffering terribly from the cold and feeling drowsy 'probably from hunger' stands there until 8 a.m.

Paul de Bourgoing has fought in Spain and witnessed the appalling vestiges of Borodino. But this, he realises, is going to be his first real battle. And as ADC to General Delaborde, commander of the Young Guard's 1st Division, he must live up to his romantic role.[19] Before riding out of Krasnoïë on a captured mare he has re-christened Grisélidis, he has therefore shed his thick fox fur and entrusted it to his plucky little servant Victor:

'The battlefield was an immense snow-covered plain, crossed by a long and deep ravine, almost parallel with our front. On this escarpment's very steep bank, fading away in the distance, were placed, to our left, a Hessian brigade, by now reduced to 500 or 600 men. Our line extended for about a mile and a half almost parallel with this ravine, its right resting on Krasnoïë. In the centre, two regiments of the same strength, the 1st Tirailleurs and the 1st Voltigeurs. Then, to our right, a battalion of the Dutch [3rd] Grenadiers. Mortier, his staff, his escort of Red Lancers and his squadron of Portuguese cavalry commanded by the Marquis de Loulé had placed themselves out in front of this long line of infantry.'

To impress, if possible, the Russians the front has been

'extended out of all measure by placing our men in two ranks instead of three, thus presenting to the enemy a line of battle lengthened by one-third, but proportionately weakened in the event of a hand-to-hand fight'.

A few yards away from the Hessians are the Fusiliers-Grenadiers:

'To our left and behind us a ravine lay athwart the highway. This hollow sheltered all those who were near it. On our right were the Fusiliers-Chasseurs, with the head of their regiment a gunshot from the town. In front of us, 250 yards off, was a regiment of the Young Guard commanded by General Luron. Still farther to our right were the Old Grenadiers and Chasseurs, commanded by the Emperor, on foot.'

Chlapowski too, in his escort, sees how

'the whole mass was commanded by the Emperor himself, on foot. Walking with firm steps, as if on a grand parade day, he placed himself in the centre of battlefield, facing the enemy's batteries.'

164

Always, on days of battle, Dumonceau seems fated to enjoy some perfect vantage point. As it has grown light he has seen how the Young Guard's regiments, 'supported by a few guns' already in position, are fringing the Losima's semi-circular valley. And how, somewhat nearer the town's exit, the heads of the Old Guard infantry columns are drawn up. Out ahead of them, 'detached at the bottom of the ravine, at the village of Ouwarowo, whose defence had been confided to it and recognisable by their sky-blue greatcoats' over their white and scarlet uniforms, are the Dutch (3rd) Grenadiers.

Now an hour has gone by. And at about 9 a.m. Roeder sees some Russian units, mostly artillery, approach and draw up in front of his Hessians. All along the line it's the same. Artillery, artillery, artillery. The Russian plan is simply to wipe the Young Guard out with cannon fire. And after half an hour more the Russians open up at the Hessians across the snowy plain with

'about ten guns and two howitzers. We were especially exposed to the fire of a battery of some six pieces lying a little to the left, which never stopped firing at us and with great violence.'

Within half-range of the Russian artillery almost the first Fusilier-Grenadier to fall is the man who's always enjoyed making life hell for everyone else – the sadistic Adjutant-Major Delaître. 'He was leading his horse, the bridle over his right arm' and Bourgogne and two of his friends are immediately behind him:

'A roundshot had taken off his legs just above the knees and his long riding-boots. He fell without a cry. Didn't utter the least sound. We halted. Since he was blocking the path we were walking on we were forced to step over him to get on at all. I, the first to do so, looked at him as I passed on. His eyes were open and his teeth were chattering convulsively. I came closer to listen. Raising his voice, he said: "For God's sake take my pistols and blow my brains out!" No one dared do him this service. Without replying we went on our way – most luckily, as it happened: for we hadn't gone six yards before a second discharge carried off three of our men behind us, and killed the Adjutant-Major.'

Of all the cavalry regiments, the Polish Guard Lancers, Zalusky notices, are the most numerous. The rest, all that still have mounts, are standing beside their horses, 300–400 yards away behind them and their Dutch colleagues,

'in columns of fours. Like ourselves they were on the crest of the plateau, so as to stand out at a distance. Seen in flank they seemed to be a considerable mass of cavalry. Finally, ahead of them, to our left rear, was the Viceroy's corps, massed at the limit of the plateau, facing the point at which the road debouched along which the retarded corps should be arriving. All we could see of the enemy was some isolated horsemen in the distance, criss-crossing the vast snowy plain that spread out in front of us like an amphitheatre. As yet their masses were hidden from our gaze by some folds or other accidents of the terrain.'

It's on the Smolensk road and the high ground in front of Krasnoïë, of course, that Napoleon's and his staff's telescopes are focused. Surely the head of Davout's column must soon appear?

'But instead of seeing the Marshal arrive all we saw in the direction of Smolensk were deep columns of the Russian army. They were beginning to surround us to the south, while the Russian cavalry was already showing itself beside and behind us.'

'Under a sombre sky' Dumonceau sees the fighting commence over at Ouwarowo, 'against which the enemy directed reiterated efforts'. Now the Russian sharpshooters are 'advancing in great numbers toward the ravine, and they'd already carried a small village on our right flank'. At this Murat – he no longer has so much as a brigade of cavalry to command – rushes up to Chlapowski and orders him

'to follow with one squadron at the trot. The snow being deep, it was hard for our horses to do so. Halting with us in front of the little village the Russians had occupied, the King of Naples said to me: "Get into it!" This was an extraordinary order to give to cavalry, but we had to obey. As you'll believe, I didn't stroll through the village! Yet the snow, which almost came up to our horses' girths, didn't enable them to gallop.'

Chlapowski enters the hamlet by its main street:

'Russian chasseurs fired at us point-blank out of the houses' courtyards. Four lancers fell – Murat has them on his conscience. We also had six wounded. The Russians didn't flee, anyway they couldn't get out of the courtyards quickly enough to escape behind the hedges.'

The Polish lancer squadron emerges on its far side. Reforming his squadron in front of the Russian line 'about 600 paces away', Chlapowski notices

'a company of Guard Grenadiers that the Emperor, probably in view of Murat's extravagant order, was sending to seize the village. They occupied it without firing a shot. The Russians hardly had time to fire once. Some of them managed to withdraw by crossing the ravine. The others were taken prisoner.'

Returning to his starting-point, he finds Napoleon still

'on foot in front of his Guard. I came back to take my place near him. He was furious with Murat. Addressing me, he said: "How could you listen to that fool?" At each moment the shells were beginning to fall more thickly and were throwing several of our men to the ground. The Guard stood immobile as a wall. Our guns placed on the ravine's edge were hardly replying. The Emperor wasn't allowing them to, saying that the Russians were firing from too far off. But their *unicorns* were reaching us.'

If the Russian 'unicorns' – howitzers (Chlapowski explains) 'whose axle trees are decorated with unicorns' – are striking at unusually long howitzer range, it's thanks to their long barrels and 7–10-pounder calibre. Dumonceau, now standing by his horse, now 'running to and fro to keep warm', notes how much of the Russian artillery though 'mounted on sledges and manoeuvring swiftly' is, as usual, firing too high. Even so

'the Russians were smothering us with projectiles. Fortunately most of them ricocheted on some slight undulation of the terrain and then bounced well over our heads, or else, merely rolling up to us, were spot-

166

ted and easily avoided. His shells exploded with a crash the more sonorous for the repercussions from the frozen ground.'

Having stood his youngsters up in a thin wall against this storm of shot and shell, Mortier has promised Napoleon to hold up the Russians until nightfall. Then, if Davout still hasn't appeared ...

More and more enemy guns, 'hastening to line the slope of the high ground opposite', are being brought into action. Never have the Hessian Footguards

'had to stand up to a cannonade of such long duration, not even at the great battles of Wagram and Aspern. I left my place for a moment to have a word with Captain Schwarzenau, and just before I got back to it a ball passed terribly close to Lieutenant Suckow,[20] who'd stepped in, killing outright the men who were standing in the second and third rank to the right. The first of these was my old cook, Heck, an honest fellow, who died a noble death. Another shot, passing close to my eyes, passed through a gap in the ranks without doing any damage but struck the hand off a drummer in the 4th Company. Unfortunately the Prince's Own, which was close to the Russian cavalry, had to form square, and in a short time it lost ten officers and 119 men dead and wounded.'

The French are utterly outgunned. And even some of those guns they do possess, Bourgogne says, 'were soon dismounted'. Everyone agrees that to stand up to short-range cannon fire without being able to reply is worst of all. Yet the Young Guard's 18-year-olds, now undergoing their baptism of fire, are suffering terribly: 'Our men died without budging.' At first the Russians bombard Delaborde's division with 30 guns; then with more and more:

'It was the first time our young soldiers had heard the sharp snoring sound of roundshot and the more accentuated sound of shells, ending their flight with the crash of an explosion. My old general passed slowly down the battle front saying: "Come on, my children, noses up! Now we're really smelling powder for the first time." Joyful shouts and *vivats* met these words.'

Yet despite his notable sangfroid in critical situations, even Delaborde's evidently beginning to be a bit worried. And rides over with his staff to join Mortier's:

'One of the old captains said that the three regiments placed out on the ravine had been put there "like a bone for the enemy to gnaw on".'

Feeling the battle must soon reach its crisis, Delaborde gallops off again across the snow and places himself in the midst of the Hessians, who're still receiving the full force of the enemy fire. Paul de Bourgoing follows him. Finding 'the young prince [Emil], then 20 years old and of heroic valour, surrounded by dead and wounded', Delaborde congratulates him on his men's staunchness. Gallant compliments are exchanged, Delaborde declaring – somewhat gratuitously – that 'complete equality between French and allies is the custom on the battlefield'.

After a couple of hours a third of the Fusiliers-Grenadiers have been killed or wounded:

'But the Fusiliers-Chasseurs were worst off of all. Being nearer to the
town they were exposed to a deadlier fire. For the last half-hour the
Emperor had drawn back to the high road with the Old [Guard]
Grenadiers and Chasseurs. We [the Young Guard] remained alone on
the field, with a very few men from various corps, facing more than
50,000 of the enemy.'

But what's this? Dumonceau pricks up his ears. Beyond the roar of the
Russian guns battering away at the long thin infantry line he hears another
more distant, more feeble but more welcome sound. It's the 'intermittent
cannonade, coming ever closer' of Davout's few and Miloradovitch's many
guns exchanging salvoes. And at about 11 a.m. Reviews Inspector Denniée
sees Napoleon, 'confident that his repeated orders had reached Davout
and Ney and they they'd be joining us that evening or night', get into his
carriage. 'Ordering the Old Guard to resume the retreat toward Liady', he
returns to Krasnoië.'

It had been shortly after dawn that the 30th Line, advancing along the
Krasnoië road, had run into Russian guns mounted on sledges, and after
losing several officers and 82 other ranks had beaten a hasty retreat. Captain François' left arm, badly bruised by a shell-burst, aches horribly:

'At 6 a.m. we advance slowly, because the Russians are cannonading us
from all sides at once. At the village of Katowa a Russian corps debouches
and comes marching down on us. A moment later three other enemy
units appear in front of Waskrenia. The Guard is opposite this village,
which gives us some hope. Marshal Davout prepares us for a fight. Despite
the enemy grapeshot, we take up position to the left of Waskrenia, and the
engagement becomes brisk. Our regiment's out in front, only 600 feet
from the Russian batteries.'

Lejeune sees General Compans, commander of the 5th division, in the
thick of it. He's

'as smiling and cheerful as if in his own garden, where he liked to take
long walks. His cheerful face was making his men forget the danger they
were in.'

The forenoon wears on. Doesn't the Russian command realise how frail are
the Young Guard's thinning ranks as they stand staunchly to be decimated
in the snow? Why don't the Russians launch a general attack? 'While we
stood thus exposed to the enemy's fire,' Sergeant Bourgogne goes on, 'our
numbers continuously diminishing, we saw to our left the remainder of
Marshal Davout's army corps calmly marching toward us, in the midst of a
swarm of Cossacks.' Calmly? They may look calm at a distance. In reality
they are anything but.

Finally, at about midday, François catches sight of 'several French divisions being sent to our aid'. General Friederichs, halted to the right of the
road at the head of his division's column, orders it to form up in half-com-
panies. Since roundshot are already rolling among them from the Russian

batteries on the high ground to the left, he tells Colonel Marguerye of the 33rd to send out two companies of voltigeurs to clear a path:

'But these two companies not being numerous enough, Lieutenant-Colonel de Jongh, commanding that Dutch regiment's 1st Battalion, is sent to support them. Then the entire regiment has to do so, with orders to charge the artillery in open order. We were fortunate enough to be able to carry out this order so completely that we made ourselves masters of the highway.'

Whereupon the Russian guns withdraw to almost harmless distance. 'In this fight our regiment had two officers and some 60 men wounded or killed.' And now here are some 'divisions' coming to meet them, among them the pitiful remains of IV Corps, with the 'debris' of the Guardia d'Onore, 4,000 bayonets at most, so François thinks. But it's enough. And I Corps breaks through, taking the rest at a run:

'We joined up with them; but having to march in square and close columns and under the enemy's roundshot and grape we'd lost a lot of men.'

From his unchanged vantage point Dumonceau sees Davout's men 'pour past [s'écouler] in a compact mob [foule] – François says 'en masse with IV Corps' which, its mission accomplished, no doubt also hastily retreats to the town. Wilson is there:

'The enemy passed like flocks of sheep without even offering to fire at us. It was then the Cossacks came to us and said: "What a shame to let these spectres walk from their graves!"'

What neither Dumonceau nor Wilson see is the much-wounded Dromedary of Egypt

'unable to march as fast as the others on account of my wounds in the confusion of this precipitate retreat [sic]. Suddenly I can't see the flag in the middle of the regiment. Can the man who'd been carrying it have been killed? No question but that our standard's been left behind on the battlefield! No sooner has this thought struck me than, without a thought to the danger or bothering about the Russian sharpshooters who're advancing on the line just abandoned by our division, I about-face and hobble back. At last I see the Eagle; pick it up; and, walking as fast as I can, carry it off, despite the shots being aimed at me. Several musket balls pass through my fur! The Russians too are hastening their march, all the while firing grape. In the end I'm hit by a piece of shell which carries away the skin on the back of my right hand and gives me a nasty scar on my right buttock.'

Luckily François still has

'the strength and presence of mind not to succumb to this accursed misfortune of war. My left arm's in a sling, my crutch has been shattered, but I don't abandon the Eagle. So absorbed have I been in saving it I get into Krasnoië without even feeling any pain.'

But now he does. Since there's neither water nor linen to dress his wound he asks a comrade to 'snap off the flagpole, lay the Eagle in its tasselled cravat, and hang it around my neck'. Then he rejoins the 30th in the rear of Krasnoië, where he finds his batman and his two horses.

But all's far from well with the heroic – but by now badly mauled – Dutch Guard Grenadiers. No sooner have Davout's units broken through than Dumonceau sees they're abandoning

'the important position entrusted to them, which the Russians instantly occupy with their artillery, and direct its fire against us. After this our own position was untenable. A regiment sent to recover the ground is forced to retire. Another moves forward as far as the foot of the batteries, but is stopped by a regiment of cuirassiers. Retiring to the left of the battery, the 3rd Dutch Grenadier regiment forms square. Again the enemy's cavalry come on to the attack, but are received by a heavy fire, which kills a great many. A second charge meets with the same reception. But a third, supported by grapeshot, succeeds. The regiment's overwhelmed. The enemy breaks into the square and finishes off the remainder with their swords. Powerless to defend themselves, these poor fellows, nearly all very young, having their hands and feet mostly frostbitten, were simply massacred. We witnessed this scene without being able to help our comrades.'

Among the few survivors 'flowing back to us' Dumonceau recognises an old friend, Captain Favauge, 'supported by a grenadier'. Hit in the small of his back, he's suffering so terribly Dumonceau fears he won't survive:

'Only eleven men came back. The rest had all been killed, wounded or, if taken prisoner, were being driven away by sword-thrusts into a little wood opposite. Colonel Tindal himself, covered with wounds, was taken prisoner, with several other officers.'

But in all essentials the operation has succeeded. And at long last as the daylight fades Mortier gives the long-awaited order to retire. As the intrepid Delaborde's surviving youngsters about-face and march for Krasnoië he says to them:

'Do you understand, soldiers? The Marshal orders you to march at the usual pace. *At the usual pace!*':[21]

All his life Bourgogne will broken-heartedly remember

'the terrible and sad scene as we left the field and our poor wounded, surrounded by the enemy, saw they were being abandoned, above all those of the 1st Voltigeurs, some of whom had had their legs shattered by grape'.

After making several probes near a wood to see if the Russians are strongly supported (they are), the Hessians, too, retire, 'covered by one weak division'. Only at 4 p.m., just as the last light fails, do the Russians launch a truly furious onslaught. The 1st Tirailleurs, who've lost two-thirds of their men and are still out on the crest of the ravine, are also ordered to retire. In the end only the 1st Voltigeur Regiment's still out there. Paul de Bourgoing can distinctly hear its 20-year-olds, now bearing the whole brunt of their first and last battle, shouting *"Vive l'Empereur!"* as they're scythed down by Russian grapeshot. And when at last another ADC is told to 'make for a white-ish point where the smoke of the combat can scarcely be made out in the evening mist' and order them to retire, all he finds when he gets there are 'a few scattered groups here and there, still resisting the Cossacks and the Novgorod Dragoons'. Where are all the rest, he asks one of their lieutenants whose face is covered in blood:

'They no longer exist.'

Lieutenant Vionnet, who's had two horses killed under him but escapes with only two light bruises and five Russian musket balls in his greatcoat, sees that the 'first two regiments of Tirailleurs and Voltigeurs had been entirely wiped out. Of those two units not 120 men were left.' The Fusiliers-Grenadiers see

'many of them painfully dragging themselves along on their knees, reddening the snow with their blood. They raised their hands to heaven, uttering cries which tore at one's heart and imploring our help. But what could we do? At each instant the same fate awaited us too; for as we retired we were also having to abandon those who were falling in our own ranks.'

But Delaborde, sitting his horse at the town gate, goes on 'encouraging and directing the men who were defending the entrance'. As he's waiting to retreat through the gateway 'with the last companies to pass through Krasnoïe', Bourgogne sees

'some pieces of artillery on our left, firing at the Russians for our protection. They were being served and supported by about 40 men, gunners and light infantrymen – all that was left of General Longchamps' brigade. He was there himself with the remnant of his men, determined either to save them or die with them. As soon as he caught sight of our colonel he came to him with open arms. They'd been through the Egyptian campaign together. They embraced as two friends who hadn't met for a long time and perhaps wouldn't ever meet again. The general, his eyes full of tears, showed our colonel the two guns and the few remaining men: "Look," he said. "That's all I've left!" General Longchamps, with his poor remainder, was forced to leave his guns, all the horses being killed, and follow our retreat, taking advantage of what cover he could find behind houses or earthen banks as he went.'

Soon the Russian roundshot, fired at close quarters, is 'going through this little country town's wooden houses, killing several soldiers of our rearguard. Shortly afterwards,' Paul de Bourgoing goes on, 'the main street is swept by musketry, and it's at this moment I come across Victor, no less exposed to the keenest fire than the most valiant of our infantrymen'. All this time his faithful 'guttersnipe' has been admiring his lieutenant as he'd galloped about out there on the snowy plain!

'He'd been waiting for me to give me my fur, which he hadn't wanted to leave behind.

'"Quick, lieutenant, take your fur. I can't march as fast as the rearguard and we'll have to get a move on if we're not to be left behind."'

But 'the officers of the 30th, assembling in Krasnoïe, are regarding Captain François as

'a lost man, so covered am I with wounds. However, I don't despair. I've
still got a good appetite, little though it's excited by any succulence in
the dishes making up my meals.'
Although his exploit's been quickly reported to his colonel, who reports it
to General Morand, and he to Davout,
'who engages my colonel to write him a report on my conduct, and
though the report was written, certifying my feat of arms and telling me
I'm being recommended for the Cross of the Legion,'
nothing, sighs François, ever comes of it.

All day Boulart and his gunners and men of the Train, parked beside their
lake, have been listening to the sounds of battle,
'all in a state of acute anxiety, an anxiety aggravated by the incessant passage of non-combatants and vehicles through the town'.
After what seemed an interminable waiting with his slimmed down
artillery, Boulart had seen the head of the Guard column appear:
'Debouching from Krasnoïe and without halting, it continued its march
towards Liady. I followed its movement.' Every house in Krasnoïe and its
big monastery have been filling up with the Young Guard's wounded. But
now Larrey sees his surgeons, too, falling under the roundshot or Cossack
lances. And not only his surgeons, either. But also women:
'The Frenchwomen who'd left Moscow with us were carrying their devotion to the point of heroism. They came out and bandaged our wounded
under the fire of the Russian guns. Above all the directress [sic] of the
Moscow Theatre, Mme. Aurore Bursay, distinguished herself.'
As usual the Surgeon-General has himself been operating on many of the
gravest cases. To Lejeune, coming in with I Corps,
'nothing was more afflicting than to see all these rooms encumbered with
fine young soldiers aged 20 to 25, who'd only recently joined and who'd
seen action for the first time that day, and who, within the hour, were
going to be left in the enemy's power. All who could walk after their
wounds had been attended to were making haste to leave. All the others
stayed there without surgeons and without help. There were perhaps
3,000 of them.'
As evening has come on, 1,200 others have been evacuated from the town.
Krasnoïe itself is 'intersected by a deep hollow' crossed by another 'little
trembling bridge'. Going on ahead in his carriage Mailly-Nesle has seen
men who'd fallen from the bridge lying dead in the half-frozen river, at the
bottom of which Bourgogne is astonished to see
'a herd of oxen, dead of cold and hunger. Only their heads were visible,
their eyes still open; their bodies were covered in snow. They belonged
to the army, but hadn't been able to reach us. They were frozen so stiff
our sappers could hardly cut them up with their hatchets.'
But now Larrey even has to leave behind the 1,200 he'd evacuated from the
battlefield amid Krasnoïe's splintering and crumbling timber houses – 'for
lack of transport we could only take a very few with us'. And the deepen-

ing dusk is rent by the 'piercing cries of hundreds of seriously wounded youngsters' as they realise they're being abandoned to the 'brutality of a savage and pitiless enemy, who were already stripping them without regard to their situation or their wounds'.

I Corps' rearguard consists of 390 Dutchmen of the 33rd Line. Davout, on the spot, orders its Colonel de Marguerye to send a strong detachment to occupy some ruined houses to the left further along the Liady road. But then, just as all the rest of I Corps is already crossing a street to his right, the Marshal comes back with a new order: to draw off the whole regiment 'broken up into echelons'. Major Everts listens

'attentively to the Marshal's orders. For many years his military reputation had stood on solid foundations. But on this occasion experience once again told me that in unforeseen situations even great men of that stamp can make mistakes.'

If they remain scattered like this among houses so widely detached, Everts sees, they'll neither be able to keep on the move nor put up a resolute or vigorous rearguard action. 'We'd be beaten in detail at all points.' Already the rest of I Corps is more than 300 yards away and the Russian cavalry's coming on quickly toward them. So he advises de Marguerye to ignore Davout's orders, concentrate his men, get out into the plain, and form square. All the 33rd's other senior officers agree:

'But having advanced a few hundred paces in column, we heard a vigorous hurrah behind the regiment. At which the colonel ordered us to halt and form square to sustain the Russians' charge. But the mass of Cossacks noticed our movement and faced about. A few moments later four hostile squadrons of Cuirassiers of the Guard appeared and flung themselves flat out at us.'

Although the 33rd's muskets are 'in bad shape after the bivouacs', they keep up a well-nourished fire, killing or wounding a lot of the cuirassiers. A second charge also fails, and the survivors make off to attack isolated men and units. But then, seeing Friederichs' division has now left the 33rd behind, Everts realises his men are isolated:

'The cuirassiers came and drew up in front of our square's left face. While they were doing this, six guns were placed to their left and in front of them. They opened up a heavy fire of grape at us. The colonel still wanted to send some skirmishers against this artillery. But the regiment's effectives were too reduced. It could do no more.'

Once again the Russian cuirassiers attack. Once again they're repulsed. But then two battalions of Chasseurs of the Russian Guard come on in open order, keeping up a well-nourished fire, and by now very few of the Dutchmen are still on their feet, 'least of all on our left face, the one facing the artillery'. Colonel Marguerye orders all his officers to take up muskets and do what they can to fill the gaps:

'At that moment he himself was hit by two musket balls in his neck, and began losing a terrible lot of blood. I quickly handed him my pocket handkerchief to stem it.'

A third time the Russian cavalry charges – and this time breaks into the shattered square. Just as Everts is about to take command, the 33rd is charged by Russian infantry,

'furiously striking with bayonet and sword, pointing and slashing in all directions, and terribly augmenting the numbers of our killed and wounded. The colonel suffered two more wounds in the lower part of his body. Fifteen officers were killed, 20 wounded, some very gravely. In all, only six officers remained unscathed. I was one of these privileged men. Of our rankers only 66 were still on their feet. Thus the square was as it were framed in corpses.'

Taken prisoner, all the survivors are 'stripped of everything we had on us or in our clothes'. Violent rows break out among the Russians, accompanied by fisticuffs, 'because each wanted to take everything. As I personally experienced. Having taken everything off me, down to my shirt', two Russians dispute the capture of Everts' gold watch. Even so, he counts himself lucky not to be among the wounded:

'Thus undressed, they took me to General Roozen [sic] who was so courteous as to believe what I told him of my rank, etc., and spontaneously even had the goodness to have me at once given an old Russian overcoat and something strong to drink. In addition to all this, at my request he had the humanity – most essential of all – to order an end to the massacre of my unfortunate comrades. To do this he sent an adjutant and two drummers, who made a roll, and put an end to it. At the same time several of our officers, who were in a most precarious situation because of their wounds, were being carried to the general. One of them, Captain von Ingen, made him a Masonic sign. At which the general gave him a few paper roubles, which he took out of his portfolio. From every point of view I cannot pay homage enough to the generous and loyal conduct of the enemy general who'd commanded there. May Heaven reward this brave man!'

While their former subordinates are marched off naked into captivity, some senior officers are even buried with military honours. 'The unit was led to the grave (in which the officer was to be placed without any coffin) by a platoon of their men, escorting it with reversed arms, and a drum beating a kind of funeral march.'[22]

Only after they've left Krasnoië a quarter of a league behind them do the surviving Fusiliers-Grenadiers

'calm down a bit, sad and silent at the thought of our own position and of our unhappy comrades we'd been forced to abandon. It seemed to me I could still see them begging us to help them.'

Looking behind they see some of the least severely wounded, almost naked, coming after them, and hurriedly give them whatever can be spared to cover their nakedness.

But back in Krasnoië after Davout had left, they're being told, some 3,000 unevacuable wounded are simply being thrown out of the windows into the streets and (so Chlapowski'll hear) being massacred by the returning inhabitants.

CHAPTER 11

MARCHING, MARCHING, MARCHING ...

Getting out of Krasnoïe – Louise nearly dies – the cavalry's last charge – 'As long as your sacred bloody persons get through' – 'the Old Guard passed through like a 100-gun battleship through fishing boats' – Napoleon skids into Liady – live Jews and chickens – where's Ney? – 'We must get to the Berezina as quickly as possible' – 'For the first time he struck me as worried'

For the thousands of stragglers getting through Krasnoïe has been a nightmare. Carriageless, all alone in the mob, Louise Fusil had asked an officer how she was to join IHQ.

'"I think it's still here," he said, "but that won't be for long. Because the town's beginning to burn." The fire was spreading fast – the little town was all of timber and its streets exceedingly narrow. I ran through it, burning beams threatening to fall on my head. A gendarme was so kind as to help me as far as to the exit where a dense crowd was jostling one on all sides.'

'"The Emperor left long ago," he tells her. "You'll never be able to catch up with them again."

'"Very well, then," I said. "I'll just have to die, because I haven't the strength to go any further."

'I felt the cold was numbing my blood. This asphyxia, they say, is a very gentle death; and I can believe it. I heard someone or something buzzing in my ear: "Don't stay here! Get up!" Someone was shaking me by the arm. I found this disturbance disagreeable. I was experiencing the sweet self-abandonment of someone who's falling peacefully asleep. In the end I understood nothing, lost all sensation.'

But when she comes out of this benumbed state she's in a peasant's cottage, with a lot of officers standing around her. 'They'd wrapped me up in furs and someone was feeling my pulse.' It's Napoleon's personal surgeon Desgenettes:

'I thought I was coming back from a dream, but was so weak I couldn't stir. I scrutinised all these uniforms. General Bourmann, whose acquaintance I so far hadn't made, was looking at me with interest. Old Marshal Lefèbvre came forward and said: "Well, how are things with you? You've come back from very far away." They told me they'd picked me up out of the snow.'

Only Desgenettes has saved her from being placed close to their big fire. "Don't do anything of the sort!" he'd shouted. "You'll kill her on the spot! Wrap her up in all the furs you can find and put her in a room where there isn't one." By and by she begins to thaw out and Marshal Lefèbvre brings her 'a big mug of very strong coffee. "Keep the mug,"' he tells her. '"It'll be historic in your family." But adds more softly: "If you ever see it again." And takes her into his carriage, which is soon rolling on behind a Guard detachment. Her fellow-actress Madame Bourcet hasn't been so fortunate. Dedem sees her perched on a gun-carriage in the costume she'd worn in the comedy *Ma Tante Aurore*, 'the only one she'd saved from the pillage'.

Griois hasn't a single gun left. On its way down the slope out of Krasnoië behind IV Corps, his group (Berthier's son among them) see 'our troops at grips with the enemy'. It's Davout's rearguard.

Now all sorts of people have neither horse, cart, carriage nor wagon to carry their effects. Von Muraldt's horse has given up the ghost, leaving him to struggle on under the weight of his iron cookpot. After grabbing a riderless one and 'galloping' into Krasnoië, Lieutenant Sauvage joins I Corps just as it's 'descending the slope' beyond the town. But the horse is recognised as belonging to a Polish general. And he has to dismount and walk.

Once again guns are being left behind – even the Guard's. General Lallemand approaches Pion des Loches and authorises him in the Emperor's name to abandon any he must, but on one condition: that he bury them deep in the ground and burn their gun-carriages,

> 'though to do that we'd have needed spades and pickaxes, and they'd been lost with the ammunition wagons. I left four pieces on their carriages, had the lashings cut, and some spokes broken.'

But Boulart's guns are rolling along down 'the great broad road straight to the horizon and planted on both sides with three rows of magnificent silver birches' that had provided shade against the appalling August heats. 'An hour and a half beyond Krasnoië' some Cossacks, pressing in from the left, carry off General Desvaux's wagon, and Boulart's guns, preceded by a horse battery, have to fire some shots at them.

> 'Three miles beyond Krasnoië, a new ravine, a new mêlée. My first gun gets jammed in it, I can't get it out. So, even though it brings me close to the Cossacks, I direct the rest of my column a little further to the left. To avoid breaking up the ground I recommend that no vehicle shall follow in the tracks of the one ahead. This succeeds admirably, and I have the happiness to get back to the road without being held up at all, and leave behind me all this scrum the Russians are already firing their guns at.'

Once again Boulart, by superior management, has saved his guns – all except one. Regretting its loss, he goes back to see whether anything can be done about it. Just as he's deciding it can't, he witnesses a painful scene. A Russian roundshot carries away the jaw of a fractious donkey, ridden by well-dressed young woman, a fugitive from Moscow. Although he realises this means she'll soon be the Cossacks' prey, probably their victim, 'my artillery was already beginning to be far away, and I'd no means of saving this unhappy woman'. Farther on, at a new jam where the road narrows to cross a swamp and is only viable to one vehicle at a time, he's shocked to see even superior officers – 'almost all stripped of any resources and reduced to an extremity more painful than the men's' – pillaging the bogged-down vehicles.

For still the Russians aren't giving the column any peace, and the survivors of the Young Guard (Vionnet contradicts Pastoret) haven't so much as a single gun to oppose them with:

'We had to pass through a hollow road under the fire of four guns and two howitzers, which made extraordinary ravages. Not a shot failed of its effect. One can imagine the carnage caused by this battery.'

To keep the Russians at a healthy distance on a line of high ground to the left, Colbert's lancers are riding across thick snowy fields, flanking the Old Guard. Just then a cannonball from that quarter kills an infantryman at Dumonceau's side, causing his horse to shy and fall on top of him. 'The shells which went beyond us were bursting around the Emperor without his even appearing to notice them.' Suddenly Pastoret's group see

'the enemy unmask a battery he'd been concealing on our left flank. He sends some parties of cavalry to support it and lets his cavalry appear on our right and ahead of us. At the same time he attacks our rear on the paved highway. Instantly the Emperor changes his battle front, and to keep the Russians at bay throws the Young Guard and the heavy cavalry to the right, leaving the stragglers, whose numbers make them look like a considerable corps; sends a reinforcement to the rear; and with the Old Guard marches in line to the left. At a signal the officers gather and form a circle. Napoleon tells them "it isn't me you're to serve. It's us. It's the Empire, it's France. Remember, the safety of one is the safety of all."'

The column advances to the attack. Colbert's lancers and the rest of the Guard's light cavalry under Lefèbvre-Desnouëttes, called in, charge together and disperse the Russians. Now only some 2,000 cavalry are left. And when another Russian battalion makes a determined effort to come down from the high ground and block the road, it's ordered to stem it. The charge is hit by a storm of fire. The relics of the 23rd Dragoons, says *Pierre Auvray*, are

'obliged to charge home. So great was the mêlée, not to be stabbed by their bayonets we could only get clear by separating their weapons with our hands. In that moment, just as I'm about to sabre my Russian, he jabs his bayonet at my left side. My sabre belt parries the blow.'

Holding his horse's reins with his right hand Auvray tries to fend the man off with his left. 'His musket shot goes off in my hand, taking off my forefinger and the ball ripping the front of my coat.' And that makes one more non-combatant to add to all the thousands of others. He has great difficulty in finding the 23rd Dragoons' surgeon to amputate the stump of his finger. Very few of his comrades return from that charge.

Meanwhile the Russian gunners, it seems to Pastoret, are aiming directly at Napoleon:

'Upon a shell falling quite close to the Emperor, he struck it with his riding whip saying: "Ah! What a long time it is since I've had a shell between my legs!" The shell exploded, covering the Emperor in snow, but without hurting anyone.'

177

Berthier urges him to leave the spot and move further off to the right. As he's doing so, an officer who's just stepped forward to take orders – he's standing exactly where Napoleon was a moment ago – is hit and killed by a roundshot. A French battery unlimbers and silences the Russian fire. Noticing that fresh Russian troops – far too numerous for Davout to contain – are all the time being thrown in, Napoleon concludes that III Corps has probably been forced to capitulate 'or perhaps is making a great detour around the Russian army to rejoin him'. This time there can be no turning back. 'We marched,' says Chlapowski,

'in close columns headed by the service squadrons, the Guard artillery on the road, then the infantry, and finally all the Guard cavalry'.

Pastoret sees the Guard's close-packed column go by:

'To right and left rode the cavalry, with orders to scout for us. In front of us two battalions of infantry with two guns formed the usual advance guard and preceded the Emperor's carriage, under the Master of the Horse, that of the Prince of Neuchâtel, and that of Count Daru. All the others had been consigned to the rear. After this advance guard came the combat corps.'

It's a sight he'll never forget. Nor will the Russians:

'The Emperor was marching first, alone, followed by the Major-General [Berthier] and the *Intendant-Général* [Daru], walking together, and by the Grand Marshal of the Palace [Duroc], who was driving his own sledge. Behind him, sword in hand, came the Marshal Duke of Danzig [Lefèbvre] commanding the Guard; and after him the Guard itself, as if on parade. Each divisional general was at the head of his division, each brigadier at the head of his brigade; each colonel led his regiment, and each captain his company. No officer could under any pretext whatsoever quit his particular post. The men, brought back to discipline, marched in their ranks and in perfect order. A uniform and equal step seemed to unite so many movements into one, and the deep silence reigning in this immense body of troops was only disturbed by the firm curt cry of command, repeated by the officers at regular intervals from rank to rank, and which, from the Guard, passed on down to the various corps following it. The enemy observed us from afar.'

In his place at the head of his company of the 1st Foot Chasseurs, 'marching almost all the time in square' is Captain Lignières:

'In the middle of the square the Emperor marched with his staff, his carriage, his wagons, the artillery. We were forbidden to let anyone, no matter whom, enter the square. All round us was a mob of stragglers, an innumerable mob we rejected with blows of our musket butts. Each time we changed direction we had to pass through this mob. Marshal Lefèbvre, in command of us, said: "Chasseurs, you must pass. I insist your sacred bloody [*sacrée*] persons shall be respected. As long as your sacred persons get through I don't give a damn for the rest."'

Never as long as he lives will Denis Davidov, head of a band of Russian partisans, forget that sight. As 'the Old Guard, with Napoleon himself in its centre' approaches,

> 'we jumped on our horses and placed ourselves close to the main road. Noticing our noisy bands, the enemy cocked his muskets and proudly continued his march, without hastening the pace. All our efforts to detach a single soldier from his closed columns were in vain. The men, as if carved out of granite, scorned all our attempts and remained intact. I'll never forget the free and easy air and the menacing attitude of those warriors who'd been tried by death in its every aspect. With their tall bearskins, their blue uniforms with white belts, their red plumes and epaulettes, they looked like rows of poppies in a field of snow. Our Cossacks were in the habit of galloping around the enemy, snatching his baggage and guns if they straggled, and circling scattered or detached companies. But those columns remained unshakeable. In vain our colonels, our officers, our NCOs or simple Cossacks thrust themselves at them. The columns advanced, one after the other, driving us off with musket shots and scorning our useless raids. The Guard with Napoleon passed through our Cossacks like a ship armed with a hundred guns passes through fishing boats.'

'This calm regular march so impressed the enemy,' Pastoret is no less amazed to see, 'that for several days he no longer attacked us.'

That evening Sauvage strays from one bivouac to another, vainly searching for his Captain Houdart. But what's this? An abandoned wagon, full of shoes! Nearby, lying on the snow, is a Polish lancer's portmanteau. Taking out several pairs, he puts them into it; and shortly afterwards has the luck to fall in with – though not exactly be welcomed by – the officers of his division's artillery train, who've still got their wagon and are making some soup. Sauvage is just turning in for the night when the enemy guns open up again. And all the French scatter, despite their officers' attempts to hold them together. At that moment Davout

> 'hastening to the danger point, managed by his example and exhortations to gather round him those who scorned the Russians' 20 or 25 shots at us. In this way the Marshal hid his army corps' disorder from the enemy and prevented them from attempting any other movements.'

From Smolensk to Orsha is 123 kilometres. From Krasnoië to Orsha some 50 miles. Half-way between them, everyone remembers, is the little town of Liady, the first in Lithuania. How long they seem, these sixteen leagues! Mailly-Nesle, no longer singing as he walks along beside his imperial carriage, is feeling sad:

> 'Each of us, his head lowered, his hands hidden in his clothes and his eyes fixed on the ground, sombre and silent, was following the unfortunate man in front of him. The plaintive cry of the wheels on the hardened snow, and the croaking of constellations of rooks, the northern crows, and other birds of prey which always followed our army, were the

179

only sounds heard, unless the Cossacks came to shake our poor French soldiers out of their melancholy apathy.'

Today (18 November) a thaw has set in; and the fog's 'so thick we could see nothing'. Sergeant Bourgogne is

'terribly tired. Our men were still in some sort of order. But the previous days' fighting and having to abandon their comrades had demoralised them. They were thinking the same fate no doubt was in store for them.'

Towards nightfall it begins freezing again

'and the roads were so slippery we kept on falling over, and many were seriously hurt. I marched last of the company.'

As darkness falls they drive some German, Italian and French stragglers out of a church:

'Unfortunately for them the night grew much colder, with a high wind and a fall of snow, and when we came out next morning we found many of the poor wretches dead by the roadside. Others had dropped farther on, while trying to find somewhere to shelter. We passed by these dead bodies in silence. No doubt,'

he goes on, with a retrospective twinge of bad conscience,

'we ought to have felt guilty at this sad sight, of which we were partly the cause. But we'd reached that point of indifference to even the most tragic events that we told each other we'd soon be eating dead men, as there'd be no more horses left.'

This is one hour before reaching the village of Dubrovna. Until now I Corps, too, has been marching in quite good order; but partly as a result of that night when the officers had pillaged the abandoned vehicles, it's become 'almost completely disorganised'.

And now and again everyone looks back over his shoulder.

What's become of Ney?

At first, while Davout had still been at or near Krasnoië, Napoleon had told Berthier to order him to fall back to Ney's assistance. But then thought better of it:

'For Davout to have lingered at Krasnoië would have jeopardised the army without serving any useful purpose. To return there, as certain persons proposed, was quite pointless. Ney's fate was already sealed, one way or the other.'

Caulaincourt forbids us – his future readers and armchair strategists – to pass judgement as between Ney and Davout. Still less so on Napoleon. But his own verdict is unequivocal:

'The fact is, of course, the pace ought to have been accelerated all along the line, and Ney should have left Smolensk on 16 November. But the Emperor could never make up his mind when it came to ordering a retreat. We knew nothing definite about III Corps, of which I Corps had had no news since the 16th. Not a single officer had returned.'

Altogether communications have virtually broken down:

'The dispatch of orders and reports was all but impossible, or else so slow they were rarely arriving in time to be any use. Staff officers, having

mostly lost their horses, were on foot. Even those who still had them couldn't make them walk on the ice, and so got there no sooner than the others. Braving every kind of danger, they were often captured. To make any progress at all they had to attach themselves to some unit, halt when it halted,, and advance to join another unit when it advanced. Had those sent with messages even reached their destination? The Emperor was lost in conjectures.'
When he'd left Smolensk he'd believed for some reason the Russian army was to his right. Now, hearing from a peasant and from contingents familiar with the locality that there's a lot of Russian cavalry to his left, he realises it must be Kutusov trying to steal several marches on him.[1]

Cold and sunny the weather may be, but the whole landscape's an ice-rink. Just before Liady, eleven miles from Krasnoië, the great plateau comes abruptly to an end; and there's a steep descent. How is IHQ to get down it? Eblé's three companies of sappers are already at Orsha, having made 'all necessary repairs to the bridges along the road'. But evidently Jomini's report hasn't come in yet. If it had, Berthier's headquarters guides would know that the slope
    'can be turned by a road to the left. I've got the commandant of that place to promise to point it out to the whole Train. The two slopes between Dubrovna and Orsha, of which one goes up and the other down, are no less bad and will cause a great delay in the march. There are two or three very steep slopes and very dangerous to the artillery teams. It seems to me there's nothing to do about it, except the descent at the entrance to Liady.'
where Eblé, he says, has thrown down some fascines so as to be able to turn it a bit further on. From the sublime to the ridiculous – Napoleon will soon be telling Caulaincourt, is but a step:
    'It descended so steeply, and a large part of its frozen surface had been so polished by all the horses and men that had slipped on it that we, like everyone else, we were obliged to sit down and slide on our backsides. The Emperor had to do the same, as the many arms proffered him didn't provide enough support.'[2]
After a few miles the Russian pursuit has faded away. The Lancer Brigade's been able to leave the fields' deep snow and – Dumonceau says nothing about the slope – ride straight along the road and, wary – as back in August[3] – of its single street's transverse logs, so dangerous to their horses' legs, right through it.
    Amazing! Not since leaving Moscow has anyone seen any inhabitants. But here they are:
    'Almost all Jewish, they'd stayed behind their filthy window panes, with an air of consternation watching us pass. From the lights in the windows we realised the houses were full. A profound calm reigned everywhere.'
Castellane, arriving with IHQ, is delighted to see them. Perhaps even more so the chickens and ducks, real live ones, which 'to everyone's

great astonishment are running about in the town's streets and yards!'

'Every face cheered up, and everyone began to think that our privations were at last at an end. Liady's modest resources, combined with such things as money could buy in its neighbourhood, enabled a fair number of men to take the edge off their appetites.'

Caulaincourt adds these details, he says, somewhat solemnly, 'because small things have great influence on Frenchmen, whose spirits are quick to rise and fall'. There's even wine to be had, at least for the first comers, and 'a good bedroom with windows, a wooden floor to sleep on and a stove to heat the air'.

Boulart says nothing about chickens or ducks – perhaps by the time he gets there they've all found their way into IHQ's cookpots. Nor about how his guns and caissons have negotiated the slippery slope – perhaps Jomini's report has caused them to take the circuitous road to the left. But at the bridge at the town entrance reasonably good order prevails, for once. Boulart is standing there with his batteries, 'shivering and impatiently waiting my turn' to cross it, when he's summoned to Davout – who tells him I Corps, too, is to march straight through without halting. Since some Cossacks – evidently they've appeared again – are being supported by infantry he needs Boulart's guns to disperse them. Boulart waits until 4 a.m. – all he gets to eat is some biscuit and sugar 'hard as stone, which spoiled my teeth and lacerated my gums' – before he can get moving again. Then he puts his guns into battery, and drives off the Cossacks.

Griois and his friends have done considerably better for themselves. Arriving at Liady towards nightfall 'at about the same time as the Emperor' they've found

'this little town's houses full of military from all corps, pressed together there *en masse*. An emotion [*mouvement*] reigned there which, without being one of gaiety, had something less lugubrious about it than the usual sight presented by our bivouacs. It's true' [he goes on sombrely]'the inhabitants were all Jews whose hideous squalor in any other circumstances would have shocked us. But by dint of threats and blows we, for gold, were able to get some potatoes out of them.'

Louise Fusil is more considerate, more humane: 'They were Jews, but at least living beings. I'd gladly have embraced them!' Squeezing himself into a room 'which was already housing more people than it could reasonably contain' Griois sees Dr Desgenettes, who'd saved her life. Luckily, one of Griois' party finds another, less crowded house to spend the night in, and they 'replace the insipid and detestable broth by our potatoes'. Franz Roeder, now feeling very ill, gets here too, and Prince Emil gives him back a slice of his Göttingen sausage, which is so much the more welcome as he has lost his boy-batman Dietrich; and notes in his diary: 'Musketeer Alt, with the furs, fodder and cooking pot, may well be utterly lost.' Next morning, finding his feet so swollen he can't pull his boots on, he has to turn to one of his Hessians to lend him a pair of soldier's shoes, even if they're two sizes too big for him.

But for 300 men of I Corps that night Liady is the end of the road. In the cold foggy morning Fezensac sees how

'all had perished, burnt to death in a barn, blocking the doorway as they'd all tried to rush out at once. Only one was still breathing, and to finish him off he had to be shot twice.'

Now 'the weather, which had been cold but very beautiful' suddenly changes. And there's a thaw, so that 'a thick damp fog enveloped us' and Griois' group march on

'through melting snow. The dampness of the air and the water running away from the surface of the layer of ice covering the silver birches along the road pierced our clothing; and the cold we were exposed to, though a great deal less sharp, was more inconvenient and above all less healthy than that of the preceding days. I was promptly seized of a fierce cough, accompanied by a sore throat.'

Doubtless he isn't the only sufferer. Everywhere Castellane sees sledges being abandoned in the slush. Liady being a Lithuanian town and therefore on 'liberated' territory, the officers of the Italian Guard have assumed

'it'd be respected. But even after seeing a good part of its houses demolished to feed the bivouac fires yesterday evening and last night, we were most surprised and pained to see, as we left, what remained – sad and hard necessity – being given over to the flames to slow down the enemy's pursuit!'

Possibly only Roeder, who has a special respect for them, gives a thought to its poor Jews. They'd been right to be apprehensive.

'All eyes were now turning to Orsha, which the Emperor, like everyone else, regarded as an important base.' Halfway, 30 kilometres further on, lies the village of Dubrovna. After leaving Liady at 5 a.m., IHQ has to march for twelve hours to get there. When it does it installs itself in Princess Lubomirska's château. Like all Lithuanian villages Dubrovna is mainly Jewish. Le Roy's little group, hurrying on to keep ahead of the mob of disbanded men, have already passed through on 16 November and found

'all the inhabitants in their homes. We'd halted in my former billet where there were already two superior cavalry officers. Neither had a horse. For a while we'd chatted about our miserable state. They told me we were in danger of being cut off at the Berezina, at the big Borissow bridge. This news had made me hasten my march to Orsha.'

At Dubrovna Griois' 'little caravan' is 'happier than it'd been so far, in the fairly spacious house' of some people who provide them with 'wonderful fresh bread and a little honey and not too dirty a floor to sleep on in front of the fire'. By now Griois has run a high temperature. In the middle of the night a Cossack 'hurrah' disturbs his sleep – at the first shots all but two or three of the armed pontoneers he has placed at the door have rushed off to join the troops in the market place. But the Cossacks find they've bitten off more than they can to chew. It's Napoleon's headquarters and the Imperial Guard they've tumbled on.

By dawn it's freezing again. As Dedem sets out along the Orsha road that morning (19 November) he sees

'the Emperor trying to reorganise the Guard. He was walking along, preaching discipline. Marshal Duroc and the other generals with him had tried to halt the soldiers and incorporate them. But their efforts had been unavailing.'

Von Muraldt – his memories from Krasnoië to the Berezina will be fuzzy – will nevertheless remember one thing very clearly:

'At a fire by the roadside I saw the Emperor. He was wearing a fur-lined dark green coat and as far as I could judge doing his utmost to restore some kind of order among the pitiable mass. Yet no one was paying any attention any longer either to his commands or of his orders of the day.'

The only person in his entourage, Griois thinks, who seems to be perfectly cheerful is Murat, whom he sees arm in arm with Napoleon, who's walking with a 'long stick':

'Neither the cold nor our sad situation had taken away the air of self-assurance and gaiety natural to him. He smiled as he spoke with the Emperor, and the numbed faces of the others provided stuff for facile jokes. Walking in front of him was Marshal Berthier, wearing a blue over-coat. He seemed to find nothing amusing about his present situation. A fur, a toque and fur boots *à la polonaise* made up Murat's costume, whose elegance contrasted with everything around him.'

Where's the enemy. What's Kutusov doing? For four days, someone tells Cesare de Laugier, 'we've known nothing of what the Russians are up to. Jews, though promised rewards, can say nothing.' From Dubrovna on, Dedem thinks, it's become clear to Napoleon there's

'no salvation for him or ourselves except in the enemy's lack of audacity. He realised that sooner or later the few men under arms would melt away.'

But Pastoret notices something else:

'Having realised what a catastrophe had followed from lost time, he was now the first to insist on keeping going.'

That day the young Intendant falls in with the remnant of the Witebsk garrison. Among them are some of his own employees, with whom he offers to share his remaining 100 roubles. 'Almost all refused. Afterwards I only saw six men out of all those who'd made up the administration of a large county.' Marching on between the endless double alley of silver birches, one of his companions is kicked by a horse,

'which could have broken his leg, and in our situation this accident could have been mortal. At that moment it happened that M. Larrey had just passed us on horseback, and immediately declared: "Nothing broken. I heard the blow."'

But from then onwards Pastoret has to give his arm to his bruised friend.

As for Cesare de Laugier, he's learning a 'magic lesson about the heart of man!' He's finding it very remarkable

'that in the regiments where the colonels have shown themselves just but severe the officers are firmer in maintaining the bonds of discipline. These superiors are always respected, and above all always helped with their needs – in sharp contrast to the regiments where there reigns soft- ness, condescension and a generous negligence. There the men refuse respect, first in little groups, then in a great number and more and more often. Only a few units can be excepted from this rule, where the chiefs' vigilance is extreme. Yet even they can't prevent it altogether.'

He jots down the various corps' strengths in his diary:

'Of the Imperial Guard's original 35,000 remain only 7,000
'Of I Corps' 67,000, only 5,000
'Of IV Corps' 41,000, only 4,000
'Of VI and VIII Corps' 86,400, only 2,000'

perhaps as many or more disbanded men. 'As far as Smolensk,' he's think- ing, 'the number of combatants had exceeded those of the disbanded. Since Krasnoië it's been the other way round.'

At Orsha someone, for once, has really done his duty. This big town, lying in a bend in the Dnieper, is stuffed with supplies of all kinds: food, guns, bridging equipment, and, most important of all of course (Jomini has reported back to Berthier when he's got here on 20 November) 90,000 food rations. They've been assembled, says Pastoret – who'd had a corre- sponding task at Witebsk – by the Portuguese Marquis d'Alorna, 'a scion of the royal house of Braganza, governor of Molihew province and well-liked by its inhabitants, adored by his men and well-seen by the Emperor.'⁴ If Molihew can be guarded and the convoys protected against the soldiery by the élite gendarmes he'd met on the Liady road and brought back to Orsha, there's some hope – so Jomini has reported to Berthier – of their being properly distributed. The survivors of the Guardia d'Onore gape at the gendarmes, freshly arrived from France,

'as at something novel, extraordinary. The cleanliness of their equip- ment, their gleaming weapons, the splendour of their strappings are all in most singular contrast to the rags and tatters and the filthy state dis- played by ourselves.'

Already they'd stopped Le Roy as he'd reached the first Dnieper bridge – there's one on each side of the town – and taken him to the town's military governor:

'He put me a lot of questions, to which I replied, concealing part of the truth. But I fancy he knew more or less what was going on and what straits the army was in. But he was far from imagining how demoralised it was.'

But falling in with a friend who knows nothing of the disastrous retreat, he'd told him about it: 'He soon left me under pretext of letting me get some rest, and ran to the general to pass on the information I'd just given him.' Le Roy had just been about to stretch out on some straw when Jomini[5] had come into his room. For lack of any other superior officer, the Swiss had wanted Le Roy to take charge of a strong detachment:

'You're to take it to a point an hour's march from here on the Dnieper to defend the river passage, which, only at this point, is probably frozen over. You'll have a village on your right and a forest in front of you. But above all you must concern yourself with the passage, which must be strictly guarded. I've just got news that the Emperor's going to halt here. As soon as the Guard arrives I'll immediately have you relieved and I'll be sure to let the general staff know of your great devotion.'

So Le Roy, irritated – yet content, even so, to have got six days' rations out of the inhabitants – had left . His detachment comes from every thinkable regiment – all convalescents, a captain tells him, who've been halted and assembled at Orsha to police the town and guard its food stores:

'Having sent the town governor and the general heartily to the devil, I thought of nothing except the punctilious execution of my orders. I had my whole wardrobe on my back. I was leaving nothing in the rear. My faithful Guillaume was going with me. And, lastly, I had enough food for several days. So I wasn't worried.'

Taking up his position overlooking the Dnieper, he places lookouts. 'At about 9 a.m. the corporal in charge of an outpost on the river comes and tells me a flag-of-truce wants to speak with me.' He turns out to be 'a Russian officer, very well horsed and speaking fluent French'. Le Roy hears his proposal:

'"We're on both flanks of your army, which has just been crushed at Krasnoïe. The Imperial Guard is blocked at Dubrovna. We've just cut communications between that town and Orsha. So your Emperor can retreat no further. So, go and see if you wouldn't like to surrender. In that case you'll be received as prisoners of war and well treated in Russia." He paused a moment, and seeing we were making ready to drive him off with musket shots, vanished into the woods. But during the forenoon, fearing I'd be forgotten, I sent back an old sergeant to the main headquarters to remind them of our existence. The river was frozen hard enough to support men and horses, but Cossacks were beginning to appear on the other side. Towards evening I went up on to the high ground dominating the village to try and see what was going on around Orsha, only five versts or a good hour's march from me. I saw fires all around it and could even make out the sound of vehicles crossing the river,'

presumably Boulart's cannon. Le Roy's about to fall back when

'my old sergeant returned with verbal orders to abandon my post, retire on Orsha, and send back the men in my detachment to their own regiments'.

But having already sent out a patrol over to the opposite bank he has to await its return.

That afternoon (19 November) IHQ has installed itself in the town's big Jesuit building. En route Pastoret has seen

'the Emperor, indignant to see so many of our guns and ammunition wagons being abandoned for lack of horsepower, while a multitude of infantrymen and stragglers were insolently riding the horses they'd stolen from them'.

Now he sees the Emperor station himself at the bridgehead, where he

'for two hours, a stick in his hand, functioned as a baggage master-general. One by one the carriages reached the bridgehead. He asked who they belonged to, with his inconceivable memory remembered how many belonged to each, let some go on, had others burnt, and sent the horses to the artillery. There a Marshal was allowed two vehicles, a general officer one, M. le Prince de Neuchâtel six, and so forth with the others. All men who were on horseback but had no right to be were obliged to dismount.'

This piece of accounting, Pastoret thinks, if rigorously carried through, would be almost enough to rehorse the artillery. But at the end of two hours Napoleon

'found it tedious, went off and left it to the Prince of Neuchâtel, who even more quickly became bored with this novel occupation. This task descended from one level to the next, until in the end it was confided to a staff officer. Night came down. Everyone passed unhindered. And the disorder began afresh.'

There are fierce disputes over lodgings. Entering a house, Captain Lignières of the 1st Foot Chasseurs finds his way blocked by an ADC who claims it's his general's:

'He was a foreigner, and so was his general. We replied that there was room for everybody. There were about 30 of us, officers and chasseurs. The ADC tried to prevent us staying. One of our officers fell into a violent dispute with him. I kept on telling him: "Oh, my dear fellow, let Monsieur alone, if he troubles us too much we'll put him out of the door."'

Finally the two officers call each other such names they've no option but to fight it out with cold steel:

'It was evening, very clear because of the snow. They went behind the house. Our comrade passed his sabre through the body of the ADC, who fell on the snow and stayed there. We hadn't so much as seen his general. Several generals were far too egoistic.'

For his part Boulart has been assigned a place on a bearskin

'in a vast courtyard of an immense building on the left as you come in. I was on the snow, but two walls were sheltering me, and I wasn't too badly off. I had the pleasure of again meeting Lieutenant Lyautey.[6] In a word, our position seemed to be improving. But we were intensely worried over the fate of Marshal Ney and his corps, whom we believed had been captured.'

Lieutenant Sauvage gets to Orsha at about 2 p.m. and finds the town

'already encumbered by the Imperial Guard and the various corps trying to reunite all the isolated men. Distributions of bread, meat and brandy were being made there. There I again find M. Mabru, Captains Houdart and Bergeret, as well as a dozen gunners of the company. From Captain Houdart I hear that after unheard of efforts the two sapper companies have been almost totally destroyed by the Russians' ball and grapeshot.'

Parked on some high ground are 36 new guns. Elsewhere there's a bridging train.[7] Even in the best of circumstances each of its pontoons needs a dozen big cart-horses to pull it. Surely they can be put to better use? Seeing it's freezing again, Napoleon, concerned as always for his artillery, makes what will turn out to be a near-fatal decision. To burn the Bridging Train.

On the other hand Fain notes that

'everything that may be useful for constructing trestle bridges – tools, iron clamps, nails, forges, coal, ropes – are being loaded on to the carts, passably well teamed, that are to go on with General Eblé.'

Like Jomini, Colonel Séruzier of the horse artillery finds himself attached to Eblé's party and from now on 'with what remained of my guns' is

'at the head of a body of pontoneers, charged with the task of securing the crossings for the army's return, just as I'd had to during our victorious march on Moscow!'

Nor is it only pontoons that are to be abandoned here at Orsha; but also 500 sick, 25 (presumably less serviceable) cannon, and several hundred Russian prisoners. In the morning Griois is sent for by Prince Eugène:

'He received me with his usual kindness. He told me the Emperor was going to divide up several batteries that were at Orsha among the various army corps, and he ordered me to distribute them to IV Corps' artillery companies, adding that it was crucial to the army's salvation to keep these guns until the moment, not far off but decisive, when they'd have to be used.'

Going up to some high ground

'where the park was set up, I found the Emperor's first *officier d'ordonnance*, Colonel *Gourgaud*, who gave me the guns allocated to IV Corps. I gave some to the Italian Royal Guard's gunners, and the rest to the French companies. These guns had no horses; and to harness them up we had to take those of a bridging unit, whose vehicles and boats were being burnt.'

Napoleon will soon be wishing he'd kept his bridging equipment, no matter how many horses would have been needed to draw its pontoons on their massive drays, and had jettisoned some of his guns instead.

A few futile efforts are being made to reform units or build new ones out of the human debris. Lefèbvre tells Pion des Loches – over and above his well-stocked wagon he only has four guns left – to join them up 'with those of Colonel Drouot, commanding the Guard reserve batteries', collect all the gunners and any Line and Guard pontoneers who no longer have any *matériel*, form them into a battalion and continue the march at their head, behind the Old Guard infantry:

'"There are 1,500 of them," the Marshal said, "all armed. You'll form
them up in companies and you'll be commanding a tiptop infantry battalion. Do you really know your infantry drill?" I knew them better than
His Excellency, and that wasn't saying much,'
claims Pion who always knows everything better than anyone else, but for-
gets that Lefèbvre had risen from the ranks of the old Royal Guard. 'Yet I
didn't manage to bring up a single one of those 1,500 men.' V Corps, too,
is reinforced by 'garrisons from Orsha and its surroundings, among them
a depot of Polish cavalry, a most useful help in our pressing state of equine
penury'.

The Dnieper being very wide, everyone's astounded that the Russians
haven't even tried to bar it. 'In our disordered state,' Labaume sees, 'the
most formidable of armies would never have been able to force it without
exposing itself to total ruin.' Dedem too notices:
    'the whole army's surprise at the Russians' complaisance. So we crossed
    the Dnieper on two hastily constructed bridges. Marshal Kutusov had
    left us with the flattering prospect of seeing Victor's and Oudinot's
    corps turn up.'
This puts Napoleon into a good mood – the least thing, Caulaincourt's
noticing, suffices to spark off his optimism. On the other hand, Rapp sees,
he's 'lost all hope of seeing the rearguard again'. There's a massive distribution of food and new clothing, at least to the Guard, which by this time,
according to Bourgogne, consists 'only of 7,000 or 8,000 men, the remnant
of 35,000'. 'We've said good-bye to the Dnieper,' Fain jots down in his journal, 'by burning on its banks[8] carriages, baggage, papers, and everything
we could lighten ourselves of to double up the teams we were conserving.'

Now it's the morning of 20 November. After waiting for his patrol to return
from the Dnieper's far bank and having heard 'from the old sergeant that
the Emperor, the Guard and several corps were already setting out for
Borissow', Le Roy, judging he has no time to lose, has reunited his detachment and marched it back to town, where he finds I Corps has arrived –
but not before the wretched and heroic 30th Line has lost three more officers and seventeen men before getting to the bridgehead and the protection of some guns placed on a hilltop. Sending his men back to their units,
Le Roy finds the 85th
    'bivouacked on the crest of a hill dominating the town, where it had
    taken shelter against the walls and gardens which in happier times had
    been Orsha's ornament'.
Sad news. Poor resourceful Sergeant-Major Ballane – he who'd pinned all
his hopes on his officer's insignia but had them stolen at Smolensk – has
died the previous day. The 85th's Major Frickler, too, seems to be sicken-
ing after stilling the pangs of hunger with hemp seed. None of this pre-
vents the lucullean Le Roy and Jacquet – presumably Guillaume too –
from sharing 'a well-cooked ham'. That morning, after marching for an

hour and a half with the Hessian Footguards, Roeder ('very ill') too arrives and rides

'straight over the Dnieper bridge, 125 paces long. On a hill on the far bank I found Colonel Follenius. Mustered all those of our men who'd gone on ahead. On this hill we were told the army was to take three routes: via Minsk, Vilna and Witebsk. We were to take the first route.'

Just as Roeder's jotting these words down in his diary, Berthier, perhaps, is reading a report which, dated that same day, is from Jomini and mainly concerns the state of the routes westward,[9] particularly to Minsk. But his letter opens, almost offhand, with a rumour which, if true, is devastating indeed:

'*Monseigneur. I heard yesterday that the enemy has occupied Minsk with a corps of regular troops. Because of this I feel I must remind Your Highness, who has not followed that route, that from Bobr to Minsk there are 34 leagues of continual forests, constituting a defile where a little infantry troop with cannon could hold up the march of an army. Throughout the whole extent of this road it is impossible to pass either to right or left of it.*

'There is also an error in the distances marked on the map. Semolevice is eleven leagues from Minsk and ten from Borissow ... The map shows five to six leagues less. That road is bare of everything except woods and swamps.'

Minsk – with all its stores, enough to feed 100,000 men for six months, clothe and rearm them – taken? It's incredible. Even more than incredible, it's terrifying. Surely it can't be true? How can Schwarzenberg, whose prime task has been to keep it secure, have been so remiss?

No sooner has IHQ tumbled to the disaster which must be befalling III Corps than everyone from Napoleon down sets about washing his hands of it:

'The Prince of Eckmühl [Davout] wasn't generally liked. The Prince of Neuchâtel [Berthier], rather as if he wanted to clear himself in advance, was showing everyone the General Staff's orders to the Prince of Eckmühl. He showed them to me. The outburst of fury against Marshal Davout was the more general in that the Emperor publicly charged him with being responsible for all the dangers that might overwhelm III Corps. Great and small alike seized the opportunity of casting their stones at him, without finding out whether the orders he'd received, the advice he'd given to Ney, or the circumstances of the moment, didn't justify him.'

Yet in some obscure way everyone's pinning his faith on Ney. 'To his everlasting glory', Caulaincourt goes on, the army has only one opinion about him:

'To catch up with us on the Krasnoïe road was regarded as an impossible task. But if anyone could make the impossible possible, Ney was the man. Every map was in use, everyone pored over them, tracing out the route he'd follow if courage could open a way for him. "He'll retreat through Kiev rather than surrender," was the general view.'

The only fear is that at the sound of IV Corps' guns at Krasnoïe Ney may have got himself killed while trying to fight his way through. As IHQ leaves Orsha at noon on 20 November, the Master of the Horse observes Napoleon,

'dressed as usual in his chasseur officer's coat and a great overcoat, on foot at the head of his guards, surrounded by a numerous staff. He seemed to be most uneasy, and was marching hesitantly. At each moment he halted, and only after doing so for a quarter or half an hour did he resume his march. Doubtless the purpose of these repeated halts, which seemed to surprise everybody, was to wait for the rearguard, of which we still had no news, and give it a chance to rejoin us. Consternation stood painted on every face.'

Some twelve miles further on IHQ halts again, this time in 'a miserable peasant village', before finding lodgings in Baranouï manor house, a couple of miles from the road.

For several days now there's been no courier. No news from Victor's operations on the Dvina. Or from Schwarzenberg, who should be making Tchitchakov's presence on the Berezina impossible. Napoleon speculates:

'"No doubt Tchitchakov intends to join up with Tormassov, and they'll send an army to the Berezina, or rather to join Kutusov in this hilly country. As I've always thought, Kutusov's leaving us alone now so as to get ahead, and is going to attack as soon as these reinforcements have reached him. We must hurry. If my orders have been carried out I too will have my forces assembled on the Berezina. We've got to get there as fast as possible, because great things may happen there."'

'For the first time,' says Caulaincourt, 'he struck me as worried about the future.'

As for what's happening to Ney, that's anyone's guess.

CHAPTER 12

NEY'S AMAZING EXPLOIT

Ney leaves Smolensk – a naked man runs twelve miles – 80,000 Russians to 6,000 Frenchmen and Württembergers – 'we marched across ploughed fields, suffering horribly from hunger' – General Henin's obstinacy – 'We were still eight leagues from Orsha' – 'Our position isn't brilliant, Marshal' – 'Go and tell your general a Marshal of France never surrenders' – a tragic lieutenant of Voltigeurs – 'Ney's calmness kept the men to their duty' – 'Qui vive?' – 'France!' – 'there was a joy hard to describe'

Of the 11,000 men of III Corps who'd left Moscow only 3,000 had reached Smolensk. 'Nothing was left of the Württemberg division or the cavalry. The artillery had only retained a few guns.' Fezensac had admired his men's staunchness as they'd slowly withdrawn through the eastern suburbs into the Old City. His 500 men of the 4th Line had been the last to withdraw from the burnt-out ruins beyond the Dnieper. 'During the three days this affair had lasted,' he assures us, 'no notice had been sent to Ney of the danger' about to engulf him.

In the city, reinforced by the 129th Line, the Illyrians and I Corps' 2nd Division – of which the 2nd and 3rd Battalions[1] of Joseph-Napoleon's Spanish Regiment form part – Ney had 'assembled all the isolated detachments and united them with his own corps, reorganising a battery of six guns' (to which 20 men of Lieutenant Sauvage's company have been attached, though Sauvage himself, as we've seen, had marched on ahead with I Corps). Then, in the afternoon of 16 November, one of Davout's ADCs, a Major de Briqueville, had come back to tell Ney that I Corps was ordered to hasten its steps and recommended he do likewise. Ney – according to Caulaincourt, who'll hear about it afterwards, presumably at the Baranouï manor house – receives Briqueville

'ungraciously enough. The two marshals didn't like each other. They'd just had a difference of opinion about the pillage of Smolensk.'

In fact there'd been a blazing row. Ney had accused Davout of stripping the magazines, leaving nothing for III Corps. ('When I in my turn entered the town,' Bonnet had written in his diary, 'I could find nothing for my regiment or myself.')

In the evening a second messenger had arrived. Since he, Davout, was going to force the pace to support Eugène, who was at grips with the Russians outside Krasnoië, he advises Ney to leave forthwith. To this Ney, who only has a few hours to provision his corps and is forced to choose between starving en route and being cut off, replies arrogantly that 'all the Russians on earth and all their Cossacks won't be strong enough to prevent me passing through them'.

'Of the last orders sent to him, one never reached him, and the other only arrived in the evening of 16 November, when it was too late. These delays were due to the state of our communications.' Communications now so bad as to be non-existent:

'A lieutenant and twelve men who'd been sent back to Smolensk for food were all captured by the Cossacks as they tried to return. Only a drummer got back – leaving 43 of the 67 men to answer roll call that morning.'

That evening, as he retires through what's left of this city which he (like Le Roy) had known as a prisoner of war in 1807, Fezensac sees

'the doors and windows of what remained of its houses shattered, the rooms full of corpses, in the middle of its streets carcasses of horses, all of whose flesh had been eaten by the soldiers and even by some of the inhabitants.'

Major Bonnet realises that the town's 'on fire for the second edition [*sic*]'. 'The fire', says General *J.-D. Freytag*, whose division leaves at midnight, 'was so violent that the bright light of its flames in the midst of a very dark night lit up our way for us for 12 miles.' Fezensac will

'never forget the impression of sadness I felt that night, in the deserted streets by the light of the fire reflected in the snow and contrasting singularly with the soft clarity of the moonlight'.

Colonel Schmidt of the Illyrians is carrying out his orders to blow up the medieval walls and ramparts, and as Bonnet marches out with Razout's division at 3 a.m., he sees

'one of the towers of the rampart, standing up on the horizon against the glow, leap up and lie down, overthrown by the mine laid underneath it'.

It's the so-called Royal Citadel.[2] Just as he's leaving, Fezensac hears 'several strong explosions'. But then Miloradovitch's Cossacks come bursting in and prevent his men from doing more damage: 'Their many guns killed or wounded more than half his Illyrians.' Luckily Schmidt himself, against his own gloomy forebodings, finds he's unscathed.

Ney's battalions are now massed in bodies 'three or four times greater than before Smolensk'. And march on, undisturbed by Cossacks. Major de Briqueville is with them, but his message, it seems, has been forgotten. No one realises that III Corps is cut off. But when Freytag's division is 'half-way to Krasnoïe' and has 'halted briefly to wait for daybreak' something astounding happens:

'We saw running toward us a man who'd been stripped of all his clothes, having absolutely nothing on but his shirt. It was a sergeant-major who'd been in hospital at Smolensk. At the height of the fire this unfortunate man, forgetting his sickness and the terrible cold then prevailing, had run through the flames and ruins, and having done twelve miles, he'd reached us, still running. Unfortunately we couldn't lend him the least scrap of clothing, we had none ourselves.'

Tragically the sergeant-major 'having escaped from the enemy, the flames and his fatigue after covering such a distance at such a speed' expires of cold 'in the midst of his own men'.

All day their march goes on. And when, as they're advancing quietly along the Krasnoië road at dawn on 18 November, they 'hear a lively cannonade' in the distance ahead of them, everyone assumes it can only be Victor's IX Corps, sent to their assistance. On the other hand they keep seeing 'traces of bivouacs obviously not French'. Between 1 and 2 p.m.

'we were approaching Krasnoië, when, as a tailpiece to these reflections, some roundshot reached us from our left; and soon we were filing past some rather well-nourished gunfire. Colonel Reissenbach was sent forward with some voltigeurs in line of skirmishers against these pieces.'

But what unit is this in the morning fog 'to the right of the road, less than a league from Krasnoië' which Bonnet sees 'rallying, not having been able to force its way across the Krasnoië ravine'? It's Ricard's brigade[3] – seconded from I Corps at Smolensk – that's run into

'the enemy drawn up in battle order not far from that town. Now it was our turn. He presented long lines of cavalry, several infantry corps, and his left extended to a short distance from the highway. A rather deep ravine separated us from the Russians, who were opening a cannonade and deploying some formidable artillery.'

Major Faber du Faur, commanding the remaining three 12-pounders of Ney's reserve artillery, sees

'swarms of Cossacks approaching to within 4,500 paces and crossing the road in all directions. Their artillery saluted our column with a murderous discharge of roundshot and grape. Scarcely had we made the painful attempt to take the guns off their limbers than most of our teams were blasted to pieces by the enemy fire, and we saw ourselves unable to advance our guns.'

So they spike them and leave them to the Cossacks. After which his surviving gunners, 'the armed men at our head', join the compact mass of unarmed men.

Only now, it seems, as Ricard's survivors come staggering back to the right of the road to take refuge with Ney's three divisions, do they realise that it's not Marshal Victor's army corps that's come to meet them:

'It had been the Prince of Eckmühl who'd come to grips with the Russian army and tried to force his way through to Krasnoië. The enemy had been waiting for us on the heights, to cut off our retreat. The Russian army, ranged in line of battle, was barring the route.'

Ney, in observation on the other side of the ravine, has only 6,000 combatants, six cannon and his personal escort of 'two squadrons of Polish lancers' plus the usual horde of stragglers and camp-followers to embarrass his movements. There's a thickish morning mist. But through it he sees he has against him Miloradovitch's 80,000 men, drawn up in front of the forests away to the left and across the road. Forming up his line of battle in the plain, Ney assembles 'all the sappers, and adding to them 100 of the most determined men,' entrusts their command to Colonel Bouvier of the Engineers:

'Supported by a few guns and the rest of our rearguard, he had to attack and punch a hole in the enemy; but at the height of the action this brave officer was felled by a roundshot and his troops were repulsed by cross-fire from an enemy anyway vastly superior in numbers.'

At this moment one of Miloradovitch's ADCs approaches under a flag of truce. He tells Ney he's confronted by an army of 80,000 men. If the Marshal wants to convince himself of the truth of this statement he can send an officer to see with his own eyes. Miloradovitch, he says, admires his talents and courage; and this doesn't permit him to propose anything unworthy of so great an officer as Marshal Ney. But the fact is he's been abandoned by the rest of the French army. And has no option but to surrender. – 'For sole reply, taking a few salvoes of gunfire as a pretext, the Marshal took the spokesman prisoner,' confiding him, says Tschudi, to the 48th Line.

Bonnet's colonel, commanding the brigade that's come to include the 'Illyrians, the 4th Line's two battalions, and ourselves, also two battalions strong', leads the attack and charges with the 4th Line. To the right, Ricard's already in action again:

'The 48th were ordered to cross the ravine, follow the highway in closed column and then abruptly change direction to the left, to charge the Russians with the bayonet as soon as parallel with their flank.'

But the moment the enemy see what they're about, the 48th are

'crushed by the Russian artillery. No one had ever seen such dense or continuous grapeshot. Even so, these soldiers, dying of hunger and cold, charged so vigorously that we twice saw the enemy's guns beat a retreat and form battery again. Both the general of brigade and the colonel, several paces ahead of the first platoon, were gravely wounded.'

His arm shattered by a fragment of grape, the 48th's colonel realises that

'this rumour, spreading through the ranks, seemed to be worrying the rank and file, but went on marching at the head of his unit, and didn't leave the field of battle until he'd been hit in both legs by two pieces of grapeshot. The regiment, which had only 650 men under arms, lost 550 of them and had to recross the ravine.'

Fezensac, marching at the head of the 4th Line along the road criss-crossed by cannon fire, sees how every cannon shot is

'carrying off whole files. At each step death was becoming more inevitable. Yet our march wasn't slowed down for a single instant.'

'Favoured by the fog,' says Bonnet, the 18th Line cross the ravine,

'but amidst a hale of grape. Climbing up its other side I was hit in the cheek by a fragment which almost made me lose consciousness. I left my rank. The regiment impetuously continued its charge and, taking off to the right, threw back a line of infantry; but enveloped by numerous cavalry it was itself annihilated, except for two or three officers who'd been wounded early on, and the colonel, Reissenbach, the officers of his company and myself. The Eagle was left there.'

The leading 'division'[4] of Fezensac's regiment, 'utterly crushed by grapeshot,' is thrown back on to the one behind it,

'carrying disorder into its ranks. The Russian infantry charged us, and the cavalry, falling on our flanks, threw us into a complete rout. For a moment a few well-placed skirmishers halted the enemy's pursuit. Ledru's [10th] division was put into the line, the six guns replied to the numerous Russian artillery. During this time I rallied what was left of my regiment on the highway where roundshot was still reaching us. Our attack hadn't lasted a quarter of an hour, yet the 2nd Division no longer existed. My regiment was reduced to 200 men. The Croat [Illyrian] regiment and the 18th, which had lost its eagle, were even worse treated.'

For the 2nd Division, which also includes Colonel Tschudi's Spaniards, 'it had been impossible to reconnoitre the enemy lines because of the fog,' its Commandant Lopez will remember:[5]

'We'd crossed the ravine, swept by grape from the enemy batteries, of which we captured two guns. General Ricard, wounded in the head at the action's outset, had still gone on giving orders. He was everywhere at the same time, electrifying the men with his shouts of *"Vive l'Empereur!"*'

By now the Joseph-Napoleon's two battalions are 'only 35 files strong, having had 76 men killed or wounded in this affair, eight of them officers'.[6] More than half the Croats, too, have been put out of action, and Colonel Schmidt's been wounded in the leg. Ricard's men have made

'an impetuous attack without artillery, unsupported by I Corps' other divisions and, despite the fire of 50 pieces of cannon placed in an advantageous position, had thrice overthrown the Russian line.'[7]

It's also been the end of the 18th Line. 'So,' Bonnet, his cheek streaming with blood, realises, 'the road to France was cut off for us.' 'While we were ranged in order of battle in the plain,' Freytag goes on,

'all the time standing up to a terrible and continuous fire, our carriages, our horses, part of the artillery and all the unarmed men, the stragglers and the sick who'd remained on the road, fell into the power of a "hurrah" of Cossacks. All the food and the few resources still remaining to us were lost. Marshal Ney gave orders that if possible the fight should be sustained until dusk, in order to retreat by the Dnieper.'

Thus begins Ney's ever-famous night retreat.

At first he thinks he'll make a detour southwards and aim for Molihew. But the wounded Colonel Pelet of the 48th Line (so Captain François will hear), points out to Ney (who'd 'bitterly' complained that the Emperor 'was abandoning the rearguard, what will become of us?')[8] that the Russians are stronger on that side. So perhaps it'll be better to cross the Dnieper on its ice and get to Orsha that way? The Dnieper lies only nine miles away; but to find a road to it means retracing their steps for three miles. Fezensac relates 'verbatim, a singular dialogue':

'Ney's self-confidence equalled his courage. Without knowing what he meant to do nor what he could do, we knew he'd do something. The greater the danger, the prompter his determination; and once having made up his mind, he never doubted he'd succeed. His face expressed neither indecision nor disquietude. All looks were fixed on him, no one dared interrogate him. Finally, seeing an officer of his staff beside him, he said to him:

'"We're in a bad way."

'"What are you going to do?"

'"Cross the Dnieper."

'"Where's the road?"

'"We'll find it."

'"And if the river isn't frozen?"

'"It will be."

'"*Well, the best of luck to us!*"'

It's about 4 p.m. and dusk is already falling as Fezensac's men, 'suffering horribly from hunger', march off

'across ploughed fields. I was on foot, like any ranker. At the beginning of our attack on Krasnoïe I'd had a horse killed under me and it was impossible to find another.'

'At about 9 p.m.' Freytag goes on, 'we reached a village on the banks of the Dnieper. All we found in the way of food was a drink made of beetroot.' The village's name is Danikowa. Pretending to bivouack there for the night, Ney lights fires and places outposts. Meanwhile a lame peasant is 'found and used as a guide to tell us where the Dnieper's most likely to be frozen. Led by this peasant we set off.' By and by they come to a second village – François calls it Gusinoë – where the Dnieper has steep banks.

'It was Marshal Ney's intention to wait for dawn before crossing the river. Since it wasn't entirely frozen over despite the extreme cold, it was crucial to be able to see clearly so as to find those points along it where the ice was thick enough to bear the weight of men and horses.'

While the surgeons give what first aid they can to the wounded, Ney snatches some sleep.

'Ney alone, oblivious of the day's and morrow's dangers, slept deeply. But at midnight a message arrives of the enemy's approach. Cossacks have even been seen in the village. Marshal Ney at once ordered the crossing to begin – the guns and their ammunition wagons were abandoned.'

Likewise the non-walking wounded.

'Disorder and confusion were extreme. Everyone tried to get across first. We slid down very gently one after another, fearing we'd be swallowed up under the ice, which was cracking at every step we made. At every moment we were between life and death. But apart from the danger to ourselves we had to witness the saddest spectacle. All around us we saw unfortunates who'd fallen into the ice with their horses up to their shoulders begging their comrades for a help they couldn't give. Their complaints tore at our hearts, already overwhelmed by our own perils. Reaching the other side we had to clamber up a very steep bank, twelve feet high. It was all slippery from those who'd gone before us and made the ascent impracticable'

– in a word, the same situation as at the Wop.

'Three times I'd reached the top, and three times I fell back into the river. My strength was beginning to desert me when I heard the voice of Marshal Ney telling me to make haste and come up. "I can't", I said, "unless someone helps me." Instantly the Marshal used his sabre to cut a branch off a tree, reached it down to me and in this way pulled me up. Without his aid I'd infallibly have perished.'

So thin is the ice that 'very few horses were able to get across'. Fezensac confides 'the Duke of Piacenza to two sappers, who finally saved him and M. de Briqueville who'd been dangerously wounded the previous day and who crossed the Dnieper by dragging himself on his knees. The troops formed up again on the other side of the river.' 'In the midst of such disorder', Freytag goes on,

'it was very hard to rally the scattered troops, discouraged as they were and almost succumbing to the intense cold. The cavalry, above all, delayed us. It was impossible for it to cross at the same point as we had. So it had to go a long way to find a more solid passage. At last it rejoined us, and we set out.'

But Fezensac sees little if anything of it:

'Success had already crowned the Marshal's first plan. We were over the Dnieper. But we were more than 15 leagues [45 miles] from Orsha. And must get there before the French army had left it. We were going to have to cross unknown districts and stand up to enemy attacks, with only a handful of exhausted infantrymen, without either cavalry or artillery.'

Next day, surprisingly, those who've got across find themselves unmolested. They pass through a village full of sleeping Cossacks, whom they take prisoner:

'At first daylight on 19 November we took the Liubavitschi road. Only for a few moments were we held up by a few Cossack outposts, who fell back as we approached. By midday we'd reached two villages on high ground, whose inhabitants hardly had time to flee and abandoned their provisions to us. The men were falling into the joy caused by a moment of abundance when we heard the shout: "To arms!"'

The Russians are pushing back their outposts:

'The troops came out of the villages, formed up in a column, and got going again, the enemy being in presence.'

Even if it's only Cossacks there are entire squadrons of them

'manoeuvring in an orderly manner, and commanded by General Platov himself. Our sharpshooters contained them, the columns quickened their pace while preparing themselves to meet cavalry.'

If Ney's men aren't afraid of them it's because 'Cossacks never dared drive home against an infantry square'. Much more serious, Platov has some guns on sledges. At 3 p.m., just as the few survivors of the 18th Line are halting in a village, they see some Cossacks:

'Three masses appeared, of about 100 horses. We took up our weapons and marched against them. As the hostile cavalry retired it led us on to a dozen guns which briskly saluted us. By marching to the left through shrubs and bushes we supported ourselves on the bank of the Dnieper.' They manage to march past them. 'Until nightfall Marshal Ney fought unceasingly against so many obstacles, availing himself of the least accidents of the terrain.' But as darkness falls he has to turn his column off to the left, 'along the woods which fringe the Dnieper. The Cossacks had already occupied them.' The 4th and 18th Line, led by General Henin, are ordered to throw them out. 'Meanwhile the enemy artillery took up position on the other side of a ravine we'd have to cross. It was there Platov was counting on exterminating the whole lot of us.'

Fezensac leads his regiment into the wood and the Cossacks withdraw; but so dense and black is the forest his men have to face in all directions at once:

'Night came down, we heard nothing from around us. Ney, as likely as not, was still marching on. I advised Henin to follow his movement. To avoid being reproached by the Marshal for leaving the post he placed him in, he refused.'

At that moment they hear loud shouts at some distance, indicative of a charge being made: 'So it became certain our column was continuing its march and we were going to be cut off.' Fezensac assures Henin

'that the Marshal, whose way of doing things [*manière de servir*] I knew very well, wouldn't send him an order. It was up to each unit commander to act according to circumstances; and anyway he was by now too far off to be able to communicate with us. The 18th had certainly left long ago.'

So he should follow on. But all Henin agrees to, at the utmost, is to join up with the 18th and so re-unite the two regiments. But the 18th has already left the scene, and 'instead we ran into a squadron of Cossacks'. But though Henin, too late, tumbles to his situation, and 'though we searched the woods in all directions' they can no longer find their road:

'The fires we saw lit on various sides still further helped to bewilder us. The officers of my regiment were consulted, and we went in the direction the majority suggested.'

With only 100 of his men left to him, Fezensac is more than an hour's march behind the column. He has to march as fast as possible, while fighting off Cossacks

'who kept shouting at us to surrender and firing point-blank into our midst. Those who were hit were abandoned. A sergeant had his leg shattered by a shot from a carbine. He fell at my side, and said coldly to his comrades: "Here's a man done for; take my pack, it'll be useful to you." Someone took his pack, and we left him in silence. Two wounded officers suffered the same fate. Yet I noticed uneasily the impression this state of affairs was making on my regiment's men, and even on its officers. Then so-and-so, a hero on the battlefield, seemed worried and troubled – so true it is that the circumstances of danger are often more frightening than the danger itself. A very small number preserved the presence of mind we were in such need of. I needed all my authority to keep order as we marched and to prevent each man leaving his rank. One officer even dared give it to be understood we'd perhaps be forced to surrender. I reprimanded him aloud, so much the more sharply as he was an officer of merit, which made the lesson more striking.'

Finally, after over an hour, they see the Dnieper to their left. Fezensac's men recover their spirits. And Henin makes them march along the river bank, so the Cossacks shan't outflank them. And though Platov's cannon open fire at them, their aim in the darkness is chancy. Over the plain, over ravines whose sides are so steep they can hardly clamber up them, wading half-frozen streams up to their knees, they march on. Not a man quits the ranks:

'General Henin, hit by a fragment of casing from a bursting shell, wished to say nothing about it, for fear of discouraging the men, and went on commanding with the same zeal. Doubtless he could be reproached with obstinacy for defending the Dnieper wood too long; but at such difficult moments error is pardonable. What no one will deny him, at least, is the bravery and intelligence with which he guided us as long as this perilous march went on.'

At last, just as Ney's about to set out again, they see, ahead of them, his campfires. So, though utterly exhausted, the men of the 4th march for yet another hour, until they come to a village where there are some provisions and they can rest up. Yet

'we were still eight leagues from Orsha, and Platov would unquestionably redouble his efforts to carry us off. At 1 a.m., the fall-in was beaten.'

Freytag, too, though with the main body, has been having a nightmarish night. Forced to cross a swamp where the rearguard was being ravaged by grapeshot, he'd only managed to do so by clinging to a horse's tail:

'Although it was the darkest of nights we rallied and formed up in line of battle. A senior Russian officer came quite close to shout to us: "Surrender, surrender – all resistance is useless." "Frenchmen fight but don't surrender," replied General Ledru des Essarts, and ordered us to fire by platoons. We'd shared out the cartridges left after the battle at Krasnoïe. We marched on, always harassed by the enemy. The third day [20 November] at about 3 p.m., Marshal Ney made us take up a position with our backs to a forest.[9] We had a great deal of difficulty in scraping together 1,500 men who were in a state to hold their arms. But the monstrous cold made them incapable of using them.'

'To present a more imposing front we formed up in two ranks. All who'd lost their weapons or thrown them away when crossing the Dnieper were placed behind them. In front of us we saw a swarm of Cossacks, whose skirmishers came to within pistol-shot range. Nevertheless our troops stood with arms shouldered, and for lack of cartridges only pretended to fire when the Cossacks advanced by troops. Whereupon they retired and contented themselves with manoeuvring in front of us.

It was at that moment that Marshal Ney came up to me and said:
'"Well, Freytag, and what d'you think of this?"

'"That our position isn't brilliant, Marshal. But even that wouldn't be too bad if we only had some cartridges."

'"True; but it's here we must know how to sell our lives dearly."

'At nightfall the Marshal had fires lit at distances, to make the enemy think we were going to spend the night in the forest. At the same time he told us unit commanders to prevent our troops from giving themselves over to sleep, because at 9 p.m. we'd be breaking camp. In this interval the Russian general commanding-in-chief sent a flag of truce to summon Marshal Ney to surrender with his feeble army corps which, he said, couldn't fight the 100,000 Russians who surrounded it. I was present at the interview, and this was Ney's reply to the spokesman:

'"Go and tell your general a Marshal of France never surrenders."

'An hour later a second came to us, with the same purpose:

'"As for you, monsieur," the Marshal told him, "you'll stay with us. I'd very much like you to see for yourself how French soldiers surrender."

'At 8.45 a third came to claim his predecessor, and put the same proposition to the Marshal.

'"That makes two of you", he said again, "to see for yourselves in what fashion I'm going to surrender to the Russians."'

'While this flag-of-truce was speaking to Marshal Ney,' (Captain François will hear afterwards),

'the Russian kept throwing glances in all directions. The Marshal had him blindfolded and put under guard of a few troopers. The officer's protests were of no avail. Yet it was true. The Russians surrounded us on all sides. At 9 p.m. exactly the Marshal gave the order to fall in without making the least noise. He advised us[10] to make our troops march in close formation and without uttering a word. We set off and with the greatest sangfroid and in the deepest silence passed through the Russian camp. However, the enemy noticed it. But before they could start shouting their hurrahs we were out of their camp. It was so dark and we marched so fast they couldn't get at us. Not that they didn't send many cannon shot after us or capture some stragglers, if one can apply this name to unfortunates who'd have needed supernatural strength to escape their destiny.'

By this time Henin's brigade has rejoined. The column trudges on undisturbed until daybreak. Then the Cossacks re-appear, taking advantage of its having to cross a plain,

'Platov advanced on sledges the artillery we could neither avoid nor get at. And when he thought he'd thrown our ranks into disorder, ordered his Cossacks to charge home. Marshal Ney swiftly drew up each of his two divisions in square. The 2nd, commanded by Henin, being the rearguard, was the first to be exposed.'

Fezensac has to use the strongest threats to force all isolated men who still have a musket to join the ranks. The Cossacks, 'feebly contained by our sharpshooters and driving before them a mob of unarmed stragglers, tried to reach our square. At their approach and under the gunfire the men forced the pace. Twenty times I saw them about to disperse and run on all sides, deliver themselves and us to the Cossacks' mercy. But Marshal Ney's presence, the confidence he inspired, his calm at so dangerous a moment, kept them to their duty. We reached some high ground. The Marshal ordered Henin to make a stand there, adding that it was a question of dying for the honour of France. Meanwhile General Ledru was marching for Jokubow [Teolino], a village with its back to a wood. When he'd established himself there we went and joined him. The two divisions took up position, each flanking the other. As yet it wasn't midday and Marshal Ney declared he'd defend this village until 9 p.m. A score of times General Platov tried to carry it. His attacks were constantly driven off and, in the end, weary of so much resistance, he took up position facing us. Already that morning the Marshal had sent off a Polish officer to Orsha.'

When the time comes to resume the march Ney's men are so weary he has to set fire to the 'big village' to get them to leave its houses. In the fire's lugubrious light Fezensac contemplates the spectacle of Ney's rearguard:

'The previous day's fatigue and the water filling my boots had brought back all my previous sufferings. Hardly able to march, I leant on the arm of M. Lalande, a young voltigeur officer.'

Earlier, Fezensac has had occasion to reprimand him. But now, very pleased with him,

'I felt the moment had come to promise to make it up for him, and promised him he'd be the first in the regiment to be promoted captain.'

Tragically, the voltigeur lieutenant too falls; 'but I like to think that the hope I'd given him sustained his courage for a while and perhaps softened the horror of his last moments.' 'But the enemy wasn't in force,' Bonnet sees, 'and despite their demonstrations, their bivouac fires, which seemed to have been lit by 10,000 men, we passed through their lines at 9 p.m.'

It's a bright moonlight night. At Orsha, Davout's been ordered 'incessantly to send back scouts along the Smolensk road' and Eugène too has been told to wait for Ney until midnight. 'If we didn't get any news of him by then we must go on our way and give up all idea of ever seeing him again.' But who's this officer coming across the endless expanse of snow towards the 1st Guard Lancers' outposts, commanded by Chlapowski?

'In the distance we take him for a Russian. But soon he's recognised as a Frenchman [sic]. We go to meet him and are overjoyed to learn that Marshal Ney and his men have escaped by a miracle and are only a league away.'

By and by Chlapowski and his Poles make out

'the brave Marshal himself, riding a wretched horse, followed by a few hundred men under arms, and an almost equal number of disarmed soldiers who'd thrown away their muskets out of exhaustion. The Marshal's officers told us what had happened during their painful march.'

The incredible news is sent instantly to Eugène, some of whose units have already set off down the Bobr road. Griois, with his fresh artillery from the Orsha depot, is

'already at some distance from Orsha when Prince Eugène, retracing his steps, told me we were going to turn back to meet Marshal Ney, of whom there'd just been news, after several days of cruel anxiety'.

Other units of IV Corps, after being regaled to something so rare as a distribution of rations, superintended by the Royal Guard, 'which had produced a better effect than threats, also – rare indeed – a roof to sleep under,' are 'reposing calmly in the warmth. At the news of Ney's being in peril,' Cesare de Laugier goes on, 'everyone's on his feet'. 'Nothing less than this motive,' Griois confirms,

'was needed to make us, without regret, turn back in the middle of the night and in a very sharp cold mount the Dnieper again without even knowing how far we'd have to go.'

Laugier:

'Retracing our steps, we did two leagues [eight miles] in the dark, often halting to listen. The Viceroy, for lack of any means of communication in this sea of snow, had a few cannon shots fired.'

Griois:

'then we drew up in position, and at the Prince's order, I had my guns fire three shots, to notify III Corps where we were'.

Laugier:

'to which Ney's force replied with some platoon volleys. From that moment the two corps marched to meet each other.'

Thus it comes about that Freytag, Fezensac and Bonnet are struggling over the last lap towards Orsha and 'the Cossack posts along the road are falling back before us' when they see 'a division' of IV Corps, led by the Viceroy himself, has come out 'a whole league' to meet them:

'After the *"Qui vive?"*, to which the answer was *"France"*, he and the Marshal embraced. Immediately there was a joy hard to describe, which somewhat revived our flagging morale.'

Laugier:

'Ney and Eugène were the first to meet, and threw themselves into each other's arms. At this sight everyone broke ranks. Without recognising each other, everyone embraced everyone else – Württembergers, Illyrians, Frenchmen, Poles, Tuscans, Genoese, with Italians clustering around the newcomers, we listened to their Odyssey. We overwhelmed them with our praises, our attentions, and in this moment forgot past ills, men's egoism, the cruelty of fate and future perils.'

Among joyful reunions those of the fourteen officers and 50 other ranks of the 2nd and 3rd Battalions of the Joseph-Napoleon Spanish Regiment – all who're left – are probably not the least emotional. For the first time during the campaign they meet their slightly more fortunate compatriots of the 1st and 4th Battalions. Even Le Roy, five versts [more than three miles] away, hears the shouts of joy coming from Orsha. Laugier writes in his diary that morning:

> 'Pell-mell, forming so to speak only a single family, we've come back to Orsha, where we're helping these unfortunate men to restore themselves and rest, guarded by ourselves.'

The news, of course, has been instantly transmitted to Napoleon at Baranouï – by Gourgaud, who's been left behind at Orsha to supervise the town's evacuation, probably also its destruction. Reaching the Baranouï manor house, he finds Napoleon dining with Berthier and Lefèbvre. Breathlessly he announces the splendid, the amazing news. 'At once,' says Fain, 'the Emperor got up, and grabbing both his arms said with emotion: "Is that really true?"' Several staff officers are sent back to 'tell the Marshal to hasten his steps'. And by and by 'Major de Briqueville, who'd been wounded by a roundshot in the thigh when fighting with III Corps', arrives with all the details. Never has the Master of the Horse known

> 'a victory in the field cause such a sensation. The joy was general. People were drunk with delight. Everyone was on the move, coming and going to tell of this return. It was impossible to resist repeating it to anyone one met. Such a national occasion had to be announced even to the grooms. Now officers, soldiers, everyone was sure we could snap our fingers at misfortune, that Frenchmen were invincible!'

By and by Ney himself appears. 'Never', Chlapowski notices,

> 'was the Emperor more expansive than in this interview. Going to meet him, he told him "I'd have given everything not to lose you."'

But at first Ney, Planat de la Faye notices, is

> 'in a very bad humour, complaining that we'd abandoned him. But when he knew the details of our retreat, he saw very well we'd done everything humanly possible. His gaiety returned, he jokingly uttered one of those soldieresque wisecracks which ran through the army like a powder train: "Anyone who gets back out of this'll need to have his balls tied on with iron wire."'

'Thus,' Captain François, the Dromedary of Egypt, concludes proudly,

> 'was executed one of the finest and most courageous movements ever attempted by so feeble a corps. And it would be to show oneself lacking in the esteem every military man ought to have for Marshal Ney not to recognise his rare talents; also those of Colonel Pelet, who together saved the debris of twelve regiments and a great number of wounded, of employees and non-combatants in the army's extreme rear.'

CHAPTER 13

THE TERRIBLE NEWS AT TOLOCZIN

'We had to keep marching, marching' – good-bye to the Dnieper – the unspeakable Drouot – terrible news at Toloczin – 'this is beginning to be very serious' – 'never was there a more critical situation' – 'people recalled the long wooden bridge at Borissow'

'No more rearguard duty for us,' Bonnet observes with relief at 8 a.m. on 21 November, as he makes ready, despite all promises of ample rations, to leave Orsha without any. All that's left of III Corps,

'some sappers, one or two battalions of Poles and the fragments of 30 different regiments who, unwilling to be captured, have melted together like a snowball',

are being hustled on ahead by Davout's rearguard. Awakened at dawn by the sound of Russian guns – 'the storehouses, very much exposed', have become targets for Russian artillery fire – Lejeune has his pockets filled by a young cousin who's been in charge of the Orsha hospital,

'with sugar and ground coffee. I urged him to flee, go on ahead of our retreat. But he wanted to go indoors again to fetch his money and his overcoat, probably got delayed, disappeared in the crowd, and I've never seen him again.'

As Fezensac marches down the 'fine broad highway, one of the loveliest one can imagine' with its 'magnificent avenues' which Dedem has found 'so beautiful at other times' but where the birches' filigree hangs down in silver veils of icicles, he's wondering how he's going to conserve 'this little handful of men who couldn't be granted a moment's rest'. Only 80 of them are still under arms. 'I was pained to see what a bad state their equipment and shoes were in, how thin they were, and the air of dejection on their faces.' His only consolation, if it is one, is that 'III Corps' other regiments were perhaps in an even worse state than mine'.

Le Roy, who'd woken up in the small hours and, fortified by a 'well-cooked ham', had left with Jacquet and their trusty Guillaume, after cleansing Schmidt's leg wound sustained at Krasnoïe with 'brandy and salt mixed with luke-warm snow water'. At all costs 'they're determined to get to the head of the column.' Oddly enough, Schmidt's wagon – it must have been marching with I Corps – has turned up, and they've been treated to some of its contents. Just beyond the town is the bridge over the Dnieper – 'the natural frontier', Pastoret thinks, 'between Poland and Russia'. As Daru crosses over he remarks to him: 'I've crossed many rivers in my life but never one with such pleasure as this one!' But for much of the day Bertrand's battalion of the 7th Light Infantry remains

'in position on the Dnieper's left bank, our mission being to hold up a cloud of Cossacks as long as possible. Their cries and gallopings hardly scared us. We made this mass respect us until the few guns found at Orsha and the other troops had crossed the bridge. Then it was our turn

to cross over, and the Marshal [Davout] didn't do so until after the battalion's very last voltigeur.'

Once again the straight broad highway with its double lines of silver
birches stretches interminably ahead. 'Beyond the town,' Bertrand goes
on,

'the road was solid ice. We could no longer stand up. Anyone who fell
over dragged down others with him. Many, not being able to get up
again because of the atrocious cold, were left behind at the discretion of
our barbarous adversaries. Sometimes we heard these unfortunates calling out to us, but couldn't go back to help them. All the time we had to
keep marching, marching, to avoid the cannon and irreparable losses.'

Fain and IHQ may have 'set off more cheerfully, the name of Marshal Ney
on everyone's lips'; for Labaume and the rest of Eugène's staff the fine
highway is

'only a place of tears and despair. All we heard on all sides was complaints and groans. Some declared they could go no further, lay down
on the ground and with tears in their eyes gave us their papers and
money to give to their family. A little further on we saw a woman who'd
fainted; others were holding children in their arms, imploring all the
passers-by to give them a bit of bread.'

Colonel Drouot, commander of the Guard's reserve artillery, will one day
impress Napoleon.[1] But just now Pion des Loches is discovering he's 'a
kind of military Tartuffe. Cold and reserved, he's sacrificing everything
and everyone to his own promotion', and taking care neither of his men
nor his *matériel*. Pion knows he's got some supplies hidden away in his
light travelling carriage and invites him and his officers to set up a joint
mess with the 'ten or twelve around the fire'. Drouot turns up alone.
Where are the others? His officers, Drouot replies, aren't in the habit of
eating with him. And when Pion suggests he take some of his provisions
into his carriage, Drouot says he has no room for them. Anyway he still
has a keg of wine intact, and doesn't need them, 'and that'll be enough
for the two of us':

'A few paces away I saw Adjutant-Major Bitche and Surgeon Aide-Major
Boileau sitting near a campfire with a depressed air of "supping by
heart". These poor devils, belonging to no company, ought to be eating
with their colonel.'

So Pion calls them over and promises to feed them daily as far as the
Niemen if they'll guard his wagon with their lives.

Ever since Smolensk Maurice Tascher has been looking after his
younger brother Eugène, a 20-year-old *sous-lieutenant* of artillery, wounded
in one foot near Kolomna, but now with both feet frost-bitten. Eugène –
it's his first campaign but his brother's sixth (the two brothers are nephews
of the ex-Empress Josephine) – is riding on Maurice's sole remaining
horse. During the course of the day, as they and everyone else make for
Toloczin,[2] the tiny relic of Maurice's chasseur regiment sees a Cossack 'hurrah' carry off two companies of cuirassiers.

Before getting there IHQ halts briefly at the village of Kamienska. While trying to find quarters for some wounded men Daru has bumped into a Polish officer who has some news. News which, if true, is very worrying indeed. 'Admiral' Tchitchakov and his part of the Army of Moldavia, which should have been fighting the Turks[3] or at very least Schwarzenberg's Austrians, is in fact advancing on Minsk – with its immense stores of food, clothing and weapons. How can that be? What's Schwarzenberg doing?

Napoleon's plan now, protected by II and IX Corps and with the great Minsk depot as his supply base, is to halt the retreat behind the Berezina. But he's worried. As well he may be.

Toloczin, reached at nightfall, turns out to be
    'a country town of 250 timber houses on a little river crossed by a timber bridge. Two windmills. Continuous plain',[4]
– 'quite a defensible town', Maurice Tascher thinks it when he gets there. The morning's ice has turned to a thaw and hundreds of heavily laden sledges which have gradually been replacing carts and wagons are getting stuck in the slush and having to be abandoned. Here too are stores. Thanks to his commissary's uniform Kergorre, conducting a Treasury wagon, gets hold of a sack of flour and a huge bottle of brandy:
    'By gathering all my strength and despite the crowd of bayonets I managed to drag a sack as far as our house. But General Lefèvre-Desnouëttes had expelled our comrades and put his horses in the barns. Fortunately our industrious friends, profiting from whatever lay to hand, the many wooden fences and a little straw, had prepared the best bivouac in the world. There we found an excellent fire, beds prepared on the snow, but under shelter; the whole as well-arranged as a bivouac can be. The joy was general when they saw our flour and enormous bottle of vodka.'
Kergorre has even obtained some bread. Among the masses of men who've been fleeing on ahead he finds two Königsberg peasants. They have a sledge and two good horses, and are making tracks westwards, having been forced to follow the army all the long way from Königsberg. He and his friends bribe them to take them along with them.
    'Never would they have consented to let us get on to it for mere gold! We had to give them a bit of bread. All the debris of the Polish army were fleeing in sledges. There were several thousand of them, each containing two, three or four officers or soldiers. Soon the crush was such that we had to abandon our Prussians and resume our way on foot.'
IHQ itself lodges in 'some kind of a convent'. And it's here that Napoleon gets some very terrible news indeed. The worst possible news.
    Minsk has fallen!
    All its immense stores 'which the Emperor had been counting on since he'd left Smolensk to rally and reorganise the army' are lost. Its garrison, 4,000 Poles, mostly Lithuanians, under General Bronikowski, have been turned out head over heels by Tchitchakov's 30,000 Russians.

The French *émigré* General Lambert had captured '5,000 invalids and any amount of gunpowder and cannon barrels'. Even more disastrously, the Russians had seized two million rations (40 days' supplies for 100,000 men), 30,000 pairs of shoes and any amount of clothing – everything, in a word, the retreating ragged army's in such desperate need of. How can such a thing have happened? Haven't a total of 80,000 allied troops, notably Schwarzenberg's Austrians and Reynier's Saxons, been more than enough to prevent such a catastrophe?

'It also meant that he must face the disturbing certainty that the Molda-vian Army might already be massed in our rear, instead of, as he'd all along been hoping, trying to join forces with Kutusov on our flank.'

Caulaincourt can't help admiring the way Napoleon takes these shocks:

'The Emperor's character, like steel by fire, was tempered anew by these reversed circumstances, this vista of danger. He immediately made up his mind to hasten the retreat, reach the Berezina if possible before Kutusov, and fight and vanquish whatever stood in his way. He was sure he'd find the Berezina bridge well guarded. That was the main thing. On that point he had no qualms.'

Yet waking up suddenly after a brief doze while keeping Daru and Duroc beside him to chat with him, he 'asks these gentlemen, waiting to withdraw till he was asleep', what they're saying.

'"We were wishing", Daru replies, "we had a balloon."'

'"What ever for?"'

'"To carry off Your Majesty."'

'"Heaven knows, things are difficult enough. So you're afraid of being made prisoners of war?"'

'"No, not prisoners of war. They won't let Your Majesty off as lightly as that."'

In the small hours he sends for Caulaincourt. Says:

'"This is beginning to be very serious."'

The Master of the Horse has spent four winters at Petersburg as his ambas-sador. Does he think it's cold enough for the rivers and Berezina marshes to freeze hard? Ney had had to abandon his guns. Yet he'd crossed the Dnieper on the ice? And he goes on 'jokingly':

'"Their balloon isn't to be laughed at. Here's an occasion when only brave men will have a chance of saving their skins."' Once across the Berez-ina, he assures Caulaincourt, he'll again be able to control events:

'"Together with my Guard the two fresh corps I'll find there'll be enough to defeat the Russians. If we can't, we'll have to see what our pis-tols can do. We must be ready to destroy everything, so as to leave no tro-phies to the enemy. I'd rather eat with my fingers for the rest of the campaign than leave a single fork to the Russians. We should also make sure my weapons and yours are in good condition, because we'll have to fight. But are we going to get to the Berezina in time?"'

he muses, asking rather himself (Caulaincourt thinks) than his inter-locutor.

'"Will Victor have resumed the offensive in time to drive off Wittgenstein? If the Berezina passages are closed to us, we may be forced to cut
our way through with the Guard cavalry."'

Almost more than by the military situation he's worried by the lack of any
news. Malet's conspiracy is still festering in his mind. Is France aware of the
disaster that's befallen the army? And he repeats his idea of Caulaincourt
and himself leaving for France. Meanwhile everything superfluous, everything that can bog them down – forks for instance – must be got rid of.
Caulaincourt has a word with Daru, and they agree that

'henceforth everyone who fed in the Emperor's mess should be responsible for his own cup, plate and cutlery if he wanted to keep them'.

The pretext they'll give is that Ségur's canteen mules are giving out.

Morning comes, and Jomini and Eblé hear the terrible news confirmed.
Soon similar details are reaching Labaume at IV Corps headquarters:

'Dombrowski had been ordered to raise the siege of Bobruisk, go to
Minsk and hold it. But the bad dispositions taken by the governor of that
place caused it to be surrendered before help could come. Whereupon
Dombrowski had moved back to Borissow, where he'd found the debris
of the Minsk garrison.'

Secretary Fain reflects in his journal:

'The army is cooped up in a cramped space of fifteen leagues, between
Kutusov, Wittgenstein and Tchitchakov. We're encircled by 140,000 Russians, who hold almost all the outlets. Never was there a more critical situation! Some high-ups are murmuring about memories of Toloczin and
Charles XII. Some are even speaking in low voices of capitulating.'

Nor can the situation be concealed from the troops. An ADC to General
von Ochs of the Westphalians, a Captain Johann von Borcke from Magde-
burg, hears a dark rumour spreading that

'two new armies were threatening our line of retreat. On the march
these rumours steadily gained substance, and the names "Tchitchakov"
and "Berezina" were passing from mouth to mouth. At the time of our
advance, four months earlier, the river had looked very insignificant to
everyone. But now it seemed possible that the crossing might be fiercely
contested. People clearly recalled the long wooden bridge at Borissow
and the black marshy bank. And these recollections were enough to
make us shudder at the prospect of having to fight our way across in the
teeth of a fresh Russian army.'

Cesare de Laugier, too, hears how

'Generals Zayoncek, Junot and Claparède are to burn half the wagons,
luxury carriages and all kinds of small vehicles which have accompanied
us this far, and send the horses to the Guard Artillery. A staff officer and
50 gendarmes are seeing to it that this operation is carried out, on pain
of death.'

Anyone under colonel's rank is only allowed to keep one vehicle. The
horses of the Train, too, are to be sent to the artillery. Evidently it isn't
only the horses pulling the guns and caissons of the Guard Artillery that

are giving out, but also those drawing its treasure chests. Its paymaster Eggerlé opens them and gives everyone advances. Pion, in his turn, opens his wagon and has all his 'candles lit'.

But IHQ's 24-hour halt at Toloczin, Fain notes in his diary, has done its 'men and horses the greatest good'. Just as Pion and his group are about to set off again,

> 'an *officier d'ordonnance* comes to tell us His Majesty's finding the conduct of his Guard's artillery officers scandalous, abandoning guns and ammunition wagons and harnessing their best horses to their wagons to save their personal effects'.

But Pion replies abrasively that *his* officers aren't undressing at bivouacs, like Gourgaud's subordinates are. As for his wagon, it contains food, and 'we prize our lives more than our guns, which are useless anyway, for lack of ammunition wagons and gunners'. But when the *officier d'ordonnance* warns them that the Emperor's just had the wagon of an officer of the Train burnt 'without letting anyone extract any of its contents', second thoughts prevail. Pion's party realises that the same thing can happen to their own wagon. Anyway its horses are obviously unlikely to drag it much further. So they off-load its most valuable foodstuffs on to the animals' backs:

> '"It's all over with us," said Bitche. "In a week we'll all be dead." I emptied my trunk into a travelling-bag I'd had made at Moscow out of one of Prince Bayetinski's tapestries. I gave my sword to Lagrange, who'd lost his. I put about 100 pounds of biscuit and a loaf of sugar into my sack, and four bottles of rum into my canteen, loading myself with a fifth. I distributed a quintal of very fine flour to my comrades, together with my supplies of tea and coffee and the rest of my sugar. There remained more than 150 bottles of wine and liqueurs which we drained off during a large part of the night. Thus a few hours destroyed resources which would have kept us alive a fortnight longer.'

In his much regretted wagon – the one he'd filled so methodically with victuals in Moscow but which they now leave standing by the roadside – Pion also says adieu to

> 'a magnificent spyglass, a pretty little mahogany desk and my box of books. But I kept another box containing a superb Chinese porcelain dinner service which I placed in an artillery wagon.'

Drouot's egoism appalls them. 'Pretending to eat a bit of biscuit and then slipping off aside to drink a few gulps out of a bottle that he was carrying between his greatcoat and his coat', he's not sharing anything with anyone:

> 'Bitche and I never took our eyes off him. More than once we caught him red-handed. I admit he once offered me a long sausage. I cut it into two parts: one very small, which I gave him back, the other very big, which I shared with Bitche and Boileau. I was delighted by my prank,'

but he doesn't get a chance 'to commit a second mistake'. Drouot's superior, 'Old Thunderer' General Sorbier, commander of the Guard artillery, isn't exactly a charming character either. 'A man of medium height, thin and sallow', the sensitive Planat de la Faye finds his face 'cantankerous and repulsive'. He too is 'what's called a bad bedfellow'. Yet even he scorns Drouot, keeps on sending him back to make sure their rearmost *matériel* is keeping up, etc. And finally tells him not to present himself before him unless summoned.

After 'marching with great difficulty along a thawed, muddy road' the Fusiliers-Grenadiers had reached Toloczin at about midday on 22 November and have been 'halting on the far side of the town, drawn up by the roadside'. Alas, Bourgogne's pack – so weary or thoughtless he's becoming – has been abandoned on a sledge to the Cossacks:

> 'So good-bye to my knapsack and its contents, which I'd so set my heart on taking back to France! How proud I'd have been to say "I've brought this back from Moscow!" I saw Cossacks in the distance carrying off their prisoners – and no doubt my poor knapsack too.'

All of a sudden who should he see in the crowd, a basket on her arm, if not the very woman who'd saved his life in that den of thieves at Smolensk? And she too recognises him – 'by my bearskin'. Yes, she tells him, all the brigands who'd beaten her for refusing to do their washing had been killed at Krasnoïe, 'fighting desperately to save their money, for they had a lot of it, above all gold and jewels'. Now she's all on her own:

> 'But if I'd take her under my protection she'd take good care of me. I consented at once, never thinking of the figure I'd cut in the regiment when I turned up with a woman.'

If only Bourgogne can find a house or a stable to change in, she'll give him some fresh linen out of her basket. 'I accepted joyfully. But as we're looking for a suitable place I hear the drums beating.' So telling his new-found 'wife' to follow on and wait for him on the road, he falls in:

> 'Just then the Emperor came past with King Murat and Prince Eugène. Placing himself among the Grenadiers and Chasseurs, the Emperor made them a speech. He told them the Russians were waiting for us at the Berezina, and had sworn that not one of us should get across. Then, drawing his sword and raising his voice: "Let us all swear to die fighting rather than never see our country again!" The oath was taken. Bearskins and shakos were waved on the points of bayonets, and shouts of *"Vive l'Empereur!"* were heard. Marshal Mortier made us a similar speech, received with the same enthusiasm, and similarly with all the regiments. It was a splendid moment, and for the time being made us forget our miseries.'

As for his 'wife', she's been

> 'engulfed in the torrent of Prince Eugène's thousands. They and the corps belonging to Marshals Ney and Davout were in complete disorder. Three-quarters of them were sick or wounded, and the rest utterly demoralised and indifferent to everything.'

Only the Poles of V Corps – after a fall from his horse at the beginning of the retreat Prince Poniatowski's had to hand it over to Zayoncek, a senior guards officer – and Claparède's Vistula Legion seem to be coping.

Claparède himself – his Poles don't like him a scrap – has fallen into despondency. Dedem van der Gelder, indeed, is often finding the Poles so obliging as to 'swap my horsemeat for mutton cutlets and *kacha* soup'. In general, he says, 'the allied troops were finding them much more amiable than the French'.

Amazingly, Le Roy, who's glad to find 'the road firmer than it was yesterday, though the wind and snow seem to want to bring us to a standstill', has a bit of luck. While passing through a hamlet, what does he see abandoned in the middle of the road but a big bear's skin! Picking it up, he puts it on his horse and tells Guillaume to take good care of it. Once again he and his friend Colonel Schmidt of the Illyrians are keeping each other company. Yes, Schmidt agrees again, they're worse off as superior officers than they'd ever been as subalterns. But to Captain François, aching from his multiple wounds, in Davout's rearguard, it's obvious all such distinctions have long ago been lost:

'For a long time now officers of all ranks and the men had the same accoutrements. Nothing more extraordinary than our half-burnt sheepskins and greasy leather garments. Our long beards had icicles hanging down from each hair. Everyone was walking along, speechless, haggard-eyed, stunned. Whenever a man fell, those who could open their mouths said: "There's yet another who's *done a bear*" – *faire l'ours*, such was the expression. And a few instants afterwards one of those who'd just said this *did a bear* in his turn. Some were wearing a beggar's scrip or haversack with a little flour in it hung over their shoulders, with a pot hanging at their side by a bit of string. Others were leading shadowy horses by the bridle, carrying a few victuals and kitchen utensils. If one of these horses fell, we sliced it up and put the flesh on the backs of those that remained, to nourish us.'

Private Jakob Walter, trudging onwards with a *konya* whose unshod hoofs, he's pleased to see, aren't having any trouble with the ice, is noticing that hardly one man in a hundred has a cookpot. To belong to a group, now, is a man's only salvation:

'The units were more or less dissolved. Their wreckage had formed a great number of corporations of six, eight or ten men who marched on together, having their reserves in common, repulsing all outsiders. All these unfortunates walked huddled together like sheep, taking the greatest care not to break up amid the crowd, for fear of losing their little group and being maltreated. Did a man get lost? In that case another corporation took any victuals he might have and pitilessly drove him away from all the fires – if the wind allowed any to be made up – and from any spot where he wanted to take refuge. He didn't cease to be assailed until he'd rejoined his comrades. These men passed in front of the generals, and even of the Emperor himself, without paying more heed to them than they would to the least man in the army.'

Images of ontological catastrophe which will fix themselves in François' mind forever:

'Our heads were hideous, our faces yellow and smoke-begrimed, filthy with the soil of our bivouacs, blackened by the greasy smoke from conifers; eyes hollow, our beards covered with snot and ice. We couldn't use our hands or button our trousers, which many had fastened with a bit of string. Like my comrades, I'd opened mine at the back, but often did my business in them. On all the roads we heard the sound of corpses being ground to pieces under the horses' feet or the vehicles' wheels. On all sides we heard the cries and groans of those who'd fallen and were struggling in the most terrifying death-throes, dying a thousand times while waiting to die.'

Where the route crosses the Molihew road, surgeon von Roos sees

'a Westphalian soldier sitting on the ground. He was holding a big ingot of silver in the shape of a rectangle. Weighing 15–20 pounds, it probably came from a church ornament. He was offering it in exchange for food. But no one wanted it.'

Returning from Molihew whither he'd been sent from Smolensk to order the units stationed there to fall back on Borissow, *Roman Soltyk* of the Topographical Department rejoins the column; and is devastated to see how things have changed in the meantime:

'The infantry, accompanied by the little country horses the French called *konyas*, laden with various objects, was marching all pell-mell with them. The cavalry was almost wholly dismounted, and our troopers were walking painfully on foot. In general the men's clothing was in the worst of states. Their torn coats didn't keep out the cold. Some were covered in women's opulent furs; others in velvet mantles looted from the Kremlin. Others had found nothing to protect them against the rigours of the season but cloth-of-gold or silver chasubles. The men's footwear was in an equally wretched state. Many had wrapped their feet in linen and the bark of trees, tied with bits of string.'

As the cold becomes more severe he often sees

'soldiers, stupefied – or, rather, inebriated by the freezing weather – fling themselves headfirst into a campfire and so die consumed by its flames, without it even occurring to their comrades to drag them out'.

Only when he catches up with IHQ does Soltyk see

'the units we'd rallied in Lithuania and the Guard, above all, marching in good order. The latter was setting an example of devotion and subordination. Harassed by such long marches and such severe privations, its men were marching and dying in their ranks. Although bent under their weight, all were carrying their weapons and packs,. Frequently one saw one totter, fall and expire on the road.'

Next comes Bobr. En route for it, Schmidt, realises his wagon is no longer an economic way of transporting his provisions; and distributes

'biscuit and rice for two days to each man who'd been escorting it, which, with the bread they should have received at Orsha, should suffice for them for several days'.

He also makes them a present of the wagon and its horses. The rest of its contents are distributed among the party and its servants. Le Roy's pickings are some clean underclothes, a shirt and 'a brand new flannel waistcoat, mine being in shreds' – to keep his *embonpoint* warm. Also a couple of pocket handkerchiefs to protect his ears from frost-bite. Le Roy's amazing memory of every meal he has ever eaten will recall that evening's

'rice and a bit of beef, the last we still had, and which we ate with pleasure, despite the mob of people who were resting up and warming themselves in the room. After we'd dipped into the pot, spoonful by spoonful, we gave the rest to our servants.'

But only a bit of a wall of a burnt house provides shelter against the wind. That night (23 November) he and his friend and his servant lie down

'on some still warm cinders. The bearskin sheltered us. We lay pressed against each other to avoid a cold which had resumed with new strength.'

Upon the Illyrian regiment's surgeon suddenly appearing, Schmidt decides to travel on in his cabriolet. And Le Roy returns to him the notes and silver he'd entrusted to him at Smolensk,

'though he made difficulties about taking them, saying that being wounded he was afraid he mightn't get out of the danger we were all in'.

Having no taste for painful *au revoirs* that may turn out to be *adieux*, Le Roy leaves early next morning. And Franz Roeder, sick but no longer able to ride in Colonel Follenius' chaise because of the extreme cold, has to walk for seven hours to get to Bobr. 'Searching for water, my horse broke the ice, stumbled into a water hole and I fell in up to my stomach.' And the horse drowns. The dysentery-ridden Roeder studies his frost-bitten feet, but sees he

'must go on stoutly or perish. I pulled myself together with all the strength of my body and soul and did seven or eight hours on swollen feet.'

Once again his Sergeant Vogel has disappeared. The Hessians' neurasthenic Major Strecker has had some kind of stroke. Only Mailly-Nesle still rides on in his carriage

'in a very sad state of mind. The discouragement was growing daily. They told me they were going to burn our calèche and that I'd have to make do with a horse.'

So taking with him the basic necessities – they include 'one spur' – he too tells his servant Louis to do what he likes with the rest.

Marching for Bobr, Napoleon sends off an order to Oudinot. While Victor goes on manoeuvring his IX Corps to stave off Wittgenstein, II Corps is to come and form the column's rearguard. Clearly, now, only one thing matters. The bridge at Borissow. At all costs the army's last link with France must be saved.

PHASE THREE
ACROSS THE BEREZINA

CHAPTER 14

STRUGGLES FOR THE BORISSOW BRIDGE

Oudinot resumes his command – 'the very type of a light cavalryman' – 2nd Battle of Polotsk – two Marshals at loggerheads – how Minsk was lost – 'they lay down on their faces and no one could lift them up from that position' – Corbineau's long march – racing for 'that accursed bridge' – 'come and take coffee tomorrow at Minsk' – could Marbot have done better?

It had been in the last days of September, while being nursed back to health by his young wife at Vilna, that Oudinot had heard about the burning of Moscow and immediately 'realised what a catastrophe must ensue. All these items of news, his indefatigable artist-batman, Grenadier *François Pils*,[1] saw, had thrown him 'into a state of indescribable agitation'.

Although the doctors had done all they could to keep him there a fortnight longer, on 28 October he'd left to resume command of II Corps. From Borissow, where those wounded generals in Nansouty's convoy able to do so had come to pay him their respects, he'd gone on to Orsha. And on 9 November, in wild country overrun by Cossacks, his party had been met by a detachment of Colonel *Marcelline Marbot*'s 23rd Chasseurs,

'waiting on the road to escort him. The day was so sombre one could

hardly see any longer. But since the Marshal didn't want to hang about,' they'd pushed on to Czéreia to reach Partonneaux's division, IX Corps' largest. And it had been 'at the gates of that town we met a courier bringing the bad news from Borissow' – i.e., of the loss of Minsk.

After the First Battle of Polotsk (18 August), when Saint-Cyr had taken over, II Corps had at first done very little fighting.[2] But its French, Swiss and Croat regiments, almost as much as the Bavarians of Wrede's VI Corps, had been terribly ravaged by sickness. Of the 12,626 Bavarians – half of Saint-Cyr's VI Corps – whom Wrede had mustered on 15 June before crossing the Niemen, only 4,557 were alive in September; and on 15 October only 1,622. Forced marches, typhus, homesickness and, above all, dysentery had killed most of the rest; likewise any number of men in II Corps. The Swiss Lieutenant, *Thomas Legler*, smitten like everyone else, had had to relieve himself 'up to 60 times a day. The doctors were invisible.' He'd been so weak he'd had to cling to the walls of the Jew's house in Polotsk which served for a hospital for himself and five other officers. Finally he'd cured himself by putting hefty doses of 'pepper, cinnamon and nutmeg in my soup'.

From time to time reinforcements had arrived. For instance to the 20th Chasseurs in Corbineau's light cavalry brigade. On 21 August their highly efficient little major *Jean-Nicholas Curély*, fresh from France, had turned up with some 100 troopers. Three days ago the regiment had even fled from the enemy, leaving some Bavarian gunners to be sabred by Russian cavalry, and Curély had had to bear the entire army's reproaches. Self-educated son of a labourer, a real republican of the old stamp who (like Le Roy) regards Napoleon's self-coronation as 'an act of weakness', in the eyes of his comrade de Brack[3] the 38-year-old Curély is 'the very type of a light cavalryman'. His party had formed a brilliant contrast to the rest of the regiment, most of whose horses had no shoes and whose harness was all in pieces. Instantly he'd deployed an activity worthy of Napoleon himself in his best days. The regiment's Colonel Legrange having been sick almost throughout the campaign, Curély had taken over as its effective commander: set the 20th Chasseurs' bakers to baking, its shoemakers to making shoes, and those men who couldn't do anything else to taking turns at grinding corn in a nearby mill. Meanwhile, as always, he'd been tirelessly making good the gaps in his own education, both practical and intellectual, each evening copying out what he'd read during the day. Soon each trooper had his four spare horseshoes and 50 nails. 'As for meat, there was no shortage, the countryside having an abundance of cattle.' So the 20th Chasseurs, at least, hadn't starved.

More substantial had been the 5,000 newcomers, among them 1,000 more recruits, which the four Swiss regiments of the ailing II Corps, now only some 6,000 strong and forever manoeuvring and fighting Wittgenstein's Russians, had received on 12 October. Three days after their arrival, the same day as Murat 500 miles away had been fighting to rescue his advance guard at Winkovo,[4] Wittgenstein had begun his general offensive. The Second Battle of Polotsk had been a most sanguinary affair. To his intense chagrin Legler, though recovered from his dysentery, hadn't been allowed to take part – it had been his day for police duty:

'The enemy column marching at us was said to consist of 20,000 men, the one aiming at our right wing of another 20,000, and the one which on the evening of 17 October had crossed the Dvina at Drissa, of 8,000 men. Thus we had to do with 40,000 men in whose camp there'd been no lack of anything, while a third of us looked like skeletons, and we could only put up 25,000 men to resist them. "Now at last the turn has come to us," everyone was saying, squeezing each other by the hand. "We'll resist to the last man. *Schweitzertreu ist alltag neu* [Swiss fidelity renews itself daily]."'

At nightfall the Swiss grenadiers had broken out from a surrounded churchyard at bayonet point, but when they'd got back to their camp

'150 grenadiers were missing at the roll-call, among them our Captain Gilly, whose corpse was buried with military honours at 11 p.m. in front of his battalion and all the brigade's officers'.

But Curély had been the hero of the occasion, momentarily even capturing Wittgenstein himself. By the end of the day, when Saint-Cyr, himself wounded in the knee, by an elaborate feint managed to evacuate his hospitals, all his provisions, artillery and parks from Polotsk and cross the Dvina, both II and VI Corps had suffered terribly. Of the 2nd Swiss' 1,200 men, for instance, 37 officers had been killed or wounded and 600 other ranks had been left on the battlefield. But it had also been largely Swiss staunchness that had secured the corps' retreat – the one Pouget had been notified of at Witebsk. In one of the three Swiss light infantry companies that have also been covering the heroic retreat is little voltigeur *Jean-Marc Bussy*.[5] Saint-Cyr had told them:

'I know you Swiss. For the attack Frenchmen are brisker. But if it comes to a retreat we can certainly count on your courage and coolheadedness.'

At the Bononia defile Wrede's Bavarians, too, had made a heroic stand, preventing a Finnish-Russian corps from taking II Corps in the rear. 'They showed great bravery,' thought Curély, who'd also participated in the fight with 50 of his 20th Chasseurs and himself been wounded by a lance-thrust in the shoulder. 'We killed all the horses drawing the enemy's guns and caissons, not being able to carry them off.' Even if these Swiss are largely conscripts[6] they have a military tradition all their own. Used to selling their superfluous young men dear (*'pas de l'argent, pas de suisse!'*), they've always been famous for their loyalty to their employers.

Meanwhile Victor's IX Corps, '30,000 strong and consisting of Germans' – apart, that is, from Partonneaux's division, which is mostly French – 'had come up from Smolensk' though not in time to hold the Dvina line. Among its German units are the conscripts – if any are still alive – whom the kindly Duchess Augusta of Saxe-Coburg with heavy heart had seen march out from Coburg last summer.[7]

'For the first time since 17 August we now also saw Marshal Oudinot again, who'd resumed command of II Corps. With this reinforcement we'd have thrown the enemy back over the Dvina if Victor hadn't had other orders in his pocket. These, to us, were an enigma.'

So far Victor's corps hasn't been in any battle. As for what's left of VI Corps, with his wounded knee as 'pretext' (Marbot) Saint-Cyr has handed it over to General Count Wrede.

From the moment when Oudinot had resumed his command he and his fellow-Marshal, the 47-year-old *Claude Perrin Victor*,[8] Duke of Belluno, have been at loggerheads. 'The great fault,' Oudinot's chief-of-staff and newly fledged brother-in-law Lorencez is seeing,

'had been not to give superior command of all the corps on the Grand Army's flanks to one Marshal alone. The Duke of Reggio had tried to get the Duke of Bassano to adopt this measure, but that minister hadn't dared to.'

And from the moment when Oudinot's resumed his command there's been trouble. 'At that epoch,' writes Marbot,

'all the Marshals of the Empire seemed determined not to recognise any rights of seniority among themselves, because none of them was willing to serve under one of his comrades, no matter how grave the circumstances'.

Victor isn't one of Napoleon's favourite marshals. A jaunty perhaps rather shallow personality with a baby mouth, his sunny nature has earned him the sobriquet *Beau-Soleil* ('beautiful sunshine'), causing Napoleon, so it's rumoured, to give him his ducal title (lit. 'beautiful moon') in mockery of his slightly bandy legs. But he's an efficient field commander. Pils goes on:

'*M. le Maréchal* went to see Marshal Victor, whose seniority had given him command of both corps. On 13 November the two Marshals spent two hours in conversation to decide on a common course of action against Wittgenstein.'

That day it's bitingly cold – for the first time Pils and his *patron* have just seen 'a man drop dead not far from a bivouac fire'. But evidently it isn't cold enough to freeze Pils' water-colours, for his brush memorably captures the two marshals' postures where they sit their horses amid the gloom of the Russian winter afternoon, trying to concert their incompatible plans.

Both II Corps and IX Corps, however – some 25,000 Swiss, Portuguese, Illyrians, Bavarians and Frenchmen, all in fairly good fighting trim – are intact fighting forces. II Corps' morale, perhaps, is the better of the two – they've even added twelve captured Russian guns to their own '60 well-harnessed pieces'. But Victor is far from pleased with his.[9]

The two marshals' failure to see eye to eye is causing a serious lack of co-ordination.[10] Marches and counter-marches have followed, which neither Legler nor anyone else among the Swiss can see any sense in. Nor do they see any more of Victor's men – though on one occasion, at least, they've had to come to II Corps' assistance. But II Corps' retreat south-westwards, albeit arduous, has been nothing to compare with the Moscow Army's sufferings. Of *that* neither Oudinot, Victor nor anyone else has the slightest inkling.

But now Minsk has fallen. And the bridge at Borissow must at all costs be secured.

It hadn't only been Bronikowski, the Minsk governor, who'd been in complete ignorance of Napoleon's and the Moscow Army's whereabouts, still less its dilapidated state. So were the Russian commanders in the south. It had been in the first days of October that the fetchingly handsome young French *émigré* Count *L.-V.-L. de Rochechouart* (yet another of the Tsar's many ADCs) had joined Tormassov in Volhynia. A month later it had been decided to split the so-called Army of Moldavia in two:

'The first part, 40,000 men strong under the orders of Admiral Tchitchakov, was to take the road for White Russia and recapture Minsk and Vilna. The second, with the remaining 30,000 men, commanded by General Count Sacken, to stay where it was and go on playing at prisoners' base with Schwarzenberg. We were in utter ignorance of what had happened since the French had evacuated Moscow. Our continual marchings and counter-marchings had deprived us of all regular communications and we were far from envisaging the enemy armies' deplorable condition.'

Tchitchakov's men, on the other hand, are in a 'magnificent state'. Kossecki's Polish brigade, reinforced by 300 troopers of the 18th Dragoons under their Colonel *Lafitte* – a man Bronikowski will afterwards praise for his singular presence of mind – had made a 4-day fighting withdrawal in front of Lambert's advance guard until, on 15 November,

'assailed in open country by cavalry very numerous compared with our own, and ten pieces of artillery, we ended up by suffering considerable losses. Two battalions of the new Lithuanian levy threw down their arms and refused to fire; or rather, they lay down face to the ground and nothing could lift them out of that posture.'

This left Kossecki with only

'a very small battalion of the 46th and about 250 troopers still left to myself. After surrounding the 46th's little square the enemy charged. I hurried to its assistance, charged three times. The mêlée lasted more than ten minutes.'

All in vain, Colonel Lafitte will write three days later from Borissow: 'I've only saved about 100 of my cavalry.' 'Our advance guard', Rochechouart goes on,

'was commanded by Lieutenant-General Count Lambert, a French gentleman who'd come to Russia with his brother. After several wearisome marches and a few days rest,'

Lambert's force had suddenly appeared in front of Minsk, taking Bronikowski, governor of the province,

'wholly by surprise. Amazingly, even one day before we got there, Bronikowski didn't even know our army was at his gate.'

This in spite of several warnings from both Dombrowski and Oudinot. Bronikowski's unpreparedness, not to say nonchalance, had amazed everyone at Tchitchakov's headquarters. Having 'hardly 2,000 men to oppose to 30,000 Russians,' Rochechouart goes on,

'not merely had he not organised any defence. He hadn't even tried to put up any resistance, which anyway would have served no purpose. Why hadn't he foreseen our army corps' march? Why hadn't he sent out a few scouts, if only to know what Prince Schwarzenberg was doing and where he was, etc., etc.?'

Rochechouart (writing in 1842) hazards an explanation; ascribes

'without a doubt Bronikowski's sense of security to the mendacious reports inserted into the Grand Army's bulletins, announcing victory after victory on all sides and at all points, also the annihilation of all the Russian armies. Hence, apparently, his confidence, his easy-going attitude which would cost Napoleon so dear.'

In fact it's cost him the 'immense stores of clothing, equipment, provisions and all kinds of ammunition' he at such vast expense and trouble has accumulated there. Fleeing from Minsk, Bronikowski has

'withdrawn in all haste toward Borissow, in hopes of defending the bridgehead on the Berezina. There he was met by the remains of Dombrowski's division, with some soldiers from the Spanish and Portuguese depots who were in that little town.'

Part of Nansouty's convoy of wounded officers had just left Borissow when it had been obliged to turn back; and Artillery-Inspector *H.-J. Paixhans* had actually been on his way to Minsk when he'd met 'several couriers coming back in all haste' who'd told him it had fallen into the enemy's hands. Leaving him, too, no option but to turn back.

In Minsk, 'after spending two days resting up the troops and supplying them suitably, even lavishly, with anything they might need,' Tchitchakov holds a council-of-war to decide what to do.' March on Vilna, which will probably fall into his hands no less promptly then Minsk has? Or on Orsha and, after destroying the Dnieper bridges, join up with Wittgenstein? The choice falls on Vilna,

> 'but only after we'd have seized Borissow and its bridgehead. The operation was entrusted to General Lambert, colonel of a superb 800-strong regiment of Russian hussars, whose five squadrons were on full war footing. He was given a few heavy-calibre guns, thus raising the number of troops under his orders to about 10,000 men.'

Lambert's own ADC having fallen dreadfully sick at Minsk, he's only too happy to accede to Rochechouart's request to be taken on instead:

> 'I'll be needing an infantry officer on hand to direct this army, which isn't my own.'

And next day Tchitchakov's advance guard had begun its march on Borissow.

Bronikowski, says General *Guillaume de Vaudoncourt*, 'had drawn up no plan of retreat, given no orders, so most of the garrison troops, without either a general or any orders, had moved mechanically toward the main army, which by this time we knew was retreating.' Seeing some 1,500 men bivouacked at nightfall at the corner of a wood on the Borissow road, Vaudoncourt takes charge of them. 'In two days' march we reached the Berezina. Rejoining us at Borissow, Bronikowski, who'd lost his head,' (but not to the point of omitting to take a roundabout route via Molihew to put his wife in safety)

> 'wanted to leave again [for Bobr] next day, thus abandoning the bridge. The Portuguese General Pamplona and I were opposed to this; decided to wait for General Dombrowski, and send word to Oudinot.'

In Nansouty's convoy there the 2nd Vistula Regiment's wounded adjutant-major Captain *Heinrich von Brandt* sees how the town's least corners are

> 'full of riffraff – people of all kinds in the most varied costumes – debris of troops chased by the enemy – cadres of regiments which were just getting themselves organised – fugitive patriots, and those good-for-nothings who make a vile business out of the finest sentiments, and under the most noble appellations make a habit of following armies and fouling them, everywhere causing pillage and theft. The ragtag and bobtail of gentlemen, scribes, servants, cooks, bailiffs and gardeners who've gathered here from Warsaw and the neighbourhood, with the old Polish nobility's gilded ideas of liberty, its ferocious indocility. All the tobacco shops and inns are full of these men who, day and night, are playing cards and drinking.'

The town itself, whose 300 houses are 'built on an amphitheatre against a hill dominating the whole of the Berezina's left bank', is easily defensible, especially from the west. Less so from the east. 'The long bridge crosses over lake and swamp, and at the entrance of the town are two marshy rivers.' When Dombrowski gets there with his intact division he occupies 'as best he can' the fortifications on the right bank – one of a chain begun but not finished under threat of a French invasion. Dombrowski himself is one of Napoleon's oldest officers, having served under General Bonaparte in Italy in 1796. Major Everts of the 33rd had seen him

'very simply dressed in a middle-class overcoat, with a wretched cap on his head, but on his chest the great star of the Order of Poland, surrounded by a brilliant escort of Polish lancers. The general's tall stature, together with a certain dignity and his way of speaking to me, made a good impression.'

However, Brandt goes on, 'since no staff officer had been sent to mark the position, the result was that Dombrowski didn't cover the bridge.'

And now it's the evening of 20 November. Reaching what Rochechouart calls 'the entrenched camp' on the right bank, Lambert's force bivouacs

'in front of the enemy's outposts. During the night Lambert made his preparations for a dawn assault. As soon as we could see to put one foot in front of the other we took up arms to form assault columns, throwing out skirmishers to reconnoitre the position and our adversaries' strength.'

'Shortly before daybreak', Vaudoncourt goes on, 'the enemy attacked us briskly,' quickly driving in Dombrowski's outposts,

'who promptly fell back on the small number of men they had in line. These troops, we could see, belonged neither to the same corps nor to the same nation. This cast doubt on their ability to put up a defence and deprived it of the redoubtable dash of French troops. Thus no sooner had a few squadrons of our numerous cavalry deployed in the plain than it was abandoned to us, and the enemy all fell back into the entrenchments at the bridgehead. Whereon artillery fire began that cost us some men and several horses.'

The first volley shatters the arm of Lambert's Piedmontese chief-of-staff, whose wound is 'so serious they had to amputate on the spot, cutting off the arm as close as possible to the shoulder'. Rochechouart has been given the extreme right. 'On that side the entrenchments, which seemed to me to be in a very bad state of repair, abut on the river's very steep banks.' Lacking men to storm them, he leaves his men under cover in a dip in the ground and, unscathed by a volley of musketry from the entrenchments, gallops over to Lambert and asks for a battalion of infantry. Having very little of it, Lambert orders 300 of his hussars to dismount, take their carbines and 'pretend to be grenadiers'. Then, after giving Rochechouart and his three troops time to get back, he orders an attack all along the line. Everyone's in a state of high excitement. But 'a few cannon shot aimed by the guns on top of the entrenchments sufficed momentarily to calm the general impatience.' On the extreme right Rochechouart has no difficulty in storming

'the badly defended barrier. Our skirmishers, followed by a few other soldiers, got in through this egress. Thus we were the immediate cause of the bridgehead being abandoned. For the enemy, finding themselves subject to an improvised attack from within their entrenchments, fled by the long bridge that leads over to Borissow, hoping to be in time to burn or cut it.'

But victors and vanquished entered the town pell-mell, and this, for the moment, saves the bridge. That, anyway, is how Rochechouart will remember things. For Vaudoncourt they're all a good deal more complicated. The fight has lasted all day:

'A French battalion guarding the bridge had been overwhelmed and the Russians were already masters of it when a German battalion, close at hand and under arms, drove them out.'

Shortly before dusk Dombrowski, who 'together with the Minsk garrison had about 7,000 men against Tchitchakov's [total of] 30,000', finds he has more than 2,000 men out of action, is himself almost out of ammunition, and has to think of retreating.

'He did so in good order. The valorous Poles crossed the bridge in closed ranks and sustaining the enemy's reiterated attacks. Dombrowski took up a position immediately behind Borissow on the high ground on the river's left bank. The enemy tried in vain to dislodge him, and night put an end to the fighting. Thus was lost the bridge over the Berezina.'

Lambert himself has been shot in the shoulder at the head of his hussars. 'As soon as a modicum of order had been restored in the little town, which the French had precipitately evacuated' Rochechouart installs himself in a house 'of good appearance on the square, which had just been occupied by the Minsk governor'. There the two French émigré officers get the shock of their lives:

'In this house there was – an extreme rarity in Russia – a fireplace. It was in the drawing-room. I shouldn't mention this detail if it hadn't had a most extraordinary result. A good fire was still burning in the fireplace, which had doubtless been lit so as to hastily throw various papers into it. Among those not yet consumed I noticed a letter signed *le Maréchal le duc de Bellune* and addressed to Bronikowski, governor of Minsk.'

The letter – which Rochechouart will always remember verbatim 'because of its being so interesting to us' – had been brought by one of Victor's ADCs and been on its way to Bronikowski at Minsk with various orders that its bearer, a Prince Sulkowsky, was to have supervised. It contains some shattering news:

'His Majesty the Emperor Napoleon should arrive the day after tomorrow, 23rd, at Borissow, and on the 25th will be at Minsk.'

And they, who've been assuming the Grand Army is hundreds of miles away! 'Judge our surprise at learning we'd tomorrow have to deal with the entire French army!' Victor's next sentence is even more puzzling:

'The long marches his army has had to make, together with the numerous and glorious combats it has delivered, make rest and food imperative.' Lambert instantly sends Rochechouart to Tchitchakov with the letter, telling him to point out how small his detachment is to be able to defend Borissow. Since he no longer can walk, let alone mount his horse, he has entrusted the vanguard to General Count Pahlen[11] 'one of the bravest and most intelligent of officers. All the rest will immediately advance along the Orsha road.' Leaving his Cossack servant, his carriage and all his equipment in the town, Rochechouart dashes off and 'at the bridgehead with his whole headquarters staff' finds Tchitchakov who naturally hurries to Lambert to discuss the alarming situation. And Rochechouart goes off to get some much-needed sleep.

Vaudoncourt, meanwhile, aware that the fate of the bridge and therefore of the Grand Army is in his hands, is spurring for Bobr,

'to try to get some reinforcements to Dombrowski during the night. Not having occupied Borissow until after dark, the enemy hadn't been able to distinguish one thing from another, or establish himself in solid military fashion. The Poles were still masters of the windmills and the narrow paved road which crosses the bank of the stream and by means of which one could easily debouch on to the castle. A brisk attack, made a little before daybreak, could still chase the Russians back over the bridge and regain possession of it.'

A mile and half before reaching the village of Natcha he bumps into II Corps' artillery park,

'camped end to end in column. Its guard had been confided to a Portuguese regiment, and I'd reached it without noticing any sentries. II Corps was turned to face the Grand Army as it arrived, with its back to the enemy, who were only nine miles away!'

He hastens to warn the park's commanding officer – according to the army list a Colonel Levavasseur – 'of the danger he was in of being surprised if, at daybreak, any parties of Cossacks, after overtaking Dombrowski, should throw themselves upon him'. But the officer's sceptical:

'He seemed extremely astonished at an event which apparently didn't trouble him greatly, and on which he even seemed to wish to cast doubt. Anyway he hadn't been notified of it, he said. Nor had he heard the gunfire (of 100 guns nine miles away and for eleven hours on end!) and was awaiting his Marshal's orders. I confess that if he hadn't been commanding Frenchmen [sic] I'd liked to have seen Tchitchakov turn up at that very moment. We'd have had a pretty collapse!'

When an exasperated Vaudoncourt finally gets to Natcha and passes on Dombrowski's message to Merle, Merle too, surprisingly – according to Napoleon he's 'worth four Marshals'[12] – is sceptical. Hurrying on to Bobr, where he knows Oudinot to be, Vaudoncourt's aghast to see the first fugitives from Moscow,

'some pale and exhausted cuirassiers walking painfully on bare feet in the mud. A stick in their hand they were driving their horses on before them, laden with their cuirasses and hardly even able to support so slight a burden.'

Nor is he even immediately admitted to Oudinot:

'At 9 a.m. someone came and told me the Marshal was expecting me. It was certainly high time. I couldn't contain my indignation, and replied by sending both the messenger and his superior to the devil.'

Despite Oudinot's at times leisurely way of making war,[13] the news is at least not lost on him. Is the bridge still intact? Can it be recovered? Perhaps. And when, later in this morning of 22 November, at Natcha, the 46-year-old Portuguese general-of-brigade Emmanuel-Ignace de Pamplona confirms the same dire news, Oudinot takes energetic action. Riding forward, he meets Dombrowski with 'only 300 infantrymen and 500 cavalrymen' at the village of Kroupki a little further on, and forms – and personally accompanies – a powerful advance guard. Placed under the command of General Legrand, it consists of Corbineau and Castex's light cavalry brigades

'together forming about 800 horses, reinforced by Dombrowski's 2nd and 7th regiments of Polish lancers, and two battalions of the 26th Light Infantry,'

supported by Doumerc's division of cuirassiers. Its orders: 'March against Pahlen and recapture Borissow!' The rest of Legrand's own division and of II Corps are to follow after.

That Corbineau's 6th Light Cavalry Brigade happens to be available is a story in itself and an important one.

After the Bavarians' heroic fight at the Bononia defile, Saint-Cyr had ordered VI Corps' new commander, Count Wrede, to retire to the large town of Glubokoië, not far from Vilna.[14] And though Corbineau's brigade (7th and 20th Chasseurs, 8th Lancers 'mostly Poles') actually belong to II Corps, he'd assigned it to Wrede as a rearguard. Lorencez had countermanded the order, but Wrede

'turning a deaf ear refused to rejoin us, manoeuvred as he thought fit, and made his retreat in the direction of Vilna'.

When Corbineau and his officers reach Glubokoië (according to Curély) they feel they've had enough. And when moreover on 17 November an order comes from Oudinot for them to return to II Corps, Curély tells Corbineau:

'"With 800 sabres one can go anywhere. Let me have the advance guard and we'll march over the enemy's stomach and rejoin the Grand Army."'

Reluctantly ignoring other and more senior officers' advice, Corbineau says he 'wants to share II Corps' great dangers' and obtains the permission of Wrede 'who'd just been reinforced by both infantry and cavalry' from Vilna, to leave him:

'With his brigade, still 1,500 men strong we crossed a countryside unknown to us but swarming with enemy troops, a twelve days' march, that separated us from II Corps.'

En route for the small town of Pleschenkowiczi, not far from the Berezina, they nearly bump into a Cossack regiment on its way to join Wittgenstein –

and which, incidentally, has just freed Winzingerode and another captured Russian general, on their way to captivity in France.

'Arrived on the banks of the Berezina, we hear a violent cannonade coming from the direction of Borissow. The enemy were attacking and seizing the bridgehead occupied by Dombrowski's 4,000 Poles. This disagreeable event we learned of from fugitives who joined us. But the news didn't deflect Corbineau from his project of joining up with II Corps and either conquering or dying with our brave comrades-in-arms.'

Spotting a peasant riding a horse that's 'wet up to its belly', Curély deduces the existence of a nearby ford, and sends him to Corbineau to guide them to it. By now, Curély goes on, Corbineau, regretting having taken his advice, has become extremely disgruntled:

'Usually he sent for me to give me his orders himself. But since the moment when he'd decided to fall back he hadn't spoken a word to me.'

The ford lies opposite a hamlet named Studianka. Near its 25 timber cottages on a low hill stands the even smaller hamlet of Weselovo. Reaching the ford 'in faint moonlight' at midnight of 21 November, Corbineau's chasseurs and lancers form up 'in close column, eight men abreast' on the low marshy ground:

'At the moment before crossing, faint-hearted men embraced one another, said good-bye and drank a drop together, they said, for the last time, adding that Curély would be the death of them.'

At 2 a.m. they splash out into the Berezina's darkness and force their way through 'ice floes 20 feet in diameter'. Luckily, even in mid-stream, the water, flowing rather slowly, is only 3½ feet deep. 'The horses only swam twenty paces' before struggling up the steep eastern bank, 'without losing a horse or a man'.[15] Riding on towards Kostrizza, (a pleasant surprise) they run into the 6th Polish Lancers 'apparently part of Bronikowski's command, who presented an effective of almost 500 men'. Only then does Corbineau come riding up to Curély, still commanding his advance guard:

'"Brave men never perish, do they, Curély?" he says, half-apologetically.
'"No, never."'

After which they speak of other matters. Crossing the small Natcha stream, they suddenly emerge on to the main Smolensk road, where Oudinot welcomes them with open arms. Lorencez also hears Oudinot

'praise the resolution, the presence of mind, of the 6th Lancers' Colonel Sierawski in having successfully got out of so delicate a scrape. This unit had also profited from the Studianka ford pointed out to us that very morning by Corbineau, and where he'd crossed the Berezina en route from Veleika via Zembin. It was the concordance of these reports which decided the Marshal to propose that point to the Emperor for the army to cross at, in the event of the more direct Minsk route being shut off.'

So perhaps the discovery of the Studianka ford won't have all been Corbineau's – or Curély's – doing?[16]

But now it's Corbineau and Castex's brigades who're leading the dash for Borissow. Not that Oudinot has many illusions about the outcome. Already he has written to Berthier:

'*Monseigneur.* Unless ordered to the contrary, I shall attack the enemy at Borissow tomorrow. Yet I must draw Your Excellency's attention to the fact that, even if I should manage to drive him out of the town, it's probable he'll burn the bridge, whose re-establishment would be absolutely impracticable. This will be confirmed to you, Monseigneur, by all who know the Berezina's swampy banks and Borissow's formidable position.'

Having himself crossed over the long wooden and easily inflammable bridge in early November and just listened to Corbineau's account, Oudinot's already searching the map for some alternative crossing:

'To find a ford one has to go four leagues upstream abreast of Weselovo. The road that crosses that ford leads to Zembin. I impatiently await new instructions. For the rest, the road from Zembin to Pleschenkowiczi and Veleika or Smorgoni is itself very good. I speak of it as one who has twice passed along it.'

Legrand's advance guard is marching at top speed for Borissow when 'at three-quarters of a league from Loschnitza' he runs headfirst into Pahlen's men. 'He was immediately attacked.' Marbot, prancing about at the head of his 500 chasseurs, is in the thick of it:

'It was at nine miles from Borissow, in the plain of Loschnitza, that Lambert's advance guard ran head on into our cuirassiers, who, having fought very little during this campaign, had solicited the honour of being placed in the front line.'

At the sight of Doumerc's

'magnificent and still strong regiments, the sunshine sparkling on their cuirasses, the Russian cavalry stopped dead. Then, getting back their courage, they were just advancing when our cuirassiers, charging with fury, overthrew them and killed or captured a thousand of their men.'

According to *Drujon de Beaulieu* it's at 4 p.m. that 'the 8th Polish Lancers and [Berkheim's] 4th Cuirassiers make their brilliant charges' and take all these prisoners. The 24th Chasseurs' Piedmontese regimental sergeant-major *Jean Calosso* says they and Marbot's regiment, too,

'fell furiously on the enemy. Having sabred some squadrons of dragoons with the aid of a light battery which was following our swift movements, the regiment fell on the regiment of Finnish foot chasseurs,[17] defending the town's approaches, rolled it up, and with no very great losses to ourselves took them all prisoner.'

After 'less than two hours' marching' Legler sees the Swiss infantry, coming on behind, who've been surprised to hear

'sudden musketry. One or another gun, too, was being fired. At first we didn't know what was going on, or whether it was we who were being attacked. Suddenly the order "At the double!" was given behind us. We began to run, while some light cavalry, riding past our flanks at their fastest trot, as it were dragged us with it.'

After running for a quarter of an hour they're ordered to halt in a clearing:

'In front of us on the ground lay 600 captured Russians, many of them wounded. We also saw some dead. We couldn't grasp what had happened until the enigma was solved for us. As soon as we'd got our breath back, curiosity attracted us to the prisoners.'

One of them's a captain who speaks good French:

'He told us we were cut off and that he belonged to Admiral Tchitchakov's army that had come up from the Turkish frontier and occupied the Berezina's right bank at Borissow. They'd been its advance guard. He added that this was the second time he'd been a prisoner of the French, but this time he didn't think he'd have to go to France.'

Tchitchakov's officers meanwhile have spent the day

'assembling the troops and discussing what was to be done. We were impatiently awaiting news from our advance guard, which must have spent the night at Loschnitza, six versts away. After which it was to march for Bobr.'

When a messenger comes and tells him that Pahlen's men have run into superior forces just beyond Loschnitza, Tchitchakov simply doesn't believe it. To make things worse, his baggage train, glutted with the spoils of Minsk, has already gone on across the bridge and is packing the town's streets. Marbot goes on excitedly:

'Not merely had Tchitchakov made the blunder of going on ahead and running into Oudinot's corps. To it he'd added another – of having all the vehicles of his army follow him.'

Unlike the French and their allies who'd been strictly forbidden to bring any woman of higher social status across the Niemen, Tchitchakov's Russians have been marching in almost 18th-century fashion. This afternoon Rochechouart's dining lavishly with the wife of his supplies Intendant Rochmanoff 'in charge of our army's provisions', who had filled at least 300 carts with the fruits of Minsk. Marbot continues:

'Everyone knows that after delivering a charge the heavy cavalry's big horses, and above all those of the cuirassiers, can't go on galloping very long. So it was the 23rd and 24th Chasseurs who got the order to pursue our enemies while the cuirassiers, at a moderate pace, came on in the second line.'

Oudinot, meanwhile, hurries off another dispatch to Berthier:

'The enemy's been pushed back from one position to the next as far as Borissow, where our light cavalry, supported by a regiment of cuirassiers, made an extremely brilliant charge. Upon which he withdrew in disorder into the town, which we'd have entered together with him if he hadn't set fire to a bridge which lies at its entrance.'

This, however, makes all the difference. Lorencez:

'Wishing to put the river between himself and us, the enemy didn't dispute the entrance to the town. He hastened to get over the little bridge, which he blew up, leaving a few hundred prisoners and some of his baggage in our power. This obstacle[18] made us lose precious minutes wondering what to do, just when the least instant was so precious!'

The disorder during the Russians' precipitate retreat onto Borissow,' Marbot goes on,

'was so great that the two regiments of Castex's brigade often found their march entangled in these abandoned carts'.

'Two marshy streams' at the entrance to the town are also holding things up. And together with the enticements offered by the carts cause the whole prompt action to go agley.

The handsome young Rochechouart's making pleasant small talk with Mme Rochmanoff when

'In the middle of dinner we saw some Russian hussars, part of the advance guard, their horses bathed in sweat, so fast had they galloped. Shouting "The French are here!", they were making for the bridge. Luckily for herself Mme Rochmanoff took fright, wanted instantly to recross the river and make for Minsk; and despite all I could say to reassure her, she put this project into immediate execution. I remember I insisted on having some coffee.'

'Come and take it tomorrow at Minsk!' cries his fleeing hostess. The fugitives' numbers are growing every minute and out in the street Rochechouart tries to question some. In vain. 'Yet these were the same soldiers who'd behaved so bravely the day before yesterday!' Whatever can have happened?

'Prey to what's called panic fear, all these men could say was "*Frantzousi! Frantzousi!*" They were drunk with fear, if I so may put it. Some guns, followed by their caissons, passed through the town flat out, overturning and crushing anything in their way.'

Moving with the tide toward the bridge, Rochechouart catches sight of Lambert's Russian wife. Bareheaded, she's appealing to some of his hussars: "Lads, are you going to abandon your wounded commander?"

'Being Russian, she'd been able to make herself understood. They dismounted and lifted him on to their shoulders. Four mounted hussars, leading their comrades' horses by the rein, put themselves at the head of this cortege to clear a path for it as far as the end of the interminable bridge. Tchitchakov, too, who'd just been about to sit down to table with all his officers, had been obliged to leave his dinner there, ready to be served up and, like myself, cross that accursed bridge on foot.'

'Within the space of half-an-hour' Rochechouart realises it's all over:

'Of the advance guard of 6,000 men with twelve guns, only about 1,000 and two cannon had recrossed the bridge. All the rest had been dispersed or captured. The wretched Pahlen had never been able to get 100 men together. Having only yesterday taken over command, he was unknown to the men under his orders. Nothing equalled his despair.'

As a party of Calosso's chasseurs enter the town, dismount, establish themselves in its first houses, and wait for the light infantry to arrive, Calosso sees how Pahlen's men have 'abandoned to our advance guard a great number of wagons laden with victuals. In view of our penurious state, this was truly a windfall.' He even sees Pahlen's own abandoned carriage 'fully harnessed up. I let my troopers pillage it, reserving for myself some biscuit, salt meats, tea, rum and other delicacies. Unfortunately the Russian infantry, protected by some houses from which was coming an incessant and well-nourished fusillade, had halted us, and were having time to prepare the bridge's destruction, meanwhile sending enough shells to dislodge us by setting fire to the houses we'd occupied.'

Marbot, this time, really is at the hub of events. A charming, handsome self-centred braggart he may be; but he's also a very capable and intelligent officer:[19]

'As soon as we'd got into the town the confusion had become even worse. Its streets were encumbered with baggage and draught-horses, and the Russian soldiers, having thrown away their weapons, were slipping by between them as they tried to rejoin their units. Nevertheless we reached the town centre, albeit only after losing precious time which the enemy had profited from to cross the river. The Marshal had ordered his light cavalry to reach the bridge and try to cross over it at the same time. But to do that he'd have had to know where this bridge was.'

Surely, one thinks, it can't be all that difficult for a colonel of light cavalry, formerly ADC to Marshal Lannes, to find his way down to a river bank? Can he be unaware of so elementary a piece of topography? 'None of us was familiar with the town.' And hasn't Oudinot himself only recently spent four days here? Can it be that Marbot, in his vivid and circumstantial story, is trying to explain away why the bridge's seizure, the whole point of the operation, is coming unstuck?[20] At length Marbot's troopers bring him a Jew:

'I questioned him in German, but either because this joker didn't understand that language or pretended not to, we couldn't get anything out of him. I'd have given a lot to have my servant Lorentz by me, who habitually served as my interpreter. But as soon as the fighting had broken out that poltroon had stayed in the rear. Yet it was necessary to get out of the impasse the brigade was in. So we had the streets swept by several platoons, who at long last caught sight of the Berezina.'

To carry it they need infantry. Just then Oudinot himself appears on the scene and orders Castex to dismount three-quarters of his two regiments' troopers and with their carbines attack the bridge:

'Leaving our horses in the charge of a few men in the neighbouring streets, we hastened to obey, led by Castex, who, in this perilous enterprise, wanted to march at the head of his brigade.'

On the far bank Marbot sees

'masses of fugitives fleeing into the countryside. Although it's virtually impossible for dismounted cavalry to carry a bridge and establish a bridgehead without bayonets, I was beginning to have hopes things would turn out all right, since the enemy was only opposing us with a few skirmishers.'

The 'interminable ... accursed' bridge, as Rochechouart calls it, is about 180 feet long and commanded from the right bank by 18–20 Russian cannon, 'which looked decidedly impressive'. Marbot has just ordered his chasseurs to seize the first houses to left and right at the bridge's far end and hang on until some infantry turns up, when suddenly

'the guns of the fortress roar out, covering the bridge's surface with a hail of grapeshot. This throws our feeble battalion into disorder and momentarily forces it to fall back. A group of Russian sappers carrying torches profit from this instant, and set fire to the bridge. But as their presence prevented the enemy artillery from firing, we threw ourselves at them! Most are killed or thrown into the water. Already our chasseurs have put out the fire that's hardly been lit; but a battalion of grenadiers, arriving at the charge, force us at bayonet point to evacuate the bridge, which in no time, covered with flaming torches, becomes an immense brazier, so hot that both sides have to withdraw to a distance.'

'Able to contain us at his leisure,' Calosso sees, 'the enemy had been able to set fire to the bridge.' While Pils is making the sketch of the fateful con-flagration which he'll one day turn into a much-admired oil painting, Calosso, less interested in the aesthetic aspect, is relieved to see

'the 11th Light Infantry turn up and replace us; and we made our bivouacs to the rear of the main road and astride it'.

With II Corps surrounding Borissow on three sides and the uncrossable river on its fourth, Castex's men are free to attend to provisioning their wagons and saddlebags:

'By the usages of war the enemy's baggage belongs to its captors. The officers of Tchitchakov's corps had done themselves handsomely. So Castex authorised the chasseurs of my regiment and those of the 24th to possess themselves of the contents of the 1,500 carriages, wagons and carts abandoned by the Russians.'

(Marbot multiplies the number by five. Legler, a matter-of-fact Swiss, sees only 200.)

'The booty was immense! To forestall all discussion Castex had planted alignment posts dividing the immense quantity of captured carriages into two portions. There was a hundred times more than the brigade could carry off. Never has such a profusion of hams, *pâtés*, saveloys, fish, smoked meats and all sorts of wines, plus an immense quantity of hard tack, rice, cheese, etc., etc., been seen in an army's rolling stock! Furs and shoes abounded, which would save many a man's life'.

Not to mention horses:

'Almost all were good ones. We selected the best to replace those our troopers were complaining about. The officers also took them to carry the foodstuffs. Each took an ample provision.'

Efficient regimental officer that he is, Marbot assembles his men and stresses to them that with a long and arduous retreat ahead of them what they'll be needing is food and warm clothes, and warns them

'overladen horses don't last long; furthermore I'd be holding a shake-down inspection and everything that wasn't food, footwear or clothing would be pitilessly thrown away'.

Is it Mme Rochmanoff's dinner, getting cold but still on table, or Tchitchakov's, that *maître d'hôtel* Roget takes over as Oudinot sets up his headquarters in the house on the main square? Aware of the danger of packing the town with his troops, he sends back an order for his other divisions

'to bivouac between Loschnitza and Nemonitza. Only Castex's brigade remained in Borissov, forbidden to communicate with the other units, so as to hide the fatal news from them as long as possible.'

Which certainly won't be very long – for all news spreads like wildfire – especially as Oudinot (says Marbot, contradicting himself) allows each regiment to send in a party to take its share of Pahlen's victuals. And 'at dinner-time' the Swiss come marching in. Their prisoners join others 'huddled together in abandoned houses' whom Oudinot – the temperature falling sharply – has ordered 'to be assembled around great fires in the main square' in the custody of 100 Württembergers of Bronikowski's division 'who can't be better employed'. ADCs are sent off into the night to check on the state of the roads up and downstream.

But what to do now? Chief-of-Staff Lorencez goes on:

'We had three crossing points reputed to be fordable: Oukholoda, two miles[21] downstream; Stadkov, one mile upstream; and lastly Studianka. We had these points reconnoitred as far as the night's darkness permitted. We found them all guarded. Anyway, the first two were too easily seen by the mass of the enemy's forces to tempt Marshal Oudinot, who never varied in his preference for the last.'

Already Oudinot has sent off two officers to Berthier. At 4.45 a.m. on 23 November, he sends off a third, with a new message. The concentration of the enemy at Beresino, he writes, is partly due to Tchitchakov having been reinforced there. He, Oudinot, has been intending to commence operations at Studianka at 6 p.m., 'but this seems to me to be of too serious consequence not to defer it and await His Majesty's orders'. So deferred it has been. 'As was his duty,' Lorencez goes on, 'he let the Major-General be aware of this danger. As we know, when it came to obstacles, the Emperor wanted to hear of none except those that appeared to himself.' It's only three leagues to Studianka, so Oudinot thinks he can afford to wait a little longer. One league further upstream from Studianka there's yet another ford, deeper and less practicable, it too guarded by Russian cavalry and infantry. At 5.30 a.m. he sends Corbineau's report on to Berthier, saying he has sent him to Studianka to seize the ford there. And writes:

'There are two more passages: one at Stadkov, a mile upstream, and the other at Oukholoda, two miles downstream from Borissow. The aim of the movements noticed yesterday evening on the enemy's two flanks was to occupy these crossing points, which are all guarded. During the night it has not been possible to carry out any reconnaissances exact enough to be sure which is the most favourable point for throwing a bridge.'

He's going to probe them all and

'during the night throw my bridge at the one I shall have chosen. I have 20,000 men in front of me which will no doubt move to the point where I try to make my crossing. So I do not dare guarantee the success of this enterprise, though thoroughly resolved to try everything to make it succeed.'

Next day, Lorencez goes on,

'the whole of the cuirassier division marched off pompously toward Oukholoda, where the ford had been ostentatiously sounded and materials amassed. None of these movements could escape the Russians' notice.'

To reinforce the feint

'we assembled some Jews in the town and interrogated them minutely on the road between Borissow and Beresino and from there to Ighumen and Minsk. We pretended to be convinced that this route was the one that presented the fewest obstacles. Some of the Jews we kept by us to serve as guides. The others we let go and had them taken beyond our outposts, making them promise to come back from the direction of Beresino to inform us of the enemy's movements. We knew enough of their evil [sic] dispositions to flatter ourselves they wouldn't be discreet.'

At 1 p.m. Oudinot sends off a new dispatch to Berthier saying he has in fact decided on Studianka, but that 'the enemy, on his side, isn't ignoring the strong demonstrations' he's making at Oukholoda and Stadkov. 'His troops are in continual movement. But the most pronounced of these, though we all think this is concealing some other project, is the one he's making on his right, toward Beresino.' (Beresino, where Kutusov thinks Napoleon will try to cross so as to recapture Minsk, lies downstream at a distance of 42 miles from Bobr.) Upon his artillery commander returning from Studianka at 4.45 p.m. Oudinot writes again:

'"*Monseigneur.* Your Serene Highness will see from the report of General Aubry who at this moment has just got back from Studianka at the moment I've received your latest dispatch, that the passage is far from being assured. The enemy doesn't seem to be at all being put off the scent and it is certain it's Steingel's troops, coming via Beresino, who are facing that ford. This explains the movement to the right made by the enemy yesterday. A peasant who yesterday served as guide to a column of about 6,000 Russians and who escaped from their hands, has told us that column has today made a movement in the opposite direction. But despite the obstacles presented to crossing at Studianka I think we should manage to overcome them provided I am promptly supported, for, within a few hours, I shall find myself between two hostile army corps. The river at that point is deeper than it was three days ago,"'

i.e., when Corbineau had forded it. Aubry, however, has already begun making his preparations for a crossing at Studianka. 'By 9 p.m. twelve trestles will be ready, with timber collected for the table'. Rising ground on the left bank is enabling him to do this out of sight of the Russians:

'The river is 35 to 40 *toises* [70 to 80 yards] wide at the ford, which three days ago was at most 3½ feet deep, but is deeper now, if the inhabitants are to be believed, who assure me the waters have risen. The access on this side won't be difficult. When one reaches the other bank there's a straight paved road which crosses a marsh that's impracticable except during times of hard frost. It's still broken at a few points because of the very nature of the ground."

But a few fascines will fix that. Aubry has seen cavalry and infantry on the move in the village which is in the centre on the far side, and seen cannon being established on the paved road,

'or at least in its direction and on the village's flanks, to cover the bridge. The right bank slightly dominates this one and above all has the advantage of thoroughly concealing our works when we begin them. There's no doubt that during the course of the day it'll be covered by numerous artillery which will make the passage very difficult,'

the more so as Corbineau has seen some 8 to 9,000 men arriving on the scene from Lepel and lighting their fires. Aubry adds a PS to his sketch, detailing the positions of the Russian guns, 'both on the low ground and in a clearing in the forest, between the road and the village'. He's sure the plateau to the left of the village will soon also be covered with them.

To tell Berthier, i.e., Napoleon, verbally about all this, Oudinot sends off another of his ADCs, a Major Lamarre.

Whose fault is it the Russians have had time to burn the bridge? Jean Curély, that exemplary light cavalryman, wasn't on the spot – he was pursuing Pahlen's 7th, 14th and 38th Jäger Regiments, cut off while foraging, in the direction of Staroï-Borissow. But when he hears about it all he's sure Castex's chasseurs can't *really* have charged home. Not as *he'd* have done! On the other hand, if the cavalry hadn't been in quite such a hurry to intervene or if the supporting infantry hadn't been left so far in the rear – and above all if Castex's chasseurs hadn't been so greedy – crucial minutes could have certainly been saved:

'If it had charged home, it would have prevented the bridge being burnt. It wasn't its fault, but when it's a question of saving an army one must do more than we dared at that moment.'[22]

CHAPTER 15

'HOW EVER SHALL WE GET THROUGH?'

'Burn all the documents of State!' – the Sacred Squadron – Oudinot utters only one word: 'Poltava!' – 'Then came the Emperor, a stick in his hand' – 'our soul was invaded by an infinite sadness' – 'they passed us pell-mell in their thousands, didn't even dare look at us' – 'they were alive, we were shadows' – 'it had never crossed our minds that the Emperor could be defeated' – 'The Emperor walked to within 50 paces of the Russian sentry' – 'our position was horrible, perhaps unexampled'

At all hours of day and night anyone with a dispatch from another corps is always instantly admitted to Napoleon's presence. Major Lamarre finds him 'alone in a timber hut' not far from Toloczin, en route for Bobr,

'with only one grenadier sentry outside. He was asleep on a map of Russia spread out on a table.'

Awakened abruptly by Oudinot's ADC, his first words are:

'"How shall we get through? How ever shall we get through?"'[1]

'Then, wide awake, while consulting his map, the Emperor made his interrogations and calculations, and gave his orders with his usual lucidity.'

Everyone at IHQ instantly grasps the full horror of the situation. Among them Rapp:

'Napoleon had every reason to worry. We had neither bridging equipment nor food. The main Russian army was advancing. Wittgenstein was coming closer, and the Moldau troops were barring our way. We were surrounded on all sides. Our position was horrible, perhaps unexampled. Nothing less than the Emperor's head and strength of character was called for to get us out of such a fix.'

Anyone else, Caulaincourt is thinking, would be shattered:

'But instead of making him lose heart, these misfortunes brought out the energy so characteristic of him. Hope, the merest suggestion of success, raised his spirits higher than he was disheartened by the worst setbacks.'

Clearly the crisis is at hand.

That 'Admiral' Tchitchakov should be at the Berezina is no surprise. But Wittgenstein's presence seems inexplicable. What's Victor doing? Next day several staff officers are sent off to locate him. When one finally returns, it's to report that instead of heading Wittgenstein off 25 miles away to the north, he's at Lochnitza, not far from the Berezina. Opening the dispatch, Napoleon declares: "The evil's irremediable. And it'll only increase the crowding." And Victor receives an angry reprimand. Various officers are sent for and consulted. Among them Pajol, whose light cavalry division had formed I Corps' advance guard in this area in August. He recommends that II, VI and IX Corps shall fling themselves on Wittgenstein and defeat him, thus leaving the army to retire unmolested to Vilna by some circuitous northern route. But his ADC, Captain Biot, hears 'Napoleon, after reflecting a moment', say:

"That could be done if all my Marshals hadn't lost their heads."

Which is hardly fair. It's the Russians who'll shortly be losing theirs. [2]

Jomini too is sent for. Not so much, as he'll claim, for his strategic insights, as for his supposed knowledge of the area. He finds Napoleon in the same wretched room where the big campaign map, stuck with Berthier's black and red pins, lies spread out. Murat, Eugène and Berthier are likewise present. As Jomini enters, Napoleon even comes a few steps towards the door to meet him. Says:

"We're in a tight spot. When one isn't used to setbacks they seem heavy. But I still have high hopes. The enemy's divided. I'm going to manoeuvre as I did in Italy. The troops I've brought from Smolensk are going to join Victor's corps on the Dvina. First we'll fall on Wittgenstein, then turn back and attack Kutusov. What do you say to that?"

Upon Jomini pointing out the grave dangers involved in this plan, Napoleon (no doubt cutting short his sententious and generally superfluous remarks)[3] goes back to the map table and together with Berthier again studies the position:

"At all events we must shake off Wittgenstein. If we wait for him, he could interfere with us on the Vilna road."

What to do?

Jomini credits himself with having closely reconnoitred the district during the summer and autumn, and also recommends the Studianka ford, already chosen by Oudinot. At that moment one of Victor's staff officers, a General Dode, is announced. Like Jomini, he declares Napoleon's plan of attacking Wittgenstein to be impossible. Victor, he says, has had no option but to fall back in front of the Moscow army. With the result that Wittgenstein is now safely ensconced behind the Tchaniki marshes.

Dode too watches as Napoleon studies the map. In the Kremlin de Bausset had always seen *The History of Charles XII* lying on his desk and even on his bedside table. Now, as Dode sees him searching for a suitable crossing point, he hears him mutter:

"Podoli! Ah yes! The Podoli! Charles XII!"

Then, after throwing Dode a look of consternation, he stares up at the ceiling and begins whistling to himself. Coming up to Jomini, Murat, delighted with his advice, takes hold of his side-whiskers, embraces him and says in his cordial way:

"Thank you! Oh, what good you've done! You'll save us all if you can deflect him from this fatal idea."

All according to Jomini. Caulaincourt too sees Napoleon hesitate about where to cross the river:

'Minsk attracted him more and more because he hoped Prince Schwarzenberg would have made his way there, and that, by means of a double manoeuvre, the Russians wouldn't have been given time either to evacuate the town or destroy its supplies. He'd also made particular inquiries about the route through Oukholoda [south of Borissow]. But the reports of General Corbineau, who'd arrived in person towards 1 p.m. [23 November] decided him.'

Writing his orders in the shorthand of his own devising, Fain sees his plan is to cross at Studianka, march down the Berezina's right bank, chase Tchitchakov away from the Borissow bridge, restore it, and then march for Minsk. Alternatively, he'll follow the Studianka–Zembin road to Molodeczno, where it joins the Minsk–Vilna highway.

At 4.30 a.m. Eblé receives orders to leave at 6 a.m. for Oudinot's head-quarters and

'work on establishing several bridges over the Berezina for the army to cross. You will divide yourselves in two, and if all your men can't leave promptly enough, you'll take with you the best marchers, so as to get there during the night and be at work tomorrow at daybreak, while the other party can be at work tomorrow before midday. Take care to leave working groups along the route to repair bridges and the worst bits of road. I'm giving the same order to General Chasseloup',

commander of the Engineers. Possibly as an afterthought he tells him to 'take Jomini along' with him. And shortly thereafter Cesare de Laugier notes in his diary that

'they've left at 6 a.m. with all their sappers and such tools as they still possess, to proceed at once to Borissow and re-establish various bridges over the Berezina at points to be shown them by the Duke of Reggio'.

And here's another dispatch come in from Oudinot. He's had the ice – presumably on the marsh opposite Studianka – tested: "Infantry will undoubtedly be able to act and deploy on either side of the road after crossing the river." But he'll need to be supported at the very moment when the bridges – he's planning to throw three – are ready, and has sent Cor-bineau to Napoleon to describe everything in detail and the various approach roads. These supports will have to deploy to the right of the road while II Corps attacks the plateau to its left. And where's his ADC, Colonel Hulot, who'd carried his second dispatch informing Napoleon that he's waiting for orders before setting the movement on Studianka in motion? Has he reached IHQ? If so, why hasn't he come back? He's beginning to be worried, Oudinot's written again at 2.30 a.m. (25 November): "Meanwhile the troops are standing by, ready to march."

But what's Schwarzenberg doing, away to the south-west? For four days there's been no news of him. All that's known for certain is that on 12 November he'd been at Slonim. Surely he must be drawing closer, is even perhaps hot on Tchitchakov's heels?

Wherever the Austrian corps may be, Napoleon is only too well aware of his own desperate situation. Alone again with Berthier, he tells him to order *Intendant-Général* Dumas to 'burn all my papers without any exception whatsoever, to abandon my wagons and send the horses to the artillery'. Zayon-cek, the senior Guards officer commanding V Corps, is to burn half of all the carriages, 'before 9 a.m. this morning, so as to give General Sorbier 120 horses and about 80 *konyas*, and more if he can.' A staff officer is to employ 50 gendarmes to ensure the order's carried out. A similar one is sent to Victor, who's to report back on how many horses he can provide Sorbier with:

> "No individual of colonel's rank or higher may have more than one vehicle, whether carriage, cabriolet, chaise or wagon."

Not only are all IHQ's remaining papers to be burnt, but also all the State papers. If there's to be a *Götterdämmerung*, nothing, nothing at all, must remain for the Russians to publish![4]

Dedem van der Gelder, sent with a message to Berthier and recognising some carriages as belonging to General Daendels, commander of Victor's 26th Division, realises it can only mean that IX Corps is somewhere close at hand. He notices an officer whisper something in another's ear. And hears the reply: "So we're cut off on all sides."

That evening Dedem sees his friend Daru burning the Emperor's papers, 'even including the most secret treaties'. Showing Daru one of these documents in a beautiful silver-gilt case, one of the four secretaries says mournfully: "There's no copy in Paris." "That's all one," Daru replies. "Burn it!" Still later that evening Daru tells Dedem in confidence that tomorrow will decide their fate: "Perhaps I'll never see France, my wife or children again." As for his friend, the former Dutch diplomat, Daru says he's sure his Russian connections will stand him in good stead: "For my part, the fate of Count Piper awaits me." Taken prisoner at Poltava, Charles XII's prime minister, who was with the Swedish army, had died miserably in Siberia. 'Yet no one could have shown more calmness or activity in his master's service than M. Daru did in these circumstances.'

Still doing his best for his poor brother Eugène, Maurice Tascher that night hears an appeal go round. 'All officers who've still got horses are to form a guard for the Emperor.' Still having his, he puts his brother in his servant's care and joins what will be known as The Sacred Squadron. François, who's just sold off one of his two to one of General Morand's staff officers for 120 francs, sees

> 'such officers as had retained their horses assemble and form into four companies of 150 each, to escort the Emperor. The King of Naples commanded in chief,'

anyway nominally. Actually Grouchy.[5] Belliard, Murat's chief-of-staff, notes and will preserve their names. The Squadron, says acting-adjutant-major *J. L. Henckens* of the 6th Chasseurs, had first been formed at Orsha by Berthier who

> 'in the Emperor's name had charged Grouchy to collect all the cavalry officers who hadn't lost their horses into a squadron of four troops, in cadres, and commanded by generals and colonels.'

'Of my regiment,' Henckens goes on,

'only Colonel Talhouët[6] and Lieutenant Berger were still horsed and therefore entitled to belong to it. Colonel de Talhouët, who didn't want to be separated from me, presented me to Marshal Berthier, explaining that I was acting as adjutant-major.'

Berthier had accepted him despite his non-commissioned rank and notified Grouchy. Thirion of the 2nd Cuirassiers is among those who're immediately sceptical about its value:

'Doubtless it was good to watch over the Emperor's safety as head of the army. But it was to take the superiors he was used to from the already demoralised ranker – men who'd led him under fire, with whom he'd been victorious, and who enjoyed his confidence. This measure could only increase the demoralisation and be harmful when we had to fight.'

Henckens disagrees. Reminds us that

'Platov, commanding the Cossacks, was said to be extremely rich and to have promised his only daughter in marriage to anyone who seized Napoleon's person, and we were so to speak surrounded by Cossacks. I believe few people have understood or wanted to understand its great value. A special guard was more than necessary.'

But it's immediately 'the object of jealousy, especially on the part of the Guard'. Also invited to join are the group of officers from the 2nd Prussian Hussars. 'But no one could make up his mind to leave his comrades to get himself admitted into a circle of officers wholly foreign to him.' But their major points out that they're the only Prussian unit in the army, and such a refusal may be prejudicial to their future. So next morning, at the village of Kroupki, Kalckreuth and two other lieutenants present themselves to Grouchy:

'All the officers, from all the cavalry regiments – French, Bavarian, Württemberger, Poles and others, some still in uniform, others dressed like peasants – were drawn up in a single rank on some flat ground. A general passed along the front, which was rather long, counting it. Only when he'd got to the middle did he begin a second rank, to place itself behind the first.'

The three Prussians stick together, in the second. Then the squadron's

'divided up into four troops. Generals commanded them. The colonels, in the guise of NCOs, rode on the flanks. The remaining officers, of all ranks, were the troopers, simple soldiers.'

Ordered to count themselves off by fours,

'our companions being Poles who knew little French, we had to do so several times before things were in order. Finally, at the signal "By the right, march!", we left in a column of fours and took the Borissow road.'

After kicking their heels for six days at Borissow, Nansouty's convoy of wounded officers have retreated precipitately to Bobr. And it's there, to his dismay, Brandt sees 'the first bizarre phantoms' of the Moscow army. Outside his lodgings, though the Emperor hasn't arrived as yet, he notices two headquarters gendarmes and a lot of men without weapons. For a while he and his comrade gape at the painful, desolating spectacle:

'Lieutenant Gorszynski said to me: "Most of these stragglers are strong and healthy. I don't get it. They must have been sent on ahead from the camp on some fatigue duty. So certainly it's somewhere in the offing." While giving free rein to our observations, we see groups gathering at street corners to read some placards. We go closer. An order of the day has in fact been stuck up which most energetically blames the stragglers' and isolated men's behaviour and orders them to rejoin their units and their division without delay and tells them where these are. The military police are ordered to intervene resolutely to restore order and discipline. Finally, mutineers are threatened with a drumhead court-martial.'

But the placard doesn't seem to make the least impression on its readers. Only one thing consoles the two Polish officers:

'In this Babylonian disarray there wasn't a single soldier from the Vistula Legion. What was really terrifying was that these men, the Grand Army's strange advance guard, lacked weapons. Yet most of them didn't seem to have suffered much from exhaustion or hunger!'

In fact it's the army's huge van of stragglers, those bands of marauders who

'without attaching themselves to any definite unit and seeming to have no other goal but to get back safe and sound, only using their weapons to pillage with. A long while I wandered about among this mob, vainly asking for news of the army and above all of my own division. Finally I got hold of an officer of the Guard, who told me Claparède's division was escorting the Treasure and the trophies, and he supposed he'd soon be here.'

In return Brandt tells him that to all appearances the Russians are masters of the Borissow bridge.

Then, suddenly, an assortment of officers of every rank turn up, with pretensions to clear out the inn and its stable for Berthier and his suite, even threatening to throw out the wounded by force:

'But the Frenchmen among us refused to submit. "You're being cruel," they shouted. "We're poor wounded men and we'd sooner be killed than thrown out of our lodgings."'

In the midst of this odious scene Berthier arrives, says one room's enough for him, and a corridor for his staff. Napoleon, meanwhile, has occupied a

'low, one-storeyed building, our former shelter, with a small porchway held up by two wooden columns. On each side of the door is a vast room with a chamber. They've wanted to lodge Berthier in a neighbouring house, but have had to give up the idea since the roof has fallen in and made it uninhabitable. It's thanks to this circumstance we have the honour of having him as our neighbour.'

Not a very agreeable honour, even so. 'Continual comings and goings are preventing anyone from getting a wink of sleep.' But in the morning some officers of the Vistula Legion appear, announcing its imminent arrival. Outside the Emperor's lodging Brandt sees 'some 40 to 50 soldiers bivouacking. A picket's encamped in the market place. In front of the house two Old Guard grenadiers, musket on shoulder. How everything's changed since I last saw the Guard in the Kremlin! Then it was in all its strength and splendour. Today, decimated by its marches and sufferings, its coats torn, it has lost a lot of its self-assurance.'

Yet, he notices,

'the old browned faces still present a quite special and martial imprint, and these men, who are anyway always surly, are more laconic, more scowling than usual. Nor have they been forgotten at distributions, as can be seen from their well-garnished cookpots and full water-bottles. We don't see the Emperor.'

That evening there's a sudden severe freeze-up after the thaw, and a heavy snow begins falling. As the Lancer Brigade reaches Bobr the mush is turning into 'rough-surfaced ice which tore at our feet and in which we often sank so deep as to be utterly weary, and made worse by a fresh thick layer of snow'.

Leaving Bobr at 8 a.m. on 24 November, IHQ marches for Loschnitza, 32 kilometres away. The ever-privileged Mailly-Nesle's beginning to feel quite *démoralisé*, but before leaving is given one of the Emperor's stable horses. Reaching Loschnitza 'a village of 30 houses in dense forest' at 6 p.m., Napoleon is met by a 'Polish gentleman from Vilna' bearing a letter from Maret, Duke of Bassano, who describes him as

'"very wealthy, head of a distinguished family, a man wholly devoted to Your Majesty's service. I've already entrusted him with a similar mission to Oudinot and Victor. He has successfully carried it out and at peril to his own life. He has been captured and maltreated by Cossacks, but still he got there. Despite his own wishes the Emperor of Russia had nominated him gentleman of his chamber. He would be the happiest of men if Your Majesty would attach him to your person."'[7]

Count Nicolas Abramovitch, though 'hardly recovered' from his rough treatment at the hands of the Cossacks, and disguised as a peasant, has brought a coded letter dated 22 November which when deciphered announces what at first glance seem happy tidings. The day he'd left Vilna everyone had been rejoicing. Schwarzenberg has beaten the Russians! 'News of this victory', Caulaincourt notes,

'has at once spread among our bivouacs. Yet from the date [16th] and place of the battle on the Bug it's instantly obvious it's irrelevant to the present situation.'

All Sacken's 25,000 Russians have done is lead Schwarzenberg a wild-goose chase to the Bug – in exactly the wrong direction – thus freeing an unthreatened Tchitchakov to advance on Borissow. 'Schwarzenberg', a depressed Fain notes in his journal, 'has made a thorough cock-up of everything, exhausting his 50,000 men in marches and counter-marches'. On the other hand Tchitchakov's force is thought to amount to no more than 20,000 and thus be insufficient to man all the Berezina's possible crossing points.

But miracles do happen. If not big, then little ones. That day (24 November) 'an officer I hardly knew by sight' runs up to Lejeune,

'begging me, with a gracious smile, to accept a parcel about the size of two fists. And refusing to explain himself, ran off again. Intrigued and mystified, I put the parcel to my nose. I felt how it gave off a delicious smell of truffles. In effect it was nearly a quarter of a pâté of duck's liver from Toulouse or Strasburg! I never saw this officer again.'

In view of the sudden urgency of reaching the Berezina, the Lancer Brigade has been ordered not wait for the rest of the Guard, go to the head of the column, and march out from Bobr forthwith. Colbert orders the 'trot', but Napoleon soon overtakes them at a gallop with his usual chasseur escort. And at about midday, in a field in the forest to the right of the highway, Dumonceau's men, catching up, see him standing by a fire. Called over, Colbert paces to and fro with the Emperor. Both lancer regiments have dismounted and are awaiting further orders. Although at the time they'd hardly even noticed so trivial an obstacle, and Dumonceau doesn't know it, what Napoleon's asking Colbert is, exactly where his Red Lancers had forded the Berezina on 13 July. At the same Weselovo ford, Colbert tells him, as Corbineau had used. Evidently Napoleon explains the exact situation; for going back to his men Colbert has the word passed round that a new Russian army has come up from Moldavia under Tchitchakov, and that worrying circumstances lie ahead. After which, still at a trot, the Lancer Brigade pursues its way westwards. Only later in the day, hearing that the Borissow bridge has been broken and that all their haste has been in vain, does it fall to 'a more ordinary pace'.

At nightfall IHQ reaches Loschnitza where it's 'very badly lodged', and where Oudinot has come to meet Napoleon. 'The sight of the disorder, which hit his eyes for the first time,' Lorencez sees,

'but even more so Napoleon's state of mind and the Prince of Neuchâtel's tears, told him what he must reckon with. He saw only too clearly he'd just have to shut his eyes and abandon himself to Fortune! On his way back from this visit he clapped me on the shoulder, and said this one word: "Poltava!"'

For several days Sergeant Bourgogne's been straying about in the forests.[8] But now, on the morning of the 25th, after meeting up in the most extraordinary circumstances, fighting a single-handed battle with Cossacks and being sheltered by Lithuanian peasants, he and his fellow-sergeant Picard emerge unexpectedly on to the main road:

'It was maybe about 7 a.m., not yet quite light. I was deep in my own reflections when I saw the head of the column approaching. I pointed it out to Picard. The first men we saw seemed to be some generals, a few still on horseback, but mostly on foot, as were many other superior officers. They were the debris of the Sacred Squadron, formed on 22 November [sic], but which after three days so to speak no longer existed.[9] The

242

ones on foot, virtually all of them with frost-bitten feet wrapped up in cloths or bits of sheepskin, and dying of hunger, were dragging themselves painfully along. After that we saw some cavalry of the Guard.'

But then he and Picard see a sight they'll never forget:

'The Emperor, on foot, a stick in his hand. He was wrapped up in a fur-lined greatcoat and had a puce-coloured velvet cap with a band of black fox fur on his head.[10] On his right, also on foot, walked King Murat. On his left, Prince Eugène. Then Marshals Berthier, Ney, Mortier, Lefèbvre and other Marshals and generals whose corps had been partly wiped out. Hardly had the Emperor passed us than he mounted his horse, as did some of those who were with him. Three-quarters of the generals no longer had one. My poor Picard, who hadn't seen the army for a month, looked at all this without saying a word. But it was all too obvious from his convulsive movements what he was feeling. Several times he struck his musket butt on the ground and his chest and forehead with his fist.'

Bourgogne sees

'great tears running down his cheeks and falling on his moustaches, hung with icicles. Then, turning to me: "In truth, *mon pays*, I don't know whether I'm asleep or awake. I weep to see our Emperor marching on foot, a stick in his hand, he who's so great, he who has made us so proud!" As he said these words Picard raised his head and struck his musket, as if to give more expression to his words. And went on: "Did you notice how he looked at us?" And in fact, as he'd passed, the Emperor had turned his head in our direction. He'd looked at us as he always looked at the men of his Guard when he met them marching alone, and above all in this moment of misery, when he seemed by his look to inspire you with confidence and courage. Picard alleged the Emperor had recognised him, which is quite possible.'

The whole, Bourgogne concludes,

'was followed by 700–800 officers, by NCOs marching in order, and in the greatest silence, carrying the eagles of the regiments they'd belonged to and which had so often led them to victory. These were the debris of more than 60,000 men. After them came the Imperial Guard on foot, always marching in order.'

'Gloomy, silent and with downcast gaze,' writes General *von Borcke*,

'this rabble of dying men walked from Orsha to the Berezina like a funeral procession. Preoccupied only with oneself, feeling the seeds of death in one's enfeebled body, and only reminded that one was a human being because of one's instinct of self-preservation, one was no longer capable of conversation. We'd sunk to the level of beasts.'

'Imagine', says Le Roy

'a mass of individuals traipsing along without any order, like a flock of sheep urged on by a shepherd to avoid a storm, saying nothing, or very little. Our hair, side whiskers and moustaches were frozen and glued to the cloths and furs we'd wrapped our face and ears in. We couldn't help the tears running from our eyes and down our nose, where they mingled with the aqueous humours coming out of it, ran down together on to the chin, and there congealed, forcing us to hold our necks stiffly. If any of us said anything, it was without looking at each other, the least movement being difficult. The wind and the snow prevented us from turning our heads.'

Anyone who's so strong, healthy or warmly clad that he's 'spared the torture of walking in a single block' can count himself happy.

And yet – now and again amazing things can happen. Straying from the highway, von Muraldt and his little group of 12–15 Bavarian chevauleger officers have 'the unexpected luck to find a big house no military had yet visited and whose proprietor was still at home'. Astoundingly, he 'serves them all a splendid meal of bread, meat, chicken, etc!' Is it all a hallucination? No. And if they want further proof – they've only got to feel its 'disastrous effects' on their weakened stomachs.

That afternoon Victor's IX Corps debouches on to the main Orsha–Borissow road, 'goal of all our efforts'. Hardly has the 36th Line's newly promoted Sous-Lieutenant Honoré Beulay of its 4th Battalion (Partonneaux's division) ordered his grenadiers to stack their muskets than

'we're ordered to take them up again. The main army's advance guard, on its way back from Moscow, was announced. At its approach an enthusiastic shout of *"Vive l'Empereur!"* went up from all our regiments, expressing our joy at feeling ourselves so close to Victory's favourite.'

Surely their troubles are at an end? Surely luck's going to change and smile on them again?

'At last we were going to avenge ourselves on the these accursed Russians who'd been giving us such a tough time! In the Emperor's stores we were going to find new clothes, soft and warm, to replace our coats, full of holes.'

Soon they'll be eating flour bread again, the very taste of which they're beginning to forget!

'Our joy grew as our comrades came nearer. We had all the difficulty in the world to keep the men in the ranks. Every one of them would have liked to run to meet the men of the Grand Army from Moscow, press them to their hearts, carry them in triumph!'

Marching down the highway with Murat's staff, Rossetti hears Victor's men shouting as they come closer:

'Some of us thought we were being attacked. But it was Victor's army corps. It was waiting for Napoleon to pass. Seeing its Emperor again, it was receiving him with long-forgotten acclamations.'

'When they were no more than a few hundred metres away,' Beulay goes on, 'all the shakos were on our musket barrels. It was a delirium!' – But then they get a horrible shock:

'What wasn't our stupefaction when, instead of the haughty, vigorous, disciplined army we were expecting to see, all we saw was a mob of stragglers – emaciated, in shreds, without weapons, marching any old how,

with a ferocious and desperate air. We stood rooted to the spot.'
Are these men with hardly human faces really Frenchmen?

'Most were got up in strange tatters. Some had brilliant- coloured ori-
ental carpets hung round their necks. Others were invisible under rich
furs. The infantrymen had taken dying troopers' great white or blue
mantles. Many heavy helmets had been thrown away and replaced by
Cossack or peasant bearskin or dog-skin caps, or even by cotton bonnets
or common handkerchiefs. Most of these poor devils had wound bits of
cloth or sheepskin around their feet, so as not to walk barefoot in the
frozen snow. Ashamed and confused they didn't dare halt, or say one
word to us, or even look at us. Nor did it occur to us to put them any
questions, or ask for explanations.'

Although Beulay sheds a tear at the sight of 'an old white-haired general,
dragging himself painfully along on an officer's arm, exhausted, his face
contracted with pain', soon he's 'no longer counting the degraded generals being swept along by this human torrent.

'In the presence of this shipwreck we forgot our own ills and our soul
was invaded by an infinite sadness. So when the Emperor appeared,
framed by the remains of his Guard, which no longer formed more than
a handful of men but which had at least kept their weapons and military
air, our regiments were struck dumb; and it was only with great difficulty
we made them, by order, utter a few cries of "*Vive l'Empereur!*"'

It's the first time Beulay's ever set eyes on

'this hero, this demigod, who'd made the world tremble. Poor man, it's
not with this worried brow, this extinguished glance, this back bent
under the weight of bad luck, I'd imagined him!'[10]

To Caulaincourt, marching at Napoleon's side and staring back at Victor's
men, it seems he's never seen what a proper army looks like before, or has
totally forgotten it:

'Our men, though vigorous on the march and full of dash when under
fire, were emaciated, bloodless, filthy as chimney-sweeps, and as feeble
as spectres. To us these others, less exhausted and better nourished, less
begrimed by bivouac fires, seemed like men of another race. They were
alive. We were shadows. The contrast in the horses was even more striking.'

Victor's men are particularly aghast to witness something never before
seen in a French army: senior officers being jostled in the mob and not
even protesting! Also to see 'the mob, not to have to step aside, trampling
on those who fell, without heeding their groans'. But most perhaps of all
to see

'the Emperor himself turning his back to the enemy. Then we too
became demoralised. The monstrous disaster had been hidden from us.
The idea had never crossed our minds that Napoleon could be
defeated.'

To offset, if possible, the effect of this nightmarish scene, General de Blamont, commanding the 12th Division's 2nd Infantry Brigade

[125th/126th Line], 'seeing consternation on every face' has the presence of mind to harangue his officers. Then he orders them to go back to their units and 'tell the cowards to join the runaways and stragglers, but the brave men to prepare to show the world what a French soldier is capable of!' These rousing words, Beulay sees, do the trick:

'That evening the veterans, having seen Napoleon go by, felt themselves cheered up. While savouring a beefsteak of dead horse, they joked into their moustaches: "The Emperor's got more than enough men to play these Russian rascals a trick or two! Just let him get busy and you'll see!"'

But they've also heard from fugitives how 'since Moscow they'd lost more than 100,000 men, all the baggage, almost all the artillery, a number of flags, and that the Emperor, a few days before, had collected on to one bonfire all the Eagles that had escaped the enemy and burnt them.[11] Only seven or eight thousand brave men remained to assure the Emperor's safety.' And Beulay, like Oudinot, knows enough history to compare the army's predicament with 'Charles XII's a hundred years ago, on the eve of Poltava', where the Swedish army of 25,000 men had been wiped out, all save 1,200 men.

The contrast may even have affected the Guard. For shortly after this Lignières is among a group of its officers who've bivouacked for the night:

'The Emperor was on horseback. We were scarcely a dozen officers in a circle around him. This, more or less, is what he said: "It pains me to see that men of my Old Guard are straggling. Their comrades should bring them to justice [*les claquer*]." And he repeated: "*Les claquer!* I'm counting on my Old Guard. It should count on me and the success of my projects." He repeated the same words several times, looking at us with a sad face which had lost its composure. Few grenadiers or chasseurs heard this discourse. The men of the Old Guard who were falling behind were those who, really sick from hunger, their wounds and cold, absolutely couldn't keep up.'

Caulaincourt sees how its veterans cheer up 'as soon as they saw the Emperor, and each day the duty battalion was maintaining an astonishing standard of smartness'. As for the Sacred Squadron, Lignières sees it's becoming scattered:

'Those officers having no units, marched in isolation, trying to find themselves and their horses something to eat. I never saw them united. I knew many of them. I always met them alone. This squadron never figured except on paper.'

Captain François agrees: 'They didn't respond to the confidence placed in them. In a few days they'd melt away.'[12] 'Since Toloczin,' Maurice Tascher, who still belongs to it, scribbles in his diary,

'we've been marching through a continual forest. Today, having done three leagues, we've halted in a hamlet close to road. Cruel situation of my brother Eugène, whom I'm obliged to leave alone with a chasseur, close to the Emperor's château. Slept on the snow, no fire, extreme cold. Left at 4 a.m.'

Besides the Guard certain other units are retaining a modicum of morale. Colonel Dubois is constantly and energetically urging on his dismounted cuirassiers – of Thirion's regiment – carrying

'carbines, to which was attached a bayonet as long as on a voltigeur's or dragoon's musket. Every morning he put his feet on men who wished for nothing better than to go on sleeping, beginning with myself, who always slept next to him.'

Lejeune and Haxo, commander of I Corps' engineer corps, spend the night in a forest, both rolled up together in their bearskin 'which was rather more than 3 square metres in extent'. The Lancer Brigade has just occupied a large, long village, to the right of the highway beyond Loschnitza, 'a village of 30 houses in the depths of the forests', when IHQ turns up there and establishes itself there for the night – so that Dumonceau's men have to give up half their 'excellent shelter' to the *Chasseurs à Cheval*. 'The whole population was there and keen to succour us.' Next day, en route for a rendezvous farther on, Dumonceau's shocked to see

'in a field to our right a fine battery of artillery, seemingly brand-new, so well was it preserved. Though parked in perfect order, no personnel or team was with it. It seemed to have been abandoned.'

But shortly afterwards he's encouraged to see one of Oudinot's regiments march by in good order. Compared with the Moscow army its turnout is 'a delight to behold'. And Le Roy, marching with Davout's 1,200 men between Natcha and Kroupki, is struck by the good shape II and IX Corps seem to be in, and above all by their

'numerous and well-horsed artillery. Unfortunately they had too many vehicles in their wake and were jamming up the road.'

At 4 p.m. on 25 November 'before nightfall', Napoleon enters Borissow, whose '350 timber houses' are packed with Oudinot's troops. Seeing the Emperor get out of his carriage and mount his horse to reconnoitre, Intendant Pastoret, sits down dejectedly in the main square and contemplates

'the horror of our situation. Our men were ready to drop with exhaustion, discouraged by hunger. Half of them no longer bore any weapons. The cavalry was destroyed, the artillery altogether lost, and there was no gunpowder. It was in these circumstances we, after a five weeks' march, were going to have to cross a difficult swift-flowing river, carry positions, and triumph over three armies who were waiting for us, sure they could give us the *coup de grâce*.'

A few moments later Regimenttal Sergeant-major Calosso, with the 24th Chasseurs down by the broken, still smouldering bridge, sees the Emperor halt

'a few paces away from us without dismounting, and train his spyglass on the enemy camp. Its various arms could be made out by the naked eye on the high ground opposite, where there was considerable activity.'

Dumonceau, who's also there, notes their 'considerable state of agitation' on the high ground on the other side. 'Our own bivouacs were peacefully concentrated around the town.' Thomas Legler too is driven by curiosity to 'follow his staff, which halted about 60 paces from it. Alone, the Emperor walked along it as far as to our farthest sentry, who was standing hardly 50 paces from the Russian one.'

The bridge, he sees, is broken

'in three places, the Russians not having been able to destroy it in its entirety. On their side only about 40 feet of it had been torn up.'

So fascinated is Legler to see Napoleon out there on the bridge, he fails to notice that Caulaincourt's there too. Obviously what Napoleon is contemplating is whether 'a straightforward attack might enable him to get control of the bridge and thus more easily cross the river' – an idea he's earlier discussed with Caulaincourt.[13] But, like Legler, both Napoleon and Caulaincourt are impressed by the

'18–20 cannon commanding it from much higher ground on the far bank. The Russians could easily have reduced the town to a heap of ashes,'

thus obviating, before it can even be organised, any chance of being outgunned by Oudinot's 60 cannon, whose ammunition wagons would be blown sky-high in the ensuing inferno. But though Borissow's so packed with men and weapons that 'one could hardly find one's way about', the Russians, oddly enough, aren't firing a single shot. Calosso can only conclude that Tchitchakov's waiting for Kutusov to come up and take Napoleon in the rear.

The Studianka ford – if still fordable – lies a little over six miles upstream; and Corbineau has already seen some of Tchitchakov's units lining its western river bank. Only a large-scale feint can save the situation. A few moments later Calosso sees

'ADCs taking fresh orders to the various divisions. The 1st Cuirassier Brigade, which had bivouacked behind us, mounted and took the road that follows the Berezina downstream. A few battalions, followed by a lot of military baggage, marched off in the same direction.'

Seeing these 'detachments and various transports moving off to the left', Dumonceau naturally assumes – as Tchitchakov, too, hopefully does – that this betokens some projected operations on that side.[14] And in fact the cuirassiers have been ordered to halt with their baggage train at Oukholoda village, where there's another ford, and there 'make a great deal of noise' as if preparing for a crossing. Meanwhile all Oudinot's other units are to march for Studianka. But before they do so Napoleon makes no bones about granting all his requests for promotions,

'something that had rarely been the case in earlier wars where the Emperor himself hadn't been present, so that many desserts had gone unrewarded'.

Legler himself gets the Cross. For the 1st Swiss there are thirteen more Knight's Crosses; the 2nd get eight; and the 3rd and 4th Regiments six apiece. As the scarlet ribbon and heavy gold epaulettes are being attached to one of his comrades in a room at Borissow, the recipient remarks:

'It all looks very pretty. If we were at home one could just be proud of it, but we aren't there yet. There'll be many empty shakos before then.'

CHAPTER 16
TWO FRAGILE BRIDGES

Who's to build them? – Dumonceau sleeps under a snowdrift – 'We're all dead men' – 'His eyes lit up with joy and impatience' – 'the bridge wasn't particularly solid' – 'his velvet mantle was flung carelessly over one shoulder' – 'he looked tired and worried' – 'the horses sank up to their knees in mud' – 'You shall be my locksmith' – 'it was like being in a wine press'

Already at nightfall on 24 November Castex's brigade had 'silently left our bivouacs and marched up the left bank', followed by Oudinot and his staff. Like most Lithuanian country roads this is 'a difficult one' of transversely laid logs, now knee-deep in snow. For a guide Oudinot's taken one of the local Jews he'd 'retained'. Half-scared out of his wits, no doubt, they can't get any sense out of him; and the usually so bluff and good-natured Oudinot suspects him of trying to lead them astray. Loses his temper. And sends him 'to General Aubry, who immediately had him shot'.

When Castex's men get to Studianka at daybreak they find Corbineau's already there. After defeating the Russians at Loschnitza at 9 p.m. on 23 November and, pursuing them, they'd

'ridden as far as to a hillock near Weselovo and heard the Russians swimming the Berezina to rejoin their main body on the right bank'.

Curély had been all on fire to pursue them; 'but Corbineau had just made himself comfortable in an old hut and wouldn't allow it'. Ordered to take a look around in the immediate neighbourhood, about six miles from Borissow, some fifteen of his troopers had come upon a big farm still occupied by some Cossacks, the manor house of Staroï-Borissow. Lying a couple of miles east of the river, it belongs, like many other estates in this area, to the immensely rich Prince Radziwil, currently serving with the Polish Guard Lancers. Turning the Cossacks out head over heels, Curély's men had seized ten of the Cossacks' horses and found 'victuals of all kinds, more than 200 sacks of flour, and brandy for the whole brigade. I had some bread baked and took away some of the flour.' Back at Weselovo in the morning Curély had seen, on the far bank, 'considerable numbers' of Russians, passively looking on. A little way downstream, on some high ground overlooking the ford which at every moment is becoming less fordable, stands Studianka village. Since a bridge was obviously going to be needed, and so as not to signal his presence to the Cossacks – prowling about on and beyond the marshes, Corbineau had hidden the bulk of his brigade behind a fold in the ground near some woods half a mile to the east. They'd 'destroyed several ammunition wagons to provide clamps and nails, and pulled down several huts' to provide the necessary planks:

'Hidden inside the houses, they were beginning to work on the construction of materials for trestle bridges. Our chasseurs made bread out of the flour we'd taken and the pontoneers worked ceaselessly all day and night.'

Just now, with the cold severe if not yet intense, the Berezina should be freezing solid. But when Calosso gets here with Castex's brigade he sees 'only a few rare ice-floes'.

At this point, Marbot notes, the river's no wider than 'the Rue Royale in Paris, opposite the Ministry of the Marine, i.e., about twelve *toises* [24 yards]'. But because of the flat and marshy right bank the flood waters have effectively increased it to 40 [200 yards]. And if the half-frozen marshes are added, the obstacle it now presents is even greater. Not that it's particularly deep – about the same as the Wop. But at least at the steep left bank its waters are swift-flowing. And in mid-stream the flood has doubled its normal 3½-foot depth.

Which makes all the difference.

Meanwhile, throughout the moonless night, the rest of II Corps has been marching for the crossing point. Among other things little voltigeur Jean-Marc Bussy and his comrades in the 3rd Swiss have seen 'a lot of carts, halted at the roadside, their shafts in the air,' captured by Pahlen's men, but

'the first troops to arrive from Polotsk had retaken them. We're told they'd been made in Switzerland to bring us some effects. Each of us is given two pairs of shoes and two pairs of gaiters.'

The march along the 'hardly distinguishable track being followed by a long file of wagons and stragglers', Legler's finding, is taking four hours. Captain *Abraham Rosselet* of the same regiment, is impressed by the

'strictest order and profound silence this movement upstream was being made in, in closed ranks, and without permitting anyone, on any pretext, to leave them. Although we were all shivering under the rigour of an icy temperature, we were forbidden to light fires.'

Now it's the early hours of 25 November, and the first of Oudinot's infantry and his pontoneers are beginning to turn up. En route, too, Bourgogne and Picart have seen a detachment of about 30 of Eblé and Chasseloup's pontoneers and engineers, under three officers: 'Having formed part of the Orsha garrison, they looked strong and well.' During the forenoon Calosso sees the rest of II Corps' infantry and artillery arrive:

'Without delay we got busy demolishing the best preserved houses to obtain the materials needed to build a bridge. The Sailors of the Guard and the Pontoneers got to work on it. Whereupon we were allowed to light fires.'

Soon Eblé and Chasseloup's men appear on the snowy scene. With them, snatched from the premature burning of the bridging train at Orsha, they've brought six wagons full of tools, nails, iron clamps, plus two campaign forges and all the iron items needed for constructing one or more trestle bridges. Likewise two carts loaded with coal. For appearance sake Chasseloup has left one of his pioneer companies at Borissow. But the others have been marching non-stop for 48 hours. Eblé examines Corbineau's construction and finds it's not solid enough. Although Oudinot's pioneers have also made a few trestles, their work too is found unsatisfactory. So all has to be begun again. There's even a professional flare-up, Marbot says, between Oudinot's gunners and Eblé and Chasseloup's men:

'Unable to moderate or even bury their differences in difficult circumstances, each came with pretensions to build the bridges unaided, so that they mutually brought everything to a standstill and nothing was getting on.'

But it's Eblé's pontoneers, most them Dutchmen,[2] who're the experts at making trestle bridges. At first the plan is to throw three bridges. But then it's realised the available materials won't suffice for more than two. One for the infantry. The other, the left-hand one, some 200–300 yards downstream, for the cavalry and wheeled vehicles. Each is to consist of 23 heavy trestles of varying height, placed in the river at 12-foot intervals:

'All the works were being done with timbers from the demolition, already carried out during the night of 25 November, of the houses of Weselovo. The trestles' height was from 8 to 9 feet, and the length of the caps 14 feet.'

Soon, the pontoneers know, they'll have to go down into the icy water to plant them in the soft muddy bottom – something which will become progressively harder because of the 'immense ice-floes' swirling downstream from right to left. Though half of Eblé's men are allowed to get some sleep, the others have to busy themselves immediately.

For time presses. At any moment Tchitchakov may appear in force on the opposite bank. Pils – equipped as usual with his sketchbook and watercolour box – sees

'the preparatory work and the trestles' construction hastened on by Eblé being done behind a fold in the ground encasing the river and so preventing enemy scouts from seeing the workmen as they moved about'

– the same hollow, that is, that has been hiding Corbineau's men. Opposite.

'On the right bank, the very swampy terrain was frozen, and it was thanks to this the vehicles would be able to get across.'

Fortunately the thermometer's still falling. But it'll only have to rise a couple of degrees to melt that thin crust of ice. And then anything that moves on wheels will sink into the morass.

Napoleon had left Borissow at 10 p.m. yesterday evening. As he'd reached the town's outskirts on the Orsha road, Fain had noticed how he followed the 'first cross-country road to the left, the one leading to Studianka'. Some way from the town the road forks. Both branches lead to Weselovo and Studianka; but while the left-hand one follows the river bank, the other climbs upwards towards Staroï-Borissow. Earlier in the night Colbert's lancers, going on ahead, have recognised its great barns as the same ones they'd occupied on 13 July after fording the river at Weselovo, en route from Zembin to Borissow. Now, in pitch darkness and the icy wind, Dumonceau finds the great farm (already visited by Curély) deserted, and under thick snow. Why doesn't Colbert allow his lancers inside its buildings, Dumonceau asks himself. Doubtless to save the contents for IHQ, the Sacred Squadron and the rest of the escort. 'This was discouraging. Even so, we killed some cattle and had a distribution of fresh meat. It was a detestable night,' for Colbert insists on reserving 'the farm's abundant resources' for IHQ 'and only accorded us strict necessities'.

At about 11 p.m. IHQ turns up. But even Rapp and Mouton, still suffering from their Borodino wounds, only have a little straw to sleep on: 'We were thinking about the troubles of the morrow, and our observations weren't cheerful.'

The army's chances of getting across, they realise, like everyone else who still has his wits about him, (but thousands, like Griois, are too stunned and exhausted even to think about the matter) are slim indeed. There's no longer any likelihood of Schwarzenberg coming up behind Tchitchakov's army – perhaps he's even joined forces with Wittgenstein? A report even comes in – happily it turns out to be false – that 'due to Victor's negligence' one of Tchitchakov's units has crossed the Berezina and already made liaison. With one army ahead of them, ensconced behind a river, and another – soon two others – in their rear, only IX and II Corps, the Poles and the 8,500-strong Imperial Guard are still capable of putting up a substantial fight in this desperate situation.[3] At 4 a.m. Berthier sends off a dispatch to Davout, still at Loschnitza, telling him that the enemy's on the right bank at Studianka, and that the Emperor's going to have to 'carry the passage by main force'. 'Ney took me aside,' Rapp will remember:

'We went out, and he said to me in German: "Our position's unheard of. If Napoleon gets away with it today he's the devil himself." We were no little worried, as we unquestionably had every reason to be. The King of Naples came up to us. He was no less worried: "I've suggested to Napoleon," he told us, "that he save himself and cross the river a few miles away. I've got Poles who'd answer for his safety and take him to Vilna. But he won't hear of this proposal. For my part I don't believe we can escape." All three of us had the same thought. Murat went on: "We're all dead men. Because there can be no question of surrendering."'

By now the moon's come up and the night's cold and clear. Crossing fields to attend to some wounded men, Larrey notices

'how serene the sky was and the cold rather sharp. I couldn't help being struck by the appearance of a comet, situated due north. It seemed to be going down toward the Pole.'

While Berthier's been writing his dispatch to Davout the Sacred Squadron is passing through Borissow in pitch darkness. On the far bank Maurice Tascher sees 'the whole line of Russian campfires. Turned off to the right,' he notes in his diary. 'Followed the Berezina. Bivouacked at Klein [*sic*] Borissow.'

'For greater safety,' Mailly-Nesle sees, 'the Emperor's horses had been sent off early in the morning.' But at Borissow, to his exasperation, IHQ's cooks are still asleep:

'I left without getting anything to eat. It was infinitely painful to go about among all Bonaparte's domestics like a beggar, asking for something to eat. Overwhelmed by the importunities of all these unfortunates perishing from hunger around the kitchen whose exhalations filled the bivouac, they took me for a simple soldier and sometimes let me go away empty-handed.'

But his footman Mouet's in worse case – his carriage burnt, he's been 'put on foot'.[4] And Private Jakob Walter, like thousands of other conscripts wandering about in the chaos, is in still worse – 20 dead cows he's found in a yard at Borissow are so hard-frozen nothing at all can be got off them. And everywhere slivers of half-frozen horseflesh have to be fought for and cut off amidst 'scuffling and slugging'.

By the time Tascher gets to Staroï-Borissow Rapp and Mouton have already left:

'Before long, riding in one of the Emperor's carriages, we came within sight of the enemy's camp fires. They covered the far bank. Forests and swamps swarmed with them, as far as the eye could see. The Emperor conversed with Ney awhile, had something to eat, and gave his orders.'

As it begins to get light Napoleon arrives at Studianka.[5] 'Hearing guns firing at Borissow' at dawn, the 20th Chasseurs assume it's a feint attack. 'A moment later we saw the Emperor and his staff arrive, followed by a column of infantry.' Napoleon goes straight to the timber cottage at Weselovo where Oudinot has his headquarters. And 'between 7 and 8 a.m.' just as Pils is

'opening its door, which was fixed by a tourniquet, the Emperor bumped up against me and said: "Is Oudinot there?" Recognising Napoleon's voice, *M. le Maréchal* came hurrying out. His Majesty was wearing a fur and a green velvet cap, lined with furs which came down over his eyes. The Prince of Neuchâtel, who was with him, was wearing the same costume, albeit of a violet colour. The Duke of Reggio took them down to the Berezina's banks. After going upstream as far as Studianka, the Emperor examined the area, visited the works, and asked what state II Corps was in.'

Oudinot tells him he still has all his artillery, 'thereto the fourteen [*sic*] guns he'd taken from the Russians on the banks of the Drissa'. His men are raring for a fight as soon as they've crossed over. 'Napoleon rubbed his hands together, and said: "Very well! You'll be my locksmith to open the passage."'

And now, as if by magic, something utterly improbable happens.

'While we were talking in this way,' Rapp goes on,

'we saw the enemy march off. His masses had vanished. The fires were going out. All we saw were the tails of his columns losing themselves in the woods, and 500 or 600 Cossacks spread about the fields. We examined the matter more closely through our spyglasses, and became convinced he'd really broken camp.'

To Lieutenant Thomas Legler, rejoining Oudinot's other divisions with the 1st Swiss at dawn, it seems as if

'they'd had orders to let us pass unhindered; the building of the bridges could have been put paid to without firing a single shot. On the opposite bank I saw with my own eyes some 1,500 infantry filing by, taking with them two field guns and between 600 and 800 Cossacks. The Russians seemed to be nothing but passive spectators.'

What's Tchitchakov doing?

On 24 November few of Lambert's Russian hussars, Rochechouart says, had failed to reply at the roll-call on the west bank at Borissow:

'But even when a big detachment that had been posted along the left bank as far as the little town of Beresino, where there was a bridge, had rejoined, six of our twelve guns hadn't reappeared.'

Then, towards evening, one of Kutusov's officers, Colonel Count Mikhail Orloff, had turned up. With him he'd had the young and strikingly handsome Lord Tyrconnel, Wilson's ADC, newly arrived from England. Also a letter from Kutusov containing 'all sorts of details about the French effectives' and describing the appalling state they're in. It had urged upon Tchitchakov the importance of 'putting every imaginable obstacle' in Napoleon's path, in order to prevent him from getting 'as many of his men as possible across the Berezina. But take care.' (Rochechouart will always remember the exact words)

'"You have to do with a man as clever as he is cunning. Napoleon will make a demonstration that he is going to cross at one point, to draw your attention to it, while most likely doing it on the other side. Prudence and vigilance!"'

And this, Rochechouart goes on, was why Tchitchakov, when he'd been warned by a

'detachment of light troops sent upstream on observation and to try to establish contact with Wittgenstein had sent to warn him that the French were preparing to throw a bridge at Studianka, had assumed – the place being so swampy and thus ill-suited to throwing a bridge – it was a feint; and that the French would profit by it to make the true crossing at some opposite point. At Beresino, for example.'

Eblé's bridge-building operations at Studianka, so far from alerting Tchitchakov to what was really going on, have caused him to give 'the whole army the immediate order to march for' Beresino. Only

'Count Langeron was sent with 4,000 men and eight guns to a point facing Studianka, to observe the enemy's movements. Another detachment

254

under that general's orders had been left to guard the [Borissow] bridgehead and prevent any attempt to re-establish the broken bridge.' Between them Napoleon and Kutusov have really and truly '*donné le change à* [bamboozled] Tchitchakov!' So that in the dawn light Calosso's troopers of the 24th Chasseurs, 'massed in a fold in the ground between the river bank and the village, but in full view of an enemy who didn't pursue his march the less for that', see

'the Russian columns on the opposite bank marching for Borissow. Over and over we said to each other: "We'll just have to believe those imbeciles don't grasp the advantages of their position."'

Rapp goes to Napoleon,

'whom I found deep in conversation with Marshal Oudinot: "Sire, the enemy has quit his position." "It can't be possible!"'

Ney and Murat – Rossetti presumably with him – come and confirm the incredible report:

'Whereon Napoleon rushes out from Oudinot's headquarters. He looks and can still see the last files of Tschaplitz's column moving farther away and disappearing into the wood. Transported with joy, he threw a glance to the other side of the river. "I've fooled the Admiral" (he couldn't pronounce Tchitchakov's name).[6] He thinks I'm at the spot where I've ordered the feint attack. He's hurrying off to Borissow!" His eyes lit up with joy and impatience.'

Soon all they can see – and hear – on the far side are a few Cossacks who've come out of the forest to

'gather some forage from the hay stacks scattered about the meadows. He gave orders to drive them away. And immediately some Polish lancers swam the ford',

with voltigeurs riding up behind them:

'Colonel Jacqueminot, ADC to the Duke of Reggio, and the Lithuanian Count Predzieski were the first to throw themselves into the river and reach the opposite bank despite the ice-floes which cut and bloodied their horses' chests.'

'The Emperor passed close by us,' Calosso goes on,

'to mount a small hillock that dominated the river on our side. All our eyes were fixed on him. Not a sigh, not a murmur arose from our ranks. The pontoneers throwing the bridge were up to their necks in water. They were wholly unopposed. It was exceedingly cold. The Emperor was generous with encouragement.'

Now the Lancer Brigade, too, has reached the river bank. Zalusky, feeling hungrier than any day since the campaign opened ('unless it had been at the battle of Mojaisk' i.e., Borodino), watches as

'under our eyes the Berezina ford was tried out by an officer of the 8th Regiment, aided by a few lancers,'

– 'about 60 of them,' Rapp specifies, from the 8th Lancers of the Vistula, under Colonel Thomas Lubienski. With them, Calosso sees, are the debris of the 7th Polish Lancers,' 'who knew the neighbourhood better than we did. As the Emperor wanted some prisoners to be brought to him for questioning, our brave allies flung themselves on the tracks of the Cossacks and, seizing two of them, brought them to headquarters.'

Rossetti sees 'Squadron-Leader Sourd and 50 chasseurs of the 7th carrying some voltigeurs on their cruppers followed them. Likewise two frail skiffs, which in 20 voyages carried over 400 men.' When 50 of Curély's chasseurs, too, are sent swimming across, each trooper has an infantryman riding up behind his saddle: 'These few infantry were put into a wood to drive off the few Cossacks who'd been left to observe,' and who're seeking refuge from the chasseurs and lancers behind bushes. All, however, escape: 'Except one,' says Rapp, 'whom M. Jacqueminot took prisoner and brought before His Majesty.' A young artillery lieutenant in Merle's division, *F.-N. Lassus-Marcilly*, has been standing there admiring General Jacqueminot as he

'having left his horse, had reached the far bank and seized a Russian infantryman [*sic*], whom he brought back at a gallop on his crupper to the Emperor's bivouac. I'll live for centuries before I forget that brief apparition. Clad in his brilliant uniform, Jacqueminot halts his horse and dumps his prisoner, just like a horseman might throw a truss of hay to the ground, and then went off, doubtless to change his clothes. Stupefied, the wretched soldier has difficulty in getting up, and blinded by the brightness of the fire puts his hands in front of his eyes. "How many men in your battalion?" the Emperor asks, a question translated by Prince Poniatowski or General Krasinski. Someone replies: "He doesn't know." Same answer when he asks: "In your company?" Finally, "In your squad."'

Dumonceau, too, can scarcely believe his eyes. All he sees on the far bank, 'a low-lying marshy swamp rising farther off to slightly higher wooded ground that bounded it a thousand paces away, were some groups of our horsemen who had just swum the river and were moving about in the distance to reconnoitre its limits. All eyes were fixed on them, anxiously waiting to see what they might find, for each of us appreciated the importance of the enemy not being there to dispute our crossing.'

Rapp, however, disapproves of all this 'unnecessary chasing of Cossacks', because one of the lancers, too, is taken prisoner;

'and it was when examining him that the Russians tumbled to Napoleon's whereabouts.'

Calosso, though no Napoleon-worshipper, confesses that:

'In such critical circumstances we still had faith in his genius. On his way back, his reconnaissance over, he passed close to us. We thought he seemed more satisfied. He was chatting and gesticulating vivaciously with his generals. We couldn't hear what he was saying, but we realised he was congratulating himself on having lured the Admiral into making a mistake. Shortly afterwards a double battery was set up on the hillock the Emperor had just left. And we were allowed to go there to see the march past of the enemy whose rearguard frequently kept turning round to keep an eye on our operations.'

Seeing '30 pieces of artillery retreating' on the high ground beyond the marsh, Rossetti reflects:

'A single one of their roundshot would have been enough to annihilate the single plank we were going to throw to join the two banks and save ourselves. But that artillery was falling back as a battery of ours was being set up. Farther off we could see the tail of a long column which, without looking back, was moving off toward Borissow. However, a regiment of infantry and twelve guns still remained in presence, but without taking up any position, and we saw a horde of Cossacks wandering about on the forest fringe. It was the rearguard of Tschaplitz's division which, 6,000 men strong, was thus moving off, as if to make us a gift of our crossing.'

The French artillery commanding the river and the marsh from either side of the bridgehead, Legler sees, consists of 'two batteries of twelve guns each to left and right'. 'At that moment', Rossetti goes on, 'two enemy guns reappeared and opened fire.' As it happens we know who they're commanded by. Seeing the bridge-building operations commence and 'hoping to fire on the workmen as soon as they reached the middle of the river' *Ivan Arnoldi,* an officer of the Russian horse artillery, has sited his four guns in the marshy terrain, as close as he can bring them:

'But hardly had we fired our first salvo than we were saluted from a hillock by a battery of 40 guns. I saw my men and horses falling in a whirl of dust.'

Faced with such heavy calibre long-range artillery fire, Arnoldi has to beat a hasty retreat. Whereon Rossetti hears

'the Emperor order the guns to remain silent for fear of their recalling Tschaplitz, as the bridge had hardly been commenced. It was 8 a.m., and the first trestles were still being sunk.'

The French battery, Rapp will afterwards remember[7] is 'commanded by a brave officer with a wooden leg' – doubtless Captain Brechtel, 'who did the whole campaign with a wooden leg, which didn't prevent him from mounting his horse'.

'During the action a roundshot' (evidently from one of Arnoldi's guns) has 'carried it away and thrown him over. "Fetch me another leg out of wagon No. 5," he told one of his gunners." Strapped it on, and went on firing.'

Among the units standing by the river bank waiting to cross are the 500 troopers of Marbot's handsome 23rd Chasseurs – 'the colonels of our corps' other regiments could only muster 200' – and it must be about 8 a.m. For he, like Pils, is admiring the pioneers as they 'throw themselves completely naked into the Berezina's cold waters, though we didn't have a single drop of brandy to give them' and begin

'placing out their trestles at equal distances in the river, with its huge ice-floes, and with rarely exampled courage going out into the water up to their shoulders. Some fell dead and disappeared, carried away by the current; yet their comrades' energy wasn't the less for seeing them come to this tragic end. The Emperor stands watching these heroes; doesn't leave the river bank.'

Dumonceau, who reckons the distance between the two bridges as being about 200 yards, sees him 'walking to and fro along the shore from one bridge to the other'. Of the two it's the left-hand bridge, designed to carry artillery and vehicles, that must be the more stoutly built. Oudinot, Murat and other generals are standing there with him,

'while the Prince of Neuchâtel, seated on the snow, sends off the correspondence and prepares the army's orders. Since the engineers didn't suffice for such gigantic work, General Aubry sends for men from several infantry regiments to make fascines to support the bridge's table.'

The bridges have

'the structure of sloping saw-horses, suspended like trestles on shallow-sunk piles; on these lay long stringers and across them only bridge-ties, which were not fastened down'.

Progressively as the left-hand bridge is completed its table is strewn with straw and horse dung to minimise the wheels' bouncing and bumping. While waiting for it to be completed so that II Corps can cross, Marbot too sees Napoleon walking about talking both to officers and men, with Murat at his heels. Just now that glamorous personage seems 'eclipsed' – but brightens up at the sight of Oudinot's cavalry, which is still in such excellent order. Napoleon too is 'delighted [*s'extasia*] at the fine state of preservation of these troops in general' and, Marbot preens himself, 'of my regiment in particular.' But who's this he, overjoyed, sees coming toward him, if not his brother Adolphe's devoted servant Jean Dupont?

'His zeal, courage and fidelity had stood up to all tests. Left alone when my brother had been captured at the campaign's outset, he'd gone with the 16th Chasseurs to Moscow; done the whole of the retreat while looking after my brother's three horses; and despite the most seductive offers had refused to sell any of them. After five months of fatigues and miseries this brave lad was coming to join me, bringing back all my brother's effects. But in showing them to me he told me with tears in his eyes that, having worn out his footwear and seeing himself reduced to walking barefoot on the ice, he'd permitted himself to take a pair of his master's boots.'

For a moment Napoleon also halts in front of the 20th Chasseurs. And Oudinot wants to present – the desperately shy – Curély to him. And Corbineau tells him he's promoted colonel.[8]

While all this is going on, thousands of individuals are still struggling on towards Studianka, alone or in groups. Griois, like Le Roy, keeps falling in – for the last time, as it'll turn out – with acquaintances. Is it these chance encounters that will have some sinister influence on his friends' fates? For most will perish. And Le Roy and Jacquet, struggling to catch up with the Guard where they feel they'll be safer, try to save an officer who's lost all his horses, wants to go no further, and is obviously at his last gasp. He turns out to be a man named Albitte, who during the Revolution had been a member of the Convention and one of its most zealous commissioners, 'which by no means diminished his merit in my eyes'.[9]

    'A little sooner, a little later,' Albitte tells them, 'there must be an end to it. In France I'll leave a name,' he murmurs as they leave him to die, 'that'll one day be appreciated.'

Farther on, propped in a seated position against a pine tree, they come across the 85th's Major Frickler: Le Roy goes up to him, asks: 'What the devil are you doing there beside a fire that's gone out?' But Guillaume tactfully plucks at his sleeve: 'Leave him, he's dead.'

    'I had to put my hand on his face. Found it cold and frozen. The eyes were open. As yet the snow, because of the fire, hadn't covered him. He'd died for lack of food. I still seem to see that unfortunate young man, with ebony black side whiskers, ivory teeth, the most robust, the most handsome man in the regiment. "Poor boy, may God comfort him,"'

says the deistic major, weeping. 'He'd just been pillaged. His pockets were turned inside out.'

    Struggling on among III Corps's stragglers and amidst this vast swill of a stunned and disintegrating humanity toward Studianka 'where the indescribable horror of all possible plagues awaited us', Private Jacob Walter, buffeted like thousands of others by the icy swirling snow and all alone in this vast but ever-dwindling host, can only trust to his own resourcefulness. Not that he isn't still always keeping a weather eye open for his Major von Schaumberg, whom he has lost, then – to the latter's great joy – found; but will lose again. By now Walter's had to leave his horse behind; likewise the sledge in which, ever since Smolensk, he'd been dragging the major's possessions. And when he does find a friend, what does the latter do – if not accuse him of stealing a bit of his bread. 'Which broke my heart.' But now here's another fellow-Württemberger coming toward him. Outside Smolensk he'd nobly shared a 2-pound loaf with him: 'Laying it on the ground, he'd cut it in two with his sabre'; and Walter had been so moved that he'd said he'd never forget it as long as he lived

    'because you've treated me like a brother. This second meeting, with both of us in the most miserable condition because no aid was available, caused a pang in my heart which sank in me unforgettably.'

But soon they too are separated – for ever.

    Jakob Walter's recently published account, though often hopelessly confused as to times and places, is in some ways the most affecting of all. Like most conscripts who'd been torn from their homes all over Europe, he has no emotional investment whatever in politics, military glory or strategies. Only in survival, to which he is helped, he says again and again, by his trust in God. In general the Germans are religious, the French not.

    Now it's broad daylight and only three of Studianka's 25 timber houses are still standing. At 9.30 Pils returns with Napoleon and Oudinot to II Corps' headquarters cottage:

'He was served a cutlet, which he ate standing. When the *maître d'hôtel* presented him with the salt cellar, which consisted of a screw of paper, His Majesty said to him: "You're well mounted. All you lack is a white saddle,"'

a pun on the words *sel* (salt) and *selle* (saddle). Oudinot shares 'his few remaining provisions' with the top brass, 'who'd been putting up with great privations for several days now'. For II Corps still has lots of the loot from Minsk taken, first by Pahlen, then by itself. It's even for sale. Here are some victuals for Captain Josef Zalusky and two of his lieutenants

'which helped me and provided me with provender for a long time to come. We bought a pig, some geese, and had eleven big round rye loaves baked. For a gold coin, a napoleon or a ducat, one could purchase a lump of sugar, a packet of tea and a litre of rum.'

Ever since Smolensk Victor Dupuy's shoulder bag has been hoarding a deep-frozen chicken. Now he too decides to contribute it to some other officers' rice stew. Paul de Bourgoing (his general, like many another middle-aged man, is on the verge of despondency) has been 'present at a village's complete demolition'. On the high ground where it had stood Fain sees how the 'double battery' commanding the marshes on the opposite bank now consists of 40 guns. And Dumonceau how 'the parks and baggage, arriving incessantly from Borissow' are building up. Hearing that 'the Emperor was by the riverside' and despite the strict orders against leaving one's unit, Captain Rosselet wants 'to see the great man at close quarters in the situation we found ourselves in'. Slipping along past the Swiss he gets down to the waterside:

'I saw him at close quarters. His back was resting against some trestles, his arms were crossed inside his overcoat. Silent, having an air of not paying attention to what was going on, only fixing his glances from time to time on the pontoneers a few paces away, sometimes up to their necks amidst the ice-floes, busy placing the trestles, which they seemed to have the greatest difficulty in fixing deeply, while others, as soon as they were in place, were laying the planks on them.'

General Roguet sees him 'put his foot on each plank as it was laid'. All Rosselet hears him say for quite a while 'in a bad-tempered impatient tone to the superior officer in charge of the works' is that 'all this was taking too long'. Captain *Louis Begos* of the 2nd Swiss, who hears it too, thinks he's no longer

'the great Emperor I'd seen at the Tuileries. He looked tired and worried. My friend Captain Rey of our 1st Regiment was in a good position to study him at his leisure, and like myself he was struck by his worried expression. Having dismounted, he was leaning against some beams and planks, looking down. Then, with a preoccupied impatient air, he lifted his head. Turned to General Eblé and said: "It's taking a very long time, General. A very long time." "You can see, Sire", replied Eblé in a vivacious and self-assured manner, "that my men are up to their necks in the water, and the ice is holding up their work. I've no food or brandy to warm them with." "That'll do," the Emperor replied. He stared at the ground. After a few moments he began complaining again. He seemed to have forgotten what the general had said.'

This must have been at the left-hand, larger bridge. For at about 11 a.m. Pils sees an officer come and tell him the other one is ready: 'His Majesty immediately gave his orders.' First to cross is the 1st Battalion of Albert's brigade:

'Placing himself at its head, *M. le Maréchal* directs the advance guard. Napoleon, who'd placed himself at the bridgehead, his feet on an ice-floe, tells him: "Don't go over yet, Oudinot. You'll only get yourself captured!"

But Oudinot points to his men:

'"Amongst them, Sire," he replied, "I'm afraid of nothing;" and, his horse being led by a chasseur, he set off quickly, with General Albert at his side.'

Is Albert's brigade really the first to cross? Or has Pils overlooked Castex's 23rd and 24th Chasseurs? Or is Marbot's memory determined to take pride of place? Anyway Castex hastens to join up with Corbineau:

'We in our turn followed the Polish cavalry. The 23rd Chasseurs followed next. The bridge wasn't particularly solid, so we had to cross it on foot, and, to be on the safe side, preserve a certain distance between one horse and the next. This slowed down the brigade's crossing. Once on the right bank each of us mounted independently, and each squadron, as soon as it was assembled, advanced along the Borissow–Vilna road, which wasn't far away.'

Scarcely are the scouts across than carbine shots are heard on various sides:

'Then the voltigeurs deployed in open order and, marching straight ahead, had to cross a marshy area before reaching the hillside, which they climbed. One by one the Cossacks, protected behind some bushes, were flushed out. During this fusillade the Marshal was on foot, the horses sinking up to their knees in the mud; but as soon as he'd reached more solid ground he galloped off to rejoin the voltigeurs who were reaching the Minsk road, in the forests,'

i.e., the 'long road, straight as an avenue' over to the left, down which Tschaplitz's rearguard has disappeared:

'During this short ride he met with the corpses of many Cossacks. All had been shot through the head.'

Aware of the extreme danger of an enemy unit seizing the series of highly inflammable little bridges between the marsh and Zembin, chief-of-staff Lorencez has sent Marbot there to seize them. Nothing, Chambray realises, 'was more important than to occupy the road leading us to Zembin because six miles from Studianka it crosses a marshy woodland, impracticable for vehicles except when frozen hard or in very hot weather.' Unbelievably, it's wholly intact.[10] Pils goes on:

'As soon as the whole of the first brigade had reached the Minsk road, *M. le Maréchal* ordered it to halt and wait for the rest of Legrand's division.

He placed himself in observation with General Albert, following the movements of a strong party of Cossacks. In the same moment two roundshot flew by to his right. One of them knocked General Albert over. Jumping up at once, he exclaimed: "That scum haven't any good powder, or I'd have been cut in two!"'

After Albert's infantry comes Legrand's; then Maison's French division; then Merle's Croats and Swiss. Two guns are also 'very carefully taken across' the infantry bridge. When at 1 p.m. Caudras' brigade begins crossing over, Napoleon is 'still in the same position where I'd left him, just as taciturn, with the same pensive air'. The Swiss shout '*Vive l'Empereur!*' as they go by, but without Napoleon 'paying us the least attention'.

Not until about 3 p.m. is the artillery bridge almost ready. And still there's no sign of Tschaplitz coming back! Among Merle's divisional artillery, queued up at the bridgehead, are two guns commanded by Lieutenant Lassus-Marcilly. Who's in a state of ecstasy: 'My captain had brought me, together with a little bit of ribbon, the news of my nomination to the Legion of Honour.' Standing by his bivouac fire only a few feet away, Napoleon tells Lassus-Marcilly they must hurry up:

'I replied that we were waiting our turn behind the other batteries. And as he turned to go back to the fire, a clumsy gunner trod on his foot. The Emperor gave him a gentle shove between the shoulders, saying calmly: "What a clumsy b*****r he is! [*Que ce bougre-là est lourd!*]"'

What in fact are the Russians up to? Caulaincourt is one of those at IHQ who're lost in speculation:

'The Admiral's inaction baffled everybody. Why hadn't he, who'd been able to observe our tactics for the last 36 hours, burnt or dismantled the Borissow bridge, so as to be easy on that score? How come he hadn't made a quick sally with perhaps 80 guns and blown us to smithereens while we were crossing the river? Was he waiting for Wittgenstein? Nor was it any easier to understand the slow pace of Wittgenstein's pursuit. Had Kutusov joined forces with him? Was he manoeuvring in our rear?'

No one knows, or can even guess, the answers to these questions. It's all a riddle – but one that Rochechouart could answer: 'Reaching Beresino in the morning of 25 November we'd seen no trace of the French army, and this had begun to make us fear we'd made a very false move, as useless as it had been wearisome.'[11] And this is why the day, Pils notes in his diary,

'is passing in great tranquillity. The army's gone on crossing. The snow's falling so thickly the daylight's obscured by it.'

Back from their feint in the direction of Beresino, even Oudinot's magnificent cuirassier regiments have crossed over 'without any difficulty – even our sutlers were getting across with their carts'. This gives Marbot an idea. Why not unharness a few such carts, tie them together and fix them in midstream? Wouldn't it make an extra bridge for the infantry?

'This idea seemed to me such a good one that, though soaked through up to my waist, I re-forded the river to pass it on to the generals at IHQ.

My project was found to be good, but no one lifted a finger to go and put it to the Emperor. Finally General Lauriston, one of his ADCs, said to me: "I charge you with carrying out this footbridge, whose usefulness you've just explained so well.'"

But of course Marbot has neither sappers, infantrymen, tools, stakes, nor ropes to do it with. Nor can he leave his own regiment, already on the right bank. So nothing's done about it.

Late in the afternoon the last of the red-coated Swiss arrive. As the 'little élite battalion of united grenadiers and voltigeurs (four companies, of which two of the 3rd and two of the 4th Regiments) crosses the left-hand bridge' Jean-Marc Bussy notices that Napoleon's wearing *both* his hat *and* 'a fur cap under it'. At this critical juncture that potent symbol, unique in the army, is obviously needed.[12] 'Wretched though we are,' Bussy goes on, 'we don't give it a thought. We shout *"Vive l'Empereur!"* at the tops of our voices.' 'As soon as our horse artillery had reached the right bank,' Legler goes on,

'a considerable swarm of Cossacks came out of the wood where they'd been hiding, intending to cut it up. But the chasseurs quickly formed up and opened fire in two ranks, which our two batteries on their flanks could support with no danger to themselves. Whereupon the Cossacks fled. Meanwhile the general crossing had begun, and there'd begun to be continuous shouts of *"Vive l'Empereur"*. When the turn came to us, and we had to halt near the bridge, some words from the Emperor's mouth reached our ears, directed to General Merle:
'"Are you pleased with the Swiss, General?"
'"Yes, Sire. If the Swiss attacked as sharply as they know how to defend themselves, Your Majesty would be content with them."

'"Yes," Legler proudly hears Napoleon reply: "I know they're a good lot [*des braves gens*].'"

Just how brave they'll shortly have to show, as they're the army's prime bulwark. 'When we'd crossed the bridge at last,' Legler goes on, 'we sent up a ringing cheer for the Emperor.' Then they too turn off left 'if possible to throw the enemy back on to his fixed position opposite Borissow.'

At 4 p.m. Oudinot's guns begin to cross the left-hand bridge – Rossetti says 4.30, Denniée, 5 p.m. The captured Russian ones are left behind on the left bank. As each 12-pounder crosses over, what Caulaincourt calls the bridge's 'matchwood' construction sways and shakes wildly, and the weight thrusts its trestles ever deeper into the river's muddy bottom. Soon both bridges' platforms are hardly a foot or two above the swirling waters. Neither has a rail. Gourgaud, who'd been one of the first officers to swim his horse across the river and back, sees how everything's being promptly repaired under the Emperor's eyes by the pontoneers, sailors and sappers. And Fain, also standing near the bridgehead, notes in his journal:

'Braving the cold, fatigue, exhaustion, even death, they're working ceaselessly, water up to their shoulders. The death they must find under the ice-floes is not less the death of brave men for that.'

Ahead of II Corps lies a pine forest – the Brill Farm Wood. Through it runs the main Borissow–Zembin road, down which Tchitchakov's army, estimated by Napoleon as only about 25,000 men but in reality some 35,000, will surely at any moment come hurrying back to remedy its disastrous mistake.

'However, our division didn't see the enemy that day. The first two divisions drove him back without loss. While marching for two hours along the country road at the first division's heels we didn't even see a single wounded man coming back.'

By and by an orderly officer comes riding up, orders them to form up in assault columns to left and right of the road. And there, with Legler's regiment to the rear, they make ready to spend the night.

Meanwhile, on the left bank, the Guard has turned up. And after it III Corps – 900 men all told, so Major Bonnet estimates. Ney's men are immediately sent across to support Oudinot. As soon as the 4th Line has bivouacked as best it can in the Brill Wood beside fires that 'scarcely served to warm us' Fezensac decides to count his effectives. 'Since Smolensk I'd had neither the time nor the courage to study my regiment's destruction at close quarters.' Summoning his officers he compares the roll-call with

'the list I'd brought from Moscow. But what changes since that time! Of 70 officers hardly 40 were left, most of them ill or exhausted. I spoke with them at length about our present situation. I praised several whose truly heroic conduct deserved it. I reprimanded others who were showing more weakness, and above all I promised always to try and encourage them by my example.'

Worst of all,

'almost all the company cadres had been destroyed at Krasnoïe, which made it much more difficult to maintain discipline. Of the remaining men I formed two platoons, the first made up of grenadiers and voltigeurs, the second from the centre companies. I designated officers to command them, and ordered each of the others to take a musket and always march with me at the head of the regiment. I was myself at the end of my strength. I'd only one horse left. My last portmanteau had been lost crossing the Berezina. All I possessed was what was on my back – and we were still 50 leagues from Vilna, 80 from the Niemen! But in the midst of such sufferings I counted my own privations for nothing.'

Even Ney himself has

'lost everything. His ADCs were dying of hunger, and more than once, I remember, they had the goodness to share with me what little food they'd been able to get hold of.'

But what's that up there in a tree? Honeycombs!

'Difficult and dangerous though they were to get at, some of the men, thinking they might as well die of a fall as perish from hunger, managed to reach them with the aid of a rod. They threw that honey down bit by bit and their comrades threw themselves on it like famished dogs. The cold had started up again, the snow was falling furiously.'

Late into the freezing night the icy north wind, sweeping ever more fiercely across the marshes, whines and soughs in the Brill Farm Wood's conifers. Having 'established its outposts at nightfall' Castex's light cavalry brigade, too, joined after dark by the 1st Infantry Brigade and by Doumerc's cuirassier division, bivouac

'in the great forest. The rest of II Corps, by now reduced to about 12,000 men, camped in the little plain, around a hamlet. The thatch of the roofs served our poor horses for nourishment.'

When men from the Moscow units come begging the Swiss for 'something to relieve their sufferings' in the intense cold, all they have for them is 'a little food, to save them from starving to death'. Regimental Sergeant-Major Calosso's comrades want to drive away a wounded Italian officer 'wrapped up in a little fur, partly grilled by the camp fires and belonging to some Russian peasant', from their big camp fire; but he manages to obtain a place for him. 'Observing him closely' as the Italian uses his sword for a skewer, he notices the bullion of its sword-knot:

'This detail enabled me to recognise in this unfortunate man a senior officer. All I could see of his uniform was a filthy collar, turned down, and of doubtful colour. On his head he had a grey astrakhan cap.'

The officer turns out to be a colonel of one of the regiments of the Italian Royal Guard. Oudinot himself, sheltering from the gale in a shack where he has set up his headquarters, sends off a report to Berthier. He has thrown the Russians back, but at a village whose name he thinks is Stakhov he's run into the enemy ensconced 'behind a ravine, where he has placed some more cannon this evening, over and above those he'd shown during the day'. And it's been impossible to drive him out. 'If I'd had some cuirassiers we'd have done something brilliant.' Meanwhile he must have some orders for tomorrow. If he attacks in the morning and drives the Russians still further back, how far is he to pursue them?

'On this point I should observe to Your Highness, that if we get engaged in the Minsk road, which is a continuous defile through forests, we shall absolutely lack for everything, and the enemy will be able to hold us up at each step.'

Precisely as Jomini had reported at Orsha. Oudinot adds in a PS that he hopes the rumour he's heard of his Polish supports being taken away isn't true? Or anyway not the lancers 'because I need them'. Yes, and then there's the 124 of his men he'd left at the Borissow bridge. He'll be needing them too. And even the 150 Württembergers in charge of the prisoners (who, like his captured Russian guns, have been left on the eastern river bank). Captain Begos of the 2nd Swiss will never forget that bivouac,

'which did little to restore us, as we'd had practically nothing to eat all day, and above all because the Russians were so close. The forest consisted of full-grown trees, rather dense, both the ground and the pines being thick with snow. At nightfall, each soldier took his pack as a pillow and the snow for his mattress, with his musket in his hand. An icy wind was blowing hard. To keep each other warm our men lay closely huddled together. The biggest pines weren't shedding their snow, and under this kind of umbrella we suffered less. Our vedettes were at their posts, and the officers, most of them leaning against a tree for fear of a surprise, didn't get a wink all night.'

Legler counts only 300 men still under arms in his company. But they're raring for a fight. To its intense regret the 1st Swiss have had to leave their Colonel Raguettli at Borissow:

'several of us had offered to stay behind and help him, but he'd rejected all such offers. "Gentlemen, other duties call you. You must attend to them first, and if you manage to get across – as I hope you will – we'll soon see each other again."'

Raguettli's place has been taken Commandant Blattmann, the elder of his majors: the other, Commandant Zingg, 'as we didn't need two commanders', remains in the rear:

'Having crossed the Berezina and thrust back the enemy we breathed more freely. Now the road to Vilna was open – even if it wasn't the right one.'

Conditions on the left bank are no more comfortable. Getting there earlier in the day, von Muraldt's little group of a dozen Bavarian light horse officers had found the terrain

'covered as far as the eye could see with cannon, ammunition wagons and all kinds of vehicles, where fires had been made up, and a variegated mass was crowding together. Among this mass of warriors of all ranks and arms one seldom saw anything reminiscent of a complete uniform.'

Arriving at Weselovo in Follenius' carriage, Franz Roeder has rejoined his company of the Hessian Guards. Although they've brought some meat and flour from Borissow, they've only one cookpot between them; so it's impossible to cook it all, and 'my turn never came'. More and more irritable as he grows weaker, Roeder has to lie down supperless for the night:

'In the darkness my greatcoat was stolen from me by one of my batmen, my jar of honey was pilfered by another, and my coffee got left behind.'

The crossing's still going on when, at 8 p.m., three of the left-hand bridge's trestles collapse and are carried away, together with such vehicles as are just then passing over them. So in the darkness and icy gale the heroic pontoneers have to wade out into the river again, smash the ever thickening ice-floes with their axes and, in 4 to 5 feet of water, reset the trestles to a depth of 6 to 8 feet. Fortunately the right-hand bridge, not having to support such weights or sustain such shocks, is still intact. And the thousands of disbanded stragglers who've already assembled in the bridgehead area are free to cross over.

But few do.

Why leave their camp fires? Even if II and III Corps' fires are beckoning to Mailly-Nesle 'like an illumination at the château of the Tuileries', the rest of the swamplands beyond the river are a pitch-black icy darkness swept by the freezing wind. How hope to survive in such a night without a fire? So almost everyone stays put. Von Muraldt's group force their way into a half-demolished barn that's already packed full with shivering men and have to defend themselves all night against 'those outside, who were trying to carry away the beams still left, to keep up their fires'.

Now it's 27 November. At 1 a.m. Oudinot sends off a new dispatch to Berthier. He's just heard that 'the enemy has placed six more guns in front of his position'. His units are asking for more ammunition, which can't be supplied: 'the main bridge not having been repaired at all, the caissons can't be brought across. The same is true of the rest of the artillery.' The forest being 'very sparse', he's had to extend far to his right and left. After the Croat regiment's losses yesterday Merle's division has only 800 men left. And from what prisoners have said he'll shortly have 40,000 Russians to deal with. Oh yes, and in his first report he'd forgotten to mention that he'd sent a reconnaissance party out along the sensitive causeway that leads to Zembin, 'which I only found occupied by a few Cossacks'.

An hour passes. At 2 a.m., the artillery bridge again begins to give way, this time in mid-stream. Even the half of Eblé's men who've had the chance of a little sleep are getting to the end of their tether. Eblé, though himself a man of 50, hasn't slept at all; but encourages them by himself several times going down to the river. And by 6 a.m. the bridge has been repaired.

In the grey dawn light 'the Sacred Squadron again assembles and remains in battle order, close to the bridgehead'. Beyond the Brill Wood the Swiss, too, have been standing to arms since dawn. But today, '27 November, everything was quiet on our side. The cannon's thunder was only heard in the distance,' Legler will recall. Le Roy, who has a fever, has spent the night in a ditch on some high ground, wrapped in his great bearskin. Only at 9 a.m. does he wake up. Feeling very poorly, he climbs up to the brink of the ditch, and finds

'the cold very sharp. We had a perfect view of the troops as they were crossing over, slowly, because of the jam of men who, loath to cross during the night, had come rushing in a mob at the bridgehead and all wanted to get across at once. They were shoving and crushing one another. It was the beginning of that disorder that reigned and would only go on getting worse until next day.'

Seeing the Old Guard still bivouacked where it was yesterday evening, he and Jacquet decide to wait until it stands to arms and then cross over in its wake.

At daybreak the Vistula Legion arrives. Ever since he'd been picked up at Bobr by his comrades of its 2nd Regiment, the wounded von Brandt has been riding in a carriage drawn by 'mouse-sized horses' and is

'in paradise. What joy to find oneself among regular troops again! The regiment's surgeon's been taking care of our wounds. We've been getting plenty of bread and gruel and tea morning and evening.'

Claparède's Poles, at least, are in good fettle:

'I can't say I found any difference between the Old Guard's and our men's turnout. On the contrary, they were more cheerful – when a Pole sees his superiors sharing his difficulties he doesn't become so easily downcast.'

Not that any one likes Claparède himself – arrogant, heartless, always looking for someone to blame,[12] the Polish officers had quickly come to detest him 'as had their forerunners in Germany and Spain': Relieved only yesterday from having to escort the Treasure – a burden that's been hanging round the Vistula Legion's neck since Smolensk – his men are going to be badly needed in the coming fight on the right bank. Now, after a difficult, frequently impeded night march they 'halt by the forest fringe' at Studianka:

'In front of us and to our left we saw some bivouac fires. Then, as soon as we could look around, on the slope of some high ground that surrounds it like an amphitheatre, a miserable village of about 25 houses – Studianka – and around it several units. We also saw a bridge had been thrown and that some of our lot were already over on the other side. Our mood changed as if by magic. The battalions drew up alongside one another in battalion columns. We must have had a good 1,800 to 1,900 men under arms.'

After a while Brandt sees

'the Emperor suddenly came out of a house. He was surrounded by a crowd of Marshals and generals. He was wearing a grey pélisse which he threw back with his left hand, and we could clearly see his shining boots and white breeches. As always, he was wearing his little hat. His face betrayed no sign of any emotion. He was talking to old Eblé who was respectfully holding *his* hat in his hand. Beside him, unless I'm mistaken, was Murat, wearing a grey fur cap surmounted by a heron plume, a pelisse and a sabre hung by the kind of cord known as Egyptian. Berthier and Eugène were wearing furs.'

Near the bridge Brandt also sees many others of the top brass:

'the excellent Duroc, whose life presents the image of a perfect knight – Ney, *figura quadrata firmisque membris* [with his firm square-set features], in a light overcoat, of sombre green – Mortier, *ipse inter primos prestandi corpore* [standing out among his peers by dint of sheer physical size] – the noble Narbonne with his bizarre, old-fashioned hairstyle, and many more. Most of the adjutants and senior staff officers only had riding-coats or light overcoats. That morning the temperature could have been between 2 and 3 degrees. The snow was no longer falling, and it looked as if we were going to have a fine day.'

The Vistula Legion having done much to pull Murat's chestnuts out of the fire at Winkovo on 18 October, the King of Naples comes over to speak to Brandt's colonel,

'whom he'd taken a liking to ever since the Tarutino affair. Exchanging a few indifferent words with him and pointing to us he said: "What are you thinking of doing with your wounded?" "Faith!" the colonel replied, "they'll follow on behind us as best they can."'

Brandt notices how 'a wound Murat had sustained at Aboukir' [in 1801] 'and which had broken his jaw at the moment when he'd captured the Turkish army's *seaskier* but which usually was hardly visible' is reddened by the cold.

'"I present you," said my colonel, indicating myself, "the commandant who valiantly led the attack at Winkovo. I've done all I can to bring him with me." "It was a fine feat of arms," replied the King, "a heroic attack, and I shan't fail to remember it. Meanwhile I grant him the decoration of the royal order."'[14]

At about 10 a.m. the order comes for Claparède's men to cross over, 'the baggage, the wounded, etc.' – Brandt among them – to stay where they are to await instructions – 'naturally that pleased us no end.' Claparède's men will bring Ney's effectives up to about 6,000. As Brandt approaches the bridgehead he sees Napoleon still standing there,

'as impassive as at the Kremlin or the Tuileries. He was wearing a half-open grey overcoat, through which one could see his ordinary campaign uniform. That day Murat, whom no circumstance prevented from showing off the effect of *his* uniforms, was wearing a fur bonnet with a big heron's plume in it.'

'The élite gendarmes,' Brandt goes on,

'in full uniform and thereto clean, but mounted on very emaciated horses, had formed a wide circle around the avenue leading to the bridge, and weren't letting any unarmed man through. Between the battalion's intervals we had plenty of time to view the entire scene. It must have been about 10 a.m. when the division was ordered to cross the bridge. Yet the gendarmes still repulsed us: "Only combatants to pass!"'

Since no carriages are being allowed over, Brandt and Lichnowski ('we'd been expecting this') have already got out of theirs 'and abandoning our vehicle and the mouse-sized horses which had brought us from Smolensk, followed the regiment on foot'. Brandt protests furiously but in vain at being taken for a mere straggler. Luckily, at that moment, a superior officer comes to his aid by pointing out that he belongs to the corps that's just crossed over. So the gendarme lets him through. The river, 'flowing very fast in a swampy bed', Brandt estimates, is '150 to 160 paces broad' and 'in certain places a good 8 to 10 feet deep:

'There'd been a massive thaw, and many an ice-floe must have measured 10 to 15 square feet. Nowhere did the bridge's surface offer a perfect surface. Little by little the planks were being pressed down; above all at the end near the other bank, part of the bridge was even covered in water which wetted us up to our ankles.'

As to its construction and solidity, Brandt as he crosses over thinks

'it certainly wouldn't have found grace from an expert. But if one bears in mind that there'd been no materials at all, and that of the entire [bridge-building] equipment only a few wagons filled with clamps and nails, two campaign forges and two coal carts had been saved, that the neighbourhood's houses had had to be demolished and trees felled to get the necessary timber, that the pontoneers were working with the water up to their necks while the cold formed crystals all over their bodies – then one will certainly regard this construction as one of the most glorious of all warlike actions in this campaign which counted so many.'

'Not far from the bridge on the far side' the Legion halts in a small wood where it's 'superbly sheltered'. Some time during the forenoon Napoleon – accompanied by Caulaincourt – crosses provisionally to reconnoitre the position on the other side, particularly 'the road leading to Borissow'. Altogether he's going to have some 11,000 Poles, Swiss, French and Croats to stave off Tchitchakov's 35,000 Russians until the rest of the army and its 20,000 stragglers, protected by Victor's IX Corps, have crossed over.

Alone, IX Corps hasn't as yet been in a full-scale battle. En route from Borissow with the Treasure, now being escorted by some men of IV Corps, Kergorre admires

'the Duke of Bellune's guns, these ammunition wagons drawn by fine horses, their harness in good condition. It was a long time since we'd seen anything of the kind – such of our own few caissons and baggage wagons as still existed being drawn by wretched little horses with their ragged rope harness.'

But when some of Victor's men, halted near a little village before reaching Borissow, stare at Griois and his friends, the latter, so far from blushing with shame at own ragged appearance, had smiled 'at the thought that they'd soon be on the same level as ourselves'.

Of his three divisions Victor has left the largest – Partonneaux's 12th, 4,000-strong – at Borissow, with orders to stay there at least until IV Corps and the huge mass of stragglers and wounded have got across the Studianka bridges.

Which makes Partonneaux's division the army's extreme rearguard.

Some time during the forenoon Victor's other two divisions – Girard's 28th (Polish) and Daendels' 26th (Berg, Badener, Hessian, Dutch, etc.), adding up to some 9,000 infantry and the 7,800 troopers of Fournier's cavalry division – begin to turn up at Studianka and crown the high ground to the east of the bridgehead. And Napoleon, feeling the situations on both banks to be reasonably well established, and having ordered IHQ to be set up near the hamlet of Brillowo, about a mile from the river, has come back to the left bank. And immediately the Sacred Squadron, after hanging about near the bridgehead until 2 p.m., gets the order to 'see whether the bridge was free enough to allow the Emperor to get across if we cleared a path for him'. Like so many others, von Muraldt's little group, riding down from their barn, see him 'standing by the left-hand bridge, surrounded by his suite, personally to supervise the crossing.' Inching her way forward in Lefèbvre's carriage, Louise Fusil, too, is able to

'examine him closely, standing at the entrance to the bridge, to hasten the march. To me he seemed as calm as at a review at the Tuileries. The bridge was so narrow our carriage almost touched him: "Don't be frightened," Napoleon said. "Go on, go on. Don't be frightened." These words, which he seemed to address more particularly to me – no other woman was present – made me think there must be some danger.'

Murat is looking his usual spectacular self:

'Holding his horse by the bridle, his hand was posed on the door of my calèche. He looked at me and said something polite. To me his costume seemed utterly bizarre for such a moment and in -20 degrees. His neck was open. His velvet mantle was flung negligently over one shoulder. His hair was curly. His black velvet toque was adorned with a white feather. All this gave him the air of a hero in some melodrama. Never before had I seen him at such close quarters and I couldn't take my eyes off him. When he was some distance behind the carriage I turned round to look him in the face. He noticed it and saluted me graciously with his hand. He was a real flirt and liked women to notice him.[15]

Louise goes on:

'Many superior officers, too, were leading their horses by the bridle, because no one could cross this bridge on horseback. It was so fragile, it trembled under the wheels of my carriage. The weather, which had grown milder, had somewhat melted the ice on the river, but that only made it more dangerous.'

Roustam, standing as usual a few feet away from Napoleon with his immediate necessities, sees Caulaincourt

'getting the Household carriages and the artillery over one after another. He was recommending to their drivers to go gently and keep their distances, so as not to fatigue the bridge excessively. At the same time he was making the Grenadiers and Chasseurs of the Old Guard cross in single file on either side.'

Fain sees Marshal Lefèbvre,

'that old warrior, who hadn't shaved for several days, adorned with a white beard and leaning on a traveller's knobbly stick, which in his hands had become a Marshal's baton, tirelessly active.'

And at the far end of the bridge Pion des Loches sees him

'transformed into an overseer, between two hedges of the Old Guard, directing the carriages of the Imperial Household, close to their owner, who that day were judging it prudent to do a few more leagues than the rest of us,' –

i.e., to make for Zembin as fast as ever they can go. Colonel Victor Dupuy, in the Sacred Squadron, is told by Squadron-Leader Offier of the 1st Carabiniers that its members are to try to cross individually. Offier himself, riding a big powerful horse 'still very vigorous', tells Dupuy to hang on to him:

'Reaching the level of the bridge, he made a right turn with his horse and continued advancing. Rather slowly, amidst curses and shouts flung at us, we managed to reach the bridge to safety. The access to it was so blocked that the bridge itself was almost wholly free. Near it and on either hand many unfortunates were still struggling in the river and it was impossible to help them! Once we'd got across we found an officer stationed there to indicate to survivors the place where the Sacred Squadron should muster.'

Evidently Maurice Tascher and some others of its mounted officers 'go off on their own'. The crush, not only at the bridgehead but even on the bridges themselves, is stifling. Lariboisière's inspector of reviews Paixhans gets across among the Grenadiers 'without touching the ground'. The Sacred Squadron pushes its way through the mob, 'even a trifle roughly, being nervous ourselves'. As nervous, Henckens thinks, as Napoleon is: 'He realised that each moment lost could mean utter complete ruin.' As soon as the Squadron's on the other side, says Henckens, 'the Emperor crossed over with his suite'.

There's nothing of imperial etiquette about Napoleon's crossing of the Berezina. All ranks are confounded. Mailly-Nesle, himself following on 'after them as closely as possible'- with his companions in their carriage as usual – sees even Caulaincourt 'shoved and hemmed in on his horse, having the greatest difficulty in getting the Emperor's horses over'. Crossing in the crowd at the same time as Napoleon is one of Captain von Suckow's Württemberger friends, a M. de Grünberg:

'Under his coat he was holding a little greyhound bitch that was shivering piteously. Napoleon offered to buy it. M. de Grünberg replied that the animal had shared all his sufferings, but of course he'd place it at Napoleon's disposition. The Emperor, visibly very much moved, replied: "I understand your attachment to this animal. Keep it. I wouldn't want to deprive you of it."'

Henckens sees 'several women crossing over with their children, of whom I recognised some as the ones I'd seen at the theatre in Moscow.' And reflects sadly: 'They'd have done better to have stayed in Moscow instead of following the army. The Russians wouldn't have avenged themselves on them for the Emperor Napoleon's mad enterprise.' 'A short while afterwards,' Dupuy goes on,

'the roll-call was called in each company [of the Sacred Squadron]. No one was missing.[16] Formed up in close column of companies, we were placed in front of the cavalry of the Imperial Guard. The Emperor was between the two bodies. It was in this order, it was being said, we were going to pass through Tchitchakov's army. Resolute as we all were, no one doubted we'd succeed.'

After he'd crossed over,' Henckens concludes,

'we surrounded him, both when he was resting and when he was on foot or horseback, watching the troops cross, which was going on in a fairly orderly fashion'.

At about 2 p.m. it's the turn of the Guard foot artillery. Pion des Loches has to set his remaining gunners to the task of removing, by brute force, the file of carriages and carts that are keeping the head of his column from the bridgehead. But so compact is the mob that neither Muraldt nor anyone else can move an inch forward:

'A few élite gendarmes who still had horses had been ordered chiefly to turn away non-combatants (a description applicable to almost everyone) as they swelled forward, so that the Guard could pass unhindered. A task they flung themselves into heart and soul, without distinction of rank or person, receiving all who tried to thrust themselves forward – efforts which for every moment that passed were becoming less and less fruitful – with violent blows of the flats of their swords.'

Despite the appalling jam and 'although mishandled by the headquarters gendarmes', von Muraldt and his sick friend Knecht – who'd given him his second horse at Krasnoïë – manage to squeeze in between two of the Guard's cannon. By now Pion des Loches' first vehicle is 'at the tail of Boulart's teams, whose head was at bridge's abutment'. The odious Drouot 'like many others' has gone on ahead and crossed on his own account, leaving his carriage in the care of the resentful Pion, who has it immediately behind him. 'Despite the press of soldiers of the Train and gunners trying to get over', he's obliged to get it across for him. Just ahead of him Boulart, busy getting his teams methodically across one by one, is finding the bridges 'not very solid' and having to be 'incessantly repaired' by the indefatigable Eblé's pontoneers 'who had the courage to put themselves into the water and work there despite the cold. They behaved admirably.'

But November days are brief. By 3 p.m. dusk has begun to fall. From a few hundred yards away on the hillside Le Roy, Jacquet and Guillaume, seeing the Guard's preparations to cross over and 'fearing with reason that in such a mêlée as we were going to find ourselves in we might become separated or stifled', have divided up their 'remaining assets'. Le Roy exacts a promise from Guillaume that, if he himself doesn't get across, he'll go home 'to our beautiful country' and tell his family what became of him. But if they should both get home, then, he promises, Guillaume will always find in him a good friend:

'We embraced, weeping, and together made for the bottom of the slope where the Guard must assuredly pass by to present itself at the river crossing.'

For a while they stand warming themselves at a fire beside four cavalry troopers who seem to be waiting for someone whose orders they are under and who, Le Roy assumes, belongs to the Guard. But though one of them has seen the Emperor himself having the devil's own job getting through the crowd, they themselves, one of the troopers explains, belong to Fournier's cavalry division of IX Corps. They're going to rejoin it and stave off the Russians.' It'll be another story tomorrow morning,' one of them adds grimly, 'when we have to evacuate our position and retire, burning the bridges.' That, for Le Roy, is enough:

'I didn't listen to any more. My legs gave way beneath me. A cold sweat rose from my feet to my head, and I felt a strangely violent thudding in my chest and around my ears. I fell, rather than sat down. My eyes filled with tears and I could no longer see clearly. All these symptoms gave me

a presentiment that my end was at hand. I sat there as if turned to stone, my head on my knees.'
Only Guillaume can shake him out of his stupor.

Zaniwki, about a mile and a half from the river, is a hamlet of three cottages. And it's here, in a 'little white house', IHQ installs itself as best it can. The 'Palace', Secretary Fain notes, has only two rooms:

> 'The inner one's been reserved for the Emperor; the other's been instantly occupied by his suite. There we lie down pell-mell on top of one another, like a flock herded together in the narrowest of sheepfolds.'

Since the three troops of the Sacred Squadron are surrounding it, the Guard has bivouacked at the village of Brillowo, a little to the south. Its last unit to cross the river has been the Lancer Brigade. After a forenoon idled away in their comfortable billets upstream at Troanitze, they'd been briefly disturbed at about midday by Cossacks and ordered to stand to arms. Then the regiment's silver trumpets had cried 'To horse!' And the two Guard lancer regiments had moved off down towards the bridge:

> 'Most of our various army corps had crossed already, likewise the whole Imperial Guard. Only part of the parks and vehicles had remained to follow on with us; but the mob of disbanded men were creating an obstacle to this by turning up from all quarters, interfering everywhere, encumbering the terrain over a considerable extent and refusing to let us through. The detachments of pontoneers and the military police at the bridgeheads were struggling violently with them to contain and regulate their passage.'

By now the confusion and attendant struggle is beyond belief:

> 'We saw there a compact agglomeration of several thousand men of all arms, soldiers, officers, even generals, all jumbled up, covered in the filthiest rags and grotesquely disposed to protect themselves against the freezing weather, swarming with vermin and – over and above these accoutrements indicative of their extreme misery – faces downcast by exhaustion, pale, sinister, smoke-blackened, often mutilated by frostbite, the eyes hollow, extinct, hair in disorder, the beard long and disgusting.'

In the end the Red Lancers have to draw their sabres to force a way through and

> 'behave like lunatics, knocking down anything in our way and, striking out with their flats, thrust back all those who, pushed by the multitude in the opposite direction, were hemming us in from all sides, as in a wine press. In this way we managed to get through, followed by thousands of enraged yells.'

Zalusky's memory of the 1st Regiment's passage will be less ferocious. But even they have to

> 'turn our lances point downwards. In this way our regiment, by dealing out harmless blows to right and left, slipped through softly and easily.'

Do they cross on horseback, or on foot and leading their mounts by the bridle? Zalusky won't afterwards be able to remember. But Dumonceau will. When at last his Dutchmen get to the bridge itself they're

'ordered to dismount and cross over, one by one, holding our horses, to avoid shaking the bridge. It had no rail, was almost at water level, covered with a layer of horse dung. It was already badly damaged, dislocated, in parts weakened and swaying in every direction. Some pontoneers, in the water up to their armpits, were busy restoring it. Among them were some Dutchmen who welcomed us and made haste to ease our passage by tossing into the river a broken cart, some dead horses and other debris of all kinds that were obstructing it.'

After debouching from the bridge and remounting, Colbert's men ride across the marsh:

'We found it broken up in several places, so that despite the freezing cold we got bogged down. Then we mounted the high ground bordering the forest and, facing left, were placed in support of the whole Young Guard infantry, united in a massed column and still forming an apparent body of three or four battalions along the roadside. The rest of the Imperial Guard could be seen farther off, formed up behind us in reserve.'

Finding that his two servants are missing, Zalusky 'with some difficulty' goes back and fetches them across the river while the Young and Old Guard, drawn up in that position, hear Oudinot advancing – evidently against the first units of Tchitchakov's army to be returning to the scene –

'by the echoes of his fusillade, witnessing to his successes. As night began to fall this noise ceased little by little. Then we got busy making our bivouacs. The Emperor, who until then had remained near a fire at the head of the infantry of his Guard, retired and went to lodge in an isolated farm, the hamlet of Zaniwki, situated behind us by the roadside, at the entrance to the woods.'

Only the Lancer Brigade is 'led about three miles from the rear to Kostuikoi', where Colbert hopes to find some forage. Unfortunately that village has already been 'invaded and demolished by the multitude' of stragglers clustering round IV and VIII Corps. 'We could hardly even find any stakes to tether our horses to. Nor was there any firewood.' So Poles and Dutchmen have to lie down in the freezing mud beside smoking fires of snow-laden green conifer, with nothing to protect them from either mud or wind. Already, during the forenoon, Caulaincourt has

'personally examined all the paths through the marshland. The soil was marshy, trembled beneath one's feet. If the cold, which had grown less during the three preceding days, hadn't yesterday become very much keener again we shouldn't have saved a single gun or its carriage.'

Now it's on this trembling surface of 'marshy but frozen ground' that Boulart, reaching the western bank apparently without mishap, 'has the good sense' (the usually so self-complacent and critical Pion des Loches amiably concedes) to park his artillery, about three-quarters of a mile from the river. 'We had no firewood. The night was cold and hard.' Caulaincourt sees how

'the last ammunition wagons cut or broke through the crust of hard-frozen grass which served as a sort of bridge, and got bogged down. Their wheels had nothing to get a grip on and sank into the bottomless mud.'

Arrived at this disconsolate Slough of Despond, where his gunners are bivouacking in the thickening darkness beside damp smoky fires that merely blind them, Pion listens sardonically as Drouot, 'a trifle ashamed of himself, tried unsuccessfully to get us to believe he'd done his best to get back to us'. This, as far as Pion's concerned, is the end of the man who will seem to Napoleon in retrospect to have been his 'incomparable' artillery officer. But at least 'no fewer than 300 vehicles belonging to General Niègre's main park, among them 50 reserve cannon' – i.e., 12-pounders – have crossed over in the wake of IHQ and the Old Guard. This, Fain notes, means that altogether 250 guns with their equipment are on the right bank. 'As for the carriages and light carts piling up around Studianka, their number is incalculable.'

Eugène, ordered to cross over with the remains of IV Corps, leaves I Corps to follow on at daybreak tomorrow. But though the pitiful remains of the Army of Italy have been ordered to cross at 8 p.m., Labaume hears their officers think it'll be easier to cross by daylight tomorrow morning; and remain squatting beside its fires:

'Only Prince Eugène and some staff officers crossed the river at the hour they'd been ordered to.'

What an accusation! The loyal-hearted Cesare de Laugier indignantly and circumstantially refutes it:

'The debris of the Royal Guard, about 500 men, follow immediately behind the prince. Hardly has Eugène set foot on the right bank than, turning to General Théodore Lecchi, its commander, he tells him: "Leave an officer here to show Broussier and Pino's divisions the way to follow so as to reach that burning village where we're going to bivouac." In my capacity of adjutant-major, I've been detailed off by that general for this painful task.'

Will he be able to rejoin his comrades in the darkness?

'The bridge remained free about twenty minutes. Then the 1st and 2nd Divisions arrived together. They crossed the bridge by sections of five to six men abreast, and after a quarter of an hour, during which the bridge was free again, Pino's division arrived.'

Only IV Corps' artillery, such as it is, has been intentionally left on the eastern bank to reinforce Davout's. At the Viceroy's bivouac in a burnt out village Labaume finds

'the darkness horrible, the wind frightful. Blowing violently, it flung icy snow in our faces. So as not to freeze, most of the officers, chilled to the bone, ran or walked to and fro, stamping their feet. Wood was so hard to come by, we could hardly light a fire for the Viceroy. To obtain a few sparks we had to remind some Bavarian soldiers that Prince Eugène had married their king's daughter!'

It's a veritable swamp. IV Corps' Italians, Frenchmen, Croats, etc. seek out frozen patches to lie down on. Then fresh orders come. Tomorrow, still escorting the Treasure and the convoy of wounded generals, they're to form the army's advance guard and, after occupying the vital little bridges of the long Zembin causeway, be at Zembin itself (nine miles away) at dawn.

Once again nightfall clears the bridges. And anyone can walk over who cares to. Although Claparède's men send back for their vehicles and find one of them quite clear, 'the carriages were so entangled and the men so closely squeezed together, there wasn't the least hope of extracting the platoon that was escorting them'. Once again most of the crowd on the left bank prefer to remain where they are – among them von Suckow. Almost unable to walk because of his frost-bitten foot, and though he realises he'll have little chance of surviving in the mob tomorrow, he prefers to pass the night's freezing gusty hours in the company of a small party of French stragglers beside camp fires 'abandoned by some Bavarian light horse' – von Muraldt's perhaps?

'Suddenly my attention was distracted by a cannon shot which had gone off at a certain distance from us. Who were these people announcing their approach? Immediately, thousands of men rushed toward the bridges, shoving and crushing each other to get across that same evening. Seeing this happen, I decided to remain that night near my fire with the Frenchmen, and I soon saw we had plenty of emulators. As night fell thousands of fires were lit and the cannon fell silent.'

So grateful is one of the Frenchmen – the young son of a Lyons master-tailor attached to the military bakery – to von Suckow for assuring him that Napoleon won't be marching on Petersburg in the spring that he gives him half a piece of bread.

Not until 9 p.m. – and by now of course it's pitch dark – has I Corps got to Studianka. 'The mass of vehicles encumbering the road', its chief-of-staff sees,

'was immense. There were all those that had escaped the order that they should be burnt, plus all those of Marshals Victor and Oudinot's corps, which had joined us.'

Lejeune spends the night

'putting things in order, first, to get the ammunition wagons across, then to repair the bridges, which were frequently breaking down under theirs and the guns' weight. The night was black, and at each step they took in this village, Dutch, French, Spanish or Saxon officers and men'

keep tumbling into those insidious Russian and Lithuanian wells which, lacking parapets, for weeks have spelt death to the unwary. 'Their cries of distress called out to us to help them, but we had neither ropes nor ladders to get them out.' I Corps too remains on the left bank to support Victor in tomorrow's struggle with Wittgenstein. After 'exchanging a few shots with the enemy' – i.e., with its most advanced units – the relics of the 7th Light Infantry have lit their bivouac fires 'on the fringe of a big wood. There we had some big old oaks to heat us, but nothing to eat.' Whereupon Sergeant Bertrand, 'as my habit was', goes off to take a look around. He knows that

'in the neighbourhood of the *cantinières* one could often come across a "Jew"[17] who only sold between four eyes and secretly; but at this moment I couldn't find one.'

Instead, his 'good star' arranges for him to fall in with 'a friend I hadn't seen since Wagram, a sapper sergeant-major of the Engineers, who was working on the bridges'. After he's told him how hungry he is his friend gives him a biscuit, saying:

'"It's been cooked in fat, you'll find it's good." I found it delicious, and didn't fail to give part of it to Sergeant Durand, my *alter ego*. Just as I was getting ready to sleep in front of a good fire, they tell me Louise, one of our *cantinières*, is on the point of giving birth, and is suffering badly. All the regiment is moved and finds ways of running to this unfortunate woman who under a sky of ice has nothing to eat, has no shelter. Our Colonel Romme sets the example. From everyone's hands our surgeons – their ambulance stretchers had been left behind at Smolensk for lack of transport – are receiving shirts, handkerchiefs, everything we could give.'

Although Bertrand himself has nothing to contribute,

'close to us I'd noticed an artillery park belonging to the Duke of Bellune's corps. I ran to it and taking a blanket from a horse's back ran back as fast as ever I could go to carry it to Louise. I'd done a bad deed, but I knew God would forgive me in view of the motive. I got there at the moment when our *cantinière*, under an old oak, brought into the world a shapely male infant.[18]Thus – in one of the debris of the Grand Army's most critical moments – our brave Louise gave the Fatherland one more defender. Marshal Davout distributed praise to everyone for our generous behaviour, and especially to our surgeons.'

Those who cross the bridges in the darkness and swirling snow this second night – and many isolated men do – are wise. For the congestion at the bridgehead is only growing worse. Yet the day, from a military point of view, Pils notes in his *Journal de Marche*,

'has passed in great tranquillity. The army has moved onwards. The snow's been falling so thickly that the daylight's been obscured by it. The paths traced yesterday by the infantry and artillery have been covered over again to a depth of a foot and a half.'

And all this time the Russians have hardly been heard from! But tomorrow?

CHAPTER 17

PARTONNEAUX SURRENDERS

*Where's Partonneaux? – a letter of resignation is ignored - 'it's as if they were mad-
dened by the gleaming gold' – a coward – 'standing out all round us in sombre lines
we saw the enemy masses' – 'since we were as incredulous as St Thomas' – Beulay's
last fight – Castellane at Zaniwki – Marbot is indignant*

At the Zaniwki cottage, meanwhile, some worrying news has come in.
Kutusov's advance guard has just appeared on the Orsha road.[1]

Other news, still more worrying, follows.

Wittgenstein isn't where he ought to be. Already he's somewhere
between Borissow and Studianka!

But it can't be true! Hasn't Victor left Partonneaux's division, his
strongest, at Borissow to hold him at bay? At once, as if by premonition,
everyone at IHQ feels extremely anxious. And Gourgaud's sent back across
the river to find out what's afoot. Two and a half miles from Studianka on
the Borissow road he runs into one of Partonneaux's units, the 4th Battalion of the 55th Line, under its Major Joyeux. Where, he asks him, is the rest
of his division? Joyeux's reply makes Gourgaud's blood freeze:

'It can only be somewhere ahead of me.'

Ahead? But it can't be! Hasn't he, Gourgaud, just come down a road
where he's seen nothing but stragglers? The 55th had been left behind to
be chopped to pieces if necessary, an embittered Joyeux explains, until a
staff officer should come and relieve them. The officer had come. And
here they are, en route for Studianka. Reaching the fork in the road and
unsure in the darkness which way to go, he'd heard some vehicles moving
along the road branching off to the left:

'I spurred my horse, and caught up with them. Asked the men around
them what division or army corps they belonged to. None of them
wanted to reply. The whole lot were stragglers.'

Whereafter some peasants 'who hadn't even wanted to be paid' had guided
him this far along the road that follows the river line:

'"We're the last rearguard", says Joyeux. "We've only Russians behind us."'

How can a whole division of 4,000 men, artillery and 500 cavalry, have
vanished? Yet it has. Partonneaux's division, the whole army's rearguard,
can only have branched off to the right, up toward Staroï-Borissow! And
what's happened to it since is anyone's guess. Dashing back to Studianka, a
panicky Gourgaud crosses the empty bridge. His return, Fain sees, 'throws
the Emperor into a great perplexity'. And Rossetti hears him exclaim:

'"Why, just when by a miracle everything has seemed to be saved, does
this[2] have to come and spoil it all?"'

If there's one man who understands instinctively what's happened it's Rossetti – yesterday he'd made the same mistake himself. Left behind at Borissow with 'two horses from the Emperor's stable' and orders, after he'd

picked up any of Murat's other staff officers who might turn up, not to leave until nightfall on 26 November,

'my route illumined by the enemy's fires which covered all the high ground on the right bank, I'd set out at the prescribed hour, taking with me the ADCs Pérignon and Bauffremont and all members of the King's household who'd managed to get as far as Borissow. After an hour the road divided and as the Berezina flowed on my left I didn't hesitate to take the road on that side. But after marching for a while I'd noticed that this road wasn't trampled down and that the snow covering it was virtually intact. So I turned back and took the right-hand route. The night was very dark; yet I'd noticed that it was insensibly bending to my right and that I'd necessarily turn my back on the river.'

Whereon Rossetti had halted his 'little column. At about 2 a.m. the sound of wheels heralded an artillery park coming up behind me.' Part of Victor's corps, it too was supposed to be making for Studianka. Its colonel, having closely studied the map before leaving Borissow, is sure he's on the right road, and refuses to turn back. 'At dawn he stumbled on the Russians. As for me I lit a fire, and at first light, having realised I was on the wrong track, I'd reached the bank of the Berezina cross-country.'

Surely Partonneaux can't have done the same?

Ten days have passed since 17 November when the 42-year-old Partonneaux had written a despondent letter to Berthier, asking to be relieved of his command:[3]

'"Up to now courage and zeal have kept me going. But my physical strength has abandoned me. I can no longer stand up to the pains being caused me by the rigour of the season and my wounds. The very service of the Emperor may be compromised by my no longer being able to be as active as before."'

Although originally 'made up of young soldiers, many of them refractory conscripts', his division – his letter had gone on – was now in excellent shape, though like himself it needed to rest.

Berthier hadn't replied.

Perhaps things would be turning out differently now if he had?

At Borissow Sous-Lieutenant Beulay and his 36th Line had managed to save 'a long file of stragglers whom we afterwards had all the trouble in the world to prevail on to evacuate Borissow, where they'd been retained by hope of sleeping in the warm under a roof'.

For Borissow, as yet, has plenty. When the artillery staff had got there Planat de la Faye's servant,[4]

'a big Hamburger, very soft and very heavy, though very clean and very meticulous on the job, had lain down in the house of some Jews, and refused to leave it. He seemed neither to be sick nor suffering from frost-bite. But he was beyond measure demoralised and in a state of terrifying stupidity.'

Griois too might easily have ended his life at Borissow, if the newly promoted Squadron-Leader Bonnardel of the 1st Horse Artillery 'more fortunate than I and in the best of health' hadn't seen his house was on fire in
the small hours and raised the alarm. 'Could anyone who'd seen us breakfasting together have guessed it would be Bonnardel, so robust and full of
life, who'd succumb that very day and I, whose pale and cadaverous face
heralded my approaching end, who'd survive?' When the time had come
to leave, Griois had urged him to get going. But Bonnardel, 'confident in
his strength and his horse's health, preferred to stay and rest a little longer
and let me leave on my own. It was these short moments of repose that
caused his loss.' Bonnardel and 'his gunner, who cooked for him' had
fallen to the Cossacks.

It's to prevent this sort of thing that Victor had entrusted the rearguard
to Partonneaux when he'd left for Studianka with his two other divisions in
the afternoon of the 27th. That afternoon Honoré Beulay had seen something strange, novel and upsetting

'beside the Studianka road where it comes out of Borissow. Several
wagons filled with gold and silver coins had been abandoned, either
because their horses had been killed or because the Emperor, afraid
his military treasure might profit the enemy, had preferred everyone
to take a fistful as he passed by.'

It can only have been left there by Claparède's '50 most reliable' Poles or
by Eugène's men who'd taken over from them:

'The wagons had been opened, revealing their gold, brilliant as a sun.
At once all these unfortunates who hadn't strength enough to carry
their weapons flung themselves on the spoils. Men who hadn't even
been able to drag themselves along became as agile as monkeys, strong
as bulldogs disputing a bone! There was a senseless shoving and pushing, a general battle. Everyone wants some of this gold, plunges his
hands into it, fills his pockets. And all those who've managed to clamber
up on to the wagons are loth to cease dipping into them as long as
they've a pocket left. It was as if the gleaming gold had driven them
mad.'

Even when the Russians bring up some cannon and fire on them at short
range – so that Partonneaux orders one of his battalions to drive them off
with volleys of musketry – it makes no difference.

'We were counting on rejoining the Marshal that same evening. It had
been agreed. Alas, Providence had decided otherwise.'

Then something even more unusual had happened. 'After coping with the
stragglers', the division had just been forming up to march for Studianka,
and Beulay's battalion was

'just coming back to resume its place in the column, when we heard
some veritable howls coming from the town side. Everyone spun round,
expecting an attack. We were mistaken. The mob of defeated men was
still trailing miserably by. But in their midst two horsemen who seemed
to be warmly wrapped up in numerous greatcoats were emerging; and it

was at them the men were shaking their fists, a gesture they accompanied with a flood of insults.'

Their officers try to restrain them, but mingle their shouts with their men's. One of the horsemen is their own lieutenant-colonel, who on some pretext had deserted them earlier in the campaign. The other's his batman:

'He seemed less then enchanted to see us again and was trying in vain to hide under his hat brim and pull up his collars to his nose.'

When they'd seen the colonels and generals of the Moscow army stumbling along behind carts on the Orsha road they'd been

'seized by compassion, even to the point of tears. But now, seeing this coward who'd run away at the first cannon shot and abandoned a still intact regiment, a shiver of rage ran from one end of the column to the other.'

With the word 'coward' and sarcasms of every kind hailing down on him 'like the rumbling of thunder', the wretched lieutenant-colonel, 'livid as an exhumed corpse, with haggard eyes lost in the distance, without trying to defend or excuse himself' trots on past the column, 'thinking only one thing: how to save a life he'd degraded'.

But then something very unfortunate had happened. At 4 p.m. (according to Beulay) Berthier's ADC Mortemart had arrived with orders to Partonneaux

'to spend the night at Borissow, to continue to draw Tchitchakov's attention and facilitate the passage of as many victims of the rout as possible. Tails between our legs, we went back into Borissow just in time to catch Tchitchakov's chasseurs, who were trying to cross the Berezina, one by one, on the bridge's half-charred timbers.'

After which the division, always on the *qui vive*, had spent a last miserable night there. At crack of dawn Partonneaux had sent

'several companies toward the Orsha road. But now the stragglers were only turning up in dribs and drabs, at wide intervals. Impatient, M. Partonneaux went on ahead of them, leaving our battalion's voltigeur company at the Borissow bridgehead. He led his division on to the main road, trying to collect the 5 or 6,000 stragglers the Emperor had specified.'

The cold, Beulay goes on,

'was becoming intolerable. Our men could hardly load their weapons, so painful was the contact with the iron. It was snowing. Great flakes were mercilessly swirling round our faces and blinding us. We couldn't see so much as 50 metres ahead of us. But in front of us we could hear musket shots which told us Kutusov [*sic*] was approaching with giant strides.'

Seeing no more fugitives coming down the Orsha road, Partonneaux had withdrawn the battalion into Borissow:

'Hardly have we got back there than General Platov's cavalry, detached by old Kutusov, charged our rearguard. On another side Wittgenstein's men, profiting by our absence, had slipped into the suburbs and, hidden in enclosures, were attacking us with a well-nourished fusillade. Without replying to this musketry, we put our bayonets on our musket-barrels and butchered our adversaries.'

Unfortunately, Beulay goes on,

'even before we'd left Borissow, their regiments had got ahead of us and were occupying the slopes which dominate the road we were to follow. We cross the town at the double in the direction of the Studianka road. But so encumbered is this highway with wagons, corpses, stragglers, we can hardly get on. The wind, whistling from the North Pole, pierces us. The snow never ceases falling. There are hardly 3,000 of us left, and we've only three guns to face the entire Russian army, united against us!'

Yet they've no alternative but to advance. Now the division, reduced to three-quarters of its strength, is marching in brigade columns. Parton-neaux himself is with the right-hand, i.e., most exposed one. The Russians, who've crowned the heights towards Staroï-Borissow, open fire. By now they're too numerous even to reply to:

'We move on at the double, always hoping Marshal Victor, attracted by the crackling of the fusillade, will hasten to our assistance. We've not gone very far when it seems to us heaven has heard our prayer. Straight in front of us, athwart the road, we see a major troop movement. Alas, it isn't Victor. It's the Russian artillery taking up position to bar our path. As soon as they're within easy range, all these guns converge their big mouths on to the middle of the road, and let fly at us a discharge which wipes out our leading ranks. After the first, a second; then a third. No sense in being stubborn! The Russian infantry to our right, too, had maximised its fire. To the left we were hemmed in by a river we couldn't cross. Ahead, a cloud of roundshot was crushing our column from one end to the other. So we'd have to retreat. But just as we're about-facing, Platov's 10,000 horsemen fall on us like a hurricane, sabring everything that comes to hand.'

'The situation,' Beulay goes on with dry understatement,

'was becoming complicated. More than half of us were reddening the snow. Night was falling. We didn't know where we were. General Par-tonneaux hastily assembles a council-of-war. It's decided we're to break up into brigades and, silently, under cover of darkness, try to slip between the enemy units. It was excessively audacious. There was little chance of success. But what else could we do?

'The general took command of the first brigade and went off to our right. The second brigade, which I belonged to, remained in the mid-dle. The third moved off to the left, on the river side. 'M. Partonneaux tried to climb the hillsides, hoping to find a break in the mesh of light infantrymen that was tightly hemming us in. But he ran into an enemy force which threw him back into the valley. Wherever he presented him-self he was hemmed in in the same way. Suddenly, there's a free space opening in front of him. Overjoyed, he enters it. But the ice breaks under the weight of his men, and while they're trying to get out of the swamps they've been pushed into, the Russians take them prisoner. The third brigade, on its side, ran into the deep masses which were pressing down on us, thus opening the banks of the Berezina.'

It was this movement, Beulay supposes, that allows his battalion's voltigeur company, left behind at Borissow, to slip through:

'At nightfall these brave fellows, realising no one was bothering about them, had finished off burning the Borissow bridge's half-burnt girders, and set off, without drums or cornets, along the river, just in time to find the road open,'

and – evidently unnoticed by Gourgaud – reach Studianka. After it had left Borissow, Beulay goes on, 'the fire put to the bridge, aided by the wind, had spread to a whole quarter' of the town:

'Soon, against the vague glow of this distant fire, we saw the enemy masses standing out all round us in sombre lines. At the same time it gave the Russians an exact idea of our position and our formation. For three hours Wittgenstein, thus informed, pierced us through and through with projectiles. M. de Blamont had sent several patrols to try and find a way out. All had come back empty-handed. But one of them told our general that a short way away, behind a little wood, there was a fold in the ground where we could take cover. M. de Blamont took all that was left of the 2nd and 3rd Brigades there. Only my regiment stayed on the plateau to keep the Russians at a distance and prevent them from setting up their batteries on the edges of that ravine. At about 10 p.m., while we were still serving as a target for the enemy, my battalion commander, who was commanding the regiment since the disappearance of M. W***, asked me to go and find the general and tell him there was only a handful of us left; that we'd run out of ammunition, and ask him to relieve us, if possible.'

The Russian outposts fire several salvoes at Beulay's 'thin figure' as he runs, 'but not a musket ball hit me'. Soon he's with the divisional staff. Alas,

'in the midst of the senseless disorder reigning at the bottom of this hole it was impossible to reconstitute any unit whatsoever, regiment or battalion, to take our place. "If you can't hang on any longer," the general replied, discouraged, "come down to us. As for relieving you, you see it's nothing to count on." As he said these words he gave a cry of pain. He'd been hit in the knee by a stray musket ball. We no longer had any generals or colonels. From that moment it was some rare commandants and captains who took over their functions.'

On his way back Beulay runs into his comrades 'running like a flock of sheep' at the edge of the plateau and thus increasing the confusion down in the hollow. Whereon the Russian guns approach and level themselves at what's left of the brigade:

'It was a veritable butchery! I was spattered from head to foot in my neighbours' blood. Maddened, stunned by this horrible uproar, by the cries of the wounded, the rattle of the dying, the whistling of musket balls, the snoring of roundshot, the roaring of the guns,' he wonders whether he's still even to be numbered among the living. Forming a kind of square, the 36th throw themselves at the Russians. By now it's about 10.30 p.m. Except for the flash of firearms and the distant glow of the Borissow fire it's pitch dark:

'Finally Wittgenstein, ashamed of this slaughter, ordered a cease fire and sent a flag of truce, charging him to tell us that Partonneaux and the 1st Brigade had laid down their arms; that it was madness to try and resist hundreds of thousands [*sic*] of men; that we'd given sufficient proof of our valour; and that the time had come to stop getting ourselves massacred to no purpose. But no one believed our divisional general had capitulated, so, without our listening to any more the Russian officer was sent back where he'd come from.'

Beulay's account becomes more and more tragic:

'We'd had nothing to eat since yesterday, our clothes were in shreds and the temperature was so cruel that those who escaped the bullets were succumbing to the cold if they remained immobile even a few instants. Marvelling at such courage, the Russian general lost no time in sending us a second flag of truce. Since we were as incredulous as St Thomas, this officer invited us to send one of our own people to assure himself that M. Partonneaux had in fact been taken prisoner. It was my friend M. Taillefer, the lieutenant of grenadiers who'd been promoted at the same as myself, who was charged with this mission. He went to the Russian headquarters, where in fact he found General Partonneaux in a state of utter despondency. When he asked him for orders, the general replied that he had no more orders to give, he left it up to us what to do. Then Wittgenstein summoned M. Taillefer to him and told him that if we didn't surrender instantly he'd kill the whole lot of us to the last man. He declared we'd violated the laws of warfare, that it was inadmissable that 200,000 men [*sic*] should be held up in their pursuit by the shadow of a brigade, that such a thing was folly on our part to attempt, and a culpable weakness on his own part to tolerate.'

Taillefer comes back. A new council of war is held. And it's generally agreed that Wittgenstein's right:

'Only eight or ten men were left per company. Even so, we decided to temporise, wait for daylight. We couldn't believe that the Emperor, who'd been so concerned over the fate of some miserable stragglers, should have allowed Marshal Victor to consent to sacrifice a whole division without trying to do something to save it from the trap they'd sent it into.'

The Russians, sure of their prey, also cease firing. Many of Partonneaux's men die of despair and inanition the moment they've nothing more to do. Beulay himself, stumbling about among the corpses and wounded, only survives by resisting a longing for sleep. Meanwhile his enterprising batman is determined to make him some breakfast. Rifling a nearby abandoned wagon, he finds in it 'something more precious than all the gold we'd seen glittering yesterday: a superb loaf of delicious barley bread, which we shared secretly with a few intimate friends'.

The batman also roasts some horse steaks over a fire made of the butts of the muskets everywhere littering the ground. One of the muskets is loaded, goes off as he breaks it, and the ball passes so close to Beulay's ear that it begins to bleed:

'Then the dawn appeared on the frozen horizon. Soon reveille's sounding on all sides in the enemy camp. A great movement begins. In the front rank we see the mouths of the guns of the [Russian] Imperial Guard trained at us. The gunners were lighting their matches, ready for the first order. Instinctively the few brave survivors form square. But while they're feeling for ammunition in their empty pouches the Russians fling themselves on us from both sides. We're prisoners!'[5]

At Zaniwki, meanwhile. Castellane – like other staff officers – isn't being allowed a moment's rest. 'Since no one foresaw this fight,' he'll jot down in his diary eventually, 'several officers of our staff have gone on ahead.' All the time, this horrible night, he's being sent on mission to the various corps. Lots of IHQ's horses have been stolen – including six of Lobau's and his wagon:

'Our men have [got into] a horrible way of stealing things. At our bivouac someone steals Chabot's hat. He had his head lying on it. A fur's been taken from one of my horses. More than one officer, believing his horse is following him, is getting here with only its cut reins around his arm. If he turns round, it's to see his horse already killed, cut up and shared out.'

At 'the Palace' Napoleon never ceases 'asking each officer arriving from Studianka whether the poor people and baggage were still crossing'. And is told, correctly, that the bridges are free, but that few if any of the estimated 20,000[6] wounded, *cantinières*, women, camp followers and refugees from Moscow huddled there around their campfires are in a hurry to profit from it. 'All night and until daybreak,' says Lejeune,

'the army's passage over the bridges had been going on without too much disorder, and I myself had been able to cross to and fro several times to place those things which were most in the army's interests in safety on the right bank'.

Marbot, going back to fetch 'the horse which carried the war squadrons' little cash box and accounts' is utterly critical of the general staff's failure to exploit these night hours:

'Having well and truly established my regiment at the Zaniwki bivouac, I galloped back. And imagine my amazement when I find the bridges completely deserted! Just at that moment no one was crossing over! Yet only a hundred yards away, in beautiful moonlight, I see more than 50,000 [*sic*] stragglers or isolated men of the kind we called roasters [*rôtisseurs*] seated in front of immense fires, calmly grilling horseflesh, as if unaware they've a river in front of them they could cross in a few minutes and finish preparing their supper on the other bank.'

It's his first sight of the debris of the Moscow army, and it comes as a terrible shock:

'Not one officer of the Imperial Household, not an ADC of the army's Major-General [Berthier] nor any Marshal was there to forewarn these unfortunates and, if need be, drive them toward the bridges.'

What Marbot evidently doesn't notice is the heroic Eblé going about in the moonlight among the torpid stragglers, trying to get them to bestir themselves while there's still time.[7] Another officer who, half-dead from hunger, crosses unhindered is the Polish Captain *Boris von Turno*:

'A vague instinct, one of those prophetic impulses one has in one's youth, turned my thoughts to General Dombrowski's division. His troops, who had come from Molihew, might have some provisions. By giving me hope this idea gave me courage. I went to the bridge, where all I heard was the monotonous bumping together of the ice-floes being carried along by the Berezina. No one was going over it.'

Reaching the other side Turno finds he's in luck. Turning left toward the Brill Wood, where little voltigeur Jean-Marc Bussy and his colleagues of the Swiss infantry are doing 'nothing but run about in the forest, in the snow, to pick up firewood and keep our fires alight for the sake of the poor wounded, who've all been attended to by our surgeon,' Turno chances upon

'four Polish artillery officers gathered around a big fire. The captain, who recognised me, exclaimed: "My dear friend, you're in luck! He offered me his water-bottle, whose contents I swallowed at a single gulp. Galvanised by this dose of alcohol, like a man waking up, I looked around me. In front of their hut a really nice-looking duck was turning on the spit, the bubbling of two saucepans emitted to my ears a culinary harmony which was making our eyes shine with savage brilliance.'

And he quotes to his 'Amphytrion' the words of Sancho Panza, 'greatest of philosophers: "It's not the man who makes the stomach, but the stomach that makes the man."' But not very far away Brandt and the Vistula Legion's other wounded have heard

'late into the night the cannon thundering on the other bank. It was the fighting that was deciding the fate of Partonneaux's division.'

CHAPTER 18

HOLOCAUST AT THE BEREZINA

'Throughout this horrible day we saw the human heart laid bare. We saw infamous actions and sublime ones, according to differences in character.' (Rossetti) – 'Napoleon was never better served by his generals than he was that day.' (Caulaincourt)

Some time after midnight, Fain has noted in his journal:
'The day now beginning is likely to be a tough one. But we hold the passage.'
And Napoleon has sent off the devoted Abramovitch to Vilna, to tell Maret the army's across the Berezina; though not all of it is. 'More than 60,000 men,' Rossetti realises,
'properly clad, well-nourished and fully armed, are about to attack 18,000 half-naked, ill-armed ones, dying of hunger and cold, divided by a swampy river and embarrassed by more than 50,000 stragglers, sick or wounded and an enormous mass of baggage.'
Already on his feet at 5 a.m., Oudinot, wearing a 'brown fur *witschoura* and an astrakhan bonnet turned down over his ears', shares some onion soup with his staff, Pils among them:
'Each of these gentlemen were placed under contribution so that the cook could do his business. One supplied the bread, another the onion, a third the fat. It didn't take long to share it out.'
Pils, no doubt savouring his share, is thinking that if his *patron*'s
'two motley legs sticking out of the *witschoura* weren't sheathed in a special pair of boots, well-lined with fur on the inside but on the outside only revealing striped blue and white feather-lined drill, he'd look like a well brought up bear'.
Tchitchakov's attack is expected at dawn. And sure enough, at 7 a.m. the 'the sound of the guns in the direction of Borissow' tells Fain he's 'attacking II Corps in the woods. The Emperor mounted his horse and galloped off.' Castellane, in his suite as it passes 'in front of Razout's division in reserve behind III Corps', sees that it amounts to perhaps half a battalion; Fezensac's regiment to a platoon. And that Ney's been 'reinforced by Claparède's division, by 12,000 men of the 15th Polish Division and by some other troops of Zayoncek's.'

A moment later Wittgenstein's guns too begin firing from the direction of Staroï-Borissow. 'At about 7 a.m.' Pils, at the shack which has been Oudinot's headquarters, sees
'Captain Cramayel arrive at a gallop to warn us that the enemy's attacking and that the Cossacks are already at blows with the outposts. This officer has hardly said what he had to when a shell, passing through the pine branches, falls noisily on the shack and shatters it. At once *M. le Maréchal* mounts his horse and orders Merle's division to advance. The

2nd Swiss Line marches at its head; a second shell carries off eleven of its men. The 11th Light and 124th Line follow on.'

So begins the Battle of the Berezina.

Thomas Legler is noticing that 'a little snow was falling', and at about 7.30 he and his Commandant Blattmann are strolling to and fro on the road and Blattmann reminds him of 'a favourite song of mine, *"Our Life is like a Journey"*' and asks him to sing it for him. 'I started to at once, and when I'd finished it, he heaved a deep sigh. "Yes, Legler, that's how it is. What splendid words!"' Other officers join them and spend 'the morning's early hours singing and chatting'.

Evidently Tschaplitz's attack is taking some time to materialise. Because it's already '9 a.m. when suddenly a roundshot passes overhead with a horrible loud noise' startling Legler's colleagues:

'We couldn't understand how we could have been standing so near the enemy without any outposts. Now we heard heavy cannon fire in the distance; and to our right musketry seemed to be coming closer. An orderly officer came galloping up from that direction: "Our line's been attacked!"'

Hardly have the group of Swiss infantry officers taken 100 paces to their right than 'to our great astonishment an enemy came forward'. The Swiss scouts 'quickly spread out backwards and sideways', keeping the enemy at a distance by a well-nourished fire until the regiment has rejoined 'the division that united us to our brigade's two other divisions, which we'd lost sight of. On the road both sides' artillery were facing each other, but the enemy's so much aslant it we could now and again trace the damage their roundshot were doing.'

The Croat Regiment having been stationed elsewhere, Merle's four Swiss infantry regiments, 'these four units together perhaps amounting at most to 2,500 men', only have the French 123rd Line to support them. 'Behind us a few small Polish infantry units, a squadron of chasseurs and one of lancers formed a second line.'

By now it's growing light and the 3rd Swiss, with the 4th Swiss to their right, are firing volley after volley, 'fighting without budging'. Yet all the time

'it seems to us the enemy's being reinforced. His firing's becoming livelier. Suddenly we're thrown back, we retreat some 50 paces. The chiefs shout: "Forward!" Everywhere the Charge is beaten. We're flung at the enemy, cross bayonets at point-blank range. Slowly, the Russians retire, still firing.'

Soon the Swiss are held up by cavalry, 'which makes a charge through the sparse snow-laden pines. But all this has been no more than a *passade*. In no time our battery and the 4th's dismount the Russian battery, which is abandoned on the road.' But the Swiss are suffering heavy casualties. The 2nd Regiment, only a few yards away, is

'the most advanced of all. After a first, very successful charge, our commandant Vonderweid, from Seedorf, was following it up vigorously',

and Captain Begons orders his adjutant,

'an NCO named Barbey, to go and get some cartridges. He was obeying when he was hit mortally. I gave the same order to a certain Scherzenecker. He too was hit, in the right arm. I was just going to send a third officer, when I saw that the Russians, protected by numerous light infantry, were still coming on ever more thickly. Although our regiment scarcely had 800 men, it was well-equipped and aware of the importance of the position entrusted to us. We heard a formidable noise of gunfire and hurrahs. It was the Russian army which, knowing our army corps had crossed the river and to dispute the passage with us, was coming on in ever greater numbers.'

Now the Swiss – the 1st Regiment has spread out *en tirailleurs* – are beginning to run out of ammunition:

'On both sides the firing was murderous. It wasn't long before General Amey and several staff officers had been wounded and several killed, among them our commandant Blattmann. A bullet went through his brain. General of Brigade Canderas and his adjutant had fallen too; a roundshot had taken off the latter's head.'

By now Legler – he's taken cover behind a tree – is estimating the number of men – 'it was growing every minute' – standing idle for lack of cartridges to be at least 300. 'All these were coming and placing themselves calmly behind the line of officers.' When he asks them what they're doing there, they simply reply "give us cartridges". What can he reply to that? At that moment he sees Merle 200 yards away. Runs over to him. Asks leave to attack the advancing Russians at bayonet point. Merle tells him to run back and, in his name, order the firing to cease and to charge with the bayonet. Legler insists that the drummers 'since we'd ceased fire' shall take the lead:

'But this they all refused to do. So in the heat of the moment I seized the first one to hand – a Swiss from the Glarus canton, by name Kundert, living at Rüti, something I didn't notice in the heat of battle – by his collar and threatened to run my sword through him if he didn't follow me. After which I, at a run, dragged him behind me to the front line, while he beat the attack with one hand. However, just as I let go of him a bullet hit him in the right jawbone.'[1]

All his long life[2] the 23-year-old volunteer *Louis de Bourmann* will remember and celebrate the 2nd Regiment's homeric struggles. He too has seen 'the intrepid Fribourgeois' Vonderweid fall:

'He'd just given his horse to his adjutant, who'd been wounded in the leg, and was fighting on foot at the head of his braves when a Russian musket ball went through his throat. He gave a cry, stifled by blood, and fell backwards into my arms. After the first moment had passed, he, without losing consciousness, said these simple words to his fellow-citizen: "Bourmann, I've died here as a Christian."'

And is carried to the rear by his men, 'hardly to survive for forty-eight hours'. At last cartridges have arrived and been distributed to Legler's men. Not enough to keep up a heavy fire however. So a second bayonet charge is launched. 'Twice at a hundred paces' distance we forced him to retire.' With some grenadiers Legler goes to the rear to get more ammunition, 'but had to search about for a powder wagon for a good half hour before we found one'. Just as they're going back to the firing line with as many cartridges as they can carry, they see Commandant Zingg, who insists on taking over now that Blattmann is dead. But as they approach the regiment they see, 'about 300 paces to the left of the road', another Russian column advancing and outflanking them. 'Already it could take us in the rear.' Being only a cannon-shot from the bridge on the forest fringe, the Swiss can't see very far ahead. And Begos assumes the 3rd and 4th Regiments must be somewhere to his right,

'almost opposite the bridge. For the rest, it was hard to grasp the army's overall movements. In such moments each man feels how important it is to stay at his post. It was a question of preventing the Russians from approaching, so what was needed was a heroic defence, no more, no less! Not for a single moment had we nothing to do. Swarms of Russians were aiming such a well-nourished fire at our regiment that after an hour of combat we'd lost quite a lot of ground.'

Legler's men, however, have been following up their bayonet attack 'for the best part of half an hour', and the Russians have turned and fled – as troops almost always do when seriously threatened by a bayonet charge –

'when we were swept up in the flight of the lancer squadron on our right flank. Looking back as we ran, we saw Russian dragoons at our heels, and some enemy infantry advancing with them. Again I yelled out to halt and form up. Those who heard me did as I'd ordered, and our well-aimed shots at the nearest dragoons, felling them from their horses, had such a good effect that the others galloped back, leaving the infantry standing.'

By now, through thickly falling snow, the Russian artillery's enfilading the road at short range. It's causing such slaughter among the Swiss that Oudinot, sitting his horse amidst the swirling snowflakes, orders Merle's division to move off to its left. Thus placing it under cover of the forest, he brings up two of his own guns. And Pils, in the saddle beside his Marshal, and clasping his first-aid box, sees how,

'before they've had time to be ranged in battery, one of them is carried off by the Russians, whom we hadn't realised were so close. We couldn't see farther than 30 paces for the snow.'

For all their staunchness the Swiss, Fezensac realises, are losing a lot of ground:

'Only three weak battalions placed on the road – all that was left of I, III and VIII Corps – served as their reserve. For a while the fight was sustained; under pressure from superior forces II Corps was beginning to sag. Our reserves, hit by roundshot at ever closer range, were moving towards the rear. This movement put to flight all the isolated men who filled the wood, and in their terror they ran as far as the bridge. Even the Young Guard was wavering. Soon there was no more salvation except in the Old Guard. With it we were prepared to die or conquer.'

But then, in a jiffy, everything changes aspect. 'What were to have been the scenes of the Grand Army's tomb became witnesses to its last triumph.' Oudinot, 'indignant at such audacity' on the Russians' part, 'remains in the middle of the road without bothering about the bullets whistling by on all sides.' The moment has come, he decides, to send in his heavy cavalry; and sends his last ADC, M. de la Chaise, to General Doumerc, ordering him to advance his cuirassiers' – the 4th, 7th and 14th Cuirassiers, that is, who've already done such splendid service after Polotsk and in front of Borissow. So impatient is Oudinot 'while waiting for his order to be carried out that he stamps his foot', asking Pils as he does so whether he hasn't got a drop of brandy to warm him:

'I'm just searching for it in my bag, paying no more heed to what's going on, when, having found some dregs of brandy, I offer them to him. In the same instant I see M. le Maréchal put his hand to his side and fall from his horse, which instantly bolts,'

dragging with it its rider (according to another eye-witness) hanging upside down. Pils, 'alone beside him' struggles to dismount,

'but couldn't extract my right shoe from the stirrup. The illustrious wounded man gave no more sign of life. But then a young voltigeur whose right fist had been carried away and who was holding his musket in his left hand came to my assistance, freed me and helped me to lift M. le Maréchal. We raised him to a sitting position.'

At this moment Captain de la Chaise comes back to report his mission accomplished:

'Supposing his chief to be dead, he threw himself upon him and embraced him. Between the three of us we placed him on the voltigeur's musket and took him away from this spot where the musket balls were still whistling. Then Lieutenant-Colonel Jacqueminot appeared, bringing back a Russian officer, whom he was grasping by the collar. Finally General de Lorencez, chief-of-staff, and some other officers had rejoined us. We got busy making a stretcher out of pine branches.'

Napoleon, meanwhile, has returned to his headquarters at the Zaniwki hamlet, only a cannon shot away, and is standing

'on foot at the forest fringe on the right of the road, surrounded by his staff. Behind him the Imperial Guard, drawn up in battle order,'

amounts in all to some 5,500 men – Mortier's Young Guard (2,000) Lefèbvre's Old Guard Infantry (3,500), and Bessières' 500 Chasseurs and a handful of Horse Grenadiers:

'Informed of the Duke of Reggio's condition, the Emperor immediately sent his own carriage, escorted by some Horse Grenadiers. But M. le Maréchal, who'd recovered consciousness, declared he couldn't stand the jolting, and so we went on carrying him.' Bonneval, sent with a dispatch to Ney to take over command of II Corps as well as his own, sees 'Jacqueminot following after, all in tears.'

As the men carrying Oudinot pass before him, Pils goes on, 'His Majesty took a few paces toward us and said:

'"Well, Oudinot, so you no longer recognise me?"'

Seeing that Oudinot has fainted again, he turns to Corvisart and Larrey and tells them to attend to him.

'The Horse Chasseurs of the Guard were drawn up to the left of the road. Captain Victor Oudinot, the Marshal's son, sees the convoy passing, has recognised his father, jumped the ditch and come to him. We laid *M. le Maréchal* down on a mattress in the Emperor's hut. There he was given first aid. Some linen, eau de cologne and Bordeaux wine had been put at his disposal, rare though such things were at that moment.'

Coming to, Oudinot says he has every confidence in his own chief surgeon. It's he – Capiomont, not Desgenettes – he wants to operate on him; indeed Bonneval, returned from his mission to Ney, hears Capiomont insist on it 'as his right and privilege'. Upon his 'refusing to be tied down', Pils gives him a napkin to bite into. And the operation begins. 'If he vomits,' opines Desgenettes, 'he's a dead man.' But though the probe goes in 'to a depth of 6 or 7 inches', he doesn't; and 'the ball was never found or extracted'. Desgenettes asks Intendant-Général Dumas, himself ailing, to look after him. And Pils, with an obviously very agitated pencil, captures the moment when Napoleon is informed that his Marshal's condition isn't desperate.

Bonneval, coming with the order to Ney to take over, has found him

'on a little white horse, surrounded by his whole staff. There he was, in the midst of a very well-nourished fire, as calm as at the Tuileries. He had, I remember, a singular habit. Each time musket balls or a round-shot whistled in his ears, he shouted: "Go past, rascals! [*Passez, coquins!*]"'

The Brill Wood's pine trees, though heavily snow-laden, are 'very sparse'. And upon Doumerc's 3rd Heavy Cavalry Division coming up, Ney orders Colonel Ordener of the 7th Cuirassiers, supported by the 4th, '200 cuirassiers at most', to charge through it. Within sight of Thomas Legler and his men – they're about to be taken in the rear by yet another Russian column which 'advancing with loud shouts' – has just forced some French or Swiss infantry to give ground', the cuirassiers are ordered to charge:

'The brave cuirassiers of the 4th and 7th Regiments, who were standing only 1,000 paces away from us, had seen the enemy too. We clearly heard the word of command: "Squadrons, by the left flank, march!" As soon as the cuirassiers had crossed the road they went in to the attack.'

In front of them is a huge Russian square. Nearby is Rochechouart, who's 'marched for the Studianka ford with everything we could collect'. Langeron has invited him to come with him

'into the forest with the grenadier battalion and a good regiment of Don Cossacks. No sooner have we got into the said forest than we're vigorously charged by a regiment of cuirassiers, such as we certainly didn't expect to meet with on that kind of battlefield'.

Legler sees only 'four shots fired; then the enemy fled'. The great Russian infantry square is shattered and dissolves:

'Our grenadiers, taken by surprise, were sabred and routed, while our Cossacks made a show of resisting, which thanks to our horses gave us time to escape.'

No sooner have Legler's Swiss seen the cuirassiers charge than

'we threw our ammunition to the ground and all ran forward with a single shout: "The cuirassiers are attacking the enemy in the wood to our left! Forward at the bayonet!" Some were shouting *"Vive l'Empereur!"* and I myself, *"Long live the brave men from Polotsk!"* The assault was general and this time succeeded so well that we took 2,500 [*sic*] prisoners, two-thirds of them wounded. Many dead and badly wounded men were lying on the ground.'

After this catch, says the breathless Legler,

'followed a calm that lasted for a quarter of an hour at least. Now, at long last, our other column, the Poles, advanced, and we were issued with cartridges, which had finally arrived in sufficient quantity. The oddest thing about this bayonet attack was that though we'd lost many dead and wounded during the firing, we ourselves hardly lost anyone at all. The enemy's second line, which now engaged us, hadn't been firing at us for half an hour before the Poles were forced back on top of us. We absorbed them into our line and resumed our firing. We were amazed how accurate the enemy shots were; if it had been sharpshooters we'd had in front of us they couldn't have done us worse damage.'

But Tschaplitz's men are falling back head over heels onto Stavkowo. Rochechouart the émigré is half shattered by his compatriots' achievement, half proud of it: 'The French and Polish infantry seconded the cuirassiers' efforts. The prize of their victory was 4,000 [*sic*] prisoners and five guns.'[3]

As they come back, driving before them 'a long column of prisoners, most of them slashed by sabre cuts', Doumerc's victorious cuirassiers are welcomed by Fezensac's men 'with transports of joy'. Rapp sees them ride past in front of the Guard 'still beautiful and to be feared, in battle array at the forest's edge'. And Fain hears how the Russian square had consisted of no fewer than 7,000 infantrymen. From a Russian officer he interrogates through his Polish interpreter Napoleon hears that all 'are from Army of Moldavia'.

It's been the battle's turning-point, at least on the right bank. 'Tchitchakov, who hadn't expected to come upon such redoubtable enemies, didn't renew his attack.'

Castex's light cavalry brigade is pursuing the enemy toward Stavkovo, when another of Berthier's ADCs arrives with an order – addressed presumably to Castex but which Marbot claims was to himself.[4] Its bearer is a young aristocrat of a very fine family indeed. Alfred de Noailles, 'heir to the Dukes of Noailles', is 'a fine officer', cherished by his ex-colleague Lejeune 'for his virtues and fine character' and 'esteemed and respected by everyone', including Bonneval, as 'a loyal and brave officer, infinitely religious and charitable'. On top of his splendiferous uniform[5] Noailles is also wearing a pair of Napoleon's own epaulettes, given him only three days ago 'at the Borissow bivouac by Angel, the usher of Napoleon's office'. Before reporting back to Berthier, he feels he ought to take a quick look at what's going on at Stavkovo. He's approaching the village and chatting with a certain Sous-Lieutenant Hippolyte Dessailles, commanding a party of II Corps' skirmishers, and Dessailles is exhorting him not to needlessly expose himself under fire – ('he'd do better to go and look for the Marshal') – when 'a ball hit him in the head. The French skirmishers, forced to withdraw from the position, abandoned M. de Noailles.' He was at once surrounded, Marbot goes on,

'by a group of Cossacks who, having thrown him off his horse and seized him by his collar, dragged him away, hitting him! The superb furs and gold-covered uniform he was wearing had probably tempted their cupidity. I instantly sent a squadron to rescue him, but this effort was fruitless, as a lively fusillade from the houses prevented our troopers from getting into the village. He was probably massacred by those barbarians.'

But soon Dessailles' light infantry, 'reoccupying the high ground, find his body again, stripped and motionless'. And when young de Noailles doesn't re-appear at IHQ, Berthier sends de Courbon, yet another of his ADCs, to look for him. And here accounts begin to differ:

'Near our tirailleurs I found a dead man, bearing a strong resemblance to M. de Noailles. He'd been hit in the head by a bullet.'

Since it's disfigured him, Squadron-Leader Courbon needs other items of evidence:

'I looked for them in a mark on his shirt and a professionally made cotton waistcoat, the only clothing left on him. But as I took them off I noticed that this dead man had a cauterised wound on his arm.'

Having lived with Noailles, but never noticed such a scar, he goes on looking elsewhere. But finding no other suitable corpse, returns to IHQ, where, however, he's told about the cauterisation. 'Others who knew him more particularly and said that he'd had just such a mark' regard it as proof positive. Lejeune will hear he'd been 'disfigured under the horses' feet and could only be recognised by his tall stature [5 feet 8 inches], the whiteness of his linen and its mark.'[6]

And still everyone's expecting Partonneaux to turn up.

'Even his rearguard battalion had arrived without any difficulties. No sounds of any fighting had been heard. The road, according to a reconnaissance party which had come back, was still free'

– a road, Captain *Roland Warchot*, bringing up the extreme rear with only a single company of the 8th Polish Lancers, is finding

'paved with transversely laid tree trunks. Under my orders I had some 500 horse. Against me I had perhaps about 10,000. But the accidents of the terrain were making it impossible for the Russians to deploy into columns of platoons, but obliged them, much to their annoyance, to stick to the timber road. This enabled me, with a single troop of twelve to sixteen files, to contain them and bar their passage.'

'Up to now,' Warchot goes on,

'they'd not had any guns with them, and I wasn't afraid of their charging me as long as I didn't find myself obliged to beat a retreat. But from the moment I had to retire and thus lose some ground I suffered considerable losses. Generally the Russians are terrible the moment one no longer stands one's ground. They fall on you like madmen. My horses were poorly shod, or not shod at all. Finally, quite close to the village of Weselovo, I had to abandon my lieutenant who had at least 30 sabre cuts and lance thrusts.'

At that moment Warchot – the lances are jabbing at his left shoulder – sees a barrier across the road. Tries to leap it. Fails. And has to leave his horse astride it – but not before repaying another lance stab in his back with a sabre slash across his enemy's face. But then another lance thrust goes through his chest 'and came out between my shoulders'. And he loses consciousness. 'The 20 or 30 lancers still with me shared my ill fortune and were either killed or taken with me.' (Not surprisingly the rest of Warchot's account is rather confused!)

But where is Partonneaux? Surely a whole division simply can't vanish, least of all on a day of battle?

'The uncertainty had only increased at about 9 a.m., when Wittgenstein's force was seen to be preparing an attack.'

Always it seems to be Dumonceau's singular good luck to be able to view great actions from some optimal vantage point. Before dawn Colbert had led the Lancer Brigade back to the same position behind the Young Guard as it had occupied yesterday. 'We dominated, as in an amphitheatre, the entire intervening plain, so we could see what was going on,' on both banks. At about 8 a.m. he'd heard the fighting start up again,

'this time not merely ahead of us but on both banks of the Berezina. The sky was sombre. At first, as yesterday, a compact crowd had accumulated at the bridges and was causing a dreadful tumult without being able to cross them in an orderly manner. All the while it was being swollen by a broad column intermingled with carriages or carts which we saw still turning up over the hills there. Behind it Marshal Victor's IX Corps, our rearguard, its right leaning on a wood which it doubtless still occupied throughout its entire extent, and its left extended by some cavalry squadrons in the direction of other woods as it arrived fighting at the hill's crest, was occupying them along its whole length and maintaining itself there all day long. Now our eyes were being drawn to this line, now to the bridges. Through the smoke we confusedly made out the former's successive movements, marked by the direction of the firing, at times flinging itself down the reverse slope in front of some enemy assault; then, having repulsed it, returning to re-occupy its former position.'

The sky is sombre; but the situation of all the thousands still on the eastern bank is even more so. A dawn fog has played its part, 'causing the crowd to take the wrong direction, force it to retrace its steps and form a kind of reflux that augmented the confusion.'

Several times during the night the wounded Lieutenant Auvray had gone down toward the crowd at the bridgehead, only to give up, dismayed at its size. But then,

'at about 3 a.m. I'd heard a murmur that the enemy was attacking the tail of the column. Despite the pain my wound was causing me, I'd thrown myself into the crowd; and there I'd stayed for three hours without being able to get on. However, at 6 a.m. I'd managed to reach the far bank; and two hours later, in a village where they were waiting for me, was so fortunate as to meet my dragoon Ducloux and Médard Chagot, who'd got across the previous evening together with my horse and effects.'

Franz Roeder, desperately ill now with dysentery and pleurisy, has been hoping to cross over in Colonel Follenius' chaise; but found it already occupied by Captain Schwarzenau – an officer who always arouses his special antipathy. Stamping off in a violent rage, he'd mounted his pony, which he'd found 'without a bridle and with one stirrup two spans too long'. But though he'd got to the bridgehead early, he too had been dismayed at the size of the terrible throng already jammed there. Just as he'd been about to give up in despair he'd heard a familiar voice shouting to him through the throng:

'"Cap'n Roeder, Cap'n Roeder, Sir. Don't you worry, Cap'n. Leave it to me, Sir. Just you lean on me, Sir."'

It's his Sergeant-Major Vogel, an ex-tailor whom he, on the outward march, at Vilna, had stood up for against the insults of his good-for-nothing popinjay of a lieutenant and saved from a lashing. Now justice and humaneness have their reward:

'He led my horse by the mane and forced his way through, while I, like a poor sinner, clung to its neck.'

Half an hour farther on from the bridge Roeder bivouacks, always in the terrible freezing wind. 'Fortunately,' he scribbles in his diary, 'I've got some good hay for bedding. The right side of my chest is giving me great pain each time I cough.'

'At about 8 a.m.,' writes Lejeune who's there with I Corps,

'when the return of daylight had enabled us to see spread out before our eyes the immensity of everything that still had to cross over, each man had hastened to get closer to the bridges, and the great disorder had begun.'

Bidding a little group of Frenchmen a curt adieu, von Suckow, who has been on his own since the dissolution of III Corps' Württemberger division, is one of thousands who suddenly decide that if he isn't to suffer all the horrors of imprisonment in Siberia the time has come to try to get across.

Le Roy is another. Though near despair, his Guillaume is sure *le bon Dieu* will help them get across and back to *la patrie*. But this morning it's taken him all of three hours to get his master even to wake up. Though it's no longer snowing, the cold's very keen. Already, Guillaume points out, all the camp fires have been abandoned, and everyone's rushing towards what seems to be the sole remaining bridge. Le Roy rubs the sleep from his eyes. Much as he hates 'theologians', he hastily agrees about *le bon Dieu* 'because we're really in a very tough spot'. And though both Guillaume and Jacquet try to support him, it's as much as the fanatical deist can do to totter two or three steps. Where have the cavalry troopers they'd seen the previous evening gone to? They've rejoined the rearguard, Guillaume says, which at any moment now will be cutting its way through the struggling mass beneath them! At this terrible news Le Roy falls on his knees:

"You know what calamities are crushing me just now," he admits silently to the God he has 'often offended but always honoured'. "Be favourable to me, and I'll do my best to improve. Or else strike me down in this moment when my repentance is sincere!" 'During this fervent prayer,' he goes on,

'I'd fallen to my knees, my arms stretched up toward the sky, my face turned toward the side where the crossing was painfully proceeding. This black mass, mobile as the waters of the sea lashed by an impetuous wind – this sight brought me to my senses. One can smile even at the grave's edge! At this supreme moment the smile on my lips seemed to censure my lack of courage since yesterday. What had really been going on in my furtive individuality, for it to be making me, all unbeknown to myself, so timid and pusillanimous? Me, an old soldier who'd stood the test of twenty battles! The lion had become a miserable roe-deer! Could the devil, or rather my good angel, have been meddling in my business? If so, they could clear off and leave me in peace.'

He doesn't need Their Lordships, he tells himself, to take so much trouble over him and make him

'commit stupidities, to spy on my actions and be my accusers and informers at the sound of the famous trumpets, so promised by Christ-ian preachers and so little desired by their flock. I blushed with shame at all these theatricals before God and this one man who'd been witness to them. At all costs I wanted to repair my mistake. So I immediately quit my chicken-hearted cowardice.'

Whereupon, head held high and 'mounted on my spurs like a village curé's cock', he braces himself for the ordeal ahead. Before he does so he makes Guillaume a present of his silver watch, tells him to secure it under his greatcoat and advises him, if their pony should become an embarrass-ment, to abandon her; 'likewise my gun and the precious possessions from Moscow'. All he asks of Guillaume, should he survive him, is to tell his fam-ily how he'd perished.

The basic trouble, Sergeant-Major Thirion sees, is that

'as only the first ranks could actually see the two bridges, the mass behind them, who couldn't, was pushing and shoving for all it was worth and thrusting the first ranks into the river'.

Thirion himself, with the 2nd Cuirassiers' Eagle still in his pocket, crosses by the right-hand bridge with his back to the mob, 'the better to resist any shove from behind which might have flung me into the water'. At the same time he's 'half-carrying, half-pushing' a comrade named Liauty,

> 'wounded in the night by a sabre cut near his buttock, and, I fancy, in the joint, which he'd sustained while struggling to demolish a hut where some other men had taken refuge'.

Grabbing a horse from a recalcitrant soldier, Thirion loads Liauty on to it and gets across.[7] Many are unable to so. One of them is IV Corps' elderly inspector of reviews, M. de Labarrière, who's come the hundreds of icy miles from Moscow in a sledge. Seeing a friend, a wounded officer, he runs up to him. 'Leaning on each other,' Labaume sees, 'they got lost in the mob, and he's never been heard of since.'

Griois too will soon be in the thick of it. With the rest of IV Corps' officers who've just spent a comfortable night in their barn

> 'we'd ridden down as quickly as our horses' sad state permitted towards the bridges, which we couldn't see because of the mist but which were no more than two miles away. The weather was sombre, the cold piercing, and some snowflakes were falling.'

At first they suppose the vast jam is due to some temporary hold up; and wait for it to clear:

> 'But fresh masses of isolated men are arriving on every hand, and only swell it further. No more movement. No one can budge. At each instant the obstacle's growing. After waiting for three-quarters of an hour we decide to go ahead; and do so, albeit slowly, thanks to our horses which strike and overthrow the wretched footfolk.'

To Griois it seems the disorder's beginning

> 'with the retrograde movement of some horsemen of II or IX Corps, who cut their way through, overthrowing everything before them. Doubtless it was some ill-conceived order, too strictly enforced, that caused much of the day's disasters.'

The distinction between the two bridges' purposes avails nothing without proper military order:

> 'vehicles, horses, pedestrians were following the same route. Getting to the bridge, vehicles and horses were refused access. An attempt was even made to send them back. The thing was impossible, and soon the paths were obstructed.'

Griois is riding a little two-year-old Polish pony he'd bought on the way to Moscow but which has become so weak it can hardly carry him. And in no time his companions have left him behind. Soon he's regretting even plunging into this ocean of desperate human beings. How dearly he'd like to get out again! 'Not to be thought of.' As yet it hasn't fallen prey to panic – not as a whole – though the weaker are crying out against the stronger, who're everywhere using brute force. As before, certain hardy individuals are trying to swim the river. And one or another even succeeds. Fain and his colleagues see them among the bushes and 'scarcely recognise Colonel

V***t in his savage nakedness'. Another is a comrade of Pion des Loches named Béranger. Fezensac has seen

'a *cantinière* of the 33rd Line, who'd given birth to a girl at the campaign's outset and carried it all the way from Moscow, cross the river with water up to her neck, leading her horse with one hand and with the other holding her baby on her head'.[8]

Others, less resourceful or more patient – or despondent – or less conscious of the impending danger – are just sitting there on the snow, head in hands, waiting to see what'll happen. Rossetti, no doubt on mission to Victor, sees 'above all the sick and wounded renounce life, go aside and resignedly sitting down stare fixedly at this snow that was to be their tomb'. Everyone who's on his own is having similar experiences. And by no means all are even getting as far as the bridge. At last, getting into the column, von Suckow finds he's

'surrounded on all sides, caught in a veritable human vice. The moments I spent after entering this *closed society* until the one when I set foot on the right bank were the most terrible I've ever known. Everyone was shouting, swearing, weeping and trying to hit out at his neighbours.'

Himself struggling in the mob, he sees a friend, wounded at Mojaisk, on a *konya*, being attacked by a French infantryman

'with formidable blows of his musket butt; but though only a few paces from him I could do nothing to help him. So tightly pressed were we one against another, it would have been impossible even to reach out my hand to him. Again and again I felt myself lifted off the ground by the human mass, squeezing me as in a vice. The ground was littered with men and animals, living or dead. Every moment I found myself stumbling over corpses. I didn't fall, it's true. But that didn't depend on me. I know no more horrible sensation one can feel than treading on living beings who cling to your legs and paralyse your movements as they try to get up again. Still to this day I recall what I felt that day as I stepped on a woman who was still alive. I felt the movements of her body and at the same time heard her calling out, croaking: "Oh! Take pity on me!" She was clutching my legs when, suddenly, as a result of a thrust from behind, I was lifted off the ground and freed from her grasp. Since that time I've often reproached myself for involuntarily having caused the death of one who was so close to me.'

'Up to now,' Cesare de Laugier assures us,

'the crossings over the bridges had been made with the greatest regularity. But as soon as the guns were heard again and with the Partonneaux battalion's arrival it had become known that his division had fallen into the enemy's power and that Wittgenstein was advancing, then men, women, baggage, light carriages, guns, ammunition wagons, heavy coaches – all rushed toward the bridges' narrow approaches.'

These first roundshot are being fired by a Russian battery which is boldly advancing 'under cover of some light infantry amidst the snow-covered bushes' along the Borissow road. At this moment the vehicular bridge breaks and has to be repaired. Which of course causes a panic rush toward the other one.

After striking his miserable bivouac in the marsh 'not everywhere equally frozen' at daybreak, Major Boulart, on the western bank, has had to abandon quite a few of his vehicles,

> 'and with them a good number of gunners who'd only been able to keep up with our march thanks to the vehicles (each time a vehicle was abandoned we reckoned that six times as many men perished with it)'.

After this he has 'gained the neighbouring high ground, where I was placed in battery on the Borissow road where it emerges from a wood'. From there, looking out over the situation on the far bank, he realises almost at once that things over there are likely to get desperate:

> 'Everything indicated I'd have to open fire. I entrusted Captain Maillard with 2,000 francs in banknotes, which I asked him to keep for my wife in case anything should happen to me. I was ready for anything, though not without turning over sad thoughts in my mind. The Emperor was near my artillery almost throughout the day.'

By and by Napoleon, who seems to Boulart to be in low spirits ['abattu'], orders him to open fire across the river at the Russian battery that's unleashing panic at the bridges. Depressed or not, Boulart's relieved to see that the ex-gunner emperor makes nothing of a little incident which might normally have unleashed his wrath:

> 'This is what happened. Though we didn't realise it, one of my guns was loaded. Assuming it had some stones at the bottom of its barrel, I ordered them to be burnt out by putting some powder into the vent. But a violent detonation and the whistling of the roundshot showed we'd been mistaken. The Emperor merely said, with a kindly air: "What a nuisance. That could give the alarm where they're fighting, and above all in front of us."'

All this Captain Dumonceau, that predestined observer of battles, also sees from a distance:

> 'Napoleon had ordered a battery of the Imperial Guard to take up position on our left near the river bank. By aiming its fire across it, it took the enemy battery on the other bank obliquely, thus forcing it to withdraw to a distance. At the same time it turned back a column that was preparing to deploy from the wood on which IX Corps' right was resting. Then we saw infantry skirmishers who'd just been driven out of the wood return with élan, throw out the enemy's, who in their turn emerged from it and thus under our eyes restored IX Corps' support. On the far left we could see repeated cavalry charges which didn't cease to maintain their superiority there.'

No doubt the four troopers Le Roy had spoken to yesterday are playing their part in them. For it's Fournier's cavalry which, flinging itself repeatedly at far superior numbers, is holding Wittgenstein's right wing in check.

'In the distance away to the right, a slight depression in the terrain exposed part of the Russian army, deployed in front of ours. From there it in turn could see our multitude gathered at the bridges, at which it had begun to aim the fire of one of its batteries.'

It had been 'shortly before dawn' that the remains of I Corps had also deployed. Coming out of their wood on the left bank, the 7th Light had formed up in line of battle. Even at that early hour Sergeant Bertrand had noted that Russian roundshot was beginning to fall on them. 'We go into action, and, a strange thing, we beat the Russians, taking from them some guns and prisoners.' But it's not until now, some time between 10 and 11 a.m., that Wittgenstein, with some 30,000 men and 'numerous artillery', as well as Miloradovitch's, Platov's and Yermolov's 10,000, sent on ahead by Kutusov, unleashes his first real attack on Victor's remaining two divisions, deployed on the low line of hills. Against him Victor has hardly 11,000, mostly Poles, Bavarians and Dutchmen, plus – to his left – Fournier's 800 cavalry, facing much larger numbers of Russian horse. To strengthen his line Daendels' 26th Division – men from Berg, Baden and Hesse – after crossing the river, has been ordered back again.

At 11.30 a.m. Tascher sees the first cannonball come rolling along the ground. And it instantly unleashes panic. 'To escape this artillery fire,' Dumonceau sees how

'the multitude rushes in all directions – running from bridge to bridge in hope of getting across – being thrown back by those who're flowing in the opposite direction, and thus forming two opposed torrents, clashing against and violently repulsing each other. Then we see the shells bursting among them – the roundshot tracing broad holes in this compact mass – new torrents being caused by their terror. One of the bridges, foundering under the mob that's flung itself on to it and carried away by the waters, was gradually vanishing into the depths. Other unfortunate individuals were risking their lives in the river to find a ford, or save themselves by swimming. Together with all this we heard, like the roaring of a distant storm at sea, cries, yells, the crashing of vehicles, an undefinable uproar. It filled us with horror. And with all this we heard, like the distant roarings of a tempest at sea, cries, yells, wagons exploding, an undefinable uproar which filled us with terror.'

IHQ's watches are showing 1 p.m. when Napoleon at last learns that Partonneaux has surrendered. No details of course are known. But it comes as a great shock. An 'infuriated' Emperor inveighs against Partonneaux's 'cowardice':

'If generals haven't the courage to put up a fight, they can at least let the grenadiers do it!' he declares. 'A drummer could have saved his comrades from dishonour by sounding the charge. A *cantinière* could have saved the division by shouting "Every man for himself!" instead of surrendering.'

At the same time he orders the news to be kept secret – or rather, only com-
municated officially to the hard-pressed Victor. But soon even Labaume,
marching for Zembin with IV Corps headquarters and the Treasure, hears
that the army, at the critical moment, has lost its rearguard:

'3,000 infantry and two squadrons of cavalry had surrendered after running towards the Russian campfires which they'd taken for our own.
Everyone was furious with Partonneaux for his "cowardice", which was
contrasted with Ney's brave resolution.'

At the bridgehead, meanwhile, the crush is becoming more and more
nightmarish. Everyone who'd been making for the broken bridge now
turns and makes a rush for the other. But though everyone's having similar dreadful experiences by no means everyone's getting as far as the
bridge. Nor is it the Russian roundshot that's causing the worst slaughter.
'The enemy', Kergorre and his companions, who're also there, realise,

'was aiming at this mass, but, true to his habit, was firing too high. The
danger from the projectiles was the lesser. No one bothered about them.
The most dreadful thing was what we were doing to ourselves. For a distance of more than 200 paces the bridge was ringed around by a semi-
circle of dead or dying horses and by several layers of men who'd been
thrown down. One couldn't afford to make a false step. Once you'd
fallen, the man behind would put his foot on your stomach and you'd
add yourself to the number of the dying. Forming a platoon to help one
another, and holding our horses by the bridle, we'd hardly launched out
into the mob than we were scattered like sand before the wind. I was carried off my feet and lost my horse.'

Having weighed up his chances of swimming the river, but reflecting
that he hasn't any change of linen or a fire to dry himself 'so I'd indubitably perish when I got to the other bank' – as against being stifled in this
crush, von Suckow too, recommends

'my soul to God, gave a last thought to my own family, and braved all the
perils. Behind me as far as the eye could see was a column of fugitives,
every moment being joined by more. In front of me was a carriage which
in the present circumstances could be described as elegant. Drawn by
two horses, it had reached the end of the queue and was trying to pass
through it. Inside was a lady and two children. Suddenly a Russian
roundshot, falling in the team, smashes one of the animals to pieces.
The mother jumps out of the post-chaise, and holding her two little ones
in her arms begs those who are passing to come to her aid. She prays,
she weeps, but none of these fugitive passers-by, prey of panic terror,
bothers about her, wants to listen. I've just left her a few paces behind
me when I no longer hear her groaning voice. I turn round. She and her
children have disappeared; or rather, she's been knocked down by the
human flood, crushed and pulverised by it.'

Quite close at hand and 'not far from the bridge we were to cross by' Surgeon Roos, also of the Württembergers, sees on a horse another

'beautiful lady of 25, wife of a French colonel who'd been killed a few days ago. Indifferent to everything that was going on around her, she seemed to devote all her attention to her daughter, a very beautiful child of four, whom she was holding in front of herself. Several times she tried to reach the bridge, and each time she was repulsed. A grim despair seemed to overcome her. She wasn't weeping. Her eyes fixed now on the sky, now on her daughter, at one instant I heard her say "O God, how unhappy I am not even to be able to pray!" Almost instantly her horse was hit by a bullet and another shattered her left thigh above the knee. With the calm of silent despair she took her crying child, kissed her several times and then with her bloodstained skirt, which she'd taken off her broken leg, she strangled the poor little girl; and then, hugging her in her arms and pressing her to herself, sat down beside the fallen horse. Thus she reached her end without uttering a single word and was soon crushed by the horses of those pressing forward on to the bridge.'

Several hours of this Dantesque nightmare must be endured if one's to get across. But slowly, very slowly, Commissary Kergorre sees, the bridge is coming closer:

'My two furs had been torn off in strips, only my greatcoat remained. Three times it was taken off my shoulders. It was my salvation. I kept it at peril of my life. Three times I halted to put my arms back into it. A few people in the midst of this crush were still holding on to a horse.'

He too loses a friend – a Monsieur Pichault – in the mob. They can only exchange a last parting glance. From time to time great surges go through the crowd. A series of shocks turns Griois' pony round so that it's facing in the wrong direction; and there – so it seems, for more than an hour – he sits with his back to the bridge 'in this desolating position which finally took away all hope'. But then he catches sight of his regimental sergeant-major, a man named Grassard. Tall, young and vigorous, he no longer has either horse or effects, only a *konya*. But when, finally, he hears his colonel shouting, he turns it round, gets to him, and 'bridle in one hand and sabre in the other, he began pushing forward, shoving aside or overthrowing everything in his way'. Griois' own sabre has snapped in half. But though he's 'a miserable scarecrow' with hardly strength enough to hold it in his hand, he does his best to co-operate:

'The crowd was so dense one couldn't see the ground, and it was only from how my beast, more or less sure of itself, was putting its feet down that I could judge whether it was walking on earth or corpses.'

Suddenly he's thrown off into the wreckage of an overturned wagon. But, to his own amazement, by a convulsive effort finds himself back again in the saddle, unharmed! As they at last approach the bridge

'the overturned or abandoned vehicles, the horses raising their heads amid the debris that was crushing them, the corpses – all this seemed like an entrenchment impossible to surmount'.

But then some of the pontoneers, still faithfully at work repairing the bridge, notice his gunner's uniform and help him to get up on to it. And

Napoleon and Caulaincourt walked out along the long timber bridge over the Berezina at Borissow to within 50 paces of the Russian sentry. Not all Marcelline Marbot's dash had been able to prevent the Russians from firing it in three places – his 23rd Chasseurs had been too busy looting Count Pahlen's 300 carts, filled with provisions taken from the immense stores captured by Tchitchakov at Minsk. Copper engraving from Lieutenant Honoré de Beulay's memoirs.

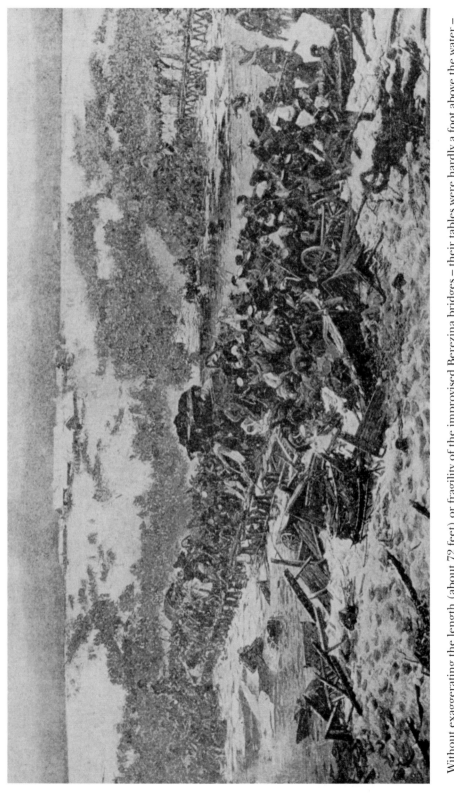

Without exaggerating the length (about 72 feet) or fragility of the improvised Berezina bridges – their tables were hardly a foot above the water – this anonymous artist's picture of the troops crossing the infantry bridge shows the appalling crush on the eastern bank.

Above: 'Around 10 a.m. the cavalry and artillery bridge caved in under the latter's weight. A number of men sank with it, and most of them perished. This led to a rush for the other, infantry bridge', seen in the background. Nineteenth-century steel engraving.

Below: The Berezina's flood waters, swept by ice floes, had effectively increased the passage to 'well over 200 yards' and doubled its normal depth of 3½ feet in midstream – which made all the difference. V. Adam's famous lithograph of the scene from the high ground where Lieutenant-Colonel Le Roy woke up on the morning of 27 November, considerably exaggerates the overall effect.

Opposite page, top: The heroic General Eblé vainly exhorting stragglers to bestir themselves in the night of 27 November and cross the remaining bridge before it is too late. Pils' untutored watercolour brush captures all the drama of the scene. On 30 December the middle-aged Eblé, 'no more than a shadow of himself' and 'in a state of utter dejection and exhaustion', would die at Koenigsberg.

Above: Standing up to the Cossacks 'in the outskirts of Ochmiana, 4 December 1812'. By now almost everyone had several weeks' growth of beard. Like thousands of others, the dying man in the foreground has already been stripped of his shoes and greatcoat. Engraving by Faber du Faur .

Left: At Zaniwki hamlet, Napoleon's headquarters on the Berezina's right bank, III Corps headquarters staff assembled for the night of 27/28 November. Note the infantrymen stripping the three houses' roof timbers: 'Next day Zaniwki had almost wholly vanished, having been taken away for the bivouac fires.' Faber du Faur.

Above: 5 December at Smorgoni. Of the 266 troopers of the prestigious Polish Guard Lancers who escorted Napoleon's 'hermetically sealed' carriage on runners as he left the army, only 36 would reach the first staging post; and only 8 of Murat's Neapolitan Guard Lancers who took over from them would get as far as Vilna. Staff captain Eugène Labaume would see their bodies littering the route, 'showing Napoleon had passed that way'.

Below: Vilna's 'long, low and narrow' Medyn Gate where thousands of survivors trampled each other to death on 9 December and 'for ten hours on end and in -28° of frost thousands of soldiers who'd thought they were saved fell frozen or stifled while other entrances were completely free' – Cesare de Laugier. The gate still exists. Sepia drawing, 1785.

Above: Governor Hogendorp's placards – or were they Roch-Godart's? – tried ineffectually to direct each corps to one of Vilna's huge monasteries, which had all been earlier converted into hospitals. 'No one could stay in those halls without fumigating them,' writes the 13-year-old son of artillery surgeon Déchy who died of the typhus while heroically tending his patients there, 'so fetid was the air. There was no bedding'. Reaching this 'Tartar hell' on 12 December, Rochechouart would try to save some of his compatriots from being thrown out of the windows to make room for Russian sick and wounded. Nineteenth-century engraving.

Below: Lieutenant-Colonel C. F. M. Le Roy's new shoes hindered him from keeping up with the scanty remnants of the 85th Line as he slithered along this road out to Ponari Hill. It was here the Fusiliers-Grenadiers' 'handsome poodle' Mouton stood up to a Russian cuirassier and Sergeant Bourgogne admired Ney's adroit handling of the rearguard. Nineteenth-century lithograph.

Vilna's Lichtenstein Coffee House, invaded by famished survivors. During the night of 9 December the Württemberger Captain Karl von Suckow was aroused by a violent kick in the ribs 'from Monsieur Lichtenstein in person, who'd earnt so much money from us and

who'd always received us with the deepest and humblest bows. Now he shouted at me: "Get up, you dog of a German! And get the hell out of here!"'

'From all the town's streets and alleyways people were already crowding across the square en route for Kovno.' A nineteenth-century artist's impression of the chaos outside Vilna town hall in the evening of 10 December, after Murat had given orders for the retreat to go on. Captain Josef Zalusky of the Polish Guard Lancers (left), assuming it to be at an end, had even donned his new parade uniform. But had to take it off again. Lithograph by J. Damelis. By kind permission of Vilnius Museum .

Above: Ponari Hill, about 5 km long and 2 km wide, rises some 160–180 metres to the plateau leading to Kovno and the Niemen. The road's gradient in those days was much steeper than it is today and nothing that moved on wheels could get up its 'icy slope... polished like marble'. At its foot, friend and foe together pillaged the Imperial Treasure's gold millions, and all the remaining guns were lost. No one mentions the chapel at its base. Sepia drawing, 1786.

Right: The news reaches Paris. Having crossed Europe with unprecedented speed in the company of his Master of the Horse, Armand de Caulaincourt, Napoleon got there only two days after the publication of his ever famous and unusually truthful XXIXth Bulletin. Engraving by Opiz, 1814, Bibliothèque Nationale.

his pony, in turn, is the means of helping a *cantinière* who's carrying her child in her arms, and who clings to its tail:

'What a weight fell from me as I crossed it! My feeling was like that of a condemned man who'd been pardoned on his way to execution. On the bridge itself I was almost alone, so congested was its access. It was hardly above the water, in such fashion that the corpses being carried by the current were held up there among the ice-floes. A great number of horses whose riders had drowned came and leant their heads against its table and stayed there as long as they had strength to. They garnished one side of the bridge for almost its whole length.'

At the far end Griois is effusively thanked by the *cantinière*, who insists on sharing her last remaining bit of sugar with him. 'I reproach myself for having accepted it.'

For their part Le Roy, Jacquet, Guillaume and their *konya* Bichette have been making for the upstream edge of the struggling mass. Reaching it, Le Roy notices that the hard-frozen river bank, being 'a little higher than the current, could bear the weight of a man'. And standing with his right shoulder against Bichette's left, and holding the bridle short at her mouth, he mutters in her ear:

'"Come along, my beauty. Maybe today means eternity for both of us. Who knows where we're going? Neither of us. But we mustn't let this painful uncertainty scare us!"'

He's counting more on her, he confides to the mare, than on either his guardian angel or his patron saints, 'who, I fancy, are wringing their hands very little over my cruel plight'.

To reach the bridge has taken Kergorre two hours and now his last strength is giving out:

'If the struggle had lasted another quarter of an hour I'd have gone under. Despite the cold my face was bathed in sweat. I was no more than two paces from the bridge. I put out my hand. I begged those in front of me to lend me theirs. I gripped one of the trestles ... but I'd overlooked human egoism. People just looked at me and passed on. A raging horse which had been thrown down was the last obstacle. Finally Providence came to my aid. A violent shock threw me over this horse. And in an instant he had ten people on top of him, pounding his head and belly. As for me, I was thrown between him and the bridge. I was saved. The bridge was a bit higher than my stomach.[9] Gathering the little strength I had left, I threw myself at it and managed to clamber up. Since there were no dead men or horses on it, people were passing along it in an orderly fashion, like a big crowd does when it's in a hurry.'[10]

There, at the far end of the bridge stands Sergeant Bourgogne, shivering with fever. Ever since yesterday evening he's been stationed there by his colonel to direct any of the Fusiliers-Grenadiers' stragglers:

'At its outlet was a marsh, a slimy, muddy place, where many of the horses sank and couldn't get out again. Many men, too, who were being dragged into the marsh by the weight of the others, sank down exhausted when left to themselves and were being trampled by others coming on from behind.'

Bourgogne tries to dissuade a corporal named Gros-Jean from going back to the left bank to look for his brother. Points out

'how many dead and dying were already on the bridge and preventing others from crossing by clutching their legs, so that they were all rolling together into the Berezina, appearing for a moment amid bits of ice, only to disappear altogether and make way for others.'

But Gros-Jean won't listen. Handing Bourgogne his pack and his musket, he says 'there are plenty of muskets on the other side'. At that moment he fancies he sees

'his brother on the bridge, struggling to clear himself a path through the crowd. So, listening only to the voice of despair, he climbed over the dead bodies of men and horses which blocked the way from the bridge and pushed on. Those he met first tried to thrust him back; but he was strong, and succeeded in reaching the unfortunate man he'd taken for his brother.'

But alas, it isn't. Nothing daunted, Gros-Jean reaches the far end only to be knocked down at the water's edge; trampled on; almost falls in. He clutches a cuirassier's leg,

'who, in turn, grabbed another man's arm. Hindered by a cloak over his shoulder, he staggered, fell, and rolled into the Berezina, dragging after him Gros-Jean and the man whose arm he was holding.'

Even so, Gros-Jean manages to clamber up by his knees on to a horse that's floating against the bridge; and by and by some engineers, hearing his shouts, throw him a rope,

'and thus from one support to another, over dead bodies and lumps of ice, he was drawn over to the farther side. I didn't see him again.'[11]

Although an hour has passed since Le Roy's got to almost within reach of the bridge, he hasn't advanced ten paces. But then 'some very lively firing started up on the right bank, causing the bridge and what was going on on top of it to stand out starkly against the flashes'. Jumping on to Bibiche, he finds the half-frozen water only comes up to her hocks. Yet between them and the bridge there's still a 'hole or ditch, whose depth I don't know, filled with ice-floes'. He tells Guillaume, who's still just behind him, to pull the horse out of this hole if he should drown in it. At that moment a shell falls into the water beside him:

'Fortunately it didn't explode. But my God! what an uproar this projectile caused in this confused mass of men from eighteen different nations, each swearing in his own language. The most vigorous grabbed the bridgehead, having crushed the feeblest, and got across first.'

The ditch isn't deep 'but the bottom not being firm, Bibiche was plunging about in the mud, shoving aside the ice-floes and all the while getting nearer to the bridge'. Suddenly, just as Le Roy's about to undertake the perilous leap from her back on to its timbers, 'my poor beast, finding some firm ground under her hoofs, leaped in one jump out of the hole and fell like a second shell into the mob around the bridgehead, and, guided by instinct, followed some horses pulling a gun – so that I crossed this dangerous passage as if by magic. Whew!'

Once on the bridge's timbers men are finding that it's not too difficult to get to the other side, albeit followed by 'benedictions' from the less fortunate ('kill him' – 'stick a f*****g bayonet in that brigand's guts!' – 'fire a shot into his arse!' 'chuck that f*****g mongrel into the water!' etc.). Von Suckow too is getting close:

'Hardly had I climbed up on this mass of men and horses than I saw at a glance there were a few corpses that had been thrown down on to the first ice-floes. Anyway those poor fellows had all been drowned.'

The bridge itself, he sees, is

'built of such pitiable materials that it was swaying to and fro in so terrifying a fashion that at any moment one expected to see it collapse. I despaired utterly of being saved. It was my first and only fit of discouragement throughout the campaign.'

And still, as they'd done yesterday and the day before, the military police are striking out to right and left with the flats of their swords. Finding himself standing on a horse – 'it was a chestnut' – that's lying on its side, panting convulsively, von Suckow gets another violent shove from behind, and almost falls to

'share the fate of this poor beast. At that moment I mentally said good-bye to the joys and sufferings of this earth, yet involuntarily stretched my arms out before me. My hand desperately clutched the collar of a blue cape. The man who was wearing it – a French cuirassier officer of prodigious stature who still had his helmet on his head – was holding an immense cudgel and using it with utmost success, pitilessly striking out at all who came too close to him. After long admiring this man's efficiency in shaking off all troublesome neighbours, I had only one thought: "You're not going to quit this fellow." And not relinquishing my lucky hold on the collar I let myself be taken in tow by its wearer.'

But the cuirassier notices what's happening:

'To get rid of me he had recourse to his cudgel, whirling it about behind him. But his efforts were to no avail. Seeing the blows as they came, I did my utmost to avoid them without letting go of his collar – so adroitly, he didn't once touch me. Seeing he wasn't getting anywhere like this, he ceased whirling his stick and adopted a new tactic, letting out formidable oaths. And when this didn't work either, he says to me: "Monsieur, I adjure you, let go of me, for if you don't we're both lost."'

But Suckow only holds on all the tighter. And, with the cuirassier swearing and cursing and trying to shake him off, reaches the bridge. Finally, realising they'll never get on to it like this, von Suckow lets go of the cuirassier's mantle – jumps for it, and finds himself up to his knees in the icy water.

'Even today, sitting by my stove, I shiver when I think of it.' By and by he too scrambles up on to the bridge.

Le Roy too struggles over the sharply tilted bridge, only pausing at its far end to see what's become of Guillaume. But there's no sign of him. Exhausted and frozen, Le Roy warms himself at a fire fuelled by several looted wagons, abandoned – like Boulart's – for lack of teams in the frozen swamp. But still sees no sign of the irrepressible, the devoted Guillaume! So, hearing a drum beating not far off and suspecting frost-bite in one foot, Le Roy makes off, alone, in that direction. 'You couldn't see ten paces ahead of you, the snow was coming down so thickly.'

But now the short day's ending. Dusk has put an end to the fighting along the eastern ridge. All that remains now is for Victor's men to effect their retreat. At about 8 p.m. 'illumined by the enemy's shellfire' Eblé – it's his *sixth* night without sleep – and his pontoneers and some gunners (among them Chambray's unit) begin clearing 'a kind of trench' through the rampart of corpses and dead horses encumbering access to the bridge. While the military police stave off the mob, Captain François, approaching with the 30th Line, now numbering only 143 men, sees

'horses, baggage, artillery trying to cut a path. A terrible struggle begins among these despairing men. I, who love extraordinary things, was horrified by this scene. To all the noise was added the whistling of round-shot, the explosion of shells and ammunition wagons.'

As the 7th Light cut a way through the mob and approach the bridge, Sergeant Bertrand too sees 'a spectacle of such horror' as his pen, even after half a century, will almost refuse to describe: 'scattered heads, arms, legs, a bloody slush!' What's more, such survivors as are closest to the 'trench' try to thrust themselves in among the ranks. But to yield to them out of mere humanity, the officers realise, will be to wreck everything:

'First and foremost we had to save everyone still grouped around the flag. Our salvation lay at the tips of our bayonets. Just as our column is passing very close by this mass of victims, I hear my name being called out, and in this sad confusion see the wife of one of the regiment's NCOs, holding her dying child in her arms. This sight made the most atrocious impression on me I've ever felt. Always I shall have before my eyes the expression on this mother's face, with her lost and supplicating look. But my duty as a soldier, though it tore my heart in two, came before all feelings of commiseration. In any other circumstance I'd have given my life to save this woman and her child. May God be my judge! All these unfortunates remained in the enemy's power.'

Ordered to take the place of the NCO bringing up his company's rear, he's just hurrying back to do so, when one of General Gérard's ADCs, taking him for a runaway, smacks his face. Bertrand raises his musket to his cheek and his finger's on the trigger, when he tumbles to the misunderstanding. Even when they get to the bridge his men see two horses are blocking it and want to heave them into the water:

'But being told they belonged to superior officers, we didn't; but the poor beasts were driven on with bayonet jabs. At last here we are on the bridge. The flooring having given way on one side, we were marching along a very steep slope. Several of us fell into the water. I saw some of them going by on enormous ice-floes, trying to reach the other shore, among others an officer who, stricken by another ice-floe, vanished under the waves. However, some others were luckier.'

A staff officer has indicated the assembly point on the other side; but at roll call the 7th Light have trouble lighting their fires. Bertrand goes to his colonel to report the smack in the face he'd received:

'He'd already been informed about it, and sent me, together with an adjutant-major, to the ADC who, having said how sorry he was, shook my hand, saying: "let's forget it, my old comrade, and let's close our ranks, because tomorrow we'll be needing them."'

Although Captain François' wounds have 'reopened and begun to bleed again', he too manages somehow to get through and rejoin his division:

'My comrades had thought I was one of those crushed underfoot. They made me share their black soup and the regimental surgeon-major dressed my wounds for the first time since I'd left Moscow.'

On the bridge, without even noticing it, he has lost his blue cape with silver clasps. And even when his servant – for 48 hours they've lost touch – turns up and 'bursts into tears, seeing me saved yet again' he's failed to save any of his horses,

'which didn't surprise me. But one of them had been carrying twelve soup spoons, thirteen forks, a ladle for stew, a soup ladle, a pair of silver spurs and a large sum in roubles. In the morning a soldier brought me my *konya*, albeit stripped of its bags.'

Even when they've got across, the refugees are by no means always out of trouble. At Brillowo, Castellane, on mission as usual, sees

'men of I Corps using violence to strip them of their packs. I forced two of them to cough up. They'd taken a straggler's portmanteau. The latter told me what was in it. Making them open it I furiously hit the thieves, who pretended the portmanteau was their property, with the flat of my sword.'

By about 5 or 6 a.m. all of Victor's IX Corps has crossed, except for Fournier's cavalry, now only 200 out of 600 troopers, mostly Baden hussars, who're to bring up its rear. Eblé's been ordered to fire the bridge at 7 a.m. or even earlier, and has already had inflammable materials placed on the bridge's transverse logs, ready to be ignited at the first sign of the Russians approaching. An order he has passed on to Colonel Séruzier,

'to break the bridges and blow them up as soon as Victor's corps and such vehicles as had been preserved should have reached the other side. I was charged to hasten the latters' crossing; and I put all possible firmness and celerity into this mission.'

Eblé pays a last visit to the stragglers huddled or asleep round their bivouac fires. Urges them for the last time to bestir themselves while there's still time. During the night Roman Soltyk too had seen

'staff officers being repeatedly sent to these unfortunates to urge them to cross the bridges at once. But these orders and threats were in vain. No one stirred. Most had fallen into such apathy that they listened indifferently to the words being addressed to them.'

'We knew the Russians were getting close,' Séruzier goes on,

'but I couldn't get the drivers of the baggage, the *cantinières* or the *vivandières* to listen to reason. In vain I told them everyone would be saved if only there was a little order; that their safety depended on crossing at once, and that our troops' salvation would depend on the bridges being broken. Only a few crossed with their light vehicles. The greater number lingered on the left bank.'

Some distance from the other bank Le Roy pauses to bind up his frost-bitten foot in some rags and bits of string:

'Daylight appeared on the horizon. The wind was still very strong; but the snow wasn't falling any longer. A few cannon shots and a fusillade were heard to our left, on the side where the Emperor and his Guard were. I was surprised by the deathly silence reigning on this side of the river.'

The musketry volleys are coming from the Brill Farm Wood, where Tchitchakov's men are tentatively – very tentatively indeed – returning to the attack. 'Seeing the dense line of marauders hastening on up the hillside,' Le Roy, not doubting that the 'rearguard was at grips with the enemy', gets going again.

Now it's past 7 o'clock. And still Eblé hasn't given the order. His tender-mindedness is saving many a life. Among others Jomini's. Suffering, like Griois, from bronchial fever, he'd managed yesterday evening to squeeze himself and his two ADCs, Liébart and Fivaz, into one of Studianka's three remaining timber cottages, occupied by Eblé and his staff. And found some straw to sleep on. But now morning – in the shape of a Russian shell[12] – awakens Jomini by setting fire to it. Where's everyone gone? Where's Eblé? Have they abandoned him? Held up under his arms by Fivaz and Liébart, the future great writer on the so-called art of war, too, makes for the bridge. And already the crush has recommenced and when at last Jomini reaches it he's pushed off into the ice-floes. In front of him a cuirassier's riding a *konya*. Gaining sudden strength from some quinine he's been taking, Jomini clambers up on to its rump and seeing some Bavarian infantry crossing, calls out to them – in French – in German – but is ignored by everyone – until an NCO he'd known at Smolensk reaches him down his musket and hoists him up, enabling Liébart to help him over to the opposite bank.

Séruzier's position is becoming anguished. Eblé has waited and waited. Now it's long past 7 a.m. Eight o'clock passes, and still he waits: 'Again the enemy appeared, the danger was growing from minute to minute.' The first enemy units, even so, are only Cossacks, and they, as usual, are much more interested in plunder than in forcing the bridges:

'It was then the drivers of the vehicles still on that bank realised what danger they were in. But it was too late! The carts, carriages and artillery wagons carrying the wounded got jammed at the bridge's entrance. Men began cutting their way through at bayonet point. Several men flung themselves into the water to swim across – and perished. The enemy, who was saluting us with cannon fire, sent us any amount of shells and put the finishing touches to the disorder. The jam destroyed all hope of getting across. A mob of men and women were going to be sacrificed. But it was certainly their own fault.'

Already Bourgogne, at the bridge's western end, has seen

'numbers jumping into the water, but not one was reaching the shore. I saw them all in the water up to their shoulders. Overcome by the terrible cold, they were all perishing miserably. On the bridge was a sutler carrying a child on his head. His wife was in front of him, crying bitterly. I couldn't stay any longer, it was more than I could bear. Just as I turned away, a cart containing a wounded officer fell from the bridge, together with its horse.'

Eblé can no longer put off the fatal moment. Séruzier:

'It was only at the last extremity, i.e., when the Russian guns were harassing me from all sides, that I, with keen regret, decided to carry out General Eblé's order, which was the Emperor's.'

Fuzes and powder trains under the transverse planks are fired. And the bridge bursts into flames. Bourgogne turns away from the scene of horror that follows. As the flames leap up a howl goes up from the far bank, the like of which no one who hears it will ever forget. Even on the Zembin road, several miles away, Louise Fusil hears

'a scream, a single cry from the multitude. Undefinable, it still resounds in my ears every time I think of it. All the unfortunates who'd been left on the other bank were falling, crushed by the Russian army's grapeshot. Only then did we grasp the extent of the disaster.'

Tragically, ironically, the Berezina – at last, but too late – has begun to freeze over:

'But the ice not bearing, it broke, swallowing up men, women, horses, carriages. A beautiful woman, caught between two ice-floes as in a vice, was seen clutching her child in her arms. A musket butt is held out to give her something to hang on to. But soon she's swallowed up by the very movement she's making to grasp it. General Lefèbvre [the Marshal's son], who wasn't exactly tender-minded, was pale as death. Kept repeating: "Oh, what a dreadful disaster! And those poor people who've been left there under the enemy's fire."'[13]

To Colonel Séruzier it's

'the most afflicting spectacle anyone could see. The Cossacks flung themselves on these people who'd been left behind. They pillaged everything on the opposite bank, where there was a huge quantity of vehicles laden with immense riches. Those who weren't massacred in this first charge were taken prisoner and whatever they possessed was falling to the Cossacks.'

From somewhere in the vicinity of the Brill Wood, the Polish Captain Turno, no less appalled, sees 'whole ranks of desperate men being pushed onwards by masses of other unfortunates coming on behind', hears 'their piercing screams' ... witnesses

'the terror of those being hit by enemy roundshot ... ammunition wagons and shells exploding in the midst of this shouting, groaning mob. My heart was torn with grief. The Russians, who've crowned the high ground beyond, are sowing terror and death amid the 10,000 sick or wounded soldiers and a multitude of carriages or wagons, most thrown on top of one another and broken.'

Looking back from the high ground towards Zembin, Le Roy sees the guns' smoke as they fire, but – so violent is the whining of the north wind – hears no explosions. Taking refuge in a half-demolished house, he looks out over the 'narrow space of a mile and a half, half of it taken up by the river, and is sure

'a clever painter, had he been at my side at that moment, could have made a beautiful picture! He'd have painted a still-life [*une nature morte*]. Trees laden with hoar frost, snow and icicles. In the foreground the village of Weselovo. In the background, between white-powdered conifers, would be seen perfidious Bashkirs,[14] waiting keenly for a favourable moment to throw themselves on their prey. The river itself would play the chief role and, at a pinch, could represent Acheron, the river of Hades in the fable. The damned on the left bank. The elect on the right.'

Yet the elect, Le Roy muses, are hardly happier than the damned, except insofar as 'the latter have the repose of nothingness, while a large part of the elect would succumb to the same fate'. Even as he drags himself toward Zembin, looking everywhere for Guillaume and Jacquet, no other sound strikes his ear except that terrible howl of despair. And there it'll go on resounding, he says, 'for thirty years; and, I feel, until my natural heat is extinguished'.

CHAPTER 19

TWO PRISONERS

Surgeon Roos seeks another way over – a Cossack – 'we're going to take the bird with the nest' – 'screams, lamentations, tears, supplications made themselves heard' – 'men were praying in all languages' – Beulay is driven like a beast back to Witebsk

Among 'the damned' left on the eastern bank is Heinrich von Roos. Having taken one look at the struggling masses at the bridges and seeing no chance of getting across, he and several others – like Muraldt's group before him – have wandered off upstream. Perhaps, after all, there's another, more practicable ford higher up? The results are fateful. Seeing a group around a campfire, he'd approached them

'with a view to warming myself and drawing up some new plans. They were Polish grenadiers, guarding some bits of rotten butcher's meat. They confirmed for a fact that there was no bridge higher upstream. After resting up a little, we decided to go back to the village, no matter what fate might be waiting for us.'

Emerging from the woods, they come across a flock of soldiers of all arms being driven to the rear by a swarm of Cossacks:

'I was turning off to my left to get back into the wood when a Cossack grabbed the collar of my cape: *"Tu officier?" "Oui!"* No matter how great my terror, I felt truly relieved not to feel his iron pike instantly penetrate my body. As is often the case with prisoners, I, who thought that after coming so far I could courageously and coolly face all the evils that were threatening us, felt very humble. The Cossack, a young beardless man of about 24 years, was pocked with smallpox, yet was neither ugly nor was his face disagreeable. Taking me aside, he made me understand I must empty my pockets and share with him everything I owned.'

It takes Roos a certain amount of time to get at his pocket under cape and overcoat.

'But at length I pulled out a piece of paper containing fourteen ducats, which I handed over to him. He contemplated them with pleasure, pocketed them, and by putting his two fists against his right ear and clucking with his tongue got me to understand he wanted to know whether I had a watch. I shook my head. Without showing any anger, he took the musket that was hanging from his shoulder, cocked it, and aimed it at me. This time both courage and sangfroid deserted me completely. I fell on my knees, and involuntarily, trembling all over, cried out: *"Pardon!"* I don't know whether he understood. Anyway he didn't fire. He uncocked his musket and I got up. He searched me in the region where he'd seen me take out the ducats, found my Leipzig watch, and immediately put it to his ear. Despite the joy he was getting from his catch, he went on looking at me with a threatening air.

'Not content with ducats and my watch, he searched me again and found my decoration, wrapped up in some paper. As yet I'd never worn it, because with us Württembergers decorations are worn on the uniform jacket but not on the greatcoat. Seeing it, he was delighted and seemed to regard me with greater goodwill. From my cartridge pouch he took the thalers which I'd been keeping ever since the battle of Borodino,' [on the eve of which the Württembergers had received arrears of pay], 'together with the silver roubles the Poles had given me at Ljasna. Finally, he took my instrument case. In vain I implored him to give it back. All he left me was my pipe, some scissors, some first-aid things and my powdered coffee. The Cossack was already wearing a Cross of the Legion of Honour on his chest. He immediately added my decoration. Then, without doing me the least harm, he took me to the rear. To our right a serious engagement was going on; and I soon realised I was behind the Russians' battle line. They were assembling prisoners, and among them I recognised a young officer of our Württemberger infantry regiment. I beckoned to him. He came over. I took him by the arm and from then on we never separated. He'd been treated worse than I had. But they'd left him his uniform, his boots, and his trousers, but taken his hat, his cape, and everything he had on him. He told me his name was Schaefer, and he was a clergyman's son. I, in turn, told him my story while we were being put together with another group of prisoners. My young Cossack rejoined his detachment and we were confided to others to be transported.

'We were made to march forward behind the Russian battle line. To our right the cannonade was violent. The road we were following went through a wood. Schaefer wanted to take his own life. He suggested I should buy some brandy, drink ourselves asleep with it, and then lie down in the snow, never to wake up again. I found his project good, but replied that neither of us having any money, nor any other means whatever of getting hold of any brandy, we'd have to try and replace it with water – in our exhausted state, and with the cold getting worse, it would produce the same effect.

'We met many Russian troops belonging above all to the militia, in great greatcoats and round hats ornamented in front with a yellow cross. The men had muskets and black belts and straps. The officers were wearing a green and red uniform, with caps of the same colour. We admired these peasant-like soldiers' thoroughly military order as they marched in closed columns. Many of the French, above all some officers, wanted to complain to the Russian officers of having been despoiled; but the officers they spoke to just went on marching by, and the Cossacks, with blows of the knout, forced back into the ranks anyone who'd left them.

'Still holding on to each other's arms Schaefer and I walked on without anyone doing us any harm. The order was given: "Officers to the front!" We obeyed promptly, and didn't budge again from the place assigned to us. But the French malcontents drew fresh blows on themselves.

'Some women were weeping and lamenting. Either because of our obedience or disciplined spirit, or for some reason to be explained by events still to come, an old Cossack came and offered to let me mount a horse he'd taken from the enemy. I got on to it, and the Cossack led me by the bridle. Schaefer had the same good luck.

'However, my Cossack who, despite his grey hairs and beard, looked every inch a military man, wanted to get into conversation with me. To everything he said I replied yes or no, in German, accompanying this word with a gesture of approval or negation. I think I got the sense of some of the words he was addressing to me: "Isn't it true the Cossacks are a decent lot?" He proffered me his water-bottle of brandy. He'd already given me some bread, and later he even gave me some sugar.'
But there's a reason for such generosity:
'He thought I had some money in my black silk cravat. Twice he probed my neck, and ended by appropriating it. He also exchanged his crude cape for mine, which was more refined. He'd also taken a great liking to my velvet-lined boots, and made me understand he'd give me his own in exchange. But things went no farther.

'However, we'd reached a village where there were already a lot of prisoners. Some Russian troops were drawn up in lines. To our right the musketry and cannonade was still going on. There was a Russian officer on horseback there who seemed to me to be of German origin. I asked him where this road led to. "To Borissow!" After an exchange of questions and answers, he said to me: "Probably this war will end today. We're going to take the bird with the nest."'

'It was getting colder. It was snowing. Soon the snow was coming down in whirlwinds. Then night fell. Schaefer, without hat, without gloves and without cape, felt so cold that he dismounted. He preferred to walk. Gradually our Cossack detachment dwindled. My old Cossack, in his turn, pushed off, and I had to start walking again.

'We'd passed through some woods where, here and there, some abandoned fires were still alight. The road wasn't clear, the cold was atrocious, and a violent wind was blowing. The snow got thicker and thicker. Enfeebled and starving as I was – I hadn't eaten anything all day except what the second Cossack had offered me – worried about the future and without any money, I felt utterly demoralised and thought I was going to die.

'In the distance, on some high ground, we saw an enormous conflagration. We supposed it must be Borissow on fire. It was late at night when we got there. We'd reached the goal of our day's march and were going to be able to rest, but were asking ourselves what fate was reserved for us.

'For a long while they marched us through the streets until the Cossacks had found the man who was to take command. Finally, we halted in front of a little house. One of our guides went inside, another stayed outside the door as sentinel, and the others surrounded the group of prisoners, which might well have totalled three to four hundred men. Some French officers wanted to enter the house, but were forced back into the ranks by blows of the knout.

'After an hour's wait we were directed towards a row of houses that were on fire. At once the rumour went round that we were going to be thrown into the flames. Immediately screams, lamentations, tears, supplications made themselves heard. The women were particularly vehement. "If we're to die by fire, let God's will be accomplished," I told myself, joining my fate to that of my companions.

'Utterly exhausted, shivering with fear and the cold, we were being guarded by some infantry from the Tobolsk Regiment. We lay down on some ground the fire had dried out. At first our guards, wanting to appropriate whatever the Cossacks might have left us, prevented us from going to sleep. Those men who still had their packs were obliged to hand them over; if they didn't they were crudely reprimanded. I noticed that these packs, after a hasty examination, were often being handed back to their owners. One of the Cossacks came up to me: *"Tu Capitan?"* "Yes," I replied. But even if I'd answered No, it wouldn't have helped. This time I was stripped of everything the Cossacks had left on me, though – I must say – without their using any brutality.

'The loss of my pipe caused me as much pain as the loss of my instrument case. I'd bought it at Vienna, after the battle of Wagram. It was decorated with an image of Emma of Falkenstein at the moment when she pours oil on the wounds of her knight, who's taken refuge in the cloister, where they've recognised each other by their rings.

'Separated from everyone I loved and belonged to, stripped of everything that could have been any use to me, alone amidst thousands of unknown people, I, like them, felt poor, poverty-stricken, and deeply unhappy. All round us the silence was profound. And for the first time in my life I heard soldiers praying. There was so little space, we were lying on top of one another, in an inexpressible confusion. A Pole was stretched out on my legs, I had an Italian to my right, a Spaniard or a Portuguese to my left, and my head was resting on a Frenchman. Men were groaning and praying in all languages. Catholics from all countries were saying the *Ave Maria*. Certain passages from Gellert's *Canticles* came to my mind and brought me some consolation. Finally I fell asleep.'

But after only two hours von Roos wakes up again. From among the sleeping prisoners he seeks out four chasseurs of his Württemberg regiment. He also sees men of Partonneaux's division 'who'd been allowed to keep their baggage and packs'.

Among them is Lieutenant Beulay: 'So it's been to end up like this,' he's thinking to himself,

'we left France, crossed Europe and, for several months now have been putting so much energy into fighting a conspiracy of men and the elements! We were prisoners of people we'd ruined, exasperated ...'

316

He wonders why Partonneaux's officers have been singled out and brought into town, the men having been abandoned out in the fields. Why this apparent favour?

'They parked us in the heart of the town, like a vile herd of cattle inside a big hovel whose roof and all doors and windows had been devoured by fire. Between these four walls, because of the draughts, it was colder than out in the countryside, and we didn't even have the recourse, left to our men, of cutting themselves beefsteaks from dead horses.'

Towards dawn several NCOs, who've managed to join them, are horrified to find their superiors in such abject misery. Discovered, they're sent back, escape, are recaptured and slaughtered. For five days Partonneaux's officers won't be given a mouthful of food. Then a tender-minded sentry lets Roos slip out to buy himself a bottle of brandy and some biscuit. 'All down the street Russians wearing the most varied uniforms were walking about.' Some hit him with the flats of their swords. But he gets what he's looking for. Others follow his example. They've just finished their 'feast' when

'in a temperature of -33°, with the north wind cutting our faces and our moustaches bristling with icicles, a Frenchman, completely naked, presents himself at our door. He claimed to be an adjutant-major. For a lark some Russians who'd been drinking had burnt down the hospital where he'd been left, stripped its patients to their shirts and thrown them, dressed like Adam, into the street. He begged us to give him something to put on against the cold. In vain. We ourselves were shivering under our threadbare clothes with holes everywhere! To rid ourselves of his useless tears and supplications we put him out of the door. After ten minutes his complaints had ceased. Death had put an end to his misery. So exasperated by suffering were we that none of us, alas, felt any remorse at this abominable behaviour, nor did it in the least degree trouble our digestion.'

On the fifth day, 'at 4 p.m.' the Cossacks come and haul them out of their prison, where the French and their allied prisoners are leaving behind so many dead comrades it's more like a cemetery. Then they're driven on by blows of the Cossacks' *nagaïkas* (leather knouts) along an icy road through the freezing night – 'we'd never known such cold'. When the whips don't suffice

'the Cossacks took their lances, as if they had to do with cattle. But at the end of a few hours neither whip nor lance availed. Many of us, exhausted by cold and fatigue let ourselves drop and were crushed under the escort's horseshoes.'

Beulay only survives by staying in the thick of the column and taking tiny sips of his brandy.[1]

Surgeon Roos has been much luckier. Typhus is raging at Borissow and after some days he's allowed to report for medical service. Wittgenstein isn't accepting any French medicos – only Germans. Roos, taken on in that capacity, sees 300 women and girl prisoners shut up together in a freezing cold storehouse for their protection. Perhaps some of Louise Fusil's fellow-actresses are among them? Not all of them have managed to get across – Langeron and Rochechouart have 'captured actresses of a troop of the *Comédie Française*' meaning certainly the Moscow troupe. 'Also Italian singers belonging to Murat's musicians.'

PHASE FOUR
BEYOND THE BEREZINA

CHAPTER 20

CORTEGE THROUGH THE SNOWS

The Zembin bridges – 'a single bale of straw and a spark from a Cossack's pipe...' – Victor reprimanded – where's Guillaume? – plight of the women – Ney's hard-heartedness – Oudinot's private battle – 'Good-bye, my friends, you must march as far as you can' – Shedding the prisoners – Bausset's gouty leg at 'Miserowo' – Marbot fights the Cossacks – the Poles feel at home – IHQ no longer recognisable

From the Berezina to Vilna is 54 leagues, to the Niemen, 80. Which is a long way still to go.

Tchitchakov, repulsed by Ney, had quite simply given up. And in the evening of the 28th Fain and the rest of IHQ had moved from the Zaniwki hamlet,

'almost completely destroyed during the day. In the evening we only found three barns standing, of which two were occupied by the Emperor and his household, the third by the King of Naples and Prince of Neuchâtel's officers.'

But now a new day's dawning. It's 29 November:

'We left the banks of the Berezina, pushing in front of us the crowd of disbanded men and those marching with Victor's already disorganised corps.'

For disorganised it is:

'Yesterday evening, together with II Corps and Dombrowski's division, it had still presented 14,000 men. But already, except for some 6,000, the rest no longer had the shape of a division, brigade or regiment.'

Evidently Victor feels he's done enough. Half his men have been left behind, dead or wounded. A brigade of light cavalry which Napoleon has demanded and been duly sent on ahead to IHQ, 'consists only of 60 troopers'. Yet all the thanks he gets for his resolute stand (Deniée is shocked to hear) is a severe reprimand for not having attacked Wittgenstein at Tschereia and so perhaps have made

'the fateful crossing unnecessary. It had reduced our reserve corps to the same state as those which had gone all the way to Moscow. Hardly had the march been opened than Victor declared he could no longer form the rearguard. He even tried to pass on ahead and leave III Corps exposed to the Russian vanguard's attacks. This led to a rather brisk exchange of words between him and Marshal Ney.'

Both marshals appeal to Napoleon, who tells Victor to do his duty. But the demoralisation's already beginning to spread to

'these fine troops, who're beginning to feel the effects of our propinquity. The unlucky carry misfortune with them! Only a few regiments of German cavalry preserved the most exact discipline, at least as far as such a thing was possible at this fatal moment when all subordination was extinct, even among officers.'

The army may have won a tactical victory, but not much of it is effectively left. It's being seen off by all three Russian armies: Tchitchakov's, as advance guard, following along the same main road. By Kutusov, some-where on its left. And, by Wittgenstein marching parallel to its right. Both at Chotaviski and Molodeczno, Fezensac will hear, the rearguard, Victor's IX Corps, is energetically attacked and completely routed. Riding on with Murat's staff, Rossetti sees Victor's men

> 'amid the mass of disbanded men who'd come from Moscow. There were still 60,000 men, but without any cohesion. All were marching pell-mell, cavalry, infantrymen, French, Germans, Italians. There was no longer either wing or centre; the artillery and the vehicles rolled on through this confused mass, their only orders being to get on as well as possible.'

Long before dawn Le Roy has woken up under six inches of snow, but found himself 'sound in mind and body'. Just as he's searching about him for his Bibiche – he finds her nibbling at some fruit trees – someone seizes his arm: What joy! It's Jacquet. Immediately Colonel Piat of the 85th invites them 'to share their soup *en famille.*' Then, at 4 a.m., the remains of I Corps – according to Captain François' probably exaggerated estimate, 8,700 men – 'led by the Duke of Eckmühl in person, had set off via the village of Zawitchin to march for the little Jewish town of Kamen' via Zembin. The Swiss have left the battlefield with particularly heavy hearts:

> 'We took our farewells of the poor friends from the homeland who had to be left behind by the fires, awaiting their fate. We got under arms without tap of drum, the enemy was too close. Nor had we noticed the Russians taking any of us prisoner.'

Marc-Bussy's Major Weltner, his thigh carried away by a roundshot, had been carried to

> 'a little house close to the Berezina. At all costs he'd wanted to leave with us. So we, six voltigeurs, are sent to look for him. He wants to get on horseback. Impossible to remain in the saddle with the newly operated stump of a thigh half a foot long! So he has to stay where he is. A trum-peter of our company was also left on the battlefield.'

'So here we are on the road,' voltigeur Bussy goes on,

> 'in a tightly closed up column. It'll make a very small square, all that's left of our two [3rd and 4th] regiments. We daren't speak to each other, for fear of hearing of our comrades' deaths. Yesterday morning we were 87 voltigeurs in the company. This morning we only find seven safe and sound! And everywhere it's the same tale, more or less.'

With IX Corps, II Corps is making up the rearguard, Castex and Cor-bineau's light cavalry brigades bringing up the extreme rear.

But where's Guillaume? Is he one of the 'damned', Le Roy's wondering – pillaged, stripped, being driven along stark naked, with a Cossack lance at the small of his back or even killed by those 'archers of death' the Bashkirs? That his Guillaume, so young, so lithe and vigorous, hasn't got across the river somehow is more than he can believe. So great is his faith in him, he keeps turning round to try and make out

'the ugly face of this poor fellow I was sending to all the devils each time my hopes were disappointed. In the fierce cold wind we didn't *march* to Zawitchin; we ran, without halting. My foot was painful, my hand cured – by rubbing it with snow.'

'The Borissow–Molodeczno road via Zembin', Lejeune knows,

'was the only one we could hope to take. A very narrow paved road, it was raised above the water, and at every step cut by little bridges to allow the waters of the immense marsh it crosses to flow away. These little bridges are thrown at quarter-hour intervals across broad and deep streams with muddy banks; and the Cossacks would only have had to break one of them, to bring the entire army to a halt.'

How is it possible they haven't? 'The army,' Rossetti goes on,

'crossed over three consecutive bridges 300 fathoms long with an astonishment mingled with terror. A spark from a Cossack's pipe would have sufficed to ignite them. And from that moment all our efforts, our passage of the Berezina, would have been in vain. Cooped up without food, without shelter, between these swamps and the river, in the midst of an insupportable hurricane, the Grand Army and its Emperor would have been forced to surrender.'

One of the longest of the '30 or 40 little wooden bridges' is more than ¾ of a mile long. Caulaincourt, crossing it with IHQ and Napoleon, has the same thought: 'A match set to a bundle of straw would have been enough to cut off our retreat.' 'If the Russians had been in our position and we in theirs,' Boulart reflects grimly, trundling his guns and ammunition wagons along the Zembin causeway, 'not a Russian would have escaped.' Nor, if Junot had had his way, would a single Frenchman or ally, nor even the Emperor himself. Having himself crossed this long bridge yesterday with his advance guard of 800 Westphalians – so Intendant Pastoret's shocked to hear – Junot had ordered the bridges

'to be burnt. Grouchy had been sent to prevent him. The Duke of Abrantès had replied coldly that it'd be safer for himself that way, and he didn't give a damn for anything else. M. de Grouchy insists, and while they're discussing the matter the first men of the fighting corps arrive; and at the Emperor's approach the Duke of Abrantès gives way. One trembles to think of the horrible disaster such an action would have caused. It'd have been all up with us. Not one of us would have seen France again!'

That the Cossacks haven't set fire to what Dumonceau calls this 'long dike across swamps covered with a vast forest of conifers' seems miraculous.

Somewhere towards the rear of this Dantesque procession across the swamps ,the Grand Army's official historian[1] is struggling along. That morning Jomini, all his precious campaign notes lost in the Berezina's waters, has woken, coughing and spitting blood, in one of the three remaining Zaniwki huts to find himself alone. Once again he's been abandoned. Evidently even his ADC Liébart has given him up for dead. Luckily, just then, Victor's chief-of-staff General Château had come in. After sharing some *pâté de foie gras* with him and washing it down with a bottle of Bordeaux, Château had placed him in Victor's carriage. For a while this had been fairly comfortable. But upon its being threatened by Cossacks, Jomini's had to bundle out again into the icy north wind, trusting to his Astrakhan fur – soaked in the Berezina but dried out at Berthier's campfire – to serve him as a cuirass against it. After a while, again, he drags himself over and seats himself on one of the rearguard's gun-carriages, jolting on along the log causeway. But then the gun has to be placed in battery, and he has to move over to an ammunition wagon's canvas cover. But the cold's getting worse and worse and, in the end he has to get down and walk. Jomini's by no means the only invalid in the throng. Wracked by coughing but supported by Sergeant-Major Vogel (someone's just stolen their horse), Franz Roeder too is stumbling along the Zembin causeway:

'I can hardly walk for the pain in my right lung. Found a wretched pony by the roadside. Was lifted on to it and so rode on for about an hour and a half on the beast's jagged back. My sergeant-major is making himself of indescribable service to me. Am I going to get as far as Vilna?'

Le Roy and Jacquet, meanwhile, have soon found Colonel Piat's and his entourage's company disagreeable and pushed on by themselves:

'For vigorous individuals the weather was supportable. As we marched we talked of the perils and privations that had overwhelmed us. We were sure we'd be finding food and reinforcements at Vilna that would enable us to resume the offensive.'

Then, halfway to Zawitchin, Le Roy feels a clap on his shoulder. And there he is – his Guillaume, but without the pony. He'd lost her at the bridgehead. When Fournier's rearguard cavalry had come slashing their way through the crowd he'd waited for a gap to arise between it and Victor's slower moving artillery horses, and slipped in between. What's more important, Guillaume has a bottle of wine and a little rice and biscuit: 'I knew you'd be needing them,' he says. So delighted is the once so portly Le Roy, he tells him to his face, in front of Jacquet:

'"Since you've been with me I've never had the least reason to complain of you."'

The bottle, opened with his penknife's corkscrew, is found to contain excellent Madeira.

The Zembin causeway is 6½ miles long. So narrow and so crowded are its bridges and everything's going so slowly that some impatient individuals are trying to outflank them and are getting stuck in the marshes. General Preyssing, von Muraldt's former brigade commander, is one of them. Heedless of his subordinates' warnings, Preyssing leaves the causeway – and both horse and rider sink into the swamp. Unable to extricate him in the biting cold, everyone passes on, leaving him to his fate. But 'Old Thunderer' Sorbier, commander of the Guard Artillery, resorts to a more effective way of getting ahead. Although he has managed to get most of his artillery across the Berezina, he's had to leave his own effects on its left bank:

'Whereupon he'd taken out his handsomest uniform, with gold lace on its every seam, and donned it. Trotting along on a little Polish horse, without overcoat or fur, but armed with a long rod with which he pushed aside the stragglers, he kept shouting "Out of the way! Out of the way!". And everyone mechanically stood aside! In this way he got as far along the road in two hours as was taking us all day.'

In similar vein, Berthier's ADC Bonneval finds himself walking along beside Marshal Lefèbvre:

'Like all the rest of us he was on foot, a long stick in his hand, and we were pushing on side by side. Arriving at a bridge encumbered with baggage and troops that were making it virtually impossible to pass, the Marshal sees a huge figure of a man, 6 feet tall, in front of him, wearing a cuirassier's cloak,'

– the very man, perhaps, who'd involuntarily been of such help to von Suckow on the Berezina bridge? But no – 'Administering two or three blows of his stick on his back, Lefèbvre shouts in his German accent: "Co on, zen, co on, vot ze tevil, you're in my vay!" The other man turns quickly.' And who should it be if not his fellow-Marshal Mortier!

'"Ah! my gomrade," Lefèbvre says, confused, "if I't known it vos you, I vouldn't have hit zo hart!"'

Pausing after the first of these bottle-necks to rally his few men, Fezensac is shocked to see

'officers of all ranks, soldiers, servants, a few troopers scarcely able to drag their horses along, wounded and cripples mutually supporting one another, all pell-mell. Each was telling of the miraculous way in which he'd escaped the Berezina disaster and congratulating himself on having saved his own life by abandoning everything he'd possessed.'

Even more pitiable, as usual, is the women's plight. One wife is walking along beside her husband, an Italian officer who, carried by two soldiers, is obviously breathing his last:

'Acutely touched by this woman's trouble and the care she was lavishing on her husband, I gave her my place by a fire we'd lit. She needed every illusion bred of tender feeling not to perceive how futile her cares were. Her husband was no longer alive, but she went on calling to him up to the moment when, no longer able to doubt her misfortune, she fainted across his corpse.'

Corbineau, Castex and Séruzier aren't being guilty of the same oversight as the Cossacks. Curély – his inept and ailing Colonel Lagrange has found himself a sledge and has handed over to him – is making sure the 20th Chasseurs burn each little bridge as they leave it behind. Useless, says Marbot:

'The burning of these bridges served no purpose at all. The rigorous cold which, at this time of year, so easily could have turned the Berezina into a highway, had come down and frozen the waters hard enough to support cannon!'

At the bridge over the Goina stream Dumonceau's men are overtaken by the Sacred Squadron, 'assembled under the pretext of guarding IHQ, but

in reality to provide a refuge for isolated officers, 200 to 300 cavalry officers under General Grouchy's orders'. Among them Dumonceau espies
three old comrades. One, Sloet by name,

'officer of the 11th Hussars, was walking alone at the foot of the dike
among the trees, in a state of complete marasma, foaming at the mouth.
A mere shadow, he was carrying a phial of I don't know what elixir with
which he kept trying to revive himself.'

Dumonceau gives him a piece of biscuit, is thanked profusely – and never
sees him again.

Zembin, where Napoleon is meaning to spend the night, is reached by
IHQ at about 10 a.m., and turns out to be a village swarming with people.
After breakfasting 'in the neighbourhood of the Russian prisoners' he
changes his mind and goes on to Kamen. IV Corps, escorting the Treasure,
has been at Zembin since yesterday evening. Only after nightfall does Griois get this far and find

'an agitated multitude moving in all directions. The bivouac fires
touched one another and were being fed by the village's houses, almost
all of which had been demolished.'

But he's lucky. Falling in with one of his group who've already been there a
long time, having probably arrived with Eugène's staff last night, he lets them
take him to a still intact cabin. 'I was received like a friend everyone had
thought was lost. They embraced me, tears in their eyes.' Griois' group of officers even accept his RSM – who'd saved his life – as one of themselves. Everyone's been telling everyone else of how he got through across the Berezina:

'On a spontaneous impulse we were embracing those who'd come back
and whom we'd never expected to see again. We congratulated each
other in the most natural way on having escaped from a day more terrible to us than the bloodiest battle.'

Bourgogne, who can only be kept from falling asleep by kicks to his behind
from an officer named Favin, who also pulls him by the hair, sees

'many whom we thought had perished coming on from the Berezina.
They were embracing and congratulating one another as if it were the
Rhine they'd crossed, still 400 leagues away.'

On the other hand, Griois is astounded to find he's been robbed en route:

'When I, on getting there, wanted to take the bread and tea I'd bought
yesterday out of my saddlebags, I found there was nothing in them. To
empty them someone had cut them open from end to end, even while
I'd been on horseback, under my eyes, without my seeing it.'

All he now owns is a little portmanteau 'which I lost soon afterwards'.
There's the usual struggle for lodgings. Some infantrymen who try to
demolish their cabin for firewood and smash its doors are supplanted by
some grenadiers who declare it's needed by General Friederichs' staff. Griois' group, 'though numerous' offer to accommodate them 'even if we
should suffocate'. In vain. The pitiless Friederichs chucks out the first comers and even orders his grenadiers to put a wounded officer out of the

house 'despite his groans and our remonstrations. Doubtless the night and the cold put an end to his sufferings.'

The plight of the women is really piteous. Most, like Louise Fusil, have got here last night. Among them is the beautiful blonde wife of the French librarian in Moscow 'whom Rostopchin had taken away to send to Siberia'. She's in despair. One after another the generals' carriages she's been travelling in have broken down and since the Berezina she's been walking on foot and had to carry her child in her arms. Wrapping them in a wolf skin and several lengths of silk, Lejeune seats her on one of his horses.[2] Kergorre, too, sees

'some beautiful women who'd all the while been under Marshal Mortier's protection. They were in rags. These ladies' situation gives some idea of the state of those women who hadn't had the same advantage.'

And in a carriage with Grimblant (the gendarme who'd dissuaded him from returning to Moscow after Winkovo) Mailly-Nesle again sees some ladies who've come all this way in their white silk slippers. 'Almost unrecognisable, swathed in chiffons scorched by campfires, wholly smoke-blackened', they dine with him and give him

'some pink taffeta used for making cravats and handkerchiefs. Mlle Eléonore's elegant turnout existed only in memory. Clad in hitched up strips of clothing, they had the air of gypsies fallen on evil times.'

Many of the Berezina survivors, perhaps most, are mourning some friend. But only now does Fezensac hear of the death of Alfred de Noailles, his personal friend and former colleague on Berthier's staff:

'Up to that moment I hadn't lost any of my friends, and a sharp pang of grief went through me. But all the consolation Marshal Ney gave me when I spoke to him of it was to say: "Obviously it was his turn, and when all's said and done it's better we're mourning him than for him to be mourning us."'

In such circumstances, Fezensac adds, Ney

'always showed the same lack of feeling. Another time I heard him reply to a poor wounded man who asked him to have him carried: "What d'you expect me to do about it? You're a victim of war." Certainly it wasn't because he was ill-natured or cruel; but he'd become so habituated to the evils of warfare that they'd bitten into his heart. Obsessed with the notion that all military men ought to die on the battlefield, he found nothing simpler than that they should fulfil their destiny. He made no greater case of his own life than he did of others, as we've seen.'

All in sharp contrast to Berthier, whose self-pity when verbally flagellated by his endlessly exacting taskmaster also extends to his fellows, whatever their rank. Dumonceau's just seen him

'giving a bit of sugar to a poor dismounted cuirassier who, dying of hunger, was begging for charity as he dragged himself painfully along the road'.

Here at Zembin Jomini's sharing 'his last 20 peas' with Prince Eugène's chief-of-staff Guilleminot. Always someone's in luck. Tonight it's Gourgaud, whose sole but obsessive extra-military ambition is to get married. Although he has cast his somewhat protruding eyes on the 'neither young nor beautiful' daughter of Senator Roederer, the father, so far hasn't accepted him, he being merely the son of a violinist at the *ci-devant* Versailles court. But who's this, if not Roederer's eldest son? The poor fellow's in an utterly lamentable state. A musket ball has 'passed through his lips, removing his teeth down to the very gums'. Gourgaud takes him to Dr Yvan, who attends to his mouth. And thereafter the *premier officier d'ordonnance* doesn't let this prospective brother-in-law out of his sight.[3]

But Lieutenant Tascher, happy to have come across his wounded brother again, is noticing an odd fact. Coffins, at Zembin, are nothing but 'a bit of wood between two stones'.

The Treasure too has crossed the Berezina and its 'eight or nine vehicles, containing four millions in gold' are lumbering and slithering along the 'sheet of ice' which is the Kamen road. In the evening Berthier writes to tell Davout it's got there; but since IV Corps, now the army's advance guard, is having to keep the road clear of Cossacks, it's Davout who's to 'take the Treasure under your protection. Send one of your staff officers to the Viceroy to reconnoitre or park the Treasure.'

Far from lucky are the 2,000 or so Russian prisoners. No one's maltreating them. But no one has anything to give them either. During this cruelly cold night of 29/30 November Sergeant Bertrand and the 7th Light, around their fires which, 'lit on the snow, sink into the sand and are as it were at the bottom of a well', have to guard some:

'At about midnight the cold increases. Our prisoners either die or escape, we're too few to look after them.[4] The sky, sombre until now, clears, and the icy north wind begins whining. At the bottom of our holes it whips up particles of burning sand which fly at our eyes like silver spangles. By morning many of us had gone blind. Those who'd been spared by the burning sand lead those comrades who couldn't see. For my part, being only slightly affected, I was leading an adjutant-major, M. Rougeaut.'[5]

Kamen, 'four to five leagues further on', where Napoleon had first heard the sound of the guns en route for Witebsk in July, is 'a village of 50 timber houses in a continuous forest'. After passing through 'defiles, conifer forests, very narrow country roads', IHQ after doing 'altogether seven leagues in one day' has reached it at 5 p.m. on 29 November. Lodged 'in a baron's château', Castellane notes in his diary,

'we've found some potatoes; it's an event. You should see us in the Emperor's courtyard, all with potatoes on the tips of our sabres. We've eaten our fill. I'm to sleep in a sort of room on good straw. It's not a beautiful spot, but to be under a roof means a great deal; one night, at least, not spent under the bare sky!'

There, around their campfires in the courtyard, the staff officers are hearing the details of how Partonneaux's division, '4,000 infantry and a light cavalry brigade strong', had gone astray:

'The 29th Light Infantry, a handsome regiment made up of officers and veterans recently returned from English prisons, was part of it. These unfortunates, it must be admitted, are toying with misfortune. A fair number of them had been in the San Domingo expedition. Only one battalion of the 55th, the last left at Borissow, arrived,'

an item of information doubtless contributed by Gourgaud, who'd run into the 55th on the Borissow road. Is he too roasting a potato on the tip of his sabre?

Oudinot had left the battlefield early on the morning of the 29th, well ahead of IHQ 'so as to avoid the scrum'. Despite his pains from the unextractable musket ball in the small of his back 'which had grown worse with the inflammation and fever', he'd been placed in his carriage and, escorted by his ADCs, some military police and a troop of Horse Chasseurs commanded by his son Victor, had gone on ahead. 'Toward 1 p.m. we'd reached Pleschenkowiczi', a village of 30 timber houses. 'His officers suggested he lodge in a château we could see a musket shot off to our left', where, as it happens, the insouciant Mailly-Nesle, after admiring the timber manor house's charming French-style garden, has just passed a pleasant evening listening to one of Gourgaud's subordinates 'singing very well and very gaily'. Evidently the imperial household, too, has come on from Kamen, for

'the bread they were baking *chez l'Empereur* was of rye, hardly ground up at all and very poorly leavened. It tasted of mildew. Although I was almost dying of hunger I could hardly bring myself to eat it. It was also said to cause dysentery.'

But Oudinot's unwilling to leave the road, and one of his aides, M. de la Chaise, goes into the village where he chooses a Jew's house instead. The wounded Marshal's anxiety turns out to be justified.

For things have been happening at Pleschenkowiczi.

Only yesterday the Russian General Lanskoi had fallen on it and captured the Polish General Kaminski. He'd also attacked its château and captured some of the *fourriers* [quartermaster sous-lieutenants] who'd come on ahead to prepare 'the Palace'. No sooner has Oudinot been installed in the Jew's house and his wound attended to by Dr Capiomont and he's trying to get some rest, than his son Victor rushes in. '"My dear father," he cries. "We must accept it! We're all prisoners!" "What!" Oudinot replies, in a terrible voice, forgetting the state he's in. "Get the hell out of here and fight!"' At 10 a.m., so Lejeune'll hear afterwards,

'a Cossack officer had come with 200 men to surround the house where Oudinot and Pino were with 25 or 30 officers or soldiers of their suite and addressing them in good French had summoned them to surrender.'

Pils, of course, is there:

'Through the windows we saw some Cossack lances. The Duke of Reggio, who was only wearing a simple pelisse, sat up and said to me: "Hand me my great ribbon [of the *Légion d'honneur*]. At least if they take me alive they'll see who it is they have to do with."'

After putting his pistols and a hunting gun beside him, Pils, like everyone else, rushes out to the horses. 'Hastily I bridle one, grab up a sabre and bring it to him, leaving its sheath behind. Meanwhile M. Jacqueminot [still clad no doubt in his 'magnificent uniform'] has run out into the square, shouting in a loud voice: "Everyone rally around me!"'

'Quickly a troop was formed up and fell on the Cossacks with its sabres, who fled away down all the streets that abutted on the square, charging and pursuing them until they were out of the village. The greater part of their regiment took refuge in the château we'd seen on the left of the road, where they captured several of the Emperor's carriages which, commanded by an officer of the Horse Grenadiers, were just then arriving.'

Other Cossacks are still glimpsed roving about. And after placing scouts around Pleschenkowiczi in case they should come back, M. Le Tellier and Colonel Jacqueminot come and fetch Oudinot, lift him into the saddle, and take him

'to a house at the end of the village, already occupied by the Italian General Pino and able to sustain a siege. All the mounted men surrounded this fortress and those who were on foot went inside. A big fire was lit in the courtyard to pass the night while awaiting an attack.'

According to Cesare de Laugier, who'll soon be somewhere in the vicinity, the house has a gate barred by a timber grill and is 'guarded by some carabiniers of the 3rd Italian Regiment, commanded by a Lieutenant Catilini.' Besides Pino, Oudinot's companions include General Anthouard (IV Corps' former artillery commander whom Griois had replaced after he'd been wounded just before the Wop crossing), General Fontana and various other Italian officers who've just installed themselves in the house. – 'But the Russians,' Pils goes on faithfully in his *Journal de Marche*,

'probably thought we were far more numerous than we really were, and began attacking us with their cannon. A roundshot, passing through the roof, broke a truss, a splinter of which hit *M. le Maréchal* and knocked him over backwards. Surgeon Capiomont, who was at his side, was immediately able to dress this new wound, which had no serious consequences. Two Russian guns were firing grape at the six horses harnessed to the Marshal's carriage. The two shaft horses were killed by the same fragment.'

Afterwards Lejeune will hear how,

'between salvoes the Marshal himself, though suffering greatly and lying on his mattress, fired his pistols at the Cossacks through two or three little openings, and didn't miss. Already four roundshot had made holes but not wounded anyone. In the Spaniards' fashion our officers immediately used these holes to aim at the enemy. A fifth roundshot came and smashed the pallet where the Marshal was lying and at the same time shattered the wall of an oven where five or six little children of the Russian peasant whose dwelling it was had hidden themselves. Terrified to death, these little mites scattered through the room amidst all the smoke and the combatants, who were greatly surprised to see them there.'

After a considerable affray, during which Cossack 'hurrahs' are repeatedly repulsed by volleys of well-aimed musketry, the assailants,

'charged by our mounted men, are driven back on their units. In one of these pursuits a Chasseur of the Guard even managed to capture a Cossack he'd just wounded with a pistol shot and brought him back to us.'

But help is at hand:

'Finally, at about 4 p.m., we saw on the horizon a line which seemed to grow as it came closer. Accompanied by a trumpeter, Captain Delamarre galloped off in that direction.'

It's some of General Hammerstein's Westphalian cavalry, from VIII Corps.[6] 'Soon the Duke of Abrantès arrived and the Marshal embraced him as his liberator.' It's the only useful thing Junot has done throughout the campaign. The two corps commanders go back to the Jew's house, where they spend 'almost the whole night talking together'. Interrogated by an officer of the 7th Polish Lancers who's serving as Oudinot's interpreter, the captured Cossack tells them how after Lanskoi had ordered his regiment to capture 'a wounded general', they'd been expecting some Russian infantry to come up in support and seize Pleschenkowiczi during the night.

Now other units are beginning to arrive at Pleschenkowiczi, and several circumstantial accounts of Oudinot's private battle immediately begin to circulate. 'Having hastened our steps at the sound of the gunfire' Lejeune gets there with I Corps: 'The Cossacks, with some 50 wounded and a few dead, not daring to continue, fled at our approach. What a good thing we'd turned up.'[7] Also reaching Pleschenkowiczi in the evening, von Muraldt's little group of Bavarian chevauléger officers spend the night in the very same cabin where Oudinot had fought his private battle. 'An infantryman showed us the wretched bed from which the Marshal had led its defence and where he'd been wounded' by the splintering roof truss.

As Delaborde's group approaches the village, Paul de Bourgoing sees coming towards him – in the wrong direction – 'an officer on a handsome horse, followed by a trooper leading another.' Who can it be, if not his own brother, an officer in the no longer extant 4th Chasseurs! Hearing of Oudinot's plight, he'd decided to retrace his steps, bought a horse off Jacqueminot and is going to offer him his services. Not half an hour ago he's met Napoleon, 'accompanied by Berthier, Sébastiani, Grouchy and several other generals', complaining bitterly about Partonneaux's surrender and

'reflecting how easy it would have been, but for this, to have made the crossing of the Berezina one of the finest and most glorious military operations ever undertaken – rumours were current that Partonneaux hadn't been with his troops, but had been marching by himself.'[8]

Napoleon had called him over and asked him:

'Where are you off to like this?'

Asked for details of Oudinot's condition, he'd told the Emperor all about the Marshal's fight. And Napoleon had exclaimed 'with emotion':

'"Brave Oudinot! Brave Oudinot! Always the same!"'
And to his informant:
'"At least you aren't losing courage."'
Then the Bourgoing brothers part, each in his own direction.

But here's a surprise. When IHQ stays in the 'rather pretty château Oudinot hadn't dared to occupy, someone comes across 'Baraguay d'Hilliers' portfolio and uniforms' in one of its attics. Sick and disgraced and en route for France after his court-martial at Smolensk, he has felt he'll never again be needing either.[9]

That Sunday evening Le Roy gets there too and lodges together with several other of the 85th's officers

'in a house occupied by its proprietor, a German national, who received us in Austrian fashion, with plenty of bowings and scrapings. That was all we could get out of Baron de Rudorf, a big talker and in supreme degree a braggart. We'd have been only too happy to listen to him if a starving stomach hadn't had first call on our ears. All these fine promises turned into some potatoes and a half-firkin of fermenting red beetroot juice, of the kind used for colouring vodka.'

One officer gets the crimson liquid all over his nose and moustaches. The juice is also a powerful laxative, and will act as such for several days. 'Eight days later Captain Mabou, our newsmonger [*fureteur*], died of it, victim of his own greed.' Kergorre, for his part, spends the night in just such a house as Oudinot's 'fortress':

'We were very snug. However the great numbers of mice which kept scurrying over our faces all night were a nuisance, though I'd taken the precaution of covering mine with a handkerchief.'

At 2 a.m. Berthier again writes to Davout. The halt for the Treasure and the prisoners on 1 December is to be at Stagenki 'if you find nothing inconvenient about doing so and the day's march isn't excessive'. He asks for an officer to be sent to him to say where in fact Davout will be stopping. At 6 p.m. he writes again, from Staïki, exhorting Davout to leave next morning 'at 6 a.m. precisely with your army corps and your prisoners' and to follow Junot, who's following Eugène. There's to be about a league's interval between the corps. The order to 'march closed up and in good order' is again reiterated. 'His Majesty will try to go and spend the night at Selitchi, which is about half-way between Iliya and Molodeczno.'

The morrow is an icy sunny day. In a temperature of -25° Réaumur [-15.6° C] Marbot's gallantry in a violent clash with Don Cossacks almost costs him his life.[10] Dumonceau, less impressed by the heroic qualities of Oudinot's fight than by what it implies, is finding it

'most unpleasant, proving as it did that the Cossacks, whom we'd been hoping we'd seen the last of, weren't yet counting on leaving us in peace'.

Which they certainly aren't. Pion des Loches sees they've

'dressed themselves up in gold-braided hats and coats they'd found in the many artillery vehicles, wagons and generals' carriages that had been left behind, and were pursuing us in this grotesque getup'.

But for most of the thousands in that sad cortege the time for heroics is over. 'Yesterday evening,' an unhappy Franz Roeder notes in his diary,

'Vogel and I pilfered a loaf of bread and, this morning, a copper saucepan. Overmastering need! We've had to do as everyone else is doing!'

After seven or eight hours on the road, leaning on his sergeant-major 'who's endured everything for me', Roeder 'without knowing it' again catches up with the relics of his Young Guard division, bivouacked in a village to the left of the road. And at 4 a.m. 'after another sleepless night' is heartily glad to get going again, naturally in pitch darkness. – Tascher, 1 December:

'Heavy snowfall. Thick flakes all day. Road hardly discernible, no longer flanked either by trees or ditches. The countryside is savage, deserted and covered in forests.'

Castellane too is finding the Lithuanian countryside 'vile. All we have to cheer us up are conifers by the wayside.' All that first December day the snow falls heavily. Nevertheless as Brandt sets off for the next little town the temperature is still going down. The road, marked by corpses around campfires, goes through a forest. Under a sky of glittering stars from time to time Brandt and his companions halt

'at bivouac fires. But we seemed to be among the dead. No one stirred. Sometimes an unfortunate fellow would raise his head, throw us a glassy look and lie back again, doubtless never more to get up. What above all made this night's march disagreeable was the glacial wind that was lashing our faces. At about 8 a.m. we saw a church tower: "It's Molodeczno!" we all exclaimed with one voice. Imagine our amazement when we learnt on reaching it that it was only Iliya, and that we still hadn't gone more than half way to Molodeczno.'

Although the loss of so much baggage has 'considerably lightened the army's march' and it's less encumbered now by stragglers, it has, by the same token, very few horses left to eat. Le Roy's carefully organised pocket larder has long been empty – and neither he nor anyone else has any hope of getting a mouthful for days to come, 'the whole countryside having been ravaged by both armies for 20 miles around'. Yet amazingly, all along the narrow icy-surfaced road with its endless forests, many *fricoteurs* are still plodding on with 'their immense booty'. Now and then Mailly-Nesle – still in his carriage of course – sees

'a man leading three heavily laden unnourished horses which can hardly stand up. To have less trouble leading them, he tied them to one another's tail, only concerning himself with the first. Now someone would cut the rope holding the horses together, and some robber profit by it. Now a movement of impatience caused one of these innocent animals to be killed, and sometimes even the driver would be felled to the ground.'

Suddenly whole rows of demoralised soldiers, clinging to one another, fall like packs of cards, or 'turn and flee if the tip of a lance appeared or the word 'Cossack' was repeated two or three times'. 'Bands of marauders' are still being formed, Caulaincourt notices, 'in full view of everyone, so as to recruit fresh stragglers'. Marc-Bussy's little band of Swiss runs into just such a small private army

'from all the corps: the Imperial Guard, light infantry, troopers, marching like demons. The colonel of the 123rd Line, who knows what such marauders go for, shouts to us: "Soldiers of the 3rd Brigade, distribution time!" We leave our ranks, the colonel among us, and fling ourselves on them as if they were an advancing enemy column. All had food and effects they'd pillaged.'

Bussy, for his part, fills his pocket handkerchief with valuables, and gets

'a Russian woman's overcoat of thick white cloth which one of these marauders had let fall from his shoulders. The colonel, seeing one of them, fine as if on parade, with the cross of the *Légion d'honneur* on his coat, rips it off him, calling him a straggler, a marauder. The other doesn't answer a word. This body is twice as numerous as our brigade. The grenadiers of the 123rd furnished themselves with fur bonnets of the Guard in exchange for their own, which were worthless.'

But now even the staunch Swiss are beginning to melt away:

'Often we hear someone say: "*Ma foi!* it's all up! We can't do any more. We're always getting fewer. I'm going to do as the others." Of all the brigade we're only fifteen in the ranks, all Swiss! The colonel of the 123rd tells our Major Graffenried: "Major, I put you in command of the brigade. I'm pushing off too." The major replies: "I shan't be commanding it for long, shall I? You see what's left!" Whereupon Graffenried makes us all present arms, and says: "Good-bye, my friends. You must march as far as you can." I think they left together. The night was so dark we couldn't see them leave, and on the snow you can't hear horses' footfalls. Each of us is trying to get on as best he can, without losing his comrades for fear of the Cossacks. At 8 a.m. there are still a few of us together.'

But later that day (2 December), lingering too long in a village but – unlike many others – still clinging to his musket, the little voltigeur from the Vaud suddenly finds he's all alone.

Throughout the retreat the white-haired 57-year-old Narbonne's behaviour at IHQ has been impeccable. Although 'used to enjoying all the ease and pleasures of life' he's been showing 'all the activity and ardour of a young man'. 'In the midst of our disasters,' attests his ADC Castellane admiringly – and Gourgaud and Ségur confirm it –

'his courage, his gaiety were remarkable. He wore the "royal bird" hairstyle, had himself powdered in the mornings at the bivouacs, often seated on a roof-beam, the steps of some house or a bench, even in the nastiest weather, as if he'd been in the most agreeable boudoir. During this operation he amused the bystanders with his jokes.'

If it weren't for Napoleon's marble features (every morning he shaves himself while Constant holds the mirror), Narbonne's clean-shaven face would be almost unique. Castellane hasn't shaved for two weeks and Kergorre for six. But Daru is no less imperturbable than Narbonne. According to his valet, 'he made almost the whole route from Moscow to Posen on foot and shaved himself every morning with as carefree an air as if we'd been at the Tuileries.'

Not that IHQ is immune to alarms. One at least, turns out to be a comic mistake. Someone starts shouting for an officer whose name is Ozanne. The cry is taken up by others, and immediately turns into '*Aux armes!*' which brings the whole Guard to arms! Even Napoleon comes out to ask what's going on. At IHQ things are happening that have never happened before. 'Two mules from the Emperor's transport wagons which had fallen behind,' it's reported to Caulaincourt, have been stolen

'while their driver was a little way off. No one knew who'd taken them. I mention this insignificant event because it's the only one of its kind to have happened throughout the campaign.'

Roustam says the thieves, starving soldiers, had taken the canteen, carried on the backs of the three mules which, under Ségur's command, always followed with wine, bread or biscuit and provisions in baskets on their saddles, and was always conducted by three gendarmes and two of the kitchen and table staff:

'The soldiers could see, written on it, who it was for; but stole it even so. The Emperor excused these men. Yet he wanted to know which regiment they belonged to. "A day will come when they'll have plenty of food and I'll review them on parade. But no, the reproach would be too cruel: On such or such a day you stole your Emperor's bread!"'

'On the last of these mules', Roustam explains, 'was the little iron bed which we erected everywhere and which was folded up with a mattress.'

Now even the Old Guard's beginning to disintegrate. The Master of the Horse keeps on coming across its veterans

'who'd succumbed to frost-bite and fallen to the ground. Should one help them along, which meant laboriously carrying them? They begged you to let them be. Should one take them to one of the bivouac fires which lined the route? Once these poor wretches fell asleep they were dead. If they resisted the craving for sleep, some other passer-by would help them on a bit further, thus prolonging their agony a little while, yet not saving them. In this state the drowsiness brought on by the cold is irresistible. Sleep comes inevitably; and to sleep is to die. In vain I tried to help several of these unfortunate men. The only words they uttered were to beg me, for pity sake, to leave them to sleep a little. Alas! It was the poor wretch's last wish; but at least his sufferings were over, without pain or death-throes. Gratitude, a smile even, was imprinted on his discoloured lips.'

For Pierre Auvray the first two days of December are

'days the like of which has never been seen. The cold had become so bad that the hoar frost, attaching itself to one's face, formed on it a 2-inch icicle. We marched through forests amidst the most terrible sufferings.'

And all the time the snow falls steadily. Dumonceau's lancers are finding it 'hardly possible to make out the road. Its whereabouts is no longer marked

either by rows of trees or ditches.' Of all the survivors of the Berezina cross-
ing, only the Polish Guard Lancers, who are taking 'the wars of Batory,
Zamoyski and Chodkiewicz for our models', are feeling quite at home.
Indeed more and more so:

> 'From day to day our march was getting easier. Order, morale, the lan-
> guage, all were facilitating everything for us in this fraternal country. For
> us the winter, though harsh, was in no way extraordinary. Above all when
> marching in the evening or in extreme cold we were in the habit of dis-
> mounting and, holding our horses by the bridle, singing march tunes or
> "Cracow songs", as much to relieve the horses as to keep our men warm
> and prevent them from falling asleep on horseback. It's an officer's duty
> to keep up a spirit of gaiety and confidence in his subordinates. Sup-
> ported by the example of the French veterans we persevered in sup-
> porting our own.'

Griois too is noticing that

> 'virtually all our army's Poles were using such means that their knowl-
> edge of the country and the language facilitated for them, and they felt
> little of our terrible distress.'

By and by orders come to V Corps for all Poles to branch off left toward
Olita, where it has its depots. All dismounted cavalry, on the other hand,
are to make for the big remount depot at Merecz.

And still no one has anything to give the Russian prisoners, most of them
bleeding from Doumerc's cuirassiers' long sword-thrusts and slashes. All
day Lejeune and his party are

> 'passing through an immense forest with difficult defiles at every step.
> In these woods we lost almost all our prisoners. The two to three thou-
> sand we were taking with us were a great source of embarrassment to us.
> We hadn't a scrap of food to give them, and I was happy to shut my eyes
> when they took their chance and escaped while we were passing through
> some forest. Because I couldn't be so cruel as to let them be maltreated
> into going on with us.'

Le Roy too sees the futility of keeping a 25-year-old Russian who's been
allotted to him. As evening begins to fall he makes a sign to his prisoner,
seated beside him on some pine branches; and together they get up and
walk a few paces away from the fireside:

> 'I showed him where the rearguard was: "*Franzozi, Rusqui!*" Then I
> showed him the forest, crooking my arm, my hand pointing toward the
> Russian army that was behind us, saying: "*Nein franzozi.*" Then, putting
> my hand to my mouth: "*Nein cleba, niema mieuza*"[neither bread nor
> meat]. I put a little bit of biscuit into his hand, saying: "*Pachol*" [March!]
> – a word I'd remembered from the time I was myself a prisoner [in
> 1807]. This poor young man understood me perfectly. He threw himself
> on my hand, which he kissed several times.'

Jacquet praises Le Roy for his action. At least one person's happy! Only the
men of Morand's division evidently have greater resources. Captain

François, too, is in charge of some prisoners. 'We shared everything with them. Afterwards they were very useful to us in procuring us some food.'

The row between Ney and Victor is inspiring little confidence in IX Corps' support. And Ney 'wants to set the remainder of III Corps, i.e., a few officers and the regiments' Eagles, at a distance'. Ney's personal escort against the Cossacks, 'a little sacred squadron, scarcely 100 men still under arms, and all the eagles', is provided by one of Fezensac's subordinates, a Captain Delachau:

'A drummer of the 24th Line marched at our head. He was all that was left of III Corps' regimental drummers and musicians.'

The rest of the corps tries to catch up with IHQ, which isn't easy, since it's already a whole day's march ahead.

'For two days and three nights we marched almost without halting; and when excessive fatigue forced us to take a moment's rest we all gathered in a barn with the regiments' Eagles and some soldiers still under arms, who watched over their defence.'

But when an order comes to break all the Eagles and bury them Fezensac simply can't bring himself to obey. 'I had the pole broken and the Eagle put into the pack of one of the Eagle-bearers who was always marching at my side.'

The second manor house to provide overnight quarters for IHQ is at Staïki (fifteen houses, plunged in the depths of an endless forest). Although

'the barns attached to it are full of forage, so far we haven't had so miserable a lodging. The Emperor and staff officers each had a little corner measuring 7 or 8 feet square. All the rest were packed together in another room. It was freezing so hard that everyone took shelter in this little hole of a place. When we lay down we had to lie on top of one another to save space. A pin couldn't have been dropped between us.'

Least of all is Napoleon's plump major-domo ever likely ever to forget his night here:

'All the way from Moscow M. de Bausset, suffering from gout, had been in a carriage. Someone, moving about in the dark, trod on his foot. The wretched cripple began screaming "Monstrous! I'm being murdered!" Those of us who were awake shouted with laughter, which woke up those who were asleep. And everyone – including the unfortunate invalid himself – paid tribute to this momentary foolishness with roars of laughter. We nicknamed Staïki "Miserowo".'

When morning comes, Larrey's scientific eye notes how the night's freshly fallen snow is

'crystallising in six-pointed stars, of various sizes. In the little stars the same distribution as in the big ones, and the same symmetry of the crystals was to be seen.'

CHAPTER 21

THE EMPEROR QUITS

'They danced while others froze' – a bulletin that doesn't lie – 'Sire, I'm old. Take me with you' – 'One must always trust one's luck – 'Kill me rather than let me be taken' – a hermetically sealed carriage and its escort – 'they'd been dancing while others froze' – 'the Emperor was shivering as with the ague'

Now IHQ's making for Molodeczno, near the junction with the Minsk–Vilna highway. This day, 2 December, is a double anniversary – of Napoleon's self-coronation, and of Austerlitz, that great victory only eight years ago which had 'rolled up the map of Europe'. But this freezing day no one feels like celebrating either. Left behind at Sedlichë to communicate with Victor, Castellane places himself under a tree, where

'all day, near a campfire on the highway, I've had the spectacle of the stragglers of all nations, all arms, most of whom have thrown away their muskets, the men of the Old Guard excepted. They're keeping theirs. All this forms a close column of twelve to fifteen men abreast.'

From a disgruntled Marshal Victor, when he turns up, he hears how IX and II Corps had taken up position to protect the stragglers as they'd passed through the narrow passage across the swamps near Ilya, and how the same disorder had reigned as at the Berezina. His colleague d'Aremberg has been sent on the same mission; but somehow they've missed each other. At 7 p.m., after passing the Vilna–Minsk junction on foot, Castellane gets to Molodeczno 'and the Emperor's headquarters, set up in a house which almost has the air of a proper château.' Molodeczno is quite a large town, but most of its timber houses, 'following our men's praiseworthy habit', are already in flames.' As for the château,

'standing by itself to the left on some high ground at the entrance to the bridges, it's a fine timber manor house, the property of Count Oginski. The King of Naples had his campfire a few paces away from us.'

The sheet ice has prevented no fewer than twenty couriers from coming further. Fourteen of the leather dispatch-cases all, Fain notes (sent between 1 and 19 November, Caulaincourt sees), are from Paris; the rest 'from all along the line'. They don't only contain official correspondence. Castellane, who hasn't had any letters from home for a long time and has 'been deprived of news from Paris since Krasnoië', now gets nine. Several others, he gathers from their contents, must have been captured by Cossacks.

The most important dispatches are from Maret, at Vilna. Some report on Schwarzenberg's now useless advance. More relevantly they tell Napoleon that twelve battalions of Loison's [34th] division[1] had reached Vilna on 21 November and been ordered forward to Ochmiana, the last town before it, to cover the last stage of the army's retreat. Loison himself is still at Königsberg, organising the rest of his scattered division.[1] To send forward Loison's untried Neapolitan and Bavarian conscripts from the Confederation of the Rhine has been Hogendorp's idea. And Napoleon immediately tries to inhibit it. Writes to Maret:

'"The 34th Division's movement must be stopped. If it has left, how shall we feed it? It will become disbanded, like the rest of the army."'

Some of his ministers he declares himself pleased with. Others not. Particularly not – indeed very far from pleased – with his ambassador-extraordinary at Warsaw, Abbé *D.-G.-F. de Pradt* who – he's been telling Caulaincourt over and over again – has ruined all his plans.[2] Where, for instance, are the 'Polish Cossacks'? There quite simply aren't any. And it's all Pradt's fault! The fact is, however, as Maret writes, the Grand Duchy's finances are exhausted. So is Lithuania. And Caulaincourt, listening no doubt to Napoleon's comments as he rips open the leather dispatch-cases and glances at their dates of dispatch, realises that from now on

'we'd have to make do without all the other supports the Emperor had been counting on. Obviously neither Vilna, nor even the Niemen, would be the end of the army's retreat, and therefore of our troubles either. The Emperor busied himself reading his dispatches from France, and everyone was glad to have news from home. In Paris there'd been some worry about news from the army being interrupted, but no notion of the extent of our disasters.'

Also shivering at Molodeczno is a M. de Forget, Councillor of State, with the ministerial portfolio. Napoleon questions him on the state of the roads, etc. Is anything known of the army's catastrophe? Nothing? Well, that's just as well. The main thing now is that the Austrian, Prussian and American ambassadors who've been at Vilna all this time are on no account to be allowed to witness the débâcle.[3] And an urgent message is sent off to Maret to clear the diplomatic corps out of Vilna post-haste.

Ever since the Berezina, Caulaincourt's been aware that Napoleon's preparing a bulletin. And this evening at Molodeczno he dictates its text. For an Imperial Bulletin the 29th is quite exceptionally candid.[4] It dates the catastrophe from 6 November ('*until which time the weather was perfect ... the army's movement had been carried out with greatest success*'), and goes on to describe how '*30,000 horses perished in a few days, those of the cavalry, artillery and the Train were perishing every night, not by hundreds but by thousands*', how much of the artillery and 'munitions of war and mouth' had had to be abandoned for lack of teams; and how, as the result of the sudden cold of 7 November, '*this army, so handsome on the 6th, was already very different by the 14th*', and had been unable to risk a battle for lack of artillery:

'"*The men seemed stunned, lost their gaiety, their good humour, and dreamed only of misfortunes and catastrophes. The enemy, seeing on the roads the traces of this terrible calamity that was striking the French army, tried to profit from it. He enveloped all the columns with his Cossacks who, like the Arabs of the desert, carried off the trains and vehicles that were following on.*"'

In sum, the largest army ever raised in Europe no longer exists. What a shock it's going to be for the Parisians! For France!

Already, yesterday evening, Castellane's friend Quartermaster Anatole de Montesquiou has been sent on his way to Paris with eight captured Russian flags and orders to everywhere spread news of the victory won on the banks of the Berezina and insert it instantly in the Vilna and Mainz newspapers. Above all he's to tell Marie-Louise all this verbally, before the terrible news becomes public:

'The Emperor's idea was to prepare public opinion. He was determined to hide none of his disasters.'

Boulart's among those who profit from the courier's departure to send a letter to his wife.

But Napoleon has reached an even more important decision – to leave the army. He tells Caulaincourt:

'"With things as they are, it's only from the Tuileries I can keep my grip on Europe." He was counting on being able to set out within 48 hours. He was eager to start, so as to forestall the news of our disasters.'

As soon as contact's been made with Loison's fresh division, based at Vilna – where 'as he saw it the army would no longer be at risk' – he'll be off. Caulaincourt is dubious. Obviously Napoleon still has no real idea of the completeness of the catastrophe. But when he says he doubts that the army'll be able to make a stand at Vilna, Napoleon merely replies: "You're laughing at me!"

On another important point, however, he affects to listen to Caulaincourt's advice. To whom should he hand over supreme command – Murat or Eugène? Caulaincourt, in his blunt frank way that so often gives offence, repeats what he's already said several times before. The army has more confidence in Eugène. Murat, though a hero on the battlefield, isn't generally thought to have either the force of character, the sense of order or the foresight that'll be needed to save or re-organise what's left of the army. People are even accusing him of

'having instigated His Majesty to undertake the Moscow expedition and of having lost the magnificent cavalry force there'd been at the start of the campaign.'[5]

Well, that's true, Napoleon agrees. But a king can't serve under a viceroy; so for reasons of rank it's not possible for him to hand over to Eugène. As Berthier, Caulaincourt adds, agrees.[6]

'Certain other remarks he'd made earlier, and which I recalled because they recurred during this conversation, gave me the idea that he'd prefer to leave to his brother-in-law the honour of rallying the army, and that he was loth to let his stepson have the credit for this further achievement,'

a typical instance, Caulaincourt thinks to himself, of Napoleon's distrust of anyone who enjoys a well-deserved personal reputation. His impending departure, Napoleon goes on, is to be kept secret for the time being. Caulaincourt's preliminary preparations likewise:

'Under pretext of making arrangements for officers to be sent with dispatches, I gave orders to the post-stages. But our troops soon disorganised these relays and I had to make other arrangements by sending several transport detachments on ahead whose horses would serve our purpose.'

Then there's the question – which is the Master of the Horse's business – of transporting Napoleon himself. *Quâ* organiser of all headquarters transports Caulaincourt's to accompany him to Paris:

'Our situation was such that if steps weren't taken well in advance the least trifles were liable to place obstacles in our way, even insurmountable ones. We wouldn't be able to use our relays to get along the highway, for instance – it was like a sheet of glass – if I hadn't kept a sack of coal under lock and key, to forge shoes for the horses. We'd only been able to do our forging at night, the transport wagons being on the move for 12–15 hours every day. The cold was so severe, even beside the forge fire, that the farriers could only work in gloves and even then had to rub their hands together at every moment so they shouldn't freeze.'

Who else is to come? Not Berthier, anyway. Roustam is eavesdropping 'in the next room. I heard loud words being spoken. It was the Emperor reprimanding Berthier at the top of his voice for wanting to go with him.

'"I'm going to France because my presence is indispensable."

'"Sire, Your Majesty has known for a long time I want to leave the service. I'm old. Take me with you."

'"You'll stay, together with Eugène and Murat. You're ungrateful. You're a coward! I'll have you shot in front of the whole army!"'

Berthier, Roustam hears, was weeping and sobbing. It seems he isn't the only one listening through the half-open door – or else it's thanks to him that a Major Dariale, Commandant of the Palace, knows how Berthier has pleaded in tears to be allowed to come too, pointing out that he'd never yet abandoned him: 'That's not possible,' Napoleon had replied, so Dariale tells Castellane.

'"It's necessary you remain with the King of Naples. I know very well, I do, that you're good for nothing.[7] But no one believes it, and your name'll have some effect on the army."'

So long as Berthier remains with the army it'll at least *seem* to have a headquarters. Murat is least of all an administrator. And Berthier's routines will be necessary to re-organise the army when it gets to Vilna.

This scene, Roustam declares, 'took place on 3 December. Next day Berthier had become resigned.'

Tascher. 4 December:

'Rigorous cold. Silent road. Thoughts worth remembering. Anniversary of my birth. Memory of my mother ... tears, agony. Did six leagues, lodged in a village, half a league ahead of headquarters. Fever and diarrhoea. Eugène's sufferings.'

But miracles do happen, if only petty ones. By now Sorbier's taken a complete loathing to the miserly sycophantic Drouot (who incidentally is also shaving every day), even forbidden him to appear in his presence unless summoned – but the thick-skinned Drouot appears even so. Again and again he's been sending him back to make sure his guns (which he, Sorbier, anyway doesn't think he'll be able to save) are following on. But today is St Barbara's day – a day for gifts. And Drouot astounds everyone by making 'a generous gesture. From his ammunition cart he took out his wine keg and a few bottles of wine', and distributes them to his fellow-officers. Peering into his wagon, Pion and Boulart both see in it a whole ham; and consider pinching it. But desist. Which is a pity, because in a few days it'll go the way of all the other wagons. The wine, however, will be enough to sustain their little group for more four days. That day the Guard artillery, following on, is attacked by Cossacks, who among other booty relieve it of Boulart's wagon:

'A real catastrophe for me. The cold increases to -20° [-12.5° C]. Fire breaks out in the next house to mine. Had to flee hastily, portmanteau under my arm.'

En route Castellane, too, bumps into his 'dragoon', who tells him his servant boy and horses have fallen to the Cossacks. 'The only fur I've got left is a woman's fox pelisse. I've been marching all day with holes in my boots.'
But I Corps' little party is lucky. It runs into

'some vehicles of a convoy coming from Germany which had got as far as Markowo, a little village, just as we were about to enter it. They'd brought an abundance of fresh and varied foods, and our brave soldiers were able to eat bread, butter, cheese and drink a glass of wine. What a repast, after 40 days on short rations!'

For once something has been rationally arranged:

'General Guilleminot and his division [sic], who'd got there first, had taken measures to see to it that these vehicles' contents shouldn't be wasted. He invited the men to dine at the village's little château. On fine tables of chestnut there was an enormous soup tureen, all the china of a tea service, many white loaves and several baskets of Breton butter. At this sight, so novel for people who for two months had been living under the most frightful privations, our eyes, our nostrils, opened like those of an Arab horse that hears the trumpet. Each of us ate enough – not for two, but for ten. Afterwards it was painful to leave this comfortable place with its warmth and food to go on and lie out in the open at a bivouac near Smorgoni in 25 degrees of frost.'

Leaving Molodeczno at 9 a.m., IHQ reaches the village of Bienitze, halfway to Smorgoni. Here it's met, as protocol requires (but also in response to an order sent off to him at 1.30 a.m., 2 December), by General Dirk van Hogendorp, governor of Vilna province. A bluff, square-minded 51-year-old Dutchman who'd once had been governor of Java then Dutch ambassador at St Petersburg, Hogendorp enjoys the enviable status of ADC to the Emperor.[8] Now, leaving Loison's lightly clad division behind him at Ochmiana, he has come to report on the state of affairs in the rear. He finds IHQ lodged in Count Zoçal's manor house, whose barns are yielding any amount of 'oats, flour, peas, potatoes and oatmeal'– all of which are being distributed to the Staff and the Guard. After being cross-examined by

Napoleon, Hogendorp sets off back again, to prepare the unsuspecting Vilna to receive the wreckage of what had been the Grand Army.

Another major worry is the Treasure. Ever since the Berezina, order after order, inquiry after inquiry, has been sent back to Davout and Eugène, whose officers and NCOs are escorting it. While IHQ had been at Molodeczno, the convoy – which also comprises Pajol's convoy of carriages containing wounded generals – has been attacked by Lanskoi's troops, together with 600 Cossacks. In the affray Generals Pino and Fontana are gallantly defended by three Italian carabiniers. So far Pajol's convoy has managed to survive by always keeping ahead of the column,

'ignoring such habitations as the route offered. From time to time we ran into magazine guards, employees of the Administration, who'd remained behind during the campaign. To them, they who'd lacked for nothing, the tale of our sufferings seemed a fable!'

Tascher. 5 December:

'Reached Smorgoni, little town; lodged there. Resources here which we have the misery of seeing pillaged without being able to profit from it. Found a detachment of the regiment. Amazement at seeing clean well-turned out men.'

Also getting to this major 'country town [*bourg*] of 200 timber houses with a number of villages within reach' where Charles XII's army had gone into winter quarters for the last time in 1708–9, Boulart finds

'some horses come from France, which are being distributed among the various batteries of the Guard. My battery still being the best mounted, I'm not given any.'

Noting that the thermometer on this upland has fallen to -20° Réaumur [-12.5° C], Cesare de Laugier, as he trudges on along the 'good road' that leads to Smorgoni, is struck by 'some birds falling from frozen trees' a phenomenon which had even impressed Charles XII's Swedish soldiers a century ago:

'The ground no longer presents anything but an enormous crystallised and impracticable surface. No one who still has a horse can any longer make use of it. In the air a great silence. Not a breath of wind. Anything that lives or stirs, even the wind, seems to be pierced through, frozen, stricken dead. Those of our men who've so far been able to preserve the greatest constancy are at the end of their tether.'

Many men remember Smorgoni very well, having been there in early July. It's

'a long village strung out along the road and situated in a region of immense forests. Its inhabitants hunted bears, sold their furs, and trained the young bears to do gymnastics in Europe as a spectacle. Not waiting for us they've fled with their merchandise and their pupils.'

Continuous suffering can be relieved by weird, almost surrealistic outbursts. A good comrade of Griois', a Colonel Cottin, still has his servant. The party have just reached Smorgoni and are having to defend the house they've occupied, and Cottin's

'threatening to run our assailants through with his sword and lunging
out with great thrusts through the crack of the door and windows.'
He's just giving orders to his servant when, for the first time, he notices the
man's face is as smoke-blackened as everyone else's. 'What shocked him
most was the dirtiness of the man's ears.' His arms flailing 'like two
telegraphs' Cottin shouts at him:

"How dare you present yourself in front of superior officers, colonels,
with your face and ears smothered in filth! Have you forgotten the
respect due to them? Since we left Moscow I've lost part of my belongings and my horses by your fault, and I've never reproached you. *But to
present yourself with a dirty face like yours, that's the limit!* Get out, go and
wash, and for God's sake *wash your ears!*'

Everyone, not least the servant, who's 'stupefied', thinks Cottin must be
joking. But he isn't. 'Probably it was the last straw.' The party doesn't think
poor Cottin who, for all his firmness of character, is coughing 'mouthfuls
of blood' where he lies on the ground at nights, will even get as far as the
next bivouac. But he does. And one day distributes to them all he has left:
'For my part I got a shirt and four blocks of chocolate.' Cottin himself will
live to laugh at his own strange outburst.

This isn't an army where secrets can be kept; and by now almost everyone,
at least on the staff, knows what's in the wind – that the Emperor's leaving.
At 2 p.m. on 5 December IHQ reaches Smorgoni. 'One hour after his
arrival,' Napoleon says to Roustam:

'"Roustam, fix everything in my carriage. We're leaving."'

They're to take all the cash they can – Roustam's to ask First Secretary
Méneval to supply it. Upon Méneval's applying to Paymaster *Guillaume
Peyrusse* – who, unlike himself, is still in the best of health – Peyrusse gives
him 60,000 francs in gold. Of this Méneval passes on 14,000 francs to *Constant Wairy*, the chief valet. As for the remainder, Roustam divides it up into
three parts: 'one-third in a compartment of the carriage, one-third in a silver-gilt chocolate pot, and the last third, in rolls, in the double-bottomed
case'. Everyone's asking him what's afoot. Castellane, in the *salon de service*,[9]
is 'greatly astonished to hear that the Emperor's leaving'. But not, among
others, his valet:

'About half an hour later the Emperor sent for me in his room and said
to me:

'"Constant, I'm leaving. I thought I'd been able to take you with me;
but on reflection I see that several carriages would draw attention. It's
essential I'm not held up. I've given orders for you to be able to leave as
soon as my horses get back. So you'll be following me at a short distance."

'I was feeling very ill,'

which, Constant thinks, is 'why the Emperor didn't want me to leave on the
box, as I asked to, to give him all the care he was accustomed to.'[10]

All the army corps commanders – Murat, Eugène, Ney, Mortier,
Bessières, Lefèbvre and Davout – have been summoned to a meeting at 7

p.m. Only the wounded Oudinot, who's gone on ahead, and Victor, some miles behind with the rearguard, are absent. For form's sake Napoleon pretends to seek the marshals' advice. Of course everyone knows it's a foregone conclusion. But Bessières has been ordered to take it upon himself to broach the matter. Should not His Majesty leave for Paris?

'No sooner had the first words been said than he flew into a violent rage, saying that "only my most mortal enemy could propose I should abandon the army in its present situation." He even went further, for he made a movement to draw his sword and throw himself at the Marshal.'

Whereupon Bessières (so at least he'll tell Baudus afterwards) replies 'with studied coldness':

'"Even when you've killed me, it'll be no less true that you no longer have an army, that you can't stay here because we can no longer protect you."'

Pure amateur theatricals, says Baudus, 'because we have proofs that his project to leave had already been decided on'. However, the ritual has to be gone through. And Napoleon, who's not above such amateur theatricals, pretends to let himself be convinced. Only his choice of Murat to take over as commander-in-chief causes universal dismay. Least of all does 'King Murat' want it. Ever since the Winkovo camp only his wife's urgent warnings have dissuaded him from emulating Jérôme Bonaparte,[11] quitting the army, and going home. Now his presence of mind deserts him completely. In vain he invokes his ignorance of army administration. As for matters of protocol, he protests, he'll be only too glad to waive them and step aside in favour of Eugène (whom he openly detests). Napoleon tells his 'Neapolitan *pantalone*' sharply do as he's told. Meeting over. To Rapp he says:

'"Well, Rapp, I'm leaving tonight for Paris. France's welfare and that of this unfortunate army necessitate my presence there. I'm leaving the King of Naples in command."'

When Rapp objects that his departure will depress the army, he replies:

'"I must keep an eye on Austria and keep Prussia under control."'

Rapp, aware of the intensity of Prussian hatred from his time as governor of Danzig, says he's sceptical about the latter possibility. For a while, hands clasped behind his back, Napoleon paces to and fro. Says nothing. Then:

'"When I'm at the head of the 120,000 men I'm going to organise, the Prussians will think twice before declaring war on me."'

To Rapp it's obvious that Napoleon's still labouring under a delusion that the army only has to go into winter quarters at Vilna to be able to put up a firm resistance. Finally Napoleon orders him to second Ney.

Soon the rumour has reached everyone. Told by his servant Louis that things are being prepared for the Emperor's departure ('which at first I didn't believe') Mailly-Nesle – 'for the first time during the retreat' – is stricken by anxiety. What if he can't get his promised certificate to allow him to take the waters in France?

'But a few moments later a page told us the Emperor's carriage was ready, and that he was leaving for Vilna to prepare victuals *for fear of wastage*'

– the explanation, so Dariale's told Castellane, that's to be put about, 'I know very well he's going further than that.' This is the moment, Mailly-Nesle feels, to turn to one of his fellow-aristocrats. Slipping in among the top brass, he gets Narbonne to promise him he'll have his certificate. Narbonne also sends for his ADC Castellane and tells him he's to be sent on mission to Berlin. The suave, well-liked diplomat of the *ancien régime* is to do what he can to play down the news of the Grand Army's destruction – which will certainly throw King Frederick William's subjects into transports of joy – and keep him faithful to the French alliance. Not that Narbonne's leaving right now. He and his aides still have many icy days marching ahead of them.

General Delaborde still has his carriage, but his supply of candles has run out. Dryly humorous as usual he, told he'll soon be receiving an official proclamation, merely tells Paul de Bourgoing to keep their 'spluttering light of a splinter of resinous wood' burning, to read it by:

'"You see, my friend, it's a vestal's job I'm entrusting you with. Bear in mind it's to read the Emperor's order that you're going to keep the sacred fire burning. It's said he wants to talk to some of his generals this evening. Perhaps he'll summon me. I must be able to read his orders on the spot. Under such circumstances I shouldn't like to be a moment late."'

Whereupon Delaborde quietly takes a nap.

Evidently Caulaincourt has prepared everything for immediate departure and the meeting with the marshals can't have taken long. Under its commanding officer, Szeptycki, Zalusky's squadron of Polish Guard Lancers, 'bivouacked along an enclosure', is on duty. 'A brazier was burning in front of us.' A relative of the same name, Lieutenant Adam Zalusky, is standing at the head of 'a column of dismounted cavalrymen'. The two officers are enjoying

'a honeycomb for dessert and it was getting rather late, when suddenly we were told to order the squadron to mount.'

Some Cossacks in the offing? Zalusky, not regarding his cousin or another officer as fit for such a foray, leaves them in charge of others of the same ilk, and

'the squadron assembled. We were ordered to go into the courtyard of the château, a vast antique timber building. We found the courtyard's right wing already occupied by the Horse Chasseurs. Extremely curious to know what was afoot, we drew up to their left.'

It's between 8 and 9 p.m. Suddenly Zalusky sees

'two coaches with lanterns lit come forward. The Emperor, with a numerous suite, appeared on the steps of the house.'

Henckens, in the Sacred Squadron, standing there beside his superb steed Cerberus and unfamiliar with these personages' appearance, asks his aristocratic young Colonel Talhouët – who until Moscow had been one of Napoleon's adjutants – to identify them for him.

'The Emperor came out of the house where the conference had taken place. His air altogether pensive and with his characteristic cowlick hanging down on his forehead, he sat down on a milestone.[12] As we made to mount, he gave Grouchy the order to leave the officers standing by their horses. After quite a long wait General Caulaincourt turned up with four sleighs, very well harnessed up.'

After which everything goes at its usual breakneck speed:

'The Emperor took his seat with Caulaincourt in the first carriage. Lobau, Duroc and Lefèvre-Desnouëttes in the second. And in the third two other persons of his suite.'

So quickly is it all happening that Castellane sees how Count Lobau,

'hasn't even time to speak to his nephew. The carriage had already been brought out when he was told to get into it.'

Captain Count Wonsowicz, 'a Polish officer who'd been through the whole campaign, a man of proven courage and devotion', is to ride at one side of the first carriage, as guide and interpreter. Roustam on the other. Fagalde and Amodru are to be outriders. A footman and a workman are to follow in a barouche on runners. The second carriage is to leave a few minutes later. The 'personages' in the third, Fain, Bacler d'Albe,[13] Doctor Yvan, and Baron Mounier (Third Secretary), are to follow on. Paul de Bourgoing sees the first carriage get under way,[14] escorted by *Chasseurs à Cheval.* 'The Chasseurs set off,' Zalusky goes on. 'Our squadron followed the carriages at a gallop.' Outside Smorgoni, Colonel Szymanowski, meeting the first carriage with another squadron of the Polish Guard Lancers, notices on its doors the letters 'SA':

'The French, not losing their sense of sardonic humour even now, said they stood for '*Sans adieu'* ['without so much as a good-bye'].'

And as it flits by, Roman Soltyk's friend Grabowski, also of the Polish Guard lancers, thinks he hears some of the 'old grumblers' muttering: 'Ah yes, it's *Colin-qui-court* ('Colin who's running away'), a sarcastic pun on Caulaincourt's name:[15] About one mile outside Smorgoni', Brandt, with the few survivors of the Vistula Legion,[16] is overtaken by

'a big vehicle, a sort of coach, on which a front seat had been improvised, arriving at a considerable speed through the mass of fugitives. It was preceded by a horseman [Amodru] wearing a green riding-coat and who'd taken no other precaution against the unspeakable cold than to wrap his ears in a small shawl. I don't know what happened; but suddenly I saw him draw his sword and strike out at a man who was on the road and who tottered and fell over backwards. The carriage instantly passed on. Later it was said that it was the Emperor's carriage, that the man was an orderly officer, and that the soldier who'd been corrected in this way had probably said some unsuitable word.'[17]

In a long village beyond the town Dumonceau, too, has been ordered to be ready to leave at 9 p.m. in command of an imperial escort. To go where? No one tells him. But since it's not his turn for duty he, 'pleased to escape a nocturnal ride which looked like being most painful', lets his friend Captain

Post command it instead. ('Though I afterwards regretted having been excused when I became aware of the mission's importance.') And at 10 p.m. Napoleon's carriage turns up[18] and Post's escort replaces the Chasseur detachment. That Colbert's men – by now most of them are Poles – are to escort the carriage is explicable. Already some 500 Chasseurs have died en route. But the Poles, as we've seen, are in good trim. And they've just been joined by their '5th squadron, newly formed at Danzig'. But, says Zalusky,

'it was fitted out in its parade uniforms and made up of young, still inexperienced men. So it was suffering greatly from the sharpest cold (-22°) of the whole campaign.'[19]

By midnight Napoleon, 'sound asleep' in his carriage, reaches Ochmiana; but by now the night's so cold that one-third of its escort has fallen behind. Getting down 'to heed a call of nature' Roustam sees

'a light, quite close to me, in a hut. I go inside to light my pipe, I see some people lying on straw. I recognise an officer of the Gendarmes of the Guard, who seemed astounded to see me, and said. "What chance brings you here?" I told him the Emperor was there. "How lucky he didn't get here earlier!" he said. "An hour ago the Cossacks were here. They made a *hurrah* on the village.'

Roustam realises the party isn't yet out of trouble. Far from it. For only a quarter of an hour ago two light infantry regiments and a detachment of Loison's Neapolitan cavalry have been attacked by 600 Cossacks under the Russian Colonel Seslavine, together with regular cavalry and light artillery on sledges. The Russians are only a few hundred yards outside Ochmiana. So cold is the night that Loison's men (so Kergorre will hear next day) 'hadn't been able to fire their muskets'. Even so, they've driven off their assailants by sheer weight of numbers. Hogendorp's idea of sending them forward to Ochmiana may prove fatal to Loison's men. But it has saved Napoleon – so far – from falling into Russian hands! When Caulaincourt sees them he notices that

'these troops, believing the main army was covering them, were so full of confidence that, the cold being so extreme, they hadn't even posted proper outposts'.

The night is extremely cold and pitch dark. The carriage has drawn up – an hour will pass before the second will arrive – in the main square, where two fresh detachments of Polish cavalry, 'one of Guard Lancers, the other of the 7th Regiment of Lancers of the Vistula', are 'drawn up in line of battle'. Among the officers who place 'themselves in a semicircle around the carriage door' is General Gratien, commanding Loison's division in Loison's continued absence. Another is a Saxon surgeon named *Geissler,* who notices that the carriage, 'drawn by six little Lithuanian horses, is draped in furs'. Utterly impressed by this man whose word has made and unmade most of Europe's states and monarchs, Geissler studies his features:

'His face hadn't changed at all since 1807, 1808 and 1809. We closely considered this powerful mortal from distance of a few paces. He wore a serious air and seemed to be in very good health.'

The troops' acclaim has to be suppressed – the local situation, everyone's aware, is utterly precarious. What are His Majesty's chances of getting through? One in three? One in ten?

'Such a secret couldn't be kept for long, and already the Russians might well have sent troops to intercept him. Going into the house of the local military governor, he studied his map of Lithuania, examining it very closely. His generals tried to dissuade him from going on. But he rejected their advice. To set off in broad daylight, indeed, seemed the most dangerous of all expedients.'

Wonsowicz is amazed at his determination to press on. And when he asks Wonsowicz whether he has any escort for him, Wonsowicz says there are 266 lancers. That'll do, says, Napoleon. He'll take them:

'"We're leaving at once. The night's dark enough for the Russians not to see us. Besides, one must always trust to one's luck. Without that one gets nowhere."'

So the fresh lancers are ordered to mount:

'But before leaving again he summoned his orderly officer, took a pair of pistols into his *coupé* and gave them to him, recommending that he place himself on the seat with General Lefèvre-Desnouëttes. The mameluke Roustam got into a sledge immediately following the Emperor's carriage; and Colonel Stoïkowski, commanding the escort, was given orders to keep close to the carriage door. Here are the ever-memorable words the Emperor, after all these preparations, addressed to those around him:

'"I'm counting on you all. Let's go! Keep a sharp lookout to right and left of the road."'

Then, turning to these devoted and fearless men, to whom he'd given his pistols, he added:

'"In the event of certain danger, kill me rather than let me be taken."'

'Count Wonsowicz, deeply moved at an order no one would have obeyed except in the barbarous ages of paganism, said:

'"Does Your Majesty permit me to translate what I've just heard to our Poles?"'

'"Yes, let them know what I've said."'

'Those words were repeated in the Polish language, and the lancers shouted with one voice: "We'll rather let ourselves be cut in pieces than allow anyone come near you." All this happened at 2 a.m. on 6 December, at a time of year and in a latitude where the nights last seventeen hours. And Napoleon was prepared to confront such dangers! The Russians had only withdrawn a short distance.'

Roustam returns to the carriage. A crack of the whip, and off it goes again 'at top speed' into the black icy night. Outside the town the Cossacks are only a few hundred yards from the road:

'Where the mist was thinner their lights could be seen on the skyline just outside Ochmiana, especially to the left of the road. The silent procession could even hear the voices of the enemy sentries.'

But nothing happens. The Cossacks don't spot the carriage. Are left behind.

It's one of those fiercely cold nights one gets in the north. No snow is falling. So extreme is the cold that after a few miles 50 at most of the Poles are still with the carriage: 'The horses kept falling, and as a result, the riders having no remounts, at the second relay we'd none left.' Only a small advance guard's been sent ahead to the next post- house, at Rownopol, reached at dawn. Two others have been placed out in echelon along the road:

> 'By the time they reached Rownopol there were only 36! These were divided, half going before and half after us. Of all the detachments there weren't fifteen men still with us when we reached the relay.'

There, in a temperature that's fallen to -28° C, new horses are waiting, and the remaining Poles are replaced by a detachment of Neapolitan Horse Guards, under the Duke of Rocca Romana, who'd got there with Hogendorp. 'Some of these Neapolitan troopers, dressed in [sky-blue and yellow] parade uniforms, froze during the transit and littered the route with their corpses' – tomorrow Labaume will see them lying by the roadside 'showing that Napoleon had passed that way'.

The third relay post is at Miednicky. Here the Duke of Bassano himself, alias Foreign Minister Maret, has been waiting for it. Getting into Napoleon's carriage he gives Caulaincourt his own in exchange – and the Master of the Horse goes on ahead to Vilna which he reaches almost simultaneously with the returning Hogendorp. Going straight to his headquarters, he finds the Dutchman

> 'having to rouse to action people who were just leaving M. de Bassano's ball. They'd been dancing while others froze.'

Caulaincourt asks Hogendorp urgently to obtain some post-horses for the next stage of the imperial transit.

At 10.15 a.m. Napoleon's carriage reaches Vilna. But doesn't enter it. Circumventing the town wall, it halts at 'a country house half-destroyed by fire' in the Kovno suburb. Now there are

> 'barely eight of the escort left, including General Lefèbvre-Desnouëttes. Such of the Neapolitans as were still acting as escort had frost-bitten hands and feet.'

Just then or a moment later Caulaincourt comes out from the town, where he has bought fur-lined boots for the whole party. To his alarm he sees the Duke of Rocca Romana

> 'pressing both his hands against the stove. I'd great difficulty in making him realise he was risking losing them, and in making him go out and rub them in the snow – a treatment which so increased his pains that it was more than he could do to persevere in it',

so that Rocca Romana loses several fingers and toes. Meanwhile Hogendorp, in response to Caulaincourt's urgent request, has ordered the governor of Vilna city, General Roch-Godart to provide 27 relay horses, 'which I was so very fortunate, albeit only with great difficulty, as to find in the midst of a mob of troopers who were in the main square. I also managed to assemble some 60 mounted men to escort the carriages, so great was the disorder beginning to be.'

Having furnished the escort and the relays with six of Maret's horses and his own postilion, Hogendorp, *quâ* ADC to the Emperor, wants to go to him. But now it's nearly midday. And Napoleon has gone – at 11.30 a.m. 'Such had been his haste, he'd already left. Just as we were leaving' the second carriage, with Duroc and Lobau in it, had caught up.

An hour and a quarter has sufficed for Vilna. In no time Napoleon is speeding westwards toward the Niemen – which no doubt he's privately regretting ever having crossed.

Throughout that day and the following night, the carriage flies on over the snowy plains. Never will Caulaincourt

'remember suffering so much as on that journey between Vilna and Kovno. The Emperor was wearing thick wool and was covered with a good rug, with his legs in fur boots, thrust into a bearskin bag. Yet he complained so of the cold that I had to cover him with my own bearskin rug. Our breaths froze on our lips, forming small icicles under the nose and eyebrows and around the eyelids. All the carriage's upholstery, particularly its hood, was frozen hard and white from our rising breath. When we reached Kovno, two hours before dawn, the Emperor was shivering as with the ague.'

That's at 5 a.m. on 7 December. They halt at 'a kind of tavern kept by an Italian scullion who'd set up in business since the army had passed that way' where Amodru, riding on ahead, has had a fire lit. 'The meal seemed superb, simply because it was hot. Good bread and a fowl, a table and chairs, a tablecloth – to us all these were novelties.'

But dare they pass through Prussia? Napoleon insists it's Caulaincourt's sole responsibility to decide which route to take to Warsaw – 'which, I confess, seemed to me a heavy responsibility, and worried me a lot'. He decides to chance it, and they set off. Crossing the Niemen bridge they turn left for Mariempol and Gumbinnen. Climbing the

'the almost perpendicular slope which one must surmount en route for Mariempol, we were forced to get down. At every moment the horses kept falling or losing their foothold and the carriage was on the verge of slipping backwards and tumbling over the precipice. We heaved at the wheels; and at last reached Mariempol.'

And all the time Napoleon is talking and talking – an endless monologue which Caulaincourt scribbles down at their overnight halts while he snatches a few moment's sleep...

CHAPTER 22

'THE VERY AIR SEEMED FROZEN'

Reactions to Napoleon's departure – a splendid dawn – 'we were completely iced up'
– 'I've seen soldiers carrying officers on their shoulders' – 'only a very few were still
themselves' – 'they couldn't even assemble the Old Guard's service battalion ... a sen-
try had frozen solid on his feet' – 'but Ney was there!' – not a very cruel death? – Le
Roy's prayer – 'We've done everything humanly possible' – 'they told us it was Vilna'

The army, Paul de Bourgoing thinks, reacts to the Emperor's departure
'differently as between the regiments and the staffs, according to the character of each'. Emerging from the last Imperial Headquarters at Smorgoni
just as it's being dissolved, Philippe de Ségur, Assistant Prefect of the
Palace, runs into

'Colonel Fezensac with his regiment's eagle, escorted by some officers and
NCOs, the sole remains of his unit. In a voice full of emotion I told him:
"the Emperor's leaving us." After a moment this colonel, at first silent and
pensive, replied: "He's doing the right thing!" Fezensac's position and
mine were different; but this firm word, said in passing, restored my firmness of will. Such sangfroid gave me back my own. I tacitly accepted this
noble example, to which it today pleases me to bear witness.'

But to Roman Soltyk, that ardent Polish patriot and Bonapartist in the
Topographical Department, Napoleon's departure seems to be the signal
for the army's complete dissolution. 'Everyone', says Fezensac, 'did whatever came into his head.' 'A great man cannot be replaced,' Ségur thinks.
'The Guard's veterans fell into disorder. It was a general *sauve-qui-peut*. 'As
long as he'd stuck with us,' Dumonceau confesses,

'our total confidence in him had helped to reassure and support us in
our resignation. Now he was abandoning us, and all hope of any happy
outcome vanished with him.'

Even the Old Guard seems smitten. 'No one was expecting Napoleon to
leave us,' least of all Dr Réné Bourgeois:

'He'd left the army about a quarter of an hour and I'd gone up to one
of the Guard's bivouacs where there were some senior officers, when a
major of the Grenadiers came up to me and addressing one of them,
said in a loud voice:

'"Well, there you are then. So the brigand's gone, has he?"

'"He's just gone by," the other replied, "same as in Egypt."

'Astonished at this expression – "brigand" – and not knowing whom
it referred to, I paid close attention, and as a result of this conversation
learnt that it was Napoleon who was being spoken of.'

Captain François, who'd himself been in the army General Bonaparte had
abandoned in Egypt in 1799, is categorical:

'This news destroyed what was left of the army's courage. The men were
sombre, and lost all hope of ever seeing their own country again.'

351

But others, perhaps most, are already too stunned for it to have much effect one way or the other. On Griois' party for instance it makes 'little impression'[1] Many, like Griois, Dupuy and Vionnet, realise on reflection that it's the only thing Napoleon could have done: 'He had to think as much about his empire as his army.' Others again are philosophical. When the remains of I Corps reach Smorgoni next day (6 December) and hear that the Emperor's gone, Le Roy, Guillaume and Jacquet take it for granted

'he'd be collecting fresh troops to come to our aid while we were at Vilna or on the Niemen. Soon we didn't bother our heads any more about it. We had other things than politics to attend to!'

They're only kept going by thinking how nice it'll be to get home. It's the only thought that's keeping up their courage. To von Muraldt, too, it seems that though the Emperor's departure 'soon became known, it made no particular impression on the great majority. Each was too preoccupied with himself and his own misery.' But Castellane has a private grief. He'd spent

'part of the night copying out the 29th Bulletin from the draft corrected by His Majesty's hand. It had been passed to me by the amiable and witty secretary Baron Mounier. The words "gèle difficilement" [incorrect French for 'it's freezing badly'] were written in His Majesty's handwriting.'

From Narbonne he's heard that, like the Emperor's other ADC's, he's been given 30,000 francs and been promoted. But while Gourgaud and the other officiers d'ordonnance have been given 6,000 francs a head, the adjutants 'have been overlooked' though 'they've done quite as much service'. The oversight festers.

Dumonceau, 6 December:

'Even before dawn we were on the march again in a beautiful winter twilight under a splendid starry sky. The atmosphere was calm and limpid but the cold more rigorous than ever. It was said to be touching -30° Réaumur [-18.75° C]. Even the very air seemed frozen into light flakes of transparent ice which were flitting about in space. Then we saw the horizon gradually lighting up with a burning red, the sun appear radiant through a light misty radiation its fires set fire to. The whole snowy plain became splendid with purple, and scintillated as if sown with rubies. It was magnificent to behold. The road wasn't encumbered with its usual crowd. We marched at our ease, though always tiringly because of the ice.'

Some debris of a convoy of biscuit intended for the army's rearguard, scattered over its surface, looks repulsive, but is avidly consumed by all who're passing by. Tascher:

'Excessive cold. Great number of men dropping dead on the road, sometimes stripped before expiring and left there naked on the snow, still alive. Bivouacked with the Army of Italy, 2½ leagues behind headquarters.'

In the breathtaking cold Lejeune, like everyone else, sees

'the road littered with dead men. The carriage wheels, turning with difficulty, caught up these ice-covered corpses and dragged them along, sliding. Haxo and I were marching arm in arm to support each other on the ice. A soldier and an officer were marching beside us. The soldier took a bit of Russian black bread somewhat bigger than a man's fist out of his pocket and greedily bit into it. The officer, surprised to see this bread, offered the grenadier a 5-franc piece for it.

'"No," replied the soldier, biting furiously into his bit of hard bread, like a lion jealous of its prey.

'"I beg of you, sell me your bread. Here's 10 francs."

'"No, no, no!" And the bread dwindled by half.

'"I'm dying. Save my life. Here are 20 francs."

'At this, with a savage air, the grenadier's teeth took away another enormous mouthful. He took the 20 francs. and gave away what was left, regretting the deal.'

'We were completely iced up,' Lejeune goes on:

'The breath coming from one's mouth was thick as smoke, and attached itself in icicles on our hair, our eyebrows, our beard and our moustache. These icicles became so thick they intercepted our vision and respiration. Breaking the ones which were getting in my way, General Haxo, seeing my face and nose were discoloured and waxen, told me they were frost-bitten. In fact I felt nothing at all. I had to make haste to rub them with snow. A minute or two's rubbing got the blood circulating again. But the reaction of the heat after the cold on the hand I'd used to do it with caused me horrible pain, and I needed all my willpower to stand it. A moment later Engineer-Colonel Emi had the same pains for the same reasons. He threw himself down and rolled on the ground in despair. Not wishing to abandon him, we had to hit him violently to make him get up.'

Constant, the Emperor's abandoned valet, sees 'gunners putting their hands under their horses' nostrils, to try to get a little warmth from those animals' forceful breathing'. Dysentery, too, – or anyway diarrhoea[2] – is ravaging the column:

'Its victims were promenading their frightful skeletons, covered with a dry and livid skin. The nakedness of these unfortunates, who had to halt at every step, was the most terrifying picture death could show us. Others, almost all of them cavalrymen, having lost or burnt their shoes, were marching with bare legs and feet. The frozen skin and muscles were exfoliating themselves like successive layers of wax statues. The bones were exposed, and their temporary insensitivity to any pain in them sustained them in the vain hope of again seeing their own homes.'

Le Roy, getting to Smorgoni, sees

'several soldiers and officers unable to do their trousers up. I myself helped one of these unfortunates to put his *** back and button himself up. He was crying like a child. With my own eyes I saw a major make a hole in the seat of his trousers so as not to have to undress to relieve himself. For the rest, he wasn't the only one to take this disgusting precaution.'

Franz Roeder, too, is heeding a call of nature in the bushes when some Cossacks ride up. They immediately strip him of his fur coat – the one that had belonged to the voltigeur officer killed at Krasnoïe – torn and blood-stained though it is. But then, to Roeder's amazement – and also Sergeant-Major Vogel's, who's staring helplessly from another bush – the raiders suddenly desist and gallop away. What's happened? Luckily they've mistaken Roeder's Hessian Order of Merit for the Order of Vladimir, which has the same ribbon! 'Now, Vogel,' declares Roeder, 'I'm really beginning to believe it's God's will we shall get to Vilna!'

But the equally faithful Guillaume has caught cold – last night he seemed to have a slight temperature. How's he feeling? Get up, let's go, says Le Roy when morning comes and all the others in their group have already left Smorgoni. Guillaume takes the reins of horse and pony, but 'the poor devil couldn't stay on his legs, kept falling down'. Le Roy suggests he get on the horse he'd provided them with, and ride on ahead to the next overnight halt. He and Jacquet will follow on, leading the pony: "Get on with it, then! There's the rearguard firing!" But the end has come for poor ever-faithful, ever-resourceful Guillaume. Both his feet are frost-bitten. He has a splitting headache. The fever's strangling him. If he goes on it'll only be for them helplessly to see him die en route. They're just passing Smorgoni's last houses when they see an open door:

'"Carry me inside," says Guillaume, "and get going."'

But at least they can leave him the pony, the bearskin rug and the food bag? 'If you can't catch up today, try to make it tomorrow!' Guillaume's just protesting he's still got the money Le Roy had entrusted to him at the Berezina, when one of Ney's ADCs comes by and – though Le Roy protests he can't leave his brave servant – drags him out into the street:

'It was then, seeing the road deserted, I got going. And I did well to, for I hadn't done one league before I saw Cossacks behind me trying to carry off the rearguard. But Ney was there!'

One man sorry to leave Smorgoni is Brandt:

'It was the first place where we could get something for money. We'd also found some troops there who were in quite good order. We bought some bread at not too excessive a price, as well as some rice and a little coffee, from an old Jewess. It seemed to break her heart to separate herself from her victuals. It was the first coffee I'd drunk for several months [Brandt had only briefly halted in the Moscow suburbs] and though there was neither sugar nor milk it was a great comfort to me.'

Then Smorgoni too is left behind.

From there to Ochmiana, as Napoleon's escort had found out, is 24 versts (fifteen miles). An 8-hour march for what until yesterday was IHQ. To have been overlooked while Gourgaud and the other wearers of sky-blue and silver uniforms have each been accorded 6,000 francs, is evidently causing resentment. Ever since Moscow, where the egocentric Gourgaud was made a baron of the Empire, Castellane, who's merely been promoted, has been finding the arrogance of this 'bad bedfellow hard to live with' insufferable. Now, this night at Ochmiana ('nasty little timber town') the staff officers are 'piled up on top of one another in a wretched barn' and Gourgaud's 'leaning against a barrel, violently complaining of there being no room for him on the floor. His stupid monologue irritated me. Since his Moscow nomination his pride knows no limits, I reproached him for it. One word led to another, I got up, grabbed my sabre, he his; we went outside to fight.'

Their comrades protest that this is neither the time nor the place for a duel. But it's the cold that

'did more to send us back inside. We couldn't hold our sabres. To risk one's life for a place on the ground after escaping so many dangers proves the extent of our recklessness and indifference.'

Also no doubt the dissolution of headquarters morale. Now

'we're often being refused any water. Because of the cold the Grenadiers of the Guard, [though] well paid [to do so], often prefer not to go and look for any. Then we have snow melted in our pannikins.'

That night Prince Eugène and his remaining 500–600 men bivouac in a church. Hitherto the wives of Colonel Dubois of the 2nd Line and of the intendant-commissary of Pino's division, who'd joined their husbands in Moscow, have been travelling, well wrapped up in furs and straw, in a sleigh. That morning they'd left Smorgoni and, as usual, gone on ahead. But now the Réaumur mercury falling to -24° has been too much for them. Both are dead when their husbands catch up with the sleigh at Zapray. But hard-frozen corpses are part of the landscape. Le Roy's just about to lie down supperless to get some sleep on the earthen floor of a cottage where there's at least a stove burning, when he sees two corpses underneath it. They smell so nasty he goes out and sleeps in some hay beside a bivouac fire instead:

'Anyone who wanted to profit from it had to keep it going. They did this so well that all the horse cloths and timbers went into it.'

At Ochmiana Dumonceau and the rest of the Lancer Brigade come upon Loison's division – some 10,000 men, he thinks, in summer uniforms. Also some squadrons of no less lightly clad Neapolitan cavalry. And hears about the previous evening's clash with the Cossacks just before Napoleon had got there, during which part of the town's large supplies of provisions had gone up in flames. Even so, the lancers get a more than welcome ration of meat, flour and brandy. As for Loison's men, when Fezensac gets there he's shocked to see how

'after only two days of bivouacking, the cold had reduced them to almost the same state as ourselves. Finally the other regiments' bad example had discouraged them. They were being swept away in the general rout.'

To Kergorre the division seems to have been

'wiped out by the cold during the night. These troops were totally useless and even harmful, since they swelled the number of the famished and the disbanded. The men could no longer hold their muskets with their frozen hands, even though they'd taken the precaution of wrapping them up in linen.'

For General Count *Wilhelm Hochberg*, future Margrave of Baden, commanding a unit in what had been IX Corps, 7 December is 'the most terrible day in my life. There were 30 degrees of frost. I could only assemble 50 of my men; the others, 200 to 300 of them, lay on the ground, frozen. The last remains of IX Corps were annihilated. Doumerc's cavalry, which had made up the extreme rearguard, was destroyed, it too, during that unhappy night of 6/7 December.'

On the other hand the wind, when morning comes, isn't quite so strong and Colbert's men are entertained to another brilliant dawn. But soon they're shocked to come across more detritus of Loison's ill-fated division, left behind while advancing along the Ochmiana road:

'We found the sides of the road littered with dead soldiers whose regular turnout and fine clothing contrasted with the rags we were used to seeing. Coming as they had out of good cantonments and consequently less acclimatised than ourselves, they'd seen themselves instantly decimated.'

All along the roadside Cesare de Laugier keeps seeing

'the corpses of the Neapolitan vélites. Recognisable by their rich brand-new clothes, they showed the Emperor had gone this way.'

Kergorre, sharing some potatoes with his three companions and General Grandeau, notes that the thermometer has fallen from -16° to -28° Réaumur:

'That morning the snow had a sharper sound than usual. The sun was so red you could look straight into it, as you do the moon, though the sky was cloudless. An icy mist swathed us, we could only breathe by putting some cloth over mouth and nose.'

That day Berthier sends off a dispatch to the Emperor that won't reach its addressee – so fast is his transit – until he's in Paris. Line by line, wasting no words, he details the catastrophe:

'Almost all the men of the Train have disappeared ['*disparu*' also means 'dead']. Only the gunners, out of a sense of honour, are leading horses, but many are succumbing, not even being able to hold a bridle. The Young Guard is completely disbanded. The Old presents scarcely 600 men together. The cavalry is almost completely disbanded. I've had all the vehicles carrying the trophies burnt, except one that carries everything that's most precious. The whole of Rapp's face is frost-bitten. Three of your muleteers have just been found dead. Last night 20 of the horses pulling the Treasure died. We've taken horses belonging to individuals in hopes it will reach Vilna.'

Catching up with the 85th toward evening at Polé, Le Roy bivouacs almost alone with Jacquet in a barn full of grain, straw and hay. For 10 francs they buy a chicken, mix it with some beef that's been left over and make soup:

'Ah, what a soup! Poor Guillaume, I said at each spoonful. If you could only have such a beef-tea you'd soon be well again!'

All night he can't sleep for thinking of him:

'Poor lad, he was so attached to me! Took such care of my interests! He's certainly the only servant I've had who never deceived me.'

356

Every evening Paul de Bourgoing's teenaged servant Victor, also so gallant, so cheerful, so devoted, has always been turning up – even if half an hour late – at Delaborde's bivouac. But now an evening comes when the lad doesn't show up at all. 'I inquired after him in vain. And I've never seen him since.' So ends the epic of the heroic little Parisian street-urchin who'd so desperately wanted to be a drummer-boy but who'd been turned down because of his puny physique.[3]

Berthier has got over his fit of despair and is riding with 'King Murat in the Emperor's berline, surrounded by 200 grenadiers of the Guard'. The adjutants, among them Castellane and Flahaut (promoted general of brigade at Napoleon's departure), are 'taking turns to sit on the box behind':

> 'I did one league like this, then I went ahead on foot. No better proof of our misery, as Flahaut caused me to observe, than to see a general and a superior officer count themselves happy to be able to sit up behind a carriage! For the rest, the greatest personages were regarding it as a stroke of luck. M. de Narbonne and others of the Emperor's ADCs took turns to sit up behind his Majesty's carriage.'

Murat has immediately shown his strategic, logistic and administrative ineptitude by wanting to send the feeble wreckage of III Corps, now march-ing with the Guard, back to support Victor. An order impossible to imple-ment. And therefore quite simply ignored. 'General Ledru, who commanded us, just continued his march.'

Now no one's riding a horse. Hardly anyone has one, even at headquar-ters. And those who have one can't use it. All those belonging to Murat's chief-of-staff Belliard have long since died and been eaten. For three days now Belliard himself – still suffering from his Borodino wound – has had to be 'carried on the backs of a 27-year-old ADC, Colonel Robert, his inten-dant Pierre Aumann, and his foster-brother'. Cesare de Laugier admires other instances of such devotion. Though himself feverish with 'dysentery', Surgeon-Major Filippi of the Royal Italian Guard has flown to the assis-tance of several officers and

> 'without a thought to the musketballs flying about his ears, given first-aid to the wounded, put them in a carriage, and with great difficulty didn't rejoin his regiment for a long while, without anyone giving a thought to him in the meantime. At last he rejoined us, and his comrades, who'd thought he was lost, welcomed him with delirious shouts of joy.'

Then there's Major Maffei, who, like several other officers, is being carried by his men (but will die at Kovno). In this most desperate of straits Larrey's still being accorded special treatment by one and all:

> 'In the midst of the army and above all of the Imperial Guard I could not perish. And in fact I owe my existence to the soldiers. Some ran to help me when, surrounded by Cossacks, I was about to be killed or taken prisoner. Others made haste to pick me up and lead me on when, my physical strength having abandoned me, I fell down in the snow. Others again, seeing me tormented by hunger, gave me such food as

they possessed. And if I presented myself at their bivouac each made room for me and I was immediately wrapped in some straw or their clothes. How many generals or superior officers were repulsed or pitilessly sent packing by their own men! But at the name of Larrey everyone got up and acclaimed it with friendly respect,'

he'll write proudly to his wife in January. Not that officers and generals, as Labaume sees with more jaundiced eye, aren't for the most part being avoided, 'so as not to have to serve them'. Generals, officers, NCOs, rankers, are all one. Bonnet comes across a grenadier sergeant named Logeat commanding

'ten or twelve men of the regiment, guarding a cart at the roadside, in full dispute with General Ledru, commanding a division of our corps. This general had taken a great fancy to what was on this cart, and Logeat was defending himself with very disrespectful words. I took his side and the general had to make do with treating us as pillagers. That evening, to console him, I sent him half a turkey and some bread the little detachment had been bringing back.'

But the adjutant-major of what once was the resplendent, the privileged Guardia d'Onore[4] sees even more shocking sights:

'I saw soldiers of the Imperial Guard stripping Intendant Joubert, who they thought was dead, while he was crying out to them: "At least let me die before you strip me of my clothes!"'

But, Cesare de Laugier consoles himself in his diary (can it be he's keeping it, like Labaume, with 'crows' feathers dipped in gunpowder'?) 'I've also seen soldiers carrying their officers on their shoulders.' The Swiss regimental doctor Heumann is such a hero. When others – among them, regrettably, Thomas Legler (but he's promised his fiancée first and foremost to look after himself) – abandon his acting-colonel Zingg, he refuses to leave him. And then there's Berthier, always charitable to beggars along the route.

Such devotion from men for their officers has been hard-earned by years of campaigning. 'All honour to the nation that could produce such men,' writes Caulaincourt in an unusual outburst of emotion, 'and to the army that can boast such soldiers!' Perhaps it's Labaume, among others, Caulaincourt is thinking of when he adds:

'And shame on the scoundrels and disloyal Frenchmen who've in any way tarnished a glory so valiantly acquired!'

Tascher. 8 December:

'Extreme fatigue forces us to make an early halt by the wayside. Did four leagues; bivouacked in a hamlet on the road, sixteen miles from Vilna. Alacrity in all eyes. Hopes of Vilna!'

The cold, it seems to Boulart,

'has become more intense. I sleep in a church, on a pew and close to a nice fire which brings on the most acute pains in my feet. The nave is packed, lots of men are dying there. Terrifying cries of "Run away! Get out! Everyone here's dying!" awaken me. I'm in a maddening state of exhaustion.'

Jomini's suffering from pleurisy. Before reaching Ochmiana the intense cold had forced him to get down from Eblé's travelling coupé and bivouac, together with the Duke of Piacenza, inside the hard-frozen cadaver of a horse, where he'd paid 3 ducats for as many spoonfuls of honey. Even so they'd had to drive away marauders armed with axes. Buying a sledge off a soldier, together with the little pony that's drawing it, he'd stipulated as condition that the soldier should take him as far as Vilna. Dozed off in the sledge. But been woken up abruptly – in a ditch. The soldier had simply tossed him into it! Now a gigantic Swiss drum-major is shaking him by the shoulders and a familiar voice is asking in a Vaudois accent: Does he really intend to end his brilliant military-literary career in a Lithuanian ditch? Helped on to Ochmiana by the drum-major, he finds a fine house intact at the entrance to the town which is in flames. The drum-major hammers on the locked door. And who should come and open if not General Barbanègre, he who five months ago had been governor of Vilna town and welcomed him as his successor? 'Along a road marked only by rigid frozen corpses' Vilna's two ex-governors pursue their way in the latter's carriage.

There are occasional Cossack incursions. Already Caulaincourt has noticed that, glutted with booty, they're neither bothering to kill men nor even take prisoners. At one point Paul de Bourgoing sees some and some Russian hussars lying dead by the roadside. But is too cold to pay much attention. And in fact the Russians are finding the going almost as hard:

'The Russian general headquarters wasn't able to follow the French as swiftly as we were, the route being so pillaged, burnt and devastated that there was no means of engaging any other troops.'

All along the road Rochechouart and Wilson have been seeing

'both sides littered with dead bodies in all postures, or with men expiring from cold, hunger and fatigue. Each of us could individually take an incredible number of prisoners. Most, stripped of their clothes by the Cossacks, were wandering about half-naked, begging us, for mercy sake, to take them prisoner. Some said they knew very well how to cook, others that they were clever hairdressers, valets, etc. We were deafened by those cries: "*Monsieur le Baron*, take me with you. I can do this, I can do that. For the love of God a bit of bread, of anything at all.'

As for the body of the Russian army, it has

'spread itself out to left and right, where it at least could subsist, even though submitting to the effects of the lethal cold which was falling equally on us all'.

In a tavern at Ochmiana the French *émigré* sees something which

'put the finishing touch to the picture of the horrible sufferings the most beautiful, the most valiant army in the world was having to endure. Two big thin faces, with no flesh on them.'

They're two Portuguese officers, stripped of their uniforms by Cossacks. One of them is

'dressed in the most bizarre fashion, long underpants, torn stockings, shoeless, a wretched waistcoat, a shirt in shreds, and for head-dress only

a black silk stocking whose foot dangled negligently behind his head.'
To their astonishment Rochechouart, who'd spent some time in Portugal
in 1801–2, addresses them in Portuguese. The man so oddly dressed turns
out to be 'the Viscount d'Asseca, from the house of Souza', from
d'Alorna's Portuguese Legion. Only by threats can he prevail on the Jewish innkeeper to provide them with sheepskins; and provides them with 'a
pair of boots taken at the Berezina and destined for myself'. They'll serve
for both of them until they get to Vilna with him. Just as they're about to
leave Ochmiana

> 'a skeleton of a woman presented herself to our shocked eyes, asking for
> something to eat, and adding after having devoured what we'd given
> her: "Messieurs, take me with you. I'm young and beautiful, I'll do any-
> thing you want." Poor woman, we left her there.'

And all they can do while passing through 'the miserable town of Ochmiana' is to get the town's *starotz* (elder), against payment, to light a fire in
the town gaol, where

> 'a hundred or so prisoner officers were behind bars, in their shirtsleeves,
> having been stripped of their coats, trousers, etc., by Cossacks and Jews'.

From the barred unglazed windows they call out to Rochechouart and his
three companions that they're dying of cold and hunger,

> 'adding to their screams signs that were well understood by my com-
> rades, who hastened to given them what was left of our provisions,
> adding some clothing'.

His companion Wlodeck explains that they're Freemasons, 'and that being
Freemasons like them and being able to do so they had to come to their
brothers' help'.

Miedniki, 'a village of 40 houses, with a brick manor house, 28 versts (17½
miles) from Vilna', is the Lancer Brigade's goal for the day. There Dumonceau catches up with his fellow-captain Post and the remains of his detachment that had escorted Napoleon. The road is hilly. Castellane's following on:

> 'The King's headquarters goes on to Miednicky (thirteen miles). Leav-
> ing at 9 a.m., we get there at 3 p.m. Horrible day. We've seen lots of
> corpses of the Neapolitan division. First it had come to meet us, then
> fallen back toward Vilna. Its soldiers fall. A little blood comes out of
> their mouths, then it's over. Seeing this sign of imminent death on their
> lips, their comrades are often giving them a blow on the shoulders,
> throwing them to the ground and stripping them before they're quite
> dead. Any number of frost-bitten feet, hands, ears.'

During that terrible night, Larrey's little Réaumur thermometer, still hanging from his coat lapel, falls to -26°, -27° and -28° (-16.25°, – 17.5° C). Afterwards he'll realise that 8/9 December had been the coldest days of the
entire retreat.[5]

Griois' misery is at its height. His clothing 'suitable at best for a mild
southern autumn, is wholly inadequate in a Russian winter'. Ever since the
Winkovo camp back in October it' has consisted of

'a gold-laced red kerseymere waistcoat, a tailcoat of light cloth, over it a one-piece riding-coat, a pair of cloth trousers buttoning up on the side, no underpants, very tight Suvarov-style boots and woollen socks. However, it had been impossible to change it, and the bearskin I'd got hold of was no substitute for the mantle-style overcoat I'd been robbed of when crossing the Berezina.'

Excellent to sleep in at nights, his bearskin is far too heavy for the road, and he has to drape it over his horse. Cutting some strips from it he's made himself

'a kind of sheath, 7 or 8 inches long, attached at the ends by a string I passed round my neck. When on the march I thrust my hands into it, for lack of gloves, and made a kind of sleeve. But when on horseback I put it in my stirrups, and it was then my feet, more sensitive to the cold than my hands, that profited from it. From another strip of bearskin I'd made myself a chin-band which covered the lower part of my face and which I attached behind my head.'

It's in this 'singular getup, my head sheltered by a tattered hat, my skin chapped by the cold and smoke-blackened, my hair powdered by hoarfrost and my moustaches bristling with icicles', he's struggling on toward Vilna. Yet he's one of the few

'whose costume still kept something of a uniform about it. Most of our wretched companions seemed to be phantoms dressed up for a carnival [en chienlits]. One day I saw Colonel Fiéreck wrapped in a soldier's old greatcoat, wearing on his head over his forage cap a pair of trousers buttoned up under his chin. All these grotesque accoutrements were passing unnoticed. Or if anyone did notice them, it was only to profit from such inventions as seemed most appropriate to keep out the cold.'

The future Margrave of Baden, with IX Corps, sees

'a cavalry general on a konya, his legs wrapped in tatters, enveloped up to the ears in a fur. A cuirassier officer in a fur-bordered satin mantle on a similar horse, trailing his feet along the ground. A civilian employee with a gold-embroidered collar, wearing a woman's hat and toddling along in yellow pantaloons, etc.'

Surgeon-General Larrey, just as exposed to the cold and to hunger as everyone else, is keeping himself alive by noting, scientifically, the exact effects of extreme cold on starving men:

'The deaths of these unfortunates was preceded by a facial pallor, by a sort of idiocy, by difficulty in speaking, feeble-sightedness or even the total loss of this sense. And in this state some went on marching for a while, longer or shorter, led by their comrades or friends. The muscular action became noticeably weaker. Individuals staggered like drunken men. Their weakness grew progressively until the subject fell – a sure sign that life was totally extinct. The swift and uninterrupted march of men en masse,'

he goes on remorselessly,

'obliged those who couldn't keep up with it to leave the centre of the column to get to the roadside and flank it. Separated from the closed column, abandoned to themselves, they soon lost their balance and fell into snow-filled ditches, which they found it hard to get up out of again. Instantly they were stricken by a painful stupor, from which they went into a state of lethargic stupor, and in a few moments they'd ended their painful existence. Often, before death, there was an involuntary emission of urine. In some, nasal haemorrhages, something we'd noticed more particularly on the heights of Miednicky, one of the points in Russia which seemed to me to have the greatest altitude. I have reason to believe the barometer, in this high region, had fallen considerably.'

Such a death doesn't seem to Larrey to be a cruel one:

'The vital forces being gradually extinguished, they drew with them the overall sensitivity, and with it disappeared any awareness of the sensitive faculties. It seems probable that at the last moment the heart became paralysed, and at the same time the vital organs ceased to function. The fluids, already reduced in volume by privations and the lack of calories, promptly coagulated. We found almost all the individuals who'd perished like this prone on their stomachs. Their bodies were stiff, their limbs inflexible. The skin remained discoloured and apparently without any gangrenal blemishes. In general, death was more or less prompt, according to whether the subject had suffered from a longer or shorter abstinence.'

All this he's noting with scientific eye though

'we ourselves were all in such a state of prostration and torpor that we could scarcely recognise one another. We marched in a depressed silence. The organ of life and of the muscular forces was enfeebled to a point where it was very hard to keep a sense of direction and maintain one's equilibrium. Death was heralded by the pallor of the face, by a sort of idiocy, by difficulty in speaking, by weakness of vision.'

Lejeune, like Bourgogne before him, like thousands of others, has an irresistible desire to sit down. And does so. He's just letting the blissful torpor of death overcome him when his comrades at Davout's headquarters force him to get up and keep going. At every step Kergorre's seeing men drop:

'The habit of seeing them grow weaker enabled us to predict the moment when an individual would fall down and die. As soon as a man began to totter you could be sure he was lost. Still he went on a little way, as if drunk, his body still leaning forward. Then he fell on his face. A few drops of blood oozed from his nose. And he expired. In the same instant his limbs became like bars of iron.'

Von Muraldt's companions are

'giving vent to our pain in various ways. Some wept and whimpered. Others, totally stupefied, didn't utter a sound. Many behaved like lunatics, especially at the sight of a rousing fire or when, after starving for several days, they got something to eat. Only very few indeed were still themselves.'

That day Castellane, for the first time but for a very good – or rather, painful – reason, ceases to make entries in his journal. His swollen right hand isn't merely useless. It's agonising. At the evening meal he can't even raise it to 'dispute the morsels' of food. But one of Berthier's ADCs, d'Hautpoul[6] 'an excellent comrade, took my plate and had the *maître d'hôtel* put everything into it.' That night of 7/8 December d'Hautpoul is his bedfellow. 'Some thirty of us were heaped up in that barn: generals, ADCs to the Emperor, officers.'

Now despondency has even hit a member of the marshalate. At 8 a.m. on 8 December the *générale* was being beaten in the King's courtyard. Castellane, helped to attach his last portmanteau ('my servants, chilled, frost-bitten, demoralised, were telling me it was impossible') by Augustin, the only one of Narbonne's domestics who's still 'quite healthy', hears why:

'It's due to the arrival of the Duke of Bellune, who's abandoned his two army corps. He only had 50 men under arms, and therefore has chosen to return in person to general headquarters. The Prince of Neuchâtel, who'd lost his head, came into the room where we were having our breakfast, shouting at us that we were dishonouring ourselves by finishing it and pointing out that the stand-to was being beaten. We didn't pay him much attention. They weren't even being able to assemble the Old Guard's service battalion. It was leaving its dead at its bivouac and a sentry frozen to death on his feet. The cold didn't permit the men to hold their muskets.'

Berthier's been unnerved by Victor's attitude. 'Having asked him where his corps was,' he'll write in his next report to Napoleon,

'he replied that it was several leagues away. I told him that when one has the honour of commanding the Grand Army's rearguard one should be with those of its men who are closest to the enemy. To this he countered that he only had 300 men left.'

Murat and Berthier tell Victor he's 'a miserable wretch' [*le traitaient en misérable*]. All he replies is

'"Don't attack me. I'm quite unhappy enough as it is."'

How are things with the Treasure? That morning Davout writes to Berthier:

'*Monseigneur*. I have the honour to inform Your Highness that the Treasure is having the greatest difficulty in keeping up. The wagons are too heavily loaded and won't move at all. At every moment it's being cut off without any human strength being able to prevent it. It seems to me necessary to replace the wagons by sledges which we would use our authority to seize in the columns or obtain in some other way. If this measure isn't taken the Treasure will never be able to keep up and be lost at the first slightly steep hill.'

'One Treasury wagon was looted by stragglers,' Berthier will write, passing on Davout's report to Napoleon, now far away:

'Only 12,000 francs were saved. We've done everything humanly possible to save the other wagons. But each hill is an obstacle. On the downward slopes, despite putting the brakes on, the cannon carry away the horses. Yesterday six out of a post of eight men of the *Chasseurs à Cheval* died.'

Only yesterday their Captain Dieudonné (ever-famous from Géricault's heroic masterpiece, just now being exhibited at the Paris Salon) was seriously wounded, evidently in some affray with a Cossack.

But in spite of everything, Captain Duverger, I Corps' paymaster, has managed to keep his Treasury wagon on the move. Now he's only got three more hours to go to reach Vilna. Alas, just then another wagon, containing 2 million francs, gets stuck in a deep snowdrift. Least of all does Duverger want to spend another horrible night under the open sky. His comrade who's in charge of it implores his help. Only when the Paymaster-General himself implores him to give a hand does he do so. And he and his fellow-treasurers have to pass the night in a little shed. There, sharing some provisions filched from the Paymaster-General's cook, whose wagon's been looted by Cossacks, they find 'an old sapper'.[7] He could symbolise the whole vanished army:

> 'His long red beard, sprinkled with icicles, flashed like diamonds. A bear's skin, fixed by a rope on his right shoulder, draped part of his bust. Aslant his head he was wearing his regulation bearskin, but it been shaved bare on one side by being habitually rubbed against the ground as a pillow, and on the other preserved only a few short hairs. The old sapper was pale and shattered. A deep bleeding wound furrowed his brow. His grey sombre eyes wandered mournfully around him.'

And when they try to wake him in the morning he too is dead.

That last night, only six miles from Vilna but in a temperature of -28° Réaumur (-19.5° C), Boulart too, whose feet are hurting so much that he's travelling 'in the cart of a *vivandière* of my artillery – though deep in its straw, I'm suffering cruelly from the cold' – has to sleep 'in a wretched forge, without a door or windows, open to all the winds'. Le Roy too, after the house where he and Jacquet have spent that icy sleepless night has nearly burnt down, spends its last hours going over his experiences in detail. Only the reflection that very likely his sergeant son would have succumbed during this – at last he gets the word out – 'rout' if the Cossacks hadn't captured him outside Moscow[8] consoles him for his probable death. As for Vilna, which is now so near, he's fearing it may be 'Smolensk all over again'. At this thought the convinced deist and hater of all priests and theologians is reduced to again praying to that God he believes in, but who, he assumes, takes but scant interest in the sufferings of mortal men. "My God," I said fervently,

> "'I who find such happiness in living and admiring your beautiful sun, accord me the mercy of once again being warmed by him [*sic*] and not leaving my wretched remains in this barbarous icy country! Let me see my family again for one hour! only one hour! I'll die content. I've never asked anything of you, God, as you know! I've only thanked you in all circumstances, happy or unhappy, as they've befallen me. But this one's beyond my strength, and if you don't come to my aid I'm going to succumb under its weight."

'Jacquet, who'd heard me, said: "*Mon major,* your prayer goes for both of us. I ask half of it. I've been listening and, *ma foi,* if these gentlemen aren't asleep they must have heard you too, as I've done. But believe me, with such courage as ours I've got it into my head we're going to get out of Russia safe and sound."'

Now it's morning. And they've only gone a few yards along the road when they come across someone who's evidently had neither their faith nor their strength. 'Where the road leaves Rokow it makes a little right-angle bend, after which it makes straight for Vilna.' Inside the elbow of this bend they see

'a Negro, a musician of the 21st Light Infantry. Probably he'd sat down on the edge of the ditch; then, trying to get up again, had used both hands to do so. But lacked the strength. The cold had gripped him. His arms were stiff. His legs stretched out. His knees weren't even touching the ground, only his stomach seemed supported by the road. His neck and head were arched up, as if he'd tried to sit down. His face was turned toward the town. I touched his face. It was frozen, frozen in this position! A child of a burning climate, it was as if he'd been struck by lightning, killed by 26 degrees of frost. I heard several passers by laughing at this unfortunate's eccentric posture.'

Victor Dupuy and his Major Lacroix, walking together along the highway, count up to 900 rank and file, almost all Bavarians or Württembergers, who 'within a very short space of time had fallen dead on the road'. Out of sheer curiosity Le Roy and Jacquet too, walking on down the middle of the road, start counting the dead bodies to right and left. Near a little village just outside Vilna they see nine men seated around a dead fire. Six have just died. Three others are already covered with snow. This depressing sight puts an end to their counting. 'In a little under a league and a half [4½ miles] 58 corpses.'

As Lejeune, Davout, Haxo and Gérard reach the hills outside Vilna they see that only 300 men of the once resplendent I Corps, mostly officers, are still with them, 'and the colonels and generals were reduced to carrying the Eagles'. A single drummer, the only one they have left, marches at their head.

'At 2.30 p.m.,' Jean-Marc Bussy notes, his feet soaked and frost-bitten, 'we enter a big town full of unfortunates like ourselves. We're told it's Vilna.'

The extreme limit of human endurance has been reached – and passed.

CHAPTER 23

PANIC AND CHAOS AT VILNA

A city of hospitals – another governor with a gammy leg – 'from time to time one changes hand, step and lady' – 'all vanished in the twinkling of an eye, as if by enchantment' – a general sauve-qui-peut *– a long narrow gate – restaurants and cafés – 'confusion had reached its peak' – 'I'd only enough strength left to eat' – Murat loses his head – 'Napoleon's cipher seemed covered by a veil' – 'He asked as a last favour to be allowed to embrace the Eagle' – those who could go no further*

Although otherwise intact and stuffed with stores of every kind, Vilna is already one huge hospital. Only at Ghjat, on 3 September, had Napoleon at last yielded to Larrey's appeals and ordered the War Office to send the extra surgeons and medical supplies the Grand Army had needed all along. Whereupon, says Caulaincourt, 'a certain number of surgeons had been sent, but the hospital supplies we lacked so grievously hadn't arrived; nor could they do so quickly, as the road beyond the Niemen offered no means of transporting them'. A man who'd got back to Vilna from Smolensk in September to help supply the acute want of doctors had been Surgeon *Déchy*. He and his 13-year-old son,[1] too, had found Vilna

'nothing but a vast hospital, with men arriving sick with typhus and dysentery. The former convent known as the Hospital of the Cadets, a big three-storey building, had fallen to my father's lot, with five or six hundred men confided to his care. No one could stay in these halls without fumigating them, so fetid was the air. The floors, on all three storeys, were covered with the intestinal evacuations of our unhappy compatriots, dying there in great numbers. There was no bedding, as one can imagine.'

But Déchy had been a man of action. To provide bedding

'my father had a lot of pinewood planks brought, and by having them planed down reduced them to shavings that could replace maize leaves. He had them spread out five or six inches thick, thus forming beds on which each man rested his head on his pack.'

No less devoted a doctor than a father, Surgeon Déchy had himself caught the typhus and died.

But though Vilna's fifteen hospitals and five depots crammed with sick and wounded lack for everything, any amount of other stores have been arriving from the rear. On 2 November a Polish officer named *Bangowski* had got to Vilna with a convoy of 60 wagons loaded with clothes, weapons and harness, plus 500 troopers from various regiments.[2] Hearing that the Moscow army was retreating, and some 'intuition' warning him to go no further, he'd decided to deposit his stores – actually destined for Minsk – in a Vilna church. After which he'd managed to find himself asylum in a damp and unbearably cold cellar room owned by a Jew and already occupied by 'four officers, sick or amputees'. Next day his intuition had been confirmed when the 120 survivors of the newly formed 3rd (Lithuanian)

366

Guard Lancers had come struggling back into town after two Russian light cavalry regiments had wiped out all the rest 'within the hour'. 'Vilna presents the most lamentable appearance,' Bangowski had written in his diary:

'Streets encumbered with wounded, dead and dying, ravaged by the plague [*sic*]. No room in the churches, in the hospitals. No means even of removing horses' carcasses. And ever more convoys of wounded turning up all the while from Moscow! Everyone's doing what he can to get by, without compassion for anyone else.'

Though the very first refugees' arrival on 22 October had caused a certain consternation, as yet no one had had an inkling of what was afoot. Only after the fall, first of Polotsk then of Minsk, and more especially after the annihilation of the Lithuanian Lancers, had Hogendorp and Roch-Godart, the two governors, begun to worry about its vulnerability. Vilna has a town wall, but no fortifications to speak of. So Roch-Godart had proposed to Hogendorp (who of course will claim the idea as his own) that all avenues and suburbs should be barricaded, and cavalry and infantry pickets placed out on all the approach roads. These and other dispositions,[3] Roch-Godart had thought, had done something to restore confidence. But since 1 December everyone's been getting extremely jittery. Each day Roch-Godart's been anxiously consulted by

'the chief families of Lithuania, who'd all sided with the French and were holding posts under the government. No more than they could I guess that the Grand Army had ceased to exist.'

By sending out Polish detachments he's managed to 'hasten in supplies of grain and build up stores to feed an army of 120,000 men for 36 days'. But his staff haven't had a free moment, and everything's been becoming utterly complicated. In poor health anyway, he's been finding 'the government of Vilna an intolerable burden to bear'. A man with a 'loud harsh voice' who's risen from the ranks and has a rough way with inferiors and superiors alike,[4] Roch-Godart has been wounded nine times 'with a particular attention [five times] to my left leg' – which is making it more and more difficult to mount his horse. And since the turn of the month he's been ill. His duties are crushing him:

'No hospital had any basic supplies. Men were dying in great numbers without receiving any help. Abuses were spreading rapidly in all branches of the administration. The town was filling up with people from all quarters. Vilna had become a real labyrinth, you simply didn't know where you were. But I didn't let anyone lose heart and forced myself to mount my horse and myself saw to everything.'

The anniversary of the Coronation, of course, had had to be duly celebrated. Lieutenant *Porphyre Jacquemot* of the 5th Company of the 5th Artillery Regiment had been ordered to fire a 21-gun salute at 8 a.m.; as many shots again while the *Te Deum* was being sung in the cathedral; and again the same salute at 4 p.m. By that time the whole town had been lit up. And in the evening there'd been a great ball at Hogendorp's palace, which Jacquemot had attended with a colleague:

'As usual, it opened with a *polonaise*, which is nothing but a promenade. Each cavalier chooses a lady and the most respectable person at the ball takes the lead, all the couples following after. From time to time one changes hand, step and lady. In this way one promenades for half an hour accompanied by a march, in such a way that, when it comes to an end, the last lady has become the first. It's the custom for all officers to go to the ball booted and spurred and wearing stable trousers. The women present spoke French, as they all generally do at Vilna.'

Next morning, a Thursday, Jacquemot and his gunners still had no suspicion of the disaster. But since Loison's artillery still hadn't arrived at Vilna, a battery of 6-pounders had been sent off, half of it manned by foot and half by horse gunners:

'It's being said in Vilna that this division has been sent out to prevent any Cossacks who may be marching ahead of the retreating army from seizing the Emperor, who's intending to leave it.'

On the other hand some 'very unpleasant rumours' had been spread by a courier who'd passed through the town.' On the banks of the Berezina we're said to have lost more than 20,000 men, 200 guns and a lot of baggage. The troops are in the greatest disorder.' What's happening? Rumours are rife.

Some days earlier Abramovitch had reached Vilna with Napoleon's dispatch from the Berezina and closeted himself with Maret; and Oudinot's young wife, noticing how reserved her friend's husband had become, had had her own grave suspicions that all was far from well. But then Oudinot himself had arrived. After spending two nights in Davout's bivouacs he'd slept 'a second time (1 December, 'one of the dreariest days' Pils will afterwards remember, 'the men lacked everything'),

'at Ilya. But how times had changed! The first time he'd passed through here his staff had attended a fête in the home of the *seigneurs* living in the château. Everyone had danced all night. This time the château was deserted and no one in this countryside was welcoming us.'

Determined to reach Smorgoni and, despite the loss of his coachman Chalon, who'd been so shaken by the Cossacks' roundshot hitting the coach at Pleschenkowiczi that he'd gone out of his mind, wandered off into the snow and had to be replaced on the box by Oudinot's *maître d'hôtel*, the party had pushed on. That evening Oudinot had asked his staff to get hold of some post-horses and had set off again early next morning to reach Vilna the same day. By about 11 a.m. they'd been at Ochmiana:

'Three miles further on we met a detachment of Loison's division which was marching out to meet the Grand Army. These young men, mostly fresh levies, had an air of great alacrity. They were singing to shorten their road, which was a foot deep in snow, and forget its difficulties.'

This had cheered him up. His faithful and resourceful ADC Le Tellier had gone on ahead, reached Vilna, and come back and a few versts outside the town met the party with Oudinot's great carriage:

'We were amazed to see horses in such good shape and rough-shod for ice. A few moments later we met a regiment of horse chasseurs of the

Neapolitan Guard, it too on its way to join the Grand Army. These horse-men were well mounted and magnificently turned out.'

Shortly before nightfall the wounded Marshal's carriage had rolled up and stopped in the great square in front of the archbishop's palace. To his young wife it seems his attendants are 'frozen stiff on the box. *Mme la Duchesse*,' Pils goes on,

'at the foot of the staircase, took him into her arms. Doubled up with pain, frozen, the Marshal, unrecognisable from head to foot, reached the waiting fireside,'

and at the sight of the dinner table, laid with silver, etc., exclaims:

'"It's a dream, gentlemen, is it not, to be back at a properly laid table?"'

Then, suddenly, on 5 December, all illusions had vanished. The astound-ing news spreads. The Emperor has circumvented the town and left for France, leaving behind him the frozen relics of his escort. Only five of them, Jacquemot notes in his diary, formed

'from the debris of three cavalry regiments, will ever see Italy again! They'd marched in 22 degrees of frost. Hunger and cold have totally annihilated them.'

This, even Caulaincourt had noticed during his brief visit to Hogendorp, had

'quickly became known, and been the signal for almost universal depart-ure. The Duke of Bassano with his *bureaux*, all the foreign ministers, the members of the provisional government, all the provincial authorities, the mayor, most members of the municipality – all vanished in the twinkling of an eye, as if by enchantment. I've never seen such a panic terror like the one which struck all minds at once.'

One of the first refugees to get here in advance is Dedem van der Gelder. And Maret, before quitting the archiepiscopal palace where for four months he's been the Emperor's plenipotentiary, provides him with trans-port to Warsaw. Not that he expects the Dutch ex-diplomat to get that far. Dedem seems so desperately ill that Maret privily tells the courier who's to accompany him that, if he doesn't survive, he's to obtain a burial certificate for Dedem's family in Holland. Naturally he also goes to tell the Oudinots what's happened:

'The Emperor has passed by tonight on his way back to France.'

Everyone's leaving, he tells them. They should do the same. The 'Bayard of the French Army' is shattered. 'Catastrophe,' his young duchess realises, 'was a word he didn't understand'. Two francophile Lithuanian ladies she's made friends with immediately beg to be allowed to leave Vilna with them. Few indeed are the fugitives who do so as snugly as her severely wounded husband, 'lying down and carefully wrapped up'. Her 'good coach, with its mattresses, a *dormeuse* [sleeper]', has been hastily stocked with food and is almost comically full. Also in it are four members of Oudinot's entourage, all suffering from dysentery. A fifth, his *maître d'hôtel*, M. Roget,

'to whom notably belonged the glory of having grilled the mutton chops the Emperor had partaken of shortly before crossing the Berezina, was now on his knees, now lying partly stretched out on top of the others and twisting himself into every shape, and exciting their acute compassion.'

Escorted by 20 of Hogendorp's perfectly equipped cuirassiers, wrapped in their big white mantles, the *dormeuse* rolls through Vilna's paved but snow-laden streets:

'Not a soul was to be seen, except some pale shivering Jews, on their way to their speculations, which nothing ever abates.'

Such is the state of affairs in this town that's about to be invaded – as Maret has informed Roch-Godart – by 'a troop of 20,000 fugitives who, frozen and starving, are about arrive and are intending to pillage the magazines'.

Until this moment Roch-Godart's had no inkling of the extent of the disaster. The news horrifies him. Sick and ailing as he is, he summons the mayor and chief of police and impresses on them the dangers of the situation. All householders are at once to begin baking bread and give it to any soldiers needing it. But orders are one thing. Actions another. Within 24 hours

'no one was any longer bothering about anything except their own safety. All the Polish families were leaving for Warsaw or Königsberg. The mayor of the city, the police commissary and the principal civil authorities were abandoning their functions and fleeing the country.'

So are the ambassadors of the foreign powers. General Trechkoff (Austria), General Baron Krusemarck (Prussia), the Danish envoy, and Mr Barlow, Minister of the United States (he'll freeze to death en route for Warsaw) – all are leaving head over heels.

There's no doubt about it. The greatest military force in Europe's history, the incomparable, invincible Grand Army, no longer exists.

The Napoleonic tide has turned. At last.

Vilna's 'many monasteries', Roch-Godart goes on, 'belonged to various orders' and he has 'persuaded all the monks to retire into only one of them, to avoid all danger when the army arrived in disorder' – hardly well-advised (all the monasteries and convents, after all, have been turned into typhus-ridden hospitals) the order seems to be the only feasible one. Dirk van Hogendorp, too, is taking his measures. That day, 7 December, in a temperature of -27° to -30° Réaumur (-18° to -19° C), he has big placards put up,

'showing in large letters which monastery the men of each army corps were to report to, and where they'd find soup ready made, meat, bread and warm apartments'.

And three hours after dark, at 7 p.m. on Tuesday, 8 December, the first refugees begin to arrive. The approach to the town gate, Mailly-Nesle notices, goes

'by a road through a gully in the hillside. Palisades had been erected in front of the gates and soldiers were prohibiting anyone from entering. But we passed though in spite of their jabbing bayonets.'

Soon the road's 'encumbered for a mile and a half with carts and carriages entangled in each other and unable to move'. Even while still 25 miles away Pion des Loches' usual prescience has foreseen that 'we'd have to get there in good time if we were to find lodgings and food'. Telling his servant to stick with Drouot, 'whose *matériel* had been reduced to one gun and an ammunition cart' – himself he only has three caissons left – he promises to

'come back to the town gate and wait for them. Three miles from Vilna a line of French and Bavarian soldiers had been detailed off to protect our entry; and even at that point the crush was already beginning to be noticeable.'

Reaching the gate Pion des Loches finds it blocked by

'a broken vehicle. The men on foot were going in one by one, without bothering to get rid of what was left of it to clear a path for men on horseback. These, having their feet split open by the cold and wrapped up and unable to dismount, were patiently waiting their turn. It was one of the saddest sights I'd seen in the retreat.'

Inside the town walls Lieutenant Jacquemot has been ordered to station himself at what he calls 'the Minsk Gate' with eight gunners and a corporal, to prevent artillery vehicles from coming into town and make them take a side road to go and park on the Kovno highway. But though he stays there until 5 p.m., it's no good: 'because no one listened to me'. All he gets for his pains is a frost-bitten hand.

Morning comes, and Hogendorp, as protocol requires, rides out to meet the army's new commander-in-chief. By and by, coming toward him on the road, he sees

'the King of Naples and the Prince of Neuchâtel on foot because of the intense cold. Murat was all wrapped up in huge and superb furs. A very tall fur hat added to his already great stature, making him resemble a walking colossus. Beside him Berthier, his small frame weighed down by heavy clothing, contrasted oddly.'

The town gate is 'narrow, deep and vaulted'. And outside it there's already a growing mass of freezing men. To get through it takes Griois more than an hour; afterwards he'll remember how, even though the gate's only 200 yards away, 'seeing its long vaulting packed with men and horses being pushed over and suffocated by the mob I'd have given everything in the world to still be far away from it'. Victor Dupuy – he who five months ago had galloped into Vilna to the ecstatic applause of Polish ladies watching from their open windows – has to wait for the gate to open. 'Overcome with lassitude and drowsiness, gripped by the frost', he longs to sit down. But his fellow-officers of the 7th Hussars, knowing it'll be the death of him if he does so, hold him up and walk him to and fro to get his circulation going again:

'The King of Naples was about to come by. At the head of the officers I had with me I placed myself in his path. I saluted him. He recognised me, signed to me to follow him. For him the town gates opened up. We entered at his heels.'

At last Griois tumbles into the town: 'But I was alone. I'd lost the gunner who'd been with me. There I got my breath back, for my strength had almost wholly abandoned me.'

Once inside, an amazing sight greets his eyes. A perfectly normal town, going about its everyday business! 'The houses were still intact, the inhabitants busy with their normal occupations.' Entranced, Mailly-Nesle too enters the town

'with a feeling of prodigious happiness. We saw glittering shop windows, chimneys smoking, well-dressed people. And, above all, the restaurant keepers' signs.'

Sent on ahead by Colonel Dubois of the 2nd Cuirassiers – only three have survived – Sergeant-Major Thirion is also among the first to enter. And finds the town

'very calm and well provisioned. I went into the first cafe I came to; and there, seated near a rousing fire, I had myself served *café au lait!* How many cups of it didn't I consume, and little cakes besides!'

After which he takes rooms for Colonel Dubois.

By now it's between 9 and 10 a.m. Roch-Godart, aghast, sees 'all the army's debris arriving'. Even if Hogendorp, after what he's already seen at Ochmiana, isn't quite so surprised as Roch-Godart, he's no less stupefied – some will say paralysed:

'The head of the unfortunate column began entering Vilna. In vain, efforts were made to draw their attention to the placards I'd put up to direct them to the convents. Everyone, generals and soldiers, forced their way into the first house that seemed suitable, looked for its warmest apartment, lay down, and had themselves brought something to eat. The strongest drove out the weakest. Generals and officers, if they could assert a vestige of their authority, made the soldiers give up a place to them, even if it was only a room or a bed. The town would indubitably have burnt down if all its houses hadn't been built of stone.'

Yet there's an abundance of victuals. And, so Hogendorp will protest afterwards, they're being distributed 'without any formality to the first-comer who presented himself'. This, however, isn't how von Muraldt will remember it. According to an 'order of the day as cruel as it was half-witted' – and which he ascribes, precisely, to Hogendorp – 'only men who're still with their colours' are to get any food from the stores:

'Only those with the colours! No army corps, no divisions, no brigades, no regiments existed any longer. Not even any individual troops.'

Few, it seems, see Hogendorp's placards anyway; or if they do, ignore them. Muraldt may scorn what he's heard is Hogendorp's order that rations are only to be distributed to men with the colours. But Le Roy sees in it the paradoxical reason for the catastrophe that's building up at the long narrow vaulted gate:

'Perhaps you'll ask why these unfortunates didn't try to shelter for the night, like we did. To this I'll reply that most of the men who were marching on their own had left their regiments, thrown away their arms and, for that reason alone, found themselves repulsed by their comrades, who'd often had to do service in their place. These men were driven away and banished from the distributions. That's the reason why they had to march with their unit, but nevertheless without communicating with it.'

Now, having to rejoin the mass to get into the town, they're

'afraid the superior officers detailed off to supervise the entrance would have them arrested as fugitives if they entered on their own'.

This, as Le Roy sees it, is why the *fricoteurs* and 'the army' are

'pressing one another to suffocation point, while they could have entered by a side-gate, which was free. Where one went, another followed, like Dindoneau's sheep.'

Everyone who survives the crush is making a bee-line for the nearest restaurant or cafe, above one of which Mailly-Nesle sees

'written for example in good French: "*Au Veau qui Tette*" [The Sign of the Suckling Calf] – "*A la Renommé des Pieds de Mouton*" ['Famous for Sheeps' Trotters']. First we entered a German hostelry where everything had already been demolished and where, despite our resources and pecuniary offers, it was impossible for us to get anything. So we dragged ourselves off to the "*Veau qui Tette*", which, like all the town's other inns, was packed to the roof.'

There he and his companions, 'grabbing *en passant* some boiled potatoes destined for someone else', have to make do with a chimney corner and a bottle of brandy. The Marquis de Bonneval – 'a bizarre fact' – has

'one fixed idea: to eat some *crêpes* in company with some comrade! Someone pointed out a Jew who had this as his speciality. But alas I couldn't eat in moderation.'

Dupuy and his party of 7th Hussars, for their part, dive into

'a liquor shop a short distance from the gate. There were only a few bottles, about half a litre each, at the price of a gold *Frédéric* apiece [21.50 francs]. Everyone went through his pockets, his belt. The needful sum being put together, we each took one and, drinking to a better future, we quickly drained it off straight out of the bottle. It was cinnamon liqueur, so weak it didn't go to our heads at all; yet was of such comfort to us, even so, that I felt no ill effects afterwards.'

Lieutenant Vossler's group of Prussian hussars make for the big Café Lichtenstein, as do also von Suckow and his good friend Captain von Klapp – but not before they've already eaten the largest omelette a Jew can make them. They'd been putting a glass of stout to their lips when they'd noticed, under the table, a scarlet-faced corpse, dead from an overdose of brandy. 'From his coquettish uniform I saw it was a gunner of the horse artillery.' Not that this has damped their appetite. Throwing the corpse out into the street, they've gobbled up their omelette, refused to pay the Jew more than 4 francs for it[5] – he'd wanted 7 silver roubles or 28 francs – and gone on to the Lichtenstein, where they've found the Württemberg war commissary Schoenlin, who gives von Suckow his arrears of pay: 14 ducats (about 175 francs). With this he goes out and buys himself some clothes, muffs and a fur cap. Coming back to the Café Lichtenstein he sees some of his fellow Württemberg officers throwing an insolent French hussar officer out into the street for insulting their young Prince Eugène. Then they all have a game of billiards. And von Suckow falls asleep under the billiard table. Emerging from the vintner's, meanwhile, Victor Dupuy has again fallen in with some his officers:

'I established myself in a wretched gin shop, also run by a Jew. None of us had any money. I had a few payments of arrears of pay due to me as captain. I gave part of them to Lieutenant Korte, who went and got the cash from the army's paymaster, a man named Bresson. Korte brought me back about 1,000 francs. I took 150 of them and said to my companions:

'"Share the rest out among yourselves. Here's my notebook and my pencil. Each of you can write his name and how much he takes."

'And so they did.'[6]

Some high-ups such as Lariboisière are finding a room prepared for them and their staffs, with a nice fire and a dinner

'on a little table covered with a white tablecloth. Such a sudden change seemed like a fairy tale. We thought we were dreaming. It was a delightful dream. But it had a fateful effect on several of us,'

notably on Captain Lebreton de Vanoise, one of Planat's six artillery captains,[7] who 'went out of his mind'. Like everyone else, the first thing Major Boulart has done has been to

'try to provide for myself, the lack of food having completely exhausted my strength. In this my comrade Cottin and I were rather successful, though the crowd of starving men was making it difficult. But this meal so stupefied me and gave me such an urgent longing for sleep that, forgetting to rally either my servants or my horses, I only thought of going to take possession of the billet I'd been given.'

The house, Boulart finds, belongs to a cordwainer and is already occupied by an old acquaintance – none other than Captain Lignières of the 1st Guard Chasseurs. For 20 francs Lignières has bought bread and some potatoes off some Line soldiers; and off his host, for a further 20 francs, a small pig. Boulart, 'dying of cold', is admitted.[8] Likewise a gunner captain 'whose face had been burnt by a powder explosion'. His sleep is only protected by a dragoon and one of Lignières' chasseurs, who point a loaded musket 'though a hole made expressly for the purpose' to keep out intruders. But unwonted warmth, too, if excessive, can be fatal:

'Woe to the man who, stunned by the cold and whose animal functions had almost been annihilated and in whom all exterior sensibility was extinct, if he suddenly came into too hot a room! The exposed or frozen parts [of his body], far from the centres of circulation, were stricken by gangrene, which instantly manifested itself, and developed with such rapidity that its progress was noticeable to the eye. Or else to the individual who was suddenly suffocated by a sort of swollenness which seemed to seize on the pulmonary and cerebral system. He perished as if asphyxiated.'

Larrey sees Chief Pharmacist Sureau, of the Guard – he who during the night before Borodino had been sent to the rear to fetch a plasma to help Napoleon's cough and migraine – die like this:

'He'd got to Vilna without mishap. Only his vitality was enfeebled by cold and abstinence. Offered asylum in a very hot room in the hospital's pharmacy, he'd hardly spent a few hours in this novel atmosphere than his members swelled up, became bloated; and soon afterwards, without being able to utter a single word, he expired in the arms of his son and another of his colleagues.'

But outside the city gate the scrum's becoming utterly awesome. With evident satisfaction Lieutenant Jean-Roch Coignet sees the colonel who'd looted icons from Moscow churches drop dead – and his possessions being plundered by his servants. Any number of wagons and carriages are getting stuck and having to be abandoned. Seven of the thirteen horses of I Corps' paymaster Duverger have died in the night. Now, says his colleague Kergorre, his Treasury Wagon No. 48, containing 2 millions in gold and 'what remained of the trophies which Commissary Duverger with infinite pains had brought so far' gets stuck in the jam outside the gate and is snatched by Cossacks. So, immediately behind young Peyrusse's wagon, is the section of the Treasury convoy commanded by a certain Paymaster Roulet, 'a good fellow'. Peyrusse himself, 'dead with cold and hunger', gets through – though his convoy has been scattered, Luckily Kergorre (who witnesses Duverger's disaster) has got through with his horse and even a little box full of silver

'at the heels of General Grandeau, who cut a path for himself with his cane, shouting: "Make way, make way for the General!" – even at risk of being knocked down by those he was jostling. We were all dressed in such a way no one could be distinguished from anyone else. I don't mean merely the soldier from the general, but even a man from a woman.'

Then Kergorre, with his 'six weeks' growth of beard and a face black as coal and icicles hanging from my nostrils', goes and finds his *ordonnateur* – who doesn't even recognise him:

'I had to whisper my name in his ear – for a fortnight now I'd lost my voice terribly. One hour after I'd got there they served us up some hams. I ate one almost whole. So little did I feel my stomach, the more I devoured, the hungrier I became! Joly, my comrade from Mojaisk, objected vainly. Seeing how I went on, he wrested the ham away from me almost by force.'

But the Bordeaux does him good:

'I don't understand how it was that I didn't get drunk. In a normal state a quarter as much would have turned my head.'

But in the night Kergorre vomits it all up, undigested; and two of his colleagues die.

Delaborde's carriage too has to be abandoned outside the gate. And so does that of Pion des Loches, with its superb Chinese porcelain dinner set. As he fights his way through, Fezensac, who's been given General Ledru's permission to come on ahead to find out what arrangements have been made, is reminded of the crush at the Berezina:

'No precaution had been taken to establish any order there. Yet while everyone was stifling everyone else at the gate there were other side passages open we didn't know of and to which no one was showing the way.'

Planat and several other officers have to wait nearly two hours to get in. 'We were so stunned, everyone regarded himself as lost if he separated himself even a few paces from the column.' Reaching the gate at last with Sergeant-Major Vogel, Franz Roeder too is

'threatened with a horrible death. Swept off my feet, I was flung down between two fallen horses, on top of which a rider then stumbled with a third. I gave myself up for lost. Then dozens of people began to pile up on top of us, screaming horribly as their arms and legs were broken or they were being crushed. Suddenly one of the horses' heavings flung me into an empty space, where I could pick myself up and stagger in through the gate.'

Ill though he is, Roeder isn't so shattered by his experience that he can't lament the 'loss of a splendid English lorgnette made by Ramsden'. When the Red Lancers get there, at about midday, Dumonceau is horrified to see dead, dying and struggling men and horses

'heaped up on top of one another in a little hill more than two metres high. It was a veritable moving mountain.'

Slowly, ever so slowly, his Dutchmen clamber over it,

'pushing, shoving, hemmed in on all sides, horrified at having to get over it and at each step risking being overthrown by the quiverings, the convulsive spasms of the victims we were trampling underfoot'.

Yes, it's the Berezina all over again. Or even worse. There it had been a river to get across. Now only a long deep narrow gate to squeeze through. And yet the town has other – wide open – side gates! Taking one look at the horrific scene, Davout, Haxo, Gérard and Lejeune decide they'll never be able to get through:

'I couldn't get into the town except by some gardens, where I found a ladder which fitted into another ladder, and by means of it easily climbed over the wall.'

Inside the town the first sight to meet Lejeune's eyes is

'a cart belonging to the army's Paymaster-General. Its barrels had been smashed in and partly pillaged. But this icy metal had become so painful to the touch that the passers-by, utterly exhausted and hardly having enough strength left to drag themselves along, hadn't the courage to bend down and pick up the crowns, which were too heavy for them to carry.'

Happily he comes across his sister, who's been nursing General Vasserot, who'd saved her life at the Berezina. Marshal Lefèbvre's carriage, too, has got through the crush immediately in Murat's wake; and with it Louise Fusil, who's nursing his wounded son:

'Pressing forward, the crowd seemed to fancy they'd reached the Promised Land. It was there almost all the French from Moscow perished. Fighting cold and hunger, they couldn't get into the town.'

Once through, she drives to a house where Lefèbvre 'had lodged when passing through the first time'. It belongs to the wife of a Polish francophile, Countess Kasakoska:

'But the house was all at sixes and sevens. The Count was preparing to leave. We couldn't find a servant to give us something to eat or even make us a fire. The cold was at -28 degrees and we spent a horrible night. From the agitation reigning in people's faces I could see we shouldn't be staying long.'

Neither has Fezensac, once inside the town, seen any of Hogendorp's placards:

'Arrived in the middle of the town, it was impossible to find out where III Corps was to be put up. Everything was in confusion at the governor's palace and the municipality.'

In the end, utterly exhausted and unable to find out where III Corps is supposed to go, he pushes his way into Berthier's lodgings, where he finds 'his servants scattered. Having supped on a pot of jam without any bread, I fell asleep on a plank.' Yet the notices are certainly there. For when Le Roy and Jacquet at last get through the gate they see them written up on the first houses:

'Some orderly officers guided us, each to the place allocated to him. "Such or such a unit to the Benedictines, such another the Dominicans." The whole of I Corps was lodged in a large monastery.'

When Griois sees such a notice it's in the hall of the municipal offices, where one of his group has put it up to tell them where to go. But the instruction is vague, the house hard to find, and 'most of the inhabitants had shut themselves up inside their homes, and those I met with didn't speak French'. Luckily he falls in with one of his gunners, who shows him the way to their billet,

'the ground floor of a house, truly a very small one. But there were two rooms anyway, one for us [officers] and one for the gunners and servants. There was good stove in each, wood to heat it up and a narrow courtyard for the horses.'

A bottle of Spanish wine – 'whose taste one had almost forgotten' – brings him back to life. 'You'll laugh at me and pity me when I tell you that this moment, preceded and followed by such dangers, was one of the moments in my life when I felt the most real and complete happiness.' He shaves off a month's growth of beard and throws his reserve shirt, which he's had with him in his portmanteau but is aswarm with lice, into the fire,

'refusing pitilessly to give it to the servant girl who was helping me clean myself up. Then I took off my boots which hadn't left me for six weeks. Lying down on a mattress with some other comrades I had the delicious sensation of an unfortunate prisoner from whom the irons he's long been wearing are taken off.'

The 85th Line, Le Roy goes on, 'occupied two rooms on the first floor' of the monastery assigned to it:

'There I was charged with the Eagle and policing the unit. The staff officers and the colonel had gone out to have dinner in a hotel. They were to have sent me something to eat. But either by oversight or neglect, I only got the food portion due to my rank. This meant I had to share a room with some exhausted officers, who kept me company for the last time. Most of them had made up their minds not to leave Vilna until they'd recovered.'

He counts 50 officers,

'half of whom, unable to go any further, were determined to stay in Vilna, and a little more than 200 NCOs and men, only half of them armed. I'm sure that including its isolated men, the regiment, 4,000 strong when it had entered the campaign, couldn't have assembled 300 at Vilna. And we weren't at the end of our troubles.'

Someone tells him there's a magazine full of clothing, both for officers and men:

'Someone came and advised us to go and get some of these effects. But few soldiers, I saw, loath to be disturbed, were in a hurry to do so. I'd a trunk at the depot. I had it brought up to the room where I was. I found some new effects and took what seemed needful, notably a pair of brand new riding-boots.'

After which he distributes his few remaining possessions among his comrades.

Is Vilna defensible? Napoleon has certainly thought so. Surely this is the end of the endless retreat? Certainly the Poles are assuming it is.

But what's going on at headquarters, now not even imperial? Everyone except the Poles, Chlapowski thinks, is losing his head. In the troops of the Confederation of the Rhine he sees,

'the utmost demoralisation reigned. And the best proof of it is my meeting with General de Wrede and some Bavarians.'

Little is left of them either. Withdrawing parallel with the main army from Polotsk via Veleika and Nemenczini, VI Corps too has been almost destroyed. Approaching Vilna, Wrede had been ordered to liaise with Ney, but acted insubordinately. Now Labaume sees his 'half-routed' Bavarians turn up with a few guns, whose horses can no longer pull them, after – according to Lejeune – 'all day with the few troops left him he valiantly fought the enemy, who didn't cease to cannonade us'. 'In the morning', Chlapowski goes on,

'I went to King Murat's headquarters at the château. I met a man wearing a civilian cloak, a kind of turban on his head, with a sword in his hand, gloveless, and running, followed by some fifteen men armed with muskets, with bayonets levelled as if to charge. Catching sight of me and recognising my *czapka* and my uniform, he shouted excitedly: "Where's the headquarters? The Cossacks are in town!'"

Examining him closely, Chlapowski recognises his interlocutor as Wrede, whom he'd often seen in the 1809 campaign. And answers calmly:

"'I'm just on my way there and if you permit, General, I'll show you the way there. There's no need for us to panic. The town gates are being guarded by infantry, the military police are everywhere, and I assure you there still aren't any Cossacks in the town. But General, sheath your sword, or you'll frighten King Murat.'"[9]

If only the Emperor were here! Then, Chlapowski's sure, order would soon be re-established. As it is, though Hogendorp has

'had a circular order printed and taken round to every house and posted up at each street corner, inviting the Marshals and generals to assemble there',

Berthier's being depressingly unsuccessful in assembling the generals of brigade, and even of division, at his headquarters.

'There were at least 100 generals in Vilna – but hardly ten came. Generals refused to listen to the orderly officers and the ADCs sent them by the Major-General.'

But in Berthier's house on the main square, next door to the palace – the one that was by rights the Archbishop's but by turns had been the Tsar's, then Napoleon's, then Maret's, and now, if only fleetingly, is Murat's – the Belgian Sergeant *Scheltens* and the 30 survivors of the 2nd Guard Grenadiers have broken into the Imperial Staff's food stores and are treating themselves to

'some fine flour, lard, fine oil, rice and good wine, even champagne, and some excellent cognac, baked some bread and pancakes and roasted a ham in the oven'.

If chaos reigns at Murat's headquarters, Hogendorp says his own house

'resembled a hospital. I owe it to myself to say that the enormous expense contributed greatly to the ruin of my fortune.'

Hogendorp had 'so little believed what I'd told him,' says Dedem, 'that he didn't even save his own carriages.'[10] And when Ney comes to his headquarters to reprimand him for having sent the newly raised Lithuanian regiments behind the Niemen, he finds him 'with his ADCs, eating hastily, without any crockery – he too had lost everything'. Pion des Loches, too, turns up. While Hogendorp writes out an order allocating billets for what remains of the Guard Artillery,

'I read, furtively, a pile of printed orders of the day, dated I don't know which day, announcing that the Emperor had post-haste taken the road to his capital, having handed over command to the King of Naples. So, the deserter of Egypt was deserting Russia, abandoning us to our wretched lot and to all the follies and caprices of an adventurer who'd have been the world's biggest lunatic if he hadn't been its emperor.'

Asked to explain what's going on, Hogendorp can't. But tells Pion des Loches he's welcome to take some copies of his proclamation. 'I rolled some up, put them in my pocket, and left.' His three remaining caissons will remain in Vilna.

All that Wednesday the ghastly struggle to get through the town gate goes on and on. And by now, inside the town

'the houses were full. Unfortunates who'd managed to drag themselves as far as this in hope of finding succour, fell down from fatigue in the streets and squares and soon died of cold. All the town's doorways were so packed you could no longer get in or out. In a word, it was a real débâcle. Already the Cossacks had seized several suburbs and so to speak were all jumbled up with our men.'

Lieutenant Jacquemot sees

'troops are still arriving *en masse*. I believe a small effort has been made to assemble them, but it's not been possible. They haven't been given a single loaf of bread, though all the magazines were overflowing with flour and grain. Since 6 December they've even ceased making any distributions to the garrison.'

Jacquemot himself takes a lot of artillery officers to his lodgings, but has nothing to give them, 'and they were badly off, even if warmly so'. Von Muraldt has pneumonia. All his limbs are aching, 'but otherwise I'm all right'. Once inside the town Dumonceau has found

'the streets comparatively deserted; calm reigned, the dwellings were shut up from top to bottom, as in a town taken by assault'.

Behind closed shutters the Belgian lancer captain glimpses the pale faces of invalids. Even while proud of the good order prevailing in what's left of his own regiment, he imagines how it must feel for the French who'd stayed at Vilna to see what a state the army's in. Planat too notices that the 'men who'd been at Vilna or were on their way to join the army' are almost more terrified than the locals. At the sight of

'a kind of mob, more like a legion of convicts or hideous hobgoblins than troops, they became much more demoralised than we were. When he saw the demoralised columns [*sic*] passing through the town, Roche, chief veterinary artist of the artillery parks, who'd remained at Vilna throughout the campaign – a very fine fellow, kind and obliging beyond comparison [he'd lent Planat money to equip himself when he'd first been commissioned] – had a stroke and died.'

After the tiny relics of III Corps have elbowed their way through the mob Captain Bonnet goes to an inn and buys a pound of sugar for a gold napoleon. By now stragglers from the 85th who're still rejoining at I Corps' convent are reporting that the Cossacks are already at the town gates, trying to force their way through the rearguard; and already Le Roy doesn't 'believe the army will be staying very long'. Especially as there's no sign of any fresh troops. Everywhere Fezensac sees

'our ragged and starving soldiers straying about. Some were paying for the most wretched food with its weight in gold. Others were begging a bit of bread from the inhabitants and imploring their pity. Terrified, the latter contemplated the remains of this formerly so formidable army which five months ago had stirred their imagination. The Poles were sorry because of the miseries that were ruining their hopes. The partisans of Russia were triumphant. The Jews only saw an opportunity to make us pay through the nose for everything we needed. Already on the first day the shops, the inns and cafes, not being able to cope with the numbers of clients, had closed, and the inhabitants, fearing our greed would soon bring on a famine, were hiding their provisions.'

A few distributions are being made to the Guard, but all the other army corps are so chaotic it's impossible to help them. Sent on ahead, the Guard Lancer Brigade's farriers, however, have

'obtained for us regulation billets, distributed to us immediately on our arrival. It was the first time such a favour had fallen to our lot since we'd set out from here last July'.[11]

Although given proper billets in the main street leading to the Kovno Gate and issued with food and forage, Dumonceau and Post go to a restaurant which they find 'packed with starving hungry men like ourselves, loquacious and noisy with joy as a synagogue'. Squeezed in at a corner table, they have to content themselves with 'a simple morsel of grilled meat and a bottle of mediocre wine, paid for heavily'.

Unable to get any sense out of the civil authorities, Pion des Loches and his friend Bitche push their way into a cafe where they manage to get themselves served two cups of bad coffee. Also, after insisting, a bottle of mediocre Bordeaux and 2-pound loaf which, though piping hot, isn't fully baked. Then pushing open a street door at random they enter a huge room,

'rather over-decorated, heated by a big stove whose warmth however couldn't melt an inch of ice on the floor tiles. Two ladies were there. We saluted them and took our place on a big sofa, loudly telling each other that we weren't going to be put out again at any price.'

The ladies, horrified at their appearance, give a servant some silver to get some food, regretting they can't offer the two Guards artillery officers beds. 'Beds, *Mesdames*! Since leaving Moscow we've slept on snow.' Greedy above all for eggs and meat, they're told good food is already in short supply.

'The ladies, doubtless afraid they'd be eaten up alive, brought us some wretched lukewarm soup, which we threw ourselves on avidly.'

It's now between 4 and 5 p.m. As darkness falls Dumonceau and Post are on their way back from their meagre and expensive meal and are hoping for a comfortable night in billets for once – when they hear a cannonade starting up outside the city. Good-bye to all hopes of a comfortable night!

'Fate didn't have one in store for us. Already the guns were beginning to rumble outside the town, mingled not far away with musketry. On all sides the drums were beating the fall-in. The men, grumbling, were running to arms. Others were staying where they were to get food from the magazines, which were said to have been given over to pillage. Still others were lying on the snow, against the walls of houses, not knowing whom to turn to to obtain a bed or help. By contrast, some unfortunate wounded or sick men were fleeing from homes where they'd previously been received, so as not to expose themselves to the vindictiveness of their hosts, become inhospitable at the enemy's approach.'

Orders come for Colbert's men to be ready to leave at 11 o'clock. Not daring to relax in his billet in the meantime for fear of being left behind, Dumonceau takes refuge among his stable horses.

No one at headquarters, least of all the King of Naples, is giving a thought to defending Vilna – not even for twenty-four hours – 'even though some remaining units of Loison's division are still staving off the Russians' advance guard on the heights outside'. Rapp, in obedience to his orders, has reported to Ney:

'We had a long talk. Ney too, urged the necessity of continuing the retreat. He regarded it as indispensable. "We can't stay here a day longer." Hardly were the words out of his mouth than the cannon were heard. The Russians were approaching in some strength. Fighting was going on to fend them off from the town. Immediately we saw the Bavarians. They were retiring in disarray, mingling with our stragglers. Confusion had reached its peak.'

At first, according to Rapp, Murat had hoped to make a stand. But now the reports coming in from the heights around the town 'remove all hope of doing so. He gave orders to retreat.' Telling Rapp he's to return to Danzig and resume his governorship of that city,[12] he utters the memorable words:

'"I'm not going to be taken here in this piss-pot."'

The first thing Zalusky had done had been to

'take a bath; and having got rid of the dust of our marches I dressed myself from head to foot in a brand-new uniform, made in Paris, and which I'd only put on once, in Moscow, since we'd crossed the Niemen'.

For him and all his colleagues in the Polish Guard Lancers it had been obvious this was the end of the great retreat. Resplendent in his dark-blue uniform with its scarlet facings and trimmings, its tall Polish-style *czapka* with its massive silver plaque and its silver aiguillette dangling from his shoulder, he'd gone out into the town to look for acquaintances. What a disappointment!

'I met with many friends who avoided me, partly out of shame, partly because of the jealousy Napoleon's Guard inspired. It was thought that we owed our having stood up to the privations better than others had to imperial favour, not to our own efforts.'

While he's studying the mobs swirling about the streets he's summoned to the regimental paymaster, 'who pressed me to draw my arrears, and wanted to pay me in Dutch thalers known as albertus. He explained to me that we were going to evacuate Vilna.' What a shock! Zalusky's pained and astounded:

'Our youthful Polish imaginations couldn't imagine we shouldn't be staying here. If the French leaders had done their duty as well as the Polish ones had there'd have been no question but that the army would have gone into winter quarters at Vilna. After a lot of trouble I prevailed on him not to burden me down with silver, so as not to spoil my horse. And in fact the trumpet was sounding the 'To horse!' I take off my fresh uniform, put on the one I've been marching in, with my sheepskin waistcoat and my mantle. I reach the square of alarms. I learn that King Murat wants to retreat further and that he's taking us with him. So that's how it's to be, our last hopes vanish and we must continue our peregrination beyond the Niemen!'

Orders come to the Lancer Brigade to be ready to leave at 11 p.m. 'At 5 p.m.', Rossetti notes in his diary, 'the King, the Viceroy and Marshal Berthier left the town and went on foot to establish themselves in a house on the outside fringe of the Niemen suburb.'

> 'In the midst of the tumult Prince Murat rushed out of his palace, pushed his way through the mob without his guards, and went and established himself in the suburb on the Kovno road, where, Your Majesty' (Berthier will explain to Napoleon afterwards) 'parked the artillery on our arrival in June.'

As he leaves the Archbishop's palace, Murat orders Rossetti 'to stay in town until the moment when Marshal Lefèbvre, with the remains of the Imperial Guard, should be forced to evacuate it'. Cesare de Laugier, that stickler for military honour, is utterly shocked:

> 'Who'd ever have thought that Murat, that soldier without peer for intrepidity, for courage, despising danger, accustomed to throw himself sabre in hand on the enemy – that this same Murat, no sooner than invested with high command, should be weighed down to the ground by so heavy a responsibility and become timid and irresolute?'[13]

To an indignant Cesare de Laugier it seems as if Murat's only concern is

> 'to save himself and abandon us all to our fate. Happily, it's only a question of moving his headquarters to a café on the Kovno road, a musket shot from the town.'

Murat's courage may have abandoned him, but not his customary gallantry toward the ladies. Through his secretary he has assured the Countess de Choiseul-Gouffier she has nothing to fear. Since Vilna isn't going to be defended, neither is she in danger of being taken by storm! The scene in the main square that night reminds the art-loving countess of a Teniers genre-painting:

> 'The men were lighting fires in the streets to keep themselves warm. A thousand men were to be seen spread out among the flames and leaping sparks. The Town Hall still bore some festive decorations. Looked at through the clouds of smoke rising to the sky, Napoleon's cipher seemed to be covered by a veil.'

Yes, the scene even reminds her of a yet greater artist: 'The night effects had something Rembrandt-like about them.'

Only this morning of 9 December have the imperial carriages 'escorted by the Dragoons of the Guard and which should have got to Vilna on 6 or

7 December, arrived in the greatest disorder' – Berthier writes that evening in a dispatch to Napoleon (now nearing Warsaw). They'd had immense trouble negotiating a frozen gradient:

'"Your Majesty knows the slope down into the town. It was nothing but a sheet of ice. Despite the lock-chains most of the carriages carried away and turned over on top of one another. The cold had stunned almost all the men. Most had frost-bitten hands or feet."'

Ordered to get under way again at midday

'"the élite gendarmes abandoned them. The coachmen and postilions refused to march. There was even a moment of insurrection against the stable-master.[14] They all wanted to stay in Vilna. At 5 p.m. we still hadn't got your carriages to leave. We have decided to burn some of them.'

It's from the burning carriages that some of the smoke veiling Napoleon's cipher is coming. Also (his doctor Desgenettes will tell Wilson) from 'his state tent lined with shawls, etc., all his table-linen, his state bed, etc. Here were buried or destroyed all the trophies that he took from Moscow' and of which 'he'd previously ordered drawings to be made' so that he could 'remake them in Paris'. Included among them, Bacler d'Albe had seen, 'the flags taken from the Turks during the last hundred years, old weapons, and a Madonna'. Doubtless also the cross of solid gold, 'about 10 inches high' which had been found inside the great silver-plated Cross of Ivan when it had been pulled down from the cathedral in the Kremlin. All night the countess watches

'the Emperor's carriages being burnt in the university courtyards opposite the palace, as well as a heap of other things – tents, camp beds, etc., etc. One young academician wanted to buy a magnificent gold mathematical case, bearing the imperial arms, off a sentry. But the soldier just poked the case into the flames with the tip of his bayonet.'

In the end, Berthier goes on, enough men have been scraped together to get the remaining carriages on the move:

'"But, Sire, I owe you the whole truth. The army is totally disbanded. The staff officers, our ADCs, can march no further. We're all tired out, can only walk."'

As for Murat's carriages, which had 'come from Naples under the orders of Fontanier, his stable-master' Rossetti doesn't say. But he's found 'three of my horses and two grooms who'd been in the King's convoy also waiting for me'.

Vilna's much despised Jews – a very large segment of the population – may be driving hard bargains and showing little or no compassion for the French who all these months have been behaving so arrogantly toward them. But now they're being

'very useful. When no one could supply any more bread or sugar, or coffee, or tea, etc., they brought us spiced bread. Better still, they could even un-nest – God knows where from – means of transport, horses, sledges, when there were none to be had anywhere. Thanks to them some hundreds of officers managed to escape from Russia's frozen plains. But "*le monsieur* had to have money", even a lot of money, because they were robbers beyond all expression.'

Sledges and sleighs, above all, are in maximum demand. The otherwise unprejudiced von Suckow has to pay 20 roubles for a sledge which, he assumes, 'hadn't cost our noble intermediary more than a tenth part of that sum'.

Hearing the drums sounding the 'Fall-in!', Griois and his comrades assume

'these warlike sounds only applied to the Vilna garrison, charged with driving away the enemy from the town. They troubled us very little. Nor had I paid much attention, on getting here, to Marshal Ney, whom I'd seen on the square forming up such soldiers as he'd been able to reunite into platoons.'

Fezensac says the 'officers of III Corps, like the rest of the army, had spent the day quietly enough in the houses, and troubled themselves very little when they heard the *générale* go, or about the approach of the enemy'. And Hochberg, Margrave of Baden – loth even to pause at Vilna and wanting to make a bee-line for the German frontier – sees '74 officers and doctors of the Baden troops refusing to leave'. Griois and his friends are calmly having supper when the orderly officer they've sent to Eugène's headquarters returns:

'Never in my life shall I forget how we felt when he told us the Prince, like the rest of the army, was about to get going and that Vilna was going to be entirely evacuated during the night. I was stunned. The most utter discouragement seized hold of me. Death seemed preferable to the fatigues and sufferings we were again going to have to endure.'

He longs to get a fever, as an excuse to stay. But his temperature remains obstinately normal. His feet, however, have swollen so he can't get his boots on again. 'So I was going to have to stay at Vilna or else leave in the icy cold, legs bare and with no other shoes except a pair of old slippers I'd had great difficulty in finding in the house.' 'So in this terrible cold,' von Muraldt hears to his despair,

'now at -28°, this unexampled retreat was to go on! My strength didn't suffice for me to continue the journey on horseback, still less so on foot.'

At the same time he can't bear the thought of being taken prisoner. Fortunately a Captain von Hagens 'of the Bavarian Lifeguards' [*sic*] who's just joined his group, overhears him discussing with his friend Knecht what to do now, and his own horse having just died, but who has a little cart and a servant to drive it, suggests they harness up Muraldt's horse to it, so that the feverishly coughing Muraldt can ride in it. Well, for lack of a sleigh, a cart will do. Said and done. The benevolent Hagens arranges everything. Since Knecht is to proceed on horseback with the rest of the group, they bid each other a fond farewell 'hoping to meet again in better times'. And Muraldt takes his seat in the cart. But Hagens feels he must go off and get some bread and food for the journey; and suggests they drive to the market place and wait for him there. Which they do:

> 'From all the town's streets and alleyways crowds of people were already crossing the square en route for Kovno. Already we could hear cannon-fire and even some musketry from the surrounding hills. Each moment the disorder and noise were growing worse. I waited impatiently for my fellow-traveller to come back. In vain I looked to right and left. A long while we waited; but still he didn't come. Meanwhile the cannonade was growing and coming closer to the town. From the men hurrying past us we caught the words: "We're cut off. The Cossacks have occupied the Kovno road", and so forth.'

Muraldt and the servant discuss what to do, decide to wait a little while longer. But when, after two hours, von Hagens still doesn't put in an appearance, they decide to leave without him. Bonneval for his part is still obsessively guzzling *crêpes* when 'fortunately the sound of the Russian guns wrenched us away from our feast, and we got going again'. Now it's 11 p.m. In I Corps' monastery Le Roy hears

> 'a shout of "To arms!" The drums beat the "Fall-in!" Half asleep, still not believing my ears, I'm just sitting up, when the colonel tells me to bring the regiment downstairs, says he's waiting to take us to new lodgings.'

Pushing the regiment's Eagle-bearer in front of him and lit by several fine candles, Le Roy tries to encourage his exhausted comrades of the 85th by telling them they've better lodgings waiting for them in the suburbs, where they'll be better able to defend themselves if attacked. But several officers, he sees in the candlelight, are in no mood to obey:

> 'Come along, captains! Come along, lieutenants! You who've got this far, surely you aren't going to let me leave all on my own? Are you going to abandon your Eagle just when you're getting back to a friendly country? Come, lads, just a little more courage! I'm in the same wretched state you are, and yet here you are, wanting to add to my sufferings the chagrin of seeing brave men abandon themselves to the tender mercies of a enemy who's furiously determined to ruin us. Oh, believe me, you can hope for no pity. Stay here, and you're giving yourselves over to death.'

(At least that's what he, as a grandfather, will say he said.) One of the older captains, who's been with the 85th since Egypt and fought in innumerable battles, can't resist Le Roy's stirring harangue and gets up with difficulty:

> '"Help me up, even if I'm going to die at the foot of the stairs. Help me up," he said to his comrades, "so I can die a bit further on." We set him on his legs. He couldn't take even one step. His legs, so long stiff and swollen, could no longer support him. Collapsing again into a sitting position, he asked as a last favour to be allowed to embrace the Eagle. Three of his friends and several soldiers tried in vain to come with us. Like him they embraced the Eagle and shed tears at this symbol of a distant fatherland. We left them with two sappers to look after them until the enemy got there.'[15]

The cold beer offered to Pion des Loches and his friend Bitche by the ladies has immediately given him diarrhoea. Even so, they're still at table when, at 11 p.m., they too hear the *générale* being beaten. Realising what's going to happen and afraid of waking up too late tomorrow morning, des Loches convinces the others to come with him to Murat's headquarters at the café in the suburbs, where they spend the small hours with other artillerymen and officers, most of whom have severe colds and whose coughing makes a hellish din all night:

'I was bent double on a bale of hay and unable to stretch my legs. My diarrhoea was getting worse and worse. Unable to get out, I was reduced to shoving aside the bales of hay I was lying on.'

All that's left of Pion's wagonful of provisions, wines, liqueurs, etc., so carefully stocked in Moscow, is 'a few sugar loaves'.

Rapp, his nose, one ear and two fingers frost-bitten, has meanwhile dismounted at Hogendorp's headquarters, where he inquires after Ney, to whom Napoleon had ordered him to give his support. And Ney tells him:

'I've just had the *générale* beaten, and have hardly been able to assemble 500 men. They're all frost-bitten, exhausted and despondent. No one wants to hear another word about fighting. You look as if you're in a bad way?'

That night Roch-Godart's feeling so ill he could die:

'But my worst affliction, much though I was suffering physically, was not to be able to mount a horse in these critical moments and support the fatigues and cold I was going to be exposed to.'

Many, perhaps most, of the 20,000 or so of those who can go no further are wounded men. After a few hours rest to recover from his own utter exhaustion, Larrey has made

'a quick visit to the hospitals, to make sure they were being served in those respects which concerned me. At the Hospice of Charity I gathered together the sick surgeons and principal wounded officers, whom I confided to the especial care of the good Grey Sisters. In all the hospitals, beside all such medical officers, I left a sufficient number of surgeons of all grades to treat the wounded. I left them letters of recommendation to the senior medical officers of the Russian army; and got ready to join the Guard and the staff.'

Neither is Lefèbvre's son – known to the whole army as 'Coco' – in a state to be transported any further. So at their host's house, where comfortable lodgings and a good dinner had been prepared in advance, the terrible decision is taken to leave him too behind. And Louise Fusil – remembering how the old Marshal had saved her life between Krasnoïë and the Berezina – nobly volunteers to stay on as his son's nurse:

'Late that evening the Marshal came back and told us everyone was leaving; and he wrote to the Russian general commanding the outposts that, forced to leave his son in the town, he trusted in his loyalty to treat him generously as an enemy.'

One of Lefèbvre's ADCs is sent off with the message.

Obviously Sergeant Scheltens and his 29 comrades of the 2nd Grenadiers have strong digestions; for they, at least, have survived their sudden banquet. They're just coming out of Berthier's house when Scheltens sees

'a soldier killed in a manner in which no one, perhaps, can ever before have left for the next world. Our Lieutenant Seraris was just coming out. He was carrying a ham under each arm. Appears a soldier, barring his way and demanding one of his hams. By way of reply our man instantly got a blow on the head with the ham, applied with such force it felled him to the ground. He was so weak, it's only fair to add, little was needed to slay him.'

Out there on the main square Lefèbvre has 'drawn up the 600 Grenadiers of the Guard that still remained to him in battle formation'. But Captain Lignières sees how the agonising prospect of having to abandon his sick son is causing the poor old man utterly to lose his head:

'Standing in front of us, the 1st Regiment of Chasseurs of the Old Guard – to be more correct, of the remains of the Old Guard – he said: "Look, here's this Old Guard which was the terror of Europe, of the world. Look what a state it's in! You think you'll see France again? Not one of you will ever see it again." And pointing:

'"D'you hear the guns here, d'you hear them over there?"

'A voice shouted: "Silly old fool, shut up! If we've got to die, we'll die."

'One of the King of Naples' ADCs who'd retained all his vigour and activity [Rossetti perhaps?] came to tell him to report to the king. [Afterwards] we were informed that the king had sharply reprimanded him. We never saw him again.'[16]

Although 'furiously tempted to remain behind' with his faithful servant-cum-foster-brother Louis, Mailly-Nesle too has decided he'll have to leave him behind to the tender mercies of the enemy. Reluctantly he entrusts him to the care of a Jew who at first refuses 'to take in someone who was so ill'. He leaves him all his money; 'and we parted, tears in our eyes'. Once again blue blood has recourse to its peers. Going to the palace just after Murat has evacuated it, he finds everything there in turmoil. Flouting the efforts of some officers who fail to recognise him, swear at him and try to turn him away, the young aristocrat gets hold of Narbonne[17] who at once offers Mailly-Nesle 200 gold napoleons – 'but I only accepted half'. Thanks to Caulaincourt's wise measures no fewer than 80 of the 715 IHQ horses have reached Vilna safe and sound. And once again Mailly-Nesle's given one of them.

Bumping into his brigade commander General Jacqueminot and his chief-of-staff Tavernier, Victor Dupuy hears that Sébastiani, as captain of the Sacred Squadron's 2nd Company, has occupied the palace courtyard. All its members are to assemble there at midnight with their horses. So he and his remaining officers of the 7th Hussars do so. Invited upstairs, they're officially informed of the Emperor's departure for France. 'We were told not to become disunited and that in a few moments we'd be marching for Kovno.' News which causes Dupuy – as he himself admits – to lapse from virtue:

'Coming closer to the fire in General Sébastiani's drawing-room, I saw in a corner of the mantelpiece a bottle with its cork half out. I picked it up. It was full. Stuffing it hurriedly under my cloak, I went out, signing to one of my comrades to follow me. As soon as we were in an antechamber I sampled the bottle's contents. It was excellent wine. We drained it quickly. I went back into the drawing-room, put the bottle back in its place, and left, laughing at its owner's disappointment when he found it empty.'

Boulart, meanwhile, is

'just giving myself up to the delight of being able to sleep in a good bed, when someone came and told me Vilna was being evacuated and that we'd better get going.'

A long time he lies there, trying to make up his mind whether he can't afford to sleep on until morning:

'But at length, at midnight, I pulled myself together and went to General Sorbier, where I got into Colonel Lallemand's[18] carriage, together with Captain Evain who, having been burnt at Krasnoië by the explosion of an ammunition box, had been travelling in it for several days.'

Neither has Griois, with his swollen feet still in slippers, been able to face up to the prospect of having to resume the march. Come what may, he has decided he's going to stay where he is. But then, suddenly, a fellow-officer, 'a M. Guyot, who'd left from Verona with a detachment of remounts and conscripts and been kept at Vilna by the governor' and who'd been lingering in Vilna for the past month, turns up. Both he and his men and horses, Guyot says, are in tiptop condition,

'and were at my disposal. With a zeal and an urgency I'll never forget as long as I live, he undertook to find a sledge, harness two of his best horses to it, and come and fetch me in an hour or two.'

Which Guyot does. What's more he brings with him a pair of his own boots, large enough for Griois' swollen feet. This gives Griois back his courage 'which, I admit, had entirely abandoned me that evening'. Some time after 1 a.m. Guyot comes back and fetches him. Others of his party have already gone on ahead;

'Only two of those who'd shared our billet, utterly worn out by fatigue and with frost-bitten feet, preferred to wait for the enemy.'

Giving up all hope of ever again seeing his adjutant-major 'M. Lenoble,[19] who'd never left my side throughout the campaign' and whom he hasn't seen since their last bivouac, Griois climbs into a sledge filled with hay. And off they go, Guyot riding and then walking beside it, followed by some gunners, one them leading Griois' horse. Rossetti's servant, too, has swapped his wagon for a sleigh, 'loading it with my effects and the new provisions of food he'd got hold of in Vilna'. Now at 2 a.m., 'an adjutant of the Guard came to warn me that Marshal Lefèbvre was getting ready to leave the town, and that Marshal Ney, who'd resumed command of the rearguard, would be following him at one hour's distance. I went to the King and spent the rest of the night at his head-quarters.'

After buying himself 'a fur hat, fur gloves and fur boots', Lieutenant Vossler together with some Prussian cavalry officers who've have placed themselves under the command of General Count Norman have decided to follow side roads to the Niemen and then each make his own way home. Unfortunately no one's been giving any orders to von Suckow. At the Café Lichtenstein he's awakened by a violent kick in the ribs

'from M. Lichtenstein in person. With a ferocious air this café-keeper who'd earned so much money from us and who'd always received us in the most flattering manner and with the humblest and deepest bows, now shouted at me: "Get up, you dog of a German! And get the hell out of here! Your comrades have already run away and are getting the treatment from the Cossacks they deserve." Yes, the Cossacks were in the streets. On all sides one heard shouts, oaths, whiplashes being applied, and groans in I don't know how many languages.'

Franz Roeder, in the home of a drunken English vet named Mr Drew who'd been his host in July, is feeling too dreadfully ill to go on. With the best will in the world neither he nor his Sergeant-Major Vogel can go a step further. Roeder, that sharply intellectual, humane if at times arrogant man, that stickler for justice who could never resist the temptation of another campaign, has undergone a religious conversion more heartfelt and deci-sive and certainly less rhetorical than Le Roy's: '10 December: I'm sitting here in Vilna! It's morning and I've slept in a bed, completely undressed!' Roeder thanks God from the bottom of his heart; prays he, even so, may reach the frontier: 'God, what appalling misery! And all this has been sur-vived by a man in failing health, with swollen feet and hands, thin as lath! But God be praised, the pain in my chest has abated.' With this pious but heartfelt reflection he falls into a kind of delirium, in which he dreams he's

'still on the icy road, where the dead, as if on a battlefield, lie in frozen ranks along the roadside, and an infinite number of horses.'

Sometimes he thinks he's going mad ...[20]

'More than 20,000 men, almost all sick,' Fezensac sums up, 'several generals, many officers, almost all sick, fell into the power of the enemy, as well as stocks of victuals, armaments and clothing.' Among them are 3,000 to 4,000 officers. Also numerous women. One, after being tragically separated from her two children en route, is Mme Marie-Rose Chalmé – she who'd been interviewed by Napoleon in the Petrovskoï Palace outside Moscow.[21] Like so many others – like Franz Roeder, almost – she'll die in Vilna – probably from typhus.

CHAPTER 24

PONARI'S FATAL HILL

Why the arsenal wasn't blown up – Ney's new rearguard – Mouton the poodle's last fight – 'he was like one of the heroes of olden time' – gold millions in the snow – 'the sharpest cry I'd ever heard him utter' – a poor Polish maidservant – Ambassador Pradt is dismissed

At 4 a.m., in a sudden brief but heavy snowfall, III Corps, a mere couple of hundred men, leaves at Murat's heels. Of the 4th Line all that's left is a sergeant and ten men. The temperature, Larrey notices as he leaves, has 'risen a few degrees. A great deal of snow fell in those few moments.' Marching out through the Kovno suburb with the Old Guard in pitch darkness and the heavily falling snow, III Corps is followed by the debris of all the others. And when at 6 a.m. IV Corps – also only a mere hundred or so men still under arms – leaves the St-Raphael monastery, Labaume and Cesare de Laugier everywhere see

'the courtyards, galleries, stairs of buildings full of soldiers. We left in silence, leaving the streets littered with soldiers drunk, dead or asleep. Neither shouts nor orders could get anyone to obey.'

Those of the 85th who'd responded to Le Roy's exhortations had made up their bivouac fires 'from newly constructed but dismantled houses in the Kovno suburb' just opposite Murat's headquarters. Leaving them, they too follow on.

But before leaving his café Murat – or is it Berthier? – has suddenly remembered something. A hundred or so miles way to the north-west Macdonald's X Corps, which has been besieging Riga but done little fighting, is still virtually intact. For some time now he's been without orders. 'Macdonald', says Hogendorp, 'had been forgotten about.' Now Berthier hurriedly entrusts a dispatch to a Prussian staff-major who's been waiting for them in Vilna. X Corps, of which two-thirds consist of General Yorck's 'superbly equipped' Prussians, is to withdraw immediately to the Niemen at Kovno. The Prussian major having been sent off with his dispatch, 'an hour before daybreak the King, the Viceroy and the Prince of Neuchâtel left the Vilna suburb and took the Kovno road.'

As a parting administrative gift to the Lithuanian capital Hogendorp has ordered Eblé to blow up its arsenal. The task devolves on Lieutenant Jacquemot, whose company of the 5th Artillery Regiment has left prematurely. This snowy or, as it soon turns out to be, icy clear morning Jacquemot's kicking his heels in the town square, longing for something to eat, when his major comes by. Why's he idling there? Why isn't he getting busy? The captain who's been charged with the job, Jacquemot replies, has gone to get orders from the Marshal. At that moment his own superior turns up and

'has the fuzes cut and placed, ready for lighting, on some planks pierced expressly for the purpose'.

By now it's 8.30 a.m., and already the Cossacks are infiltrating the town from all quarters. Some, Jacquemot's gunners see,

'together with some infantrymen, had climbed the hill beside the arsenal and would soon be reaching it in spite of us'.

And though some of his men have already been detailed off to cope with them, the others decide to light the fuzes forthwith:

'One man lights the one leading to the powder magazine, and a corporal and some gunners in my company those that led to the ammunition wagons. With my own hand I placed two on a little bag.'

But then everything goes wrong. 'Suddenly I see all the gunners who're with me in the arsenal running off as fast as their legs can carry them.' Jacquemot runs after them, shouting to them to come back. There's no danger, he shouts, the fuzes will take five minutes to burn off. Reaching the square in front of the cathedral he finds another squad posted there under a fellow lieutenant:

'He shouted to me: "Did you see them?" "No! who?" "The Cossacks, behind you, removing the fuzes you'd placed!" It was their arrival that put my gunners to flight.'

And who save the Vilna arsenal.

Now it's the Traka Gate, leading to Novo-Troki and Kovno, that's jammed with fugitives. Outside it Hogendorp, with the help of a fellow-Dutchman, a Major During, has managed to assemble a variegated battalion of 400–500 men – including Jacquemot's fugitive gunners. 'He ordered me to form up my platoon and follow on after two companies of the Imperial Guard, to protect the retreat against Cossacks who'd already circumvented Vilna to our left.' On reaching Vilna yesterday, Séruzier, too, had divided his battery into two sections and sent each by the side road that circumvents the town walls. Jacquemot remains at his new post, to let the column pass on. 'The night was magnificent,' Griois will recall,

'and the moon was shining with a brilliance reflected on the carpet of snow covering the countryside. The cold was more rigorous than ever. The ice crackled under the feet of men and horses. Everyone was pressing on, even more so as to stand up to the cold by marching quickly than to flee from the Cossacks.'

There in the moonlight the road is flanked by extraordinary and terrible sights. Bonnet and his little party of the 18th Line had only got into the town

'towards 2 or 3 o'clock – such was the encumbrance at the gate I'd lost touch with my companions but got in by dint of my elbowings, gone to a tavern, been given some food for silver, bought a pound of sugar for gold.'

But immediately leaving again yesterday evening, he had passed

'between lines of stacked muskets abandoned by men who neither would nor could stay out there in the open fields. They were fresh troops of Grandjean's or Lorge's division[1] who'd seen our rout and been stricken by our example.'

But, more terribly, Captain François sees there

'thousands of corpses, completely naked, many of them bearing marks of dagger blows. But it certainly wasn't the Poles who'd committed these crimes; they showed us great attachment. It was Platov's Cossacks who'd assassinated the sick and wounded whom the inhabitants, terrified of these brigands, had driven out of their houses.'

Now Murat and Berthier are riding in one of the few imperial carriages to have survived the night's *auto-da-fé*, followed by the men of the 85th, 'in support of the cavalry [i.e., the Sacred Squadron],

'marching just ahead of him. Murat was between the two bodies, accompanied by his staff and a feeble escort.'

With them, besides Eugène, either on foot or horseback, are Lefèbvre, shattered at having to leave his dying son, Mortier and Bessières, all accompanied by what remains of their staffs. Davout, Labaume notices, has a high fever and is travelling by sleigh. The remaining mounted cavalry are commanded by Sébastiani,[2] who 'at this moment of distress, when egoism was the order of the day' has 'generously offered the hospitality of his headquarters to Narbonne. He and his little group, too, are travelling in three sledges: Narbonne and Castellane's fellow-ADC Chabot in the first; 'I myself with Ayherts, the servant, in the second; the valet and cook in the third.' But soon the moon sets and 'in the darkness of the night' the three sledges become separated.

If Le Roy's finding the going difficult it's because of his new boots. Slithering about in the deep freshly fallen snow, he's beginning to fall behind, even by the time the men of the 85th reach the suburb's last houses.

Vilna's outskirts have already been left behind when someone on Murat's staff suddenly remembers something. What about that picket of 40 men (François says 30), half from the 29th Line and half from the 113th, who'd been guarding the long bridge over the Vilia? General Gratien sends a Captain Paolo Lapi back to bring it in. Although attacked by numerous Russian cavalry, Lapi shows a coolness and self-possession worthy of Ney himself. Withdrawing the picket from the bridge, he closes the ranks and beats the charge:

'Attacked by Cossacks and a furious mob, the men, obeying their officer, formed a ring and fired by ranks. Then, levelling their bayonets, they marched off, cleared themselves a path,'

and so rejoin the rearguard 'without the loss of a single man'.

Meanwhile Ney himself, 'destined up to the last moment to save what was left of the army', has appeared with yet another rearguard. This one is made up of 'some of Wrede's Bavarians and the remains of Loison's division', in all some 2,300 infantry and 200 cavalry. As Hogendorp moves on with his own scratch battalion, he can't help seeing how Ney

'by his extreme ability in the profession of war seemed to augment its strength. He made it manoeuvre in such fashion as to occupy the Cossacks, halt them, and attract them on to itself, and thus cover the general retreat – or rather, rout.'

Not that Hogendorp likes Ney personally: 'he thought he was the only man who was doing his duty, or even knew how to'. Nor has Wrede, 'who couldn't disguise his hatred of the French', have a good word to say for him:

> 'Marching with his staff and the debris of his cavalry under this little rearguard's protection, he kept grumbling with a morose and discontented air at what the Marshal was doing. The Marshal, he was telling his ADCs in German, was giving himself and his men a ridiculous lot of trouble and only making the retreat more difficult.'

Which certainly isn't true. Co-ordinating his rearguard's Bavarians with Séruzier's horse artillery, Ney is protecting the remaining transports. Notably the Treasure, whose wagons had been supposed to leave Vilna at midday yesterday, but in fact have only got going at 7 a.m.

Not far away in the chaotic column Sergeant Bourgogne and his fellow-sergeant Daubenton are fighting for their lives. Not against Cossacks but – a rare mention of regular Russian troops at this stage – with a Russian cuirassier. Daubenton himself, though 'half dead from cold and hunger, his face thin, pale and blackened by the bivouac fires' is 'still seemingly full of energy'. But his movements are being hampered by the regimental dog, 'a handsome poodle' named Mouton – whose name of course means 'sheep'. Sheep by name, but certainly not by nature, Mouton has been with the Fusiliers-Grenadiers ever since 1808, when they'd found him in Spain. He'd been at the battles of Essling and Wagram; gone back with the regiment to Spain; but in Saxony, en route for Russia, had gone missing, perhaps stolen. Yet in Moscow there he was: 'A 15-man detachment had left Paris some days after ourselves, and as they passed through the place where he'd disappeared the dog had recognised the regimental uniform and followed the detachment.' Out of pity for Mouton's frost-bitten paws Daubenton has attached him to his knapsack, where he's 'barking like a good dog'. Which is just the trouble:

> 'The cuirassier gave Daubenton a second blow on his shoulder, which struck Mouton on the head. The poor dog howled enough to break one's heart. Although wounded and with frozen paws, he leapt off his master's back to run after the man; but being fastened to the straps of the knapsack he pulled Daubenton down. I thought it was all over with him.'

Bourgogne takes aim, but the priming of his musket doesn't burn; and 'the man, shouting savagely, threw himself on me'. He just has time to scramble in under an abandoned wagon

> 'and present my bayonet at him. Seeing he couldn't do anything to me, he went back to Daubenton, who because of Mouton hadn't had time to get up. All the time that devil of a dog was barking and dragging him sideways.'

But Daubenton's musket goes off and the Russian cuirassier

> 'uttered a savage cry, made a convulsive movement, and at the same moment his sword fell, also the arm that held it. Then a stream of blood

came from his mouth, his body fell forward over the horse's head, and in this position he remained as if dead.'

Freeing himself, Daubenton grabs the cuirassier's horse. At that moment they hear behind them a lot of noise, followed by cries of "Forward! Fix bayonets!":

'I came out from under my wagon and saw Marshal Ney, musket in hand, running up at the head of a party of the rearguard. At the mere sight of him the Russians fled in all directions. The rearguard seized several horses, and made their riders march among themselves.'

But they're soon left behind. 'What else could we do? Never shall I forget the Marshal's commanding air at that moment,' Bourgogne concludes admiringly,

'his splendid stance in face of the enemy and the confidence he inspired in the unhappy sick and wounded around him. At that moment he was like one of the heroes of olden time. In the last days of this disastrous retreat he was the saviour of what was left of the army.'

But it's been poor Mouton's last fight. 'I never saw him again.'

Each of the remaining Treasury wagons – these caissons which Kergorre, Peyrusse and others have been conducted at such immense pains all the long way to Moscow and back – contains 12 million francs in gold; and – as Davout had already pointed out on 8 December on the eve of reaching Vilna – 'is much too heavily laden'. Together with others which have been picked up in Vilna, they too are now to meet their Nemesis.

Three miles outside Vilna, just beyond a bend in the river Vilia, there's a short steep slope. Ponari Hill.[3]

Three days ago, on 7 December, the Oudinots' carriage, drawn by its rough-shod horses, had had no difficulty in 'vigorously mounting this straight steep slope', though even then the Duchess of Reggio, peering out into the murk through its window, had

'made out some motionless soldiers scattered all over the slope they'd vainly tried to climb. Overcome by the cold, they'd collapsed; and no one who'd fallen there had got up again. A few dribbles of blood had escaped from their lungs and nostrils and reddened the snow.'

Neither do the Polish Lancers of the Guard, who're forming the advance guard, 'have the least difficulty' in climbing it. 'The first-comers,' Griois goes on,

'had been able to reach the top. The hill wasn't very high; but it was steep, and covered in ice. The greater part had halted on the road.'

But then, as the surface has become more and more slippery – 'like marble' – under successive sleighs, sledges and other vehicles, more and more have failed to make the gradient, slithered backwards, and ended up all at a criss-cross at the bottom. 'Since they were blocking it,' Griois sees,

'those coming on behind had decided not to go any further tonight. Grouped around fires fed by the debris of broken or abandoned vehicles, their drivers made a picturesque tableau as they waited for daybreak.'

Approaching in their three sleighs along the road in the darkness, Narbonne's scattered party, too, see 'the mountain covered by the campfires of drivers who'd realised it was impossible to get on.' And at once all the Grand Army's remaining artillery and its few surviving headquarters vehicles – they'd had left Vilna at 8 a.m. – get hopelessly stuck. So that by the time IV Corps headquarters arrives on the chaotic scene it finds that 'no vehicle had been able to pass for the last 24 hours':

> 'After marching for about an hour, the column came to a sudden halt and we saw in front of us a veritable sea of men. Several of us went to find out what the matter was and we reported back that the first carriage hadn't been able to climb the hill.'

Are they even on the Kovno road, Labaume wonders. 'The Poles were making for Novo-Troki.'[4] Should IV Corps have taken that smaller road which, a mile or so to the rear, had borne off to the right? But no. It simply isn't possible, Le Roy and Jacquet realise, 'to go off to right or left, the roadsides being steep and wooded'.

After two hours painful marching during which they've diverted themselves by swapping memories from Spain, Jean-Marc Bussy and his sergeant, who've long ago lost touch with any of their Swiss comrades, are also brought to a standstill by this 'mass of cannon, ammunition wagons, carts, halted pell-mell at the foot of a hill'. Obviously neither guns nor Treasury wagons are going to get up it, nor indeed anything else much that moves by horsepower. For all that moves on wheels this icy slope's the end of the road.

But sledges? All the rest of the long icy night Castellane tries to 'move my sledge on, through the guns, the wagons'. Soon the jam has become inextricable; and by the time von Muraldt gets there the gunners are already detaching their horses and spiking their guns. Clothes, uniforms, effects of every sort lie scattered on the snow. Although Paymaster Guillaume Peyrusse, who'd left Vilna at 7 a.m., no longer has his own calèche, he still has his Treasury wagon. At 10 a.m., together with the others, it reaches the foot of Ponari Hill:

> 'I spent the hours of darkness looking for roads, trying out ways through. Neither my horses nor I could keep our feet. Since it's impossible to get on, I hoped it'd clear tomorrow,'

he'll afterwards write to his friend André in Paris:

> 'That fatal day 25 degrees of frost were killing me. The reflux of men running away from the Cossacks, who'd been masters of the town since 9 a.m., was causing an appalling disorder. The blockage grew; finally nothing could get by. Already the Cossacks were reaching the summit, bringing cannon with them.'

What to do? Someone's sent to consult Murat. Who tells the emissary from the Treasury:

> '"There isn't a moment to lose to save as much as we can for His Majesty." I was ordered to take everything I could out of my wagon, load it on to my horses and reach the top of the hill, where we were to rally.

I don't know how I found the strength to do so. From all sides I took whatever sacks I could find on the vehicles. I broke open my cases of gold and put all of it, my roubles,[5] my jewels, into the sacks. Taking any men of the Household I could find, I gave each a horse to take by the bridle, took some effects, and set fire to all the rest; and there I go, walking on foot with my convoy.'

Truly Peyrusse is earning the position of the Emperor's travelling cashier, the object of his burning ambition! 'We busied ourselves thrusting aside the overturned vehicles,' Berthier will write to Napoleon,[6]

'setting fire to everything that got in the way, so as to get the rest of the Treasure through. Almost all the vehicles had only got there after we'd put 20 horses to each. Of Your Majesty's carriages only three got to the top. Your Majesty's table silver and that of the paymaster of your household was put into bags and carried on horses. None of it was lost.'

But at the foot of the hill someone breaks open one of the ordinary Treasury wagons:

'It was like a signal. Everyone flung himself on these vehicles, smashed them open, dragged out the most precious things. The men of the rearguard, passing in front of this disorder, threw away their weapons to load themselves with booty. So furiously did they fling themselves into it, they didn't even hear the whistling of musket balls or the Cossacks' howlings. One even saw Russians and Frenchmen, forgetting all about the war, jointly pillaging the same wagon. Ten millions of gold and silver vanished.'

Already the lids of several caissons – among them perhaps the two which Coignet had brought from Paris in June?[7] – have been smashed open with musket butts and are being plundered of their little casks of gold napoleons:

'Even so, we saw many men hurry by, indifferent, only being interested in saving their lives and paying not the least heed to the bags of cash being flung about on the ground. A struggle had broken out among the plunderers. Several bags full of gold and silver had fallen from hands frozen too stiff to hold them, and now the coins were rolling about on the ice.'

Among the Treasury vehicles that have to be abandoned, Kergorre sees, is the new one designated by Berthier before reaching Vilna 'for the most precious items' and into which Paymaster Duverger, at Vilna, has put the precious jewel-encrusted Madonna, worth so many millions, taken from Moscow.

Is there really no way round? Planat de la Faye recalls having carefully studied the map on his way to Vilna in June, and that there's another road 'not a mile to our rear' that leads to Novo-Troki and which mounts the hill at a gentler gradient. 'We'd be able to regain the Kovno road cross-country.' Lariboisière's carriage, Planat sees, as he stands there watching not only soldiers but officers fighting for the gold lying in the snow, hasn't a ghost of a chance of getting through this chaos, let alone up the hill. No more than Roch-Godart's or Delaborde's. 'The General hesitated,' Planat goes on:

'Honoré thought we ought to unharness the horses, load on to them all we could save of the baggage, set his father on one of the pack-horses, and try to pass through the woods flanking the road on either side.'

But Planat's sure that Lariboisière, weak and depressed as he is, isn't up to sitting a horse:

'At this moment General Pernetty, whose calèche was just behind us, having heard our discussion, dismounted and agreed with me. Without wasting more time on discussion, I took the lead-horse's bridle and turned our calèche around. Since the vehicles coming behind us had passed to right and left of us in hopes of finding a way through, we went back without meeting any obstacle; and by the end of a quarter of an hour we were on the Novo-Troki road, where we soon heard musketry and hurrahs. Vehicles, admittedly in no sort of order, were moving on along this road, which wasn't encumbered. So General Pernetty and I galloped ahead to organise two regular files of vehicles and to halt every-thing which wasn't an ammunition or baggage wagon.'

Many other individuals besides the Poles – who've taken this route as a mat-ter of course – are doing the same. Lejeune for instance.

But at the foot of Ponari Hill the jam's only getting worse, and all the time the sound of Séruzier's cannon fire and Ney's fusillades is coming closer. Likewise the noise from the ever-growing mass of men pouring out from Kovno.

How to get up this mountain of ice? Certainly not up the road, even on foot. Many individuals, among them Le Roy, still gravely handicapped by his new boots, are therefore struggling to get up through the brushwood on each side.[8] Taking off from the road, he's cut himself a stick in the woods, heavy as they are with the night's fresh-fallen snow, and crawls slowly upwards. But von Suckow's feverish legs won't even carry him. 'Thereto my driver was showing clear signs of wishing to mingle with the other plunder-ers around the bags of gold and leave me in the lurch.' But somehow or other he dissuades him; and they too keep to one side of the road:

'Thanking God and after inexpressible difficulties and at almost every moment, often having had to halt to let our poor horse get its breath back',

von Suckow gets his light vehicle up to the summit. Cursed and sworn at by the crowd all round them, Griois and Guyot, too, take off to the left and put their backs into heaving their sleigh upwards over the virgin snow:

'We were half-way up when some terrifying shouts were heard from above us and spread swiftly down to the bottom. It was a cannon which, held up at the summit and disturbed from its place by some shock, was hurtling downwards with a terrible noise, smashing and dragging with it everything it met with.'

All tangled up no doubt with its team of six or eight horses, it rushes down past them. And at long last Griois and Guyot reach the summit with their sleigh. So, at dawn, does Castellane; but without his. 'Three-quarters of the way up', fed up with his slow progress, he'd decided to abandon it and walk, leaving it with Ayherts the servant.

Still at the rear of the column – or rather the inchoate mass – Sergeant Daubenton has had the Russian cuirassier's horse snatched from him and disappeared into the crowd to assert his rights, leaving Bourgogne to suffer acutely from colic and wonder whether that Jew's wine he'd drunk yesterday at Vilna wasn't poisoned? Trudging on 'in the midst of men, women, and even some children', he looks about him in vain for some glimpse of his friend. Some Hessians – he assumes they're from Victor's IX Corps – have just tried to make a stand on a little hillock, but been wiped out by Russian cavalry:

'Behind, only Marshal Ney and his rearguard were to be seen, taking up position on a little eminence.'

And ahead of him Bourgogne too surveys Ponari Hill

'from the foot to the summit. The road about three-fourths up the slope to our left could be traced by the number of wagons, carrying more than seven [sic] millions in gold and silver, as well as other baggage and carriages drawn by horses whose strength was so exhausted they'd had to be left on the road.'

Now he reaches the abandoned bivouacs where some men are still warming themselves at the still smouldering fires. Lieutenant Jacquemot, whose horses have been roughshod ever since late November and who has therefore managed to get up the hill with his gunners, even sees

'two companies of the Guard thrown into disorder, never to reassemble. The carriages abandoned at the foot of the hill were being burnt and all sorts of things were being pillaged. The standards taken from the enemy, even the enormous cross of St Ivan, taken from the Kremlin[9] were lying abandoned on the ground.'

For Fezensac it's

'a singular sight to see men covered in gold and dying of hunger, and to find spread out on the snows of Russia [sic] all the objects invented by Parisian luxury'.

Bourgogne, all on his own now, rounds

'the hill to the right. Here several carts had tried to pass, but they'd all been overturned into the ditch at the roadside. One wagon still had many trunks in it. I should have liked to carry one off, but in my feeble state didn't dare risk it, afraid, having once got down, I'd not be able to climb out of the ditch again.'

But someone from the Vilna hospital corps 'seeing my dilemma, was kind enough to go down and threw me a box' containing four fine linen shirts and some cotton trousers. Which are almost more welcome than gold – especially as he has 800 francs on him anyway, and hasn't changed his shirt since 5 November, and his 'shreds and tatters' like everyone else's are 'filled with vermin. A little farther on I picked up a band-box containing two superb hats.' And here's his old friend and fellow-countryman

Sergeant Picard, who helps himself to a pair of Marshal's epaulettes! A little further on, through some brushwood, the path 'beaten out by the first men who'd crossed the hill at daybreak' turns left; and he rejoins the highway. Shortly afterwards little Jean-Marc Bussy – for his part he has contented himself with filling his empty cartridge pouch with cartridges – sees two men in gold-braided hats by the roadside, whom he at first takes for Russians; but then recognises as two Swiss colonels. Has he seen their carriages, they ask. He says he hasn't and, after some words of mutual encouragement, passes on. Half an hour after reaching the summit, Bourgogne hears

'a heavy fusillade, accompanied by loud cries from the direction of the wagons. Marshal Ney, seeing the booty couldn't be saved, was having it distributed among the men, and at the same time was keeping the Cossacks off by steady volleys.'

A moment later, just as he sees some Cossacks advancing towards him, he sinks 'more than five feet, up to my eyes' into the snow. Almost suffocates.

But at the foot of Ponari's fatal slope the remains of the Guard artillery, the rest of Napoleon's carriages and most of the Imperial Treasure have all been lost. Roch-Godart, too, has lost his carriage and sledges, just as Jomini, still very sick, has lost the brand-new sledge he'd just got hold of at Vilna, together with its coachman. For all his sapience Pion des Loches, too, has to abandon his last three vehicles. 'They didn't leave again. We clambered up the slope through trees and rocks.' All that's left of II Corps' artillery also gets stuck and is left behind:[10]

'It was there the remains of the army's carriages disappeared. Thus of 1,100 guns that had gone into Russia, not one would recross the Niemen.[11] As for the carriages of the Emperor and his suite, the only ones I saw after Vilna were the calèches of Generals Sorbier and Lallemand; and I guarantee each of them had cost at least 100 artillery horses. Drouot lost the two carriages left to him,'

concludes Pion des Loches with a certain smug satisfaction.

'"It was 12 millions my troops looted at Vilna,"' Napoleon will tell his minister Molé in February. Just now, however, he has other things to think about. At the Gragow post-house he and Caulaincourt have abandoned the 'hermetically sealed' imperial berline for what they've been told is

'a very comfortable one mounted on runners which the local squire had had made for his daughter, recently married. At first this Polish gentleman had refused to sell it, no matter what price was offered him;'

but on hearing who it's for has insisted on giving him it for nothing. Napoleon tells Caulaincourt:

"Hours flit by, and in my position if I lose a moment I may have lost everything," and he won't 'accept the gift, for which (according to Bourgoing/Wonsowicz) he paid 1,000 ducats (10,000 francs)'; but according to Caulaincourt:

'a few gold pieces. In view of the Emperor's impatience to reach his destination it was a piece of good luck. We left the carriage in the charge of the footman. The Emperor hardly gave us time to transfer our rugs and weapons. For lack of space in the sleigh he was even forced to abandon his *nécessaire* he found so useful,'
– a gold item of equipment which, according to Constant, contained 'everything that was agreeable or useful in a bedroom, together with a breakfast service for several persons'. – 'Uncomfortably seated and hemmed in still worse,' Caulaincourt continues, 'he was sacrificing everything that makes a long journey endurable'. At Mariempol they'd been caught up by the second carriage, with Duroc, Lobau and Lefèvre-Desnouëttes in it, but soon left it behind. And that's the last they'll see 'either of a carriage or a man of those who'd left Smorgoni'. Their new vehicle, alas, turns out to be less than cosy:

'The aged box, which had been once been red, had been set on a sled and had four large windows, or rather panes of glass set in worm-eaten frames, which didn't close properly. The joints of this hulk, three-quarters rotten, gaped open on all sides, freely letting in the wind and snow, which I had to be sweeping out all the time so that we shouldn't get soaked through by letting it melt on the seats.'

Caulaincourt has again had to sacrifice half his cloak to keep his imperial fellow-traveller even moderately warm. So far from being cast down, however, Napoleon seems to be more than a little euphoric. When Caulaincourt expresses doubts as to whether the army will be able to rally at Vilna he dismisses them out of hand: "Vilna's well-stocked with food," he tells him, "and that'll set everything to rights again. I've anticipated everything in the orders I've left with M. de Bassano."[12] And all the time he's making brilliant analyses – seen from his point of view – of the power situation in Europe: "Everyone should see the Russians as a scourge. The war against Russia is a war wholly in the interests – if rightly judged – of the older Europe and of civilisation. Europe should envisage only one enemy – the Russian colossus."

To this, Caulaincourt ventures, with his usual frankness: 'It's Your Majesty who's the cause of everyone's anxiety, which is preventing them from seeing other dangers.'

The crazy old vehicle flies on over the snow. As Napoleon blithely talks on and on, good-naturedly replying to the more pertinent of Caulaincourt's criticisms, he

'felt up for my ear to tweak it; and as he couldn't find it under my bonnet, it was my neck or my cheek that received the pinch – a kindly rather than an irritable one. He was in such a good mood that he admitted the truth of some of the points I'd brought forward. Others he refused. One would have thought he had no immediate concern in them. So far was the Emperor from checking my frankness that he listened and replied not only without ill-humour but with real cordiality.'

Only one thing – or rather, person – infuriates him. His ambassador at Warsaw, Abbé Pradt. Why hadn't he appointed Talleyrand instead? Well, it had been Maret's wife, terrified at the idea of having her husband's predecessor, that arch-intriguer, in Warsaw, who'd intrigued him out of the job. And then, Duroc and others had spoken so well of Pradt:

'"He has ruined all my plans with his indolence. He's a chatterbox, nothing more,"' declares Napoleon angrily.

By now Caulaincourt has 'dispensed with the services of our worthy [Mariempol] post-master, whom the Emperor rewarded suitably'. Some 32 miles north of Warsaw lies Pultusk, scene of the battle of 26 December 1806, reached two hours before dawn:

'A Polish servant-girl, half-dressed, poked and puffed at the fire for all she was worth and nearly burnt her eyes over the most miserable one that ever was lit. The Emperor inquired what this poor girl earned. It was so little that he remarked that the sum would hardly suffice to keep his heavy clothing in order. He bade me give her a few crowns and tell her they were for her dowry. The poor girl couldn't believe her eyes. The Emperor remarked that it was possible to make many people of that class happy with very little money. "I'm impatient, Caulaincourt," he added, "for the day of a general peace, so as to get some rest and be able to play the part of the good man. We shall spend four months in every year travelling within our own frontiers. I shall go by short stages with my own horses. I shall see the cottage firesides of our fair France."'

He goes on to dilate on all he'll do, when that day comes, for France and Europe:

'The soup and the coffee were taking time to come, and the Emperor, numb from the cold and the fire's increasing heat, fell asleep. I seized the opportunity to make some notes. When he woke up his sorry meal was soon gulped down and we clambered back into our sledges.'

Half-way between Pultusk and Warsaw

'although the snow was knee-deep, the Emperor visited the defences of Sierock and Praga. We shook the snow off as best we could before getting back into our cage – for such, exactly, was the shape of the antique box which housed us.'

But here at last is the Vistula:

'The Emperor's vanity didn't reassert itself until we got to the gates of Warsaw. On reaching the [Praga] bridge we couldn't repress a humble reflection on the modest carriage of the King of Kings. He seemed delighted to find himself in Warsaw, and was very curious to see whether he'd be recognised. I think he wouldn't have been sorry if someone had guessed his identity.'

But, even though it's 'the hour when that part of the city is at its most crowded' no one does:

'The Emperor's magnificent green velvet cloak with gold braid only drew the attention of a few humble passers-by. They turned to look, but didn't stop, being in a hurry to get back to their own firesides. Anyway it would have been difficult to recognise the Emperor, for he wore a hood, also of green velvet, and his fur cap covered half his face.'[13]

Amodru the outrider has 'only got there a few moments before', having been ordered to arrange accommodation not at the French Embassy but at the Hôtel d'Angleterre: "I refuse to stay with a man I'm going to dismiss," says Napoleon, and asks 'to be taken to the hotel by way of the Cracow Boulevard, which at that time was Warsaw's main thoroughfare.'

"'I'd like to find myself in that street again," Wonsowicz hears him say, "because I once held a great review in it."' At 11 a.m. after walking up it – 'we didn't take our seats in the sleigh until we'd crossed the main square' – they alight at the Hôtel d'Angleterre. (Pradt says it was at 1.30.) And Napoleon tells Caulaincourt to go and fetch the wretched ambassador.

It's to be a confrontation neither Caulaincourt nor Pradt will ever forget.

'The doors of my room,' Pradt begins his account of his last interview with the Emperor Napoleon,

'were flung open and admitted a tall man, who stalked in, supported by one of my embassy secretaries. "Let's go. Come, follow me!" said this phantom. His head was wrapped in a silk shawl. His face was lost to view in the depths of the fur, in which he seemed to be buried. His gait was hampered by fur-lined top boots. It was a kind of ghost-scene.'

'Dressed as I was,' Caulaincourt concedes, 'the Ambassador was no little amazed to see me. But he was even more astounded, couldn't believe his ears or his eyes, when I said the Emperor was there[14] and was asking for him.'

"'The Emperor?"' he repeats again and again, in astonishment, as Caulaincourt gives the lie to Maret's inflated reports, e.g., of 6,000 prisoners taken at the Berezina. "'Why, in such grave circumstances, write to an Ambassador as if he were the editor of *Le Moniteur,* when it's vital he should know the truth? The number of prisoners is of little import, seeing we can't keep them." Pradt flatters Caulaincourt for having been against the war from the outset: "Your Grace will have justice done you now, for it's well-known you did your best to prevent it."

No comment. Caulaincourt declines some breakfast but asks Pradt to send Napoleon a bottle of Bordeaux; and leaving the flurried ambassador to change his clothes, goes back to the hotel. While waiting for Pradt, Napoleon has been opening his other mail. One item informs him that the playboy Count Montholon – his minister plenipotentiary at Würzburg – has married the divorcée Albine Vassel (both of whom will accompany him to St Helena). Since such marriages are forbidden – except in his own case, for reasons of state – Montholon too is instantly dismissed. By and by Pradt arrives and is admitted to

'a low-ceilinged little room, freezing cold, with its shutters half-closed to prevent his being recognised and where a wretched Polish maidservant was on her knees puffing at a fire of green wood which rebelled at her efforts, sputtering out more damp into the chimney than heat into the room.'

Unadvisedly – but, Caulaincourt thinks, spontaneously – Pradt declares his concern for the health of this phenomenal man who seems to have dropped out of the sky:

'But this seemed to be even less in his favour. The Emperor would rather have been blamed, even criticised by any other man, and wasn't disposed to tolerate this man-to-man air of concern from a man with whom he was deeply angry.'

Caulaincourt tactfully tries to leave the room. But Napoleon, evidently 'to increase M. de Pradt's discomfiture by the presence of a third party', tells him to stay. Upon Caulaincourt pointing out that he must fetch His Majesty a cloak and make other arrangements for the onward journey, he's told, in that case, to summon the Polish Prime Minister, Count Stephan Potocki, and the Minister of Finance. Returning, Caulaincourt, 'as the door between the rooms didn't shut properly', can't help eavesdropping. He hears Napoleon berate the wretched Pradt 'for committing nothing but blunders' – and Pradt trying to justify himself, promising betterment, and reiterating the disastrous state the Polish economy:

'The more M. de Pradt justified himself, the angrier the Emperor became. His presence seemed to be infuriating him. His gestures, the way he shrugged his shoulders, so clearly showed the temper he was in that I really shared the embarrassment of his victim, who was in an agony of mortification. It seemed to me his remarks on some grounds weren't unreasonable.[15] Seeing a card on the mantelpiece, the Emperor stopped suddenly in mid-sentence, snatched it up, wrote a few words on it and handed it to me. It said: *"Tell Maret that fear of the Russians has made the Archbishop of Malines lose his head. He's to be sent back and someone else entrusted with his duties."*'

But by and by Napoleon's fury abates and he asks Pradt:

'"What do the Poles really want?"'

'"They want to be Prussian."'

'"Why not Russian?" Napoleon rejoins.'

'Indignantly turning his back on M. de Pradt, he told him to return in half an hour with the ministers who'd been summoned.' When he's gone, Caulaincourt points out that it's hardly the right juncture to dismiss his ambassador publicly, it'll produce a bad effect. Very well, says Napoleon, Caulaincourt can write to Maret from Posen: "Now let's have dinner, so I can see the ministers, and we'll be off." His point evidently conceded, Caulaincourt drops the card in the fire.

All this time dinner's been getting cold.

Attended by Pradt, Count Potocki and the Minister of Finance arrive. Say how worried they've been at the personal risks His Majesty's been running and their relief at seeing him safe and sound.

'"Risks? Fatigue nourishes me. Peace and rest are only for lazy monarchs."'

Outside the door as he attends to their travel arrangements, Caulaincourt hears him telling the two Poles:

'"I've committed two errors. One, to go to Moscow; the other to have stayed there too long. Perhaps I'll be blamed, but it was a great and bold measure. But it's true: from the sublime to the ridiculous is but a step. Neither French nor German soldiers are made for this climate. Below 7

degrees they're worth nothing. Up to 6 November I was master of
Europe. I am not so any longer.'"

Blatantly exaggerating the army's surviving effectives to 150,000 men, he
says that before three months are out he'll have as strong an army as when
he'd opened the campaign:

"'I carry more weight when I'm on my throne in the Tuileries than at
the head of my army.'"

Well yes, at Pradt's suggestion he'll lend the Grand Duchy "the 2 or 3
million francs in copper from the pawnshops that have already been lying
in Warsaw for three months; and 3 or 4 million in paper, drawn on the
Courland contributions" to raise the country against the Russians. For his
part, he assures the two ministers, he'll never abandon them. Is His Majesty
going to cross Prussia, they ask with obvious anxiety, as he, in the most cordial manner, dismisses them. Yes, he is. Potocki goes home, and his daugh-
ter-in-law notes how

'the fascination this extraordinary man exercised over all who heard
him was so powerful that my father-in-law, who'd been in the deepest
gloom when he'd left us, returned full of hopes'.

Meanwhile Caulaincourt, outside fixing the horses 'while the Emperor
attended to his toilet', jots down

'particulars of what he'd said to the Ambassador. As far as I'd been able
to pay attention to what was being said, I'd heard the Emperor ascribing
his setbacks solely to the climate. The burning of Moscow, he admitted,
had upset his plans.'

But as he climbs back into the sleigh Napoleon the Inexhaustible goes on
grumbling about Pradt:

"'He complains of everyone, criticises everything. What's *he* ever done to
entitle him to blame others? He's losing this campaign for me.'"

Fagalde cracks his whip. And away goes the strange old conveyance, rat-
tling down Warsaw's streets, en route for the Prussian frontier, Posen and
Dresden.[16] It'll take Napoleon and Caulaincourt precisely eight days to
reach Paris – the fastest transit yet recorded.

CHAPTER 25

NEY'S LAST STAND

Lithuania's icy plateau – What's become of Narbonne? – a diary saved, a diary lost – 'the roar of the distant artillery and the howling of the wind' – 'Ney's absence seem to be the end; his presence set everything to rights' – 'I begged every man to show zeal, man by man' – 'The King of Naples must be replaced' – I'm the rearguard of the Grand Army'

When at last they get to the top of Ponari Hill both Fezensac and Le Roy are surprised to find themselves alone. But then some of Fezensac's men catch up with him; and Le Roy, coming out of a hut he's gone into to scratch the soles of his new boots with his knife, finds himself among a dozen of the rearguard's skirmishers whose 'packs, though not full, seemed to be laden down with something very heavy'. Bourgogne, who's also on his own,[1] 'seeing some people were in it', enters the hut. Inside are

'a score of men belonging to the Guard, all with bags containing 5-franc pieces. When they saw me several began calling out: "Who'd like 100 francs for a 20-franc gold piece?"'

But Bourgogne already has '800 francs in gold and more than 100 francs in 5-franc pieces' and at this moment is 'caring more for life than for money'. Outside in the darkness Castellane, he too alone and on foot, having left his sledge to Narbonne's servant Ayherts,[2] is being approached by Ney's men,

'Frenchmen and allies who offered to let me buy looted objects, basins, sets of table silver, etc. Our men were only to happy to give 100, even 300 francs in silver for a gold napoleon [20 francs].'

Getting no offers they try to give away their loot. Some musicians, 'terribly weak and their fingers frozen', are too heavily laden to get far:

'Shaking the 5-franc pieces out of their bags, they say it'd have been better to have left them in the wagons, especially as there'd been plenty of gold for the taking. But many had sacks of double napoleons.'

Others, 'always the weakest', go on clinging to their loot, only to have it torn from them by those who've omitted to take any. Castellane decides he must get going; and Bourgogne, also trudging along on his own, is surprised to see someone he knows coming toward him. It's a comrade named Pinier 'commissioned eight months ago'. Bourgogne asks him where he's bound for. Instead of replying his friend asks him who he is:

'At this unexpected question from someone who'd been my comrade in the same regiment for five years, I couldn't refrain from tears.'

Recognising him, Pinier gives him some wine:

'I only had one free hand, so the good fellow supported me with his left hand and with the other poured the wine into my mouth. Only yesterday, and then very vaguely, had he heard of our disasters.'

Bourgogne tells him there's no army left:

'"What's that firing?"

'"That's the rearguard, commanded by Marshal Ney."

'"I shall join the rearguard,"'

says Pinier. And goes to join Loison's men, not one of whose squares (Loison will claim when he finally catches up) have been broken by Russian cavalry, 'only by grape and roundshot', they being pursued by '14 cannon, without a single one to reply with' and are making haste to join up with Ney. '"You're suffering,"' says Ney dryly, when Loison reaches him. '"You'll be better off at Königsberg. I authorise you to go there."' And Loison hands over his remaining 500 men to General Marchand.[3]

At last day dawns. Once again

'the monstrous cold was accompanied by a brilliant sun that gave only light, but no warmth. The air seemed to be filled with innumerable little icy atoms. If for a moment one closed one's eyes to protect them against the snow's blinding whiteness one had all the difficulty in the world to reopen them.'

Von Muraldt, covered though he is from top to toe in warm furs, feels frozen to the bone. 'The cold hurt dreadfully and every breath I drew made a painful hole inside my chest.' Paymaster Peyrusse's morale is only being kept up by the reflection that he hasn't lost a single one of the coins that were entrusted to him. He needs it. For the Cossacks are at his heels – 'those furious devils weren't content with their fine haul' at Ponari. Not until they've marched four leagues do the Treasury officials rally. Their immediate goal, like everyone else's who remembers the district, is Evë,[4] 44 kilometres from Vilna. In a sleigh that's taken him on board at the summit of Ponari Hill and whose two well-nourished horses are being briskly driven by 'one of the regiment's soldiers whom I'd rudely chastised at Moscow', Brandt gets there at 11 p.m. And orders him to drive straight through the town (sleighs just now being more valuable than gold) and only halts at its last house, where he finds the rest of the Vistula Legion bivouacked:

'You can imagine our comrades' joy! I gave eight napoleons to our saviour for handing over the two horses and the sleigh, but on condition that he stay with me.'

Everyone wants to buy the sleigh; but now, if ever, possession is nine points of the law. At Evë, too, Le Roy catches up with the column. But when Griois gets there it's only to realise he's lost something very precious indeed. His diary,

'which I'd been keeping meticulously ever since I'd left Naples. I'd have given all the gold I still had in my belt to get my notes back.'[5]

The gunner who's been leading his horse – a 'novice' from Vilna – has let someone cut its reins en route. The loss of his last horse – the campaign has cost him no fewer than 27 – and his few remaining effects, 'a shirt, some chocolate, my portfolio, some letters' – is nothing compared with such a loss. And he flies into a rage – a rage that goes on for several days and which he'll afterwards regret – with the gunner, who sheds tears of remorse:

> 'I could even have hit him. Each time I caught sight of that gunner it began again. What I myself, though carried in a sleigh and well covered up, had suffered along that same road should have made me more indulgent, or anyway more just.'

At 5 p.m., Castellane too, 'on foot, exhausted by the fever due to my frost-bitten hand and dying of hunger', has reached Evë, having fallen in en route with Chabot, Narbonne's other ADC, who tells him he'd seen Narbonne on the road some time before dawn, and that 'General Curial assured us he'd seen him in the rear, on foot'. They fear the worst. At 11 p.m. the groom, 'his nose and feet frozen' turns up with his sledge – but still no Narbonne. Nor is there any sign of the servant Ayherts or of Castellane's sledge. Rejoining a headquarters no longer imperial, and after a supper consisting only of 'a bit of black bread, a hunk of meat without even any water', Castellane passes another horrible night 'holding my hand in the air as I shared a bale of hay with Chabot and two of my other comrades'. But, unlike Griois, he consoles himself that when abandoning his sledge at Ponari he'd slipped *his* diary into his pocket 'together with my parents' portraits'. Next day, Friday, he lingers at Evë until 10 a.m.

> 'in hopes of seeing my general. During all that time the mob of stragglers kept passing by. The Old Guard, reduced to 1,400 men at the moment of the Emperor's departure, now counted no more than 800 under arms.'

Murat, it seems, has recovered from his panic, and is intending to make a stand at Kovno, or at very least evacuate it in an orderly fashion. So at 5 a.m. on 11 December, Berthier sends back a staff officer to Ney, asking him to 'make short day's marches to enable us to establish ourselves at Kovno'. Short marches! When Ney, pressed by some Cossacks with fourteen cannon, hasn't a single gun with which to reply! Just as Murat's leaving Evë for Kovno, Loison's division, now only 600 strong, turns up. Some of them belong to the 113th Line, of whom some are Florentines, whose uniform had struck Castellane 'in that town, by its beauty and good quality'. Now the Italian regiment has only some 120 men left, and when Castellane asks one of its sergeants how so fine a unit can have melted away so quickly, the sergeant replies:

> '"We're dying of hunger and cold. The enemy fires a few roundshot at us, we can't send any back."'

So they've melted away, like the rest of the army. Getting into Narbonne's sleigh with their cook – 'the only one of our lot who wasn't at all frost-bitten' – Castellane and Chabot make for Kovno: 'All day our anxiety for M. de Narbonne only grew.' Although his gangrenous hand aches monstrously, he consoles himself by thinking: 'We've seen a spectacle of great horrors. Nothing like it will ever be seen again.'

Now everyone's making for Zismory. Leaving their miserable bivouac at 4 a.m., Lieutenant Jacquemot's gunners, passing through Evë, see on all sides villages in flames and by the roadside, abandoned for lack of teams to draw them, unused guns and ammunition wagons that have belonged to their colleagues of the 18th Company of the 4th Artillery Regiment. This morning, travelling on in his sleigh, he fancies there are even more corpses than yesterday. At one slope he has to get out and – like Napoleon at Liady – 'despite the cold felt by the parts in contact' slide down on his backside. The Fusiliers-Grenadiers (Bourgogne has caught up with them) do the same:

> 'General Roguet, some officers and several sappers who were marching in front, had fallen over. Some picked themselves up, and those who were strong enough went down it in a sitting position, guiding themselves with their hands. Others, weaker, trusted to Providence – i.e., they rolled over and over, like barrels.'

In this fashion Bourgogne, bruised all over, reaches the foot of the hill. But he's cheered to note something not seen for a long time:

> 'The general had ordered a halt to make sure everyone was there. I remember that when a man fell, cries were heard: "Halt! A man's fallen!" A sergeant-major of our battalion shouted: "Halt there! I swear not one of you shall go on until the two left behind have been picked up and brought on." It was by his firmness they were saved.'

Altogether it seems to Bourgogne that

> 'On this march there was much more readiness to help one another than before. Probably it was the hope of reaching our journey's end. Meanwhile the roar of the distant artillery and the howling of the wind were mingled with the moans and cries of men dying in the snow.'

As for himself, however, he feels he's nearing the end of his tether. Straggles repeatedly. Sometimes, though hardly able to drag himself along, he manages to keep up with his comrades. Sometimes, when he doesn't, he falls in with other isolated comrades, most of them too at their last gasp, and they do what they can to help one another along. Again and again he's rescued by his friend Grangier, who refuses to let him make his will and give up in despair.

Somewhere between Evë and Kovno Murat sees Loison's much-delayed artillery coming towards him. To save its sixteen guns he orders it to turn back. So only the Cossacks have any cannon. And when Jacquemot at about 5 p.m. hears the sound of their approaching gunfire,

> 'our misery didn't leave us enough energy to be afraid of death or try to avoid it. The sound of the hurrahs didn't hasten our march.'

Seeing a village close to the left of the road, they hope to spend the night there. But then, seeing a party of Cossacks forcing some Guard cavalry troopers to evacuate it, are obliged to push on to Zismory. Getting there at 10 p.m., they, like Planat's group, find the village 'packed' and 'entirely devastated'. Ruthlessly, Lariboisière's servants turn out two young Dutchmen 'from the latest levy.[6] They'd formed part of one of the route columns that hadn't been through any of the fatigues of the campaign and were vanishing like smoke as soon as they came in touch with our terrifying column. One of them, who wasn't even twenty, burst into tears and begged to be allowed to stay. In vain. Anyway he was very warmly dressed.'

Jacquemot's gunners, too, have to sleep outside in the snow, with not a bite to eat except a little biscuit pillaged from the Vilna stores. And through part of the night Planat and his comrades hear the Dutch youngster's groans. 'Next morning he was dead.' So are many others who – unlike Muraldt who, though he has some brandy in his cart, wisely decides to stick to tea – have drunk themselves silly on it. 'Certainly two-thirds never saw the sun rise.' But here at Zismory, to his two ADCs' infinite relief, is the white-haired Narbonne. After Ponari he too 'had found himself quite alone, on foot, believing he'd lost everything'. Fortunately he'd confided his money, including the sums Napoleon had given him at Smorgoni for his diplomatic mission in Berlin, to a general of the Neapolitan Guard, who has looked after it for him. He and his party take refuge with 'Sébastiani's very well-composed headquarters'.[7] A Warsaw banker, a M. Bignon, 'is there with his carriage'. Even when a Dutch surgeon has treated his hand, Castellane is unable to hold the reins and has to turn down Sébastiani's offer of his own horse.

Now it's the morning of 12 December, and the first-comers are arriving at Kovno – that 'very well-built little town set in an amphitheatre of pine woods' at the junction of the Rivers Vilia and Niemen, which at midsummer had put Vossler in mind of an Italian city. Immense jagged blocks of ice that seem to Thomas Legler taller than Swiss chalets, stick up from the Niemen's surface 'everywhere frozen to a depth of 6–8 feet'. Yet yesterday evening, almost without realising it, Muraldt's group have crossed over and been received in a village whose lights they'd seen on the Polish shore. Now, recrossing the frozen river in the morning, they again make for Kovno by the Vilna road, and notice how

'since we'd left in June, this town had been provided all round with regular fortifications, with bastions and countersinks, palisaded and furnished with numerous artillery,'

all according to Napoleon's order of early July. Although 'its entrance is narrow' there is as yet no crowd, so Muraldt and his companions have no difficulty in getting in and bivouacking in the main square 'in the centre of town and near the Niemen'.

Here too are immense stores.

The garrison consists of Neapolitans, whose prime duty it is to guard them – notably the huge stocks of rum. Presenting himself at such a store, Muraldt, though confronted with a Neapolitan bayonet and volubly shouted at in an incomprehensible Italian dialect, manages to elude the guard and get himself some biscuit, fresh from the oven – only to find that in the dark he has paid not 2 francs but 2 napoleon*s* (40 francs) for it, almost all the cash he has left.

At that moment – some time around midnight of 11/12 December – Murat and Eugène arrive. And though Murat immediately gives orders that the stores be distributed 'without formalities' the pillage continues. Soon the rum is

> 'virtually flowing in the streets. Only with difficulty were the men prevented from drinking it all up, so as to keep something for the rearguard which, under Marshal Ney, was to join us tomorrow. The smell of it spreading and upsetting me, I lay down on the floor in the corner of another room to sleep'.

It's Muraldt's first night in a warm room since leaving Moscow. Here he's luckier than Fezensac. Dead with fatigue, unable to find himself a lodging of any kind, Fezensac has to sleep on the doorstep of a house already occupied by IV Corps – for soon the crowd has begun to arrive, with the usual battles to get in and keep others out. The Treasury personnel become scattered in the crush: 'Some get inside, others aren't strong enough to push through the mob.' By the time Jacquemot's gunners had got to the town gate there'd already been such a crush that it had been 2 p.m. before they could get through. And nightfall before Griois and his 'guardian angel' Guyot get here, even though they'd left their bivouac in the early hours. By now 'an immense crowd was obstructing the avenues to the gate'. Warmly wrapped up though he is in Guyot's sleigh, Griois' teeth are chattering 'so my jaw could break'. Just then, sitting there shivering in the mob, he catches sight of

> 'a man with a cadaverous face, astride a flankless horse, with a half-burnt forage cap on his head and wrapped in shreds of some bed covering. It was Major Petit, of the artillery, my adjutant in the Calabrian campaign and a comrade of mine for many years past. Only when he told me his name did I recognise him and me he'd probably only recognised from what was left of my uniform and Lieutenant Guyot's.'

Remembering how ill Petit had been when he'd left Smolensk, he's not particularly pleased to see him; 'abandoned by his men, stripped of his effects, he was reduced to the most pitiable state'. Although still accompanied by an NCO as ill as himself, neither has been able to help the other. Seeing Griois sitting there, apparently snug in his sledge,

> 'he came up to me and told me of his misfortunes and how utterly alone he was. Doubtless he expected me to offer to let him join me. And indeed that ought to have been my first impulse. I blush as I confess I didn't; and I was even afraid he'd make the request, which a shred of shame would have prevented me from refusing. But a comrade, a friend, would be only one more mouth to feed.'

Guyot, who has gone off to reconnoitre, comes back and tells Griois it's easier to turn off to the left, go to the river bank, and get into Kovno over its ice:

> 'After a cold "good-evening" I hardly expected a reply to, I decided to take this option and it was without regret, or rather with pleasure, I left M. Petit'

– an act so hard-hearted he'll never forgive himself for having committed it. 'The sufferings of six weeks had effaced all human feeling from me, a monstrous egoism had my heart in its grip.'[8] Griois finds the streets full of military men of every rank, all looking for food and shelter for the night:

'Yells, curses echoed on all sides. Barrels of biscuit and rum from the pillaged magazines were being bashed-in in the middle of the streets and each man was watching jealously over this precious loot. The uproar, the disorder was terrible.'

Peyrusse searches about in the mob for his missing colleagues – resorts no doubt to the same means as Griois, 'usual since everyone had been marching on his own: despite the din, to shout out the names of one's companions'. Luckily, an NCO recognises Griois and takes him to a house outside the town wall where IV Corps' artillery staff are being put up, quite lavishly, by a Jewish family:

'Stimulated by our generosity, they were providing us with any amount of sugar, coffee, dairy goods, potatoes, meat and above all some bread of a brilliant whiteness and an exquisite savour.'

The beer's bad but the wine good. A single largish room contains both the party of officers and their hosts,

'who, without getting in our way too much, were hardly less numerous: i.e., a dozen people, among them a swarm of children who, according to the custom of the country, spent the night above the stove.'

The Jewish family sells them sheepskins, shoes (furred and otherwise), sugar, butter and flour. Their hostess has

'a beautiful Jewish face with an aquiline nose, large black eyes surmounted by eyebrows of the same tint and whose hue stood out against a perfectly white complexion,'

which reminds Griois, that lover of Italian art and music, of 'the Rebeccas and Judiths of the Italian school'. What's more to the point, she spends the night baking for them.

At midday the Guard has been followed into town by I and IV Corps, 'represented by the Eagles, the officers, and a hundred or so men. All the rest had been disbanded.'[9*] Those of its men who, unlike Bourgogne, haven't been able to cram themselves into a room, have bivouacked in the main square. Many are hopelessly drunk on rum, 'the more dangerous' says Fezensac,

'because the men weren't aware of its effects. Only being accustomed to the country's bad brandy, they thought they could drink the same quantities of rum with impunity.'

Dumonceau's men, who've got here in advance, are billeted in a large inn with a yard; but the crush to get inside is so great that, like Fezensac, Dumonceau prefers to camp outside on the pavement. In one corner of the square a fire breaks out and two houses are burnt down.

How many people even realise they've reached the Niemen? Few, so it seems to von Muraldt, if any. Nor are they expecting any imminent improvement in their conditions. Many disbanded men, he sees, are obsessed by only one thought – to get out of Russia, that 'accursed country'. Fezensac too sees masses of fugitives passing straight through the town without even halting:

> 'Accustomed to mechanically following those walking in front of them, we saw them risking suffocation as they forced their way over the bridge, without realising they could easily cross the Niemen on the ice.'

'The Niemen had vanished,' Berthier will write to Napoleon:

> 'Everywhere it was frozen to a depth of 6 feet, and so covered in snow that vehicles were passing over it, as if across a plain. It can bear the weight of the heaviest guns. Only the map showed a river existed there.'

As for the fortified bridgehead, in which optimists at headquarters have been placing their hopes, Berthier explains why one glance at this chaotic scene is enough for the King of Naples to realise there can be no question of halting at Kovno either: 'It's only a big useless redoubt, open at the throat,' i.e., on the river side.

Lejeune's longer route along the Vilia's winding bank has taken more time, of course, than the direct one. And when he gets to Kovno it's

> 'snowing heavily. You could hardly see ten paces ahead of you. Part of Kovno was on fire. Carefully crossing the bridge in my sledge, I couldn't restrain my tears at the thought of what I'd seen at this same spot on 24 June and the comparison with what was happening here now.'

Already Berthier has notified Ney: 'II and IV Corps have at most 60 men apiece, the Vistula Legion is only a feeble detachment' (of 60 men, says Brandt). And now Ney's reply comes in. It's been impossible for him, he writes, with Loison's division reduced to a mere 500 youngsters, to hold the Cossacks at Evë, and when he gets to Kovno he's very much afraid it'll be with enemy at his heels. So he'll be needing the entire Kovno garrison to defend the town's evacuation. At midday Berthier writes to say he can have it, and that Murat is sending him six of Loison's guns. With this force he must try to hold up the Cossacks at the defile at Rumchiki, at least until tomorrow morning:

> '"We have here a kind of bridgehead or sort of entrenched camp, armed with twelve guns, a work where we can make a stand until enemy infantry appears in superior force. Here Loison's division will find everything it lacks. Thus you'll form a respectable body of infantry. The King has ordered the dismounted cavalry, the whole Imperial Guard, both infantry and cavalry, and I and IV Corps to draw food rations for eight days and move over to the left bank this evening. The twelve pieces of artillery that were here have been placed on the high ground over there. In this position the King thinks we can teach the Cossacks a lesson.'"

All of which looks fine on paper. But once again has little to do with reality. And anyway Murat has already decided to clear out – 'you've seen with your own eyes that almost nothing's left of the Imperial Guard'. A second officer is sent off to Macdonald, with new orders. He's not to retire on Kovno, but on Tilsit, 20 leagues further down the Niemen.

All day the indefatigable Daru and his colleagues are busy writing their last orders on Russian soil – for that's what Lithuania must again become. These men, at least, Berthier will certify, have lost nothing of their energy. Once again, everything useful that can't be taken away is to be destroyed. Eblé must blow up the arsenal. The chief medical officer is to evacuate the hospital. As the early night again begins to fall, as much of the Treasure as had been saved at Ponari, plus some more that's been lying in Kovno, is loaded on to new wagons 'harnessed up to artillery horses' and makes its way 'with greatest difficulty' through the crowds down to the bridgehead. There the congestion is immense ('because of the large numbers of sleighs and sledges both officers and men had taken in the villages').* Not that many of the fugitives aren't making their way across the ice above and below the town. 'On the bridge one of the Treasury wagons overturned. A guard was placed over it.'*

Murat's headquarters have already crossed over to the high ground on the left bank, together with twelve guns to command the frozen river. Likewise his Royal Neapolitan Guard which – surprisingly – according to Berthier still amounts to some 700–1,000 men. A meeting of the Marshals is called for 7 p.m. And Bessières informs his colleagues that the Imperial Guard still has 500 cavalry.

Beyond the bridge the road forks – right to Tilsit, left to Gumbinnen. Its for the latter town, the first in Prussia, that Murat intends to march at daylight, leaving Kovno to Ney, in whom 'he has every confidence'.*

Morning comes. Ney, who's had a good night's sleep at lodgings inside the town, insists that IV Corps' staff shall help him defend it:

'An earthwork, hastily [sic] thrown up in front of the Vilna Gate, seemed to him a sufficient defence to hold up the enemy all day. In the forenoon the rearguard again entered the town. Two guns, serviced by some infantry platoons, were placed on the rampart, and this little number of troops made ready to sustain the attack that was already preparing.'

Although his party has woken up at the usual early hour, ready to depart, Griois has to wait for a a pair of fur-lined shoes from a Jewish shoemaker who's been paid in advance for them. He and Guyot can't leave until he does, even though 'a sound of men and horses and some musket shots not far away announced a hurrah'. Cossacks, presenting themselves at the town's exits, are driving in their guards, 'very few in number anyway and stunned by the cold'. They too, being few in number, aren't daring to force their way in, but are

'galloping through the streets of the suburb, firing off pistol shots and pursuing any Frenchmen they caught sight of with their shouts'.

The shoemaker's fur-lined shoes 'whether from inefficiency or by design' turn out to be too small and narrow, and the Jew, 'in atrocious German', wants to discuss how they can be improved,

'certainly intending to keep me there up to the moment when the Cossacks entered the house. It was only by shoving my foot into his chest I got rid of him, and left him the shoes and the silver he'd received.'

At the sound of the very first shots Guyot has harnessed up their sleigh:

'We made haste to put the victuals we'd bought on to it. But our hosts, profiting from the danger the least delay could expose us to, were unloading our sleigh as fast as we were loading it. Father, mother, children, flung themselves at our provisions without taking any other precautions than to elude our kicks; and I still laugh when I recall our anger and oaths at seeing our sugar loaves, our hams and even our bread being whipped from under our noses.'

Now some Cossacks are coming down the street. And the two artillery officers dash off in their sleigh into the town, where all that's left of the Imperial Guard has assembled at dawn in the market place. There General Roguet has had all the trouble in the world to winkle his men out of the houses. For more than an hour a Piedmontese comrade of Bourgogne's, named Faloppa, has

'done nothing but prowl about on all fours, howling like a bear. I realised he fancied he was in his own country amidst the mountains, playing with the friends of his childhood. In short, poor Faloppa had gone mad.'

Just as he's confiding his dying comrade's money to two women who've taken pity on him, Bourgogne hears

'the noise in the street increasing. It was already daylight, but in spite of that we couldn't see much, for the little squares of glass were dimmed with ice, and the sky, covered with thick clouds, foretold a lot of snow still to come. We were making ready to go outside when, all at once and quite close to us, we heard the sound of cannon from the direction of Vilna, mingled with volleys of musketry, shouts and oaths. I thought I could make out the voice of General Roguet. Indeed it was he who was swearing and indiscriminately dealing out blows at officers and NCOs as well as rankers to make them get going. He was entering the houses and making the officers search them to be sure no men were left inside. He did right, and it's perhaps the first good service I ever saw him render the rank and file.'

"Don't you see it's that brute of a General Roguet striking at everybody with his stick?" says another of Bourgogne's comrades – one who means to stay and await his fate, as so many others have done. And fixes his bayonet: 'Just let him come here; I'm waiting for him!' Adjutant-Major Roustan, however, turns them all out. Falling in, the Fusiliers-Grenadiers march slowly through the mob; but have to wait a long time at the Niemen bridge:

'Colonel Bodelin, who commanded our regiment, ordered the officers to prevent anyone from crossing it alone. We were now about 60 men, the remnant of 2,000, all grouped round the colonel. He looked sadly on the remains of his fine regiment, probably drawing a contrast in his own mind. To encourage us he made us a speech. I'm afraid very few listened.'

In the thick morning mist the Lancer Brigade brings up the rear. Only some 600 infantry and 600–800 cavalry of the once 50,000-strong Imperial

Guard – that élite of the élite which at midsummer 'headed by its bands playing fanfares' had crossed Eblé's pontoon bridges – stumble across the narrow Niemen bridge, 'established on very tall piles that resembled stilts'.[10] In the crush someone steals Zalusky's portmanteau containing his fine new uniform 'thanks to which I'd cut such a brilliant figure at Vilna. The saddest part of it was I couldn't impute this theft to the Cossacks, who were doing their best to avoid us.' Dumonceau too notices what a host of carriages and other troops are crossing directly over the ice.

All in all the Guard column totals some 2,500 men under arms. Castellane, who's there, makes a slightly different count. He sees some 2,000 of the 10,000 of the Old Guard who'd left Moscow cross the bridge; and some 300 only, of the 8,000 of the Young Guard. After them come the tiny remnants of I, II, III and IX Corps. 'They hadn't one bayonet between them', Daru says with pardonable poetic licence, meaning a few officers only. IV Corps has 30 men. Wrede's 20th (Bavarian) Division (VI Corps) has 50. Oudinot and Victor's corps, Castellane thinks, are still in reasonably good order. 'Of those who'd reached this point,' Bourgogne notices,

> 'not half had seen Moscow. They were the garrisons of Smolensk, of Orsha, of Vilna, as well as the remnant of the army of Victor and Oudinot.'

There are individuals who nearly reach the bridge only to drop dead. One such is Colonel Widman of the Italian Guardia d'Onore, who, Labaume writes

> 'had supported our fatigues until then. Unable to go further, he fell just as he was leaving Kovno to go to the bridge and expired without the satisfaction of dying outside Russia.'

Griois is appalled by the chaos and destruction in the streets:

> 'The rearguard was still there, and the Cossacks were no longer to be feared. But what horrible spectacle didn't this unhappy town present! All the houses which the soldiers had just left seemed to have been pillaged. Stove-in casks, broken or half-burnt furniture, filled the streets. Numerous corpses added to the horror of this picture. They covered the main square. Almost all of them were Grenadiers of the Guard who, having got there first, had taken possession of the stores of rum and brandy to make good their long privations. Stunned by inebriation and gripped by the cold in the bivouacs they'd established on this square, they didn't wake up again. It looked like a battlefield, or rather a halt where harassed soldiers were lying in closed ranks.'

Bourgogne hears that 1,500 men have perished there during the night. Making for 'the gate on to the Niemen', Griois and Guyot force their way through the crowd. 'I could easily have avoided this dangerous passage by crossing the river over the ice.' But that's very dangerous too. One officer who does so in his sleigh and almost fails to reach the Polish shore is Dessaix's ADC Captain *Girod de l'Ain*. His sleigh gets stuck between two of the immense blocks of ice. Only after he has given up all hope does a passerby come to his aid. Otherwise most people are doing the same as Griois:

'Sufferings and misery had so weakened my intelligence and enervated my will that everyone was mechanically following the path traced by those ahead of him.'

Le Roy, too, is here, with his 'bosom friend' Lieutenant Jacquet:

'As early as 2 a.m. on 13 December I heard the 85th being called. I woke up the gentlemen. "Come on, my dear Jacquet, for the last time on Russian soil, let's go and see what's wanted of us."'

But it's 5 a.m. before they can cross the river.

Outside the town, meanwhile, Séruzier and his horse-gunners are helping Ney to fend off huge swarms of Cossacks – afterwards he'll remember their numbers, perhaps exaggeratedly, as about 15,000. To Grabowski their appearance seems

'very funny. They were so weighed down by loot that their horses could hardly advance. We saw many of them wearing a French general's richly embroidered coat under their cape. Their pockets were stuffed with rings and watches. Hung at their saddle they carried bags of silver and gold.'

Seeing them busy pillaging (or, as the saying goes, 'Cossacking') stragglers, Séruzier's men capture '300 good horses which I hastened to distribute to my dismounted troopers'. With Colonel Pelleport of the 18th Line, Fezensac has spent the night trying, mostly in vain, to stop their few remaining men from drinking too much liquor. Now they're at their posts on the town's defences:

'The Russians' first cannon shot dismounted one of our guns. The infantrymen fled, the gunners were about to follow suit. Any moment now and the Cossacks would be able to enter the town. But just then the Marshal appeared on the rampart. His absence had seemed to be the end of us. His presence was enough to set everything to rights. He himself took a musket. The troops returned to their post.'

'Hardly had the rearguard re-entered Kovno,' Ney will report indignantly two days later to Berthier,

'than the artillery officer ordered his guns to be spiked, thus destroying all possibility of keeping the enemy at a distance from the town'

– an act of 'ineptitude' confirmed, in his own report, by Ney's immediate subordinate General Gérard:[11]

'Towards midday the enemy cavalry approached with some artillery pieces and began firing at the works which are to right and left of the Vilna Gate. Those works were armed with four guns, which, having replied with a few shots, were spiked by the ineptitude of the officer commanding them.'

The rearguard, Gérard goes on,

'consisted of 300 of the 29th Line [Loison's division] and 80 men of a battalion from Lippe. It had been impossible for me to assemble two men from the division's other units. As soon as the Lippe infantry had received some roundshot into its ranks, it broke up, threw away its arms, and fled, without either *M. le Maréchal* or myself being able to halt even one of them'

– 'except one sergeant,' Ney conscientiously corrects him, 'whose name, I'm sorry to say, I don't know.' – 'There was a moment of terror,' Gérard goes on: 'Everyone was abandoning us, and we ourselves were obliged to fire muskets to hold up the Cossacks who were coming closer and closer.' On the high ground beyond the river, so the 'inept' commandant has told Ney, there should be the twelve guns Murat last night stationed there – or anyway eight of them; Murat, already retreating along the Gumbinnen road, has taken four of them with him. But already 'several hundred' Cossacks are appearing there, 'almost surrounding us by this manoeuvre'. Commanding as they do the Gumbinnen road, the town, the bridgehead and the bridge – on which they're already firing grape – Ney sends General Marchand with the pitiful remains of III Corps and anyone else he can get hold of to support them:

'Although we lost some men there, and only succeeded in gaining a foothold in some barns at the edge of the plateau, this movement was well executed. At the same time the enemy was cannonading the bridgehead on the right of the Vilia River[12] and threatening to carry by force the works at the Vilna Gate whose guns, as I've already said, I'd been deprived of by the artillery officer's incredible blunder. My position then became most alarming, and it was only after the greatest efforts that I managed to place some of the 34th Division's guns and make some detachments of the 29th Regiment protect them. This semblance of resistance began to contain the enemy, and by redoubling my activity, by begging each and every man, man by man, to show some zeal, I managed to last out until night began to fall, without the town being carried by main force [a threat] it had been exposed to for three hours. At 9 p.m. I began my retreat.'

By this time, Gérard adds, only 150 men of Loison's division are left – Ney says 200. Both the Niemen and the Vilia bridges have been set fire to, at both ends. All Kovno's magazines and arsenals have been blown up.

That evening of 13 December the pitiful relics of III Corps pass through Kovno amidst the drunk, the dead drunk, the dead and the dying. 'By the light of the bivouac fires still burning in the streets' Fezensac's companions

'make out some soldiers who look at us indifferently. They said nothing when we told them they'd fall into the power of the enemy, just lowered their heads and huddled together round the fire. The inhabitants, lined up to watch us pass, were regarding us with insolent looks. One of them had already armed himself with a musket. I wrenched it from him. Several soldiers who'd dragged themselves as far as the Niemen fell dead on the bridge. We in our turn crossed the river and, turning our glances toward the terrible country we were leaving, felicitated ourselves on being so fortunate as to get out of it; and above all at being the last to do so.'

But fate has something much crueller in store for the intrepid Séruzier, he who'd been in the army's advance guard all the way to Moscow and then in its rearguard all the long way back. Reaching the bridgehead, he finds there 'more than 15,000 Cossacks, who attacked us'. Seeing he hasn't a chance against such numbers and

'wishing to obtain, if possible, an honourable capitulation, I placed my infantry in a little wood and disposed myself to charge with my cavalry'.

He's hoping the Cossacks, seeing his resolute attitude, will only pillage his vehicles and let his men slip across the Niemen:

'As I was giving the order to sound the charge I saw a Russian horseman coming forward for a parley. He proposed that I lay down my arms and let myself be taken prisoner with my infantry and squadrons.'

Séruzier agrees, on condition that his men and their effects are taken to Russian headquarters. The Russian emissary returns to his commander for orders, and Séruzier goes back to the wood,

'expecting to find my infantrymen there. But found no one. While I'd been doing my best to arrange an honourable capitulation these unworthy soldiers, terrified at the swarms of Cossacks they saw on all sides on the plain, had disbanded themselves and were trying to reach the bridge and escape. You can imagine my anger! I leave the wood, gallop flat out back to my cavalry, only to find ... no one's left! My troopers had done the same as the infantry. I found myself without any troops. Only one man had stuck by me. He deserves to have his name mentioned. He was an Alsatian named Klein.'

All the fugitives are overtaken by the Cossacks, run down and stripped. In the wood Séruzier and Klein, heroically defending themselves to the last, are also attacked by Cossack lances

'which I parried as best I could with my sabre. Then their commander ordered them to fire at me. Six Cossacks fired at a range of fifteen paces, and I was hit by four of their carbines. My horse fell dead, my right leg was caught beneath him. Then these brigands fell on me, gave me 27 lance jabs, tore my clothes off me, seized my decorations, my weapons, my money, and stripped me completely.'

Only the extreme cold, by freezing the blood, saves him from bleeding to death:

'Though I'd been wounded in the cruellest fashion, the Cossack chief, seeing I'd got up and judging from the riches I'd been stripped of that I was an officer of note in the French army, was so barbarous as to force me to march, naked, for nine miles in a cold of -27 to -28 degrees, to Hetman Platov's headquarters. It was about 4 p.m.'

Rejoined by many of his men, all as stark naked as himself, Séruzier reproaches them bitterly for their cowardice. Platov examines him, wants to know who he is and what possessions he's had taken from him: 'Everything. Silver. Jewellery. Effects. Six horses, two from Limousin, two Normands and two Hanoverians.'

But Platov – he who since his son was killed near Moscow has even offered his only daughter in marriage to any Cossack who kills or captures Napoleon and whose hatred for the French knows no bounds – ignores the code of generous behaviour normal between superior officers. Taking Séruzier's horses for himself, he gives him back nothing:

'I was in front of an immense bonfire, and the warmth unfroze my wounds. My blood began flowing from all parts of my body.'

And he passes out.[13]

Ségur isn't on the spot; but in his moving but far from always accurate epic, he'll write afterwards that Ney

'passed through Kovno and crossed the Niemen, still fighting, falling back and not fleeing, marching behind all the others, sustaining the honour of our arms up to the very last'.

Most of the refugees who have recrossed the Niemen bridge have been taking the left-hand road, following the Guard towards Wilkowiski. But immediately in front of them is another hill at least as steep and frozen as Ponari and no more surmountable. At its foot, where the roads divide, Jacquemot's men see 'calèches, carriages, baggage wagons, an entire artillery park' which had been brought up from Königsberg 'completely abandoned'. Even one of the new Treasury wagons has come to grief. Hochberg can hardly believe his eyes:

'The men were throwing themselves into the wagons but, pushed by those who came after, they fell in headfirst, their feet in the air. Others were succumbing under the weight of sacks they'd filled with silver and the passers-by were maltreating them in the most shameful fashion.'

Jacquemot sees a large amount of the treasure being taken away by a German officer. Getting to the top of the hill Bourgogne realises that nothing's left of the Fusiliers-Grenadiers. And for Dumonceau, whose *konya* had been stolen in Kovno while he and his servant Jean had been snatching some much-needed sleep, there's a small but poignant tragedy in store. After waiting for Jean to catch up, following on no doubt with their last lead-horse, he's riding his favourite 5-year-old mare Liesje,[14] and tries to overtake a Neapolitan unit when Liesje's hindlegs slip as she tries to jump the ditch – and they both tumble into it. One leg trapped beneath her, Dumonceau, after calling out in vain to passers-by, is finally extricated by a fellow-lieutenant of the Red Lancers. But Liesje – she on whose back he'd trotted about so blithely and curiously not far from here on Midsummer Eve – she's done for:

'I tugged at her bridle, shook her impatiently to force her to make an effort. She did all she could to please me, and in the end managed to drag herself up out of the ditch; but that was all I could get out of her, and it was becoming obvious her back was broken. So her state was hopeless. The poor beast seemed to be suffering greatly, was groaning sadly and when she saw I'd made up my mind to go off without her several times dolorously raised her head to follow me with a sad look, her eyes inflamed with tears, expressive of her anxiety, her regrets and as if begging me not to abandon her. I was profoundly moved. I ran off as if

pursued by remorse, carrying my portmanteau under my arm. She was
the best horse I ever had in my life.'

It's the only time the Belgian captain, in his lucid but mechanical handwriting, expresses any grief.

Since all too many men seem to be turning right at the bridge, Griois
and Guyot too, without knowing where it leads to, have taken the
Wilkowiski–Gumbinnen road. Reaching the hilltop they hear behind them
'gunfire and a fusillade' from the other side of the river:

'It was our rearguard, commanded by the brave Marshal Ney, disputing
the enemy's entry into Kovno. Despite too unequal a fight he maintained
himself there until evening. These were the last cannon shots I heard.'

But to Ney, who's 'hoping to be able to retire to Gumbinnen via Skrauce
under cover of the night that hid the feebleness of my means', this new icy
slope proves insurmountable. No sooner have Ney's men begun climbing
the slope than 'roundshot from the enemy drawn up across the road' begin
falling among it. 'This last attack', Fezensac realises,

'was the most unforeseen of all and the one which most vividly struck the
men's imagination. Marchand and Ledru managed to form a kind of battalion by uniting all isolated men present to III Corps. In vain we tried to
force our way through. Since the men's muskets didn't carry that far, they
didn't dare advance. They stubbornly refused to open the passage by
force. I ordered some tirailleurs to advance. Two-thirds of the muskets
didn't go off.'[15] To advance or retreat was equally impossible, it would be
to expose themselves 'to a charge. Our loss would have been certain.'

Deaf to his appeals to them to stay and if necessary die with him, some of
Fezensac's officers,

'just embraced me, weeping, and went back to Kovno. Two others suffered the same fate. One had got drunk on rum and couldn't keep up.
The other, whom I was particularly fond of, disappeared shortly afterwards.'

This breaks Fezensac's heart. Heroism can do no more. It's the end:

'But then Marshal Ney appeared. In so desperate a situation he evinced
not the least disquietude. He decided to follow the Niemen downstream
and take the Tilsit road in hopes of reaching Königsberg by cross-country roads,'

even if it means depriving Murat of any rearguard. Nor can Ney even notify
Murat where he's gone to. But there's nothing for it. Under cover of night
Ney's party march back downstream, and though many don't realise what's
happened and wander on downstream towards Tilsit, about six miles from
the Kovno bridge they turn off left into a lane. Major Bonnet is one of
them: 'At 10 p.m., having got back some of our martial air thanks to the
29th Regiment which the Marshal had recruited I don't know where, we
halted at a fine village.'

By now Headquarters is at Skrauce, and as Murat leaves again, wondering of course what's become of his rearguard, he sends an officer back to
find out:

'Getting to the first houses, he finds a post of twelve Cossacks, who arrest him, take his money, his watch, his Cross, his epaulettes, and then let him go, together with the sledge he'd come in. They gave him back one napoleon.'

Ashamed of such humiliation, it'll be a day and more before he rejoins to tell the tale. Meanwhile Murat, still hearing nothing, has sent back a second officer, an *officier d'ordonnance* named Atthalin, who, after hearing guns firing in the direction of Kovno, returns without any news.

Deep in the night Ney's little party, struggling on through Poland's snow-laden forests, are sharing a single 'white horse, which we mounted one after the other'.

On 15 December Headquarters reaches Wilkowiski, that village where on 22 June Napoleon 'in a terrible voice' had declared war on Russia. Now Berthier writes to him: 'There were not 300 men of the Old Guard [on parade]; of the Young Guard fewer still, most of them unserviceable.' And next day, at Wirballen in a ciphered PS:

'The King of Naples is the first of men on the battlefield ... the King of Naples is the man least capable of commanding in chief. He should be[16] replaced at once.'

Himself, he possesses only what he stands up in. Even the carriage with the campaign's maps and documents has been lost. Fortunately, thanks to the energy and intelligence of its driver, it turns up next day at Gumbinnen. There 'for the first time since leaving Moscow' Larrey eats

'a complete meal, slept in a warm room and in a good bed. Lariboisière was so ill, so shattered, he could no longer speak. That evening he went to bed, never to get up again.'

Not very far away, across the Baltic, the former Marshal Bernadotte, now Crown Prince Elect of Sweden,[17] has just heard about Napoleon's disaster at the Berezina. He too adds a hasty PS, to his letter to the Tsar:

'I had expected, Your Majesty, that on being informed of your state's evacuation I should be able to congratulate you on having seized his person near Borissow. The opportunity was excellent, but it would have been to hope for too much at once.'

After unsuccessfully trying next day (18 December) to convince the Prussian provincial governor Schön at Gumbinnen (where Griois finds the heroic Eblé 'in a state of utter weakness and dejection ... no more than a shadow of himself')[18] that Murat has a whole French army at his heels, *Intendant-Général* Dumas and some friends are just

'drinking some excellent coffee when a man in a brown greatcoat entered. He had a long beard. His face was blackened. And he looked as if he'd been burnt. His eyes were red and gleaming.

'"At last I'm here," he said. "Why, General Dumas, don't you know me?"

'"Why no. Who are you?"

'"I'm the rearguard of the Grand Army. I'm Marshal Ney."'

A few hours later, 'just as the clock was striking the last quarter before midnight', a shaky old post-chaise, 'one of those cumbersome vehicles mounted on two enormous wheels and with old-style shafts', gallops into Paris. Its two occupants are Napoleon and Caulaincourt. It dashes through the still unfinished Arc de Triomphe[19] – 'only Amodru had stuck with us' – so rapidly the sentries have no time to halt it, and into the courtyard of the Carousel at the Tuileries. When they knock at the door of the Empress's apartments the Swiss porter, not even recognising them, refuses at first to admit them.

'Never in my life have I had such a sense of satisfaction,' writes Caulaincourt, who has hardly enjoyed a wink of sleep for the three weeks it's taken them to dash across Europe. At his levée next morning Napoleon tells his amazed ministers:

'"Well, gentlemen, fortune has dazzled me. I've let it lead me astray. Instead of following the plan I'd in mind I went to Moscow. I thought I'd sign peace there. I stayed there too long. I've made a grave mistake, but I'll have the means to repair it."'

And gets down to work, raising fresh armies to defend his crumbling empire.[20]

TWO EPILOGUES

In the spring of 1813, Heinrich von Roos, after spending the winter at Borissow practising his medical arts, would visit Studianka. From a Russian engineer officer who was 'cleaning out the river and extracting from it anything that had fallen in during the crossing' he would hear how 'in the nearby forests an ample harvest of watches, silver, decorations, weapons, epaulettes, etc., had been gathered from hard-frozen corpses found seated against trees'. The officer, who'd built himself some shacks out of the wreckage of the bridge which had once been the wreckage of Studianka, would make Roos

> 'a present of a sword, a sabre and an English saddle. We explored the houses [i.e., the three which had been left standing and evidently not demolished by Victor, as per Napoleon's order]. Many weapons, shreds of clothing, helmets, peaked caps, papers, books, plans were still left there. I found officers' commissions, death certificates that concerned the units I'd belonged to and which I handed in two years later to the Petersburg embassy.'

The Russian major's special business is to collect all letters, documents, maps and other papers being found there in such vast numbers, and sort them out by language. Roos helps him with the German ones, and a French sergeant with the French, which include

> 'the correspondence of Marshals, their notebooks, even some letters from Napoleon, some addressed to his wife and others to his ministers. The first proved the Emperor could be tender, and the other that despite the difficulties of this unhappy retreat he was busying himself paying close attention to everything that was going on in France.'

The sergeant weeps every time anything crops up that wounds his patriotic feelings. Roos also hears how

> 'after the army had left, the village's inhabitants had wanted to rebuild it, but were forbidden to do so by a decree of the Emperor Alexander, according to which the village of Studianka was to be utterly razed and not exist for the future. At the limits of what had been the village we saw two big sepulchres. One stood not far from where I'd spent the night of 26/27 November. It was as tall as a peasant's cottage and completely surrounded by conifers. According to the professor this tomb dated from a hundred years ago and the sharply disputed passage of the Swedes under Charles XII,'

en route for their last victory at Toloczin and final defeat at Poltava.

> 'One only had to scratch the surface to find bones. The Eastern sepulchre, which encloses our warlike companions dead of hunger, cold and exhaustion, is even loftier and takes up a larger surface area. The number of corpses buried there is estimated to be several thousands.'

In his study at Staroï-Borissow Prince Radziwil's *intendant*, a Baron de Korsak, whom Roos had helped back to health, was making a collection of relics:

'Here I saw successfully used for the first time the iron hand-mills Napoleon had had sent from France for his army. Also an incredible collection of decorations of almost all the nations that had taken part in the war. Some had been compulsorily handed over by the peasantry, some had been bought off them.'

In 1822 a Prussian engineer officer, Major J. L. U. Blesson, would visit the scene. Emerging from the dark forests between Borissow and Studianka, he'd begin to notice:

'just think of it, ten years after the catastrophe – a mass of leatherware, strips of felt, scraps of cloth, shako covers, etc., strewn on the ground and fields. As one approached the river, these melancholy relics lay thicker and even in heaps, mingled with the bones of human beings and animals, skulls, tin fittings, bandoliers, bridles and suchlike. Scraps of the Guard's bearskins had survived.'

Close to the bank where the main (artillery) bridge had been he'd be surprised to find:

'an island divides the river into two arms. It owes its origin to the vehicles and bodies which had fallen off the bridge and to the corpses which had been carried down to this point and then covered with mud and sand. We made our way with difficulty along the bank amid relics of all kinds, and soon reached the second [foot] bridge.'

Here are no more mounds of skeletons, only piles of fittings and mountings. The bodies had been swept downstream. 'Below the island three muddy mounds had formed, and these, we found, were covered with forget-me-nots.'

Revisiting Russia on business in 1828, Paul de Bourgoing, one-time lieutenant of the 5th Tirailleurs,[1] would keep halting for deep and sad reflections:

'I recognised these feeble undulations of Russia's verdant terrain, these long avenues of immense silver birches, that graceful tree of the North with its pale and lightsome foliage. I remembered very distinctly the sight of our two battalions of the Young Guard as it had windingly mounted this succession of hills, deserted now. It seemed to me these narrow valleys should have retained some faint echo of the singing of so many joyous voices,[2] of the song of that regiment which could have no inkling of the fate awaiting it. But no sound, no whisper was heard in the distance among these solitudes. The greatest number of these voices, so full of life and hope, had been frozen by the cruel onslaught of these countries' climate, so smiling and so flower-bedecked in the fine season, so deserted, so cold, so desolate in the depths of winter.'

To this day mounds can be seen along the Moscow road where the Grand Army lies buried.

NOTES

Chapter 1. 'A Word Unknown in the French Army'

1. For Albrecht Adam, see *1812 – The March on Moscow*, hereinafter referred to as *The March*, index.

2. See *1812 – Napoleon in Moscow*, hereinafter referred to as *Moscow*, pp. 218 et seq.

3. Following the fatal route a year later, when the Grand Army's 1,100 abandoned guns were on display outside the Kremlin, the English travel writer J. T. James would be told how it had been 'curious to trace, in the course of their flight, the successive diminution in size of the different pieces of ordnance which were taken; first the 12-pounders, then the eights, and then the sixes, their means of transport constantly decreasing as they advanced further on their march'.

4. See *Moscow*, Chapter 8.

5. Virtually every one of our eye-witnesses reiterates the same thing. 'Hurrah' is in fact a Cossack word, meaning 'death'.

6. See *The March*, p. 179.

7. See *Moscow*, p. 197.

8. Since the Revolution tents had not been regulation issue in the French armies.

9. For the load the ranker had to carry in and on his pack, see *The March*, p. 32.

10. This according to General *Guillaume de Vaudoncourt* who would himself be taken prisoner. 'The massacre at Moscow seems to have been very terrible,' Wilson was noting in his *Journal*: 'The captives pay dear for their master's crimes. Those are the happiest, indeed, who quit their chains and their lives together. But the Russians have great wrongs to avenge. Buonaparte was very cruel in the capital, executing many without proof of guilt, for offences which he had no right to punish with death.'

11. See *Moscow*, pp. 171 *et seq.*

12. See Moscow, pp. 202 *et seq.*

13. Marshal A.-J. Mailly had been wounded in the head and captured at Rossbach. Created a Marshal of France in 1783, he tried in vain to defend the Tuileries but resigned when Louis XVI had tried to flee the country. Arrested at the age of 86, he was guillotined on 25 March 1794 at Arras, presumably under the very eyes of the detestable terrorist-Jacobin Lebon, who enjoyed dining on a balcony opposite, watching the executions. 'Despite his 86 years he mounted the scaffold unaided and died crying *"Vive le Roi!* I die faithful to my king, as my ancestors have always been!"* Doubtless it was this that in 1815 would cause Mailly-Nesle to be raised to the peerage.

14. 'A white's always a white, a blue always a blue,' Napoleon would say on St Helena.

15. See *Moscow*, p. 228.

16. See *Moscow*, illustration facing p.141.

17. See *The March*, p. 42.

18. See *The March*, index; also *Moscow*, with Le Roy's portrait.

19. Bonnet wouldn't write anything more in his diary until Smolensk.

20. See *Moscow*, index.

21. As I pointed out in *The March*, the term 'dysentery' denoted any kind of diarrhoea.

22. See *The March*, p. 324.

23. The Portuguese Chasseurs attached to the Young Guard wore brown jackets, sky-blue trousers and Bavarian-type helmets with a heavy crest hanging down over the brow. He'd see them still in good shape at the Berezina.

24. For the 5th Tirailleurs and their redoubtable Colonel Hennequin, see *The March*, p.113.

25. Winzingerode had been an inveterate supporter of the successive coalitions and in 1806 been active in getting Prussia to declare war on France, with disastrous consequences.

26. Among them perhaps General Count *Philippe de Ségur*, Assistant Prefect of the Palace (who, Roman Soltyk says, was in charge of the headquarters mules during the retreat 'and made a very good job of

it') and – clearly – Marshal Bessières' ADC Lieutenant-Colonel Baudus, whose account of the incident is in Bertin: *Etudes sur Napoléon*, p. 163. My account fuses that of Baudus with Caulaincourt's more extensive one, and with those of Ségur, Fain, Denniée, Rapp, and A. F. de Beauchamp's *Histoire de la Déstruction de Moscoue en 1812*. All essentially agree.

27. Ségur may very well have been present and thus is exempt on this occasion from Gourgaud's scornful charge of reporting mere gossip.

28. See *Moscow*, p.198.

29. See *Moscow*, pp. 115–18. Despite Mme Anthony's tears, both actresses would get back to France.

30. Marbot, however, calls Friederichs an 'excellent, very brave officer, the handsomest man in the French armies'. He would die the following year, two days after being wounded at the Battle of Leipzig.

31. See *The March*, p. 334.

32. See *The March*, pp. 205, 207, 208.

33. Dedem saw 'the dead unburied after our first passage' and next day Captain Charles François would see several of his former companions' putrefying corpses. One of the 30th Line's captains 'still had his mouth on his own arm, eaten to the bone'.

34. See *The March*, pp. 325–6.

Chapter 2: Borodino Revisited

1. See *Moscow*, p. 235.

2. See *Moscow*, index.

3. The Napoleonic soldier measured distances in leagues. A league was about an hour's march or rather more than three miles.

4. See *The March*, p.132.

5. See *The March*, and illustration.

6. Crossing it a week or so earlier in a convoy escorted by 300 Poles of his own regiment, the wounded Polish Captain Heinrich von Brandt had sat up in his wagon and thought that 'seen in perspective from the hilltops these heaps of corpses, stripped of everything, looked like immense flocks of sheep'.

7. Von Suckow's rendering seems less faithful than Vossler's. See *The March*, p. 318 and J. T. James's illustration, p.193. By the time James sketched it, already leaning to its fall, in 1813, all the corpses had apparently been burned or buried.

8. See *The March*, pp. 299 *et seq.*

9. 'Some Baden grenadiers, who escorted Napoleon's baggage, treasure and kitchen as far as the Berezina. Later on, at Borissow, two NCOs of that regiment who, prisoners like myself, were serving me as orderlies, assured me it was Napoleon himself who'd given this order. Some officers of his staff had been of his opinion; others, like Berthier, had stood up against him. The latter had even hinted to some of the grenadiers to let their prisoners gradually escape under cover of night.' Captain Count M.-H. Lignières, of the 1st Foot Chasseurs of the Guard, says it was Spaniards and Portuguese, not Frenchmen, who'd committed the atrocity. Zalusky: 'In his critique of Ségur's *History*, p. 200, General Gourgaud exonerates us completely from the reproach made us by M. de Ségur in saying that there were some Poles among the Spanish and Portuguese escort. Never has a Pole struck his disarmed enemy!'

10. Presumably one of the five temporary bridges thrown over the Kolotchka on 6 September, not the one leading into Borodino village.

11. It's not clear to me whether François means the Kolotskoïe abbey or the village of Kolotskaya, which had been burnt down during the battle and could hardly have been rebuilt. Nor, presumably, would he have 'approached' it because his unit must have followed the main road through the ruins of Borodino village and its church.

12. Not that discipline in the French armies was always what it could have been. In 1807 the starving Guard infantry refused to share what food it had even with Murat.

13. 'This heroic carabinier', Sergeant Bertrand concludes, 'got himself another musket when we left Smolensk and was killed by a roundshot on 17 November at the battle of Krasnoïe.'

14. But a few days later the 'secretary' would be carried off by Cossacks while

foraging in a village; 'the other, ill and almost blind, got lost on the road before reaching Vilna'.

15. 'Thanks to the brave Captain Berchet, paymaster of the 18th, and to the honesty of my brave comrades, *the 120,000 francs were put back in the chest after the campaign* [Pelleport's italics]. I don't know whether many regiments were as fortunate as the 18th Line. Anyway, I'll always regard it as an honour to have commanded men capable of accomplishing such acts of heroism.'

Chapter 3: Getting Through at Viazma

1. See *The March*, index.

2. See *The March*, pp. 240 et seq.

3. See *The March*, pp. 90, 91, where Everts is wrongly ranked as sergeant.

4. See *The March*, pp. 174–5.

5. See *The March*, p. 112.

6. Rossetti says 'we', i.e., presumably Murat's staff, had got to Viazma 'towards midday', and that Napoleon had sent the Guard 'which had marched for part of the night' on ahead to seize the town, and that it had got there at 9 a.m. But Rossetti (see *The March*, pp. 110–11) isn't always too reliable about times.

7. A repeat performance, that is, of what had been done on the way out. See *The March*, p. 238.

8. Brandenburgs were tassel-ended loops, usually of black but in Napoleon's case gold lace.

9. The master of HMS *Northumberland* too would record Napoleon as having a 'loud harsh voice'.

10. John R. Elting's *Military History & Atlas of the Napoleonic Wars* summarises the movements of II, VI and X corps as follows: 'In the north, Macdonald moved on Riga, ignoring Steingell, who marched south to join Wittgenstein. The two Russian commanders tried to trap Saint-Cyr between them. Administering a bloody repulse to Wittgenstein's assault on Polotsk, Saint-Cyr successfully withdrew from that town after dark on the 19th, burning his bridges behind him, and sending Wrede against Steingell on 20 October, the Russians retreating to Disna

in disorder. (Lacking a bridging train, Wittgenstein could not interfere.) Thereafter, Saint-Cyr sent Wrede to Glubokoïe with the remains of the VI Corps to cover the direct road to Vilna. He himself retired towards Lepel to be on the flank of any advance against Wrede, but had to relinquish his command because of a painful wound. Learning of Saint-Cyr's plight, Victor marched to his aid on 20 October, reaching the crippled II Corps near Tchasniki on the 29th. Here he clashed indecisively with Wittgenstein, and retired on Sienno. Wittgenstein did not pursue.'

11. In July Jérôme, initially in command of three army corps, had gone off back to Cassel in a huff. See *The March*, index.

12. There seems to be some confusion here. The Guard had surely left on 2 November? In view of what followed and the Russians' approach, it seems strange that Napoleon did not wait for IV and I Corps to arrive. But doubtless he was anxious to secure the Dnieper bridge at Doroghobouï. In general, Caulaincourt criticises his lack of foresight during this part of the retreat.

13. Afterwards Planat would find that he had few memories of this first part of the retreat after Ghjat, because of being exposed to sudden sharp cold. 'Later I'd stand up to much more rigorous cold without my faculties being noticeably affected.'

14. See *The March*, p.128 and illustration.

15. Young Moncey 'who'd just come from the imperial pages'. See *The March*, pp. 193, 214, 374.

16. See Guesse's painting of the Russians thrusting the French rearguard at bayonet point down Viazma's main street.

17. See *The March*, p. 241.

18. Wilson even went so far as to send off his ADC to Petersburg to complain to the Tsar. A little more energy, Wilson thinks, and Kutusov might have got to Viazma still earlier – but in that case he'd have had to confront Napoleon and the Imperial Guard, an eventuality which, to judge by later developments beyond Smolensk, Kutusov was rightly scared of. My pen-friend Colonel John Elting, however, has little use for Wilson's *Geschäft*: 'Wilson was

easily taken in – in fact he probably became a catspaw in the Bennigsen (a former Hanoverian and so *almost* an Englishman) v. Kutusov feud.' Certainly he was very full of himself and a considerable knowall.

19. The Russians of course celebrated Viazma as a victory.

20. See *The March*, index, and *Moscow*, p.195.

Chapter 4: Handmills at Doroghobouï

1. Thus Ney himself, in his so-called *Mémoires*: 'A retreat *en échiquier* upon two lines may be effected according to the principles laid down in the [1791] regulations. This movement may be made alternately in the two lines, and by even and uneven battalions, during the whole time the retrograde movement lasts.'

2. My eye-witnesses' texts all describe the same developments, in very similar words. The above is from a Russian account.

3. See *Moscow*, Chapter 8.

4. For Grouchy and the semi-imbecilic Lahoussaye, see *The March*, p. 331 and *Moscow*, index.

5. Chlapowski had started the retreat with nine horses, of which seven would survive 'all in good condition'. He himself had been wounded nine times, always in the same arm. Having a very large income, he had been married off by Napoleon, but not happily.

6. 'While on campaign,' Jean-Michel Chevalier, an officer of the Guard's *Chasseurs à Cheval*, tells us, 'Napoleon ate very little. He breakfasted at 9 or 10 a.m. and had nothing more to eat until 8 or 9 p.m., and very little then. He always wore our regiment's green jacket or dress coat, with very small, general's epaulettes, without any aiguillettes, a single star, that of the [Grand] Eagle and the decoration of a simple knight of the Legion of Honour, a white cashmere waistcoat and similar short breeches, riding boots (indoors, silk stockings and slippers with gold buckles), the great red sash [of the Legion of Honour] between coat and waistcoat, his historic little hat, and a sword. When it was cold he put on the grey overcoat everyone knows over his coat. When he was riding along the route on horseback, in our midst, he had the air of being our colonel. Then nothing – rain, hail, snow, storm – nothing prevented him from pursuing his way; he paid it no attention. Prince Berthier always rode at his side, then [came] the generals, the ADCs, the *officiers d'ordonnance* and his Mameluke Roustam. If it was cold and he dismounted, the chasseurs of the escort hastened to make up a small fire. Then he would amuse himself by pushing the firewood with his feet, or turn his back to the fire, his hands behind his back. If he needed to pay a minor call of nature en route, he dismounted in our midst and did his business without ceremony. Sometimes I saw him change his linen. One can say that Napoleon, in our midst, was at the centre of his family and seemed to be quite at home [*chez lui*].'

7. See *The March*, pp. 232, 233.

8. See *Moscow*, pp. 70, 71.

9. See *Moscow*, p. 161.

10. 'That', he adds, 'is just about all I had on me when I recrossed the Niemen.'

11. A napoleon, sometimes also referred to as a *louis*, was worth 24 livres, or 20 francs, say £500/$1000 in modern money. But such calculations are notoriously problematic.

Chapter 5: Snow

1. Joubert commanded Razout's (11th) Division's 1st Brigade (4th and 18th Line).

2. Together with a few fellow-conspirators Malet, a former Jacobin who'd taken up with the Catholic reaction, had 'arrested' Pasquier, head of the Paris police and Police Minister Savary in the name of an imaginary provisional government, announcing that Napoleon was dead in Russia. Desmarest, another police officer he'd conned and arrested, had instantly imagined 'Bernadotte at the Russian headquarters, coming after the fatal blow to offer himself to our bewildered generals as a mediator, arranging with them a new government under Alexander's auspices and then, in concert with them, having sent orders and agents to Paris'. A veteran of the Paris Municipal Guard witnessed Malet's and his fellow conspirators' execution:

'The conspirators had been condemned to death. They were to be shot on the Grenelle plain. The battalion of veterans in barracks at the Rue du Foin were ordered to attend the execution, maintain order, form line ... Naturally, I went with the battalion. The condemned men arrived in cabs at Grenelle [beyond the *Champ de Mars*], where they were made to stand in a single row. I believe there were twelve of them. The platoons which were to shoot them were some tirailleurs of the Young Guard, taken from the depots. I was struck again by the spectacled man, as at the council. They fired. I hardly saw the unfortunate men fall: the smoke prevented it. I heard heart-rending cries, then a succession of musket shots to finish them off. The veterans I was with, who were at a great distance from the place of execution, said the condemned men had been massacred, the tirailleurs not knowing how to fire a shot. The troops' movements, the noise of the crowd which *we* veterans were holding at a distance, the drums, together all that suppressed emotion ... I only saw the spectacled man who'd been condemned, the smoke of the gunpowder prevented me from seeing him fall. But when I got home I was very pale, extremely agitated, and people tumbled to it that I'd gone with our veterans at Grenelle: I was reprimanded. I seem to remember that Parisian Guard, white coats, green turn backs, were present, unarmed, at the execution. It was dissolved, I believe, and its men absorbed into other regiments. The conspirators' punishment had no more effect on the lower part of the population, that of my quarter, than the conspiracy had. Everyone kept his mouth shut. As long as the Great Empire lasted I always heard people speak in very low voices, even in the family, about political events. Any individual who spoke aloud, fearlessly, was counted as a police spy.'

3. See *The March*, p. 62.

4. The troops invariably referred to the regimental eagles as '*les coucous*'. It is curious to think that the first symbol of empire to be proposed to Napoleon had been the cock – which he'd dismissed as 'ridiculous'.

5. The so-called *halte des pipes*, made normally every two hours. See *The March*, p. 28.

6. Did he? According to John R. Elting 'it was an old army yarn'.

7. Some men would afterwards forgive themselves – and one another – for such sins against the code of *camaraderie* and military honour. Others not. Bourgogne's immortal *Memoirs*, written to exorcise his horrible memories, are as much a military man's confession of human weakness as of its powers of survival.

8. Larrey himself, to judge from his portrait, was a typical Celt. His observation is correct, but not of course his explanation. As we now know, it wasn't the southerners' blood or intelligence that saved them, but their smaller heat losses, due to having less skin area in proportion to bulk. Small individuals tend to feel cold less than big ones.

9. But many would fall in battle at Krasnoië. See Chapter 10.

10. Like many other letters, Compans' to his wife from Smolensk owes its survival to its being captured by Cossacks.

11. Jean Victor Moreau, Napoleon's rival for power during the last years of the Republic, had gone over to his enemies after being exiled for plotting to overthrow the Bonapartist regime.

12. Even this incident is only mentioned in a footnote. Whether or not one agrees with the victim's assessment of Napoleon, it must be remembered that Bourgeois' book, like Labaume's, came out in 1814, under the first Bourbon restoration. Not that Bourgeois seems to have had any strong Bonapartist feelings.

13. An attitude that seems to have been spreading even as early as at Smolensk in August. Dedem is even more crushing. After the first serious snowfalls, he says, 'not a single French general was at his post' – certainly an exaggeration. And Caulaincourt adds that the 'most public-spirited' of them, seeing that Napoleon, marching along with everyone else, was all too well aware of the extent of the disaster, 'exempted themselves from talking about or indeed from taking any notice of it'.

14. This is a question I must leave hanging in the air. If I could re-read many of the memoirs I first made excerpts from before reading all the others but to which I no longer have access, I should certainly be

able to provide many a missing piece in this jigsaw puzzle.

15. Labaume, a cavalry captain on Eugène's staff, published his embittered and critical book in 1814 during the first Bourbon restoration. He sees Napoleon above all as a man who, despite all his imperial and rationalistic rhetoric, was in love with war and adventure, no matter at what cost. Labaume wrote 'to the end and the moral of rendering odious this fatal expedition which forced civilised peoples to make war on barbarians'. His history would afterwards come out in numerous editions, in French, English and other languages.

Chapter 6: Disaster at the Wop

1. During the '16-hour long night' before leaving Doroghoboui's smouldering ruins, one of Cesare de Laugier's fellow-officers, a Lieutenant Bandai, dying in a roofless stone building in thickly falling snow, foretold the moment of his death: 'At the end of 50 minutes [Raffaglia, as he'd ordered, had his watch in his hand] he asked what time it was. "11.50", came the reply. "Then I've ten more minutes, and my pains are finished. Bring me a bit closer to the fire." We saw him die at the exact moment he'd predicted.'

2. See *Moscow*, pp. 76 *et seq.*

3. See *Moscow*, p. 201 for their kindness to him.

4. Apparently he'd tried them out. His text contradicts itself.

5. Marshal Berthier's son, Anthouard, wrote his own account. See Bibliography.

6. In his *Mémoires* Ney specifies the duties of an adjutant-commandant. He was the equivalent of a 20th-century colonel assigned to staff duty.

7. See *The March*, p. 232.

8. It was Del Fante who'd led the storming of the Great Redoubt at Borodino, captured the Russian general Litchacheff and taken him to Napoleon. See *The March*, pp. 303, 305.

9. Even so it was only a dress-rehearsal for what would happen to the entire army three weeks later.

10. Ségur, with IHQ and just then entering Smolensk, would hear the details afterwards.

Chapter 7: How Witebsk was Lost

1. Elting points out that Napoleon would now and again go through the army lists looking for deserving but no longer active officers. But our memoirists' pages frequently echo the belief that absence meant imperial oblivion.

2. See *The March*, pp. 103, 104.

3. For Jomini and Hogendorp's embittered squabbles and Napoleon's order, see *The March*, p. 243.

4. For Napoleon's insoluble Polish problem, see *The March*, p. 101, etc.

5. The small country town where the campaign's first major action had been fought on 25/26 July. See *The March*, pp. 131 *et seq.*

6. For Charpentier at Witebsk, see *The March*, pp. 174, 178. See also pp. 153 *et seq.*

7. On the other hand it was partly because considerable forces had to be left in the rear that the army had lacked decisive superiority at Borodino.

8. See *The March*, pp. 174, 175.

9. 'If poor Amédée de Pastoret were one day to write his memoirs he would have a lot to tell!' – Stendhal.

10. On the eve of the campaign Oudinot had married Mlle de Coussy (who had now come out to Vilna to nurse his shattered shoulder) in a double wedding where Lorencez, his chief-of-staff, had espoused one of Oudinot's daughters. Lorencez had remained with II Corps when Saint-Cyr had taken over.

11. For Beschenkowiczi, see *The March*, index.

12. Castex's light cavalry brigade, consisting of the 23rd and 24th Chasseurs, was actually part of II Corps. After evacuating Polotsk, a badly wounded Saint-Cyr had met Victor, resigned and gone back to France. This had placed II Corps temporarily under Victor's command.

13. Taken to St Petersburg and released after the wars, Pouget, like Balzac's Colonel Chabert, would be a victim of his Bonapartist sympathies and apply in vain

to the Bourbon government for any recompense for his services at Witebsk, or even for his 'costs for espionage, which amounted to about 1,200 francs'. Napoleon's only comment when he heard of Pouget's last fight and his refusal to abandon his wretched Berg soldiers was: '*Eh bien*, he should have run off and left them stuck there.' An opinion which Pouget, writing his memoirs, would be inclined to share.

Chapter 8: Smolensk Again

1. 'The main street, the great square, all had suffered the same destruction, even the very house pointed out as having been the lodging of Buonaparte. The walls were breached in several parts, and the towers, on which batteries of howitzers had been planted, were in a very shattered state' – but that would be after they'd been partially blown up by Ney's Illyrians on 17 November. *J. T. James*, visiting Smolensk in 1813.

2. An immeasurably popular *opéra comique* by C. S. Favart (1710– 92).

3. Mainly because Murat had given orders to deceive Napoleon as to his losses by burying the French dead first. See *The March*, p. 213.

4. An old comrade in arms from Italy, the elderly and tight-fisted Baraguay d'Hilliers, Colonel-General of Dragoons, was a man on a level with Junot. Reaching Berlin, he'd die of chagrin and/or whatever illness it was he was suffering from.

5. All according to Ségur, but other eyewitnesses in the rear at Smolensk, e.g., Honoré Beulay, confirm it.

6. These were men of Platov's corps. Kutusov's main army had circumvented Smolensk to the south and gone on to try and cut off the French retreat at Krasnoië.

7. See *The March*, p. 217.

8. During the advance the invaders had found the population as far as Smolensk able to speak Polish or Lithuanian and therefore anti-Russian.

9. 'Banding themselves together, they'd been going on ahead of the army and been the first to get to any houses they found, or camped separately in villages. When the army had got there, these thieves had come out of their hiding, prowled around the bivouacs, stolen their horses as quietly as possible and the officers' portmanteaux, and set out again very early before the army started out. Such was their daily plan.'

10. 'By prodigious economies' these would be made to last as far as Bobr. Le Roy's chicken would keep him going as far as the Berezina.

11. On 6 November, in addition to his own duties as responsible for the entire Administration, such as it was, Daru had also officially replaced Mathieu Dumas, who'd been ill ever since leaving Moscow.

12. This, no more than Kergorre's statement to the same effect, isn't quite true. Getting there in September from Minsk with Partonneaux's division (IX) Honoré de Beulay had found all the hospitals full of sick men from the Moscow army 'shivering in infected and stinking barns, lying on rotten straw and devoured by fleas and lice ... dying like flies'. The former inhabitants, 'finding time go slowly in the depths of inhospitable forests, were beginning to return to their homes. We'd been described to them as bloodthirsty barbarians. They were very much surprised to find us civilised people, who liked to laugh when we weren't ill and showed ourselves amiable to women and children and paid for what we bought.' But very few had come back. When Everts had got there on 31 October he'd found the garrison 'in a kind of barracks' and the officers in some uninhabited houses abandoned by their occupants.'

13. Roustam's statement, reiterated by Denniée in his *Itinéraire*, that Napoleon, contrary to all his habits, shut himself up in the governor's palace 'and didn't come out until the 14th at 5 a.m. to continue his retreat', cannot stand up to Caulaincourt's.

14. See *The March*, p. 42.

15. It was by this road that Barclay de Tolly's army had retrograded after the battle of 14 August. See *The March*, p. 375.

16. For the Neuchâtel battalion, see *Moscow*, p. 113.

17. Paul de Bourgoing, who was certainly present, assures us that this happened at Smolensk, not during the ensuing battle

of Krasnoië, as popular historians would afterwards make out: 'How could the wretched men, even if they'd been standing to the right of the regiment, have blown down their instruments, or used their poor frost-bitten fingers? This on the other hand was quite possible at Smolensk, as there were fires where they could warm themselves.' Bourgogne agrees.

Chapter 9: The Icy Road to Krasnoië

1. 'Of these four ADCs,' Mailly-Nesle writes, 'M. Giroux died of wounds received while rejoining us, and M. de Bugueville received three musket balls in his body.'

2. Domergue was one of the French civilian hostages taken from Moscow by Rostopchin.

3. See *Moscow*, pp. 116, 117, 118.

4. See *The March*, pp. 187 *et seq.*

5. See *Moscow* pp. 149, 150.

6. See *Moscow*, p. 242.

7. The Krasnoië ravine had already played an important part at the First Battle of Krasnoië in August, when Griois' guns had got stuck in it. See *The March*, p. 172.

8. The one Napoleon had ordered to be burnt on the eve of Borodino, but which Narbonne had saved from the flames. See *The March*, pp. 251, 252.

9. J. T. James, following the route a year later, would be astonished to see how all the trees in the forests lining the road were half-burnt.

10. See *The March*, pp. 172–3.

Chapter 10: The Guard Strikes Back

1. This is Chambray's estimate in his attempt at a dispassionate and objective account of the campaign (published in 1825). He errs in assuming the Russian army had 'suffered few privations' – it too was suffering dreadfully from cold and starvation. 'Having received some reinforcements [it] was almost as numerous as when it had left Malojaroslavetz. The French army, including the debris of Baraguay-d'Hillier's division and the Smolensk garrison, added up to no more

than about 49,100 combatants, of whom 5,500 cavalry were in the worst possible state. More than 30,000 stragglers were marching with the columns, embarrassing their movements.'

2. See *The March*, Chapter 21.

3. On leaving Moscow on 19 October, according to the returns assembled afterwards by Chambray, the Imperial Guard had still consisted of 22,480 officers and men, including gunners and Train, and 112 guns. Since then it had lost horses and wagons, and certainly several hundred men.

4. Including those regiments which were sometimes classed as Middle Guard, among them the Fusiliers-Grenadiers.

5. For its latest recruits see Bourgoing and Fezensac's accounts in *The March*, pp. 22, 23, 113.

6. A *toise* was more or less a fathom.

7. Roguet says 1 a.m., Bourgogne with his column says 2 a.m.

8. But François' men had at Borodino: See *The March*, p. 282.

9. 'For almost two months', Griois adds, 'this hope of something better that never materialises prevented me from succumbing to fatigue.'

10. For Ornano's ineptitude, see *The March*, p. 293–4, and *Moscow*, pp. 195, 196.

11. Oddly enough Griois makes no mention of this famous episode. Ségur tells the same story, at second or perhaps third hand, in virtually the same words as Laugier, but puts the reply into the mouth of General Guyon, whom he makes claim to have 24,000 men against the Russians' 20,000. Laugier, too, is certainly writing at second hand and, for once, *ex post facto*, and therefore may have got it from Ségur, whose history there is other evidence of his having read. That day, as we've seen, he was in no state to report anything.

12. The Joseph-Napoleon Regiment, whose would-be deserters had caused Coignet such trouble in July (see *The March*, pp. 107, 108), was made up of fragments of Romana's corps who had failed to get themselves evacuated by the British Navy from Denmark, and of Spanish prisoners of war. Its 1st and 4th Battalions formed part of IV Corps; the 2nd and 4th

Battalions had fought at Borodino under their Swiss Colonel Tschudi as part of what had been Dedem's 2nd Infantry Brigade of Friant's 1st Division, which had now been detached to reinforce III Corps, still at Smolensk.

13. Cesare de Laugier adds in a note that Eugène honoured Del Fante's family with a pension and that a street in Leghorn (Livorno) is called Cosimo del Fante. Is it still? The francophile Laugier spells the gallant auditor's name 'Ville-Blanche'.

14. It's a curious trait of human nature that though we have no compunction in shooting or stabbing down an enemy, nothing will induce us to put a friend out of even the worst extremes of agony. We shall see this again in the case of the hated and sadistically minded Delaître. After the Second Battle of Polotsk, Honoré Beulay, too, would hear an officer of the Train 'who'd had a sword thrust through his stomach and whose guts were dragging after him in the snow, calling out to me to finish him off, to put an end to his unspeakable sufferings. I shrank back in horror from the thought of it, and while grieving for this unfortunate man with all my heart, I ran off, abandoning him to his sad fate.'

15. Grabowski assures us that if Klicki – Ségur spells it Kliski – colonel of the 1st Regiment of Lancers of the Vistula, hadn't chanced to be there, IV Corps would have had to surrender.

16. For Napoleon's dream of invading India and the rumour that he intended to, see The March, p. 31, and Moscow, pp. 146, 240. Taken to St Petersburg, Davout's bâton would be put on display at the 'victory' celebrations. Although supposedly out of reach, it vanished! A rumour that it had been taken by some member of the French theatre troupe led to a riot and the troupe was forthwith embarked for Stockholm.

17. The last we saw of Sauvage and Houdart of VIII Corps' artillery park was during the advance through Lithuania in July. See The March, pp. 68, 75.

18. In a letter to Napoleon from Königsberg, the 20-year-old Prince Emil of Hesse would receive the highest praise from Berthier for 'constantly marching with his 250 men whom he has known how to preserve, as also five guns'. Bourgoing lauds his 'heroic valour' and Vionnet admired him for 'never quitting his officers, sharing their difficulties, their privations and their dangers as if he were the least of them'.

19. See The March, pp. 155, 157.

20. Not to be confused of course with von Suckow of the Württembergers.

21. Paul de Bourgoing confirms Ségur's account on this striking detail.

22. The few survivors of the 33rd Line would be repatriated to the Netherlands after the 1813 campaign, without any representations either from the French or Dutch Ministry of War.

Chapter 11. 'Marching, marching, marching ...'

1. Actually Kutusov, under the impact of the Guard's attack at Kontkovo on 17 November, had assumed that it was acting as rearguard to the rest of the army; cancelled his projected assault on Krasnoië; and even sent orders to Tormassov to halt his march to the Dnieper.

2. What a scene to delight Gillray and the patriotic hearts of his fellow London caricaturists: 'Buonaparte, Emperor of the Frenchies, whizzing downhill out of Russia on his a**e, like a shot off a shovel!' Naturally neither Caulaincourt nor anyone else at IHQ seems to have seen the funny side of 'the grave situation'.

3. See The March, p. 171.

4. 'He joined our march,' Pastoret adds. 'This son of the princes of Lisbon came to die at Königsberg for a foreign prince.' On 27 January 1812 Alorna, wishing to 'prove to himself and his friends that he still wasn't decrepit' and to avenge insults from the British, had written to Napoleon, asking to be allowed to shed his blood for him 'the greatest man in the world' by making war in the North. Altogether it's interesting to note how well the Portuguese performed in Russia, as they were simultaneously doing – against the French – under the victorious Wellington in Spain. – See also Theotonio Banha: Apontamentos para a historia du Legiao portugueza, Lisbon, 1865.

5. Brandt, too, thought Jomini was governor at Orsha, and Labaume lists him as such. Elting points out that 'whatever army Jomini accompanied it was noted that he always meddled and interfered'.

6. Future Marshal of France. See *The March*, p. 62.

7. At Vilna on 7 July Napoleon had written to Lariboisière, telling him that Eblé had just been ordered to 'instantly organise a bridging train of 32 boats, with two companies of pontoneers and one of sailors, and place them under the orders of a senior officer'. It was to be at Murat's orders. Faber du Faur had seen part of it parked in the Kremlin. Evidently another part had been left at Orsha, or else subsequently brought up.

8. Doubtless on the broad sandy foreshore Dumonceau had noticed in August, now fringed with ice. See *The March*, p. 139.

9. The one concerning the route from Krasnoïe to Orsha had been sent off the previous day.

10. For the contretemps which could arise when dealing with French arrogance, see *The March*, p.115.

Chapter 12: Ney's Amazing Exploit

1. For these Spaniards, see *The March*, index.

2. See *The March*, p. 178.

3. I.e., ex-Friant, ex-Dufour, now being commanded by General J.-B.-L.-A. de Ricard. A returned *émigré*, Ricard was a relation by marriage to the Marseilles family of Clary, thus to the Bonapartes.

4. A division, in this sense, consisted of two companies, marching in line together.

5. His narrative is to be found in *Les Espagnols de la Grande Armée*.

6. One of them being the Provençal Major Doreille, sole support of his indigent mother at Tarascon, she who had already lost her other six sons in the wars.

7. François confirms that the 2nd Division was almost totally annihilated.

8. François himself, of course, wasn't in Ney's rearguard; he was limping on beyond Krasnoïe, after rescuing the 30th's Eagle. But to judge from the detailed

intensity of his account he seems afterwards to have heard all about it, Unfortunately he doesn't identify his informant for us.

9. François gives the name of the forest as Netinki.

10. Evidently François is identifying with his informant or repeating his words.

Chapter 13: The Terrible News at Toloczin

1. At St Helena he would declare him to have been 'incomparable for the artillery', mentioning him in the same breath as 'Murat for the cavalry'. Promoted General of Brigade, in 1813 and 1814 Drouot would provide notable services in action, accompany Napoleon to Elba and command the Guard artillery at Waterloo.

2. It was near Toloczin that Charles XII's Swedish army had won its last victory before being annihilated at Poltava on 30 June 1709.

3. For Napoleon's Turkish problem, see *The March*, index.

4. These and other town statistics are taken from a report sent in by an anonymous Polish officer, sent on ahead. It is to be found in Chuquet.

Chapter 14: Struggles for the Borissow Bridge

1. Pils too says the 23rd – see *The March*, p. 43. Marbot's tale that he rescued Oudinot in the nick of time after he'd 'barricaded himself in a stone house, adding to his ADCs a dozen French soldiers who were rejoining the army' is obviously purloined from what would happen much later on at Pleschenkowiczi. As we shall see, much of what Marbot, *raconteur par excellence*, writes does not withstand close scrutiny.

2. As I've explained in the introduction to *The March*, there has been no possibility, even within this book's fairly vast framework, to follow the doings of II and VI and then IX Corps around Polotsk; not for lack of memoirs – there are many, a whole account could be sewn together from those of Saint-Chamans, Marbot, Saint-Cyr, Legler, Pils, Lorencez, etc. – but of space. Saint-Cyr's own account of his

operations and the second Battle of Polotsk is lucidity itself, and required reading for war-gamers.

3. Antoine F. de Brack, author of the famous *Avant-postes de Cavalerie légère.*

4. See *Moscow,* Chapter 10.

5. See *The March,* p. 32.

6. See the fascinating texts of this and other 'treaties' imposed by Napoleon on his 'allies' in Nafziger's invaluable book.

7. See *The March,* p. 23.

8. See James R. Arnold's biographical study in Chandler: *Napoleon's Marshals.*

9. On 24 November Victor would write to Berthier: 'My generals of division are complaining a great deal about their troops. Generally speaking they are serving badly. It's difficult to keep them within bounds. They ascribe this to their state of indigence, but I believe it's due to their being so badly composed. The Dutch regiments, above all, are absolute nullities. The only unit which holds up and has always marched in good order is the Baden Brigade.' He had only 800 cavalry left.

10. The non co-ordination of II and IX Corps and its putative effect on the Berezina battle would provide an endless topic of debate among military men for decades afterwards. Lorencez produces documents to defend Oudinot and show that he was all the time trying to edge towards the Moscow army and was fully aware of the Borissow bridge's importance.

11. Second son of a former governor of St Petersburg, Pahlen would one day be the Russian Ambassador in Paris.

12. Having been Jérôme's chief-of-staff during the campaign's opening stages, he'd been given command, after that popinjay king's petulant departure, of II Corps' 8th Division.

13. At the campaign's outset Marbot, too, had been received with polite scepticism and a patronising clap on the shoulder when he'd come rushing with news that Wittgenstein was in presence.

14. For a brief description of Glubokoië, see *The March,* p. 109.

15. Corbineau's other two regiments may not have been so fortunate, for Fain will hear afterwards that '70–80 troopers less well mounted than the others' were lost.'

16. And certainly not Jomini's, who claims it was. At most his general knowledge of the vicinity may have contributed to the decision. Nor was Lorencez right in thinking that the 6th Lancers had crossed by the Studianka ford; in fact they used another, just north of Borissow.

17. After the Swedes had lost Finland to Russia in 1808 it had become a Russian archduchy. This explains the presence of Finnish soldiers at the Berezina.

18. Later that day Oudinot would write to Berthier: 'This contretemps has prevented us from saving the big bridge over the Berezina, which had been set fire to at three points simultaneously.' But added (as if it in any way palliated the disaster): 'We have taken several artillery ammunition wagons and are looking for six cannon we're assured the enemy have abandoned. We've already taken about 800 or 900 prisoners, among them several superior officers and we're still picking up many in the town.'

19. Napoleon would leave him a substantial sum in his will 'to go on defending the honour of French arms'.

20. Oudinot attributes the capture of Pahlen's '300 or 400 vehicles to our voltigeurs who'd crossed the stream to the left' of the small bridge at the town's entrance. 'We'd have entered it', he'll report to Berthier, 'if the enemy hadn't set fire to it.'

21. Actually 'three short leagues, i.e., about eight miles, according to General Bourdesolle, whose light cavalry had reconnoitred it and found 'narrow cross-country roads through the woods and marshes. Log bridges have had to be hastily constructed. The infantry and cavalry would only be able to make this march very slowly and with extreme fatigues and preceded by sappers. The artillery wouldn't get through.' Another officer thought the 'road through the forest is at present practicable for artillery except for certain spots which aren't properly frozen but can be turned. The approach to the village of Oukholoda is marshy.' The river's width was about the same as at Studianka. 'But the inhabitants say it isn't fordable even in summer.' On the right

436

bank, lined by trees, there were houses for the Russians to fortify, and the ground became marshy. A Polish ADC, the 32-year-old Colonel Falkowski, too, had been to Beresino.

22. 'Saving the Bridge at Borissow', it seems to me, would make a perfect war-game. Starting from the loss of Minsk and Oudinot's and Victor's strategical disputes, it would hinge around an analysis of he accounts given by Vaudoncourt, Victor, Pils, Lorencez, Marbot, Langeron, Rochechouart, Tchitchakov, Calosso and Curély.

Chapter 15: 'How Ever Shall We Get Through?'

1. *'Comment passerons-nous? Comment passerons-nous?'* All this according to Paul de Bourgoing, who however makes the error of thinking Napoleon got the news at Orsha.

2. It was particularly unfair to Davout, who was methodically commanding the rearguard against dwindling forces of Cossacks, 'accompanied as always by an infinite number of all the army corps' stragglers who, halting close to our troops when we take up a position, at the least alert rush to the rear, sweeping the combatants away with them.' Nor has Eugène, a few miles ahead of Davout, lost his head. On the contrary, bivouacked 'three leagues from Toloczin, near Jablonka', he's proving an admirable commander in adversity. Ney, who certainly isn't losing his, is in advance of him. Analysing IX and II Corps' movements, Lorencez writes: 'If Wittgenstein had marched on Bobr or some other place on the major line of communication between Smolensk and the Berezina, Napoleon would have found his Poltava long before reaching Borissow.' But Kutusov, still at Krasnoïe and 'preyed upon by theoretical as well as practical doubts concerning the Russian strategy' (Chandler) as he struggled through hardly less terrible difficulties than the French, had his most advanced units at least 40 miles to the rear. Tchitchakov, as we shall see, would be thrown into confusion by his recommendations.

3. Jomini says his words were: 'Sire, we aren't in Lombardy, nor in Swabia; but in Lithuania, 600 leagues from France, in a desert where winter has already overtaken us. What matter now the beautiful manoeuvres offered us by a divided enemy on our flanks? Any day that puts distance between the army and its line of retreat will risk the loss of such of it as is still in a state to carry arms.' In reality one doesn't exactly see even 'the insufferably conceited' (Hogendorp) Jomini lecturing Napoleon in such terms!

4. Oddly enough, it had also been at Toloczin that Charles XII had burnt all his State papers. Was there an element of suggestion involved? We know from Bausset that throughout his stay in the Kremlin Napoleon had had the *History of Charles XII* (presumably Adlerbeth's, not Voltaire's, which he had had no use for) open on the roll-top desk in the Tsar's bedroom and 'even on his bedside table'.

5. Three days later Junot would write in the most fulsomely obsequious terms: 'I haven't a single infantryman left, not a gun, and my cavalry has hardly 100 horses. Who could do it more devotedly? What general officer can date the honour of guarding Your Majesty as far back as I can? Etc.' Junot having so disastrously blotted his copy book at Valutina in August, his letter was ignored.

6. For this intelligent young aristocrat's dependence on the experienced Henckens, see *Moscow*, p. 145.

7. At Vilna Oudinot's young wife, living under Maret's direct protection in the governor's palace, had struck up a 'strong and fascinated friendship' with Abramovitch's wife, a Polish woman who'd been divorced by no fewer than 'three husbands, still living'. One of them, Eugénie de Cousset alleges, had been Montholon 'who afterwards went with Napoleon to St Helena' and, according to Sten Forshuvud's researches, finally murdered him. But as far as we know Albine Montholon was his first wife.

8. Bourgogne's unforgettable epic of his survival amidst the icy wastes should be read in his own classic pages.

9. As we have seen, opinions would differ widely about how much of the Sacred Squadron survived intact, and for how long.

10. Lieutenant J. M. Chevalier, a long-serving officer of the Chasseurs à Cheval who'd been with him in Egypt, describes

in minute detail Napoleon's and Murat's costumes at this stage of the retreat: 'The Emperor had had a cap of green velvet made, in the shape of a toque with a tassel, and a little gold tuft, the band and ear pads in black martin skin, a kind of dressing-gown in grass-green velvet like the cap, the collar in black otter, the whole lined with fur, fringed with gold brandenburgs, a white belt around it to support his sword, fur boots, big gloves and a big stick – that's how the Emperor was dressed just then. An accoutrement, for the rest, which didn't seem much to his liking, for he only wore it a few days. The King of Naples wore a huge, opulent, semi-Polish costume: a Polish-style cap with a white ostrich feather, a fur-lined Polish-style mantle, violet like the cap, baggy red trousers, boots over them, a black bear's skin (I believe) in the form of a half-mantle thrown over his left shoulder, which gave his way of walking and his physiognomy a martial and imposing air. Prince Berthier, too, in a blue overcoat and a peasant cap, was marching at the Emperor's side.' As for other members of IHQ, Chevalier adds tersely: 'general carnival'. Chevalier's own clothing at this time may be of interest: 'Here's how I was clad, a complete portmanteau on my person: 1. A flannel waistcoat; 2. a shirt; 3. a knitted woollen waistcoat; 4. a sheepskin waistcoat; 5. a coloured waistcoat; 6. a braided waistcoat; 7. a dolman; 8. a belt; 9. a riding-coat; 10. a cloak over the whole. On my thighs: 1. a pair of underpants; 2. a pair of buckskin breeches; 3. a pair of Hungarian breeches; 4. a pair of cloth trousers; 5. a pair of trousers for riding, and, on my head, a bearskin cap.' We offer these exact descriptions to any tin figurine enthusiast to try to render!

11. No eye-witness authenticates this legendary scene, depicted in the well-known painting and a thousand tin-soldier dioramas; this is the only reference to it I've been able to find.

12. But not, as we shall see, before some residue had got across the Berezina.

13. Caulaincourt (p.105) thinks Napoleon would have done better to have made for Weselovo direct from Kroupki, taking the same road as Corbineau had arrived by. 'The fact is, that if we'd taken it, we'd have gained two marches; and that by making

our manoeuvres seem to be directed toward Borissow, we could have avoided the Admiral altogether, and that all our losses might have been saved.' But, thinks Caulaincourt, 'Pahlen's defeat and other considerations' had made Napoleon opt for Borissow. 'On the whole, though, the probability is that he knew nothing of Corbineau's suggestions, since he never spoke of them at the time they were made, and even deplored the inconvenience to the artillery and transport of having to make so big a detour to reach Weselovo. He spoke to me about the matter, as well as to the Prince of Neuchâtel, grumbling that he was never told about things in time.' There is some obscurity here which it seems impossible to clear up.

14. There is a time-scale problem here. As we have seen, Oudinot, according to Lorencez, had already sent II Corps' 'whole cuirassier division' (Doumerc's) to make a demonstration downstream on 24 November. Yet both Curély and Dumonceau see the movement undertaken 24 hours later? The matter seems to me to bear on the question of whether Oudinot or Napoleon ordered the feint.

Chapter 16: Two Fragile Bridges

1. A native of Crissier, in the Vaud, Jean-Marc Bussy had been a prisoner of war in England and even joined the British army, but feigned sickness so as not to be sent to India. Returning to France, he'd tried to get himself demobbed, but been arrested and sent off to Spain ... and Russia.

2. In his book *Vers la Bérésina*, Paris 1908, B. R. F. van Vlijmen says there were 300 of them; 'those from II Corps, about 200, were mostly Dutchmen'. This is partly confirmed by Dumonceau, below.

3. In his *Campaigns of Napoleon* David Chandler suggests 'some approximations' as to the Grand Army's fighting strength at the Berezina: Guard 8,500; I Corps 3,000; II Corps 11,000; III Corps (after reinforcement) 3,000; IV Corps 2,000; V + VI Corps 1,500; IX Corps 13,500; IHQ 2,500; mounted cavalry 5,500, and some 250–300 guns. Total 49,000 under arms plus some 40,000 stragglers.

4. Castellane, at least, wasn't underestimating the efforts of IHQ's cooks and

maîtres d'hôtel. 'Since Smolensk,' he writes in his diary, 'our meals consist of a very small slice of black bread, in the morning, with a bit of cow or horsemeat. In the evening we also get some soup. Sometimes we've been given mutton.'

5. Marbot (who says Napoleon got to Studianka at midday) says he 'put an end to the dispute by ordering one of the bridges to be built by the artillery, the other by the engineers. Instantly the beams and scantling battens of the village's huts were torn off and the sappers, like the gunners, got down to work.'

6. Oddly, Napoleon always found certain French words unpronounceable, or else didn't bother to try and pronounce them properly. E.g., he always called the infantry *'l'enfanterie'.*

7. Rapp's memories tend to be sporadic, and by no means always accurate. He'd remember the battery as having only twenty guns.

8. Although Berthier, always at hand, must have noted it down in his 'little green notebook' Curély's promotion wouldn't be confirmed until 9 August 1813.

9. Albitte had been famous at Mainz for his melancholy air 'which people took for a sign of remorse' for his revolutionary zeal; obviously mistakenly. – A. Chuquet: *Feuilles d'Histoire du XVII au XX Siècle,* Paris, 1911.

10. Chandler: 'If any one Russian mistake can be singled out for special comment, it is their failure to hold or destroy the crucial causeway leading away from the Berezina toward Zembin.'

11. Next year Tchitchakov, in virtual exile in Paris, would publish a defence of his bungling at the Berezina: *Rélation du passage de la Bérésina,* Paris, 1814; and *Mémoires,* Berlin, 1855. See also Emile Charles: *Documents sur la vie de l'Amiral de Tchitchageff,* Paris, 1854.

12. No one in the army, except Berthier, was allowed to wear a Swiss civilian-style hat like Napoleon's.

13. Duverger saw him in much the same light.

14. The decoration would never reach him. 'Only too soon', sighs Brandt, 'it would enter the category of things one

doesn't even dare boast of having had. But he, the brave and chivalrous king, he'd have more unhappiness than I [for lack of] my decoration!' In 1815 Murat, like Ney, would be shot by firing-squad.

15. 'His uniforms, his plume, his boots made after an antique fashion, all appeared to him to be invaluable accessories in the art of seducing the fair sex. With this paraphernalia he really thought himself the most irresistible of men, though in point of fact he was so handsome no one needed such trappings less than he did.' Caulaincourt, of Murat.

16. It will be seen that Dupuy's account contradicts Tascher's. Perhaps Tascher himself and some others 'drifted away', while others remained?

17. He means a 'rag-and-bone man'. See *The March,* p. 111.

18. Unlike Mère Dubois' infant, this one would survive. In 1818 Bertrand would 'next meet with him as a child in the Legion of the Aube'.

Chapter 17: Partonneaux Surrenders

1. Actually Kutusov was four days' march behind but had sent on Platow and Miloradovitch to catch up with and harass the French as they approached the Berezina. Clausewitz, serving at Russian headquarters, ascribes Kutusov's dilatoriness and caution to his over-estimating the numbers of French effectives. It was also due to poor reconnaissance on the part of his Cossacks who failed to report that half the Grand Army now consisted of stragglers. Napoleon, Clausewitz says, was 'living on a capital amassed over long years'. His mere name scared all the Russian commanders.

2. Rossetti writes 'this defection', but it seems unlikely that Napoleon should already have used this word, though he'd call it that afterwards. Besides, it still wasn't certain Partonneaux's division was lost. But we have already caught Rossetti out using 'terminological inexactitudes'.

3. Partonneaux's little-known letter is in Chuquet: *op. cit.,* Series 3.

4. At Hamburg Planat had impressed on him 'the dangers and hardships of a campaign. But at that time he'd been full of health and ardour, and told me he'd all

his life wanted to go campaigning with the brave Frenchmen. The poor devil had already had enough when we'd crossed the Niemen and I'd have sent him back as soon as we'd got to Kovno, if I could have replaced him.'

5. For their fate, see Chapter 19, below.

6. Caulaincourt would specifically set the number of individuals finally lost at about 10,000. Fain says 200–300 combatants (after Davout and Victor's withdrawal) and 10 to 12,000 stragglers.

7. Pils' expressive water-colour of the lurid and dramatic scene – here reproduced, unfortunately, only in black and white – in which he perfectly captures the moonlight effect, must have been made the previous night. It is reproduced – in colour – in Gaston Stiegler's book.

Chapter 18: Holocaust at the Berezina

1. In 1816 Kundert, then a corporal drummer in the 31st Swiss Regiment in Dutch service at Duisburg, would remind Legler of the incident. 'He still had the musket ball in his jawbone.'

2. Bourmann lived until he was 89, 'the last Fribourg survivor of the Napoleonic armies. Always upright and walking lightly he seemed to defy time. Each year on 28 November' (also commemorated in '*The Berezina Song*', apparently composed soon afterwards, and still sung in Switzerland) he would make 'a distribution to charity while taking the sacrament. That service was followed by a second in memory of his comrades who'd died on that sanguinary day.' He died in 1877, having seen Napoleon III's defeated army take refuge in his canton.

3. 'As for the poor 22nd [Russian] Chasseurs, old comrades of my first campaigns, they'd been crushed by the cuirassiers on the one hand and on the other by a well-nourished fire of artillery which had taken them in flank.' That evening their colonel, all in tears, would tell Rochechouart: 'Of the 2,000 men I had with me this morning, I've only brought back 150, three officers and my flag.' 'A great part of them had been taken prisoner, and the rest were out of action, dead or wounded.' But many would return to the colours next day.

4. This isn't the only occasion where an attentive reader catches Marbot out arrogating to himself a role which certainly belonged to his superior general. He does the same thing at the campaign's outset, at the Battle of Wilkomir on 28 June, which in his own account he claims to have won almost single-handed but where Calosso and Pils' more sober evidence reduces events to their proper proportions.

5. No doubt the very one Lejeune had designed for Berthier's 'ladykillers' in Spain, or some variant of it. For details of the uniform worn by Berthier's ADCs see *The March*, pp. 44–5.

6. Certainly there's something in Marbot's version, too; for Fain also hears how Cossacks had been 'seen dragging this officer away, striking him as they did so', and that 'the 23rd Chasseurs had done what they could to rescue him. But he was never heard of again.' Bonneval's statement that he'd seen Alfred de Noailles the previous day lying dead at the bridgehead, 'shot though the head by one of our own men' is obviously aprocryphal. Even more so Mailly-Nesle's tale of de Noailles being killed at Zembin next day. What is certain is that he wasn't listed by the Russians as a prisoner. In July 1813 Flahaut would translate an official Russian letter to that effect, but that 'on the other hand, his effects and letters have been found near the Berezina'. Young Noailles' health had been severely impaired as a prisoner in Spain, where Berthier had evidently got him exchanged. See Chuquet, vol. III, pp. 370–7.

7. But a few days later they became separated and 'I never saw him again.'

8. Fezensac says the little girl got back safely out of Russia 'without even catching cold'.

9. Several of our writers mention this gap, so difficult to surmount, between the bridge and the river bank. One wonders how the carriages and artillery had got over it? Doubtless thanks to their own ramps they had with them.

10. Hardly one of our 'cameramen' but has left an equally dramatic and circumstantial account of how he got across the Berezina. These four, Suckow, Le Roy, Kergorre and Griois, must stand for dozens and for the experience of thousands.

11. 'But I heard next day he'd found his brother a little way away, but in a dying condition. Thus perished these two poor brothers, and also a third in the 2nd Lancers.' Bourgogne adds that when he got back to Paris he saw their parents 'who begged me for news of their children. I left them a ray of hope by saying that their sons had been taken prisoners, but I felt certain they'd died.'

12. It's curious to reflect that the shells were being fired at the orders of one of Jomini's most ardent readers and disciples, Wittgenstein's chief-of-staff General Diebitsch.

13. 'A few unfortunates,' Louise will hear, but not being there herself cannot vouch for it, 'nevertheless managed to walk over the ice and get across the river. Those who rejoined us at Vilna', she adds, 'told us of scenes which made us shudder.'

14. The Bashkirs had impressed themselves on the invaders' imagination – and skin – by being armed with bows and arrows.

Chapter 19: Two Prisoners

1. On 9 December, after stumbling on through a devastated countryside, what was left of the column would get to Witebsk. The monstrous sufferings of the Russians' prisoners are related *in extenso* by Roos, Beulay and Faure, *op. cit.*

Chapter 20: Cortege Through the Snows

1. Jomini, it will be remembered, had been appointed official campaign historian after Napoleon had scotched his secret plans for serving under the Tsar, where he'd hoped for more rapid promotion. See *The March*, p. 104.

2. She would survive the retreat.

3. For some reason Roederer didn't accept him even so. For Gourgaud's personality and ambitions, see *The March*, p. 360. For his growing arrogance, see below.

4. 'Almost all would perish from hunger en route for Vilna.' – As for the ones from Rochechouart's 20th Russian Chasseurs, 'the French being unable to guard these prisoners, they were able to rejoin their flags three or four days afterwards'.

5. Luckily the evil was transient. 'Two days later everyone would have got his sight back.'

6. For its virtual annihilation at Valutina, see *The March*, p. 210.

7. Accounts of Oudinot's famous private battle at Pleschenkoviczi differ. Naturally I trust Pils, who was on the spot. Marbot's version, as usual, is wildly inaccurate; he has neither the date nor the place right. Cesare de Laugier, always concerned to defend the honour of Italian arms, is annoyed with Labaume, Ségur, Cambray and Vaudoncourt for their accounts – particularly with Labaume, who, being on Eugène's staff, must have heard Captain Migliorini ('who'd distinguished himself throughout the campaign' and together with the captured Cossack been sent to Eugène on his arrival at Pleschenkoviczi to report on the affair) for not mentioning Pino's gallantry in commanding the defence.

8. Which was untrue. Partonneaux and his headquarters had been at the head of the division, and going on along the straight road toward Staroï-Borissow instead of turning off to the left he had marched with the brigade closest to the Russians. Napoleon would do him less than justice in the celebrated 29th Bulletin, issued a few days later. It was felt that if it hadn't been for the loss of his division all the stragglers and baggage might have been got across the river, and with them such stores as might have enabled much more of the army to reach Vilna. But Napoleon could also be magnanimous. On 19 July 1813 he would give Partonneaux's three sons – their father still being a prisoner in Russia – free places in the Turin Lycée; and on his return from Elba, hearing they'd been deprived during the First Restoration because of Partonneaux's political affiliations, he gave them new ones at the Marseilles Lycée, even though Partonneaux had refused to serve under him any more. Partonneaux himself would afterwards deny that he'd lost his way, claiming instead that he'd heard the bridge over the Berezina was already cut, whereupon he'd tried to find a way northwards and so rejoin the Vilna road.

9. Baraguay d'Hilliers would in fact die in Berlin.

10. It can be read *in extenso* in his *Memoirs*.

Chapter 21: The Emperor Quits

1. Loison's ill-fated division, part of Augereau's XI (reserve) Corps stationed in Germany but at Vilna since 21 November, consisted of three infantry brigades, the first nominally eight battalions strong, but in reality only some 3,000 (Castellane would estimate it at 6,000; but Berthier's figure is to be preferred) of its original 10,000. In March–April 1813 there would be an enquiry into Loison's behaviour, but though subjected to Napoleon's criticism he would be reinstated.

2. For Pradt's point of view, see *Moscow*, pp.109–11, 237–8.

3. It must not be imagined the Tsar had not hastened to inform Europe, or at all events those powers which, openly or secretly, sympathised with his cause, of his great enemy's catastrophe. In Stockholm, for instance, various letters and strangers dispatched from Petersburg and arriving in the Swedish capital had 'caused a certain amount of worry on account of Napoleon's entrance into Moscow and it was assumed St Petersburg would have to be evacuated if, as was being said, he marched against that capital with a large part of his army.' This news, Bernadotte, Sweden's freely elected Crown Prince, had written to Alexander on 25 November, had put heart into the francophile anti-Russian party. In his high-flown rhetoric Bernadotte had reassured the Tsar – and told the Russian Ambassador in Stockholm – that no matter what the war's outcome might be 'Sweden would sooner bury itself among its boulders than change sides.' Why, he'd even signed a treaty of friendship with the ex-King Ferdinand III of Spain (currently held prisoner with his obstreperous family in Berthier's château on the Loire)! On 28 October the Tsar had replied at length, recounting Russian successes from 6 October on: 'Knowing the friendship Your Highness feels for me, I hope Your Highness will be somewhat interested in this good news.' Having failed to detach the Danes from their French alliance and already planning a Swedish-Russian offensive in Germany for 1813, in the event of a catastrophe for the Grand Army in Russia, Bernadotte certainly was.

4. Madame de Staël, herself no mean exaggerator and just then hobnobbing with the Tsar at Petersburg en route for Stockholm, where she'd soon be doing the same with her old friend Bernadotte, would say of her arch-enemy that he was 'a man who so loves to cause strong emotions and who when he can't hide his setbacks exaggerates them, so as always to outdo anyone else.' *Considérations*. Here there was no possibility of exaggeration!

5. The second accusation was of course true (see *The March*, p.123), the first the opposite of the truth. Murat had never wanted any part in the campaign, and at Smolensk, in August, had even begged Napoleon to halt his march on Moscow. See *The March*, pp. 185, 201.

6. Afterwards, when Murat's lack of character and total unreliability had become evident, Berthier, 'overwhelmed by despair, reproached himself with having contributed to the selection of such a leader'. (Caulaincourt)

7. Roustam's memoirs are not perhaps the most reliable of sources. For Berthier's declining efficiency in 1812 and Napoleon's occasionally brutal way of speaking to him, see *The March*, p. 66. But at the Tuileries, hearing of the loss of Vilna, Napoleon would regret not having handed over to Eugène.

8. After Waterloo, Hogendorp would found an agricultural colony in Brazil. Napoleon would rather unaccountably leave him 100,000 francs in his will. In defiance of Napoleon's strict order that no woman should cross the Niemen, his young wife, the Princess Hohenlohe, her mother and their little girl had joined him at Vilna. On his being ordered to send them back at once (see *The March*, p. 243) he did so; but the young Duchess of Reggio (also flouting imperial orders) on her way to join her wounded husband at Vilna in early October, encountered them at their first wretched overnight stop after Kovno on their way back. The daughter seemed sickly, and indeed died six months later; and soon thereafter also her mother.

9. The outermost of the three rooms that invariably constituted Napoleon's personal headquarters. For its routines see *The March*, pp. 93–4.

10. On 16 December Castellane would see Constant and Collin, the major-domo, at Heilsberg, on their way back to France.

11. See *The March*, p. 109

12. *Une borne.* Probably one of the official milestones; but the word also means a stone sticking out from a house to keep carriages from knocking against the wall. Perhaps it was the latter.

13. For d'Albe's function as Chief Cartographer, see *The March*, p. 94. Amodru and his brother would accompany Napoleon to St Helena in the capacity of coachmen.

14. Bourgoing says at 8 p.m. Fain, also on the spot but perhaps having other things to think about just then, says 9 p.m. Roustam says between 8 and 9. Bourgoing's circumstantial account of Napoleon's departure and journey, published in 1869, has high source value, having been based on an unpublished account in Polish by Wonsowicz.

15. The jibe, if it really were made, had been revived in the Paris theatres on the eve of the war when it had become known that Caulaincourt, a friend of the Tsar's and just back from his 4-year Petersburg embassy, was a 'dove' and completely against it. Actually it had originally been invented and stuck at the time of the judicial assassination of the Duc d'Enghien. For Caulaincourt's painful position, see *The March*, p. 16.

16. At Molodeczno its wounded had rejoined its other survivors. It had been virtually wiped out in the Brill Wood, and even been sabred by mistake by Doumerc's cuirassiers, 'notably Colonel Kosinowski who'd been wearing a green pelisse'.

17. Somehow, though Brandt's word isn't to be doubted, there's something unclear about this incident. He describes it as occurring *before* reaching Smorgoni, in which case it can hardly have been after Napoleon had left.

18. Dumonceau, who is usually to be relied on in matters of detail, writes 'in a sledge'. But Caulaincourt, who after all had arranged all the details, says specifically it was a carriage on wheels. A sledge was following, with a workman in it to make any necessary repairs en route. Most historians describe the carriage as being escorted by Polish lancers, but don't mention the Dutch ones who, as we see, were also involved. Dumonceau's account was

only published in 1963. And perhaps by this stage of things, in December 1812, the original writers didn't distinguish too clearly between Colbert's two regiments, both no doubt tightly wrapped up in their cloaks. Is Zalusky's memory, too, failing him when he says that it was at the 'Ochmiana post-house the Dutch Guard Lancers relieved us'?

19. Zalusky, who notes the lowest temperature recorded as -22°, accuses the historian Thiers of exaggerating it to -30°. 'I don't know what our regiment's friend Dr Larrey, who carried a thermometer, noted. But what I know is that in our Polish countries it never falls below -24° or -25°. Around Danzig and Eylau it had frozen at least as low as this during the wars of 1806–7.'

Chapter 22: The Very Air Seemed Frozen

1. Ségur and Labaume, he says, are definitely wrong in saying the army was indignant and that Napoleon's departure put the finishing touch to its discouragement and disorganisation.

2. As I explained in *The March*, the term 'dysentery' was used in those days to cover both conditions.

3. See *The March*, p. 48.

4. See *The March*, p. 46.

5. Thereafter his thermometer would rise slightly to between -24° and -18° R (-15° – 11.25° C).

6. See *The March*, pp. 165, 319, 390.

7. 'Sappers', or as perhaps the word should be translated 'pioneers', regularly had beards, wore bearskins, white leather aprons, and in addition to their muskets carried axes.

8. See *Moscow*, p. 150. Perhaps we even owe something of the vividness of his memoirs to Le Roy's sleeplessness that night, the coldest of the entire retreat?

Chapter 23. Panic and Chaos at Vilna

1. See *The March*, pp. 36, 52; *Moscow*, p. 162. Berthier's letter, dated the Kremlin, 13 October, had arrived shortly afterwards. Sent for by a commissary, the boy had been told the Emperor had given him

all the privileges of a commissioned officer and was sending him back to France to finish his schooling at the imperial expense.

2. He'd embarked them in the yacht *Charlotte de Königsberg* at the Frische-Haf on 20 June, switched them on 30 September to seven barges on the Niemen and had all the trouble in the world reaching Kovno before the rivers froze.

3. 'All I had at Vilna were four Polish regiments made up of recruits who, though they'd officially existed since July, were still neither dressed nor armed. I had to take whatever I could find in the hospitals and stores, and within 24 hours all these men were more or less armed and clothed.' By mid-November, in a cold which had fallen from -20° to -25° Réaumur, the two governors had 'managed to assemble about 12,000 infantry and 2,000 cavalry and had sent them off in two brigades – one towards Smorgoni on the main Minsk road, the other toward Dolhinov, to support II Corps and facilitate the Berezina crossing.' Meanwhile several provisional regiments had arrived from Prussia. Also, more spectacularly, 1,200 Neapolitans, 'two regiments of Murat's Royal Guard and Guards of Honour', all volunteers. Oudinot's young duchess had seen them on parade, no doubt magnificently turned out in their yellow or pale blue and crimson uniforms: 'I couldn't refuse the Duke of Bassano's invitation to be present at a review of the Neapolitan Guard, which was passing through Vilna to go and rejoin Murat. Bright and brilliant, it manoeuvred for an hour or two under our eyes. It was its adieu to the world; a few days later, the cold having got worse, men and horses gradually melted like snow in sunshine.'

All these troops had had to camp around the town. 'From this moment the "fortress of Vilna" presented an imposing aspect.' And when, toward the month's end, Loison's division, twelve German and Italian infantry battalions, had arrived from Germany, Hogendorp had fanned them out strategically 'to support the retiring army and prevent it being surprised by the Russians. Those at Lida were to keep open communications with Reynier. Those at Voronov and Roudzicvhi with Grodno. The units at Sventsiany with Dunaborg. A big cavalry depot was established

at Merecz and the debris of the shattered 3rd Guard Lancers was at Novo-Troki. At Vilna itself 1,500 cuirassiers and carabiniers were stationed to maintain order.'

4. Roch-Godart had first met Bonaparte in 1797. The circumstance of his battalion having been the one that had been active during the *coup d'état* of 18th Brumaire, together with his distinguished service record, doubtless explains his knighthood of the Legion of Honour. By 1812 he'd become disgusted with the decline in public morals among the Napoleonic hierarchy. It was his chronically gammy leg he had to thank for his governorship. Passing through Grodno en route to join Delzons' division of IV Corps at Moscow, he'd found his leg 'was in a frightful state' and applied to be employed in the rear. And a fortnight later he'd received Berthier's orders. It had taken him 10 to 12 days to create order where evidently Jomini, that eminent theorist, had left chaos. Everything had been inadequate. (For Napoleon's orders to Jomini in July, see *The March*, p. 104.) For instance there'd been a grave lack of carts so that even as late as early October Saint-Cyr had begun complaining of II Corps not getting any supplies. – Roch-Godart would write his memoirs as a prisoner of war in Hungary in 1814, so they have a high level of memory-value. Since Hogendorp and Roch-Godart would be made scapegoats for the ensuing débâcle, both men's memoirs try to show they'd done everything they could to avert it.

5. Monetary values are notoriously difficult to render in modern terms. But 28 francs was perhaps worth some £100 or $200, a considerable price for an omelette!

6. Dupuy adds: 'And when the regiment was re-united I got back all my advances.'

7. See *The March*, p. 95.

8. Lignières says Boulart told him to visit him one day and remind him of what he'd looked like at Vilna, 'because he'd saved his life'. But when in fact, years afterwards, Lignières, during the Restoration, sent him a letter at Strasburg, Colonel Boulart never replied. Boulart himself makes no mention of this incident.

9. There are several accounts of this, but Chlapowski's is the most drastic. After-

wards there would be general tendency to accuse Wrede of radical insubordination, even of treason to the French cause, the more so as he'd go over to the Allies in 1813.

10. In Paris Hogendorp lived in Mailly-Nesle's town house. Afterwards he would be made a scapegoat for the chaos at Vilna – which he certainly couldn't have prevented.

11. When they'd had to spend the night in a downpour being soaked to the bone and up to their knees in mud in a monastery courtyard. See *The March*, pp. 74–5

12. Rapp would conduct an epic defence of Danzig throughout 1813, finally have to surrender and himself be sent as prisoner of war to the Ukraine.

13. Hearing at the Tuileries about the headlong evacuation of Vilna, he would say to Caulaincourt: 'There's no example of such a rout, such stupidity. What a hundred men of courage would have saved has been lost under the nose of several thousand brave men by Murat's fault. A captain of voltigeurs would have commanded the army better than he.' But why had he ignored his own assessment of Murat's character? (See *The March*, p. 64). 'When the King of Naples hears bullets whistle,' he'd tell his minister Molé on 13 February 1813, 'when he can see the danger physically in front of him [*matérielle-ment*], he's 12 feet tall. But when he doesn't, when he imagines it, he becomes more timid than a pregnant woman. Sees phantoms. He lacks moral courage; it comes from his lack of intelligence [*esprit*]. I've no one to put in my place and I'd been only too happy if I could make war through my generals. But they aren't used to it and there's none of them can command the others.' To Molé Napoleon would describe Eugène, who'd perhaps have done somewhat better, as 'less brilliant than the King of Naples; less eminent in one respect; even in every way a mediocre man. But there's more proportion and harmony in him. The King of Naples has lost me my army, because I still had one when I left, but haven't one now. As long as I was there people murmured, but they obeyed.'

14. Napoleon's stable-master was a M. de Saluces, formerly squadron-commander

in the Sardinian service. Next year he would be made major in one of the new Guards of Honour regiments.

15. Afterwards Le Roy would hear that 'for several days all these unfortunates had stayed there without any food, having been stripped of their belongings and maltreated. Probably all succumbed to their sufferings. Not one reappeared in the regiment.'

16. Lefèbvre's son would die a couple of days later, and after the old man had reached Königsberg Napoleon would grant him permission to return to France. For his biography, see Gunther E. Rothenberg's article in David Chandler's *Napoleon's Marshals*.

17. 'Although the traces of his fatigues and privations were strongly marked on his face,' Oudinot's duchess would think when she saw him again, 'this courageous old man had survived all the miseries of the retreat without losing, at least to all appearances, his infectious and gracious gaiety.'

18. Lallemand, though not one of those chosen by Napoleon to go with him to St Helena, would be one of the group of officers who went aboard HMS *Bellerophon* in 1815.

19. Lenoble would die, worn out, in the hospital at Königsberg.

20. All students of this or any period owe a debt of gratitude to Miss Helen Roeder for translating and so vividly presenting excerpts from her ancestor's diary, *op. cit.* The account of what happened to him and Vogel at Vilna, and their journey in May through Poland and Pomerania, where they'd be imprisoned by the Swedish authorities, but finally get home to Darmstadt, is particularly fascinating. It gives a vivid impression of the state of affairs in the region after the débâcle.

21. See *Moscow*, pp. 30, 55.

Chapter 24: Ponari's Fatal Hill

1. Grandjean and Lorge's divisions of XI Corps had also been ordered up. Caulaincourt and Napoleon had seen them at Rumchiki, a village just outside Kovno.

2. See *The March* and *Moscow*, indices.

3. See *The March*, p. 70. Strangely enough, various eye-witnesses would afterwards remember Ponari Hill as lying at quite different distances outside Vilna. Professor Algvidas Jakubcionis of Vilnius University, who has so kindly provided me with many details about and pictures of the town in those days, writes that 'the distance in the early 19th century was 6–7 kilometres'. He explains that the hill's exact gradient in those days is hard to determine, 'as the road now follows a gentler one'.

4. See *The March*, index.

5. Characteristically, Caulaincourt says, when Napoleon heard about the loss of the Treasure at Ponari he was less indignant at the loss of so much gold, as that the millions in false rouble notes he'd secretly had printed in Paris before the campaign might fall into the Russians' hands. He, the bourgeois, was worried about the scandal that might follow! Caulaincourt himself had known nothing about these mass forgeries; but doubtless they explain the care with which a Jewish banker in Vilna had scrutinised some roubles that Sergeant Bourgogne, at a heavy discount, had sold him for gold.

6. The several long letters that Berthier would write to Napoleon on 16, 17 and 18 December are in themselves a continuous and lucid account of the retreat's last days, punctuated here and there by *cris de coeur* in which Berthier's likeable personality shines tragically through. I shall acknowledge such material by an asterisk.

7. See *The March*, p. 361, note 12.

8. As at the Berezina, all our survivors either to got up Ponari Hill or had to circumvent it to find themselves, nearly 200 years later, in our book. Once again I've had to content myself with a few samples.

9. Evidently not the one lost to the Cossacks after being tipped into a lake outside Krasnoïe.

10. 'One of the sharpest cries of pain I ever heard him utter,' Oudinot's young wife would write afterwards, 'was when General Maison told him all this *matériel* had been lost.'

11. This isn't true. Poniatowski's Poles arrived in Warsaw on Christmas Day with all their 36 guns intact; and the Hesse-Darmstadt artillery brought out all theirs.

12. But afterwards he'll tell Molé he'd 'foreseen it all', i.e., the catastrophe at Vilna.

13. For brevity's and completeness sake I am here fusing Bourgoing's, Caulaincourt's and the Countess Potocki's accounts. She must have heard these details at second hand later that day.

14. Caulaincourt says repeatedly 'at the Hôtel de Saxe'. But Bourgoing/ Wonsowicz, the Countess Potocki and Pradt himself all say it was the Hôtel d'Angleterre. For Pradt's views of Napoleon and Maret see *Moscow*, pp. 110-11, 238.

15. No doubt Pradt again stressed the state of utter ruin the Grand Army's passage in June had spelt for the Poles. 1812 was a famine year, and the Continental System had made it impossible for them to export their surplus grain, the country's sole export, from the preceding six good years. And in June it had anyway all been commandeered for the Grand Army's horses. See *The March*, p. 35. Neither cash nor credit was to be had. 'Neither functionary nor priest was being paid. The Duchy's revenues amounted to 40 million francs; its expenses exceeded 100 million, etc.' Even the wealthiest Poles had been ruined. The Potockis had been the only Warsaw household able to afford to return Pradt's invitations to dinner, he says. In his book (1814) where he convincingly describes the *de facto* situation in Poland, Pradt accuses Napoleon of being *supérieurement ignorant* of everything he didn't want to know. But Napoleon, as he's just been explaining to Caulaincourt, sees everything 'from a superior viewpoint'.

16. It would take Napoleon and Caulaincourt eight more days to reach Paris – the fastest transit so far on record. And all the time Napoleon would take and talk and talk. Caulaincourt's 150-page record of his immense monologue, jotted down while he dozed for an hour or two at some staging post, is certainly the most vivid close-up of that extraordinary mind we possess. Caulaincourt's percipient, critical but also sympathetic account should be read *in toto*. No résumé can do it the least justice. Among much else he told Caulaincourt, who'd been against the war from the outset:

'Everything has turned out badly because I stayed too long in Moscow. If I'd left four days after occupying it, as I thought of doing when I saw the town in flames, the Russians would have been lost. All our disasters hinge on that fortnight [*sic*]. Kutusov's retreat [*sic*] has been utterly inept. It's the winter that's been our undoing. We're victims of the climate. The fine weather tricked me." The Emperor talked of his disasters and of the mistake he'd made in staying at Moscow in the same tone as might have been used by a stranger.'

Chapter 25: Ney's Last Stand

1. For a picture of the survivors' individual sufferings in extreme close-up, see Bourgogne's detailed account of his march from Vilna to Kovno. But his dates after Ponari are manifestly wrong.

2. Ayherts, his hands and feet frost-bitten, would be captured by Cossacks and herded back to Witebsk – 'where he turned wigmaker; he came back to France from Russian prisons in 1814, with 3 francs in his pocket'. He'd die at a ripe old age in the bosom of the Castellane family 'for whom he was always more than a servant'.

3. Loison had had extraordinary difficulties in sending forward his division from Königsberg. Only after a court-martial would he be exonerated for having joined them so belatedly at the front.

4. Today's Vievis. See *The March*, p. 63.

5. Griois' account is one of those which deserve to be translated *in toto*, together with Dumonceau's three volumes, Paul de Bourgoing's, Victor Dupuy's, Le Roy's, Louise Fusil's, Roman Soltyk's, Heinrich von Brandt's and Cesare de Laugier's.

6. Some of the 1812 Dutch conscripts were only 15 years old. See *The March*, p. 22.

7. Beyond the Niemen, Bignon would take Castellane up into his carriage 'despite the odour of suppuration' from his gangrenous hand. 'He was a man of a lively intelligence. We chatted gaily about people in Paris.' For Sébastiani's character see *The March*, p. 106.

8. Later Petit, ignored by the passers-by where he'd collapsed in the snow by the wayside, would be picked up by a compassionate colonel 'who, however, had only come from Vilna and hadn't been to Moscow'. 'When my thoughts take me

back to that epoch of my life,' Griois ends the episode, 'I tremble at the moral degradation misery can bring us to.'

9. For the rest of the chapter I shall mark extracts from Berthier's letters to Napoleon with an asterisk.

10. This would be the original Russian bridge, broken by Wittgenstein when withdrawing in June and immediately re-established by the French engineers. So Bourgogne is certainly guilty of an inexactitude when he says he marched back over 'this same bridge as we'd passed over five months before with the great and brilliant army, now almost annihilated!'

11. Readers of *The March* will recall that it was Gérard, one day to be a Marshal of France, who'd replaced Gudin, killed at Valutina in August.

12. This would be a second bridgehead, at the point where the original bridge had been destroyed in June. See *The March*, p. 56.

13. At Vilna Séruzier, in utter indigence, would appeal for help to the Tsar's brother, the Grand Duke Constantine. Before offering him any, that absurd and nugatory personage whom Séruzier had met at Erfurt in 1810 – but who in 1812 had fallen into a panic at the threat of war and begged his brother at all costs to avoid it (during the retreat Wilson had seen him actually decapitate a dying French officer with his sword) – heedless of his applicant's appalling condition would first amuse himself for an hour or so by resuming a conversation on artillery techniques they'd had at Erfurt. Only then would Constantine forward the shivering colonel's letter to Ney, who would promptly sent him some money. Both Wilson and the German patriotic writer Ernst Moritz Arndt give appalling pictures of the horrifying state of affairs in and around Vilna. Arriving in what he describes as that 'Tartar hell' on 11 January, Arndt, whose writings would play a part in the revolt first of Prussia then of all Germany against the Napoleonic regime, would see 'French cockades lying in the streets, dirty plumes, torn hats and shakos that reminded one of how the French had strutted with them through the streets five months earlier but now were humbled in the dust and trodden underfoot.'

14. For Liesje's history and equine qualities, see *The March*, p. 42.

15. '... *ne partirent pas*'. The expression is ambiguous; it could equally well mean that the men refused to attack the hill – presumably the same one from which Faber du Faur had first seen the main body of the Grand Army assembled at the bridgeheads in midsummer. See illustration in *The March*.

16. Less peremptorily, the French word *doit*, used by Berthier, can also mean 'should be'. But Murat himself had had enough: 'It's no longer possible to serve under a lunatic,' he'd rage to Berthier. 'No prince in Europe any longer believes in his word, nor in his treaties ... Oh, if I'd only listened to the proposals made me by the British! I'd still be a great king, like the Emperor of Austria and the King of Prussia!' An indignant Berthier interrupts: 'The King of Prussia and the Emperor of Austria are princes by the grace of God, time and custom. But you're only a king by the grace of Napoleon and French blood. It's black ingratitude that's blinding you, and I'll let him know your words.' At 4 p.m on 17 January at Elbing, Murat, despite Berthier's supplications, would leave for Naples and 'without orders from the Emperor but certain his decision would have his approval' be succeeded by Eugène. Eugène cancelled Murat's orders for a precipitate retreat. 'From then on everything changed aspect.' In a menacing letter Napoleon would take his *pantaleone* of a brother-in-law to task for his 'weakness of character. I imagine you're not one of those people who suppose the lion is dead. If you're counting on that, you're wrong. The title of King has turned your head.' Berthier himself would fall so ill with the lethal fever sweeping through the army that Daru had to sign his dispatches for him.

17. Of Bernadotte the ex-emperor would say at St Helena: 'I can accuse him of ingratitude, but not of treachery. In a manner of speaking he became a Swede.' And in fact he had accepted the Swedish invitation on condition that Napoleon strike out his stipulation that he wouldn't bear arms against France. In 1813 Bernadotte would play a crucial role in planning the Allies' successful strategies.

18. On 26 December at Königsberg, where Lariboisière had already died, Planat de la Faye would ask Eblé 'for his orders for me in Paris. He had none to give. He was completely demoralised. All he did during my visit was to show me his trouser belt, which had become half again too large for him.' That day Planat left for Berlin with Ferdinand Lariboisière's heart preserved in spirits of wine and his father's body 'in a kind of box in such a way that the head reposed on the cushion at my side'. Eblé would die at Königsberg on 30 December.

19. Or rather, according to *Hortense Beauharnais*, ex-queen of Holland, it had been hastily finished off in wood on the occasion of Napoleon's marriage to Marie-Louise.

20. On 11 January 1813 he'd call up 250,000 conscripts. On 13 February he'd tell his minister Molé: 'I'd have been amazed by such a spectacle if I hadn't long ago learnt to control myself. The day before [5 November] I was conqueror of the world, I'd been commanding the finest army of modern times. Next day, nothing of all that was left. I think I showed a calmness, I'd even say preserved an unalterable cheerfulness, and I don't think anyone among those who saw me could give me the lie. But don't believe I, like other men, haven't a soft heart. I'm even quite a good fellow; but since my earliest youth I've applied myself to silencing that string, and in me it doesn't give out a sound.' He admitted that he was not quite so active as formerly in his work, when he'd now and again only asked de Bausset for 'a glass of water'. Now he finds he needs a cup of coffee. The great chemist Chaptal, another eye-witness, scientifically observing Napoleon after the Russian disaster, found his ideas no longer so clear and logical and his conversation fitful and full of outbursts. 'Somnolence and the pleasures of the table gained on him.' Riding fatigued him and he now tended to drop off to sleep and waste a lot of time talking. Though he no longer worked so hard, his passion for power remained unassuaged. On 3 April 1813 he'd call up 180,000 more conscripts, In August 30,000 more. On 9 October 280,000 more. On 15 November 300,000 more. Of France's total population of 25 millions, and his Empire's 50 millions, Napoleon, in the vast struggle between the *ancien* and the post-Revolutionary regimes, would use up

an estimated 2,114,000 lives. His enemies certainly no fewer.

Two Epilogues

1. See *The March*, p. 112

2. When Napoleon reviewed the 5th Tirailleurs at the Trianon in March, only their redoubtable Colonel Hennequin, a few officers and NCOs and one drummer boy remained. Of Lignières' company of the 1st Foot Chasseurs, 245 strong at Moscow, only 52, 'and this was the strongest of all the Old Guard's companies'. Total losses of officers in Russia had been 9,380, whereof 2,965 killed or dead from wounds, and 6,415 wounded, including seven divisional generals killed and 39 wounded, and 22 generals of brigade killed and 85 wounded. Five Marshals had been wounded. Somewhere between 130,000 and 175,000 horses had perished, excluding the innumerable *konyas*. Of 826 surgeons only 175 are registered as being still alive in February: 'the paymasters have had the same fate', Peyrusse would write to his Parisian friend. Of the '600–700 handsome, powerful men' of the 4th Bavarian Chevaulegers, 'the officers admirably mounted and in brilliant uniforms, filled with vitality and courage' who'd left for Russia, a mere 40 to 50 officers, NCOs and troopers got home. Refused sick-leave, the officers were immediately ordered to form cadres of new recruits. According to the complete breakdown of killed and wounded officers, regiment by regiment, drawn up by the statistician Aristide Martinien (to be found at the end of vol. 2 of Chuquet's *Guerre de Russie*, an invaluable anthology of documents), only the 1st and 2nd Grenadiers and Chasseurs of the Old Guard hadn't lost an officer and only one in each regiment had been wounded – all in cruel contrast to the Line regiments, where an average of seventeen officers had been killed. For the expendable rankers no figures are given.

The patient reader will doubtless be wondering what happened in the end to at least some of our principal protagonists. According to Oudinot's young duchess, Narbonne, in whose company we started our tragic tale,

'had survived all the miseries of the retreat without losing, at least to all appearances, his infectious and gracious gaiety. Yet the traces of his fatigues and privations were strongly marked on the face of this courageous old man.'

But a couple of years later, when the Bourbons returned, he'd die suddenly – another victim, thinks the Swedish researcher Sten Forshuvud, of the arsenical arts of Napoleon's arch-enemy the comte d'Artois, who nursed an undying hatred of all persons of standing who'd supported the imperial regime.

The debonaire but frequently self-pitying Murat, after stupidly emulating Napoleon's come-back during the Hundred Days, would be shot by a firing-squad in Calabria. His last words are said to have been: 'Soldiers, spare the face! Fire!'

After acting as Napoleon's last emissary *vis-à-vis* an implacably united Europe in 1814 and as his Foreign Minister during the Hundred Days, Caulaincourt, Duke of Vicenza, would pay the price of his stubborn loyalty to a man whose policies he had disapproved. Implacably cold-shouldered by the Bourbons as the Duke of Enghien's alleged assassin but still befriended by the Tsar, he'd die of cancer in 1827. The publication of his incomparably initiated memoirs in 1935 would be one of the great events of Napoleonic historiography.

Berthier would desert Napoleon's cause, or rather, remain faithful to the Bourbons in 1815. He died at Bamberg by falling out of a third-storey window while standing on a chair to get a better view of Russian troops marching down the street.

Oudinot, who at Königsberg had 'put his head under his pillow so as not to be kept awake by 20 or 30 Prussians drinking to our disasters' (Pils), lived to be the Grand Old Man of the Napoleonic epoch; he became head of the Invalides in Paris, and despite his many wounds died at a ripe old age.

After promising Louis XVIII to 'bring Bonaparte back in an iron cage' on his return from Elba, Ney, whose nerves and presence of mind seem to have been overstrained in Russia, would make a mess of the conduct of Quatre Bras and Waterloo. Arrested by the Bourbons on a charge of high treason, he'd be shot by firing-squad.

Larrey, captured by the Prussians at Waterloo and already facing a firing-squad, would be recognised and saved by a British officer.

Quite a few of our officer-eyewitnesses, the all-observant Dumonceau for example, would end up as generals, and three, Lyautey, Castellane and Gérard, as Marshals of France.

While in Moscow, if Ali's memoirs are to be believed, Napoleon had one day fallen to 'discussing with Duroc the best sort of death. The best, according to Napoleon, was to "die on the field of battle, stricken by a bullet". For his part he feared he wouldn't be so happy. "I'll die", he said, "in my bed, *comè un' coglione".*' His words were prophetic. Deported to St Helena, he would finally – if the Swedish researcher Sten Forshuvud's closely argued and evidenced theory holds water (and Professor David Chandler has said that it's 'an accusation which must stand in any court of law until someone no less painstakingly and convincingly refutes it') – be poisoned by Count Montholon. Summed up by Ben Weider and David Hapgood in *The Murder of Napoleon*, NY, 1982, it is perhaps the 20th century's most brilliant piece of historical-scientific detection.

INDEX

PAUL BRITTEN AUSTIN

1812: The March on Moscow
1812: Napoleon at Moscow
1812: The Great Retreat